The Executive Guide to Corporate Bankruptcy

THE EXECUTIVE GUIDE TO CORPORATE BANKRUPTCY

Thomas J. Salerno, Esq.
Jordan A. Kroop, Esq.
Craig D. Hansen, Esq.

BeardBooks
Washington, D.C.

Library of Congress Cataloging-in-Publication Data

Salerno, Thomas J.
The executive guide to corporate bankruptcy / Thomas J. Salerno, Jordan A. Kroop, Craig D. Hansen
p. cm.
Includes bibliographical references and index.
ISBN 1-58798-026-6 (alk. paper)
1. Corporate reorganizations--United States. Salerno, Thomas J., I. Kroop, Jordan A., 1969-II. Hansen, Craig D. III. Title.

KF1544.S253 2001
346.73'06626--dc21 2001025150

Printed in the United States of America

"Bankruptcy is one of those words, like 'war,' that you have heard all of your life, and think that you understand until you actually become involved with the process the word is intended to identify."

J. Weidman
***Fourth Street East* (1910)**

AUTHORS

THOMAS J. SALERNO is a partner in, and co-chair of, the Reorganization And Restructuring Group in the Phoenix office of the international law firm of Squire, Sanders & Dempsey, and Chair of the International Insolvency Practice Group. Mr. Salerno graduated from Rutgers University (B.A., *summa cum laude*) and Notre Dame Law School (J.D., *cum laude*), where he served as an editor of *the Notre Dame Law Review*. Throughout the last nineteen years Mr. Salerno has represented debtors, creditors committees, lenders and other parties in interest in complex Chapter 11 reorganizations involving public debt and equity securities throughout the United States, and has represented parties in insolvency proceedings in the Czech Republic, Switzerland, Germany and the United Kingdom.

Mr. Salerno has authored *Appellate Structure and Procedure Under the New Bankruptcy Rules* (CLE Press 1984); and co-authored *Bankruptcy Litigation and Practice: A Practitioner's Guide, 3rd Edition* (Aspen Law & Business, 2nd ed. Rev. 1999), as well as the third edition of that work forthcoming in 2000, which is the subject of a nationwide seminar series; "Urgent Message To The Supreme Court: 'Just Do It'," *Bankruptcy Court Decisions* (LRP Publications, May 25, 1999); Pre-*Bankruptcy Planning for the Commercial Reorganization: A Brief Guide For The CEO, CFO/ COO, General Counsel And Tax Advisor* (American Bankruptcy Institute 1997) (winner of the ABI's Publication Award, 1997); "The 1111(b)(2) Election: A Primer," 13 *Bankr. Dev. J.* 99 (Winter 1996); *The Ins and Outs of Foreclosures* (State Bar of Arizona 1996); "Pre-Bankruptcy Planning for Professionals and ERISA-Qualified Pension Plans: Are State Created Statutory Exemptions D.O.A. in Bankruptcy Proceedings?" 94 *Commercial Law Journal* 229 (Fall 1989); "Environmental Law and Its Impact on Bankruptcy Law—The Saga of Toxins-R-Us," 25 *Real Property, Trust and Probate Journal* 261 (Summer 1990); and "Technology Licenses Under Section 365(n) of the Bankruptcy Code: The Protections Afforded the Technology User," 95 *Commercial Law Journal* 170 (Summer 1990); "A Prepackaged Bankruptcy Strategy," *Journal of Business Strategy* 36 (Jan./Feb. 1991); and "Making the Best of Bankruptcy," *Bankers Monthly* 21 (Apr. 1991). He also serves as executive editor of *Advanced Chapter 11 Bankruptcy Practice—2nd Edition* (Aspen Publications 1997). He is a contributor to *Norton Bankruptcy Law & Practice* and the *ABI Journal*. He is a member of the board of directors and the executive committee of the American Bankruptcy Institute and the American Bankruptcy Board of Certification, Inc., both based in Washington, D.C., and was co-chairman of the Subcommittee on Uniformity in Professional Fees in Bankruptcy of the ABI. He is a member of the faculty for McGeorge School of Law's International Law Program, where he teaches International Commercial Arbitration and Comparitive International Insolvency in both London and Salzburg, and is a guest lecturer at Arizona State University of Law. Mr. Salerno has been included in *The Best Lawyers of American* since 1992, and named as one of twelve Outstanding Bankruptcy Lawyers by *Turnarounds & Workouts* (1998).

He is a frequent speaker on reorganization matters throughout the United States and Latin America.

JORDAN A. KROOP is a senior-level associate in the Reorganization and Restructuring Group of Squire, Sanders & Dempsey L.L.P., resident in the Phoenix office. Mr. Kroop is a graduate, *magna cum laude,* of Brown University and the University of Virginia School of Law. Mr. Kroop is co-author of *Bankruptcy Litigation & Practice: A Practitioner's Guide*, (Aspen Law & Business, 2d ed. Rev. 1999), as well as the third edition of that work, forthcoming in 2000. He has also co-authored several articles on various bankruptcy topics, recently including "Urgent Message to the Supreme Court: 'Just Do It!,'" *Bankruptcy Court Decisions* (LRP Publications, May 25, 1999), and has authored extensive materials for, and spoken at, numerous national and regional seminars and symposia. He has lectured at Arizona State University on various legal topics and, as a member of the American Bankruptcy Institute, has assisted in the formulation of a new publications policy. Mr. Kroop has represented debtors, creditors committees, secured lenders, and other significant parties in interest in some of the largest Chapter 11 reorganizations in the United States. He has been listed as one of twelve "Outstanding Young Bankruptcy Lawyers—2000" by *Turnarounds & Workouts*.

CRAIG D. HANSEN is a partner in, and Co-Chairman of, the Reorganization and Restructuring Group of the international law firm of Squire, Sanders and Dempsey, LLP. Mr. Hansen is resident in the firm's Phoenix office. He has nineteen years of experience in the representation of distressed companies, creditors committees and both strategic and financial acquirers of distressed companies and their debt and equity securities in some of the largest restructuring transactions in the United States. He is also a frequently lecturer on restructuring related topics throughout the United States.

Mr. Hansen received his law degree from Temple University where he graduated *summa cum laude*. He is the co-author and co-editor of numerous publications and articles relating to restructurings including *Advanced Chapter 11 Bankruptcy Practice—2nd Edition* (Aspen Publications 1997); "Urgent Message To the Supreme Court: 'Just Do It'," *Bankruptcy Court Decisions* (LRP publications, May 25, 1999); *Pre-Bankruptcy Planning for the Commercial Reorganization: A Brief Guide For The CEO, CFO, COO, General Counsel and Tax Advisor* (American Bankruptcy Institute

1997) (winner of the ABI's Publication Award, 1997); "The 1111(b)(2) Election: A Primer," 13 *Bankr. Dev. J.* 99 (winter 1996); "Technology Licenses Under Section 365(n) of the Bankruptcy Code: The Protections Afforded the Technology User," 95 *Commercial Law Journal* 170 (Summer 1990); "A Prepackaged Bankruptcy Strategy", *Journal of Business Strategy* 36 (Jan./Feb. 1991); and "Making The Best of Bankruptcy," *Bankers Monthly* 21 (April 1991). Mr. Hansen is also a member of the American Bankruptcy Institute.

ACKNOWLEDGMENTS

The authors wish to gratefully acknowledge the review and input in this book from ***Steven Abramowitz, Esq.*** (Fried, Frank, Harris, Shriver & Jacobs); ***Paul S. Aronzon, Esq.*** (Milbank, Tweed, Hadley & McCloy); ***Douglas Bacon, Esq.*** (Latham & Watkins); ***Hon. William Bodoh*** (U.S. Bankruptcy Judge, Northern District of Ohio); ***N. Dwight Cary, Esq.*** (Murphy Sheneman Julian & Rogers; ***James C. Constance*** (Howard Wright Construction Company.); ***Michael D'Appolonia*** (Nightingale & Assoc.); ***Bryce L. DuPere*** (Carlton Cos.); ***Michael A. Jeffries*** (Unison HealthCare); ***Peter S. Kaufman*** (Gordian Group); ***Robert T. Ladd*** (Duke Capital Partners); ***G. Grant Lyon*** (Odyssey Capital); ***Nir Margalit, Esq.*** (General Counsel, Best Western International); ***Jock Patton*** (Stuart Entertainment and Unison HealthCare); ***Joseph Samet, Esq.*** (Baker & McKenzie); ***Michael S. Sitrick*** (Sitrick & Company); ***Michael A. Tucker*** (PricewaterhouseCoopers); and ***Joseph Valandra*** (Stuart Entertainment).

The authors wish to especially thank and acknowledge ***Jeffrey Werbalowsky*** of Houlihan, Lokey, Howard & Zukin for his editing and Appendix materials on *Executive Severance* and *DIP Financing*, and ***Barbara D. Clapper*** (paralegal, Squire, Sanders & Dempsey L.L.P.) for all her efforts.

Finally, the authors wish to gratefully acknowledge their families for allowing them to steal valuable time away from them to write this book.

To Our Families, Who Allowed Us To
Steal Yet More Time From Them In the
Pursuit of Ancillary Endeavors.

TABLE OF CONTENTS

APPENDICES

CHAPTER ONE

INTRODUCTION

> *"I see you stand like greyhounds in the slips,*
> *Straining upon the start. The game's afoot!"*
> William Shakespeare
> *King Henry V, Act III, i, 31* (1600)

"But I'm Not Ready To File Bankruptcy!"

We understand. The first thing most executives of troubled companies generally say is that their company doesn't need to file bankruptcy. They may be right—there are ways to recapitalize that don't require formal bankruptcy proceedings.[1] These are called "out-of-court workouts."

That having been said, these executives may be wrong, or perhaps misinformed. Bankruptcy restructuring should not be a first alternative for a troubled company unless there is a potentially irreversible, financially devastating event about to occur that requires an immediate filing (such as a foreclosure on a key plant or some other such event).

In any event, it behooves the smart executive to know his or her options. Unless you have been through this process, the prospect of a bankruptcy reorganization may seem intimidating, puzzling, and generally unpleasant. This book will lead you through that process. With it in hand, you may still find the bankruptcy process intimidating and generally unpleasant, but it will be substantially less puzzling.

The Historical Underpinnings Of Bankruptcy Law— A Very Brief Primer

Relax. This is not going to be an esoteric academic discussion of the historical underpinnings of bankruptcy law. It will be a thumbnail sketch of the last few thousand years of insolvency law development to help put this book into context.

The word "bankruptcy" is derived from the Latin *banca rota*, which is literally translated into "broken bench." The phrase is used to signify financial distress because of the practice in ancient Rome whereby merchants who were unable to pay their debts were penalized by not being able to sell their wares in the marketplaces. Specifically, when a merchant would find himself in financial difficulties and his creditors would complain to the civil authorities, the authorities would go to the marketplace where the merchant normally sold his goods and physically break the bench or stall from which that merchant would ply his trade. Hence the phrase "broken bench," from which we derive the modern word "bankruptcy." Armed with this trivia, you will now be the envy of your peers on the next Double Jeopardy showdown.

Historically, the concept of bankruptcy has always been penal in nature, and frankly remains as such throughout much of the world outside of the United States. In ancient Rome, for example, in addition to breaking a merchant's bench, failure to pay debts for reasons other than as a result of an unavoidable act of the gods would result in prison and the loss of an ear. Likewise, the concept of debtor's prison was well known in medieval England and Europe.

The counterintuitive nature of such an approach is self-evident. If a business or person owes creditors, and it is legally precluded from making money to at least repay some of that debt, while perhaps the creditors feel vindicated in that the malfeasor has been appropriately punished, the chances of recovery on the debts are obviously minimized. The ancient Roman custom of cutting off an ear is likewise interesting. At that point the aggrieved creditors would be screaming at the borrower for return of their money, and he would be blissfully unaware of all of the ruckus in his deafened state. In the immortal words of Charles Dickens in *Oliver Twist*, "'If the law supposes that,' said Mr. Bumble, 'the law is an ass, an idiot.'"

The Genesis Of U.S. Bankruptcy Law

Our founding fathers thought it prudent to have a uniform system of bankruptcy laws, and the U.S. Constitution delegates to Congress the exclusive power to "establish . . . uniform Laws on the subject of Bankruptcies throughout the United States."[2] This way, there wouldn't be fifty different bankruptcy laws operating in the different states.

The United States has had a federal system of bankruptcy law since the Bankruptcy Act of 1800 (eleven years after the Constitution was ratified by the requisite number of states). The U.S. laws have always been different than those in the rest of the world in breaking with the historically penal nature of bankruptcy laws. This really isn't all that hard to understand when one considers the historical context.

The United States was founded by English colonists who were persecuted and otherwise in the miscreant caste of English society. In fact, many of the original English settlers had themselves spent some time in debtors' prisons, and viewed the hardships of the New World as at least an even exchange for the fetid English penal system. It is not surprising that this country ultimately developed not only extremely liberal laws on religious and political tolerance, but also the world's most liberal bankruptcy laws.[3]

Bankruptcy is so prevalent in the United States, in 1995 it was reported that there was one bankruptcy filing for every four births.[4] Indeed, by 1995 there had been more bankruptcy cases filed under the 1978 Bankruptcy Code (which comprehensively revamped the Bankruptcy Act of 1898) than in the eighty years under the Bankruptcy Act of 1898. Since the 1980s, there has been a steady flow of bankruptcy reorganization filings in the United States, with 1991 being a record year.[5]

Working Definition Of "Bankruptcy" And "Reorganization"

To be an initiate into the strange new world of bankruptcy reorganization, you must know the language. Unfortunately, the secret handshake is reserved exclusively for investment bankers. The Appendix to this book contains a comprehensive *Glossary Of Commonly Used Bankruptcy Terms* to help the executive understand the language of the new world he or she is about to enter. Words in ***bold italics*** used in the book are defined in the Glossary (as well as other words or phrases not specifically used in the book, but which you may encounter in this process).

So, what is bankruptcy? Simply stated, the concept of ***bankruptcy*** under U.S. law refers to a comprehensive federal system of laws that provide for the collection, preservation, and maximization of value of a debtor's assets for the benefit of creditors.

What is ***reorganization*** under the bankruptcy laws? It is the ability of a financially troubled company (or individual) to utilize a complex set of federal and state commercial laws to maximize recovery for creditors while at the same time preserving the company's business as a "going concern." This involves a system of checks and balances by virtue of the participation of numerous special interest constituencies (such as ***Unsecured Creditors Committees, Equityholder Committees, Ad Hoc Committees, the U.S. Trustee*** and the like), all under the watchful eye of the federal ***Bankruptcy Court***. It's about as far away from the "broken bench" theory of creditor repayment as is historically possible.[6] Reorganization under the bankruptcy laws is the focus of this book.

Why Are You Reading This Book?

So why are you reading this book? You are reading this book for one of five reasons.

First, perhaps you're an executive in a company that is financially troubled. While it is not a pleasant prospect, and certainly not the topic of polite cocktail party conversation, there are certain economic realities that everyone faces.[7] A well-informed executive is an effective executive.

Second, perhaps you've been asked to serve as an officer or director to a company in financial distress or already in a bankruptcy reorganization, and are wondering what to expect.

Third, perhaps you can't help but read about all the businesses that themselves are going into bankruptcy in the retail,[8] health care, mining, gaming, telecommunication industries, securitization intensive industries (such as the sub-prime lenders), or the mass-tort-prone industries, and wonder what this is all about. Perhaps you've seen how huge companies and ones that have existed for a hundred years or more have visited their local bankruptcy judge, such as Colt Industries (maker of the famed "Peacemaker" of the old West), Texaco, Hoover Vacuums, Chris-Craft Boats, LTV Steel, Baldwin-United, FPA Medical Management, Sun HealthCare, Vencor, Dow Corning, Johns-Manville, Baldwin-United, Revco, Federated Department Stores, Finova, Drug Emporium, Planet Hollywood (even Arnold Schwarzenegger deserted them!), Macy's, TWA, Continental, America West, and Eastern Airlines.[9] The largest Chapter 11 of 1999 was the *Loewen Group International* case (involving nearly $4.7 billion in assets)—a huge chain of funeral homes. One would think if there was any industry that was safe, it would be funeral homes. People have to die, after all.

Fourth, perhaps you're an astute investor who recognizes that in adversity there is opportunity. Perhaps you're an executive in a competitive industry, and wonder if there are any acquisition or merger possibilities on economically favorable terms relating to some of your competitors that may be heading into Chapter 11 reorganizations or are already there. Perhaps you're interested in acquiring assets from troubled companies. Perhaps you wish to buy debt or equity at low prices to speculate, such as buying unsecured trade claims for 5¢ on the dollar, hoping that the bankruptcy process will return 10¢, 20¢, or 30¢ on those claims.[10]

Fifth, perhaps you're an existing creditor to a financially distressed business, have been asked to sit on a creditors committee, or are an equityholder in such an enterprise. You might want to know what the reorganization process is all about to properly perform your role in the case, or to protect yourself and your debt or equity investment.[11]

Standard Lawyerly Cautionary Information

Reorganizations and restructurings are, not surprisingly, complex undertakings. Their degree of complexity depends on the industry and economic facts involved. They are also professional-intensive (lawyers, accountants, financial advisors, and so on). This book is intended to familiarize the reader with some of the concepts and issues arising in reorganization cases, but whether some or all of them apply to your particular circumstances, company, or industry obviously requires specific analysis by qualified professionals.

This book is not an exhaustive analysis of the current state of the law with all its changes. Bankruptcy laws are changed by Congress periodically, and are subject to judicial interpretations that can and do change over time. The current state of the law is a function of where you are in the country and when you're looking at it. Rather, this book will cover, from a business person's perspective, what the reorganization *process* is all about, from start to finish. If you are one of the hardy souls that work their way through this book, you will learn what the Bankruptcy Code is all about. In addition to the reorganization process, you will learn about the new players and their roles, and the new realities for the troubled business entity. You will learn about business operations within the context of a bankruptcy proceeding before approval of a plan of reorganization. You will learn about the plan of reorganization and what is possible (and not possible). Finally, you will learn about ten myths of bankruptcy that you may have heard, and get the full story.

So read on. The game is indeed afoot!

CHAPTER TWO

THE REORGANIZATION PROCESS

"For my own part, looking out upon the future, I do not view the process with any misgivings."

Sir Winston Spencer Churchill
Tribute To The Royal Air Force
House Of Commons
August 20, 1940

In order to really understand what corporate restructuring is all about, it is absolutely essential to understand the reorganization process. It is in all respects a new world, with its own players, language, terms of art, and new realities that for the uninitiated can be intimidating. Before going into specifics on corporate restructurings (such as operations in bankruptcy proceedings, negotiations and provisions of plans of reorganization, and the plan confirmation or "approval" process), it is helpful to get a bird's-eye view of the reorganization process.

This chapter will familiarize the reader with the Bankruptcy Code, what types of entities are eligible for bankruptcy reorganization, and how the process is started. It then delves into what the "pecking order" is for creditors—this is an overriding concept that impacts all that is attempted and accomplished in a reorganization. Next, the reorganization process is explored in an overview perspective, and the statistical odds relating to bankruptcy reorganizations are examined. We will list the players in this process and their roles. Finally, this chapter will explore the crucial difference between the "proactive" and "reactive" reorganization proceedings.

The "Bankruptcy Code": What Is A "Chapter 11 Bankruptcy"? What Is A "Chapter 7 Bankruptcy"? What Do People Mean When They Throw Around "Code Sections" In Conversation?

As part of learning the new lingo, it's important to get a basic understanding of where it all comes from.

The bankruptcy laws in this country are contained in a federal law (which takes precedence over all state laws on this topic) called the ***Bankruptcy Code.*** The Bankruptcy Code (sometimes simply called the "Code") is a set of laws found in Title 11 of the U.S. Code. The Bankruptcy Code represents a major reworking of the Bankruptcy Act of 1898 that was completed in

1978. It is the end product of the Bankruptcy Reform Act of 1978, which superseded and otherwise completely revamped the old Bankruptcy Act of 1898.[12]

The Bankruptcy Code is divided into eight chapters, all of which deal with different elements of bankruptcy law. In order to avoid any confusion with the Bankruptcy Act, the chapters in the Bankruptcy Code are all odd numbered (beginning with Chapter 1), with the exception of Chapter 12, a very special provision included in 1986 to create special relief for economically beleaguered "family farmers."[13]

Chapters 1, 3, and 5 of the Bankruptcy Code are considered the "omnibus chapters" of the Code. They contain provisions that will generally be applicable regardless of the type of bankruptcy filed. For example, Chapter 1 deals with definitions, rules of construction, and other such matters. Chapter 3 is entitled "Case Administration" and deals with how cases can be filed (voluntarily or involuntarily) and other important matters of administration. Some of the more important provisions of Chapter 3 of the Bankruptcy Code will be dealt with later in this book (such as the ***automatic stay*** provisions, ***cash collateral*** provisions, ***DIP financing*** provisions, and ***executory contracts*** provisions). Finally, Chapter 5 of the Bankruptcy Code deals with matters involving creditors and their claims, a debtor's duties and benefits under the Bankruptcy Code, and defines and otherwise deals with the concept of the ***estate***. Chapter 5 contains what are known as the ***"strong arm" powers*** of the Bankruptcy Code (such as the power to bring back ***preferences*** and ***fraudulent conveyances***, and void unperfected liens), which give debtors some very powerful leverage points to be used in dealing with creditors in bankruptcy proceedings.

Chapters 7, 9, 11, 12, and 13 are known as the "affirmative relief" chapters of the Bankruptcy Code. Hence, when one hears of someone having filed a "Chapter 7," it means specifically that he or she has filed a type of proceeding under Chapter 7 of the Bankruptcy Code.

Chapter 9 bankruptcies are limited to municipalities (such as cities, towns, school districts, irrigation districts, and the like). As stated above, Chapter 12 deals only with certain types of farmers, and Chapter 13 deals with individual wage earners. None of these is relevant to the subject matter of this book.

The two provisions that are directly relevant to corporate restructurings are Chapter 7 and Chapter 11 proceedings. A ***Chapter 7 proceeding*** is a straight liquidation of the assets of a business enterprise with the proceeds from those sales being used to pay creditors in accordance with the official pecking order (otherwise known as the ***priorities***) as set forth in the Bankruptcy Code. This pecking order will be discussed below. This liquidation is conducted by a court-appointed officer called a ***trustee.*** The trustee is a person who acts in a fiduciary capacity for the benefit of all creditors.

Trustees are compensated based on a percentage of the debtor's assets that are ultimately turned over to creditors. As such, economically speaking, a trustee is motivated to sell assets quickly because, in all material respects, time is money. A debtor in a business Chapter 7 case has very little to do other than to cooperate and turn over records to the trustee and his or her professionals. Chapter 7 is a passive type of bankruptcy proceeding and is not used very frequently by large business organizations, even business organizations that intend to liquidate some or all of their assets through a bankruptcy proceeding.

A ***Chapter 11 proceeding***, on the other hand, is commonly referred to as a ***business reorganization*** but is available to individuals as well as business enterprises. It is possible to liquidate assets in a Chapter 11 just as in a Chapter 7. The primary difference between a liquidation under a Chapter 11 is that rather than a court-appointed trustee overseeing the liquidation, it is the business enterprise's existing management that supervises the process and, for the most part, wields the same powers that a trustee would have in a Chapter 7 case. Once a Chapter 11 proceeding is commenced, management of the business enterprise is referred to as a ***debtor-in-possession***, commonly shortened to ***"DIP"*** (with no pejorative connotation).[14] But as one might guess, power carries with it responsibilities and obligations, and those will be discussed below.

Who Is Eligible For Chapter 11 Reorganization?

Chapter 11 relief is available to essentially every type of business enterprise used in the United States. Corporations, partnerships, joint ventures, unincorporated associations, limited liability companies, and even non-profit entities are eligible for Chapter 11 relief under the Bankruptcy Code.[15]

Congress precluded Chapter 11 relief for certain types of businesses. For example, railroads,[16] insurance companies,[17] banks,[18] savings and loans, and stock commodity brokers may not seek relief under Chapter 11 of the Bankruptcy Code. These entities have insolvency proceedings that are controlled by other very specialized laws. Likewise, municipalities, which encompass not only traditional cities and towns, but also irrigation and school districts are not eligible for Chapter 11 bankruptcy relief but rather have their own specific affirmative relief Chapter known as Chapter 9. The most widely known ***Chapter 9 proceeding*** is the one involving Orange County, California, which went through a Chapter 9 bankruptcy proceeding that lasted many years. Perhaps one of the few actual towns or cities to have filed a Chapter 9 proceeding was the City of South Tucson in Arizona.

For purposes of this book, essentially all business enterprises are considered eligible for Chapter 11 reorganizations.

Getting The Process Started

So how is a Chapter 11 bankruptcy started? Chapter 11 proceedings can start either voluntarily or involuntarily. A ***voluntary bankruptcy*** is commenced by the filing of a ***petition*** and the payment of a filing fee for each entity that files.[19] If the business enterprise is a corporation, the Board of Directors must pass a resolution authorizing the filing of the bankruptcy petition and the hiring of counsel and perhaps other professionals to do so. In addition, public reporting companies under the federal securities laws must issue appropriate press releases and securities filings to avoid trading in the debtor's equity securities of such companies once a bankruptcy is filed.[20] Sample forms of a corporate resolution and press release are contained in the Appendix to these materials.

Likewise, a Chapter 11 bankruptcy proceeding can be commenced involuntarily against a business enterprise by the filing of an ***involuntary bankruptcy*** by one or more creditors.[21] For example, the Chapter 11 proceeding of *McCulloch Corporation*, filed in Tucson, Arizona, in early 1999, was started as an involuntary bankruptcy proceeding filed by three creditors, with the company agreeing to convert the case to a voluntary Chapter 11 bankruptcy within a few days after the involuntary bankruptcy was filed.

A Chapter 11 reorganization can be commenced by filing very few forms—essentially a petition, with appropriate corporate resolutions, and a cursory listing of creditors. A sample form of bare bones filing documents is contained in the Appendix. This enables Chapter 11 filings to be done quickly and on an emergency basis, *but that is never recommended* (see the discussion on "proactive" versus "reactive" bankruptcy proceedings below). The clerk's office at the ***Bankruptcy Court*** will date and time stamp a petition evidencing precisely (to the second) when a bankruptcy filing took place. From this moment forward the company in Chapter 11 bankruptcy is known as a "debtor," and more specifically a debtor-in-possession, or DIP.[22]

What's This "Insolvency" Thing?

A common misperception is that a company has to be ***insolvent*** to file for bankruptcy relief. Generally speaking, insolvency under the Bankruptcy Code is when a company's assets, at fair value, are less than its liabilities.[23] Of course, as any executive knows, this is at best an amorphous and imprecise definition. Does it include contingent liabilities? Off-balance- sheet items (capital leases, etc.)? It's unclear, but not directly material under any circumstance. **It is not necessary for a company to be insolvent to file for Chapter 11 relief.** The only requisite for filing a voluntary Chapter 11 bankruptcy is that the company has a place of business or property in the United States.[24] End of story. There is no need to assert that the company can't pay its debts, or is insolvent, or is being harangued by creditors. When Texaco filed its Chapter 11 petition in 1988 to avoid posting an appellate bond after being hit with an $11 billion judgment by Pennzoil,[25] the public outcry was that Texaco was not insolvent (even with that judgment, it still had a positive net worth), so how could it file Chapter 11? The answer was simple—because it could.[26]

The "Pecking Order"—Payment Priorities In Reorganization Cases

It is necessary to keep in mind the "pecking order" in any type of bankruptcy proceeding. This is important because it will affect business and legal decisions whether a business enterprise is considering a reorganization proceeding or already is in a reorganization proceeding.

In the normal corporate world, for example, the Board of Directors owes a primary ***fiduciary obligation*** to the shareholders of the company. However, once that business enterprise gets into financial difficulty, the Board's fiduciary obligations shift from the shareholders to the business enterprise as a whole, which encompasses the creditors. This shift occurs when the business enterprise enters what is called the ***"zone of insolvency,"*** although there is no bright-line test as to when that occurs.[27] More about this later. The pecking order in a bankruptcy reorganization, simply stated, is as follows:

· ***The "Secured Creditor."***

The creditor with a valid ***lien, encumbrance,*** or ***mortgage*** on assets is called a ***secured creditor*** and gets first dibs in the event its collateral is to be sold or otherwise used in the bankruptcy proceeding. The secured creditor with a lien on receivables and similar assets must be dealt with early on in the Chapter 11 process as part of cash collateral use, discussed in Chapter Four.[28]

· ***The "Administrative And Priority Claimants."***

Next in line come the so-called ***administrative and priority claimants.*** These are, effectively, the first ***unsecured creditors*** in the estate and are entitled to be paid before anyone below them is paid. Administrative claimants include certain unpaid employees, certain tax claims, the professional fees of the lawyers, accountants, investment advisors, and others (not surprisingly since, after all, the Bankruptcy Code was written primarily by lawyers), and other types of creditors (such as creditors that extend trade credit to a company after the bankruptcy is filed). These creditors are ranked, or "prioritized" in the Bankruptcy Code.[29]

· ***The "General Unsecured Creditors."***

Next in line (to the extent that there is anything left over after payment of the secured creditors and administrative claimants) come the general unsecured creditors. These are known in some circles as "the great unwashed." Simply stated, these are creditors that provided goods, services, or money to the company before the Chapter 11 was filed, and who hold no ***collateral***. To the extent there is insufficient money to pay all unsecured creditors in full, they will share in any distribution on a ***pro rata basis***. The Bankruptcy Code acknowledges and will enforce contractual ***subordination agreements*** that have been entered into before bankruptcy.

This alters the priority between creditors, and is seen with bond issuances, for example, where certain bonds may be senior and others subordinated.

· ***The "Equityholders."***

Finally, and last in the pecking order, come the stockholders or ***equityholders*** in the business enterprise. Under bankruptcy law principles, securities fraud claims against the company[30] (based on purchases of equity securities), whether threatened or actually reduced to a judgment, are automatically subordinated to the claims of creditors, and are put in the same group as equityholders.[31] The policy reason is simple—stockholders come after creditors. It's what they bargained for. If they feel defrauded in the purchase of their stock, those damage claims shouldn't elevate them to a creditor level; they're still part of the equity level.

Unlike normal corporate governance outside of insolvency proceedings, (where the Board of Directors live to serve the interests of the stockholders), in a bankruptcy proceeding the interests of the stockholders are relegated to the last in the chain to receive any benefit in the case. This is known in bankruptcy parlance as the ***absolute priority rule***, discussed in Chapter Five. Accordingly, even though preferred shareholders are senior to common shareholders, in a Chapter 11 proceeding it frequently occurs that all stockholders in a company will be wiped out or tremendously diluted absent the consent of the parties higher up in the food chain.

· ***The "Off Balance Sheet" Creditors.***

The Bankruptcy Code's definition of ***"claim"*** is very broad—it is intended to be as widely encompassing as possible. In effect, whether a debt is currently due or not, contingent, unliquidated, or even presently unknown (such as potential remediation costs for environmental contamination or potential class action claims for toxic torts or personal injury—such as Dalkon Shield or asbestos poisoning), it will be considered a claim for bankruptcy purposes.[32] In addition, unexpired long-term real property leases (where the company is the tenant) or personal property leases (where the company is the lessee) are claims that, while off balance sheet, must be dealt with in a case. There are special provisions that deal with these types of claims, and they are described in Chapter Four.

The Reorganization Process

How best to describe the ***Reorganization Process***? It is, first and foremost, a process whereby mutually exclusive competing interests wrangle for leverage and benefit. The Bankruptcy Code and bankruptcy court bring (or at least attempt to bring) some order to the chaos.

· ***"It's A Mad, Mad, Mad, Mad World"—The Reorganization Process As Popular Entertainment.***

In 1963, Stanley Kramer directed a movie that serves as an excellent metaphor for U.S. bankruptcy dynamics.[33] This would surprise no one more than Mr. Kramer. *It's a Mad, Mad, Mad, Mad World* is not a deep movie. If you want intellectual stimulation, watch *Looking For Godard, My Dinner With Andre*, or any of the thirty-eight *Rocky* movies. It's also clearly not about bankruptcy—far from it. It is a slapstick chase comedy that featured perhaps the largest cast of comedians and entertainers in movie history—including Spencer Tracy, Milton Berle, Sid Caesar, Buddy Hackett, Mickey Rooney, Dick Shawn, Phil Silvers, Jonathan Winters, Ethel Merman, Jerry Lewis, Jimmy Durante, Don Knotts, Buster Keaton, Norman Fell, Peter Falk, Jack Benny, and the Three Stooges. The basic premise, however, does a surprisingly good job of depicting the dynamics of the competing creditor concerns in the reorganization process.

In the movie's opening scene, Jimmy Durante crashes his car off a twisting mountain highway in Southern California, and passers-by in four cars stop to render assistance. Before he figuratively (and literally) kicks the bucket, Durante informs Caesar, Berle, Hackett, Rooney, and Winters that a suitcase filled with $350,000 in cash is buried under a "Big W" in the fictive Santa Rosita State Park. An initial attempt to fashion an equitable division of the loot proves destructive and divisive.

In the following dialogue, imagine these characters playing typical roles in a corporate restructuring context: Sid Caesar is the attorney representing the debtor trying to build consensus to get to plan confirmation; Milton Berle is a powerless small creditor who's willing to agree to anything; Jonathan Winters is a relatively unsophisticated trade creditor who is convinced that everyone is going to take advantage of him; Ethel Merman is a litigation plaintiff creditor whose claims are questionable but who attempts to exert unwarranted control; and the rest are angry, disagreeable creditors looking out for only their own interests:

Caesar: So why don't we do something sensible. Why don't we just discuss this thing and then reason something out—

Berle: I'm with you; I'm with you.

Caesar: Fine! And we can come to some conclusion like intelligent people.

Rooney: Yeah, that way nobody will have an advantage on one another, right? It's fair.

* * *

Merman: Now, what's with this fair shares for everybody?

Caesar: Look, ma'am, all I said was, we arrived in four vehicles, I think we should split it up in four quarters.

Rooney: Quarters? What are you talking about, quarters? You three each get a quarter and [Hackett] and I have gotta split a quarter?

Berle: Yeah, that's right, he's gotta point.

Hackett: Hey, what are you trying to pull?

Caesar: It seems fair enough to me.
Rooney: Naturally it seems fair enough to *you.*
Hackett: It just cheats us, that's all! . . . There was five of us down at the wreck, we should split it five ways.
Berle: He's right, we should split it five ways.
Caesar: Well, I'm perfectly willing to discuss it in a five-way manner.
Merman: You're overlooking one little thing. . . . We can all count, can't we? There were eight of us there!
Berle: She's right.
Caesar: Well, speaking for my wife and myself, we'd be just as happy with—
Rooney: You'd be happy with two eighths instead of a quarter? That's awfully big of you.

* * *

Caesar: OK. We give shares to every body and for every thing. Now—there were eight of us, that's eight shares for that. Then there were four vehicles— we give four shares for that. That's twelve shares. Then there were five of us that went down to the wreck—now we give five shares for that. So that makes it seventeen. Now seventeen shares, and then we add the same number of shares as there were people in each vehicle. . . . That adds up to twenty-five shares. Now twenty-five into $350,000 is $14,000 per share. Now, that would mean you would get three shares for being three people, one share for having the car, one share for going down and looking at the wreck, and three more shares for being three more people in the car, which would give you a total of eight shares.

* * *

Winters: As I understand it, I got one share for being one person, one share for going down the hill, one share for the truck, and one share for being a person in the truck. But no matter how you figure it out, I still don't get as much as anybody else!

* * *

Caesar: I give up. Anybody got a better, fairer plan, go ahead.
Merman: There were eight of us there, so that simply means eight shares. Three for us, two for you—
Rooney: Ahh, this is hopeless. We're gonna get no place if we're going to continue listening to this old bag!
Hackett: Yeah, what are you trying to do, lady, split us up so it becomes every man for himself? . . . Look! We figured it seventeen different ways. And every time we figured it, it was no good, because no matter how we figured it, some body didn't like the way we figured it! So now, there's only

one way to figure it: and that is every man—including the old bag—for himself!

Rooney: So good luck, and may the best man win!

Hackett: Right! Except you, lady, may you just drop dead!

Having failed to negotiate a deal that everyone could accept, the once law-abiding citizens, their wives, nephews, and mother-in-laws in tow, embark on a rabid race south to Santa Rosita, each in the hope of being the first to recover the money. The trail of destruction and injury left in the race's wake is astounding: planes, automobiles, jeeps, tow trucks, and taxicabs are stolen, sunk in rivers, and crashed; a hardware store, an air traffic control tower, and a brand-new service station are exploded and torn to the ground; and the decades-long career of Santa Rosita Police Chief Spencer Tracy comes to an ignominious end. Nearly everyone involved in the chase—the original passers-by and a dozen other well-meaning (and not-so-well-meaning) folk that become embroiled in the mayhem along the way—winds up gravely injured in a hospital, and the $350,000 is literally scattered to the winds.

It is this kind of unrestrained scramble to recover limited assets that the U.S. bankruptcy system seeks to avoid. If all of a debtor's creditors, motivated by sheer self-interest (peppered with a dose of retributive animus toward the debtor), initiate a race to the debtor's limited pool of assets, each creditor will end up wasting substantial resources — its own, the debtor's, unrelated third parties,' courts,' lawyers' — in an effort to be the first one to the debtor's assets. What would undoubtedly be a terribly inefficient exercise in extreme economic wastefulness is prevented by the filing of a bankruptcy petition and the invocation of the automatic stay (a crucial element of any bankruptcy case that will be explained in Chapter Three).

The reorganization process is judicially supervised negotiation. It is intended to focus efforts and give all parties involved a fair opportunity to negotiate an equitable distribution of the debtor's limited assets. Hopefully, all creditors (as a group) benefit from this process— far more than if each had tried to fend for itself—and the debtor is ideally left standing at its conclusion, rather than lying dead on the side of the road. The reorganization process dynamics involve the management of expectations of diametrically opposed groups.

· ***What Exactly Is The Reorganization Process Designed To Accomplish?***

So what precisely is the reorganization process designed to accomplish? The process is designed to accomplish at least nine things. Those are, in no particular order of priority:

- ***Allow For A Cooling Of Tempers.*** The filing of a bankruptcy will halt all collection activities, and is intended to provide a "breathing spell" for the beleaguered business enterprise. This is largely a result of the ***automatic stay***. The process is designed to take enough time during which hopefully tempers will cool and allow for a consensual, rational economic solution.

- ***Allow The Debtor's Business A Chance To Stabilize.*** Because of the automatic cessation of all litigation outside of the bankruptcy court, the process is designed to allow businesses a chance to stabilize their operations free from the distractions of lawsuits all over the country.[34]
- ***Level The Playing Field.*** The reorganization process is intended to level the playing field by taking some of the leverage from the creditors and giving it to the debtor-in-possession. This is done by not only stopping all outside litigation, but also by giving the DIP the ability to challenge creditors' claims in a centralized forum, and in some circumstances avoid liens and recover payments that were made to certain creditors before the bankruptcy. This is accomplished by using the Bankruptcy Code's strong arm provisions discussed in Chapter Four.
- ***Allow For And Encourage Financial And Operational Introspection.*** Because of the checks and balances of the numerous players in the reorganization drama (discussed below), the reorganization process encourages introspection from the financial and operational perspective. Whether management likes it or not, that introspection will either be self-initiated or will be thrust upon it by the other players in the process (see the discussion on professionals, below, and the section entitled "*Life In A Fishbowl*" in Chapter Three).
- ***Allow Alliances To Form.*** Given that all of the players are now stuck with each other for at least a period of time, the process is designed to allow alliances to form and the negotiating process to begin in order to maximize the chance of a consensual economic deal between all the players. These alliances will form and may then shift during the course of the case. It is a truism in reorganization proceedings that today's ally is tomorrow's enemy, and *vice versa*. As such, it is best never to burn one's bridges in negotiating with different constituencies as those once bitter adversaries may become your best friends later in the case.
- ***Allow A Consensus To Build.*** As much as the parties may wish to rush a Chapter 11 proceeding along, and indeed, under certain circumstances it does happen very quickly, the process normally takes time. According to one study that was done a number of years ago, the average time a business enterprise is in Chapter 11 is approximately twenty-two months.[35] In any event, the mere time delay in the bankruptcy can and does lead to "creditor fatigue." This phenomenon results in creditors that are breathing fire at the outset of

the case after a year or so being willing to take less to get a deal done just to have it finished. A good example of this is the *Elder Beerman* Chapter 11 bankruptcy proceeding, which took over two years to ultimately get resolved. Positions that were taken at the outset of the case were greatly softened by plan confirmation.

- ***Assist With "Holdouts."*** The reorganization process is also designed to resolve disputes with "holdouts" in the creditor constituencies. This design is necessary because of the concept of class voting on treatment (which is discussed in Chapter Five), as well as old fashioned "peer pressure" from other similarly situated creditors. Notwithstanding that, some creditors are the proverbial thorn in the side of a business enterprise, and have to be dealt with through litigation within the bankruptcy process.
- ***Centralize Disputes.*** While the automatic stay mentioned earlier stops litigation outside of the bankruptcy context in most cases, sometimes litigation continues within the confines of the bankruptcy proceeding. As such, ugly litigation that may have been pending outside of bankruptcy involving lender liability, for example, may continue as part of the ***claims objection*** process in the bankruptcy. Under any set of circumstances, the reorganization process is intended to, at least initially, centralize the dispute resolution process so a debtor is not being dragged all over the country.
- ***Allow For Plan Formulation And Confirmation.*** Finally, the process is designed to allow for the ultimate resolution of the case—the formulation and approval or ***confirmation*** by the bankruptcy court of the ***plan of reorganization***. This is discussed in more detail in Chapter Five.

The Odds (How The Deck Is Stacked)

As should be apparent, corporate restructuring can be a very complex undertaking. Statistically speaking, approximately 17 percent of all Chapter 11 cases filed result in confirmed Chapter 11 plans of reorganization.[36] Of that 17 percent, 22 percent were subsequently converted to Chapter 7 liquidation cases due to, among other things, defaults under confirmed plans of reorganization.[37] Even among those successful Chapter 11 cases, the incidence of so-called "serial filings" is becoming more prevalent. This has resulted in what is known in bankruptcy slang as "Chapter 22s" (that is, successive Chapter 11 bankruptcy filings). Examples include *Jartran, Continental Airlines, Unison HealthCare, Lionel Companies, Herman's Sporting Goods, Shepherd Oil Corporation,* and others. *Braniff Airlines* has the distinction of being a "Chapter 44" with each successive reorganization proceeding having fewer and fewer assets to reorganize.[38]

The economic reality is that the larger the case, the better chance it has of ultimately getting reorganized—the "megacase phenomena." Large cases have their own dynamics, and ultimately (although not always—note the demise of *Eastern Airlines*), deals will get done primarily because all parties have too much to lose by a failed reorganization. Based on the statistics, however, the message is fairly straightforward. The odds of successfully emerging from a Chapter 11 reorganization proceeding are not particularly promising. That having been said, however, it is important to keep in mind that many of the failed reorganization proceedings involve companies with no viable ***core business*** or companies that are otherwise subject to market forces that are beyond the ability of the bankruptcy laws to remedy.

Remember that Chapter 11 is a means to an end, not an end unto itself. It can assist in implementing a business recovery plan, but is not, by itself, the recovery plan. This is important. Frequently distressed business executives will look to the Chapter 11 process to solve an economic or legal problem (multiple lawsuits and the like). Chapter 11 is a tool to solve the problem but not by itself the solution. As such, a hallmark of successful reorganization proceedings is the existence of a "proactive" (as opposed to a "reactive") reorganization strategy and some concept of a viable ***exit strategy***. This is discussed below. Without a viable exit strategy or core business, Chapter 11 can be only a prolonged and costly liquidation. Chapter 11 is not a miracle or panacea, and the national statistics bear this out. It is important that an executive not be oversold on what Chapter 11 can accomplish.

The Players And Their Roles

Not surprisingly, the reorganization process has its own cast of characters, each with their own part to play in the process. Since it's difficult to remember the players without a score card, the roster of the players (along with a brief description of their roles) is summarized below. Some of these players will be discussed in greater detail in later chapters, but a quick overview may be helpful. In the unforgettable words of Casey Stengel: "All right, everybody line up alphabetically according to your height."

· ***The DIP.***

Chapter 11 of the Bankruptcy Code presumes that the best management for a debtor is the management it already has. Unless creditors (or sometimes the U.S. Trustee) convinces the bankruptcy court that there exists some compelling reason why the debtor's management should not remain in control of the debtor during the Chapter 11 case, management stays on. Unlike a Chapter 7 proceeding, no ***trustee*** is appointed; the debtor (and its management) remains in possession and control of the debtor's assets and business operations to the same extent as before the bankruptcy (although it has some expanded powers and obligations discussed in Chapter Three). For this reason, the Bankruptcy Code—and bankruptcy professionals—refers to the typical Chapter 11 debtor as the debtor-in-possession or DIP.

The DIP is not a person, but rather generically refers to the debtor's management. As such, a company's officers and directors are all representatives of the DIP. The DIP continues to operate the business of the debtor throughout the course of the bankruptcy case. This is no small feat. In addition to meeting the normal demands of an ongoing business, the DIP (that is, its management) must dispatch its obligations to the bankruptcy court and the U.S. Trustee (not the trustee appointed in a Chapter 7, but a "watchdog" as explained below) including, among other things, creating and submitting extensive and detailed monthly operating reports **and** the DIP must work constantly to negotiate with creditor constituencies in an effort to build consensus and formulate the strategy for reorganization and emergence from bankruptcy (see discussion in Chapter Three on the Reorganization Inverted Bell Curve). The DIP gets much needed assistance in the exercise of its duties and in these negotiations from its professionals—attorneys, financial advisors—but the DIP's officers and directors invariably (and accurately) consider these concurrent responsibilities to be primarily theirs.

A DIP is guided in virtually all respects, and is protected by, the ***business judgment rule***. There is nothing unusual about this—the business judgment standard is the governing principle of business management both within and outside of bankruptcy. What is unusual is for whose benefit a DIP's business judgments are made. The primary distinction is that once a company is insolvent, its officers and directors owe a fiduciary duty to creditors as well as equityholders (discussed in Chapter Three). While the full extent of this duty is a matter for some debate, it remains an uncontroversial proposition that a DIP's business decisions in a Chapter 11 case are almost always judged from a perspective of what is best for the debtor's creditors. In fact, when an insolvent debtor's management is shown repeatedly to be placing the interests of shareholders ahead of the interests of creditors, the chances that a Chapter 11 trustee will be appointed to supplant the DIP increase greatly. To be sure, the constant checks and balances by other players in the reorganization process will usually ensure that a DIP's actions remain in line with its fiduciary duties.

· ***The Secured Creditor(s).***

Creditors who hold an interest (usually a lien, security interest, or mortgage under state law) in assets of the debtor to secure the debtor's repayment of its debt to that creditor is a secured creditor. Stated differently, a secured creditor has been given an interest in collateral backing up the money that the debtor owes to the creditor. In the business context, many different types of entities may hold secured debt—trade creditors, banks, insurance companies, bondholders (almost always in project financing contexts), or state or federal governmental agencies (in the case of taxes or industrial revenue bonds). Almost always, the debtor's working-capital lender is a secured creditor—in fact, the lender usually has a senior lien on virtually all the assets of the debtor in exchange for a revolving credit line to the debtor. As will be explored throughout this book, this gives the working-capital lender substantial leverage in the Chapter 11 case in the cash collateral process (discussed in Chapter Four). Other secured creditors may include term lenders (who may be junior to the working-capital lender), equipment lessors (who take a lien on the leased equipment to secure lease payments), real estate mortgagees (who typically have a lien only on the mortgaged real estate), and commercial lessors (who retain a security deposit against unpaid future rent). In addition, various state laws regarding real and personal property taxes, *ad valorem* taxes, or similar taxes give localities and other taxing authorities a statutory lien on certain of the taxpayer's assets to secure payment of the applicable taxes. Under certain state laws, these liens are automatically made senior to other liens already existing on the same property.

Security interests in a debtor's assets "pass through" bankruptcy unaffected—that is, under most circumstances, a debtor cannot vitiate a timely, properly ***perfected lien*** on its property in Chapter 11 unless it satisfies the debt to the creditor in full.[39] Doing so terminates the lien, but not because of the bankruptcy, but rather because the debtor has satisfied the debt in accordance with its terms under nonbankruptcy law. Not surprisingly, secured creditors wield significant power in Chapter 11 negotiations. Those creditors whose liens are expressly junior to other liens on the same assets under applicable nonbankruptcy law, however, often must be satisfied to allow the secured creditors senior to them to negotiate a fair treatment of all secured creditors. Nonetheless, as long as the creditor remains secured during the bankruptcy case (that is, its collateral retains some value—and this is not always true), then the secured creditor will have an opportunity to negotiate its own separate treatment under the plan of reorganization.

· ***The Official Unsecured Creditors Committee.***

The vast majority of creditors in any business context are unsecured—they do not have a specific lien interest in the debtor's property securing payment of their debts. This category of creditor includes the debtor's many trade vendors and suppliers, as well as the debtor's landlords (except to the extent of any security deposit), entities with litigation claims against the debtor, the debtor's employees, most taxing authorities (including the Internal Revenue Service), and parties to ***executory contracts***. In addition, many companies issue unsecured debt securities (call them notes, bonds, debentures—they're essentially the same), and the issuer's obligations to the holders of those debt securities can be unsecured debts.

Because unsecured creditors are generally treated equally in Chapter 11, regardless of the size or age of their respective claims, it is often impractical for any but the largest unsecured creditors to participate in negotiations with other creditor constituencies (such as secured creditors) and the debtor in the formulation of a plan. For this reason, the Bankruptcy

Code requires under most circumstances that the ***U.S. Trustee*** (see below) appoint a committee made up of (usually) the seven largest (in dollar amount of claim) unsecured creditors that will act in a fiduciary capacity for the benefit of all unsecured creditors, large and small. The number of creditors participating can and does vary. This ***Official Committee Of Unsecured Creditors*** (or ***"Creditors Committee"***) is "official" because it is a separately constituted entity, recognized by the bankruptcy court as having standing to be heard, and to sue and be sued, in the bankruptcy case representing the unsecured creditors as a group. Bankruptcy courts listen to Creditors Committees.

The Creditors Committee (and its members) owe a fiduciary duty to protect the interests of all unsecured creditors. The Creditors Committee is entitled to retain counsel and other professionals, much to the same extent as the debtor may, and under most circumstances, the fees and expenses of such professionals are paid out of the bankruptcy estate, not by the members of the Creditors Committee individually. The Creditors Committee's professionals at all times represent it in its fiduciary capacity and may not represent the specific interests of one particular creditor or smaller group of creditors.[40]

In light of the large creditor constituency it represents, the Official Committee Of Unsecured Creditors is a major participant in plan negotiations, along with the larger secured creditors and possibly other "***Ad Hoc Committees***" (see below). Though not unheard of, it is relatively rare that a debtor's plan of reorganization is negotiated, confirmed by the bankruptcy court, and implemented without the Creditors Committee having ultimately preapproved the plan, usually through the negotiation process described in Chapter Four.

· ***The Official Equityholders Committee.***

As stated above, the interests of equityholders such as holders of a debtor-corporation's stock take a back seat (from a legal perspective) to the interests of the debtor's creditors, particularly when the debtor is insolvent. Since both non-bankruptcy law and the Bankruptcy Code require that, absent consent, all creditors be paid in full before equityholders may take a distribution from a debtor's assets, the Chapter 11 case of an insolvent debtor is not a terribly hospitable environment for the debtor's shareholders. Because equityholders generally stand to receive almost nothing from the debtor's bankruptcy estate, they are rarely even given an influential seat at the negotiation table.

Only when the debtor's assets and business prospects after bankruptcy are adequate to begin considering the interests of equityholders do such holders begin to participate in a material way in the formulation of a reorganization plan. As a practical matter, and absent special circumstances, this happens only in a small fraction of all Chapter 11 cases.[41] If the debtor's prospects are particularly good, and the interests of equityholders are particularly relevant, the bankruptcy court may recognize another "official" committee to represent the interests of all equityholders—one comprised of the largest equityholders: the ***Official Committee Of Equityholders.*** Even where the equity is clearly out of the money, Equityholders Committees may still be appointed in large cases (such as occurred in the *Caldor* and *Megafoods* cases).[42] Like other official committees, the Equityholders Committee may retain professionals and be reimbursed from the debtor's estate for the reasonable fees and expenses incurred by such professionals.

· ***"Ad Hoc" Committees***

Because the debtor's bankruptcy ***estate*** (and therefore unsecured creditors) must reimburse Official Committees for their professionals' fees and expenses, bankruptcy courts are usually reluctant to appoint too many Official Committees. In fact, in most cases, only one—the Creditors Committee—is appointed. When the interests of certain sub-groups of creditors do not necessarily align with the interests of the larger group being represented by the Official Committee, members of that sub-group may form an "***Ad Hoc Committee***" to represent its interests in the Chapter 11 case and in negotiations with the debtor and other creditor groups. These committees are not appointed by the U.S. Trustee nor sanctioned by the bankruptcy court; their professionals' fees and expenses are not automatically reimbursed out of the bankruptcy estate. Ad Hoc Committees (also called ***"Unofficial Committees"***) may seek to have their professional fees paid from the estate at the end of the case under the "substantial contribution to the case" doctrine.[43] This requires a showing that the Ad Hoc Committee's professionals tangibly and specifically added value to the case (a more stringent standard than other Committee professionals).

Common examples of Ad Hoc Committees include committees comprised of: holders of notes or bonds (whose interests would be—and often are—represented by the Creditors Committee);[44] landlords (typically in cases where the debtor is a retailer or similar business with many leased locations); personal injury plaintiffs (often in cases where the debtor has had mass-tort or other class-action claims asserted against it, such as *Dow Corning*, the manufacturer of silicone breast implants and intrauterine devices); and secured creditors (in cases where the debtor has borrowed extensive amounts of working capital at different times from a consortium of participating lenders).

Ad Hoc Committees may exert substantial bargaining leverage throughout the Chapter 11 process in light of their "united front" approach. Nonetheless, there is nothing preventing a member of an Ad Hoc Committee from negotiating separately with the debtor, and debtors are often able to "divide and conquer" an Ad Hoc Committee in this fashion.

· ***Parties To "Executory Contracts And Unexpired Leases."***

Landlords, lessors of personal property (equipment, vehicles, and the like), and parties to license agreements with the debtors are treated differently (and in many respects more favorably) than other creditors. As is common in retail cases such as *Just For Feet* or *Macy's*, if the debtor is a lessee of real property, the lessors have the right to be paid for all postbankruptcy rents as an administrative claimant. The debtor must then decide, sometimes in a fairly short time period, whether it is going to ***assume*** or ***reject*** the ***executory contracts*** or ***unexpired leases***.[45] If the debtor wants the leased property or wants to continue receiving the benefits of the contract, it must take the lease or contract (called "assumption") in its entirety, and must "cure" any monetary defaults as part of that process.[46] "Cure" means pay, in full, all past due payments. If the debtor wishes to get out of the lease or contract (called "rejection"), it must surrender the leased property or all benefits of the contract to the lessor. The lessor or other party to the contract is still entitled to be paid for postbankruptcy accruals, and then has an unsecured claim for damages for the rejected lease or contract.[47] As such, Chapter 11 can be a powerful tool for a debtor/lessee to rid itself of a burdensome long-term contract or lease.[48] On the other hand, lessors have rights to get either back payments or their property back, usually quicker than other creditors in the case.

· ***The Examiner.***

Unless the bankruptcy court appoints a Chapter 11 trustee (see below), or often as a first step toward an ultimate appointment of a trustee, the bankruptcy court may appoint an ***examiner*** to conduct investigations into the debtor's financial affairs. Typically, an examiner will be an accounting or auditing firm. An examiner's investigation will usually cover any allegations of fraud, dishonesty, incompetence, or other gross mismanagement on the part of the debtor and its management. The bankruptcy court retains discretion over whether an examiner will be appointed and the scope of the examiner's duties, considering the interests of creditor, equity security holders, and other parties in interest, but **must** appoint an examiner if the debtor's undisputed, liquidated unsecured debts (other than for goods, services, taxes, or unsecured debts to an ***insider***) exceed $5 million.[49] In practice, examiners are most often appointed when a debtor's transactions with its insiders (directors, officers, majority shareholders, etc.) are extensive and suspect. When a debtor has been the subject of a ***leveraged buyout*** (***"LBO"***), an examiner may be appointed to investigate the myriad management decisions made in the negotiation and implementation of the LBO.[50]

If the examiner uncovers tangible evidence of fraud, incompetence, or mismanagement by the debtor's current management, the bankruptcy court may appoint a Chapter 11 trustee, thereby terminating the DIP.[51] Considering that the bankruptcy estate pays the fees and expenses of the examiner (and any professional the examiner retains), creditors and the bankruptcy court often take a pointed interest in the results of the examiner's investigation.

· ***The Trustee.***

As stated above, if the bankruptcy court is presented with evidence that the debtor's current management has engaged or is engaging in fraud, dishonesty, gross incompetence, or gross mismanagement, the court will direct the U.S. Trustee to appoint a Chapter 11 trustee to take possession of the debtor's assets and business operations. The trustee must be a ***"disinterested" person*** without any personal stake in the bankruptcy case, precisely in the same way that professionals for the debtor and official committees must also be "disinterested."

Creditors may request that the U.S. Trustee conduct an election of the Chapter 11 trustee, and usually unsecured creditors (the group with the most to lose in most cases) take the lead in demanding, and voting in, such an election. The bankruptcy court will usually weigh carefully the costs and benefits of appointing a trustee to the creditors and the bankruptcy estate, both because the trustee's fees and expenses are paid out of the estate and because the removal of current management may have a devastating effect on the ability of the debtor's business to continue operating. The party seeking to displace the DIP bears a heavy burden, as the Bankruptcy Code has a presumption that the DIP will remain in control of the case. For these reasons, the appointment of a Chapter 11 trustee is not commonplace and is much more the exception than the rule for most reorganization cases.

· ***The U.S. Trustee.***

The U.S. Department of Justice maintains a branch of officials that monitor bankruptcy cases throughout the country and assist bankruptcy courts in the administration of cases—these officials are the ***U.S. Trustees***. Unlike a Chapter 11 or Chapter 7 trustee, U.S. Trustees are not compensated from the estate, at least not directly. A large portion of the U.S. Trustee's budget is provided by congressional funding of the Department of Justice. The remainder is made up of quarterly fees charged, under most circumstances, to Chapter 11 debtors during the course of a Chapter 11 case.[52] While the U.S. Trustees are empowered to be heard with respect to virtually any aspect of a case, practically speaking, the U.S. Trustees (or their deputies—usually bankruptcy lawyers) do most of their work at the beginning of a Chapter 11 case, scrutinizing a debtor's proposed ***First Day Orders*** (discussed in Chapter Four), retention of professionals, monitoring the preparation of a debtor's ***Statements and Schedules***, and appointing Official Committees. The U.S. Trustee will also evaluate professionals' applications for payment of fees and expenses and analyze a debtor's ***Operating Reports*** (discussed in Chapter Three), which the debtor must submit monthly. It is unusual for the U.S. Trustee to participate in any significant respect in the negotiation of a plan of reorganization, although in some jurisdictions it does occur.

· ***The Bankruptcy Court.***

Bankruptcy courts have been around since the beginnings of federal bankruptcy law. The U.S. Bankruptcy Court is a division of the U.S. District Court, which is the trial-level court of original federal jurisdiction. Because the U.S. Constitution provides that Congress has the exclusive right to make bankruptcy law (depriving states of any ability to do so), all bankruptcy cases in the United States are administered in the U.S. Bankruptcy Court. Each U.S. District Court has a corresponding Bankruptcy Court, which means that each state has at least one bankruptcy court. Populous states have several, since those states have more than one federal judicial district (and, therefore, more than one U.S. District Court). There are currently ninety-four districts (with corresponding bankruptcy courts) in the United States. For example, Arizona has only one federal judicial district (the District of Arizona), which covers the entire state. New York, by contrast, has four federal judicial districts, so there are U.S. District Courts (and, therefore, U.S. Bankruptcy Courts) based in Manhattan (the Southern District of New York), Brooklyn, Queens, and Long Island (the Eastern District of New York), Albany and Rochester (the Northern District of New York), and Syracuse and Buffalo (the Western District of New York). Small districts typically have one to three bankruptcy judges, often sitting in different cities, whereas more populous districts (like the Central District of California) have fifteen or more.

The bankruptcy court is the trial-level court for all bankruptcy cases. Bankruptcy judges, unlike most other federal court trial judges, are not appointed for life, but rather sit for fourteen-year terms, subject to reappointment at the end of the term. Because a bankruptcy judge has extensive control over the results of a bankruptcy case—virtually no aspect of a bankruptcy case ever involves a jury—and because bankruptcy judges vary widely in their proclivities, preferences, politics, and perspectives, troubled companies (with the help of experienced bankruptcy lawyers) often expend significant time and energy into efforts to obtain (or avoid) a particular judge in a particular district. These efforts at "judge shopping" within a jurisdiction are usually minimally effective since most bankruptcy courts have instituted a random judge assignment system for each new bankruptcy case filed.[53] However, companies do have some discretion as to the jurisdiction in which they can file their Chapter 11 (see discussion on *The Venue Game* in Chapter Four). The more "business friendly" the jurisdiction, the more effort will be made to file there. For example, Wilmington, Delaware, has been called the "Chapter 11 capital of the country" because of the business sophistication of its bankruptcy judges, although this is changing.

· ***The District Court And Appellate Courts.***

The U.S. Bankruptcy Court is not only a division of the U.S. District

Courts, but also a lower court for purposes of bankruptcy appeals. When a party to a bankruptcy court decision wishes to appeal that decision, the appeal is generally heard in the first instance in the corresponding district's U.S. District Court. If the District Court's decision is appealed, the corresponding U.S. Circuit Court of Appeals will hear the appeal. There are thirteen judicial circuits in the United States, each with a Court of Appeals, encompassing a group of federal judicial districts in a large geographical area. For example, the Ninth Circuit, whose Court of Appeals sits in San Francisco, takes appeals from the District of Arizona, the District of Nevada, the District of Idaho, the District of Oregon, the District of Washington, the District of Alaska, the District of Hawaii, and the Southern, Central, and Northern Districts of California.

Certain federal circuits also have Bankruptcy Appellate Panels, or "***BAPs,***" that are intended to replace the U.S. District Court as the first step in the appeals process from the bankruptcy court. Regardless of whether an appeal is first heard in the District Court or in the BAP, the next step, before the U.S. Supreme Court, is the U.S. Court of Appeals.

Finally, if further review beyond the Court of Appeals is desired, parties may seek a review (called a "writ of certiorari") in the U.S. Supreme Court, which may decide in its discretion whether to hear the matter or not. Each year, the Supreme Court agrees to hear (or "grants cert" in) only a handful of bankruptcy-related appeals. Unfortunately, the Supreme Court in recent years has failed to resolve important issues most relevant to corporate reorganizations and has instead focused on more finite issues pertaining largely to individual bankruptcies. Companies in bankruptcy never want to be in front of the Supreme Court. Other than a great trip to Washington, D.C., a chance to make law that students will dissect in law review articles, and a tour of a lovely historic building, the cost and delay of such an escapade is not worth the trip.

· ***The "Interlopers."***

Cynical bankruptcy lawyers—like the authors—will tell you that two things are true of certain federal agencies (such as the Internal Revenue Service, the Pension Benefit Guaranty Corporation, the Securities and Exchange Commission, and the Environmental Protection Agency) when it comes to bankruptcy cases: (1) when the debtor and other parties do not want the agencies to inject themselves into the process, they always do (usually with poor results); and (2) when the debtor or other parties want a particular agency to step in and take a position in a bankruptcy dispute, the agency seems to vanish without a trace. This behavior has nothing to do with the fact that these agencies usually do not have a direct financial stake in the bankruptcy proceedings. When they do—the IRS often has some sort of claim for back taxes—they are usually happy to sit back and allow their claim to be treated as the debtor suggests.

The SEC is a good example of this phenomenon. Unless there are serious allegations of securities fraud, the SEC has no direct interest in a bankruptcy case. Nonetheless, a relic from the old Bankruptcy Act survived Congress's enactment of the current Bankruptcy Code and debtors are still required to furnish the SEC with a copy of the ***disclosure statement*** describing the terms of a plan of reorganization. This gives the SEC an opportunity to nitpick the plan all it likes, except when the parties (and often the bankruptcy court) actually want the SEC to "bless" certain unusual securities provisions in the plan, at which time the SEC will likely refuse to take a position on anything. If it sounds frustrating, it is—and you will be able to appreciate your bankruptcy lawyer's furrowed brow when you tell him or her that the EPA just called.

· ***The Professional Team.***

It is a harsh reality that reorganization is professional-intensive, and a distressed company must accept this. Not surprisingly, bankruptcy reorganization is a specialty in the legal profession, and choosing good counsel (who will generally know the other bankruptcy professionals involved in the case, as well as the bankruptcy judges) is an important part of the reorganization process. The terms of retention of all professionals is ultimately subject to scrutiny and approval of the bankruptcy court, as are the professionals' fees at the conclusion of the case. Depending on the type of case involved, some or all of the professionals listed below may be necessary:

- ***Lawyers (And More Lawyers).*** Obviously, bankruptcy counsel will be needed. In addition, one or more "special counsel" may be needed, depending on the case. For example, special corporate counsel may be needed (for circumstances where a company's corporate or general counsel cannot act as reorganization counsel because of conflicts or lack of reorganization expertise),[54] as well as other "specialists," such as trademark, patent, or intellectual property lawyers, lawyers skilled in representation of clients before certain administrative agencies (such as the FAA, FCC, FTC, SEC or other alphabet-soup regulatory bodies), or special litigation counsel to continue with pending litigation (see the discussion in Chapter Three on who, exactly, the lawyer represents in a case).
- ***"Ordinary Course" Professionals.*** In addition, certain so-called ***"ordinary course" professionals*** may be needed. For example, if a company has numerous routine collection, employment, state regulatory, or personal injury matters in many jurisdictions, retention of local firms to assist in those jurisdictions may be (and usually is) cost effective.
- ***A Word About Conflicts.*** Attorneys can only represent a company if they have no legal conflicts of interest (which is known in bankruptcy parlance as being "***disinterested***").[55] While this is true out-

side of bankruptcy as well, in bankruptcy cases it takes on added significance because the attorney is a fiduciary of the bankruptcy estate. An integral part of getting approved to be bankruptcy counsel is the full disclosure by the lawyers (and their law firm) of all connections with creditors in the case.[56] The attorneys must disclose any prior or current connections with creditors or the debtors (or their principals). The attorneys must disclose what arrangements have been made for payment of fees, and any guarantees or other third-party arrangements on fees. The idea is that the attorneys have a duty of full and complete disclosure.

In large commercial cases, the connections between a large law firm and the many creditors and other parties can be both myriad and intertwined. A law firm with twenty offices may represent a creditor in other cases, or have a connection with financial advisors that are working with other (and potentially adverse) constituencies. The ethical rules of the legal profession are antiquated, and were promulgated during much simpler times when conflicts were more apparent. For example, it's obvious a lawyer can't represent both the plaintiff and defendant in the same lawsuit. Large restructurings tend to be more complex and involved. Parties are "adverse" to each other legally, but often not practically.

So why does a business executive care? Why isn't this just a lawyers' problem? Two reasons. First, a law firm that a company wishes to use (because of special expertise or other reasons) may have potential conflicts that may present problems. Second, if conflicts arise later in the case (after the full extent of creditors are known), they can lead to disqualification battles and other (very expensive) problems.[57] These are obviously disruptive in an already difficult set of circumstances. Much like how one wouldn't want a surgeon with marital strife weighing on her mind performing a delicate surgery, having otherwise preoccupied professionals is problematic in the reorganization process. Conflict issues should be discussed at the outset of a case.

- ***Valuation Experts.*** These can be appraisers, accountants, or other similar professionals, depending on the type of business or assets involved. Ultimately, the following types of values may be needed in Chapter 11 cases:
    - ***"Liquidation Value"*** of the assets of the debtor for purposes of the ***"best interests of creditors test"*** (which requires that in a Chapter 11, creditors must receive at least what they would get in a Chapter 7 liquidation).[58]
    - ***"Going Concern Or Enterprise Value"*** for the debtor as a whole for purposes of "cramdown" (discussed in Chapter Five). This is

usually done on a discounted cash flow ("DCF") basis or as a multiplier of ***EBITDA***, depending on the industry. Securities to be distributed under the plan may also need to be valued for this.[59]

- ***Special Purpose Values.*** Specific asset values for purposes of determining ***"allowed secured claims"*** of secured creditors. This provides that secured creditors have a secured claim up to the value of their collateral, and an unsecured claim for the deficiency. These valuations should be based on the proposed use or disposition of the asset.[60]
- ***Tax Purpose Valuations.*** Finally, valuations may be needed related to specific tax issues that arise in bankruptcy cases, such as cancellation of debt income (called "***COD Income***") and fresh start accounting (the concept that the debtor is considered a new taxing entity from the date the bankruptcy petition is filed forward).

- ***Accountants/Financial Advisors/Investment Bankers/Consultants.*** In many cases, having the services of good financial advisors, investment bankers, or consultants is critical, especially in more specialized industries (such as hospitality, airline, health care, casino, manufacturing, and retail). There are investment banking firms and financial advisory firms that specialize in the reorganization area (such as Houlihan, Lokey, Howard & Zukin, Gordian Group, Wasserstein Dresclner Kleinwort, Lazard Freres, Blackstone Group, Jeffries & Co., Chanin and CIBC).[61] Many of the large accounting firms also have this capability.[62] A competent, and well-connected financial advisor can frequently do more in one phone call to contacts in the financial and investment community than the debtor or its counsel can do in a month (such as in locating potential exit financing sources or buyers).
  - ***Clear Compensation Arrangements.*** It is necessary to be sure the compensation arrangements are agreed to and fully understood in advance. Many financial advisory firms will require a set monthly fee (usually in the range of $50,000 to $150,000 a month, depending on the case), as well as a success or reorganization fee, plus fees for refinancing or M&A work. Ultimately the bankruptcy court must approve any such fee arrangements.
- ***Accountants.*** Accountants will not only be involved as a result of having been the company's auditors, but also because they may be needed for certain "forensic" issues (such as avoidance actions, fraud analysis, and other investigations). Accountants also market a broad array of other services today, from computer consulting and employee compensation expertise, to crisis and management consulting.

- ***Public Relations Specialists.*** An often overlooked, but essential, member of the team is a "PR" firm. There are firms that specialize in "restructuring and crisis public relations," and these professionals are invaluable in industries where employee morale and public perception and confidence are critical to revenues (such as hospitality and transportation industry cases). One of the more experienced and high profile of such specialists is Michael S. Sitrick of Sitrick & Company in Los Angeles, one of the pioneers in the field.[63] In addition, having a well-defined communications strategy for reassuring employees, customers, crucial suppliers, and others critical to the continued viability of the debtor is essential. The importance of public relations professionals has been recognized by some insurance companies, such as National Union First Insurance Company, which is now offering coverage to corporate executives to combat bad publicity arising from crisis-based corporate events.[64]
  - ***The "Spin Doctors."*** While some companies have this ability in-house, few in-house public relations executives have the experience or knowledge to know what not to say, let alone what to say, in a restructuring or reorganization. The communications and public relations required are very different in these situations—even compared with other crises. A good public relations specialist will develop and implement an information campaign to assuage concerns of employees, key vendors, and customers. The specialist can become a central spokesperson to avoid conflicting public announcements. In restructurings—whether in or out of court, it is essential that whatever plan or statement is developed, it be done in close coordination with management and legal counsel, regardless of the form (whether it be press releases, "faxes on demand," employee handouts, or other methods.) The Internet is also fast becoming a prevalent means to disseminate information (and misinformation) to the public. Large Chapter 11 cases such as *Boston Chicken, Mercury Finance,* and the *Baptist Foundation of Arizona* used Web sites to disseminate information.[65] Once the initial shock of the filing wears off, the public relations specialist's role should move from active (on a daily basis) to maintenance or normalized and will probably diminish in intensity, until favorable press is needed as part of the *Confirmation Process* discussed in Chapter Five.
  - ***The Importance Of The Media.*** While all communications are important, few if any have the impact of those that appear in the media. For that reason, it is essential that a company have someone who is experienced and skilled at dealing with the press. Today, nearly everything a company does is scrutinized by the media. SEC filings are reported on such wire services as Bloomberg and

Dow Jones Newswire. The next thing you know, you open the morning paper and read that your company's bondholders agree to the terms of the restructuring plan offered by your advisors. According to documents your company filed with the SEC, your company has stated that it will have no choice but to file for protection under Chapter 11 of the Bankruptcy Code. That morning you come in and you have two dozen messages from vendors and nearly twice as many from customers. Like every other discipline in a restructuring, public relations professionals should be specialists.

- ***Third-Party Turnaround Assistants.*** And now for the "delicate" part. As difficult as this may be in some cases, management of the distressed company needs to understand and appreciate the necessity for realistic, objective, and honest assessment of the cause of the financial problems for the company, and have the commitment to do what is necessary to remedy those problems. At the outset of the reorganization process, the disheartened creditors will generally be looking to pin the blame of the financial distress on someone. That someone is generally some or all of management. To the extent that management is new to the company, obviously that stigma will either not attach or attach to a much lesser degree. In any event, the company might find itself in a position where certain creditor constituencies (or perhaps Committees or even secured lenders) are pushing it to retain a third-party independent "turnaround manager" or "turnaround financial advisor."
  - ***Objectivity Is The Key To Credibility.*** In order for the distressed company's management to have credibility with its creditor constituencies, it must recognize that credibility is tied to its objectivity. The company must ask itself whether its management is too closely tied (either emotionally or otherwise) to the financial circumstances to conduct a frank and candid assessment of the financial situation. If not, the concept of an outside financial turnaround advisor (while not displacing current management, but acting as a resource for that management) may be advisable. Of course, to the extent that management is too closely tied to the circumstances to view things objectively, it is unlikely that management will consent to such outside assistance.
  - ***Overcoming "Malaise" Or "Analysis Paralysis."*** At times in a financially troubled company, management is struck with a malaise (or "analysis paralysis") that hinders it in coming to realistic decisions. This is generally evidenced by a number of "Band-Aid" type, short-term solutions that only defer inevitable harder decisions. As such, one of the advantages of a professional turnaround manager is objectivity and lack of emotional baggage

that may cloud the judgment of existing management (some or all of whom may feel defensive or otherwise to blame for the economic problems of the company). There are numerous professional "turnaround managers," such as Jay Alix & Associates (which was brought in to manage *Maidenform Worldwide, Inc.*; one of the principals of Jay Alix, Ted Stenger, actually took over as president of that company); Buccino & Associates, Development Specialists, Inc. (William A. Brandt); Alex D. Moglia & Associates; Nightingale & Associates (which oversaw the liquidation of *McCulloch Corp.*); and Alvarez & Associates. In addition, the larger accounting firms often have business turnaround expertise in-house. The one thing that will become very clear to management in the reorganization process is that there is never a shortage of criticism or second guessing.[66]

- ***Meeting The Creditors Half Way.*** Sometimes in an effort to spare the bankruptcy estate the expense of yet another professional such as a turnaround manager, distressed companies introduce certain "half-way" measures that sometimes assuage creditor concerns about management's capabilities. For example, there are times when a company can (and frankly should) agree to allow a Creditors Committee in cases with significant unsecured debt to have nominees to be considered for positions on the Board of Directors of the distressed company.[67] Other half-way measures that have been utilized in cases involved bringing in a "restructuring officer" as part of the management team (allowing management to concentrate more on business—this was done in the *Macy's* reorganization), requiring management to give detailed reports to the financial advisors for the other constituencies (usually done under appropriate ***confidentiality agreements*** discussed in Chapter Three), and preparing prospective budgets and short-term business plans. This gives the creditor constituencies some ability to both monitor and have input into operational decisions over the short term. The extent to which outside assistance is brought in to a distressed company situation is generally a function of how entrenched management is and how closely they are identified with the financial difficulties of the distressed business enterprise.

· ***Auctioneers.*** Finally, if sales of major assets are in the company's future, there are well-established industrial auctioneers that can be very helpful in marketing and conducting the sales program (Keene Realty, Gordon Bros., Norman Levy Associates, Michael Fox International, and others are well known).[68] Sometimes they buy the assets outright and auction them (keeping any upside) or buy them and allow the company a share in sales proceeds over certain thresholds.

· ***A Word About Retainers.*** While this will come as no surprise to anyone who has ever hired a lawyer, accountant, or other professional, they're expensive. In distressed situations, aside from the usual cash crunches, professionals in bankruptcy cases want to be sure (not surprisingly) that they will be paid for their services.[69] While there are ways to give them comfort once the case is filed (see the discussion in Chapter Four on *Professional Fee Carveouts* in the section on *Cash Collateral*), most professionals will want some retainer as a cushion prior to undertaking representation. The amount of that retainer will be a function of the company's available cash and the professionals' degree of comfort that there are sufficient cash flows to pay fees (either as a result of unencumbered cash or because secured lenders will agree to the use of some of their cash collateral for payment of fees). Once a retainer amount is agreed on, how it is paid is very important. In order for a professional to be protected, the retainer must be paid either by wire transfer of immediately available funds or by cashier's check.[70] The reason for this is not because the professional is concerned your check is no good (as long as the company has a major credit card and two forms of ID), but because legally the payment of the retainer is not considered made until the bank has honored the check, which may not occur until after the petition has been filed. As such, a cashier's check or wire transfer is needed because they constitute immediate withdrawal of funds from the debtor's bank account.[71]

The "Proactive" Versus "Reactive" Reorganization Cases—The Need For A Viable Exit Strategy

A critical difference between the 17 percent "successful" reorganizations[72] and the 83 percent that die on the vine is the formulation of a well-defined "exit strategy"—what exactly does the company want from the reorganization, and how, from a business perspective, does the company plan to achieve it? All too often the company has only one desire from a bankruptcy filing: stop a pending foreclosure or other action by a creditor or group of creditors. This myopic analysis will result in the quintessential "reactive" reorganization. The unplanned, crisis bankruptcy filing is sometimes referred to as a ***"flat puppy filing"***[73] or a ***"free fall" bankruptcy***. It analogizes the crisis filing (and its odds of being a successful bankruptcy) to a young child whose puppy has just been run over by a truck. The child brings the mangled animal to his or her parents and says: "Here—fix it."

As one group of commentators has observed:

> In *The Art of War*, Sun Tzu observed that all battles are won before they are fought because of proper planning. This same philosophy also applies to a Chapter 11 filing. Prebankruptcy planning for the commercial Chapter 11 reorganization can be broken down conceptually into four distinct (although interrelated) categories which are set forth in no particular order of priority: (i) preparation of management, key employees and exit strategy; (ii) business preparation; (iii) legal preparation;

and (iv) tax preparation.[74]

Even if management is not focused on the exit strategy, good bankruptcy professionals will try to focus attention on this aspect of planning. As set forth earlier, sophisticated creditors and Creditors Committees will frequently want to know early on just what the company's "plan" is, and will want input into it as it is refined. Indeed, some of these constituencies will push an indecisive debtor.

Notwithstanding the foregoing, reorganization exit strategies can and do change over the course of the case. For example, in the *Megafoods Stores* bankruptcy filed in the District of Arizona in 1995, the initial exit strategy was an equity infusion for working capital and conversion of substantial debt to equity. Two years into the case an asset sale to a competitor was deemed the more feasible exit strategy. Likewise, *Just For Feet, Inc.'s* Chapter 11 filed in Delaware in 1999 started as a recapitalization and ended up a sale. In both events, there were exit strategies being pursued.

· ***The Three Phases Of An Exit Strategy—"Identification," "Action" Items," And "Implementation."***

While the last thing an executive needs or wants is some lawyer giving business advice, from a reorganization perspective an "exit strategy" has three components: (1) "problem identification"; (2) the "action items"; and (3) "implementation."

· ***Phase 1: Identification Of The Business Problem.***

While perhaps a matter of common sense, the first on the list is the "problem identification." **Simply stated, the "problem identification" component asks the question: from a business perspective what does the company need to accomplish to return to financial stability?** Is the company experiencing an aberrational slump, and can it handle all of its existing debt if it can have a moratorium for a period of time? Is the company too highly leveraged with non-operational debt (such as bonds or LBO acquisition debt) such that all existing EBITDA is being used to service debt, with no working capital for expansion or acquisition? Does the company have substantial long-term assets tied up in an unprofitable product line that it can't walk away from without significant liability (manufacturing facilities, capital equipment leases, and the like)?[75]

The biggest challenge in this first stage is objectivity and realistic evaluation. It is important to stress again that lack of objectivity by management will lead to loss of credibility by the other players in the process, and others in the process will be very vocal in pointing out real or perceived analytical shortcomings of management.

It is also important not to "cut to the chase"—that is, go right to implementation (using the Bankruptcy Code, discussed below) without fully identifying the business problems. **A bankruptcy filing should implement**

an exit strategy, not BE the exit strategy.

- ***Is There A Viable Core Business?***

  A critical analysis in the identification phase of an exit-strategy formulation for the non-liquidation Chapter 11 case is whether the core business is viable. What is the company's net operating income ***(EBITDA)*** available to pay debt service? Is there a realistic, identifiable, and fixable cause for the company's economic condition (such as research and development retarded by the need to make debt service, temporary industry-wide slump, a change in laws, such as the changes to Medicare reimbursement policies wrought by the Balanced Budget Act of 1997, or excessive general and administrative expenses)? If the core business is poor or suspect, a controlled liquidation may be the best exit strategy available.

- ***Phase 2: The Exit Strategy Action Items.***

Once the problem is identified and a desired result agreed upon, what are the action items needed to achieve those results? Exit strategies for distressed companies come in all variations. Experienced management (sometimes with the help of outside professionals and with proactive Committees, usually with much input—both solicited and unsolicited—from financial advisors) can usually identify the business action items needed to correct the problem. These items include the following:

- "Downsizing" the company by discontinuing unprofitable product lines, closing plants or stores, reductions in labor force or selling assets or divisions that will not be a necessary part of the reorganized company;
- Increasing operating cash flows through realistic and achievable programs (such as increased sales/reduced expenses, redefinition of market/product strategies or priorities);
- Reducing unsecured or secured debt load (such as in real estate cases or cases of overleveraged companies resulting from an LBO);
- Infusing working capital and/or equity from existing equityholders or from third-party investors (which may include public offerings, although this is unusual and invariably impractical);
- Identifying strategic merger candidates for the troubled company; and/or
- Orderly liquidation.

- ***Phase 3: Using The Bankruptcy Code To Implement The Exit Strategy.***

Once the debtor has a viable exit strategy, the company and its professional should explore how the Bankruptcy Code can assist in the implementation of the exit strategy. The Bankruptcy Code is a potpourri of interesting tools, such as ***asset sales free and clear of liens, cramdown*** (the confirmation of a plan over the objection of certain creditors as discussed in Chapter Five), ***super priority financing, rejection of contracts and leases*** that are undesirable, issuance of securities in a plan without need for registration under federal or state laws, or avoidance of state ***transfer taxes***.

· ***The Importance Of Flexibility.***

While the early identification of a potential exit strategy has considerable merits, the executive should maintain flexibility as the restructuring progresses to evaluate alternative exit strategies based upon the ever-changing circumstances. In other words, pick your horse early and ride it until you find a more attractive horse.

The Ultimate In Proactive Bankruptcies—
The "Prepackaged Bankruptcy"

Perhaps the quintessential proactive bankruptcy is the so-called ***"Prepackaged Bankruptcy."*** The term Prepackaged Bankruptcy is used somewhat loosely. What is referred to as a Prepackaged Bankruptcy runs the gamut from a Chapter 11 bankruptcy that is filed only a few days before the filing of a plan and Disclosure Statement (even if there has been little negotiation with creditors regarding the plan), to the "prearranged" restructuring, where a debtor will negotiate with one or more major constituencies out of court, but the actual solicitation process (discussed in Chapter Five) occurs in court.[76] Examples of this include *Payless Cashways, Hvide Marine, Unison HealthCare, Kroy Inc.,* and *Stuart Entertainment*. On the other end of the spectrum, there have been scores of Prepackaged Bankruptcies (such as *Southland Corporation*, the parent company for 7-Eleven Convenience Stores, and *LePercq/DBL Biltmore Associates Limited Partnership*, the public syndication that owned the five-star Arizona Biltmore Resort) where the plan of reorganization was fully negotiated and creditors had actually voted on it before the bankruptcy was ever filed. This is the true Prepackaged Bankruptcy, and is the most common restructuring technique for overleveraged junk bond deals—the "good company, bad capital structure" type of companies. Other examples include the *Penn Traffic, Planet Hollywood,* and *JPS Textiles* (both the first and second filings).[77]

The concept of a Prepackaged Bankruptcy has received quite a bit of press.[78] In essence, a Prepackaged Bankruptcy generally involves a very proactive debtor with a well-defined business plan and exit strategy. The commentators and practitioners that have been involved in, and studied, successful prepackaged reorganization cases have identified six essential ingredients to a successful attempt at a Prepackaged Bankruptcy:

First, foresight of the debtor to realistically assess the magnitude of its financial problems.

Second, willingness and ability to incur professional fees necessary to implement the prepackaged strategy.

Third, formulation of a viable exit strategy and a going-forward business plan.

Fourth, a concentrated creditor group (or groups) willing to negotiate the prepackaged plan and that finds the business plan and exit strategy (that is, the new capital structure) acceptable.

Fifth, an ability by the debtor to raise new equity capital.

Sixth, a consensus among large creditor constituencies to keep "unsolicitable" constituencies (such as trade creditors, which may be widely dispersed and unsophisticated) unimpaired.[79]

The information set out in this book is applicable to Prepackaged Bankruptcies because the players involved in that process understand that failure to reach consensus prior to a filing of a bankruptcy will lead to a less consensual Chapter 11 case (with all the strong and weak leverage points as discussed in this book).

While the speed with which Prepackaged Bankruptcies make their way through the process can be impressive, it is very important to remember that most of the hard work (and expenditure of fees) occurred prior to the bankruptcy being filed. As such, Prepackaged Bankruptcies should not necessarily be considered a cost-savings device because the professional fees may well be the same (less the postbankruptcy litigation expenses of a contested Chapter 11). Perhaps the major financial incentive in a Prepackaged Bankruptcy is that the fees spent tend to be more focused and the company can stay in control a little more.[80]

In addition, attempting to embark on a Prepackaged Bankruptcy strategy is not without some risk. It does require the company to have cash to pay necessary professional fees. Also, the negotiation of a Prepackaged Bankruptcy plan has a way of telegraphing to the business community the company's financial problems (to the extent they are not already widely known). In addition, by taking the time outside of bankruptcy to negotiate a plan, the company is providing recalcitrant or aggressive creditors an opportunity to take collection efforts in anticipation of a bankruptcy filing, or stop providing customary trade credit (thereby forcing a company to file Chapter 11). Nonetheless, there have been many Prepackaged and Prearranged Bankruptcies that have assisted companies in expediting emergence from Chapter 11.[81]

Now having completed a high level view of the reorganization process, it's time to explore the new realities of the corporate restructuring dynamic.

CHAPTER THREE

THE NEW REALITIES

"While the economic storm continues the proper tactics for possessors of capital are those of flight and self-defense. It is a cautionary experience; there are many casualties, cruel transfers of individual fortunes."

Matthew Josephson
Robber Barons: The Great American Capitalists
(1934)

Now that you have an overview of the reorganization process, but before we delve into *Surviving To Plan Confirmation* (Chapter Four) and *The Plan Of Reorganization* (Chapter Five), let's take some time to get mentally prepared for what lies ahead. This chapter will deal with the new realities of the restructuring process and dynamic.

Making The Transitions—Attitudinal Adjustments

In an executive's business life cycle, there are many transitions that have to be made to remain successful. One major transition, for example, is from a privately held company executive to a public company executive. The business-world scrap heap is littered with the carcasses of officers and directors who continued to act as if they owned the company after it went public. The first annual meeting in such circumstances can be an ugly event.

While many executives may never face this next transition, an equally important transition is going from an executive of a financially healthy company to a debtor-in-possession. There are new constituencies to whom duties of loyalty are owed, and potentially disastrous results that can come from failing to recognize these duties. The transition requires, first and foremost, an attitudinal adjustment. "It's my business judgment, dammit!" is a powerful (and legally correct) retort to questions regarding business decisions outside of bankruptcy; but in reorganization proceedings it's only one of many factors that are considered.

This chapter will attempt to help the executive mentally prepare for the task ahead, and to pave the way for the attitudinal adjustments that can help calm some potentially choppy waters.

The Reorganization Inverted Bell Curve

It is helpful to understand the reorganization inverted bell curve activity analysis. There will be frenzied activity early (usually for the first sixty-ninety days) in the case (such as "first day" orders, cash collateral disputes, DIP financing issues, and assumption or rejection of non-residential real property leases within sixty days of filing); then less activity while the debtor attempts to stabilize the business and the parties negotiate; and then more frenzied activity at plan negotiation and confirmation.

The Reorganization Proceeding Inverted Bell Curve can be demonstrated graphically as set forth below. The events depicted on the chart are explained in Chapters Four and Five, and are also summarized in the *Hypothetical Reorganization Timeline* contained in the Appendix.

The "Reorganization Inverted Bell Curve"

Time that management* can expect to devote to bankruptcy-related (non-pure business related) activities in a Chapter 11 proceeding

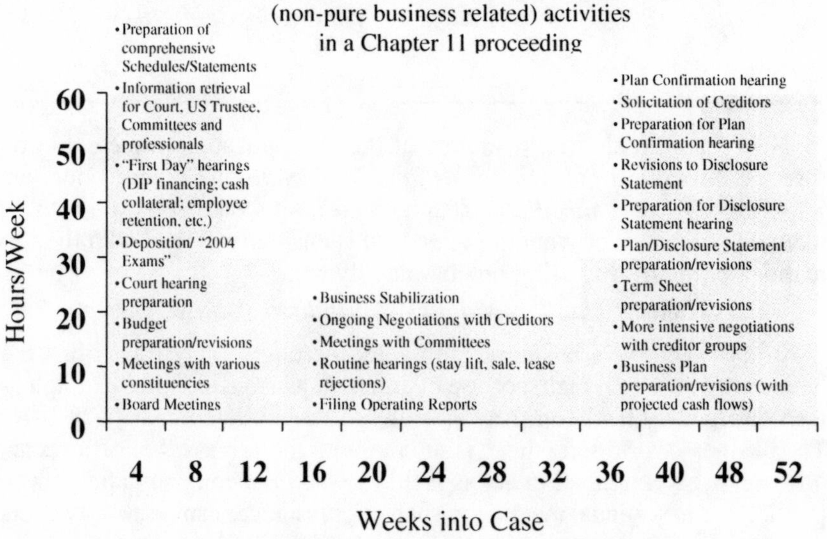

* "Management" refers to, generically and collectively, the CEO, COO, CFO, finance staff, and in-house General Counsel and staff.

· *The Elastic Concept Of Time In Chapter 11 Reorganizations.*

It is a certainty that, from management's perspective, either things will not happen fast enough to accommodate business exigencies (an emergency sale of an asset to a skittish buyer will get bogged down in the system or negotiation) or will happen too fast (litigious creditors will file litigation and get accelerated hearings when the debtor needs to catch its breath). It's imperative to understand that Chapter 11 is, in essence, a judicially supervised negotiation process. The process moves according to the timetables established and controlled by the bankruptcy court, which may or may not correspond to business realities.[82] In any event, at the risk of sounding trite, senior management must attempt to "expect the unexpected," and the best way to do this is to remain flexible in approach and outlook.

The Personal Toll

Executives preparing to embark on a reorganization are usually too preoccupied with business emergencies to think about the personal toll that the process will exact—on themselves, key people, and others. Restructuring professionals and executives who have been through the process know what to expect and become somewhat "thick-skinned." A few observations:

· ***Prepare for the Inevitable Personal Attacks.*** A word to the wise: Don't take personal attacks personally. You need to understand (if not appreciate) lawyers' tactics—innuendo, allegations of mismanagement and incompetence, and so on. It's not personal, but it has all the hallmarks of personal attacks. Be prepared to endure second-guessing by people you have never met.[83]

· ***New Stresses on Management.*** If bankruptcy isn't stressful enough, there will be many new and stressful demands made on management's time and patience. The stress and uncertainty of a bankruptcy can impact your personal lives (and can result in such unwelcome occurrences as potential marital strife). In addition to trying to keep the business ship afloat in choppy waters, you will be called upon to be the "global thinker" and provide business leadership. Demands on management's time will be higher during the crisis periods, and you will be spending time with professionals when you would prefer to spend time focusing on the business.[84] This is an area that is frequently underestimated.

· ***"Hand-Holding."*** Employees, key vendors, and others will require more "hand-holding" and strong leadership during the crisis periods. You must be prepared for key personnel to have a "flight" reaction—key, highly marketable people may wish to jump ship rather than weather the economic storm (and your competitors will certainly play to this to woo your key people). Open communication is critical during these phases to allay unfounded fears. The dilemma for management is obvious—for example, key players may need bonuses or other "combat- pay" types of perks at the very time when money is very tight and creditors aren't all that sympathetic.[85] This can create a Catch-22 scenario that can be difficult to resolve. Notwithstanding this, management must avoid the temptation of making promises to key people and vendors it might not be able to keep, other than, perhaps, as part of plan confirmation.[86] This is discussed in Chapter Four. Once a bankruptcy is filed, reasonable perks generally can be added with bankruptcy court approval if the cash flows of the company will support them. In this regard, open and frequent consultation with Committees is very helpful (see discussion in Chapter Four on *Golden Parachutes*).

· ***"A Death in the Family."*** At the risk of being accused of practicing psychology without a license, it is not unusual for management to feel depressed or defeated by virtue of a bankruptcy filing. Serious economic difficulties have been analogized to grief experienced as a result of a very serious illness or the death of someone close. Frequently, management will go through the stages of denial, anger, sorrow, and then gradual acceptance. This can create challenges to undertaking the financial introspection and objectivity that is required of the process and other constituencies (discussed in Chapter Two).

· ***Executive Compensation.*** A somewhat delicate point may be the issue of executive compensation once a bankruptcy is filed. This can be a source of creditor dissatisfaction, and early disclosure of executive compensation is important. While regular compensation is generally not subject to court approval (because it is considered an ***"ordinary course" transaction***), secured creditors with cash collateral rights, and sometimes Creditors Committees and U.S. Trustees, will likely have input into this area. This is discussed in more detail in Chapter Four. (With respect to severance and indemnification rights, see the discussion in Chapter Four on *Golden Parachutes*.)

· ***Need To Be Accessible To Your Professional Team And Creditor Constituencies.*** The CEO of a distressed company must make himself accessible and available to the professional team as much as possible, especially early in the process and as negotiations for ultimate restructuring commence and progress. For the uninitiated, bankruptcy is indeed a strange game played by seemingly bizarre rules. At least until management is conversant with the new rules, constant communication with your professional team is crucial. In addition, it is helpful to designate a "face person" to interact with the various constituencies. This is not always the CEO[87] (see the discussion in Chapter Two relating to the retention of a "restructuring officer"). Finally, it is important to the process that management establish personal relationships (if possible) with Committee members and other key constituents (major bondholders, bank lenders, etc.). This helps establish credibility (although it's not always possible) and enhances the negotiating dynamics (discussed in Chapter Five).

· ***Just Whom Does My Lawyer Represent Anyway?*** An area that can cause difficulties in closely held companies is a misunderstanding (sometimes by both the executive and the lawyer) as to who the lawyers (and other advisors) represent. As executives of public companies know, corporate counsel represents the interest of the corporation, not the individual interests of the CEO or members of the Board of Directors. For example, outside of bankruptcy if a CEO needs to negotiate an employment contract, he or she has separate counsel (who may be paid for by the company, but still represents the CEO). In reorganization cases, particularly in contentious cases, this distinction can be blurred, and can lead to difficulties.

The harsh reality is that what is in the best interests of the executive (such as, for example, keeping his or her job) may not be in the best interests of the company, particularly in an insolvent corporation scenario. This is not an academic point. For example, this can become an issue when it comes to negotiating postbankruptcy severance and change-of-control agreements in cases. The executive clearly (and understandably) wants the maximum protection, and the creditors don't always agree.[88] If counsel for the debtor points this out at a Board meeting, it is not unusual for the directors to jump down counsel's throat. However, counsel's job is to point out these types of things.

When the professionals for a company forget that they represent the company and not the individual officers or directors, and if this is apparent in actions that are taken (such as negotiating hard to obtain releases of personal guarantees by officers or directors, or arguing with a creditor constituency that the plan of reorganization should undertake to assume all of the company's prebankruptcy indemnification obligations with respect to any prebankruptcy claims), not only will the company lose credibility but the professionals will lose credibility as well.[89] The tension that results is doubly problematic for counsel who might be viewed as "disloyal" by the executives for doing his or her job, and "tainted" by creditors who believe counsel has "sold out" to entrenched management.[90]

As is discussed in *The Sacrificial Lambs* section below, it is not all that unusual for some of the senior executives to lose their jobs in the Chapter 11 process. As such, the executive needs to understand and appreciate that the professionals do not represent his or her interests, but the interests of the company. While they are often aligned, that is not always the case, and as personally difficult as that may be, acceptance of that reality is essential for a company to succeed through the reorganization process.

· ***Going to Court Early to Get the Lay of the Land.*** This last observation is from a bankruptcy judge in California, and is worth noting. While there will be extraordinary demands on your time in the Chapter 11, it is helpful to take time out early on to attend a few court sessions, particularly early in the case. This serves a dual purpose. First, it gives you a chance to assess the lay of the land and get some feel for the dynamics of the case, and second, it shows the bankruptcy judge that you are involved in the process, and begins the creation of a rapport (such as it is) between senior management and the judge.

"Show Me the Money!"

In a financially distressed environment, the creditors' primary concern is cash and short-term viability, and only secondarily are they concerned with the long-term survivability of the business. As such, concerns about research and development and other "soft costs" to preserve and enhance market share usually will not be foremost on the minds of creditors, at least not until they have a handle on the full range of business problems. Remember that the creditors' usual perception of management, at least initially, is that it is incompetent and got the company in the troubles it's in. In the world of restructuring, perception may not be reality, but management must try to recognize the perception and build credibility.[91] Managing cash flow is critical, both as a practical necessity and to be sensitive to the dynamics between the creditor groups and the company. Projecting conservatively and accurately (the former usually more vital than the latter) is critical to establishing credibility in Chapter 11. Of course, senior management must not lose sight of the ultimate goal of long-term viability, so (as with most aspects of Chapter 11) management must balance competing concerns and expectations (see discussion in Chapter Four on *Financing The Preconfirmation Operations*).

The "Sacrificial Lambs"

Another new and perhaps disconcerting reality in the reorganization process is that not everyone who starts the case as an executive with the company will be there when the company comes out of reorganization. If management is new to the company and is not directly identified with the time and circumstances leading up to the financial difficulties, the usual course of action is that they will remain with the company through the process and possibly thereafter (see discussion in Chapter Four regarding *Golden Parachutes*). Conversely, executives that were with the company when it did its public equity or debt offerings (the proceeds of which have long since gone) are often unlikely to remain in their positions as the process plays out. While unpleasant, it is a reality. Those executives will often not have the confidence of the creditor group, and the dynamics of the case will be very contentious unless and until some "sacrificial lambs" are offered. In some cases, for example, the CFO or COO may be let go (with some negotiated severance deal). Unless there are significant allegations of serious wrongdoing, the CEOs are not generally the first to leave, but they too can be a casualty of the reorganization process.[92]

As a practical matter, the most likely to survive all the way through the process are those executives that are not associated or linked (at least in the minds of the major creditor constituencies) with the creation of the financial difficulties that precipitated the reorganization filing.

"Life in a Fishbowl" (Including the Ultimate Fishing Expedition—The "2004 Examination")

Chapter 11, while providing extraordinary relief from certain actions by creditors, also creates new and unusual restraints. For example, you may be surprised to learn that consent of a lender that has a lien on receivables or a court order is necessary to utilize operational cash to pay salaries or ordinary course expenses. Moreover, the concept of a ***Bankruptcy Rule 2004 Examination*** (or "***2004 Exam***"), with its broad "fishing-expedition" scope, may well seem like a modern version of the Spanish Inquisition.

Male executives over forty that have had a prostate checkup know what a 2004 Exam is like (although generally a 2004 Exam is less sterile). The Bankruptcy Code (and Rules) allow any ***party in interest*** to examine the officers, directors, or employees (or indeed *anyone*), under oath, to get information.[93] It has been described in judicial decisions as a fishing expedition,[94] although the courts will protect proprietary or confidential trade information to prevent competitors from obtaining non-public information.[95]

Management needs to prepare for the reality that, once in a bankruptcy, business decisions will be second, third, and possibly fourth-guessed. "Transparency" of financial operations is the rule, although there are exceptions (such as confidentiality requirements for proprietary information and similar matters discussed in Chapter Four).

Your New Business Partners—Everybody's Got An Opinion

Since Chapter 11 is life in a fishbowl, you must prepare for input (whether solicited or not) from numerous third parties, including secured creditors and their advisors, Creditors Committees and their advisors, Equity Committees and their advisors, and possibly even the U.S. Trustee and the court. In addition, as a general rule you are paying each advisor for the privilege of providing that input. This reality is usually resisted by senior management at first (much like denial that one has a serious illness), but the sooner you accept it, the smoother the case will go.

· ***Keeping the World Informed.*** In a related vein, you must learn to cope with responding to incessant requests for information and reports from these business partners.

At the outset, until a manageable and reasonable protocol for information sharing can be worked out, daily demands for information will come in from all sides, some demanding "custom" reports (inventory turns, daily shrinkage reports, etc.). In the larger cases the professionals usually agree to a workable information sharing protocol, and once this is done, the demands on the company's accounting staff (which is generally already overworked) ease. See discussion below on *Protecting The Franchise: "Chinese Walls" And Confidentiality Agreements.*

· ***Working with Committees.*** While Committees can be difficult, astute management (and advisors) should learn to work with Committees (and their advisors) during the course of the reorganization case. While, at first blush, this may appear like Chamberlain in Munich, it is both a practical and legal necessity. Alienating a Committee will only make the case more contentious and protracted. If the Committee is reasonable and businesslike (and admittedly not all Committees are), then "bringing them in to the tent" is preferable to having them outside throwing rocks. Once this occurs, Committees often can be very useful in helping the company negotiate with other constituencies—such as secured creditors or the "Predatory Constituents" discussed below. A cooperative relationship with a Committee is generally much better (and ultimately less costly from a professional fee perspective) than a combative one, and Committees can be strong allies in cases where other factions are doing battle with a debtor.

The Company IS in Play—Live with it

While the Bankruptcy Code presumes existing management will lead the distressed company out of bankruptcy, it is important to keep in mind that the ultimate restructuring may not lie entirely in the hands of the debtor. In certain circumstances, a company's proposed reorganization plan might be rejected in favor of a hostile acquisition or other alternative restructuring plan supported by some constituency in the case.[96] It is important not to be oversold on what the "product" (Chapter 11) can accomplish—it is not a panacea. It is important to understand some of the limitations of Chapter 11 (such as ***credit bid rights***, ***offset rights***, limitation of ***Bankruptcy Court jurisdiction***, particularly over state governmental entities, or the "***absolute priority rule***"). These are discussed in Chapters Four and Five.

· ***The "Revlon Duty to Shop."*** In a non-bankruptcy context, courts have held that when it becomes obvious that the sale of a company (or presumably its assets) is inevitable, a heightened level of scrutiny is applied to evaluate the decision of a target's Board granting prohibitive buyer protection devices to a potential purchaser that will chill competitive bidding. In other words, once the company is in play, the Board has an affirmative duty to get the highest price—no playing favorites. In a non-bankruptcy context, the seminal case in defining the heightened scrutiny of buyer protections that would have the impact of chilling bidding is found in a case involving *Revlon, Inc.*[97] In essence, the legal duty of a Board of Directors once a decision has been made to sell the company or its assets is to maximize the value and not to grant advantages to one or more potential bidders that have the effect of stacking the deck and chilling the bidding.

The filing of a bankruptcy proceeding has the practical effect of putting the company in play whether the company likes it or not. Since the ultimate fiduciary duty of an insolvent company is to maximize the return to the various constituencies, the company needs to understand that a reorganization plan that maximizes value, even if it is a plan that is not necessarily proposed by the company, needs to be seriously evaluated much like a tender offer outside of a bankruptcy proceeding. As such, there is a duty to shop and that involves keeping an open mind to proposals even if they are not generated by the company[98] (see also the discussion in Chapter Five on "*Keeping Control—Exclusivity Rules!*").

· ***The "Predatory" Constituents.*** It is necessary to understand the ever-evolving expectations of creditors and other potentially "predatory" constituents in the Chapter 11 case. For example, distressed debt purchasers and so-called "vulture investors" may exhibit little, if any, concern for management desires and expectations, preservation of market share, employee or customer loyalties, or other seemingly laudable objectives. Well-known "raiders" such as Carl Icahn regularly buy debt as an acquisition strategy—such as in the *Marvel Entertainment* and *Stratosphere Corporation* reorganization cases. Once a creditor in these cases, the agenda is to leverage the position (through negotiations, litigation, or both) to acquire the company or its assets.[99]

That having been said, there are some protections available to companies when faced with over-aggressive raiders. In the *Johns-Manville* Chapter 11 filed in the mid-1980s, a group of investors bought large blocks of stock of the company (at rock bottom prices, naturally) after *Manville* filed Chapter 11. After years of negotiating with the various creditors, the company had negotiated a plan that would have essentially wiped out the stockholders (a common occurrence in Chapter 11 cases). The investors, understandably upset, tried to get a special shareholders meeting convened to install a new Board, which would scuttle the negotiated deal and negotiate for a return for the equity. The bankruptcy court issued an ***injunction*** prohibiting the meeting, and it was upheld all the way to the Second Circuit Court of Appeals.[100] As such, while the general rule is that corporate governance continues on in a bankruptcy, the bankruptcy court can (and does) intervene in certain circumstances.

Protecting the Franchise: Confidentiality Agreements and "Chinese Walls"

So if the reorganization process makes the financial life and times of the company a veritable open book, are there any protections available? Do competitors who may have small claims in the bankruptcy proceeding have the right to take unbridled 2004 Exams and otherwise have access to all sorts of interesting proprietary information? What about bondholders or other players that wish to continue to trade in the public debt and equity securities of the company?

In public company cases, as well as privately held companies that have proprietary and other trade-secret types of information, requiring the use of confidentiality agreements and "Chinese Walls" is not only common but is an affirmative duty of the debtor company.

Confidentiality agreements are used frequently in Chapter 11 cases when non-public information is being sought by either creditors or, more likely, Committees or potential buyers of assets. Examples include legal analyses and projections for valuation and other purposes that are not public. For asset purchasers, the due diligence type of information (which will generally include projected cash flows for income producing assets and the like) is also only provided under confidentiality agreements. A form of confidentiality agreement is contained in the Appendix to these materials.

In companies with public debt or equity, holders of those securities that sit on a Committee and would therefore be privy to non-public information often (although not always) sign a confidentiality agreement whereby they cannot trade on non-public information. There are usually provisions that would require the debtor company to "burn off" the confidential information within a specified period of time so that a holder of the security is not forever barred from trading. This is done so that large holders of securities will sit on Committees because their participation is essential to the negotiation dynamic and process. In addition, institutional holders of these securities that have both a trading desk and an investment arm where these securities are held for their own account will set up information- blocking protocols (also known as "Chinese Walls")[101] whereby the representative that sits on the committee is not allowed to share any information with the trading desk so that trading can continue to occur for the brokerage's other customers. These protocols are frequently approved by the bankruptcy court supervising the bankruptcy proceeding of the company. An example of such a protocol is contained in the Appendix.

So Explain Again Why I Decided to Make this Trip?

So with all of this having been said, why again did you decide to embark on a reorganization? The answer is because notwithstanding all of the burdens and challenges of the reorganization process, it is unparalleled as a way to recapitalize financially troubled businesses. With all of the burdens outlined in this chapter, there are extraordinary rights and remedies available to a debtor company to enable it to implement its action plan for its exit strategy.

Now that you're beginning to make the attitudinal adjustments, it's time to dive in. The Chapter 11 case has been filed. Now what?

CHAPTER FOUR

SURVIVING TO PLAN CONFIRMATION

"Victory at all costs, victory in spite of all terror, victory however long and hard the road may be; for without victory there is no survival."

Sir Winston Spencer Churchill
First Statement As Prime Minister
House Of Commons
May 13, 1940

So the petition is ready to be filed, you have your cashier's check for your filing fee, you've assembled your "team," and you're about to embark on the task of negotiating a comprehensive plan of reorganization. Congratulations. In order to avoid being in the 83 percent category of failed Chapter 11 cases, you need to survive to plan confirmation. This chapter will attempt to help you do just that.

The Venue Game

As a preliminary matter, *where* you decide to file your Chapter 11 case may be as important as when you file it. There are currently ninety-four possible districts available in the United States to file Chapter 11 bankruptcy petitions. The place where a company files its Chapter 11 bankruptcy petition is referred to as the ***venue*** of the filing.

What constitutes an appropriate venue in which to file a bankruptcy petition has always been kept somewhat vague in the bankruptcy laws concerning jurisdiction.[102] Assume, for example, that ABC, Inc., a Delaware corporation with its primary headquarters in Los Angeles, has a major manufacturing facility owned by a subsidiary in Chicago. If ABC gets into financial difficulties, and it is determined that it needs to file a Chapter 11 bankruptcy, one of the primary issues that will need to be addressed will be the jurisdiction in which to file the case. Under current bankruptcy laws, ABC could appropriately file a bankruptcy petition in Delaware (in particular, Wilmington, Delaware) because it is a corporation incorporated under the laws of Delaware. That provides sufficient basis to file in Delaware. Alternatively, ABC could file its petition in the Central District of California located in Los Angeles. This is true because it could be considered as having its principal place of business in Los Angeles. Alternatively, if Chicago were thought to be an advantageous place to file a petition, the Chicago manufacturing subsidiary could be placed into Chapter 11 first in Chicago (or more particularly, the U.S. Bankruptcy Court for the Northern District of Illinois), and then the parent company of ABC could be placed in bankruptcy in Chicago under the so-called "***affiliate rule***" of the bankruptcy jurisdictional provisions. This rule essentially provides that venue in a jurisdiction is proper if an affiliate of the debtor company has already filed in that particular jurisdiction.[103]

So what's the big deal? Why is there all of this discussion over where to file? Just like the commercial where the actor intones that "parts is parts," isn't one bankruptcy court the same as any other? The answer to this is a resounding "No!"

In fact, substantial strategy discussions *should* occur when a company is deciding where to file its bankruptcy petition. In the ABC example above, knowledgeable professionals will have to evaluate the circumstances of the filing to see what the most significant problems of the company are (to the extent they can determine it in the short period of time that they may have), and then determine if there is one jurisdiction that is more favorable than the others. In ABC's case, for example, some or all of the following strategy considerations may come into play. Delaware is well known as a "business friendly" venue. While some jurisdictions that don't get a substantial amount of business bankruptcies might hesitate to enter certain types of first day orders (discussed below), the entry of such orders in Delaware is the rule and not the exception. In fact, objections to the entry of such orders are generally not treated with too much enthusiasm by the bankruptcy judges in that jurisdiction, who for the most part understand business issues and realities, and are generally very good about giving expedited hearings on business emergencies and things of that nature. On the other hand, if ABC's manufacturing subsidiary in Chicago is an extremely large employer in the Chicago area, there is something to be said about filing the subsidiary in Chicago and then joining-in the parent corporation as an affiliate filing. While bankruptcy judges, of course, do their best to objectively look at all cases in front of them, bankruptcy filings of major area employers necessarily hit the newspapers, and newspapers are read by judges. Bankruptcy judges generally want to see Chapter 11 cases succeed, and that is particularly so where the failure of a Chapter 11 would mean hundreds (or thousands) of people being left without jobs. As such, you can't ignore either the "human factor" or the "home court" advantage in bankruptcy cases.[104]

What if the Chicago operation has substantial environmental contamination problems related to its manufacturing facility? Under those circumstances, and to the extent that those are material, ABC's bankruptcy professionals may wish to consider filing in Los Angeles or Delaware. The reason for this is that there are judicial decisions from the highest court covering Illinois in the area of discharge of environmental contamination liabilities.[105] Of course, filing in Los Angeles is always an option. Chances are that is where primary bankruptcy counsel for ABC will be located (if the usual dynamic occurs—an executive has corporate counsel that either has bankruptcy expertise in its firm or knows of good bankruptcy expertise in that marketplace). One of the considerations that may be factored into the analysis is that the Central District of California (of which Los Angeles is a part) is one of the largest bankruptcy jurisdictions in the United States. There are many judges (at last count, in excess of fourteen) that may be assigned the case. Judges (like lawyers, like accountants, like executives) are not all made equal. Some are better than others, and some judges have reputations for being hard on debtors or otherwise not particularly helpful to a reorganization process.[106] By filing in a place like Los Angeles, where a company can draw one of fourteen or so judges, the odds of getting a "bad" judge are increased. If a particular judge or judges are known to be very bad from a debtor's perspective, the safe bet may be to file in a jurisdiction where there are fewer judges and the odds of drawing a particularly bad judge are lower.[107]

In summary, there are at least six factors that need to be considered in making a venue decision: (1) sophistication of the court in the particular type of bankruptcy (for example, Delaware has seen a rash of large, industry-specific reorganizations, including the *Continental Airlines* reorganization, *T.I.E. Communications*, a radio and television conglomerate, and *UDC Homes*, a large homebuilder; it is also adept at handling Prepackaged Bankruptcies); (2) the importance of the debtor's business to a particular local economy; (3) counsel's familiarity (and comfort) with the bankruptcy judges in a particular jurisdiction (clearly preferring those who authored favorable published opinions); (4) the perceived or actual "debtor friendly" proclivities of a particular court (both the Southern District of New York and Delaware are reputed to be "debtor friendly," although this may be more perception than reality); (5) the court's willingness to entertain certain "first day orders," such as payment of prepetition suppliers; and (6) finally, all of the foregoing needs to be weighed against the potential extra expense of hiring local counsel and the time and expense of having primary reorganization counsel travel to a different jurisdiction.

Critics have looked at the analysis set forth above and have cried with alarm that it is improper "forum shopping."[108] In other words, it is nothing more than tricky lawyers playing tricky lawyer games to try and get the best judge. These same critics have attempted to limit the bankruptcy law's venue provisions to make venue appropriate only where the company's headquarters is located, or where its major assets are located. These limitations are generally viewed as anti-Delaware types of maneuvers. To date, however, Congress has not seen fit to limit the venue provisions and options available under the bankruptcy laws. As such, while the venue analysis may be disparaged as nothing more than legal maneuvering, any good bankruptcy practitioner must and should consider these issues in determining an appropriate venue for the bankruptcy filing.

The "Order For Relief"—Let The Games Begin!

The filing of the bankruptcy (which is nothing more than the physical "clocking in" of the petition and related documents and the bankruptcy clerk's office taking the filing fee) constitutes what is known in bankruptcy parlance as the "***order for relief***." The order for relief essentially means that a company is now officially in bankruptcy and subject to the jurisdiction of the federal bankruptcy courts. The automatic stay (discussed below) is now in effect, and all of the dates applicable to calculation of preference payments, fraudulent conveyances, and post bankruptcy transactions are now firmly set in stone.

The reason the Bankruptcy Code talks in terms of the entry of a order for relief is really to differentiate a Bankruptcy Code filing from the older filings under the Bankruptcy Act of 1898. Under the Bankruptcy Act, the filing of a bankruptcy petition did not automatically mean that you were in bankruptcy. Specifically, it was necessary for the bankruptcy court to "adjudicate" the company a "bankrupt." If you look at some old loan forms, you will see that this language is still included as an event of default (which just goes to show the last time these lenders revised their loan forms). In any event, under the Bankruptcy Code, there is no hearing to determine if the company should be "adjudicated a bankrupt"—that phrase and concept no longer exist. The filing of the petition, with the payment of the filing fee, gets the company the relief that it seeks immediately. It is in bankruptcy, and is subject to all of the rights and obligations that go along with that status.

The order for relief is effective when the Bankruptcy Clerk's Office file-stamps the petition. The file stamp will show the date and the time (right to the minute) that the filing occurred. This is important because it is conceivable that certain acts will occur after the bankruptcy is filed, either with or without the knowledge of the creditor that may be taking such action. For example, let's assume that a foreclosure for some real property is set to occur at 9:00 a.m. on Monday, January 10th. The debtor files its bankruptcy petition on Monday at 8:58 a.m. Even if the word of the bankruptcy filing is not given to the creditor conducting the foreclosure sale, if that foreclosure sale occurs at 9:00 a.m., it was done (albeit unintentionally) in violation of the automatic stay, which arose at 8:58 a.m. Hence the reason for precision in the time and date when filing bankruptcy petitions.[109]

The "Estate"—What Exactly Is It?

The filing of the bankruptcy petition and the entry of the order for relief also automatically creates the concept of a ***bankruptcy estate***. What exactly is the bankruptcy estate? Fair question, and frankly it's almost a little metaphysical in nature. The reason Chapter 11 debtors are called "debtors-in-possession" is because they are "in possession" of the bankruptcy estate.

The bankruptcy estate is a term of art that really means two different but interrelated things. The first (and perhaps most obvious) meaning is that the "estate" consists of all assets of the debtor, wherever they are located in the world. "Assets" are very broadly defined in the Bankruptcy Code, and consist of all property, contract rights, causes of action against all other parties, contingent causes of action against all other parties, lawsuits, legal or equitable rights—essentially almost anything you can think of is considered part of the bankruptcy estate.[110] The bankruptcy estate includes property that the debtor may have parted with prior to the filing of the bankruptcy but has a right to get back as a ***preference*** or ***fraudulent conveyance*** (discussed below). Property of the estate also includes such intangible things as rights under insurance policies, even where the debtor may not be the primary insured—such as in D&O policies (discussed below).

The second thing that the estate is used to signify is the rights of all of the creditors in those assets. Accordingly, when we talk of a DIP being a fiduciary, it is a fiduciary for the benefit of the estate. The estate under these circumstances not only means that the DIP is a fiduciary to watch over all of the property of the estate, but also the *interest of creditors in that property*. Watching out for the estate, therefore, is watching out for the interest of all creditors, with the degree of duty being dependent upon where those creditors are in the pecking order discussed in Chapter Two.

There are exceptions to what constitutes property of the estate. For example, on an individual level and by way of analogy, if your brother-in-law loans you his car on Monday and you file a personal bankruptcy on Tuesday, the fact that you are in possession of your brother-in-law's car doesn't mean that the car is automatically "property of the estate" of your personal bankruptcy. While you may have physical possession of the car, it belongs to someone else and his ownership rights are not extinguished by virtue of the fact that you simply are in possession of it. Likewise, there are certain circumstances where debtors are servicers under mortgage servicing agreements. In order to do that, they will generally be listed as the creditor under the appropriate loan and security documents. That notwithstanding, they only hold those obligations for purposes of servicing. In legal parlance, they hold the *legal* title but not the *equitable* title to those assets. Those limited ownership interests are specifically excepted out from being property of the estate in the Bankruptcy Code.[111] In any event, a good rule of thumb (and this is certainly true at the outset of any Chapter 11 bankruptcy) is to treat all property as property of the estate until it is sorted out later. It is better to be prudent in this respect rather than sorry later on.

The Automatic Stay

As we saw from our extended *It's A Mad, Mad, Mad, Mad World* metaphor in Chapter Two, it is critically important to the success of any bankruptcy proceeding that what would otherwise be the creditors' competitive, destructive, and inefficient "race" to the debtor's limited assets be stopped and that calmer heads be allowed to prevail. Unless a bankruptcy filing had the effect of halting creditor action and creating order from potential chaos, a debtor would almost never be able to prevent creditors from destroying whatever chance the debtor had of reorganizing. The Bankruptcy Code imposes an automatic stay—essentially a broad injunction—so that the debtor's bankruptcy filing can accomplish what the debtor hoped it would: keep collection efforts, litigation, and other creditor aggression from breaking apart what could be a viable going concern that, if given a chance to reorganize, could satisfy all creditors rather than just the fastest, strongest, meanest, or biggest.

The automatic stay has long been one of the cornerstones of the U.S. bankruptcy regime and, because of its scope and the many exceptions to it, continues to this day to be one of the most litigated areas of the Bankruptcy Code. This is not difficult to understand. It's not often welcomed news to a creditor that it cannot continue debt collection activities begun before the bankruptcy and that it has to wait while its competition (other creditors) catches up. Likewise, it's threatening to a debtor when a creditor believes that the automatic stay does not apply under particular circumstances. Many decades of court decisions and legislative adjustments have gone a long way to define what are now fairly clear boundaries of the automatic stay, but difficult issues remain unresolved at the margins. These marginal issues are why Chapter 11 debtors seek experienced bankruptcy counsel and why stay litigation is often a persistent feature of any reorganization case.

· ***Scope (The Good News).***

Generally, the automatic stay, which becomes effective immediately upon the filing of any petition (voluntary or involuntary), acts as a blanket injunction against all actions by a creditor that may directly or indirectly interfere with the administration of the Chapter 11 proceedings or the bankruptcy estate. The automatic stay essentially enjoins virtually all efforts by a creditor to collect on debts, take possession of collateral, enforce or create a lien, or set off a debt against the debtor. The Bankruptcy Code provisions setting out the boundaries of the automatic stay are intentionally broadly worded in order to capture as much creditor activity (and creativity!) aimed at debt collection as possible—and exceptions, as discussed below, are intended to be narrow and specific. The automatic stay prohibits a creditor from commencing or continuing any of the following: (a) judicial, administrative, or other action or proceeding against the debtor that was or could have been commenced before the bankruptcy to recover a claim against the debtor that arose before the bankruptcy; (b) enforcement of a judgment obtained before the bankruptcy against the debtor or property of the estate; (c) any act to obtain possession of, or exercise control over, property of the estate; (d) any act to create, perfect, or enforce a lien against property of the estate; (e) any act to collect, assess, or recover a prebankruptcy claim against the debtor; (f) the setoff of any debt owed to the debtor that arose prebankruptcy against any claim against the debtor; and (g) proceedings before the U.S. Tax Court concerning the debtor.[112]

Most overt creditor collection actions that one can imagine are prevented by the automatic stay. Once the debtor has filed its petition, bringing a lawsuit in state court, or evicting the debtor from leased property, or seizing the debtor's property, or foreclosing on a mortgage, or executing a judgment against the debtor are all well within the prohibitive reach of the automatic stay. The Bankruptcy Code prefers—and in most cases, requires—that the creditor file a ***proof of claim*** in the bankruptcy proceedings to collect its debt. Also prohibited are a host of other actions that may not be so obvious. For example, a creditor violates the stay when he or she contacts the debtor (by telephone, letter, fax, e-mail, telegram, Morse code, or smoke signals) in order to cajole the debtor to pay a prebankruptcy debt. This contact does not need to be particularly harassing or aggressive in order for it to be a stay violation. Of course, if the debtor is represented by counsel, the creditor (or the creditor's counsel) can always contact the debtor's counsel and threaten, scream, and yell all he or she wants without running afoul of the automatic stay.[113]

The automatic stay is much needed good news for a beleaguered debtor, as it is a powerful shield against all manner of creditor actions. The stay is also a shield against actions taken by other entities with whom the debtor does business (and who are not creditors) that could greatly harm the debtor's ability to continue operating in bankruptcy. For example, the debtor's ability to maintain adequate insurance coverage is critically important to the debtor's business, yet insurance carriers have attempted to cancel the debtor's insurance contract upon the filing of a bankruptcy petition, irrespective of whether the debtor had made all its premium payments before the bankruptcy. Doing so violates the stay, even if the insurance company is not a "creditor" (that is, is not currently owned anything) because unilaterally canceling the insurance is considered to be an attempt to "exercise control over" the debtor's property.[114] For the same reason, taxing authorities cannot hold up a debtor's tax refund, even as a setoff against other tax liabilities.[115]

The automatic stay is not only broad in scope, but in geographical reach as well. Because the Bankruptcy Code specifies that "property of the estate" includes any interest that the debtor has in property "wherever located and by whomever held," and the automatic stay applies to any act to take possession of, exercise control over, or place a lien on, property of the estate, the automatic stay ostensibly applies to everyone and every place in the world. Obviously, there are significant legal and practical barriers to enforcing the automatic stay against parties or in areas outside the United

States,[116] but it remains true at least that the automatic stay prohibits actions by any creditor located anywhere within U.S. borders.

This has been the law for many decades, yet bankruptcy lawyers are rarely surprised when a creditor somewhere in, say, Texas decides that "no bankruptcy judge in Delaware is going to tell me what I can and can't do." Making sure that far-flung creditors are not violating the automatic stay is a frequent, ongoing challenge that debtors (and their professionals) often must face during the first stages of any large Chapter 11 case. Some state court judges have been heard to scoff at the automatic stay as well, stating that "I don't care what bankruptcy this defendant has filed in Delaware, we're going forward with this here trial." While it is constitutionally improper for one court (the bankruptcy court) to enjoin another court (here, a state court), the state court trial against a debtor cannot proceed unless the plaintiff-creditor continues to prosecute the action. It is the plaintiff-creditor's action in prosecuting the claim in state court—not the state court's trial of that action—that violates the automatic stay. Any judgment obtained in such a trial may be void, since all actions taken and results obtained in violation of the automatic stay may be void (or at the very least voidable), even if the offending party was completely unaware that the debtor had filed a bankruptcy petition or that the automatic stay had been invoked. In addition, a debtor may obtain damages, including costs and attorneys' fees, for intentional violations of the automatic stay.[117]

The automatic stay, unless modified or terminated with respect to a particular creditor or certain property of the estate (see below), remains in effect until the earliest of the dates the bankruptcy case is closed, dismissed, or the debtor receives a discharge. In the Chapter 11 context, the debtor will receive a discharge as part of confirmation of the plan of reorganization well before the case is closed, so the automatic stay will remain in effect until confirmation. Once the debtor receives its discharge, the Bankruptcy Code provides for a similar injunction against all acts to collect on debts arising before confirmation that essentially replaces the automatic stay. This postconfirmation injunction is permanent (see Chapter Five, *Step Six: "Going Effective"*).

· ***Exceptions (The Bad News).***

While the automatic stay serves the debtor as strong armor against creditor collection activities, that armor is not without its chinks. While narrowly defined, there are several exceptions to the automatic stay that limit its scope and allow certain creditors to take certain actions in certain circumstances.[118] Knowing these specific areas ahead of a bankruptcy filing will help the proactive debtor anticipate creditor responses to a Chapter 11 petition and prepare for any business or operations effects such responses might have.

A criminal prosecution against a debtor is not stayed despite the debtor's bankruptcy. Such prosecutions continue unabated, even when the effect of a conviction could have a far-reaching and detrimental impact on the rest of the debtor's restructuring. For example, a prosecution against a corporate debtor for environmental crimes or antitrust violations may, in the event of a conviction and in extreme circumstances, give rise to crippling criminal fines and monetary penalties that can quickly turn a reorganization case into a liquidation case. Interestingly, criminal tax evasion prosecutions are not stayed, even when the underlying taxes would constitute a dischargeable prebankruptcy debt.

The automatic stay does not prevent a secured creditor with a purchase money security interest from taking necessary steps after the bankruptcy is filed to ensure the continued perfection of its prepetition security interest. The reason for this is obvious—it would be unfair when the Uniform Commercial Code provides for a "relation back" grace period to perfect a security interest, for an intervening bankruptcy filing during that period to prevent an otherwise secured creditor from perfecting its security interest. Perfecting a security interest is important, since a claim based on an unperfected security interest is essentially unsecured in light of the debtor's ***avoiding powers*** (see the discussion below regarding *The "Strong Arm" Powers—Speak Softly But Carry a Big Stick*).

Governments are free to enforce their "regulatory" and "police" powers without running afoul of the automatic stay. "Police power" does not really refer to "cops on the beat." Instead, the term generally encompasses a government's actions to enforce laws and ordinances aimed at the health, safety, and welfare of its citizens. But what the government says is an exercise of its regulatory or police power may not always fall within the exception to the automatic stay. An important distinction has developed primarily in environmental cases. When the state environmental agency or the EPA has sued the debtor to prevent future harm to the environment (usually, seeking an injunction to prevent the debtor from polluting further), the automatic stay will not apply and the suit may continue under the police power exception. On the other hand, when the government is really attempting to collect a prepetition debt under the guise of an exercise of its police or regulatory power, the exception will not encompass this action, and the stay will prevent its continuation. For example, if a state licensing board refuses to renew a debtor's liquor license because the debtor owes back taxes, such refusal may violate the automatic stay.[119] Recent changes to the Bankruptcy Code also establish that the automatic stay will not prevent a governmental unit from commencing or continuing a tax audit, from issuing a notice of tax deficiency, from demanding tax returns, or from assessing a tax and demanding payment of such tax.[120]

The automatic stay will not prevent a landlord from taking possession of nonresidential real property leased by the debtor under a lease that expired by its own terms before the bankruptcy. Courts have established additional exceptions to the automatic stay that technically do not appear in the Bankruptcy Code. The automatic stay will not prevent collection actions against partnership property when a general partner (but not the partnership itself) has filed a bankruptcy petition. In Chapter 11 cases, the automatic stay will not prevent collection actions taken against a non-debtor third party that is a co-obligor with the debtor on a particular debt. Under certain circumstances, however, the bankruptcy court may issue a specific injunction preventing such action if the action would affect the debtor's case—for instance, when a guarantor on the debt is entitled to be indemnified by the debtor. This arises frequently when directors and officers are also defendants in class-action lawsuits against a corporate debtor (see discussion below on *Dealing With D&O Lawsuits*).

· ***Relief From Stay And The Concept of "Adequate Protection."***

To say that the stay applies with respect to a particular creditor and particular property of the estate does not, however, end the issue. Creditors may seek ***"relief" from the automatic stay*** by asking the bankruptcy court to terminate, annul, modify, or condition the stay under certain circumstances. Essentially, there are two bases for relief from the stay: (1) "cause," including the lack of "***adequate protection***" (a concept described fully just below); or (2) the debtor's lack of equity in property of the estate, coupled with the fact that such property is not necessary to an effective reorganization. These criteria are independent of one another; either one provides a basis for stay relief.

The stakes for stay relief are high. An order lifting the automatic stay returns the debtor and the requesting creditor to the legal relationship that existed before the bankruptcy, so if applicable non-bankruptcy law would permit the creditor to take an action against the debtor or estate property, the creditor is now free to take such action, often without even supervision by the bankruptcy court. For this reason, if a debtor opposes stay relief for a particular creditor (and the debtor sometimes does not), the litigation that ensues in the bankruptcy court over the requested stay relief can be protracted and involved. Procedurally, stay litigation looks a lot like full-blown non-bankruptcy litigation (but without the jury) and often entails a trial of the same issues that separate the debtor and the creditor as would a non-bankruptcy-related trial in state court.

- ***"Cause."*** Requests to lift the automatic stay under the first criterion—for "cause"—most commonly arise in one of three situations: (1) when litigation between the creditor and the debtor in another court has progressed substantially; (2) when a debtor files a bankruptcy petition to forestall a lender's foreclosure on the debtor's primary asset; and (3) when a secured creditor believes that it lacks "adequate protection" of its security interest.

  In the first situation, the creditor (usually a plaintiff in a lawsuit pending in another court) will request that the bankruptcy court modify the automatic stay to permit the lawsuit to proceed in that other court to judgment. The creditor typically argues before the bankruptcy court that the lawsuit had been proceeding before the bankruptcy, that the lawsuit contains complex or specialized factual and legal issues, and that the debtor's defense of the lawsuit will not unduly distract the debtor from its reorganization in the Chapter 11 proceedings. The debtor will usually argue the opposite of this last assertion (that defending the lawsuit would unnecessarily divert management's attention away from the bankruptcy case, which is intended to benefit all—not just one—creditor) and that the bankruptcy court can resolve the litigated issues just as well as the non-bankruptcy court. Ultimately, however, the further along the proceedings in the other court progressed before the bankruptcy (for example, all discovery is completed, all the pretrial briefs are written, with only the actual trial remaining), and the more specialized the area of law being litigated (e.g., a patent or trademark action pending before a specialized court, or a maritime dispute), the better the chance that the bankruptcy court will prefer to have the non-bankruptcy court proceed to judgment, rather than try the same issues as part of the claim- objection process in the bankruptcy court (see discussion below on *Bankruptcy Court Jurisdiction (And Limitations On That Jurisdiction)*).

Modifying the stay to allow such a lawsuit to proceed in another court does not mean that the judgment issued in the lawsuit may be enforced beyond the reach of the automatic stay or beyond the auspices of the bankruptcy court. Almost always, a bankruptcy court order modifying the stay to allow a pending lawsuit to proceed will also require that any judgment obtained in that lawsuit be satisfied only as part of the bankruptcy case—usually as a general unsecured claim under the plan of reorganization. For this reason, and because a debtor can avoid duplicative effort and expense by finishing what has begun in the other court (as opposed to starting all over in the bankruptcy court), a debtor will often agree to modification of the automatic stay. The debtor knows that it will still be able to use the automatic stay to prevent an execution of the judgment and is assured to remain in control with respect to any judgment since the debtor will (at least during the debtor's exclusive period—see Chapter Five, *Keeping Control—Exclusivity Rules!*) be able to determine how unsecured claims are treated under the plan of reorganization.[121]

The second situation in which cause is determined to exist for the lifting of the automatic stay is in what are called ***"single-asset real estate cases"*** or, more broadly, when the bankruptcy filing is precipitated by what is essentially a two-party dispute.[122] Debtors historically attempted to counteract this approach by listing small amounts of unsecured trade debt in the schedules of liabilities, thereby making the case look more complex than just a two-party dispute between the debtor and the lender. This strategy met with middling success, and in 1994 the Bankruptcy Code was amended to provide for automatic lifting of the stay after ninety days of the petition if a "single-asset real estate" debtor fails to file a plan that has a reasonable possibility of being confirmed or fails to begin making monthly interest payments to the lender.[123]

There are other examples of when a bankruptcy petition is said to have been filed in "bad faith," giving rise to a lifting of the automatic stay for cause in favor of the non-debtor party in a two-party dispute. One such example is a debtor that files a bankruptcy petition in lieu of obtaining an appeal bond. Some such debtors have had the stay lifted against them (or their bankruptcy cases dismissed),[124] although there are notable cases—most famously, *Texaco*, which filed a bankruptcy petition to avoid having to file a multi-billion dollar appeal bond after the entry of a huge judgment in favor of Pennzoil—in which the court has refused to lift the stay in this circumstance.

- ***Lack Of "Adequate Protection."*** The third and practically most important situation in which cause is invoked for relief from the automatic stay is when a secured creditor lacks "adequate protection" of its security interest in property of the estate. The concept of adequate protection is most relevant when the debtor requests continued use and possession of a secured creditor's collateral after commencement of a Chapter 11 case (see *Financing The Preconfirmation Operations—Cash Collateral Use*, below).

In the Chapter 11 context, establishing adequate protection is most immediately relevant to cash collateral use and will be discussed below. For purposes of stay relief, it is important to understand what adequate protection is and is not. Adequate protection is a term of art in bankruptcy law that involves the concept that a secured creditor's relative position in a bankruptcy case should not change during the course of the case as a result of a debtor's use of a secured creditor's collateral. A simple example would be a creditor ("A") with a $100 claim secured by accounts receivable worth $75 on the date of bankruptcy. If the debtor wishes to continue to use that collateral, it can only do so if A is "adequately protected." In other words, A's secured claim of $75 should not decrease during the pendency of the case as a result of the debtor's continued use of A's collateral (in this example, accounts receivable). As such, if the debtor wishes to use the receivables postbankruptcy, A can be given adequate protection by: (1) periodic cash payments; (2) a replacement lien (of up to $75) for receivables that are generated postbankruptcy; (3) giving A a replacement lien on other assets (again, up to $75); or (4) other ways agreeable to the parties or ultimately approved by the court.[125]

If, on the other hand, the value of a creditor's collateral cannot be adequately protected—either because the debtor is financially incapable of providing it or because the nature of the collateral is such that it is decreasing in value too fast to compensate for—then the creditor will be granted relief from the automatic stay to execute on its collateral. Creative debtors usually will be able to fashion some sort of adequate protection for secured creditors and instances in which adequate protection is truly impossible to locate are relatively rare in Chapter 11 cases involving debtors with continuing business operations.

- ***Lack of Equity.*** The second criterion for relief from the automatic stay applies if the secured creditor is truly undersecured—that is, the value of its collateral is less than the amount of the underlying debt. If the creditor can prove that the debtor lacks equity in the collateral, it has completed the first step in establishing the second method of obtaining relief from the stay besides establishing cause. In this instance, valuation of the collateral will be an essential key to litigation regarding relief from the automatic stay. The creditor will use a valuation expert witness to establish that the creditor is undersecured, and the debtor will try to counter that testimony with its own valuation expert witness. Ultimately, the court will determine the value of the collateral based on a standard that will assess the "fair market" value of the collateral.[126]

Valuation can be a "moving target," since the value of most types of collateral changes over time. Accordingly, the timing of when this valuation battle occurs may be critical to the results of the battle. An oversecured creditor may find itself undersecured several months later, and the debtor may lose its equity in the collateral over time, making relief from the stay appropriate later in the case when it was inappropriate earlier. Valuation can also prove to be a double-edged sword, since a creditor who succeeds in establishing that it is seriously undersecured may make it far easier for the debtor to "cram down" the creditor's secured debt (get a plan approved over the creditor's objection) in a plan of reorganization (see the discussion of *"Cramdown" And The Absolute Priority Rule* in Chapter Five for a complete discussion of how a debtor's plan can force the secured creditor to take a treatment of its secured claim to which the creditor does not consent).

Once the secured creditor has established that the debtor lacks equity in the collateral, the creditor must also establish that the collateral is not necessary to an effective reorganization. It is not sufficient for the debtor to simply state that there is a conceivable possibility of reorganization and that the property will be useful to it. Rather, the debtor must show that the property is essential for an effective reorganization "that is in prospect," meaning that there must be "a reasonable possibility of a successful reorganization within a reasonable time."[127] Because courts tend to give debtors every reasonable opportunity to formulate a plan of reorganization and complete their negotiations with many different creditor constituencies, it is very difficult for a creditor to establish early in a Chapter 11 case that there is no reasonable possibility of a successful reorganization. As the case progresses, however, the debtor's inability to propose a plan capable of being confirmed will become more and more compelling evidence that a successful reorganization is not reasonably possible.

First Day Orders

If one were to follow the bankruptcy law to the strict letter, it would be true that if a check were written and mailed on Monday and a bankruptcy were to occur on Tuesday morning (when that check had not yet arrived and been negotiated), technically that check could not be negotiated without violating the automatic stay of bankruptcy, and the claim of the recipient of that check would be considered a prebankruptcy claim that would have to be dealt with in the ordinary course of the bankruptcy proceedings.[128] Although this may not be too shocking with respect to a large vendor, the same would be true of payroll checks. Imagine the extraordinary disruption to a debtor's business if its employees were told that the first four days of the workweek that they had already worked would be considered prebankruptcy claims because the filing occurred on a Friday morning.

Accordingly, in commercial bankruptcy cases, a concept of so-called "**first day orders**" has developed. If the truth were known, there is no strict legal justification for the entry of most first day orders in bankruptcy cases under the Bankruptcy Code. In fact, they really fly in the face of what the Bankruptcy Code specifically states. That having been said, however, they are also entered by most bankruptcy courts, particularly those bankruptcy courts that handle a lot of business Chapter 11 cases (such as Delaware, Los Angeles, New York City, and other places such as Phoenix). The general rationale for the entry of these first day orders is the legal premise that the payment of these claims, even though they are technically prebankruptcy claims, is "essential to the reorganization efforts" of the debtor. This is called the "***doctrine of necessity***."[129] The Appendix contains an example of a "first day package," with the "first day orders" that were entered in the Chapter 11 case of *Unison Healthcare Corp.*, a nursing home operator with operations in six states.

In essence, the whole concept of first day orders is to try to prevent the bankruptcy filing from creating such chaos with essential vendors and employees (and perhaps other constituencies) that it essentially destroys the chances of any successful reorganization before it even starts. Generally, requests for permission to pay essential vendors and other constituencies (such as employees) are understood by bankruptcy courts as a necessary evil, and after a lot of mumbling about the "necessity doctrine" and "equitable powers," most (but not all) courts will generally sign these types of orders.[130]

Of course, it is important for the debtor not to overplay its hand on this issue. It is not unusual in bankruptcy cases for a bankruptcy filing to be targeted at a specific group of creditors—such as bondholders or other similar groups. In these types of disputes, the trade creditors are incidental and usually a small percentage of the total debt in the case. Frequently, a debtor may wish to pay all of its trade creditors so that it can really focus on the negotiations with the bondholders. This may be an example of overplaying a hand and may be met with some resistance from the bankruptcy court.[131]

A debtor can't simply take the position that it wants all unsecured trade creditors paid to prevent any disruption in supply or service, the bankruptcy courts will demand a more exacting showing than that. Bankruptcy courts will generally allow for the payment of unsecured claims to the extent such creditors are essential to the operations of the debtor. "Essential" does not mean that not paying them would create inconveniences, or that you'd rather not tick them off. Essential means that they truly provide goods or services that are difficult (if not impossible) to replace or that by the time the debtor replaces such goods or services there could be irreparable harm to the business enterprise. As seen in the material contained in the Appendix, the debtor must make a factual showing as to the essential nature of the creditors and the harm to the business enterprise.

A creditor that is essential in one type of industry may not be essential in another. For example, in the airline industry fuel suppliers are understandably essential. If a fuel supplier has a huge prebankruptcy claim, it may refuse to supply a debtor airline with fuel postbankruptcy. There is no prohibition on refusing to do business with a debtor in bankruptcy—this is America after all. Jet aircraft fuel suppliers are not easily found or replaced. Likewise, in the casino industry, when a winner (yes, it happens) walks out of a casino with chips in his or her hand, if a bankruptcy were to intervene before they cashed those chips, the claim represented by the chips is nothing more than a prebankruptcy claim. The very last thing a casino wants to do is to shake the faith of the gamblers that it will honor its gaming debts. As such, in casino cases a frequent category of essential creditors are holders of gaming markers and chips. In the health care industry there are other categories of essential vendors. What is essential to the debtor is industry specific, but in all events the moniker of "essential" must be supported by a real business rationale and not just a desire to avoid a conflict with a particular group or constituency.[132]

· ***The Beauty Of "Interim Orders" And "Negative Notice."***

At the beginning of bankruptcy cases, there are a number of things that need to be determined by the bankruptcy court very quickly—indeed, sometimes in the first day of the case (hence the phrase "first day orders"). The dilemma for the bankruptcy court is that usually the other parties have not had an opportunity to figure out what's going on, retain counsel, and otherwise get the general lay of the land. There are many things that can only be done in the bankruptcy court "after notice and a hearing." If the bankruptcy court were to take a request by a debtor, such as the request to be able to pay employees for prebankruptcy wages, or to use cash collateral (discussed below), or some of the other emergency things that come up before the bankruptcy court, by the time the court gets a notice out and parties have an opportunity to come in and be heard (which could take two to four weeks), the debtor, as a business enterprise, may be dead.

Accordingly, the Bankruptcy Code provides a very loose definition of "notice and a hearing," and for good reason. The Bankruptcy Code defines "after notice and a hearing" as meaning "after such notice as is appropriate in the particular circumstances, and such opportunity for a hearing as is appropriate in the particular circumstances."[133] In addition, the Bankruptcy Code allows the court to authorize an action without any actual hearing if some notice is given and "there is insufficient time for a hearing to be commenced before such act must be done, and the court authorizes such act."[134] In practice, the bankruptcy courts and practitioners have devised interesting ploys called "***interim orders***" and "***negative notice***."

Here's how it works. The debtor will come in and ask for an emergency order to be entered (such as the honoring of prebankruptcy payroll checks). There will be no time for the court to actually send out notice and have a hearing, so the court enters an "interim order" authorizing the debtor to honor the prebankruptcy payroll checks, but then instructs the debtor to send a notice to all parties (secured creditors, top twenty largest unsecured creditors, indenture trustee, etc.) that the interim order was entered. The order is interim because, while it's immediately effective and the parties can act on it, other parties will have a chance to object later. The debtor then sends out a notice that says that the bankruptcy court has allowed it to pay its prebankruptcy payroll wages, and the debtor is going to do that in accordance with the order. If anyone has a problem with that, they need to object by filing a written statement that they object with the bankruptcy court within ten days (or perhaps twenty days).

The beauty of this is that it is perhaps the ultimate example of form over substance. By the time a party files an objection with the bankruptcy court (in ten or twenty days, or whatever period of notice was given), the debtor usually has already finished doing what they requested the bankruptcy court give the debtor the authority to do in the interim order (such as honor payroll checks or pay prebankruptcy essential vendors). As such, the interim order and negative notice process has the appearance of giving parties a chance to object and be heard by the bankruptcy judge to say their peace, but in reality there is nothing for anyone to do because the action that they are complaining about is already done. It is almost with a wink and a nod that the bankruptcy court and bankruptcy practitioners keep businesses alive during the hectic first few days of a bankruptcy case while not running afoul (at least not technically) of due process of law concerns.[135]

"Excuse Me, But Your Golden Parachute Has Some Rust On It"—Management Severance In Corporate Restructurings

Let's face it—the process you are about to embark on is going to be bumpy and not without its stress and ugliness. In a public company, the proverbial pot of gold at the end of the rainbow usually is in the form of favorable stock options and in-the-money warrants so that the company's success translates into very tangible economic perks for executives. In addition, there are performance bonuses and other niceties that comprise the economic package that the executives bargained for.

In a distressed company (and not surprisingly), the dynamics are different. The options that you bargained so hard for two years ago are now so far out of the money as to be meaningless. The company's financial performance (which may not be the fault of management or anyone, but are the result of factors beyond anyone's control) is such that creditors that are facing potentially huge write-offs and losses are not exactly going to be amenable to giving management huge salary increases. Since in many cases involving overleveraged companies, the currency to deleverage a company is the equity in the ***reorganized company*** when it emerges from bankruptcy (discussed Chapter Five), there is no possibility of repricing stock options or even granting outright shares of stock in the reorganized company to the executive other than through the plan confirmation process. As discussed in the Chapter Three section on *Hand-Holding*, key employees who may have never experienced this process before are going to want to bolt, and competitors will certainly make the most of the company's troubles by trying to lure key people to defect, thereby making it extremely difficult to keep critical people together at a time when the company will need them the most.

Herein lies the very real dilemma of management at the outset of the reorganization process. The company must survive to get to plan confirmation, but that conceivably can be a year or even two (or perhaps even three or four) in the future. Executives in better times all had severance packages and perquisite packages to fall back on. Once the executive team has met with bankruptcy counsel, it is told that since the company is insolvent, it is likely that all equity will be either wiped out or greatly diluted so that the company can be deleveraged by giving creditors stock in the reorganized entity (discussed in Chapter Five). Accordingly, for all practical purposes management is working for the creditors and for a paycheck. Most senior management find that abhorrent since the real benefit to being an executive is the upside from the equity play.

Your bankruptcy counsel will also tell you that the prebankruptcy management severance and indemnity agreements that had been so painstakingly negotiated are now considered executory contracts (discussed below) in this bankruptcy and it is unlikely that a bankruptcy court would approve the honoring of those contracts in anything other than a confirmed plan of reorganization. Finally, because the equity in the company is likely going to change hands when this company comes out of Chapter 11 (with a new board and all of the other changes that occur in change-of-control situations), there will be new negotiations with the new owners (and their board) to cut new change-of-control and management severance agreements. It is a reality in this process that executives' golden parachutes do unfortunately have rust on them.

The good news is that sophisticated creditors (such as institutional bondholders and the like) recognize that it is critically important in this process to keep management incentivised to remain with the company through the reorganization process, and (assuming the management has the confidence of the creditor groups) to remain with the company when it emerges from bankruptcy (at least for some period of time) for stability and continuity purposes. Management severance in Chapter 11 cases really needs to be viewed in three distinct phases and groupings: (1) packages for non-senior level executives; (2) preconfirmation packages for senior level executives; and (3) postconfirmation packages for senior level executives.

· ***Packages For Non-Senior-Level People.***

The area that generally tends to generate less controversy is retention (or "stay bonuses") and severance arrangements for the non-senior-level executive types. Key middle management people or sales reps are understood by all creditor constituencies (and if not, by bankruptcy courts) as being key to the survival of the business prior to plan confirmation. Accordingly, severance packages and stay bonuses are not unusual in bankruptcy cases, and are usually negotiated and proposed for approval by the bankruptcy court within the first thirty or sixty days of cases.[136] Severance and retention bonuses are viewed as even more crucial for non-senior-level people when a case will involve a liquidation as compared with a full restructuring.[137] The general arrangement for severance packages for terminations without cause for non-senior-level management range from the payment of between three and six months worth of salary upon any termination without cause. In liquidation cases, severance arrangement may be characterized as a retention or stay bonus, and is obviously payable only after the employee remains with the company after a set period.

- ***Preconfirmation Severance And Indemnity Arrangements for Senior Level Executives.***

Generally the more sensitive issue in Chapter 11 cases is what types of severance and indemnity arrangements are available to senior-level management during the Chapter 11 reorganization, but prior to plan confirmation. Senior management will generally want full indemnification for prebankruptcy acts (and lawsuits), as well as severance arrangements for changes of control or terminations without cause. The rationale for this is straightforward. If a plan of reorganization is confirmed that liquidates the assets of the company, sells the company to a third party, or converts debt to equity such that there are new stockholders with a new board, frequently the new owners of the company will want new management. This happens in non-bankruptcy situations as well. Existing management, being savvy, understands that remaining with the company through a Chapter 11 without some degree of protection is a no-win proposition for them. In effect, they are working for a paycheck with no upside, and only a downside in that their actions will be second- and third-guessed and criticized. It is a reality in a bankruptcy that usually no one is completely happy at the end of the day. As such, in order to keep management incentivised to see the process through to completion, some degree of severance arrangements are generally agreed to and approved by the bankruptcy court.[138] Preconfirmation packages for senior management generally consist of some or all of the following types of protections:

- ***Indemnification.*** Senior management will want (and should get) indemnification for any actions from the date of the bankruptcy forward. Compare this with the indemnification that existed under either the company's bylaws or applicable corporate law. With respect to indemnification for prebankruptcy actions by a board and officers (which are generally covered by a D&O policy), most bankruptcy courts will not approve those types of agreements because once they are approved, any indemnification damages would be subject to being paid in full as an administrative expense of the company. That can have a devastating effect on the chances of success for the enterprise in the Chapter 11 plan process.[139] As a practical matter, giving broad indemnification rights to senior management for postbankruptcy activities is not very expensive in any terms for creditors to give. The reason for this is simple. Any action of any degree of materiality that is done once a bankruptcy is filed is going to be subject to bankruptcy court approval. This will happen after creditors are given some amount of notice and the court will authorize and direct the DIP to do the actions that are being considered. Once a bankruptcy court approves an action, it would be difficult to imagine some party being able to sue the directors and officers for negligence because the bankruptcy court has approved it (and generally on the basis that the action being considered represents a reasonable exercise of the debtor's business judgment). With respect to fraudulent acts, the indemnifications will not cover those actions under any circumstance, so it really is not very difficult for creditors to give broad indemnifications (certainly for negligence) to officers and directors with respect to postbankruptcy activities, but before plan confirmation. In addition, and as discussed in Chapter Five under *Exculpation And Releases*, most plans contain a release of claims against officers and directors for any actions taken in the bankruptcy and plan confirmation process.

- ***Severance Arrangements.*** Management will generally also want some sort of severance arrangement to protect them from terminations without cause or as a result of change-of-control circumstances. Again, to the extent that a plan of reorganization that is negotiated results in debt being converted to equity, and the new stockholders want new management simply to "start fresh," senior management will want some sort of protection and compensation for having stuck around through the rather difficult process of getting the company to the confirmation stage. So what types of arrangements are reasonable? Two months of salary and bonus? Five years?

In reality, the packages that have been negotiated between management and creditors and ultimately approved by the bankruptcy court vary according to a number of factors. These are general and common-sense type factors, such as creditors' satisfaction with management, how easily senior management can be replaced, how loyal non-senior management is to senior management (such that if senior management were to go, junior-level but important people would go as well), and other factors. Some are also industry specific. For example, in certain high-tech industries, senior management may also be the holder of patents or licenses, or have a specialized knowledge such that they are truly essential to the operation of the company. Those senior-level people will obviously have more leverage in this process.

Contained in the Appendix is an excellent survey recently completed by the investment banking firm of Houlihan, Lokey, Howard & Zukin, which outlines the parameters of executive severance that have been approved in bankruptcy cases preconfirmation. This will be, and should be, an area of serious and deliberate negotiations with the creditor constituencies. This is also where counsel for the debtor company can find themselves in a practical conflict situation because the senior management (with whom counsel will have much interaction and dealing) will prevail upon debtor's counsel to protect their interests. Counsel generally should do this to prevent major disruption to the case.

· ***Postconfirmation Severance And Indemnification Agreements For Senior Level Executives.***

Finally, there will be a substantial amount of negotiation as part of the plan negotiation process as to what type of protection senior management would get on a postconfirmation basis. In some instances where senior management and the major creditor constituencies are not in major battles, this is the sort of thing that may be negotiated and put into the plan of reorganization. In these cases, senior management may be able to negotiate and consensually reach a deal with major creditor constituencies that they will receive a certain percentage of stock options or in-the-money warrants, as well as appropriate severance arrangements.[140] Conversely, where the creditor constituency feels that the "jury is still out" on whether or not this management team would necessarily continue postconfirmation, a plan of reorganization may provide that there will be a time period after the plan is confirmed when the new board of directors will evaluate senior management and determine at that point what type of employment contracts (with appropriate severance arrangements, stock options and warrants, etc.) will be offered to senior management. For example, the reconstituted board might have 90 or 120 days after confirmation to evaluate senior management and at that juncture decide what type of packages they may wish to offer. To the extent senior management does not wish to accept the packages that are offered, they will generally get their preconfirmation severance arrangements and be free to go.[141] Not surprisingly, postconfirmation incentives are usually tied to performance benchmarks. Again, as in preconfirmation negotiating dynamics, management may have more or less leverage depending upon the case and industry, all of which are going to impact the deals that ultimately get negotiated.

· ***Bankruptcy Court Approval Of All Severance Arrangements Is Necessary.***

It is essential that the bankruptcy court approve any preconfirmation severance arrangements with any employee (and certainly any senior-level executive). An argument can be made that preconfirmation, lower-level employee severance arrangements are in the nature of "ordinary course" activities that can be done without bankruptcy court approval (see discussion below on *Stabilizing the Business Operations*), but certainly senior-level packages must be approved by the bankruptcy court to be enforceable.

Postconfirmation arrangements will either be approved as part of the plan confirmation process, or the reconstituted board will have the authority to enter into those arrangements without bankruptcy court approval as part of the plan confirmation process. In order to obtain bankruptcy court approval, the debtor will need to submit a motion to the bankruptcy court and state with specificity not only the business rationale for the packages, but also provide the economic impact if the packages are ultimately exercised. Not surprisingly, bankruptcy courts will want to know the impact of these packages coming due because, once approved by the bankruptcy court, they will be administrative claims against the estate (see discussion in Chapter Two on the rights of administrative claimants in bankruptcy cases). Contained in the Appendix is an example of the motion and preconfirmation severance arrangements for both senior and mid-level people used in a health care reorganization.[142]

Financing The Preconfirmation Operations

In order to keep the operations going, a business needs cash. There is no charge for this extraordinary and insightful advice.

Simply stated, there are really only two sources of operational cash in the preconfirmation process. The first is to collect existing accounts receivable, and continue to create receivables in the normal business cycle. The second is to obtain or be able to access a working-capital line of credit (which may be in the form of a revolving loan or a factoring line for receivables). To the extent that the operations of the business are such that the normal collection and use of receivables in the ordinary course will be sufficient, the company will need to determine which creditors have a lien on those receivables and then negotiate appropriate arrangements under "cash collateral" use discussed below. In conjunction with cash collateral use, or perhaps separate and distinct from cash collateral use, it may be necessary for a company to obtain a new, postpetition working-capital line of credit or factoring arrangement. This is known as "DIP financing," discussed below. Other means of obtaining cash for a company, such as sale of securities are not available to a company prior to plan confirmation (understandably so, since securities should not be sold or issued other than as part of a plan confirmation process once a company is in bankruptcy). Of course, cash may also be generated by the sale of assets, but usually this is not considered part of operational cash flow (although it certainly may assist in funding the business) (see discussion on *Sale of Assets* below).

· ***Cash Collateral Use.***

A bankruptcy filing disrupts the normal arrangement of collection and use of receivables or rents. The automatic stay and other provisions of the Bankruptcy Code prevent the lender from taking a lien on newly created accounts receivable and newly acquired inventory to replace the liens it had on liquidated receivables and sold inventory.[143] If the debtor uses the cash generated from the sale of inventory and the liquidation of receivables (cash that constitutes the lender's ***cash collateral***),[144] then the lender's collateral position deteriorates and the aggregate value of its security interest decreases. The Bankruptcy Code prohibits the use of cash collateral without either the lender's consent or a court order.

To minimize disruption debtors typically seek as part of their first day orders an emergency order allowing the debtor to use cash collateral or, more often, to approve an agreement with the secured lender as to the use of cash collateral subject to whatever conditions the lender and company mutually agree upon (discussed below). In larger cases, lenders generally agree to the use of cash collateral subject to operating budgets and defined periods (usually sixty–ninety days so the lender can reevaluate the situation at regular intervals).

Failing such agreement, the debtor can only use cash collateral if the court authorizes such use after finding that the lender's interest in the cash collateral is ***adequately protected***. As described in detail earlier in this chapter, adequate protection can take several forms, and can be said to exist on its own (for example, the presence of an equity cushion) or can be created through payments of interest to the secured creditor or the granting of additional or replacement liens to the secured creditor.

The debtor's emergency motion for an order authorizing cash collateral use is more often than not an invitation to negotiate an agreement regarding cash collateral use with the lender. The lender usually does not really want the debtor's business to collapse—it's not in the lender's interest since the value of its collateral base depends on the continued operation of the business and because the debtor's chances of paying down the loan decrease substantially if the business shuts down—and the debtor knows this. As a result, the lender is willing to negotiate with the debtor on the terms of a stipulated cash collateral order that the bankruptcy court will enter granting the debtor use of cash collateral and granting the lender, in exchange, relief designed to provide the lender with adequate protection.

- ***Stipulated Or "Agreed" Cash Collateral Orders.*** A stipulated cash collateral order will usually contain these essential elements: (1) a recitation of the lender's operative loan agreements and security interests; (2) a detailed operating budget restricting and governing the debtor's use of cash collateral; (3) provisions for adequate protection; and (4) other provisions governing the ongoing relationship between the debtor and the lender.
- ***Loan Agreements And Security Interests.*** In certain circumstances, the debtor will agree to the validity and enforceability of the lender's liens on the debtor's property and the amounts outstanding under the loan. Because the debtor would be waiving valuable ***avoiding powers*** by doing this and foregoing any opportunity to attack the amount of debt owed or the validity of the lender's security interests, it is not often advisable for the debtor to stipulate to amount and validity of liens so early in the case. Even when a debtor is willing to do so (presumably, it performed due diligence before the bankruptcy and satisfied itself that no problems with the liens, perfection of those liens under state law, and the amount of the debt existed), the

bankruptcy court (often at the insistence of the U.S. Trustee or unsecured creditors) will not make the debtor's stipulation binding on other parties in interest—most notably, an Official Committee of Unsecured Creditors, which would stand to benefit greatly from an avoidance of the lender's security interests, for example. Stipulated cash collateral orders will usually provide for a deadline by which any attacks on the lender's claims and liens must be brought or then waived. This approach works even when the debtor is also unwilling to concede lien validity or the amount of debt owing; the deadline to attack a lender's security interests or object to the amount of a secured claim can also apply to the debtor as well as all other parties in interest in the case.

- ***Operating Budget.*** Many borrowers outside of bankruptcy must abide by operating budgets and similar restrictions on sources and uses of cash as part of their ongoing lending relationships with their working-capital lenders. Continuing (and tightening) those restrictions after a bankruptcy case has been commenced, or instituting such budgetary restrictions as part of agreed cash collateral use in the bankruptcy, is critical to a lender. Being able to restrict and monitor closely the debtor's use of the lender's cash collateral allows the lender to gauge the extent to which the lender must be "adequately protected" and goes a long way to assuage the lender's concerns (almost always present in bankruptcy situations) that the debtor-borrower is not carelessly squandering working capital, negligently running the business, or even intentionally diverting proceeds away from the lender.

  Budgets are as detailed as the lender needs them to be, and the level of detail is often dependent on several factors, including the industry involved, the duration of the lending relationship, the lender's confidence in the debtor's management, the nature of the collateral, the amount of cash proposed to be spent, and the duration of time covered by the proposed use of cash collateral. Because it is the lender's cash that is being used to operate the business and fund the Chapter 11 case, debtors should be prepared for the lender to take a very active role in supervising the debtor's business operations, income, and expenditures. It is not uncommon for lenders (who have previously been very "hands-off") to carefully scrutinize operating budgets, even at the most detailed level, and to haggle over specific line items with increasingly annoyed debtors. While the intrusion is never welcomed, debtors are well-advised to accept this heightened scrutiny, for without it, cash to continue operating may be very hard to come by.

- ***Carveout for Professional Fees.*** Irrespective of how detailed the operating budget needs to be for purposes of a particular cash collateral order, one expenditure will almost always be included—a ***"carveout"*** for fees and expenses incurred by professionals in the case. The carveout will be a specific maximum amount of the lender's cash collateral that the estate will be permitted to use to satisfy the claims of estate professionals (counsel for the debtor and the Committee, financial advisors, and accountants) for fees and expenses. Because professionals will typically not work unless they are assured of being paid (no shock there), the debtor will often insist on a sufficient carveout so that even if the case fails, the lender is granted stay relief, and the estate becomes administratively insolvent (that is, property of the estate proves insufficient to satisfy even administrative claims in full), the professionals will at least have the carveout to look to for payment. Lenders are usually willing to agree to a reasonable carveout, not because they love the debtor and its lawyers so much, but because unless the debtor is able to assure the professionals of payment, the debtor won't be able to retain professionals, and the case will likely fail. Recall that it is usually in a working-capital lender's best interest for the business to continue to operate since the lender's chances of being made whole are much better if the debtor reorganizes than if the business shuts down and the debtor liquidates its assets at a "fire sale." If most professionals are going to wait until confirmation to be paid any fees from the case, the carveout could and should be substantial—in very large cases, carveouts can be several million dollars. On the other hand, courts will, in certain cases, allow the estate to pay professionals on an interim basis periodically throughout the case. In such circumstances, the carveout can be much smaller, since the professionals' exposure at any one time will be much lower.

- ***Adequate Protection.*** In exchange for the debtor's use of its cash collateral, the lender will demand that its collateral position be adequately protected using one or more of the methods described above. The most common method of providing adequate protection to a lender under a working-capital revolver is to grant the lender replacement liens on newly acquired inventory, accounts receivable, or other assets to compensate the lender for the diminution in the lender's security interest resulting from the debtor's use of the lender's cash collateral. Because the debtor is granting the lender liens in property on which the lender would have had a continuing lien but for the bankruptcy, the lender is adequately protected and the debtor does not feel as though it has given up much. The only risk for the debtor is that by doing so, it encumbers assets that it may wish later were unencumbered if additional, new debtor-in-possession financing is required later in the case. If a debtor has granted liens on essentially all its assets postbankruptcy to the prepetition lender for cash collateral use, obtaining debtor-in-possession financing discussed below (because of, say, an unexpected downturn in cash flow) will become much more difficult—most likely, the financing would have to be sufficient to satisfy (or "take out") the prepetition lender completely.

The lender may also negotiate periodic interest payments or other cash payments to keep the loan "cash flowing" throughout the Chapter 11 proceedings. If there exists a significant equity cushion, or if the debtor grants the lender replacement liens, such interest payments or other cash payments may not be necessary to provide adequate protection. Because there is more than one way to provide adequate protection, debtors and their lenders spend a substantial amount of time negotiating the extent and form of adequate protection in cash collateral orders.

- ***Other Provisions.*** The lender's increased desire to scrutinize and monitor a debtor's cash flows and expenses will often motivate the lender to negotiate for certain other provisions in the stipulated cash collateral order that may not have existed under the prepetition loan documents. Most notable among these provisions are financial reporting requirements, often obligating the debtor to provide the lender with periodic (weekly, bi-monthly, etc.) reports on inventory, sales, accounts receivable, accounts payable, and other financial analyses specific to the industry, the nature of the collateral, and the agreed-on uses of cash collateral. These reporting requirements may be in addition to those already existing in the loan documents and can be made a condition to any use of cash collateral. Particularly lender-friendly cash collateral orders may even terminate cash collateral use on the debtor's failure to meet its reporting requirements. Some of the information may be covered by confidentiality agreements (discussed in Chapter Three under *Protecting The Franchise*).

Of course, if the debtor and the lender cannot arrive at a stipulated cash collateral order, the bankruptcy court will be forced to decide whether the debtor may use cash collateral and under what terms and conditions, and what adequate protection will be granted to the secured creditor. To do this, the court would have to conduct an evidentiary hearing on the value of the lender's collateral, the extent and validity of the lender's security interests, the debtor's need for cash collateral use, and numerous other issues of fact—a potentially time-intensive process. To avoid this (and the "rough justice" that could result from the court fashioning temporary or "interim" relief pending conclusion of the lengthy final hearing on all these issues), debtors and lenders typically hammer out a cash collateral stipulation, knowing that few bankruptcy judges will simply cut off the debtor's use of cash early in a case. And because interim stipulated cash collateral orders may be in force throughout the course of a

Chapter 11 case (through periodic extensions of prior orders that maintain the status quo), the debtor, the lender, and the court may be able to avoid altogether a lengthy trial of collateral valuation and lien validity issues, particularly when the Chapter 11 case results in a plan of reorganization that the lender decides to support. The Appendix includes an example of a stipulated cash collateral order featuring most of the issues and elements described above.

· ***DIP Financing.***

If a company needs to obtain a working line of credit, the Bankruptcy Code provides appropriate mechanisms to do that. This is known as "***DIP financing***" and can take one of four forms:

- ***Unsecured Trade Credit***. The Bankruptcy Code allows a debtor to incur credit in the ordinary course of its business without seeking prior bankruptcy court approval to the extent that the credit is generally unsecured. This will be treated as an administrative claim in the bankruptcy case.[145] Suppliers and trade creditors typically extend this credit on similar terms as before the bankruptcy if they are comfortable that the debtor has sufficient cash flow to pay them on a timely basis.
- ***Super Priority Administrative Claim Credit***. If trade creditors are unwilling to extend credit and rely upon a simple administrative claim (which is, in essence, the first unsecured creditor to be paid in a case—it does not take seniority over secured debts and must share with other administrative claims such as professional fees), the Bankruptcy Code allows a debtor to obtain unsecured credit that is granted a "***super priority***" ***administrative priority***—that is, it will be paid before all other (or perhaps specified other) administrative claims would be paid in the case.[146] As you might imagine, that can create some difficulty for the other administrative claimants who generally want to share equally in assets as administrative claimants.
- ***Secured Financing***. To the extent unsecured financing either as an administrative expense or a super priority administrative expense is not available, the Bankruptcy Code allows (with bankruptcy court approval) a debtor to obtain credit secured by either a junior lien on assets of the estate, or a lien on assets that are otherwise unencumbered.[147] While this is fine in theory, usually distressed businesses do not have unencumbered assets, do not have any equity in assets that are already encumbered, or all of their assets are fully encumbered by other lenders. This is a nice option to have, but usually of little practical assistance.
- ***Super Priority Secured Financing***. Finally, the Bankruptcy Code recognizes that in circumstances where a debtor is unable to obtain credit in any of the three ways discussed above, the bankruptcy court

can allow the debtor to obtain financing secured by a first lien on already encumbered assets of the estate. This means that creditors that already have liens on the assets will be pushed down or "primed." This must be done with bankruptcy court approval, and creditors whose liens are being primed must have the opportunity to object. The only way the bankruptcy court will allow such financing is if: (1) the debtor makes an appropriate showing that it is unable to obtain credit in any other way; and (2) a showing that the creditor whose ox is being gored is "adequately protected." Adequate protection is a term of art that essentially means that the creditor whose lien is being primed needs to be shown that even though its lien is being pushed down, it will not be unduly harmed by this event. This can be shown in a number of different ways.

For example, assume the debtor asserts that the collateral of a lender is worth $100, and that creditor is owed $80. The debtor needs DIP financing in the amount of $15, but the DIP financier is unwilling to lend in a junior position. By "priming" the senior lender down by $15, that senior lender is not unduly hurt because it is still fully collateralized (indeed, a $5 "***equity cushion***" still exists). Of course, there are other risks in being in a junior-lien position, but this is an example of what is sometimes shown. Another way this may be shown is to say that the loan that is going to be made on a super priority (or priming) basis will increase the value of a collateral base such that the other lender will not be harmed. As you might imagine, "priming fights" can be rather ugly.

What has occurred at times is that a prebankruptcy working-credit-line lender will agree to continue to lend postbankruptcy under the identical terms and conditions, but it will want to do so as a new postbankruptcy loan that is approved by the bankruptcy court as a super priority loan. What it is essentially doing is "priming" itself with respect to postbankruptcy advances. In addition, it will use postbankruptcy payments made on the loan to pay off the prebankruptcy amounts so that after a short while the only amounts that are outstanding are postbankruptcy advances. Sometimes companies do not have any other choice but to do this, although courts (and frequently Creditors Committees and others) will look at this with a jaundiced eye because it is a way for a prebankruptcy lender to obtain postbankruptcy money to pay off, in full, its prebankrutpcy exposure, "cross-collateralize" a prebankruptcy debt with postbankruptcy assets, and otherwise make its entire loan a postbankruptcy loan. The benefit to the lender is that this postbankruptcy loan must be paid in full according to the specific terms and conditions as part of plan confirmation. In essence, once this happens there is no leverage with this particular lender. For example, "cramdown" (discussed in Chapter Five) is not an option with respect to this lender. Sometimes simple cash collateral use is better than entering into this sort of arrangement because the debtor does not have to give up as many rights. This is something to be discussed with the bankruptcy professionals and the other parties in the case.

- ***The Interesting Negotiating Dynamic In Financing Situations.*** There is a very interesting negotiating dynamic that occurs with respect to DIP financing (and also in cash collateral use) that is worth mentioning. The debtor desperately needs the cash for continued operations. The lender knows this. The lender clearly has the upper hand in these discussions. What sometimes happens in these cases is that the debtor will cut its best deal with the lender. At that point, it must be noticed out to various creditors for approval in the case.[148] At the hearing on this matter (and prior to the hearing as part of the negotiations) the debtor is obviously bound to the deal that it was able to negotiate. The Committee and other parties in the case are not so bound, and they will use the threat of upsetting the apple cart with the lender to try and get the lender to cut a better deal. In this way, the Committee can help a debtor get a better deal even after the debtor has cut the best deal it can cut. Although this doesn't always work, it frequently is a way to re-trade a deal after it has been made. In this way, the Committee and other parties can often be a helpful ally to the debtor.
- ***"So How Much Am I Going To Pay For This Muffler"?*** So how much is the customary amount to be charged for DIP financing facilities and the like? How do you know when you're being fleeced? How do you know when you're better off going to the thug with the crooked nose who charges twenty points a week rather than deal with the DIP lenders? Fair questions.

In fact, the investment bankers and other professionals in the case can assist the debtor in finding sources of DIP financing as well as knowing when the terms are out of line. There are some fairly standard sources of DIP financing that are publicized in numerous publications.[149] In addition, experienced investment bankers and financial professionals can assist in not only the identification of sources but also the negotiation of appropriate terms. Contained in the Appendix is a compilation prepared by Houlihan, Lokey, Howard & Zukin on DIP financing point spreads, up-front fees, interest rates, unused line fees, administrative fees, and letter-of-credit fees (if applicable).[150] Note that each situation must be analyzed as a whole—what appears to be a "good deal" may be less attractive than a "bad deal." For example, a DIP lender who's an existing lender with a prebankruptcy line may require points on "rolled" exposure. As such, paying 1½ points on a new $50 million DIP facility and keeping an existing prebankruptcy $500 million secured debt in place is cheaper than paying 1 ½ points on a combined $550 million facility.[151] As a matter of fact, DIP loans are often relatively safe bets for the lender, and there are times when, with the right collateral base, some healthy competition can develop to get the best deal.

Stabilizing The Business Operations

All of the legal issues aside, from a management perspective, the number-one priority after the filing (in addition to having to comply with all of the information requests and demands on your time put on you by the professionals and the various constituencies) is to stabilize the business operations. The concept of the automatic stay is to allow the debtor to get a "breathing spell" and thereby allow it to stabilize its business operations. Of course, stabilizing business operations in a Chapter 11 bankruptcy may be viewed as an oxymoron. How do you stabilize a business when the world at large knows that you've just filed bankruptcy? The answer is that today, bankruptcy in many industries is not really viewed with any sort of stigma, and it is sometimes viewed as a ordinary course business strategy for companies. Of course, a good public relations specialist (as discussed in Chapter Two) can be very helpful in this regard.

Stabilizing the business operations can be a lengthy process, but generally entails the specific identification of what needs to be done on an operational basis to remedy the problems that the business faces. Once you're in a Chapter 11, the so-called bad news is out, so this is the time to make the required expense cuts, reductions in force, write-offs, etc. It is not a question of impacting stock prices or otherwise spooking vendors or customers because the bankruptcy filing itself overshadows these concerns. As discussed in Chapter Two under *Exit Strategies*, a key component to stabilizing the business is making a determination as to whether there is a viable "core" business for the debtor. This is not to suggest that this is something that can be done in a day or week or even a few months, but should be an ongoing process. The financial professionals and advisors can be a great help in this analysis. In addition, the other constituencies will have their own financial advisors giving assistance as well (usually unsolicited assistance but assistance nonetheless).

· ***Reestablishment Of Trade Terms And Credit.***

One of the first problems that a bankruptcy debtor faces from an operational standpoint is that many vendors will put the company on C.O.D. terms. Indeed, in certain circumstances, a company may be put on "C.B.L." terms—"cash before loading"—as in loading products on delivery trucks.[152] It is important that the company reestablish trade terms as quickly as possible to get an idea of what its stabilized cash flow would look like. One way to do this is to deal with trade vendors that may have received preferences (discussed below under *"Strong Arm" Powers*) and to otherwise entice trade creditors to continue to do business with the company. Constant and consistent communication with the trade creditors to reassure them that the company is not going to be involved in a precipitous liquidation is certainly helpful. Regular telephone and personal communication with key vendors is also important. As discussed in the section involving *First Day Orders*, above, talking with vendors about the possibility of paying some or all of their prebankruptcy claims for the reestablishment of trade credit is also helpful. In addition, having a good consensual cash collateral or DIP Financing arrangement is also of great comfort to trade creditors because they know that the company at least has a line of credit or cash available to pay for shipments (see also *Dealing With The "Special Claims"—Reclamation Claims*, below).

· ***"Ordinary Course" Transactions.***

The general rule is that while nearly all transactions are subject to approval by the bankruptcy court, in Chapter 11 cases there are certain transactions that are considered ***"ordinary course" transactions***. These do not require advance bankruptcy court approval. For example, to the extent that the business of the debtor is the retail sale of products or the wholesale of products to distributors, the debtor does not require bankruptcy court approval to engage in those transactions. Those are considered ordinary course transactions. The basic concept is that the bankruptcy court does not get involved in the day-to-day operations of the debtor's business other than with respect to the use of cash collateral or the sale of collateral outside the ordinary course of business. For example, while a debtor does not need bankruptcy court permission to sell manufactured products on the retail market, if the debtor is seeking to sell off its manufacturing equipment (see the discussion below on *Sales Free and Clear of Liens*), that sale would require bankruptcy court approval. In all events, the regular sales to customers should be an ongoing activity and do not require bankruptcy court approval, thereby helping the business to stabilize. In the service industry (such as retail, restaurants, airlines, casinos, and health care), the ordinary-course-of-business-transaction parameters are helpful in enabling the debtor to persuade customers that it is business as usual notwithstanding the filing of the bankruptcy proceeding.

There are times when debtors attempt to stretch the "ordinary course of business" rule to matters that may be outside the scope. This is frequently done in first day orders involving "cash management" activities.[153] Bankruptcy courts and certain creditors are watchful when a debtor attempts to use first day orders to expand the Bankruptcy Code's concept of ordinary course transactions.

Reporting Requirements And Other Annoyances

Unless you've skipped directly to this page without reading anything else in the book, you have by now discovered that businesses in bankruptcy may as well adopt a variation of the familiar real estate mantra, "location,

location, location"— bankruptcy is all about "disclosure, disclosure, disclosure." You can now add the reports, statements, and other informational materials described below to the long list of examples where the company in bankruptcy is essentially laid bare for all to see (truly non-public, confidential financial information, and trade secrets excepted—see discussion on *Protecting The Franchise* in Chapter Three). While preparing and submitting these materials is often time-consuming and tedious, the annoyance of having to do so can be mitigated somewhat by the benefits that a debtor can derive by making these materials further the debtor's objectives in the bankruptcy proceedings.

· ***Statements And Schedules.***

So that all parties in a bankruptcy case are able to review the financial condition of the debtor—the various types of assets and liabilities the debtor currently has—the Bankruptcy Rules require that the debtor file what are referred to in the bankruptcy lingo as the ***"Statements and Schedules."***[154] Specifically, in Chapter 11 cases, the phrase refers to the "*Schedules Of Assets And Liabilities*" and the "*Statement Of Financial Affairs*."[155]

- ***Schedules Of Assets And Liabilities.*** Conceptually, the Statements and Schedules are a combination of extraordinarily detailed balance sheets and income statements with historical information. The Schedules of Assets and Liabilities are comprised of the following:
  - **Schedule A—Real Property.** This schedule must include a listing of all real estate that the debtor owns (as opposed to leases) in whole or in part.
  - **Schedule B—Personal Property.** This schedule must include a listing of all personal property that the debtor owns (as opposed to leases), in whole or in part. For large businesses, this can be a *very* lengthy schedule, since personal property includes all tangible and intangible assets (furniture, fixtures, equipment, inventory, raw materials, cash, securities, negotiable instruments, intellectual property [patents, copyrights, trademarks, licenses, franchises], causes of action, judgments, vehicles, etc.). The official form of Schedule B that the Bankruptcy Rules require debtors to use contains thirty-three different categories of personal property in the hopes that the debtor will leave nothing out.
  - **Schedule C—Property Claimed As Exempt.** Exemptions apply only to individual debtors, so this schedule is not applicable to the business in Chapter 11. Simply putting "None" on this schedule will suffice.
  - **Schedule D—Creditors Holding Secured Claims.** This schedule is a list of all secured creditors, including mortgagees, secured lessors (like equipment lessors), holders of secured debt securities, and secured tax creditors.

- **Schedule E—Creditors Holding Unsecured Priority Claims.** This schedule lists all unsecured creditors with priority claims, including employees with priority wage claims or employee benefit plan contribution claims, and priority tax claims. Priority is determined by specific provisions in the Bankruptcy Code and for most businesses, the bulk of the priority claims on Schedule E will be claims of employees for wages and contributions to benefit plans that arose within ninety days of the bankruptcy petition.
- **Schedule F—Creditors Holding Unsecured Priority Claims.** This is everybody else—all unsecured claims, including trade claims, plaintiffs in lawsuits, landlords and other lessors—what we have referred to elsewhere in the book as the "great unwashed." In business reorganizations, Schedule F will be by far the longest list, and it is, for reasons described just below, perhaps the most important schedule to make complete and accurate.
- **Schedule G—Executory Contracts And Unexpired Leases.** This is a list of all ***executory contracts*** (contracts where both parties to the contract have yet to do material parts of what they are required to do under the contract—see *Dealing With Executory Contracts And Unexpired Leases* later in Chapter Four) and ***unexpired leases*** (leases under which the debtor is either lessor or lessee that have not expired or terminated as of the date of the petition).
- **Schedule H—Co-debtors.** In a business context, this list will include guarantors, co-obligors and co-signers on debts listed elsewhere in the schedules. Common examples include guarantors and co-tenants under a lease, co-borrowers under a loan, and guarantors under a trust indenture.[156]

An authorized officer of the debtor must execute a declaration swearing under penalty of perjury that the schedules being submitted to the bankruptcy court are true and correct to the best of the debtor's knowledge, information, and belief. To be able to honestly make that declaration, it is usually best for the CFO, controller, or similar officer of the business to participate directly in the compiling and formulation of the schedules. The debtor's counsel (or, more exactly, a younger associate or experienced paralegal in the firm—it's time intensive but not terribly complicated) will assist the debtor's financial officer in compiling and completing the schedules, but it is ultimately the debtor's responsibility, since the information needed is to be found only in the debtor's business records and institutional knowledge of its officers. **There's no need to panic if the schedules (or statements) have left something out or are inaccurate—they can always be (and indeed must be) amended and supplemented.**

Schedules D, E, and F take on a special significance because they provide the debtor with an initial opportunity to dispute claims and begin a claims reconciliation process intended ultimately to reduce the amount of debt allowed against the estate (for a discussion of the complete claims process, see Chapter Five). Each of Schedules D, E, and F allows the debtor to indicate whether a particular claim of a particular claimant is contingent, unliquidated, or disputed (or some or all of those). Generally, a claim is contingent if something needs to occur (like a judgment rendered in a lawsuit, or a guaranteed debt to default, or a claim made against the debtor's deductible under an insurance policy) before the debt matures or become due. A claim is unliquidated if liability is established, but the amount due is still undetermined. A claim is disputed if the debtor is aware that someone has or is likely to make a claim but the debtor does not believe that it is liable for the debt. Despite the debtor's belief, it is *critical* that the debtor list this claim—and all others that are contingent, unliquidated, or disputed—in the schedules. It is not an admission of liability, but rather just the opposite. Listing a claim as contingent, unliquidated, or disputed in the schedules places the claimant on notice that it must file a formal ***proof of claim*** in the case or have its claim forever disallowed and discharged (see discussion of *The "Bar Date" Order* in Chapter Five). If a claim is listed in the schedules and not designated as contingent, unliquidated, or disputed, that claim is deemed allowed in the amount stated in the schedules without the creditor having to take any further action to preserve the claim and receive a distribution under the plan of reorganization. A claimant can always file a proof of claim to correct the amount listed in the schedules, but by doing so, the claimant provides the debtor with an opportunity to object to the claim later in the case.

The importance of listing all possible claims in the schedules cannot be overstated. The debtor has entered into bankruptcy proceedings in order to clean its financial house; leaving certain claims unresolved and undischarged at the end of the case is like an exterminator killing "most" of the bugs. The ones that survive infest the house again in time. Claims that are left over after the case can seriously undermine the benefits obtained through a bankruptcy discharge. Here's why: if a debtor knew about even a remote possibility that some claimant out there had a claim and the debtor did not list that claimant on the schedules, the claimant will not receive notice of the bankruptcy case (the master mailing list for all notices is created, in part, from the schedules) or notice of the ***bar date*** (the deadline to file all claims or forever waive them), and the debtor's discharge may not be effective against that claimant. Therefore, if some mail clerk that worked for your company for three days said something about discrimination when the office manager fired him eight months ago, *put the mail clerk on Schedule F*. That way, he cannot sneak in under the radar of the bar date and claim that he never received notice of any requirement to file a proof of claim. "Overkill" in creating Schedule F—checking with human resource managers, purchasers, and other middle-management personnel to sniff out even remotely possible claims—may very well be a debtor's best weapon when the unexpected and spurious claims roll in. And they do roll in.

After the above description of how involved the preparation of the schedules can be—and how high the stakes are—it may come as a shock to the debtor that the Bankruptcy Rules require the debtor to file all schedules at the same time as the petition or within fifteen days thereafter. Don't panic!—a common ***first day order*** is an extension of time (thirty to ninety days in many larger cases) for the debtor to file the Schedules. Courts understand that in larger-business debtor cases, the financial distress and urgency that precipitated the filing of the petition does not usually afford the debtor sufficient time to engage in the substantial amounts of due diligence required to prepare accurate and complete schedules. With an extension of the time to do so, the debtor needs only to file a list of the top twenty largest creditors and a list of all equity interest holders (shareholders, LLC members, etc.) with the petition.

- ***Statement Of Financial Affairs***. In addition to the schedules, the Chapter 11 debtor must also file a Statement of Financial Affairs, a summarized accounting of all income and expense items separated into some twenty-one categories, including: gross business income from the beginning of the calendar year to the petition date and the two preceding calendar years; payments to creditors within ninety days of the petition date (this is used to ferret out ***preferences***, discussed later in this chapter); pending lawsuits and administrative proceedings to which the debtor is a party; gifts made within the last year (this is used to uncover possible ***fraudulent transfers,*** also discussed later in this chapter); casualty losses within the last year; all bank accounts and safe-deposit boxes, including those closed within the last year; prior addresses of the debtor; nature and location of the debtor's businesses; the identity of all bookkeepers and accountants that supervised the keeping of or audited the debtor's books within the last six years; the dates and values of the last two inventories taken; and current partners or shareholders owning or controlling 5 percent or more of the debtor's outstanding stock. It is imperative that the debtor be accurate in preparing the Statement of Financial Affairs as well, both because it is submitted under penalty of perjury and because it often becomes the basis for discovery and challenges in disputes with creditors later in the case.

- ***A Word Of Caution.*** While the preparation of Statements and Schedules is often left to administrative staff, it is important that some thought be given to what numbers are reported (primarily values to assets). For example, the press will pick up the "Summary Sheet" of Schedules, and if it shows $20 million in assets and $10 million in debt, this will be reported and creditors will assume they'll be paid in full (and equityholders will retain all their interests). Of course, the $20 million in assets may be the result of book values for assets and leaving $15 million of "goodwill" under intangibles. Since bankruptcy is the creation and management of expectations (see discussion in Chapter Two on *The Reorganization Process*), some thought to the values in the schedules is important.[157]

· ***Interim Operating Reports.***

Now for the even more annoying part, since the submission of these interim operating reports to the U.S. Trustee and the bankruptcy court do not, as a practical matter, provide the debtor with any strategic benefit on par with the schedules. Only occasionally does anyone (including the U.S. Trustee) ever actually read the reports, yet many case managers in the U.S. Trustee's office will raise quite a furor if a debtor fails repeatedly to file them.

Each regional office of the U.S. Trustee has its own rules regarding interim operating reports, but most require that the debtor submit the report monthly, by the fifteenth day of the month following the month covered in the report. The reports usually must contain these essential elements: accounting records, including tax receipts, bank statements, most recently filed income tax returns, and most recent Annual Financial Statements prepared by the debtor's accountant; accounting of receipts and disbursements, including reorganization expenses (professional fees, U.S. Trustee fees); accounts receivable aging; accounts payable aging; postpetition taxes; and payments to officers, directors, other ***insiders,*** and to professionals. The reports can be completed on a cash basis or an accrual basis, but are very detailed. It is usually a good idea to ensure that the completion of these reports becomes an ongoing part of the duties of the controller, CFO, COO, or similar officer once the bankruptcy case begins. The format of the reports may take some getting used to initially, but often becomes much easier to deal with as the case progresses.

. ***U.S. Trustee's Fees.***

As mentioned above, the interim reports must list the fees paid to the U.S. Trustee during the reporting period. Add these fees to the list of annoyances, as well. Ostensibly in order to partially fund the operation of the Office of the U.S. Trustee, Congress enacted a statute that requires all

Chapter 11 debtors to pay quarterly fees based on the amount of money disbursed from the estate during the calendar quarter. Currently, a minimum fee of $250 is due for every quarter if less than $15,000 is disbursed in the quarter, and fees increase incrementally to a maximum quarterly fee of $10,000 when quarterly disbursements exceed $5,000,000.[158]

Dealing With Utility Companies

Debtors-in-possession tend not to find much success running their business for the benefit of creditors when the lights go out. Congress realized that a business reorganization is doomed at the outset if utility companies—electric, gas, water, telephone/data—could unilaterally cut off service to the debtor based solely on the debtor's having filed its petition.[159] In most instances, at least some (if not all) of a company's utilities are irreplaceable—how many electric and water companies are there in your area? If a utility monopoly were to terminate service to a debtor, the effect on the debtor's business would be immediate, destructive, and irreparable. And because the automatic stay does not force creditors to continue to do business with a debtor-in-possession, a special provision was included in the Bankruptcy Code to ensure that utilities could not cut off service before a debtor's reorganization has really even begun.

This special provision prevents a utility from terminating, altering, or otherwise affecting a debtor's utility service simply because the debtor has filed a bankruptcy petition or because the debtor failed to pay for certain prepetition services.[160] This prohibition lasts only for the first twenty days of the Chapter 11 case. At any time after that, a utility can demand that the debtor provide "adequate assurance" of payment for future service (but not for prepetition service—those debts are simply general unsecured debts treated like all others) before it will continue to provide uninterrupted service. Adequate assurance can be given in many forms, but usually involves a cash security deposit, surety bond, or guaranty from a non-debtor.

In some cases, a debtor has managed to remain current with its utilities in the prepetition period, and a good payment history (even in the environment of financial distress) can itself be adequate assurance of payment for postpetition services, particularly when coupled with the administrative expense priority status to which all postpetition trade debt (utility services included) is entitled. Many debtors will include a motion among its ***first day orders*** to have the bankruptcy court determine that all utilities are deemed adequately assured of future payment based on a strong prepetition payment history, the presence of sufficient operating capital (through cash collateral use, DIP financing, or both), or already-held security deposits. Such orders typically will give any utility a limited period during which it can come into court and show that it needs additional assurance—usually no more than thirty days. The utility will not be able to alter service unless the court determines that additional assurance is warranted and the debtor failed to provide it. Squaring away postpetition arrangements with a debtor's utilities is something best done at the beginning of the case and avoids operational headaches later, when more global restructuring challenges must be met.

Dealing With The SEC

For any company that files reports with the SEC, it is important that the company's 10-Qs or 10-Ks disclose when the company determined that a bankruptcy would be filed. Failure of a reporting company to disclose the possibility of a bankruptcy filing in a timely manner will often result in an investigation by the SEC, which could lead to an SEC enforcement action such as termination or suspension of public listings. If postbankruptcy public trading in the company's securities (either debt or equity) is important, it is important to be prepared to contact the trading exchange immediately before or after filing to discuss concerns that may cause the delisting of the securities (if, indeed, it is possible to allay such concerns), and maintain open lines of communication with the SEC. As will be discussed in Chapter Five, in public companies or just large companies in general, the SEC frequently monitors major bankruptcy filings.[161] In addition, the SEC will frequently give comments on the form of disclosure statement in advance of bankruptcy court approval (see discussion in Chapter Five).

For publicly traded companies, a bankruptcy filing that is not preceded by appropriate "warning signs" in prebankruptcy press releases and Forms 10-Q and 10-K will usually bring increased scrutiny by the SEC. This could possibly result in enforcement action against individual directors and officers based on non-disclosure of material adverse information (although such action is rare). It is important to remember that the prebankruptcy disclosure will be evaluated in "20/20 hindsight." Of course, a bankruptcy filing may also precipitate action by the company's trading exchange to delist (either by termination or suspension) the company's stock or debt securities.[162]

Dealing With D&O Lawsuits

There are few certainties in life, but one of the things that most directors and officers can count on is that they can be the target of securities fraud actions whenever a company with public debt or equity gets into financial difficulties. Directors and officers are often faced with claims of security fraud based on the asserted inadequacy of prebankruptcy public disclosures, as well as breaches of their fiduciary duties in the management of the company. One of the issues in surviving to plan confirmation is protecting the directors and officers from these lawsuits to the extent that the continuation of these lawsuits would take them away from their duties in running the company.

· ***Protecting The D&O Insurance Policy.***

D&O insurance policies are considered assets of the bankruptcy estate. There is an interesting twist in the law because the actual insureds under

D&O policies are usually the directors and officers themselves and not necessarily the company. Notwithstanding that, bankruptcy courts have recognized that the policies are an asset of the estate. As such, any attempts by insurers to cancel such policies are considered a violation of the automatic stay.[163]

· ***Securities Fraud Claims Injunctions.***

The automatic stay prohibits securities fraud actions against the company, but not against the individual directors and officers. Notwithstanding that, frequently bankruptcy courts will issue an injunction to stop actions against individual officers and directors prior to plan confirmation to the extent a showing can be made that such lawsuits will take the officers and directors away from the important work of the reorganization, and that the continuation of the lawsuits may deplete the D&O policies, which are property of the estate.[164] These injunctions, however, only last until plan confirmation, and are not indefinite. That having been said, however, securities fraud claims are usually (but not always) settled as part of the plan confirmation process, settlements that generally include releases of claims against the individual directors and officers. Not surprisingly, the D&O carriers are usually at the forefront of negotiating the settlements.

Dealing With The "Special Claims"

When other legislative schemes (federal and state) intersect with the Bankruptcy Code, interesting and occasionally complex things happen. For example, issues surrounding the automatic stay and allowance of claims take on a different cast where certain governmental agencies and special legislation are concerned. From a cash management standpoint, debtors are well-advised to plan early on in the case to satisfy certain postpetition obligations and "special claims" as they come due.

· ***The EPA And Environmental Cleanup Claims.***

Orders issued at the insistence of the Environmental Protection Agency (or its state-level counterparts) seeking to remedy environmental damage generally take one of three forms, and the distinction between those forms is critically important to how such orders are treated in the context of a Chapter 11 case. Recall that the automatic stay prohibits any action to collect on a debt or execute a judgment against the debtor. Ostensibly, EPA enforcement of an order regarding environmental law violations would seem to fall within the coverage of the automatic stay. But recall also that there is an important exception to the automatic stay regarding an exercise of a government's regulatory or "police" power, and a separate exception for criminal prosecutions (see the discussion of the *Automatic Stay* earlier in this chapter). Whether the general rule or one of the exceptions apply depends on what the EPA is intending to enforce.

If the EPA has obtained an order awarding the EPA damages against the debtor for past environmental pollution, courts have regarded such orders as creating monetary claims for prepetition conduct. In this sense, these orders for monetary damages (or for reimbursement of the EPA for cleanup costs) are no different from any other claim arising from prepetition conduct or contracts of the debtor. The automatic stay prevents the EPA from enforcing such an order, so long as the order primarily calls for the payment of money.

EPA enforcement can also be in the form of injunctive relief—an order requiring the debtor either to clean up past pollution or cease and prevent current and future pollution. EPA injunctions also are evaluated in terms of the automatic stay to determine whether the injunction falls within the general rule prohibiting an enforcement of a prepetition claim or within the exception for the exercise of regulatory authority. Most courts now agree that if the EPA seeks to enforce an injunction (obtained before the bankruptcy filing) requiring cleanup of already-existing pollution, the debtor's satisfaction of that injunction still essentially requires the payment of money, since the debtor could defer to the EPA to perform the cleanup and simply reimburse the EPA for the costs. That type of injunction is, therefore, still subject to the automatic stay. An injunction that requires the debtor to cease current pollution and prevent future pollution is another matter, however. The debtor cannot simply pay money to satisfy its obligations under such an injunction, and the EPA's interest in enforcement is for the protection of the environment, not the satisfaction of the EPA's pecuniary interests (like the cleanup order essentially is). This type of prospective injunction falls within the regulatory and police power exception to the automatic stay.

Finally, egregious environmental violations may be punished as crimes. EPA prosecutions of environmental crimes against a debtor will not be subject to the automatic stay. Restitution, fines, and other monetary remedies arising from a conviction, however, would still be subject to the automatic stay to the extent that they are levied before the bankruptcy petition was filed.[165] Severe environmental contamination can cause complexities in reorganization proceedings that require serious analysis.[166]

· ***The PBGC And Underfunded Pension Plans.***

The Pension Benefit Guaranty Corporation, or PBGC, is a governmental entity that guarantees the availability and payment of benefits under ERISA-qualified pension plans—and is a huge pain in the neck for many debtors in Chapter 11 cases. The PBGC is a putative creditor in very many Chapter 11 cases—essentially any case in which the debtor has significant prebankruptcy funding defaults under its pension plan or intends to terminate the pension plan as part of an orderly liquidation or acquisition under a Chapter 11 plan—because it is the PBGC's responsibility to meet all benefit obligations under a pension plan to the extent that the employer-debtor does not.

A debtor's prebankruptcy funding arrearages can create a pension plan solvency problem in that unless such arrearages are cured by the debtor (or by the PBGC, who then would have a priority unsecured claim for reimbursement against the estate), the pension plan may not be able to pay out benefits to plan members as the need arises in the future (that is, when employees go into "pay status"). Quantifiable prebankruptcy arrearages are easier to deal with because everyone involved knows what amount will be necessary to cure those arrearages. The size of the claim for such arrearages—almost always asserted by the PBGC even though the estate will likely cure such arrearages—can be substantial, and the longer arrearages go unpaid, the more money will be needed to cure the default (since the PBGC will assert that the pension plan will not have had the benefit of investing the money that should have been in the plan). Some debtors may find it most expedient and economical in the long run to cure arrearages in a pension plan that it intends to continue postconfirmation early in the case by obtaining special permission from the bankruptcy court.

A far bigger problem arises when the debtor indicates its intention to alter its funding requirements under the pension plan, or terminate the plan outright (in the face of the debtor's liquidation or other cessation of business arising out of the terms of a Chapter 11 plan). Because the debtor no longer will be making required contributions to the pension plan (because, for example, it fired its work force), the PBGC would have to step in and fund the pension plan if current plan assets prove insufficient to pay out pension benefits as they come due long into the future. Since, presumably, the debtor terminating the pension plan has also terminated all its employees (meaning that in the future the pension plan will cover only the then-existing members), it is possible that no additional funds will be required in the future to meet pension plan obligations to members.

But the PBGC doesn't think like that. Rather, because the amount of funding for the future is not exactly quantifiable, the PBGC will take two approaches to calculating future funding requirements. Those approaches taken together typically yield an enormously inflated claim and this is where the PBGC becomes a pain in the neck. First, the PBGC will use actuarial calculations (regarding plan members' life expectancy and forecasted benefit draws) to estimate funding requirements for many years into the future, but will employ the most ultra-conservative actuarial tables, assuming that every pension recipient will have located Ponce DeLeon's fountain of youth and will live to 147 and will have no income from any other source after tomorrow. By assuming that pensioners will live to see the next millennium, the PBGC concludes that funding requirements will greatly outpace the funds already invested into the plan by the debtor. Second, the PBGC (which does not administer the pension plan) will assume that plan assets will receive an ultra-conservative investment return—something akin to the cozy two percent per year one would get with a passbook savings account at the local thrift institution. These two assumptions conspire to wildly inflate the PBGC's claim for future funding reimbursement against the bankruptcy estate to some astronomical amount—it is not unheard of for such claims to rise into the hundreds of millions of dollars.

What's more is that the PBGC—despite losing the issue at virtually every appellate court in the country over the years—will continue to argue that the entire amount of the claim is entitled to priority status as a "tax" and a cost of administration of the estate.[167] Because it is the government, the PBGC has no financial disincentive against aggressively re-litigating the priority issue in every case (it must know by now that it will never win) and causing the debtor's estate to expend significant fees in fighting what is, admittedly, a winning battle for the estate. The PBGC's claim is almost always a general unsecured claim, but the estate may have to spend significant time and fees in establishing that—and then will have to litigate (or perhaps settle) the amount of the claim. Always true is that the astronomical claims—even treated as general unsecured claims—are wholly speculative (the plan may never need additional funding), and unnecessarily and sometimes substantially dilute the recoveries for all other unsecured creditors.

· ***"PACA" — It's Not Just For Breakfast Anymore.***

Companies engaged in the grocery or food services industries are likely more familiar with the nefarious provisions of the Perishable Agricultural Commodities Act, or PACA, than they would like.[168] PACA was intended by Congress to protect sellers of "perishable agricultural commodities"—fruits, vegetables, meats, — from purchasers who suddenly file for bankruptcy protection. Because these agricultural goods are so perishable, sellers need to sell them quickly, often before they have had an adequate opportunity to gauge the purchaser's creditworthiness. Without PACA, these sellers would find themselves with a general unsecured claim for two reasons: (1) a debtor's secured lender will likely have a blanket lien on the debtor's inventory; and (2) the perishable nature of the goods prevent, as a practical matter, the seller from reclaiming the goods. Given the nature of the industry, suppliers of these goods are usually the least able to survive the delays and losses attending the typical Chapter 11 case.

PACA protects the sellers from this pitfall by providing that certain statutorily defined buyers of perishable agricultural goods hold those goods or "commodities . . . and all inventories of food or other perishable agricultural commodities, and any receivables from the proceeds or sale of such commodities or products . . . in trust for the benefit of all unpaid suppliers or sellers of such commodities. . . ."[169] Because property of the estate is defined under the Bankruptcy Code with reference to non-bankruptcy law (including traditional trust principles), goods delivered subject to a PACA trust do not constitute property of the bankruptcy estate.[170] Now, here's why you care: if the goods (or, more exactly, the cash proceeds from the sale of those goods) do not constitute property of the estate, then that cash must be paid to the seller in order to satisfy the debtor's payable to the seller. The automatic stay does not apply to the seller in recovering that cash, since the cash does not constitute property of the estate. The result: if the debtor does a lot of PACA-affected business, the debtor should prepare for a noticeable cash drain at the beginning stages of the case as PACA sellers demand payment on their invoices.

· ***Personal Liability For Unpaid Withholding Taxes.***

Companies that withhold income tax and other taxes from employee wages hold those taxes in trust for the taxing authority. These taxes do not constitute property of the estate, so any effort by the taxing authority to recover them will not be prevented by the automatic stay.[171] Worse, if the employer fails to turn such taxes over to the taxing authority, the employer's "responsible officers" (generally, any officer charged with responsibility to manage, oversee, or authorize payroll and tax withholding) may be personally liable for the taxes.[172] Financially distressed companies that handle payroll internally do funny things sometimes, and withheld tax funds have a sneaky way of "disappearing" in some cases. That can put individual officers on the hook for the liability—which can be very substantial in large companies. Bankruptcy and tax counsel will be able to help navigate the debtor through these rough waters, but the debtor should be prepared to continue paying employee withholding taxes (as well as sales taxes) as soon as they are due to the taxing authorities (see discussion in Chapter Five on *"Responsible Officer" Liability For Unpaid Withholding Taxes*).

· ***Transfer Taxes.***

We will see in Chapter Five that a debtor can use the plan of reorganization to accomplish a good many business deals related to a restructuring. A special provision in the Bankruptcy Code makes it even easier (and cheaper) to complete certain real estate transactions and other transfers of property under a plan of reorganization. In many states, there are substantial transfer taxes that are assessed when various types of personal property and real property are sold or otherwise transferred from one entity to another. These taxes can be quite high depending on the state, and substantial taxes often affect the pricing of a particular transaction. The Bankruptcy Code provides, however, that any issuance, transfer, exchange of a security (stock or bond), or the transfer of property under a Chapter 11 plan is exempt from any stamp tax, transfer tax, or similar type of tax. This provision is particularly useful when a primary goal of the restructuring is to transfer large amounts of assets to a third party—the transfer is exempt from transfer taxes, further facilitating the transfer and, therefore, the reorganization of which it is a part.[173]

· ***Reclamation Claims.***

Under state law, sellers of goods have a right to get back sold goods that were unpaid for if the buyer received the goods while insolvent—this is called ***reclamation***.[174] Where a seller's reclamation rights are interrupted by a bankruptcy filing, the Bankruptcy Code recognizes reclamation rights such that the debtor must return goods unless it provides a lien to the seller for the unpaid price of the goods or grants the seller an administrative expense for the price of the goods.[175] This is an unusual circumstance where goods will have been delivered prebankruptcy but will be treated in the bankruptcy law as having been delivered postbankruptcy such that they are entitled to an administrative expense. In retail reorganizations (such as supermarkets, clothing stores, and convenience stores) reclamation claims are a very serious issue that must be dealt with early in the case because there could be hundreds (if not thousands) of sellers that are filing reclamation notices with the bankruptcy court. A clever way that many cases have dealt with reclamation claims is to provide a protocol whereby the debtor will pay 110 percent of invoices for subsequently delivered goods until the prebankruptcy goods subject to reclamation are paid for. Sometimes they also couple this with a requirement that the vendor extend ordinary trade terms postbankruptcy (thereby avoiding the C.O.D. cash crunch).[176]

· ***Retiree Benefits And Collective Bargaining Agreements.***

In order to prevent debtor's from unduly affecting or terminating agreements that provide for benefits (including hospitalization and other medical benefits, life insurance, disability, and accident insurance) to retired workers, the Bankruptcy Code establishes a complex procedure for the suspension or modification of retiree benefit plans and programs.[177] During the course of the Chapter 11 proceedings, the debtor must continue to make payments of retiree benefits as they come due absent court authorization based on compelling reasons.[178] This is also true of collective bargaining agreements. Absent very compelling circumstances, ongoing wages and benefits payable under collective bargaining agreements must continue to be paid during the Chapter 11 case. These are both demands on short-term cash flow left unaltered by the bankruptcy filing for which a debtor should be prepared.

Sale Of Assets

As in the section on *Financing The Preconfirmation Operations* above, one way to finance the ongoing operations of the business will be to sell assets outside of the ordinary course of business. For example, if there is an operating facility that is no longer needed, or retail stores and equipment that are no longer needed, debtors will seek to sell those assets through the course of the bankruptcy proceeding. Something that the company must be aware of is that efforts made to sell large numbers of assets (or close a large number of stores, for example) will generally lead to significant anxiety on behalf of the creditor constituencies to the extent that they have not yet had an opportunity to understand the nature of the debtor's business and business problems.[179] For example, Creditors Committees would generally be very concerned about sales of assets or closure of stores on a one-by-one basis without sufficient analysis to be sure that the closures do not lead to a circumstance where, after the sales or closures occur, there are insufficient assets or operations left on which to base a reorganization. In other words, creditors are concerned about a "creeping liquidation." As such, it is generally good practice to be sure that major constituencies are in on the decision-making process to close stores or sell assets, and they are given a good overview of the business rationale behind these decisions. Once you make them part of the decision-making process, they will generally be vocal supporters of the debtor's efforts in bankruptcy court—always a good thing.

· ***Sales "Free And Clear."***

Once the decision has been made to sell an asset, the Bankruptcy Code provides the debtor with a power unique to U.S. bankruptcy law. The Bankruptcy Code allows a debtor to sell assets ***free and clear of liens*** and co-ownership interests.[180] This becomes a particularly valuable power when the asset to be sold is worth less than the amount of secured debt against it-for example, there is a piece of equipment that is no longer necessary to the operation of the business that is worth $1,000, but there is $2,000 worth of debt against it. Most courts would allow for the sale of that asset free and clear of liens and encumbrances. To be fair, there is a split in authority on this point. While most courts would, in fact, allow a sale under these cirumstances, some courts have taken the position that such a sale would be improper unless the sale would be for at least the amount of the debt against the asset. *See, e.g. In re Beker Industries Corp.*, 63 B.R. 474 (Bankr. S.D.N.Y. 1986) (allowing for a sale of assets for less than the amount of the liens against those assets); *In re Hatfield Homes, Inc.*, 30 B.R. 353 (Bankr. E.D. Penn. 1983) (same); *In re WPRV-TV, Inc.*, 143 B.R. 315 (D. Puerto Rico 1991) (same). Some courts would not allow such a sale under these circumstances. *See In re Riverside Investment Partnership*, 674 F.2d 634 (7th Cir. 1982); *In re Terrace Chalet Apartments, Ltd.*, 159 B.R. 821 (N.D. III. 1993); *In re Perroncello*, 170 B.R. 189 (Bankr. D. Mass. 1994); *In re Julien Company*, 117 B.R. 910 (Bankr. W.D. Tenn. 1990). The liens will attach to the sale proceeds. What this means is that the debtor is simply not able to sell the assets free and clear of the liens and then spend the money or use the money in operations, but rather must segregate the proceeds. So why would a debtor wish to consider such a sale? In the example given above, while the debtor may be able to get $1,000 for the piece of equipment against which a creditor has a lien for $2,000, if the debtor simply gave that piece of equipment back to the lender, the lender might foreclose on it and only end up getting $500 or $600 in a collateral sale. Using the Bankruptcy Code's sales provisions allows the debtor to maximize asset values and repay debts. Also, to the extent that there is some legal deficiency with the secured lender's lien position (such as a late recorded lien or other problem that would allow the debtor to exercise its "strong arm" powers discussed below), the sales provisions of the Bankruptcy Code are very helpful because they do not rely upon a consensual release of a lien.

· ***Credit Bids.***

The Bankruptcy Code also provides that to the extent a debtor wishes to sell assets using the Bankruptcy Code powers, creditors with valid liens against assets can "credit bid" in such sales. What this means is that in the case of the $1,000 piece of equipment against which the creditor has a $2,000 lien, when the debtor goes into court to get permission to sell the piece of equipment for $1,000, the secured lender can come in and bid $1,100 as a "credit bid."[181] This is both a benefit and a burden to a debtor. It is a benefit because to the extent that the secured lender bids (even though the bid is a credit bid) over and above the price of the asset that the debtor had negotiated, the credit bit amounts to payment (albeit, payment in kind) of more debt. That's a good thing. The burden is that every sale is an auction sale.

· ***Every Sale Is Subject To Being "Shopped".***

Credit-bid rights highlight an interesting problem with respect to negotiating sales in bankruptcy cases. It is a truism in bankruptcy cases that there is no such thing as "an exclusive offer" or an "exclusive option." As a rule, every bankruptcy sale is subject to bankruptcy court approval, and in every bankruptcy court approval situation, the bankruptcy courts will generally either ask for higher and better bids or require a debtor to go through a "shopping protocol" to ensure the asset has been adequately exposed to the marketplace. While the ordinary course of events in bankruptcy proceedings is for there to be an "auction sale" in which people bid on assets, private sales are contemplated and sometimes approved in the appropriate circumstances. For example, Bankruptcy Rule 6004(f)(1) states that: "All sales not in the ordinary course of business may be by private sale or by public auction." The concern most bankruptcy courts have under a "private sale" scenario is that they want to be sure that the asset has been appropriately exposed to the marketplace and shopped. As such, even when there is a private sale contemplated, bankruptcy courts will require that there be a showing that the assets were appropriately exposed to the marketplace. There are different ways to do this. One way is for a debtor to obtain bankruptcy court approval, in advance, whereby they set forth the specific protocol they will be following. This could include, for example, a well publicized deadline to submit sealed bids after which time the debtor will accept a bid subject to bankruptcy court approval. The bankruptcy court could approve this in advance, thereby potentially precluding bidders who come in late or don't otherwise comply with the bidding protocol from trying to upset a sale. Another way is for a debtor to implement such a protocol, and ask the bankruptcy court to approve it at the same time the sale is approved, either way precludes a general "auction." Notwithstanding the protocol approved, many bankruptcy courts will want to reserve the discretion to consider "non-conforming bids" to protect the estate in the event Bill Gates happens to show up on the date the sale is to be approved with two truckloads full of cash because he simply must have the asset. Accordingly, unlike circumstances outside of bankruptcy cases where a company can negotiate with a potential buyer and that buyer can lock the company in for a period of time, in bankruptcy it is very difficult to give anyone an exclusive right to buy before testing the marketplace. This is a burden because when assets are being ready to be sold, few purchasers have the desire to be the first offer in the door because they know that they will become the "***stalking horse***." In essence, to the extent that the asset is desirable, the first offer will be by an entity that has spent time and energy investing in due diligence, only to be outbid at an auction by other parties taking a "free ride" on the stalking horse's due diligence. As such, there are certain bidder-protection devices that are recognized and enforced in certain bankruptcy cases. In essence, the first buyer that is willing to come in the door may require as a condition to making an offer some or all of the following:

- "***Bust Up Fees***." Buyers may request advance bankruptcy court approval of a "bust up" or termination fee. What this means is that to the extent that the buyer is outbid, they will be entitled to be paid (as an administrative expense) a certain fee. This fee is usually tied to the size of the deal (1-3 percent of deal sizes), although many bankruptcy courts won't approve such fees unless they bear a relationship to the bidder's due diligence costs. Bust up fees can run the gamut, and some courts are more willing to approve them than others.[182]
- "***Overbid Protections***." Some buyers require that the bankruptcy court approve minimum overbids so that they are not engaged in a small incremental bidding war. These are called overbid protections. For example, an original buyer may make the initial bid, and request that the bankruptcy court approve an auction protocol whereby the first higher bid must be a large one (for example, it must be $50,000 over the initial bid), and thereafter higher bids must exceed the previous bid by no less than $10,000. Depending upon the type of asset and the judge, courts have been willing to approve such protections.
- "***Window Shop Provisions***." Since it is a DIP's duty to get as much as it can for the assets, a DIP must entertain any and all offers for assets once the determination has been made to sell the assets (see the discussion on the *Revlon Duty to Shop* in Chapter Three). However, the entity that makes the original offer is not excited about having the debtor go out and shop its offer to any and all parties. As such, it is not unusual for buyers to request (and obtain) bankruptcy court approval that the debtor will keep the general terms of the original offer confidential (perhaps other than the ultimate price), and

there have also been situations (although rare) where bankruptcy courts will approve a restriction on the debtor precluding the debtor from actively soliciting alternative bids, but the debtor will be able to entertain bids that are brought to it as a result of activities other than its own solicitation of the bids. These are called "window shop" provisions.[183] These types of provisions will only be approved in cases where there is a good reason to do so since it really does place a restriction on a debtor's obligations to fulfill it primary fiduciary duty to maximize the value of assets by marketing them as much as possible.[184] As a practical matter, however, even if these restrictions are put on a debtor, these restrictions would not block Creditors Committees and other parties in interest from actively soliciting offers for assets. Accordingly, while the debtor's hands may be tied, the other parties in the proceeding will not have the same restrictions.[185]

The "Strong Arm" Powers—Speak Softly But Carry A Big Stick

A good deal of the Bankruptcy Code is designed to level the playing field so that all creditors of the same type (general unsecured, priority unsecured, secured) are treated equally. As we've seen, the automatic stay does this, and as we'll see in Chapter Five, the ***absolute priority rule*** also does this. A series of provisions in the Bankruptcy Code referred to generally as the "***strong arm powers***" or "***avoidance powers***" are aimed at achieving this end while at the same time allowing the estate to marshal as much property as possible for eventual distribution to creditors and for use in a reorganization. The strong arm powers—including an ability to "avoid" (undo or reverse) preferences, fraudulent transfers, unperfected security interests, and certain types of postbankruptcy transactions—allow a debtor-in-possession the power to revoke an unfair advantage by one creditor over other similarly situated creditors, to prevent "secret" liens from bestowing an unfair advantage to a creditor, and recover often substantial funds paid to creditors prebankruptcy so that such funds can be redistributed to all creditors in a more equitable fashion.

· ***Preferences.***

When a debtor pays off (or pays down) a particular creditor's existing debt (called an "***antecedent debt***") when it is unable to pay other existing debts to all similarly situated creditors, the debtor is said to have "preferred" the paid creditor over other creditors. When this occurs shortly before the bankruptcy, the creditor that received payment has received an unfair advantage over other creditors, who must wait to receive payment on their existing debts, and may never receive dollar-for-dollar payment (like the paid creditor did). In our *It's A Mad, Mad, Mad, Mad World* analogy, it's like giving one of the motorists a head start over the others and a map to the buried money. The Bankruptcy Code allows a debtor-in-possession to recover these types of payments from the creditors who received them so that the money can go back into the estate to await an equitable distribution to all creditors equally (or ratably). A ***preference*** is defined in the Bankruptcy Code as the transfer of an insolvent debtor's property to a creditor as payment toward an existing debt that allows the creditor to receive more than it would if the creditor had not received the payment and the debtor liquidated under Chapter 7 of the Bankruptcy Code.[186] Insolvency is presumed for transfers made within ninety days of the bankruptcy filing (or one year if the creditor recipient is an ***insider*** of the debtor).[187] Preferences can be payments on unsecured or undersecured debts, or the granting of a lien to secure an otherwise unsecured debt.

What this means is that a company can pay down an unsecured debt on Monday, file Chapter 11 on Wednesday, and sue to recover that payment on Thursday. This doesn't mean that all payments made within ninety days are automatically subject to recovery. Other than the defenses discussed below, certain other payments are excluded. A prime example is a prebankruptcy payment made to a fully secured creditor. Since a fully secured creditor is entitled to be paid in full (with interest and reasonable fees) in a bankruptcy, a payment to a fully secured creditor is not a preference because the creditor isn't receiving more than it would get in a Chapter 7 case. Likewise, payments to lessors whose leases are assumed (see discussion below on *Executory Contracts*) are also not considered preferences since part of the assumption process is payment of all arrearages.[188]

If the debtor-in-possession prevails in its action to recover a preference, the creditor will be required to return back to the estate the property it received as a preference. The creditor will then have a general unsecured claim in the amount of the preference that it returned. The creditor's claim will not be allowed until it has returned the preference.[189] In this way, it is as though the creditor never received the preferential payment, and its existing debt will be treated exactly the way all other similar creditors' debts are treated in the Chapter 11 case.

- ***Preference Defenses***. A creditor can defend a preference avoidance action by showing that the debtor failed to prove one of the essential elements of a preference or by proving that the transfer satisfied one of the enumerated exceptions to avoidance.[190] The defenses most relevant to business reorganizations are commonly referred to as the "contemporaneous exchange for new value" defense, the "ordinary course" defense, and the "subsequent advance" defense.[191]
    - ***Contemporaneous Exchange For New Value.*** In order to defend (and keep) a preference as a contemporaneous exchange, the creditor must show that the payment sought to be avoided as preferential was actually and intentionally made in exchange for an extension of new credit or other value to the debtor at the same time. When a debtor pays a past due invoice for $100 but at

the same time receives in express exchange from that creditor a shipment of new inventory worth $100, that is a contemporaneous exchange of new value within the exception.[192] Another example is a company giving a creditor a lien for a brand new debt—the lien and debt are contemporaneous exchanges.[193]

- ***Ordinary Course Of Business Defense.*** The ordinary course exception is aimed at the "antecedent debt" element—the idea being that if the debtor has paid an existing debt, but the timing and terms of the debt and the payment are within the parameters of the past business relationship between the debtor and the creditor (and conforms with industry practice), then the exception will apply.[194]
- ***Subsequent Advance Defense.*** Finally, the subsequent advance defense is a way for the creditor to "fix" a preference problem before the bankruptcy by extending new unsecured credit or other value (a shipment of new inventory on credit terms, for example) to the debtor *after* the preference is made (that is, not contemporaneously). By doing so, the creditor incurs new unsecured debt to replace the older unsecured debt and is allowed to offset the preference by the subsequent new value.[195]

· ***Fraudulent Conveyances.***

Another way in which an entity can become the recipient of an unfair advantage over creditors is when the debtor transfers property of the estate to the entity for something less than fair consideration. "***Fraudulent transfers***" are not necessarily fraudulent in the normal sense—the debtor can have made the transfer with the most innocent of motives—but the effect is that the estate now has less assets than it should have because of what is essentially an unfair deal made by the debtor. At its most basic, a fraudulent transfer is a transfer of a debtor's property that either was done to hinder, delay, or defraud creditors ("actual fraud"—very hard to prove), or was done while the debtor was insolvent and where the debtor received less than reasonably equivalent value in exchange for the property transferred ("constructive fraud").[196] Transfers that are the subject of this type of analysis are those made within a year of the bankruptcy filing as well as those that are made as long as six years before the filing. Why the spread? There are two fraudulent transfer provisions in the Bankruptcy Code that the debtor can rely upon—the Bankruptcy Code's (which has a one-year look back),[197] and the applicable state law fraudulent transfer laws that are incorporated into the Bankruptcy Code.[198] Some states (such as New York) have a six-year statute of limitations on bringing actions to recover fraudulent transfers.

In the business context, most fraudulent transfers are not intentionally fraudulent (in other words, are not done with the intent to hinder, delay, or defraud creditors)[199] but rather are presumably fraudulent because the debtor received less than it reasonably should have for the transferred property and the transfer either made the debtor insolvent or the debtor was already insolvent when it made the transfer.

"Avoiding" fraudulent transfers—recovering the property transferred and placing that property back into the estate—remedies the damage that creditors would otherwise incur by not having that property for use in the satisfaction of creditor claims. Ascribing the most innocent motives to the debtor, a fraudulent transfer may be just a lopsidedly bad deal that the debtor made before the bankruptcy that arose out of the debtor's poor bargaining leverage resulting from the debtor's severe financial distress. A fraudulent transfer does not have to be a transfer for no consideration (like a gift), since the transferee can have given some value for the transfer and the transfer still be subject to avoidance. If the transferee did give some value, even if the transfer is avoided the Bankruptcy Code grants the transferee a lien on the property transferred to the extent of the value given, as long as the transferee took the transfer for some value in good faith.

A common example of a fraudulent transfer in the business context arises in the ***leveraged buyout*** transaction. A company goes private or is otherwise acquired, and the acquisition funds (in whole or in part) come from a loan secured by assets of the acquired company. The loan and security interests are often challenged in the bankruptcy context (such as occurred in the *Revco Drug Store* case) on the basis that the loan and lien are fraudulent transfers—the company received no benefit (certainly the old stockholders did), yet the company is on the hook for the debt.[200]

· ***Avoidance Of "Secret Liens."***

The Uniform Commercial Code (relating to security interests taken in personal property) and state laws relating to security interests taken in real property (mortgages, deeds of trust, etc.) are designed to give the public notice that the secured creditor has, in fact, taken a security interest in particular assets of the debtor. It is one thing to take (or "attach") a security interest in property subject to an agreement between the debtor and the creditor, while it is another thing to let the public know that the creditor has done so. Usually, the giving of public notice of a security interest involves the filing of a UCC-1 financing statement (for most personal property) or the filing of a copy of the mortgage or deed of trust (for real property) with appropriate state officials like the Secretary of State or the County Recorder. Without public notice, the security interest or lien is unknown to anyone outside the transaction—it is often referred to as a "secret lien." This public notice filing is referred to as "perfection," and it is critically important in the context of a debtor's bankruptcy case.

The reason for this is that under the Bankruptcy Code, the debtor-in-possession assumes the position of a hypothetical judicial lien creditor[201]—in other words, the DIP is assumed to occupy the position and have the rights of a creditor that obtained, at the time the bankruptcy petition is filed, a judicial lien on property of the estate. This is a powerful position for the DIP to be in, since under state law, a judicial lienholder trumps any *unperfected* security interest or lien of any other creditor. This is true even if the DIP knows of the "secret lien." If a putatively secured creditor has failed to properly perfect its lien under state law, once the bankruptcy case is commenced, the DIP (on behalf of the estate) will be able to avoid (negate) the unperfected security interest, rendering the creditor unsecured. The creditor in this instance is placed on an equal footing with all other unsecured creditors who never had public notice of the first creditor's secret lien.[202]

· ***The DIP As The "Hypothetical Bona Fide Purchaser."***

The Bankruptcy Code also places the DIP in the position of a hypothetical ***bona fide purchaser*** of real property,[203] who under state law would be entitled to take real property free and clear of any lien on the real property not properly perfected under state law if the purchaser acquired the real property for adequate consideration without notice (actual notice or constructive notice is based on proper perfection) of prior-existing liens on the property. The result is the avoidance of any unrecorded or improperly perfected liens on real property, rendering the creditor unsecured for purposes of the bankruptcy proceedings. Under the Bankruptcy Code, the DIP (wearing this hypothetical *bona fide* purchaser mantle) isn't imputed with any actual knowledge of the existence of the unrecorded lien.[204]

· ***Postbankruptcy Transactions.***

The DIP is also entitled to recover, under certain circumstances, property for the benefit of the estate that has been transferred in an *involuntary* bankruptcy case between the time of the filing of the involuntary petition and the entry of the order for relief (known as the "***gap period***"), as well to recover transfers of property of the estate after the order for relief has been issued.[205] The DIP can recover the property transferred solely under the auspices of those special provisions of the Bankruptcy Code as well as any property transferred in contravention of any provision of the Bankruptcy Code or order of the bankruptcy court. Probably the most common type of postpetition transfer that is avoidable in this context is the payment of a check issued to a creditor by the debtor before the bankruptcy was filed but not honored by the bank until after the bankruptcy commenced. Since that is a postpetition transfer of property not authorized by the Bankruptcy Code, it is avoidable. To the extent the company has outstanding payroll checks as part of its first day orders (described earlier), it will generally get bankruptcy court permission to honor those checks. Also, postpetition fraudulent transfers and preferences done during the "gap period" between the involuntary petition and the order for relief are avoidable under this provision.

· ***Limitations.***

The debtor-in-possession has two years from the date of the filing of the bankruptcy case to bring the avoidance actions discussed above.[206] Prior to 1994 there was a split in authority as to whether or not a debtor-in-possession was bound by the two-year rule found in the Bankruptcy Code (which referred only to a "trustee"). Congress amended the Bankruptcy Code in 1994 to clarify that these actions must be brought within two years of the filing (assuming no Chapter 11 trustee is appointed in the case). While this may seem like a long time, in contested Chapter 11 cases two years can go by pretty quickly and the two-year rule can "sneak up" on debtors causing a mad rush to the courthouse to get preference and fraudulent conveyance actions on file to avoid missing the statute of limitations.[207]

Dealing With Executory Contracts And Unexpired Leases

A significant part of turning any business around—and Chapter 11 is primarily concerned with rehabilitating and reorganizing a business—is evaluating all the ongoing contractual obligations of the business and deciding which ones are worth keeping and which ones are not. Companies outside of bankruptcy rarely have an opportunity to pick and choose among their various ongoing deals, but the Bankruptcy Code gives the DIP the opportunity to do just that—keep the ones that are beneficial to the estate and the reorganization and reject the ones that are more trouble than they are worth.[208] ***Assuming*** or ***rejecting*** "***executory contracts***" and "***unexpired leases***" is a critical step in putting the business back on track, but each assumption or rejection is not without its costs and pitfalls to go along with the benefits to be attained.

· ***What Is An "Executory Contract"?***

The DIP cannot decide whether it wants to continue performing under a contract or reject it until it determines whether the contract is even subject to assumption or rejection. Under the Bankruptcy Code, only executory contracts and unexpired leases can be assumed or rejected. It is not hard to understand what is meant by the term unexpired lease—it is a lease of personal property or real property that has not expired or terminated under its own terms or otherwise by operation of non-bankruptcy law as of the date the bankruptcy petition is filed.[209] Practically speaking, a debtor's current leases for equipment, vehicles, and other personal property, as well as a debtor's current non-residential real property leases (under which it is either a lessee or a lessor) are unexpired leases for purposes of assumption or rejection. If a contract or lease has been terminated or lapsed prebankruptcy, there's nothing to assume or reject in a bankruptcy—a dead contract can't be revived.[210]

The more difficult definition to pin down is executory contract. The Bankruptcy Code does not define "executory contract" (even though it does take the time to define things such as "United States" and "accountant")—perhaps Congress had as hard a time defining it as everyone else. Literally thousands of judicial opinions and scholarly articles have been written over the years regarding what is and is not an executory contract, but most everyone keeps coming back to the definition proposed by Professor Vern Countryman in the early 1970s: a contract is executory when "the obligations of both the bankrupt [debtor] and the other party to the contract are so far unperformed that the failure of either to complete performance could constitute a material breach excusing the performance of the other."[211] In somewhat plainer English, a contract is executory if enough performance remains to be done on both sides of the contract that if either party doesn't do what is left for it to do, the other party can terminate the contract for breach. Years of struggling with the question has left bankruptcy professionals and courts with a very good idea of what is and is not an executory contract, so it is unlikely that most businesses will have a contract in place that is hard to place inside or outside the "executory" box.

Contracts and leases can be—and often are—very valuable assets of the debtor's estate. A favorable intellectual property license can be critical to a debtor's operations, and a below-market lease in a popular shopping center can be one of the most valuable assets in a retail debtor's estate.[212] For this reason, decisions about how to treat these contracts and leases in the Chapter 11 case can significantly affect the debtor's ultimate success in rehabilitating its business operations and completing its reorganization.

The DIP is given three choices with respect to executory contracts and unexpired leases. It can: (1) assume and retain a contract or lease for the benefit of the estate; (2) assume and assign a contract or lease to a third party; or (3) reject a contract or lease.

· ***Assumption And Rejection.***

A contract or lease must be assumed or rejected in its entirety; the debtor cannot separate out the good parts from the bad parts and assume only those. As long as the contract or lease has not terminated under non-bankruptcy law before the petition is filed, the DIP can assume the contract or lease, agreeing to continue to perform its obligations under the contract or lease (and receive its benefits) under the terms of the agreement. Once a DIP assumes a contract or lease, the fact of the bankruptcy has virtually no effect on the ongoing relationship of the parties to that contract or lease. Any renegotiation or amendment of any of the agreement's terms is strictly up to the parties to the agreement—the bankruptcy court will not get involved.[213]

Before the DIP can assume a contract or lease, however, it must "cure" any defaults "promptly" after assumption, or at least provide adequate assurance that it will promptly cure such defaults. This means that the DIP must pay in full in cash all amounts past due under the contract or lease (all monetary defaults), and the DIP must also provide adequate assurance that it is willing and able to perform under the contract or lease in the future. A security deposit often does the trick for adequate assurance purposes, but assumptions of contracts and leases with large prepetition arrearages can be a significant cash drain.

For this reason—and because once a contract is assumed all amounts coming due for the remaining term of the contract are entitled to administrative expense priority[214]—timing issues are paramount. The DIP should generally not assume any contract or lease until a business plan has been formulated and the prospects for a successful reorganization and emergence from bankruptcy are strong. Creditors Committees will vociferously protest contract assumptions early in the case out of concern about creating huge administrative expenses if the business takes a downturn, and understandably so. The Bankruptcy Code does require the DIP to assume or reject all its executory contracts and unexpired leases within sixty days of the petition date, but the Bankruptcy Code also allows the court to extend that time for "cause." Reorganizing Chapter 11 debtors typically are granted substantial extensions both because large businesses need time to formulate a viable business plan and because it is inappropriate to force a decision to assume or reject early in the case (where the choice is either lose a potentially useful contract by rejecting or incur potentially huge administrative expense claims by assuming). Bankruptcy courts usually extend this time up to the point of confirmation of a plan of reorganization. There is a cash flow concern here: the DIP is responsible for paying all amounts coming due under a nonresidential real property lease during the bankruptcy case as an administrative expense until rejection or assumption of that lease.[215] Cash flow shortages may adversely affect the DIP's ability to do this, and may motivate an earlier rejection of certain leases more than an extended deadline the bankruptcy court may be willing to approve because courts usually (but not always) condition extensions of time to assume or reject on timely payment of postbankruptcy charges.

While the DIP is required to cure monetary defaults as a condition to assuming a contract or lease, the DIP is not required to cure any nonmonetary defaults (like filing for bankruptcy or failing to continuously operate under a lease).[216] Once the DIP assumes a contract or lease, it can also assign its rights under the contract or lease to another party, but only if nonbankruptcy law would not allow the other party to the contract or lease to refuse performance by the assignee. If state law does not require the other party to the contract to accept the assignee's performance (such as, for example, a personal services contract), and the other party does not consent to the assignment, the debtor cannot assign the contract, and indeed may not be able to even assume the contract.[217] Assuming and assigning valuable contracts and leases can be an excellent source of funds for an estate—indeed sometimes it's the *only* source of funds. If a lease is attractive and below-market, another prospective tenant may be willing to compensate the DIP for assuming and assigning that lease to it. Even for reorganizing debtors, pulling out of certain locations may not only allow the debtor to reduce overhead and return to its core business, aiding in a successful reorganization, but it may also bring additional cash into the estate to fund a reorganization in the form of payments from assignees of the leases for those locations. In this fashion, assumption and assignment decisions can be a strategic priority during the course of a restructuring in Chapter 11.

If, on the other hand, the DIP decides that a contract's burdens on the estate simply outweigh the benefits of such contract, the DIP will be able to reject the contract—unilaterally walking away from the contract, under most circumstances very shortly after the bankruptcy court approves the rejection. Rejection decisions, as well as assumption and assignment decisions, are evaluated with regard to the "business judgment" standard—if the bankruptcy court is convinced that the decision is within the reasonable business judgment of the DIP, it will approve the proposed assumption or rejection. But, rejection is **not** a "get out of jail free card." Because rejection is equivalent to a material breach of the contract or lease, the estate still may have substantial exposure to the other party to the contract or lease for state law damages of such breach, including any existing monetary defaults, all future amounts due through the term of the contract or lease, lost profits, and other costs and expenses. While it is true that all of these damages are treated only as general unsecured claims (as opposed to administrative expense claims), contract and lease rejection claims can, in many cases, constitute a very substantial part of the total unsecured claims.[218]

The good news is that the Bankruptcy Code caps certain rejection damage claims for certain types of contracts. Allowed claims based on damages arising from the DIP's rejection of a real property lease are limited to prebankruptcy arrearages plus the lesser of 15 percent of the total rent reserved through the remaining term of the lease (but not exceeding three years) or one year of rent.[219] The idea is to prevent a party to a long-term lease from diluting the recovery to other creditors by filing a massive claim (such as rents due from the twenty-year remaining term of a lease). Allowed claims based on damages arising from the DIP's rejection of an employment agreement are similarly capped at the amount of any prebankruptcy arrearages plus one year's compensation under the agreement.

· ***The "Special" Contracts.***

The legal framework surrounding the assumption or rejection of contracts and leases is already sufficiently complicated without adding into the mix special provisions for special types of contracts and leases. Unfortunately, Congress has added these provisions so we need to touch upon them.

- ***Licenses Of Intellectual Property.*** When the debtor is the licensor (as opposed to the licensee) of intellectual property (defined as including patents, copyrights, mask work, and trade secrets—but *not* trademarks), the Bankruptcy Code restricts the debtor's ability to extricate itself from the licensing arrangement with the licensee.[220] A DIP-licensor is still entitled to reject the license agreement, but the licensee is given a choice: it can either treat the license as terminated (and assert an uncapped claim for all damages arising from the licensor's breach) or retain its rights to the intellectual property by continuing to pay any royalties or other amounts due to the licensor under the agreement for the remaining term of the agreement. If the licensee elects to retain its rights under the latter choice, it is deemed to have waived a right to set off damages against future royalties and a right to assert an administrative expense claim for any postpetition damages. The DIP-licensor in this situation may not impede the licensee's access to the intellectual property, but is relieved of any future affirmative obligations or specific performance it may have owed to the licensee under the license agreement.

- ***Shopping Center Leases.*** The late 1980s and early 1990s saw a spate of retail bankruptcies, many of which affected "anchor stores" in large shopping centers (major department stores like Macy's, or hardware stores like Ernst or Rickel), which draw shoppers to the mall.[221] Shopping center landlords successfully lobbied Congress for amendments to the Bankruptcy Code that restrict a debtor's ability to assume and assign shopping center leases unless the debtor can not only cure arrearages, but also provide "***adequate assurance of future performance***." The most significant change in the Bankruptcy Code resulting from landlords' lobbying efforts is an enumeration of what "adequate assurance of future performance" means with respect to assumption of a shopping center lease.[222] In order for a retail debtor lessee to assume, or assume and assign, its shopping center lease, the debtor must show that: (a) the source of rent, and the financial condition and operating performance of a proposed assignee, is similar to the financial condition and operating performance of the debtor when it originally became the lessee; (b) that percentage rent (rent calculated with reference to gross receipts or similar operating results) will not decline substantially; and (c) that assumption or assignment will remain subject to, and will not disrupt, lease provisions regarding radius, location, and tenant mix concerns for the shopping center as a whole.[223]
- ***Airport Landing Slots.*** Partially in response to a rash of airline bankruptcies,[224] Congress enacted certain protections for the benefit of airport landlords, aimed largely at the prejudicial delay inherent in waiting for an airline debtor to assume or reject its leases. The Bankruptcy Code now provides that the sixty-day period to assume or reject contracts and leases may not apply with respect to a debtor

airline's leases for aircraft terminals, gates, or landing slots.[225] If the airline debtor is the subject of a Chapter 7 order for relief, if the debtor's case is converted to a Chapter 7 case, or if a secured creditor is granted relief from the automatic stay with respect to aircraft, aircraft engines, or other parts, the airport landlord may opt to treat the debtor's gate leases as rejected five days after such order for relief, conversion, or stay relief. If the airport landlord does so, it waives all rights to assert rejection damages. Even if the debtor remains in a Chapter 11 proceeding, the "cause" it must show for extension of the regular sixty-day time period for assumption or rejection of its gate leases must include an inquiry into the harm to the airport, airline passengers, and the public's use of and need for the affected terminals or gates.[226]

- ***Time-Share Agreements.*** If the DIP is a seller of time-share interests in real property, and the DIP elects to reject the time-share plan, the time-share purchaser may elect either: (a) to treat the time-share plan as terminated and be relieved of all obligations; or (b) retain its rights in the time-share for the remainder of the term. If the purchaser elects the latter, it may off set its rejection damages (but not damages arising in the future from the debtor's non-performance), if any, against amounts it must pay under the time-share plan for the remainder of the term.[227] Likewise, if the debtor rejects an executory contract for the sale of a time-share interest where the purchaser is already in possession of the interest, the purchaser may elect to either treat the contract as terminated, or remain in possession of the interest and continue to make all payments due, offsetting any rejection damages it may have against such payments.[228]
- ***Collective Bargaining Agreements.*** A Chapter 11 debtor may reject a collective bargaining agreement, but it must follow a specific procedure designed to ensure that the agreement is, in fact, burdensome to the estate, that the balance of the equities favor rejection (for example, the number of employees who will lose their jobs, types of benefits lost), and that the rejection will not rise to the level of an unfair labor practice under federal labor law standards.[229] The procedure requires the DIP to make a proposal to the union (or other collective bargaining unit) "based on the most complete and reliable information at the time of such proposal" with the intent of reaching an agreement by good faith negotiations with the union regarding the best way to protect all affected parties' rights. This negotiation process is a prerequisite to applying for rejection of the agreement in bankruptcy court. If the negotiation process fails—and it can be an extremely contentious and difficult process involving powerful national unions (the Teamsters aren't exactly known for being cuddly)—the DIP may then apply to the bankruptcy court for rejection

of the agreement. The hearing on the motion is held on an expedited basis, and the court must rule within thirty days of the hearing's commencement. The court is required to grant rejection of the agreement when it finds that the required proposal has been made (and negotiated if the union was willing), that the union has refused to accept the proposal without good cause, and that the balance of the equities favors rejection.[230]

- ***Retiree Benefits.*** Retiree benefits—including reimbursed payments to retirees, their spouses, and dependents, as well as direct payment to health, accident, disability, and life insurers for the benefit of retirees and their spouses and dependents—may be covered by a collective bargaining agreement that is subject to the right of the DIP to reject that agreement. Regardless of whether retiree benefits are in a collective bargaining agreement or not the Bankruptcy Code provides that if the retiree benefits are covered by a collective bargaining agreement, the union acts as the retirees' representative.[231] If the union declines to do so, the court may appoint a representative or a Committee of retirees with the same rights as Creditors' or Equityholders' Committees. The DIP must follow a procedure under which retiree benefit plans may be modified. Much like with collective bargaining agreements, the DIP must deliver a proposal to the retiree representative with all relevant information and engage in good faith negotiations before applying to the court for rejection. The hearing on the DIP's application must be held within fourteen days of the application, and the court must rule within ninety days of the hearing's commencement. Once the application is filed, the DIP and the retiree representative must continue to negotiate in good faith, and if no agreement is reached, the court will approve a benefit plan modification if: (a) the DIP has fulfilled all preapplication procedures; (b) the representative has refused to accept the proposed modification without "good cause;" and (c) the modification is necessary for the reorganization of the debtor and for the fair treatment of creditors. All payments under such plans must be made as administrative expenses up to confirmation of a plan of reorganization, but only from unencumbered funds (funds not subject to a lender's lien). Additionally, no plan of reorganization may be confirmed unless it provides for the continued payment of all retiree benefits (as is, or as may have been modified under the above procedure).[232]

Bankruptcy Court Jurisdiction (And Limitations On That Jurisdiction)

No, this is not going to be a John Housman imitation from *The Paper Chase* on the limits of ***federal court jurisdiction***. There are, however, certain aspects of the limited jurisdiction of the bankruptcy court that will affect how you deal with certain types of creditors.

· ***Jurisdiction Over Assets.***

The bankruptcy law contains an interesting (and probably unenforceable) provision that says that the bankruptcy court has exclusive jurisdiction over the assets of the bankruptcy estate wherever those assets are located.[233] This means that if a bankruptcy is filed in the Central District of California in Los Angeles, and the debtor has a piece of property that is secured by a mortgage in New York, the bankruptcy filing in Los Angeles gives that bankruptcy court exclusive jurisdiction over the property in New York, and creditors in New York are not able to disregard the bankruptcy filing and proceed to foreclose on that asset.

The reason it may be unenforceable in a broader sense arises when the debtor has assets located outside of the United States. The broad grant of jurisdiction over the assets of the bankruptcy is fine in theory, but in truth and practice, it is difficult to enforce that broad jurisdictional grant when the assets are located outside of the United States. This is becoming an interesting problem in multi-national insolvency proceedings where creditors are located in other countries as are certain assets of the debtors.[234] For example, in the *Lykes Steamship* Chapter 11 case that was pending in Miami, the bankruptcy court in Miami issued a broad order that prohibited all creditors outside of the United States from seizing the debtor's vessels (even in international waters or international ports). Seizure of vessels was allowed under the laws of various countries to collect unpaid debts. While that order is certainly enforceable in the United States, to the extent a creditor is not a creditor in the United States but is located in another country, it is (to say the least) extremely difficult to enforce that order if the creditor were to seize the ship in, say, Panama or Brazil. In the end, foreign creditors largely ignored the U.S. court's orders. Notwithstanding that, the bankruptcy laws contain very broad jurisdictional grants. Whether it is ultimately enforceable is another question. In these days of multi-national insolvencies (such as *Maxwell Communications, Lernout & Hauspie*, and *Singer*) involving assets and insolvency proceedings in different countries, international protocols are established in an attempt to try to meld and otherwise accommodate the different restructuring laws and creditor rights for different countries. In the *Maxwell Communications* case (the U.S. portion of which was pending in the Southern District of New York), there were related proceedings going on in the United Kingdom and elsewhere. The bankruptcy judge in New York, in cooperation with the insolvency judges in the other countries, prepared a form of "Protocol" which attempted to deal with competing claims to assets in the different countries. In addition, the International Bar Association adopted the "Cross-Border Insolvency Concordat" in 1995. The Concordat attempts to provide some structure or some guidance for courts having to deal with competing creditors claims and jurisdictional issues in international insolvency situations. *See, e.g., Advanced Chapter 11* at §§ 16.14 *et seq.*

· ***"Core" Versus "Non-Core" Matters.***

Most disputes that arise in bankruptcy cases can be broken down into one of three types. This is only of interest to the business executive to the extent that it affects how much the bankruptcy courts can help in streamlining and centralizing litigation against the company.

- ***Core Matters***. Certain disputes that arise in bankruptcy proceedings are known as ***core matters***. These are matters that arise directly in the Bankruptcy Code, such as stay relief matters, lien avoidance matters under the "strong arm" provisions, and the like. In these types of disputes and matters, the bankruptcy courts have exclusive jurisdiction and there is little doubt that they can and do handle these matters everyday.

- ***Non-Core Related Matters***. ***Non-core related matters*** are those matters that do not arise directly under the Bankruptcy Code but are still related to matters involving the debtor. An example of a non-core matter would be the collection of an account receivable. This has nothing to do with the Bankruptcy Code in and of itself, but rather involves an asset of the bankruptcy estate (the receivable). It is frequently very helpful for the debtor to bring actions in the bankruptcy court in which its case is pending to collect those receivables when account debtors refuse to pay. Unfortunately for the debtor, for reasons of constitutional law that are beyond the scope of this book involving the limited jurisdiction of the federal bankruptcy courts, those matters are not matters where the bankruptcy court can exercise exclusive jurisdiction. This is not to say that the bankruptcy court can't determine these matters, but the other parties to that litigation will be able to throw certain roadblocks in its way.[235] Some examples of non-core matters are actually contained in the bankruptcy laws by way of example. For example, the ultimate determination of damages for personal injury or wrongful death actions (which are very important in mass- tort-type cases, such as the *A.H. Robins, Johns-Manville,* and *Dow Corning* cases) is specifically held to be a "non-core" matter that must be ultimately liquidated in a court other than the bankruptcy court.[236]

- ***Non-Core/Non-Related Matters***

  The third type of dispute is called the ***non-core/non-related matter***. This would be, for example, where two creditors want to bring claims against each other to determine which creditor had a first-lien priority. To the extent that dispute will not affect the bankruptcy estate, the bankruptcy courts will consider it non-core/non-related, and will not hear or decide the dispute.

· ***State Entities And The Seminole Tribe Problem***

In 1998, the U.S. Supreme Court issued an opinion in a non-bankruptcy case that has had interesting implications for debtors which have disputes with state governmental agencies. In an opinion called *Florida* v. *The Seminole Tribe,*[237] the U.S. Supreme Court determined that the federal courts do not have any jurisdiction over state governments because of the sovereign immunity clause of the U.S. Constitution. Fine. What's this got to do with a corporate bankruptcy? A lot.

This decision, based on the Eleventh Amendment of the U.S. Constitution, essentially means that state governments cannot be dragged into federal courts unless they agree to go there. This has an interesting implication in bankruptcy cases. There are many times when state governmental agencies are creditors in bankruptcy proceedings—state taxing authorities, for example. In addition, state equivalents of the Environmental Protection Agency are also potential creditors, as are state licensing agencies and state regulators for nursing homes and casinos. None of the state entities can be dragged into bankruptcy court without their consent. This has created an interesting dynamic between state agencies and debtors in bankruptcy. In certain highly regulated industries (such as the casino and health care industries, for example), state agencies must be treated with kid gloves in order to avoid having them shut down the business, with the bankruptcy courts being powerless (jurisdictionally speaking) to stop them.

Okay, you've now survived to plan confirmation. You're in the home stretch. Now to finish this exercise up—the plan of reorganization.

CHAPTER FIVE

THE PLAN OF REORGANIZATION

"Make no little plans—they have no magic to stir men's blood. Make big plans, aim high in hope and work and let your watchword be order and your beacon beauty."

David Hudson Burnham
(Attributed)

You've now made it to the point in this exercise that you were wanting to get to from the day of the filing—the plan process. This is the reason for the bankruptcy—to restructure the obligations of the company. In Chapter 11 bankruptcy, this is accomplished through ***confirmation*** (or bankruptcy court approval) of the ***plan of reorganization***. The plan is the implementation of the exit strategy discussed in Chapter Two.

Simply stated, what is a plan of reorganization? In one sense it's a judicially approved contract between the debtor and all its creditors and equityholders that addresses how their debts will be paid by the company and how their equity will be treated on a going-forward basis. Unlike a normal contract, however, a plan of reorganization can be forced on creditors and equityholders even if they don't agree to it in one of two ways—by binding dissenting creditors within a class by the ***"class voting"*** rules discussed below; or by binding a dissenting class despite its negative vote. This is called "***cramdown***."

The plan process is a six-step process: (1) negotiating the plan with some or all of the major constituencies; (2) drafting the plan of reorganization; (3) obtaining bankruptcy court approval of a ***Disclosure Statement***, which is in the nature of a prospectus to solicit creditors to vote for a plan; (4) the ***solicitation process*** whereby the court-approved Disclosure Statement (with the plan) is sent to creditors for their votes (cast by ***plan ballots***) to accept or reject the plan; (5) the ***confirmation hearing*** before the bankruptcy court to obtain court approval of the plan; and (6) ***going effective*** under a confirmed plan and performing under the plan. After a plan is confirmed, the "debtor" becomes the "***Reorganized Debtor***" (much like one goes from being a student to a graduate). This chapter is written as if the plan proponent is the debtor, although as discussed below there are times when other parties may be allowed to file plans (raising the possibility that there may be multiple plans up for confirmation at the same time) (see discussion below on *Keeping Control—"Exclusivity" Rules!*) Each of these six steps will be examined in this chapter after two preliminary matters—defining "success" in Chapter 11 cases and quantifying debts against the debtor through "bar date" orders.

Defining "Success" In Chapter 11

As a preliminary matter, let's define "success" in a Chapter 11. Defining success in Chapter 11 cases can be somewhat difficult.[238] Success in Chapter 11 really is a function of your perspective—a successful Chapter 11 to a secured creditor may be a disappointment to unsecured creditors and a dismal failure to equityholders. Since Chapter 11 cases can, by design, result in an orderly liquidation of a company, having a plan of reorganization that accomplishes an orderly liquidation is presumably a success. In the *FPA Medical Management Corp.* Chapter 11 that was filed in Delaware in 1998, and which involved over a billion dollars in debt, a plan was confirmed in 1999 that paid DIP financing claims (about $53 million), and returned nothing to nearly a billion dollars in unsecured claims. Depending on one's perspective, this could be considered a successful Chapter 11 (although the unpaid unsecured creditors would undoubtedly take issue with this). Liquidation plans were also filed in the *Megafoods Stores, Nationsway Trucking,* and *Boston Markets* Chapter 11s (which liquidation will result in senior secured debt getting about 65 percent of their claim).

Conversely, there are numerous plans confirmed that sell the going concern to a third party (such as *Circle K, R.H. Macy's,* and *America West Airlines*); plans that convert debt to equity (*Stuart Entertainment, Unison HealthCare, Payless Cashways, Penn Traffic,* and *Bucyrus Erie*); plans that provide for some debt conversions plus equity infusion by existing equityholders (*Spectravision* and *Kash & Karry*); plans that implement creditor-sponsored-rights offerings (*Barney's*); and plans that provide for mergers and acquisitions combined with creditor-sponsored-rights offerings (*Mobilmedia*). The spectrum of types of exit strategies implemented through confirmed plans is as diverse as the creative minds of executives, financial advisors, and lawyers.

Success in a Chapter 11 is surviving the process and obtaining the best result possible for the creditors and even, sometimes, the shareholders (*Smith International* and *Siliconex*, as two examples). Sometimes it's a home run, sometimes a bunt single.

Quantifying The Debts— The "Bar Date" Order

As another preliminary matter, there needs to be a brief mention of the concept of the "***bar date order***" and where it fits into this process. As discussed in Chapter Four regarding *Statements and Schedules*, while debtors make every effort to be as accurate as they can in listing all of their creditors, there are times that they might not have the right numbers for claims, or they may not even know that certain creditors exist (such as potential environmental contamination claims, personal injury or product liability claims, and other claims that are not always apparent).[239] In order to get the maximum benefit from the discharge (discussed below), it is essential that the company be aware of all of the potential claims against it (and recall from Chapter Two that the term "claim" is very broadly defined so that if the company can bind these creditors to these terms of a confirmed plan of reorganization, it will also get the benefit of the discharge). What's the best way to do this?

The best way to be sure all creditors are involved in the process is to have the bankruptcy court enter a "bar date order." The debtor will file a motion requesting that the court set a bar date, and the court will then enter the bar date order. The debtor will send the court's bar date order to all creditors on its mailing list (which could be thousands of creditors). To the extent the debtor may have some of the less obvious potential claims out there, it may also request that the bankruptcy court authorize and direct it to notice the bar date order by publication. ***Notice by publication*** is allowed under the Bankruptcy Rules[240] and involves having the bar date order printed in newspapers (such as, for example, the *Wall Street Journal* or even *USA Today*) or magazines (bar date orders have been published in *Time* and *Newsweek*). In certain cases where there is concern about mass-tort liability (such as *A.H. Robins, Johns Manville,* and *Dow Corning*), notices of bar dates have been put in "infomercials" on television. The legal premise is that only creditors that are given notice of the pendency of the bankruptcy will be bound by what is done in the bankruptcy (regardless of whether they actually attend or participate in the hearings and case), and notice by publication in addition to actual notice of creditors is one way to bind people even if the company does not necessarily know that these people may assert a claim against it. Maximum notice is necessary to get the maximum benefit from the discharge, and serious consideration should be given to the proper way to notice a bar date order.

The bar date order itself will tell creditors that they must file a claim unless they agree with the way the debtor has scheduled their claim in the Statements and Schedules. Sometimes bar date orders except out certain types of creditors who need not file a claim.[241] The bar date order will state that a claim (which is a ***proof of claim*** form that is contained in the Bankruptcy Rules) must be filed by a date certain or that creditor will generally be barred from participating in the case or from receiving any distributions in the case. In addition, that creditor will also not be allowed to later bring actions against the debtor on behalf of the claim. It is essentially a judicial way of saying "speak now or forever hold your peace."[242] By the end of the bar date time period, the company should have a pretty good listing of what claims are out there (even if the claims that are filed are exaggerated in amount as frequently happens).[243] A form of bar date order used in a case involving public debt and equity is contained in the Appendix.

Step One: The Negotiation Process And Dynamics

The first step in the plan process is the negotiation of the plan with some or all of the major constituencies. While it is possible for a debtor to file a plan without having engaged in negotiations with parties, this will usually lead to a backlash of criticism and litigation against the debtor. In short, it's simply not a good way to influence people and make friends in the reorganization process. Of course, it won't always be possible to come to an agreement with all parties. In some cases, there will be battles with major constituencies, and there may not be anything a debtor can do about that. Nonetheless, it is always good to try to build a consensus with some or all major constituencies as it will help in getting the plan approved at the end of the process.[244] It is essential to have the support of at least one major constituency as both a practical and legal matter. Attempting to file a plan that has the support of no major constituency ultimately will be an exercise in futility, and will likely lead to protracted and expensive litigation in the case.[245] Notwithstanding this, sometimes it's done as a negotiating tactic.

The negotiation process and dynamic in reorganization cases is very different than the same process outside of bankruptcy. A few of the major differences are summarized below:

· ***The "Used Car" Theory of Corporate Reorganization Negotiation.***

Have you ever shopped for a used car? If you have, then you know firsthand (although you may not realize it) the tactics of car salespeople. After you've looked at the car on the lot and driven it a bit, he (the stereotypical used-car salesperson is always a "he") will take you back to his office (which tends to be a small cubicle with calendars and pictures of spouse and children who all look a little hungry) to discuss the purchase. You then tell the salesperson that you believe the sticker price of the car is too high, and you want to pay something less than that. The salesperson, being your friend, will then say that he would like nothing more than to do this deal, but of course he must check with his manager. The salesperson will then leave you in the office and disappear for about twenty minutes (give or take).

Three cups of coffee later, the salesperson will come back. His brow will be furrowed as he tells you that as much as he personally would like to do the deal at your price, the manager is giving him some difficulty. You discuss it again, somewhat conspiratorially, and the salesperson stands up and determinedly says that he will do his level best to sell this to the manager. He disappears for another twenty minutes. This process continues until you spend a minimum of three and sometimes four or five hours in this cubicle while you and your new-found best friend conspire to get your offer finally approved by the rarely (if ever) seen "manager."

As you might have surmised, the frequent excursions by the salesperson have very little to do with his efforts to sell the deal to the manager or anyone. It was simply to keep you in a room and get you to expend your time. The longer you're in that room, the more incentivized you are to have not wasted your entire day reading *Car & Driver* back issues. In fact, after a number of hours you are fairly determined that you want to cut some deal so that your time was not wasted. This has been proven in studies to be an effective means of wearing down a buyer's resistance so that a deal will be struck, and is known as "cognitive dissonance."

At the risk of offending bankruptcy professionals throughout the country, the reorganization negotiating dynamics are not all that different. In fact, the process is designed this way. At the outset of the case, creditors will be taking harsh positions with unusual vitriol in response to nearly anything the debtor wants to do. After six months or so, while there may not be any love lost between the players, they have all spent enough time together in meetings that they are getting to know each other. People will start asking questions about the other person's family, his or her kids, and the like.[246] After a year and a half or two years, people want to get a deal done. If they don't, they know that the case will likely liquidate or otherwise blow up. In addition, the major creditors are watching the effect of all of the professional fees mount.[247] Creditors know that the longer this process drags on, more and more of the value in the estate is being eaten up by professional fees.[248] This mental state on the part of the creditors is commonly called "creditor fatigue."

Other than prepackaged or prearranged plan situations (where all of the jockeying for position and other histrionics occurred in the negotiation process leading up to the documentation of the plan), the negotiating dynamics are such that some time has to pass before creditors are comfortable with agreeing to restructurings. Sometimes the faster a debtor wants to move a case along, the more suspicion there will be from the various parties that the debtor has some ulterior motive. Much like Paul Masson, the creditors will approve no plan before its time. Some players, particularly sophisticated bondholders to whom time really *is* money, do not subscribe to such maxims.

· ***You're Bound at the Wrist—Better Learn to Live With Each Other.***

In a negotiating seminar given at a large law firm many years ago, a very seasoned corporate partner was giving his views on negotiating in the corporate context. His view was that the parties should know fairly early on if they're close to a deal (or at least in some ultimately agreeable range) so they wouldn't spend too much valuable time jockeying and posturing. He stated that if it was clear that a deal was not likely, the best tactic was to get up, leave, and look for other deals.

This tactic in a bankruptcy case will simply not work. Unlike the non-bankruptcy corporate negotiating dynamic (where if this deal won't work, there is another deal with someone else that might work), in bankruptcy cases, the parties are bound at the wrists. Bankruptcy is a zero-sum game, and getting up and leaving a negotiating table, while making for good dramatics, is really not an option. In fact, if a party does that too often, the other players in the process will simply go around it. That would be true even if that party happened to be the debtor (see discussion below on *Keeping Control—"Exclusivity" Rules!*). Accordingly, it is best to understand that in a reorganization negotiating dynamic, as much as you may hate the people across the table, you're going to have to live with them. Storming out of meetings will only delay the process and is ultimately counterproductive.

· ***Keeping Control—"Exclusivity" Rules!***

Congress saw fit to give the Chapter 11 debtor the exclusive right to file a plan for the first four months of the case. If the debtor files a plan within the first four months of a case, the debtor will be given another two months for solicitation and to get it confirmed by the court.[249] This is known as the "***exclusivity period.***" The concept is that if the debtor is to be given a chance to stabilize the business operations and negotiate with the varied parties in interest to reach a consensus, the debtor needs some control over that process so the other parties don't feel they can simply go around the debtor to get a deal done. It allows the debtor to be the "gatekeeper," at least initially.

The exclusivity period can be shortened if there is good reason (which has happened, but is fairly rare), or more likely it can be extended during the case.[250] In complex commercial reorganizations, it is not unusual to see the exclusivity period extended many times. In some cases, debtors have had their exclusivity period extended for years into the case.[251] The bankruptcy courts will ask a debtor that requests an extension what progress is being made, and usually will continue to give the debtor the benefit of the doubt until a pretty good case is made to the contrary.

Exclusivity is an interesting concept. It can be used as a "shield" to protect the debtor from being picked apart by creditors that have ulterior agendas. An example of this would be a secured creditor who just wants its collateral back and really doesn't care what happens to the other creditors in the case. It also shields the debtor (and the other creditors) from the vultures and bottom-feeders (or insightful risk takers, depending on your perspective) that buy debt or equity in bankruptcy cases as a takeover tactic. Maintaining exclusivity gives the debtor the leverage to be able to deal with the single-minded creditor so the reorganization can be used for the benefit of all creditors.

Conversely, exclusivity can be used as a "sword" in certain cases. For example, there are cases where management of the debtor is pursuing an agenda that may benefit it but not necessarily the creditors (which unfortunately happens, and will generally cause serious concern among the creditor constituencies).[252] Under those circumstances, exclusivity is used as a sword to pursue an agenda that Congress probably didn't intend. In any event, exclusivity is an integral part of keeping a level playing field during the negotiating process.

- ***Understanding and Appreciating What the Constituents Want and Need.***

In order to be successful in the negotiation process it is obvious that you need to have an understanding and appreciation as to what the various constituents want and need from the process. The simple answer, of course, is that all creditors want to be paid in cash, in full, with interest; and all equityholders want to retain all their stock. That's obviously not very likely to happen, so a more in-depth analysis is in order. Every deal is different, of course, but here is a menu of common perspectives for key players in the process.

- ***The Secured Creditors.*** Secured creditors in bankruptcy cases understandably wish to retain their lien positions. They will negotiate for debt service that allows them to keep the loans on their books as performing loans. Holders of secured public debt (such as bonds) will need a debt security that will trade at (or possibly even above) par after confirmation, so interest rate, maturity, and overall size of the issuance will be an important part of the negotiations. As such, attempts at ***negative amortization*** (that is, where interest is accrued and capitalized as opposed to paid) and other attempts to deal with secured creditors in such a way that the loan at the end of the reorganization process is not something they can book as a performing loan would generally be fought. If a secured lender has marked its loan to market (that is, wrote the loan down to the extent the lender is undersecured), dealing with it may not be as difficult as dealing with some of the other constituencies in the case. Where the secured debt is public debt (such as in the case of secured bonds, which are a common means of financing casinos), the company (through its financial advisors) can generally find out what the debt is trading at and get an idea as to what the marketplace believes the debt is worth for negotiating purposes. The secured creditors can be very difficult to deal with in cases where either they are the primary debt in the case (such that they will want to retain a certain amount of secured debt in the reorganized debtor and also take all or a vast majority of the equity in the reorganized debtor), or where the players that are holding the secured debt are not the original players but strategic buyers who have purchased the debt (usually at a discount) as an acquisition strategy for the assets or the company.[253]
- ***The Unsecured Trade Creditors.*** Unsecured trade creditors for the most part just want two things. **First**, they don't want equity posi-

tions in the reorganized debtor—they would rather have cash (even if the cash is at a discount).[254] **Second**, they really want the debtor to survive. While they may be upset at having to take 30¢ on the dollar as a result of the debtor's bankruptcy, it would be adding insult to injury for these trade creditors to have the debtor go out of business so they don't have a continuing customer. As such, debtors can usually retain the support of trade creditors by ensuring that they receive some cash through the plan confirmation process (as opposed to equity in the reorganized debtor or other such currency), and through assurances that the business will survive such that they will have a customer (hopefully with a healthy balance sheet) after it emerges from Chapter 11.

- ***Unsecured Public Debt Securities.*** Dealing with holders of unsecured public debt securities is wholly different than dealing with unsecured trade creditors or secured creditors. For the most part, public debt securities are held by institutional investors that are sophisticated in restructurings. While public debt trades all the time, in distressed company situations (usually as a result of the press releases and other public filings that occur) the public debt was likely trading at discounts prior to the bankruptcy, and chances are it continued to trade even after the bankruptcy was filed.[255]

Sophisticated holders of public debt securities are generally very clear regarding what they need. While cash is wonderful, they recognize that it is usually in short supply and that the real recovery for them will usually be through currency other than cash. That customarily involves some combination of a write-down of the debt to some amount that will be tradeable and sell at par (such that the principal will need to be an amount that can be dealt with by the reorganized debtor at an interest rate that is a market rate and that has a reasonable debt-coverage ratio), and for the balance of the debt they will want a substantial portion of the equity in the reorganized debtor.

As discussed below, securities issued under a plan are exempt from registration under federal and state securities laws.[256] As such, the securities cannot be resold by the creditors receiving them unless they can find another exemption or otherwise comply with applicable securities laws.[257] To create liquidity for the plan-issued securities, and to create a market for those securities, sophisticated holders of the securities issued under plans will generally bargain for ***demand registration rights*** and exchange-listing obligations[258] in connection with negotiations with the company, and in negotiations with each other will want ***tag-along*** or ***drag-along rights*** if they are going to be acquiring minority pieces of equity in the reorganized debtor.[259] These rights are needed because while the Bankruptcy Code exempts securities issued through a plan from registration requirements, liquidity to the recipients of those securities through resale, and listing to create public market liquidity, are other matters.[260] In order for the holders of the debt or equity to have liquidity in a public market sense, these securities will ultimately need to be registered and listed on some recognized exchange.[261]

Dealing with the sophisticated holders of public debt securities can be a varied experience, often depending upon whether the holders are primarily par holders (and as such have very little chance of ever seeing a full recovery), or whether they are "vulture buyers" who acquired the public debt as an acquisition or speculation strategy. In all events, unless they are using their debt to acquire the company, holders of public debt securities are looking for an exit strategy that will involve liquidity in whatever non-cash currency is used to pay them (be it a reduced debt instrument, equity in the reorganized debtor, or a combination of both).

- ***Public Equity.*** Finally, holders of the company's public equity generally know exactly where they stand in the pecking order of payment priority. While outside of bankruptcy and in a financially healthy company the board serves to advance the interests of the equityholders, in a financially distressed and insolvent company the equityholders are generally understood to be out of the money and entitled as a matter of law to no distribution other than what senior interests (such as creditors) will agree to give them in the process[262] (see discussion below on the "*Absolute Priority Rule*").

  That having been said, equityholders generally understand that their recovery in the case will come from generally one of two sources (or a combination of both). **First**, they will be able to look to a recovery from the company's D&O policies as part of class-action lawsuits that will generally have been filed as soon as the bad financial news hits the public filings relating to damages incurred during the prebankruptcy class period. These lawsuits are often settled as part of plan confirmation with the active participation of the insurance carrier. **Second**, they will attempt to negotiate for some small piece of the equity in some form. Generally speaking, and absent unusual circumstances, the best they can hope for is very small equity allocation and/or favorably priced warrants.[263]

Step Two: Drafting the Plan of Reorganization

Once the terms of the restructuring have been negotiated, they are memorialized in a plan of reorganization and its exhibits. There are two styles of plans that you are likely to see. The first has all of the details of all of the various deals cut with different creditor constituencies put in the plan itself rather than in separate agreements that are exhibits to the plan. This will make the plan very lengthy and complex. The second type is where the plan itself is fairly simple, with major deals that are cut with various constituencies set forth in side agreements that are attached as exhibits to the plan. This makes the plan somewhat simpler since the details are in the attached agreements.

Regardless of the style used, almost all plans that you will see will memorialize one or some combination of the following seven types of exit strategies: (1) payment over time (usually through the negotiation process) of secured debt, or a surrender of the collateral to the secured creditor; (2) a sale of some or all of the assets of the debtor with proceeds used for payments to creditors, as working capital, or both; (3) identification of certain executory contracts and unexpired leases that will be assumed, and others that will be rejected; (4) infusion of equity (through rights offerings, warrant exercises, or other means) or working capital (in the form of a loan) to assist the reorganized company on a going-forward basis; (5) the issuance of some type of debt or equity securities to be used for payment to creditors in exchange for their claims (known as "conversion of debt to equity" if an equity security is given in exchange for a debt instrument); and/or (7) the dilution or extinguishment of existing equity in the company.[264] Which of the exit strategies are implemented through the plan is a direct result of the negotiations the company has with the creditors and the leverage each party has in the process.

· ***The Component Parts of the Plan Document.*** Plans are divided into either "sections" or "articles." Regardless of how it is divided, essentially every plan reads the same (because the Bankruptcy Code requires certain things be in a plan,[265] and also because lawyers drafting such plans like to follow what has worked in other cases). In any event, plans will generally contain the following articles or sections:

- ***Definitional Section.*** This section contains the definitions used throughout the rest of the document. This is sometimes put as an exhibit to the plan, and other times it is put as the first article or section in the plan. Some pretty substantive things can be discussed in the guise of definitions (such as the way a particular claim is defined and what it includes and excludes). These sections can be very lengthy.
- ***Treatment of "Unclassified Claims."*** The claims of creditors must be put into "classes" in plans. What the bankruptcy law requires is that each secured creditor be put into its own class,[266] and then the debtor may group similar claims together (such as trade creditors, bondholders, deficiency claims of secured creditors, and the like). Substantial gamesmanship and strategy can go into how creditors are put into classes (or "classified") since it affects voting on the plan (discussed below). In any event, there are certain claims that are generally understood to be "unclassified" in the sense that the Bankruptcy Code is very specific about the way they must be treated

(see discussion on *Specific Treatment Of Administrative And Priority Claims* in *Step Five: The Plan Confirmation Process*, below). As such, many plan drafters do not put them into specific classes but merely have a general section entitled "Treatment Of Unclassified Claims." Examples of these types of claims are administrative and priority claims that must be dealt with in specific ways by the Bankruptcy Code. The reasoning behind putting them as unclassified claims is that they do not need to vote on the plan since they must always be paid in full (see discussion below), nor are they part of the solicitation process (described in Step Four below).

- ***General Description of Classification of Claims and Equity Interests.*** This section describes, in a summary fashion, how the plan proponent classifies the claims and interests that will be dealt with in the plan.
- ***In-Depth Description of the Treatment of Classified Claims and Equity Interests.*** This section sets forth, with specificity, how the various classes of claims will be treated. It is in this section that the plan itself can be highly detailed as to treatment of various creditor constituencies (or "stand-alone" agreements that have been reached can be incorporated by reference and attached as an exhibit to the plan).
- ***Means for Implementation of the Plan.*** In this section the plan proponent describes how it intends to implement the plan and make payments to creditors. For example, to the extent the plan proponent is setting up a liquidating trust and transferring assets into it, this is described in this article. If there are corporate governance changes that are going to be made (such as changes to Boards of Directors), that is also described in this section. Sales of assets, a merger with another entity, reconstitution of the business entity form (for example, sometimes companies change their state of incorporation, or change from a partnership to a limited liability company), and descriptions of any working-capital lines that are going to be used by the reorganized debtor are described here.[267] This section is intended to give the reader of the plan an idea as to how the reorganized debtor is going to operate postconfirmation and perform under the plan.
- ***Description of Securities to be Issued in Connection With the Plan.*** To the extent that debt or equity securities are to be issued as part of the plan, they are generally described in a section separate from the "Means Of Implementation." The plan proponent describes the various types of securities to be issued, as well as any obligations on the part of the company to register those securities and any intershareholder rights that have been agreed upon (see discussion on *A*

Word About Non-Voting Equity Securities, below).

- ***Treatment of Executory Contracts and Unexpired Leases.*** This section will identify those executory contracts and unexpired leases that will be assumed, and which will be rejected (to the extent this has not occurred prior to plan confirmation by separate order of the bankruptcy court).
- ***Conditions Precedent.*** There are times when, in order for the debtor to be able to make payments under a plan, certain conditions must be met (such as the finalization of documentation of a working-capital line). Plans generally contain a section that sets forth, in detail, any of the conditions precedent to the effectiveness of the plan. See discussion in *Step Six: "Going Effective,"* below.
- ***Discharge and Discharge Injunction Decree Section.*** Plans also make very clear that confirmation of (or going effective under) the plan results in a ***discharge*** under the Bankruptcy Code (discussed below). In addition, most plans contain a specific ***discharge injunction*** that prohibits creditors from pursuing actions based on claims that have been dealt with in the plan. To the extent necessary, the plan will also vest title to all of the assets from the debtor to the reorganized debtor (which as a matter of law is a separate entity).
- ***The Claims Objection Process Section.*** There are two ways to deal with ***claims objections*** in a Chapter 11 case.[268] One way is to fight all of the claims prior to getting to confirmation. This is usually not viewed as an effective use of time or money, so most plans contain a provision that gives the debtor a period of time after confirmation (usually 60 and 120 days) within which to object to claims that were filed. The bankruptcy court will continue to have jurisdiction over these claims objections, and it can take years after the plan is confirmed to get all of the claims resolved.[269] This process avoids delay in the confirmation process, and lets the company get on with its business without being bogged down in this litigation. It is also possible to pursue preferences, fraudulent conveyances, and other avoidance actions postconfirmation through this process as well. Distributions can be made to claims that are not objected to, and sometimes reserves will need to be set up for claims that are in the objection process.
- ***Retention of Jurisdiction of the Bankruptcy Court.*** This is a very important provision of a plan. The plan has to state, with specificity, in exactly what matters the bankruptcy court will be retaining jurisdiction. For example, it should state that the bankruptcy court is retaining jurisdiction to adjudicate claims disputes, preferences, fraudulent conveyances, professional fee disputes, and any other expected litigation that might arise postconfirmation. This detail is necessary

because of case law that suggests that if a plan is not specific about the retained jurisdiction of the bankruptcy court, the bankruptcy court has no jurisdiction over postconfirmation litigation. If postconfirmation litigation and claims resolution is important (which it always is), attention should be paid to the retained-jurisdiction provisions.

- ***Miscellaneous Provisions.*** Plans also generally contain provisions that reserve the right of a plan proponent to proceed to confirmation by cramdown (discussed below), and also reserve to the plan proponent the right to revoke, withdraw, or modify its plan. Release provisions (discussed under *Exculpation And Releases*, below) are also generally contained here. There are other "boilerplate" types of things that are put into this section such as severability clauses, notice provisions, and the like.
- ***Exhibits.*** Finally, a plan will contain exhibits that may consist of "stand-alone" agreements with major creditors, applicable corporate governance documents (such as revised bylaws and articles of incorporation), forms of notes and indentures, and other exhibits as may be appropriate.

Contained in the Appendix to these materials are sample plans showing debt-to-equity conversions, liquidations, and sales to third parties. Obviously, those plans will all contain provisions that may have been the result of case-specific negotiations, and are intended to be illustrative only.

Step Three: The Disclosure Statement

After the provisions have been negotiated and memorialized in the plan of reorganization, the next step in the process is to draft and obtain approval of the Disclosure Statement. As discussed earlier in this chapter, the Disclosure Statement is really a form of prospectus that is used to get creditors to buy into your plan. The Bankruptcy Code is very specific that a plan proponent is not allowed to solicit acceptances for its plan without having a court-approved Disclosure Statement.[270] As stated earlier, if a debtor were to file a plan of reorganization and then begin the negotiating process for the first time, the case wouldn't go very smoothly. At the same time, filing a plan is also not the end of the negotiations. Between the time a plan and Disclosure Statement are filed and when the plan is actually before the bankruptcy court for confirmation (Step Five discussed below), significant horse-trading can, does, and should occur. Sometimes debtors file plans to break a deadlock in negotiations or to simply put a "shot over the bow" of a recalcitrant creditor group.

There is an interesting paradox regarding Disclosure Statements. There is a wealth of case law about what they must contain, and all sorts of law review commentaries on how they must be exacting and the like. In reality, many (if not most) creditors are unlikely to read a Disclosure Statement (or even the plan, for that matter). While parties may use the Disclosure Statement approval process as a way to preview plan objections, confirmation litigation, or otherwise enhance their negotiating posture, for the most part bankruptcy judges recognize that the Disclosure Statement process does not really add a lot to the process in most deals.[271]

· ***The Necessary Components of a Disclosure Statement.***

The Bankruptcy Code only tells us that a Disclosure Statement must contain "adequate information," which is defined as "information of a kind, and in sufficient detail, as far as reasonably practicable in light of the nature and history of the debtor and the condition of the debtor's books and records, that would enable a hypothetical reasonable investor typical of holders of claims or interests of the relevant class to make an informed judgment about the plan. . . . ."[272] So what does this mean?

The case law is pretty well developed as to what must be in a Disclosure Statement. While several courts have attempted to develop checklists of the information to be included in a disclosure statement, they also recognize that these checklists are not exhaustive or dispositive because Congress intended flexible disclosure requirements to be administered by the courts. Accordingly, while no checklist is dispositive, generally speaking some or all of the following information really needs to be contained in a Disclosure Statement to pass muster under the Bankruptcy Code.[273]

- The incidents leading to the filing of the bankruptcy.
- A description of the debtor's assets and their values.
- The anticipated future for the reorganized company.
- The present financial condition of the debtor.
- Discussion of the scheduled or otherwise allowed claims, including allowed amounts within each class.
- A liquidation analysis of the company to demonstrate that the plan meets the "best interests of creditors test" (that is, that creditors will get more under the plan than they would get in a liquidation of the company).
- An identification of the accounting procedures used in preparing the Disclosure Statement.
- A discussion of the qualification of future management of the reorganized debtor.
- A brief description of the plan of reorganization (which will be attached as an exhibit to the Disclosure Statement).
- An estimate of administrative expenses that will be incurred by the confirmation date.
- An assessment of the collectibility of any accounts that may con-

stitute assets of the estate.

- Risks to creditors under the plan.
- Discussion of current and potential litigation involving the debtor.
- Possible recoveries of preference and fraudulent conveyances.
- The tax effects of the proposed plan.[274]
- The relationship of the debtor to affiliates and the plan proponents, and a discussion of any plan implementation issues.
- A disclaimer regarding the ability to verify factual information and predictions and projections (this is one drafters of disclosure statements are only too happy to put in).
- Sources of information in the Disclosure Statement.
- Projections of anticipated future revenues (discussed below).

Again, there are no specific items that must be in every Disclosure Statement, but any company that has put together a prospectus knows the sort of information that is looked at and what should be included from a materiality standpoint.[275]

· ***Disclosure Statement Projections.***

One of the most critical aspects of a Disclosure Statement is the debtor's projections (to the extent the plan involves future operations as a funding source, as opposed to a liquidation). Sophisticated creditors will be very exacting on what they want to see in the nature of projections, and will want full disclosure of any and all assumptions that the debtor uses. Notwithstanding painstaking disclaimers and warnings as to the inability to guaranty or otherwise verify this information (they are, after all, only projections),[276] this is an area that gets quite a bit of attention from both bankruptcy courts and other parties in the case. It is always best that a debtor be conservative in projections.

- ***When is a Projection Not a Projection?*** Pardon the riddle, but there are many projections used in bankruptcy cases for different purposes. The projections attached to a Disclosure Statement are generally viewed as conservative estimates of future performance and are not dispositive. For example, to the extent that the plan contemplates that there will be compensation incentives for postconfirmation executives, a different set of projections may very well be used for that purpose. This makes sense because you don't want to compensate an executive for just hitting conservative base case numbers. In addition, for plan confirmation purposes and the ***"feasibility" analysis*** (discussed in Step Five, below), the debtor may "tweak" the projections up or down in order to prove the plan's feasibility (which is required in order for the bankruptcy court to confirm the plan).

· ***Valuations—When is Value Not Always Value?***

Again, pardon the riddle. Valuations of assets in bankruptcy cases are used to show different things at different times in the process. To the extent that a company values its assets, those values will vary (and potentially materially vary) based on the purpose of the value. For example, assets will generally be valued in a Disclosure Statement at a "fire sale" liquidation value for purposes of a ***liquidation analysis*** (that is, an analysis to show creditors what they would get in the event that the company was simply liquidated). Other parties in the case may wish to use "going concern" value for determining the amount of collateral a secured creditor has. Both values are legitimate because they have different uses. In any event, book values are generally not used as they often don't have any correlation to market values.[277] Whatever values or valuation methods a debtor uses, all assumptions should be clearly set forth along with appropriate disclaimers.

· ***The Disclosure Statement Approval Process.***

Once the debtor drafts the Disclosure Statement and attaches all of the exhibits to it, it is filed with the bankruptcy court, which will set a hearing (noticed to all creditors) to consider whether it will approve the Disclosure Statement.[278] The debtor need only serve the Disclosure Statement as drafted on Committees (or their counsel), the SEC, and any creditor that specifically requests a copy of it, along with the U.S. Trustee (who will likely not read it). It is generally a good idea to run drafts of the Disclosure Statement by the major constituencies, and certainly by the SEC, to get their comments beforehand. The SEC will generally review Disclosure Statements (certainly in public company cases) and give comments prior to the hearing on its approval. The SEC has been advocating the use of the "plain English" rules for Disclosure Statements.

The parties will have a period of time (usually twenty-five days, although this period can be shortened)[279] to review the Disclosure Statement and file objections. The objections should not relate to confirmation of the plan (discussed in Step Five, below), but are only supposed to address whether the Disclosure Statement contains "adequate information." As stated earlier, the Bankruptcy Code defines "adequate information" as "information of a kind, and in sufficient detail, as far as is reasonably practicable in light of the nature and history of the debtor and the condition of the debtor's books and records, that would enable a hypothetical reasonable investor typical of holders of claims or interests of the relevant class to make an informed judgment about the plan…."[280] The checklists developed by the case law are all aimed at giving drafters of Disclosure Statements at least some courts' view of what constitutes "adequate information." Sometimes creditors that will be contesting plan confirmation or are trying to get settlement leverage will use the Disclosure Statement process as a way to raise issues regarding confirmation of the plan. Most courts do not entertain those sorts of objections, nor should they at that stage of the case. Courts will generally say that such objections go to confirmation and will be heard during the confirmation hearing.

Disclosure Statement battles do not generally tend to be drawn out affairs. Since it is unlikely that creditors really read Disclosure Statements cover to cover, and it is less likely that creditors vote on a plan based on what's in or not in a Disclosure Statement, most experienced debtors' lawyers will take a very simple approach to objections to Disclosure Statements. For example, if a creditor objects to a Disclosure Statement because it wishes the debtor to disclose that, in the creditor's opinion, management of the company is incompetent and will lead the company to ruin, most debtors' counsel would advise that they will include that statement by the creditor in the Disclosure Statement (sometimes in a footnote), followed by a sentence that simply says: "The debtor disagrees with this position." Again, since in many cases few people read these things, getting involved in a protracted battle over what's in the Disclosure Statement is not a good use of resources.

After the court has a hearing on the adequacy of the Disclosure Statement, the court will enter an order (which is in many cases a form order found in the Bankruptcy Rules) approving the Disclosure Statement. This leads the way for the next step in the process—the solicitation process.

To the extent that the debtor wants to have other materials included with the Disclosure Statement (such as, for example, a letter from the CEO of the company urging creditors to vote to accept the plan, or perhaps a letter from a Creditors Committee counsel urging acceptance of the plan), the debtor may want to have the bankruptcy court approve those solicitation materials as well. While reasonable minds can and do differ on whether bankruptcy court approval of all of these other solicitation materials is legally necessary, it really can't hurt to have them approved (to avoid potential future litigation over the propriety of such materials) to the extent there is any question whatsoever. Nonetheless, some debtors take the position that they do not need to get specific bankruptcy court approval of these other materials and do not have them specifically approved by the bankruptcy court.

Step Four: The Solicitation Process

Once the bankruptcy court approves the Disclosure Statement, the real fun begins. The debtor must then get the plan and Disclosure Statement out to all creditors and parties in interest so that they can vote to accept or reject the plan.

· ***The Logistics.***

In a case where there are a substantial number of creditors that are going to vote on the plan, once the bankruptcy court approves the Disclosure Statement the debtor will go to a financial printing service (such as

Bowne or others) and have the court-approved Disclosure Statement (with all the exhibits) printed and bound. Many of these services will also handle the mailing of all of the Disclosure Statement packages. Having it professionally printed and bound by experienced financial printers ultimately saves costs and reduces bulk.[281]

· ***The "Solicitation Package."***

What creditors will then receive (either from the debtor or the financial printer to the extent they have done the mailing) will be a "***solicitation package***." What's included in the solicitation package will vary from case to case, but it will always include the Disclosure Statement, any exhibits to the Disclosure Statement (such as financial projections, or the last audited financial statements for the debtor), and the plan of reorganization (and any and all exhibits to that document to the extent they have already been prepared). The solicitation package will also contain a ***plan ballot***. The ballot, whose form may have also been approved by the bankruptcy court as part of the approval of the solicitation process, is the actual document that must be filled out by the creditor voting on the plan and returned to the debtor so that the voting results can be tabulated.

Plan ballots can materially vary as to their complexity.[282] Sometimes there are specific elections that creditors in certain classes must make on the plan ballot. An example of this would be a creditor that wishes to be treated as an ***administrative convenience claim*** (that is, a creditor with a fairly small claim that will be cashed out early on in the postconfirmation process). Generally these creditors must make a specific election on the ballot to be treated as such. In addition, with respect to public debt and equity, sometimes it is impossible to know who the beneficial holders of all of the public securities are. As such, in situations involving public debt, the street-name holders will receive a ballot, and they will then have the obligation to provide copies of the ballots to all of the actual beneficial holders of the particular security. Once they get the ballots back from the beneficial holders, they will file a master ballot that will list, with specificity, how many holders of securities have voted to accept or reject the plan, and the amount of their particular holdings.

· ***Who is Entitled to Vote?***

Not everyone with a claim in a bankruptcy is necessarily entitled to vote. Specifically, the Bankruptcy Code provides that only holders of "***allowed claims***" that are "impaired" are entitled to vote on a plan.[283]

- ***"Allowed" Claims.*** An "allowed" claim is a claim that either the debtor acknowledges it owes (such as by listing that claim in the Statements and Schedules as undisputed), or a claim for which a proof of claim has been filed by any applicable bar date (see discussion above regarding "***bar date orders***"), and to which no specific objection has been filed by the debtor.[284] The reason for allowing only holders of allowed claims to vote is simple. In a bankruptcy case, creditors will frequently file claims that may be inflated, or the validity of which may be legitimately disputed. Under those circumstances, holders of claims that are disputed should not be allowed to control the voting process as only creditors with legitimate allowed claims should be voting. In addition, the Bankruptcy Code treats secured claims in an interesting way. Under the Bankruptcy Code, an ***allowed secured claim*** depends on the value of collateral held. For example, a creditor owed $100 secured by an asset worth $80 has an allowed secured claim of $80, and an allowed unsecured claim of $20 (assuming no other disputes exist).[285]

Debtors sometimes engage in some gamesmanship in this aspect of the bankruptcy law. For example, there are times when a debtor will solicit votes, and if it gets a large number of rejecting votes, it will then file objections to the claims of the rejecting creditors. Once objections are filed, the claimants must go to the bankruptcy court and obtain ***"temporary allowance***" of their claims. This process requires the bankruptcy court to conduct a "mini trial" on the claim objections and decide, strictly for temporary purposes, how much the claims should be (if anything). For example, a creditor files a claim for $1 million and votes against the plan. If the debtor objects to that claim, that creditor's rejection vote does not need to be counted for tabulation purposes. The creditor then must come into bankruptcy court and seek temporary allowance of its claim for voting and other purposes.[286] The bankruptcy court may then conduct an expedited hearing and make a determination that for temporary allowance purposes, the claim will be counted at $500,000. At that point, the debtor must count the rejecting vote as a $500,000 rejecting vote, not a $1 million rejecting vote. The bankruptcy courts are savvy enough to look askance at a debtor filing a number of last minute objections to rejecting claims.[287]

- ***"Impaired" Claims.*** Moreover, the Bankruptcy Code provides that only creditors with *impaired claims* are entitled to vote. What this means is that if a creditor is getting paid everything it is owed in strict accordance with all of the contractual terms and provisions to which it was entitled prebankruptcy, that creditor is deemed to be unimpaired and does not get to vote on the plan one way or another.[288] Under the bankruptcy law, a class of creditors that is not impaired under a plan is conclusively presumed to have accepted the plan, and there is no need to solicit its votes.[289] Any alteration of the contractual, legal, or equitable rights of a creditor will be deemed to be "impairment" for voting purposes.[290] This includes any restriction on default interest or late charges. Conversely, any classes of claims or interests that will not receive any payment or property under a plan also do not need to be solicited because they are deemed to reject the plan.[291]

· ***The Concept of "Class Voting."***

As discussed earlier in this chapter, a plan of reorganization must classify claims. For voting purposes, bankruptcy courts are interested in how classes voted with respect to the plan. While each secured creditor is generally put in its own class, that secured creditor's vote to accept or reject will obviously carry that particular class. In classes with numerous members (such as a general unsecured creditor class), the Bankruptcy Code is specific about how the class votes to accept or reject the plan. Specifically, the Bankruptcy Code provides that a class of claims is considered to have accepted a plan of reorganization when more than one-half in number of claims and at least two-thirds in amount of claims vote to accept the plan (the "***One- Half/Two-Thirds Requirement***").[292] This requirement applies to creditors that actually vote on the plan, not all creditors. For example, assume a class has ten creditors with total claims of $310, and five are owed $10 each, three are owed $20 each, and two are owed $100 each. If only three creditors vote, the one-half/two-thirds requirement applies only to those three creditors and their claims.[293]

The reason for this requirement is straightforward. Let's assume that a class of general unsecured creditors has $10 million worth of total allowed claims entitled to vote, and ten holders of those claims. Further assume that holders of eight of those claims are owed, in the aggregate, $2 million, and the other two members hold in the aggregate $8 million in claims. If the voting were simply done on a one-creditor/one-vote basis, then the six creditors who are owed 20 percent of all of the debt in that class could impose their will on creditors that are owed significantly greater amounts. As such, the Bankruptcy Code has the dual requirement that of the claims voting, *both* more than one-half in number *and* two-thirds in amount must vote to accept the plan. In the example given above, assuming all ten creditors vote, six creditors must vote to accept the plan, and of those six creditors, their claims must equal at least about $6.7 million in order for the plan to be deemed to have been accepted by that class.

· ***"Bad Faith" Votes—The Concept of "Designation of Ballots."***

Sometimes creditors for whatever reason decide that they may wish to vote against the plan for something other than a good faith reason. For example, it is not outside the realm of possibility that a competitor may buy up claims against a debtor, and vote those claims to reject the plan proposed by the debtor for the purpose of putting the debtor out of business (because the plan might not be confirmed, and the case may be converted to a liquidation under Chapter 7 or be dismissed). Under these circumstances, where a debtor can prove that a vote has been cast in "bad faith," the Bankruptcy Code allows the bankruptcy court (upon the request of a party) to "designate" that vote as a bad faith vote and disregard it for purposes of plan confirmation.[294] The same designation could occur where another party in the case (other than the plan proponent) could show that a vote was cast as a result of an improper solicitation. For example, perhaps the debtor, needing a large creditor to vote to accept a plan so that it will carry a class, promises that particular creditor some recovery outside of the plan of reorganization. This is prohibited under bankruptcy law (and indeed may be a bankruptcy crime).[295] Under these circumstances, the accepting vote would also be stricken and disregarded under the bankruptcy law. Bad faith designations are rare, but have happened (usually in cases where creditors purchased claims under unfair disclosure circumstances—the bad faith was premised on quasi-securities-law grounds).[296]

· ***"A Card Laid is a Card Played"—Changing Votes After They're Made.***

Once a ballot is cast to accept or reject a plan, the creditor may not change the ballot without approval of the bankruptcy court. The reason for this is that it allows the bankruptcy court to exercise oversight over negotiations that occur after ballots are cast. For example, if a creditor rejected the plan and the debtor then promised something to the creditor to obtain its support, and the creditor seeks to change the ballot to an acceptance, the bankruptcy court will ask the creditor what made the creditor change its mind. The same would be true where the creditor has accepted a plan and then seeks to change its ballot to reject the plan. The debtor would have the right to ask why the creditor had a change of heart to determine if there were reasons that may not have been legitimate (such as an overture from a creditor that may be seeking to defeat confirmation of the debtor's plan and is making promises to a creditor to change its vote).[297]

· ***The Tabulation Process.***

The bankruptcy court will set a deadline when all ballots must be received. In large cases, the debtor will frequently get bankruptcy court approval to retain a solicitation agent who will receive the ballots and prepare a ***Ballot Report***. The Ballot Report will break down, by class, creditor, and claim amount, the acceptances and rejections received. In large cases, big accounting firms usually fill this role and recently, specialized claims-registration and ballot-tabulation companies have come into the market (such as Claudia King Associates). After the ballots are all received and tabulated, the Ballot Report is filed with the bankruptcy court so the bankruptcy court and other parties can see the votes of creditors. This apprises both the bankruptcy court and the debtor as to whether the plan will be in a ***cramdown posture*** or whether confirmation will be as a result of the accepting votes of all of the classes of creditors.

Contained in the Appendix to these materials is a sample solicitation package (without the plans and Disclosure Statements) to illustrate the types of materials that are generally contained in them. After the plan and Disclosure Statement are sent out and the ballots received and tabulated, the stage is set for the ultimate prize—plan confirmation.

Step Five: The Plan Confirmation Process

The solicitation package goes out to all creditors and the ballots come in. The Ballot Report is filed and it's now time to get to bankruptcy court approval of the plan—the plan confirmation process.

· ***The Thirteen Requirements for Plan Confirmation.***

The Bankruptcy Code sets forth thirteen specific requirements that the bankruptcy court must determine are met in order to confirm a plan.[298] Conceptually, they can be summarized in twelve steps as follows:

- ***The Plan Complies with the Bankruptcy Code.*** The plan and plan proponent must both comply with the applicable provisions of the Bankruptcy Code.[299] What this presumably means is that the solicitation process was done in accordance with the applicable provisions of the Bankruptcy Code and that there is nothing in the plan that blatantly violates the Bankruptcy Code (see discussion on *Exculpation And Releases* below).
- ***"Good Faith."*** The plan must have been proposed in good faith. This is really a general catch-all phrase, and in some confirmation battles the phrase "bad faith" is thrown around because there are no other substantive attacks on the plan. The case law on "good faith" was developed primarily from the single-asset cases where debtors would put overleveraged, single-asset partnerships into bankruptcy and then try to cramdown secured creditors. In large corporate restructurings it is rare (although not completely unheard of) for there to be a finding of a lack of good faith.[300] The trend of modern cases looking at good faith seems to be operating on the presumption that there is no such thing as bad faith, only varying degrees of good faith. In other words, any plan that maximizes return to creditors, avoids a free-fall liquidation, or preserves jobs will most likely meet the requirement that the plan is proposed in good faith.[301]
- ***Bankruptcy Court Approval of Payments to Professionals.*** All payments that are to be made to any persons for issuing securities or for services rendered in the case (such as professionals) must be approved by, or subject to approval by, the bankruptcy court for reasonableness.[302]
- ***Full Disclosure of Identity of Postconfirmation Officers and Directors.*** The plan must disclose the identity of all individuals that will serve as officers, directors, or in other official capacities postconfirmation, and there must not be any public policy reason why such individuals should not serve in that role.[303]

- ***Regulatory Approval.*** Any governmental regulatory agency that has jurisdiction over rates charged by the debtors must have approved any rate change that is provided in the plan.[304] This requirement would be applicable to utilities or any other businesses that are subject to governmental regulatory oversight.
- ***"Best Interest of Creditors" Test.*** With respect to each individual *holder* of a claim (to be contrasted with *classes* of claims), they either must have voted to accept the plan, or if they have voted to reject the plan, the bankruptcy court must be shown that the rejecting creditor will receive at least as much as it would receive in a liquidation under Chapter 7.[305] This is commonly referred to as the "***best interests of creditors test***." What this means is that if a creditor is in a class that has voted to accept the plan (see discussion earlier on *Class Voting*), while the creditor's *class* will be deemed to accept the plan and the creditor will be bound by it notwithstanding its rejection of the plan, the debtor must still show that the *dissenting creditor* is getting at least as much as it would get in a straight liquidation under Chapter 7.
- ***Consensual Plan.*** The Bankruptcy Code states that with respect to every class impaired under the plan, every such class must have accepted the plan pursuant to the class voting rules discussed earlier in this chapter.[306]

  To the extent a class of claims or interests has not voted to accept the plan, the plan will be in a cramdown posture, which is discussed below. To the extent that each and every class has voted to accept the plan, as you might imagine the confirmation hearing becomes a fairly simple affair.[307]
- ***Specific Treatment of Administrative and Priority Claims.*** With respect to administrative claims (such as postbankruptcy professional fees and the like), the plan must provide that they are paid in full, in cash, on the "effective date" of the plan (discussed in *Step Six: "Going Effective"*). Of course, if those creditors agree to some other treatment, that will be fine as well. With respect to certain types of priority claims (such as certain claims for unpaid prebankruptcy wages of individuals subject to certain caps, unpaid employee benefit contributions subject to certain caps, consumer deposits subject to certain caps, and certain tax claims), the plan must provide that, unless the holders of those claims agree to other treatment, they must be paid, in full, although some of those payments can be made over time at a market interest rate.[308] With respect to certain tax claims, the time period over which they can be paid cannot exceed six years from their assessment date.[309] These are the claimants that are generally put as "unclassified claims" as discussed

in *Step Two: Drafting The Plan Of Reorganization*, above.

- ***Prohibition on Total "Cramdown" Plans.*** Prior to 1984, there were situations where debtors would go to confirmation and not a single class of impaired claims voted to accept the plan. The courts were split on whether or not this plan could, as a legal matter, go to confirmation when the debtor was unable to achieve acceptance by as much as one class. In 1984, Congress changed the bankruptcy law to include a provision that says at least one class of impaired claims must have voted to accept the plan in order for it to go to confirmation.[310] The debtor cannot count the votes of any ***insiders*** in that class for this purpose (since presumably they would vote to accept the plan). The result of Congress putting this provision in the Bankruptcy Code is that classification of creditors has, in certain cases, become a strategic decision since the debtor wants to ensure that it will have at least one accepting class of impaired claims.[311]
- ***"Feasibility."*** The Bankruptcy Code provides that the bankruptcy court must find that confirmation of the plan "is not likely to be followed by the liquidation, or the need for further financial reorganization, of the debtor or any successor to the debtor under the plan, unless such liquidation or reorganization is proposed in the plan."[312] This is commonly referred to as the ***feasibility requirement***. Obviously, to the extent that the plan is a liquidating plan, the feasibility test does not apply (see discussion below on *Feasibility*).
- ***Payment of U.S. Trustee's Fees.*** Congress, trying to be sure that the government gets its pound of flesh, has made as a requirement to confirmation that all quarterly U.S. Trustee's fees must be paid, in full, under the plan.[313]
- ***Protection of Retiree Benefits.*** Finally, the Bankruptcy Code provides that the plan must provide for the continued payment of "retiree benefits"[314] (see discussion in Chapter Four on *Dealing With The "Special Claims"*).

It seems simple enough. So why are there highly contested and lengthy plan confirmation hearings? There really is no single reason—in every deal there are axes to grind (value, feasibility, classification, even the best interests of creditors test).

· ***A Word about Non-Voting Equity Securities.***

Frequently, a restructuring will involve the conversion of some or all of a company's existing debt securities to equity securities in the newly restructured entity. The "equitizing" of existing debt will either dilute or eliminate altogether existing equity in the company.

The Bankruptcy Code does not, however, give the company and its management unfettered discretion in the structure and terms of the newly issued equity securities. Specifically, the Bankruptcy Code requires that the plan of reorganization provides for the inclusion in the reorganized debtor's corporate charter provisions prohibiting the issuance of non-voting equity securities and otherwise arranges for an "appropriate distribution" of power among the classes of securities possessing voting power.[315] The new equity securities must be distributed in a manner so that the allocation of voting power (that is, the control of the company) recognizes the respective positions of the creditors converting their debt to equity and existing stockholders and management. Essentially, this provision ensures that creditors converting their debt to equity securities may participate in, and exercise some control over, the selection of the management of a reorganized debtor.[316]

While seemingly straightforward, this prohibition does present some interesting tactical decisions for management. For example, management may want to consider issuing equity securities that entitled the holder to vote only on certain "big-ticket" issues concerning the reorganized company. Such big-ticket issues may include a sale of all or substantially all the assets, mergers, and the like. Such limitations upon the voting right of equity security holders may be appropriate under certain circumstances notwithstanding the prohibition described above.[317] Moreover, there may be circumstances where creditors may not want to receive equity securities with full voting rights. For example, there are federal regulations that prohibit a bank holding company from acquiring direct or indirect ownership or control of any voting shares of any company that is not a bank.[318] There are limited exceptions to this rule, but such prohibitions will frequently impact the willingness of existing debtholders to convert their debt securities to equity.[319] Similarly, in highly regulated industries (such as the gaming industry), there are licensure requirements imposed upon holders of equity securities over certain specified threshold amounts. The debt holder debtholder may believe that the conversion of its debt securities to equity is the best way to restructure the company and maximize its recovery. On the other hand, the prospect of being subject to licensure and other potentially onerous restrictions on its ownership may have a significant impact on the willingness to convert debt to equity. In short, the structure of the equity securities to be issued under any plan should be given considerable thought, and flexibility by all parties is of paramount importance.

· ***A Word about Preserving NOLs.***

A very complex area of bankruptcy law involves the best way to structure a plan such that there is the maximum preservation of net operating loss ("***NOL***") carryforwards to reduce postconfirmation income. There are times when troubled businesses will have substantial tax losses that they have been able to preserve for future use, and it's clearly important to structure a plan in such a way that those NOLs are preserved.[320] While this is a highly specialized area in bankruptcy and tax law, generally speaking a change in ownership will severely limit the ability to use NOLs to offset subsequent income.[321] To the extent that NOLs are important and available, the postconfirmation company can pay back debt principal out of pretax (as opposed to after-tax) dollars. This means that the company (under current tax rates) saves roughly 67¢ for every dollar of debt principal that it repays that would not otherwise be sheltered by depreciation deductions. In any event, the structuring of a plan and a system of recovery to creditors will need to be crafted with the overlay of preserving the NOL. It can be a material aspect of the financial viability of a company on a going- forward basis.

· ***Feasibility.***

In large commercial cases, many of the battles surrounding confirmation revolve around feasibility (although sometimes bad faith types of issues may be raised as part and parcel of that). In the event that the plan is in a cramdown posture (discussed in the section immediately following), that will also provide fodder for significant litigation in a bankruptcy context.

Feasibility comes up frequently in contested plan confirmations because any single creditor is entitled to raise it, even if that creditor's class has voted to accept the plan. It is, not surprisingly, a factually intensive analysis and it is not unusual to have experts on all sides of the issue taking up a lot of court time. A company's representatives can also testify as to feasibility if they have prepared the projections that are used for feasibility, but in hotly contested plan confirmations where this is a big issue, debtors frequently opt for expert testimony for that added degree of credibility.

A bankruptcy court's finding that a plan is feasible does not mean that the court has found that there is any guarantee of success. Indeed, in numerous cases courts have found that plans are feasible only to have the debtor default under the plan after it is confirmed (see *Plan Defaults*, below). Instead of finding a guarantee of success, when ruling on feasibility the court must only find by a "preponderance of the evidence" (that is, that it is simply more likely than not) that a failure under the plan is "not likely."[322] When looking at feasibility, courts will generally consider the adequacy of the reorganized debtor's capital, the earning power of the reorganized debtor, the general economic and market conditions in the debtor's industry, and the ability of management and the probability of management's continuation.[323] Detailed projections that are subject to analysis by other parties and are probed for weaknesses or flaws are the cornerstone of evidence on feasibility, and this testimony can take a substantial amount of time in court.

In any event, other than cramdown litigation (discussed immediately below), feasibility tends to be the most time-consuming and factually intensive confirmation requirement in contested confirmation contexts.

· ***"Cramdown" and the Absolute Priority Rule.***

As long as a debtor has one accepting impaired class, the debtor can seek to have the plan confirmed even over the rejection of all other classes that have voted on the plan. Obtaining one accepting impaired class is generally not problematic, particularly in larger commercial cases. The confirmation of a plan over the objection of classes of creditors or equity interests is known as ***cramdown***. Cramdown must be viewed in three separate and distinct scenarios—cramdown of **secured creditors**, cramdown of **unsecured creditors**, and cramdown of **equityholders**.

- ***Cramdown of Secured Creditors.*** In order to obtain confirmation of a plan over the rejecting vote of a secured creditor, all the debtor must show is that (1) the secured creditor is retaining its lien on its collateral postconfirmation, and (2) the creditor is being paid the allowed amount of its secured claim, plus a market rate of interest, over the life of the plan.[324] To the extent that the plan calls for a sale of the collateral, the bankruptcy court will approve that plan over the secured creditor's objection provided the secured creditor retains its credit bid rights under the Bankruptcy Code (see discussion in Chapter Two under *Sale Of Assets*, and in particular *Credit Bids*).

  The litigation in a contested plan confirmation surrounding cramdown of secured creditors tends to focus on the appropriate rate of interest for the secured claim under the plan of reorganization.[325] There is no bright-line test for the appropriate rate of interest, and cases that have looked at this issue have used a combination of tests, including a prime rate plus an additional interest factor for risk. Needless to say, there is little uniformity between jurisdictions on the methodology used to calculate the applicable "market rate."[326] Financial advisors and accountants usually assist in this testimony and analysis. A common method used by experts is a "blended rate analysis," whereby an expert derives an appropriate interest rate from dividing a secured claim into traunches. For example, assume that a lender is owed $100 secured by an asset worth $80. Under bankruptcy law, the lender would have an allowed secured claim for $80, and an unsecured deficiency claim for $20.[327] Some experts have concluded that if a normal loan-to-value ratio is 80 percent, they will split the $80 secured claim into two traunches—the first would be a first- lien traunch at $64 (or 80 percent of the $80 value of the asset), and the second traunch would be secured by a second lien for $16. The interest rate on the first-lien position should obviously be somewhat lower than the second traunch since there is less risk for the first-lien position. They will then take the interest rates applicable to the first- and second-lien positions and blend them to come up with a market interest rate. This type of testimony truly involves battles of the experts. In most commercial cases, this matter is resolved through negotiation.[328]

- ***Cramdown of Unsecured Creditors—The "Absolute Priority Rule."*** Confirmation of a plan of reorganization over the objection of a class of unsecured creditors is different than cramdown of secured creditors. When a class of unsecured creditors votes to reject the plan, the debtor can obtain confirmation over their objection either by paying that class in full or otherwise providing property of a value equal to their claim (which is not very likely), or by being sure that the plan provides that no claim or interest that is junior to the rejecting class will receive or retain anything under the plan on account of that junior claim or interest.[329] This is known in bankruptcy parlance as the "***absolute priority rule***."

In its simplest form, what the absolute priority rule requires is that the pecking order of non-bankruptcy law be honored. Usually (although not always), the "junior claim or interest" to unsecured creditors that vote to reject the plan are the equityholders. In the normal cramdown battle, if a class of unsecured creditors does not vote to accept the plan, the equityholders may not receive or retain anything under the plan because of their prebankruptcy equity interests.[330] In sum, the absolutely priority rule is the Bankruptcy Code's admonition that there's no free lunch in bankruptcy—the price to pay for not cutting a consensual deal with your unsecured creditors is that old equityholders are left out in the cold. In large commercial cases, particularly where unsecured creditors are not being paid in full and where extraordinary circumstances do not exist, equity interests are usually wiped out unless something is negotiated with the unsecured creditors. What sometimes occurs is the granting of warrants for existing equity (such that they have to buy in to keep any stock). In exceptional circumstances (such as an employee-owned company where the creditors want to maintain the goodwill of the former owners/employees), perhaps some small amount of stock in the reorganized debtor will be given to those stockholders through negotiation.[331] In larger commercial cases, one doesn't see a lot of cramdown battles with respect to unsecured creditors because large companies understand that in a situation where creditors are not being paid in full the equity interests are out of the money and the last ones in the pecking order. Where these battles tend to pop up more often is in closely held companies where debtors are using bankruptcy proceedings for the benefit of former equityholders.[332]

- ***Cramdown of Equity Interests.*** Finally, if a class of equity interests votes to reject the plan, the plan can be confirmed over that objection provided that either the equity interests retain all of their rights (again, which is not likely), or that no junior interests receive or retain anything under the plan on account of those junior interests.[333] Cramdown cases with respect to equity interests do not arise too often in commercial bankruptcy cases, usually because the equity (whether preferred or common stock) is out of the money and therefore no equity interests get anything under a plan. There are cases, however, where there may be some value attributable to the old equity interests. In those cases, preferred stockholders would be senior to common stockholders, and as such there could be a circumstance where common stockholders get wiped out but preferred stockholders retain part of the ownership in the reorganized debtor.

· ***The "Holy Grail"—Discharge.***

The whole point of the plan confirmation process is for the debtor to obtain a discharge. A discharge is the release of any and all claims (as broadly defined in the Bankruptcy Code) against the debtor except as otherwise provided in the confirmed plan. It acts as a legal "accord and satisfaction." It precludes the creditors whose claims have been dealt with in the plan from bringing litigation postconfirmation based on those old claims. In a corporate bankruptcy, the claims dealt with in the plan and the plan itself provide a balance sheet of all of the claims the debtor will need to deal with on a postconfirmation basis.[334]

In corporate Chapter 11 cases, the discharge provisions of the Bankruptcy Code will not give a corporate debtor a discharge under three circumstances. **First**, if the confirmed plan calls for a liquidation of all or substantially all of the debtor's property. **Second**, if the debtor does not engage in business after "consummation of the plan." **Third**, where the debtor would not be given a discharge under Chapter 7 if the case were a case under that chapter.[335] All three of those conditions must apply before a corporation will be denied a discharge notwithstanding confirmation of a plan. The third circumstance applies to all corporations, since a corporation is never entitled to a discharge if it files a Chapter 7 bankruptcy. The corporation is dissolved, but there is no discharge given.

In a case where the debtor will continue in business as the reorganized debtor (usually with new stockholders as a result of a debt-for-equity conversion, or sale of the stock in the reorganized debtor to a third party), the corporation is given a discharge. An interesting gray area is where the corporate debtor is liquidating. Liquidations under Chapter 11 can occur very shortly after confirmation, but in more complex cases the liquidation may take a year or more.[336] Will the liquidating Chapter 11 corporate debtor always be denied a discharge? Not necessarily. Some courts have looked at the three requirements of the Bankruptcy Code and found that if the liquidation is going to take a substantial amount of time after the plan is confirmed, then the corporate debtor would still be entitled to a discharge because the debtor will still be "engaged in business"—although that business will be a liquidation of the assets.[337]

· ***Exculpation and Releases.***

In order to truly have the debtor and its officers "clean" after the process it would be really nice if, in addition to the corporation getting a discharge, any and all claims against officers, directors, and other third parties (such as, for example, guarantors) would also be discharged or otherwise released through the plan confirmation process. The Bankruptcy Code only provides that the debtor (that is, the company) is eligible to get a discharge assuming that the three circumstances discussed above are not present.[338] What happens to claims against officers, directors, and guarantors as a result of the plan confirmation process? What about claims against officers and directors who may have personal liability based on guarantees of company debts, or for environmental contamination, unpaid withholding taxes, or for securities fraud claims?

That depends on a number of things—such as in which venue the bankruptcy was filed[339] and what the plan provides. For purposes of looking at releases for non-debtors, conceptually you need to look at this issue in two distinct parts—exculpation and releases for actions done in the bankruptcy itself, and exculpation and releases for actions that predated the bankruptcy (such as potential securities fraud liability and similar matters, or guarantees).

- ***Exculpation for Actions Done in the Bankruptcy.*** Unlike releases for prebankruptcy actions discussed below, the exculpation and releases for third parties as a result of actions done in the bankruptcy is not usually very controversial. With respect to any person's involvement in the solicitation of acceptances or rejections of plans (as well as the offer, issuance, sale, or purchase of any security offered or sold under the plan), the Bankruptcy Code has a specific provision that insulates those parties from liability provided they were acting in good faith with respect to those activities.[340] In addition, most plans will contain a general exculpation and release provision that protects the debtors, the officers, the directors, their professional advisors, any Committees and their advisors, and others with respect to actions done in connection with the bankruptcy proceedings (excluding, of course, any fraud or other willful misconduct of any of those parties).[341] While there is no provision of the Bankruptcy Code that would specifically provide for these types of bankruptcy- related-action exculpations and releases, they are very common in large cases and at least provide some measure of protection to the people that are involved in the process. As a practical matter, anything that has been done in the bankruptcy proceeding that is material in any respect has been blessed by the bankruptcy court as being appropriate and proper so it shouldn't be all that controversial to provide this type of release. To the extent, of course, that any of these parties were involved in willful misconduct or fraud, the exculpation would not (nor should it) cover that conduct.[342]
- ***Releases for Prebankruptcy Acts.*** The more controversial releases found in some plans involve a release of officers and directors (and

perhaps others such as guarantors) relating to actions that occurred prior to the filing of the bankruptcy and are otherwise unrelated to the bankruptcy. For example, there are times when a plan will attempt to provide that any creditor that votes for the plan (and sometimes even those creditors that don't vote for the plan) will be deemed to have released any and all claims that it may have against individual officers, directors, or guarantors upon confirmation of the plan. Whether this type of release will be enforceable really depends upon in which jurisdiction the bankruptcy case was pending, and whether the affected creditor objected to the provision (and appealed the plan confirmation order). In certain jurisdictions, these types of releases have been routinely stricken as being unenforceable and otherwise in violation of the express provisions of the Bankruptcy Code, which only provide that debtors can obtain the benefits of discharges and releases.[343] Other jurisdictions are not so stringent, and have upheld releases of non-debtors in a plan at least with respect to creditors that specifically voted to accept the plan and provided that the release provisions are specifically and unambiguously referenced in the plan.[344]

If third-party releases are critically important in the case, this issue must be looked at very carefully and undoubtedly will be a big part of the decision as to where the case will be filed. In addition, this is an area where some tension might exist between bankruptcy counsel and at least the officers and directors of the company. Releases of third parties (such as officers, directors, or perhaps guarantors) do not ultimately benefit the debtor or the reorganized debtor. It obviously benefits the officers, directors, and guarantors. There may be extensive litigation over the propriety or terms of third-party releases that could hold up confirmation. At that point, the officers and directors (and perhaps counsel) need to make a frank assessment for whose benefit, precisely, this exercise is being undertaken.

- ***"Responsible Officer" Liability for Unpaid Withholding Taxes.*** Sometimes in cash-strapped companies where payroll is handled internally, money is "borrowed" from withholding trust funds to keep a business operating.[345] Not surprisingly, it is a violation of federal law for a company to use trust-fund withheld taxes for the business. Not only is the company responsible, but it can also subject "responsible officers" to personal liability under the Internal Revenue Code.[346] It's possible under certain circumstances for a confirmed plan of reorganization to allocate payments to the Internal Revenue Service such that the first payments go to pay off delinquent withholding taxes as a way to minimize liability or otherwise protect officers and directors.[347] In addition, it is possible during the bankruptcy process to obtain an injunction against the IRS, which prevents it from bringing assessment and collection actions against responsible officers such that a plan might be confirmed that allocates payments to unpaid trust fund taxes.[348] To the extent that the company and its officers have used trust fund taxes in the operations, it is important to look at whether an allocation can be made in a confirmed plan to minimize liability or otherwise protect responsible officers. The same issue may arise with respect to state sales taxes that are collected from sales and not turned over to the states, as the implications may carry similar consequences for officers and directors of a company.

Step Six: "Going Effective"

So now the plan is confirmed. What happens next?

· ***The "Effective Date."***

A debtor's performance is generally due under a plan of reorganization on the "***Effective Date***" of the plan. When the Effective Date occurs is a matter of what the plan specifically states. As discussed in *Step Two: The Plan Of Reorganization*, above, part of the plan will generally set forth any conditions precedent to the debtor's obligations to perform. The date when the debtor will start to perform under the plan is known as the Effective Date.

The Effective Date may be conditioned upon a number of things. It may be as simple as allowing enough time to pass such that the debtor is sure no one has appealed the bankruptcy court's order confirming the plan.[349] Accordingly, some plans provide that the Effective Date will be the eleventh day after the court enters the confirmation order. Other plans have more elaborate conditions either based upon negotiated deals with certain creditors or business necessities. For example, some major creditors may want the right to approve the form of confirmation order so an express condition to an Effective Date is everyone's approval on the form of confirmation order. Other times, the debtor may need to finalize negotiations or documentation relating to a postconfirmation working-capital line so that certain payments can be made to creditors. Under these circumstances, a condition would be the finalization and funding of that working-capital line. In certain circumstances, postconfirmation regulatory approvals may be necessary.[350]

Sometimes a plan won't go effective until an asset is sold because the proceeds from the sale of that asset are necessary to make payments. It is a requirement of confirmation that administrative claims be paid in full on the Effective Date. If a debtor needs to sell an asset so that it has the cash to pay the administrative claims, one way to deal with this particular issue is to define the Effective Date as being the date when the asset is sold so that the debtor has the cash to make the payments.[351] From and after the Effective Date, the debtor (now known as the "***Reorganized Debtor***") goes on with its business and is obligated to make payments to creditors under the terms of the confirmed plan.

· ***The Legal Effect of a Confirmed Plan.***

According to the Bankruptcy Code, the bankruptcy court's confirmation of the plan discharges the debtor (see discussion above). Sometimes the constituencies will negotiate that the discharge will occur on the Effective Date and not the confirmation date to avoid the situation where a plan is confirmed but the debtor is never able to make the payments (even the first payments) required under the plan. That scenario would create a circumstance where a debtor would technically get its discharge while never having made a single payment under the plan. As such, under those circumstances, astute Creditors Committee counsel usually require that the discharge be effective on the Effective Date and not the confirmation date.[352]

The legal effect of a confirmed plan is that it becomes (in essence although not technically in the legal sense) a binding contract between the debtor (and reorganized debtor) and all of the creditors regardless of whether they voted to accept the plan or not.[353] Accordingly, if a creditor was originally owed $100, but under the terms of a confirmed plan its claim was reduced to $20 and it also received some stock in the reorganized debtor, if the debtor defaults under the plan (see discussion on *Plan Defaults*, below), the debt that the creditor has is not the original $100 debt, but rather only $20. The creditors may not bring actions against the reorganized debtor based on the preconfirmation debts since those debts have now been substituted for whatever obligations the debtor (and reorganized debtor) has set forth in the confirmed plan.

· ***"Channeling Injunctions."***

A special mention should be made of so-called "***channeling injunctions***." This was pioneered in the Chapter 11 case of *Johns-Manville Corp.* that was filed in New York in the early 1980s. *Manville* made insulation that used asbestos, and many people were made very ill because of exposure to the asbestos. *Manville* ultimately had to file a Chapter 11 bankruptcy petition. *Manville* confirmed a plan that took all of the personal injury claims against it and "channeled" them to a special trust fund that was funded by liability insurance policies and the debtor on a postconfirmation basis.[354] The benefit this had for the company is perhaps self-evident. Rather than have the confirmation process delayed by trying to determine how many thousands of people might get ill and what those damage claims would be,[355] the company could continue on postconfirmation and people would then look to the trust and look solely to that trust for purposes of getting paid. The company then continued on without the potentially devastating effect of these lawsuits being brought for years in the future.

When the *Manville* plan was confirmed in the 1980s, it was a very creative use of the bankruptcy plan process to deal with potentially devastating liabilities (the full extent of which were not yet known at the time of the bankruptcy). Since that time, the concept of "channeling injunctions" has been used in other mass-tort types of cases, and in fact the Bankruptcy Code was amended in 1994 to specifically allow for these types of channeling injunctions and trust fund payment mechanisms in asbestos related reorganization cases as a direct result of the *Johns-Manville* case.[356]

· ***Postconfirmation Activities.***

After the plan is confirmed and has gone effective, the debtor's business continues and it must make payments or otherwise perform under the plan. As discussed earlier in the chapter, there is a lot of "cleanup" work that must be done. For example, many of the claims that were filed in the case may need to be objected to. There may be certain "strong arm" avoidance actions that must be brought against creditors to obtain more assets for the reorganized debtor (for example, if a preference is recovered, it may go into the general coffers of the reorganized debtor and be used in operations or to make payments under a plan). Postconfirmation activity in some cases can take a long time, but the concept is that the reorganized debtor can get on with its financial life while the lawyers and other professionals continue to scurry about in bankruptcy court and clean up the residual messes from the bankruptcy case.

Plan Defaults

While after the confirmation hearing everyone celebrates just having survived the process, the unfortunate reality is that, in many cases, debtors are not able to perform as they anticipated under the confirmed plan of reorganization. When there is a plan default, there are a number of things that debtors and creditors can and attempt to do.

· ***Plan Amendments and "Substantial Consummation."***

A debtor may seek to amend the confirmed plan to try to change its obligations to creditors under that plan. Under the bankruptcy law, a debtor may only amend a plan to the extent it was not "substantially consummated."[357] ***"Substantial Consummation"*** is defined in the Bankruptcy Code, but rather imprecisely. It is defined as meaning: "(A) transfer of all or substantially all of the property proposed by the plan to be transferred; (B) assumption by the debtor or by the successor of the debtor under the plan of the business or of the management of all or substantially all of the property dealt with by the plan; and (C) commencement of distribution under the plan."[358]

There has been some controversy as to when substantial consummation takes place. It is an important point because if the plan has not been substantially consummated, the debtor has the chance to go back in and try to change treatment of creditors under the plan by amending the plan. Once the plan is deemed to be substantially consummated, this option is not available to a debtor. Some cases have interpreted substantial consummation as saying that in order for a plan to be substantially consummated, the debtor must have made more than 50 percent of the distributions contemplated under the plan.[359] Other courts have held that substantial consummation occurs when the plan is confirmed as long as the assets and property that are to be transferred or distributed are those assets and property that go from the debtor to the reorganized debtor.[360]

In plans where creditors may be concerned about the possibility that a debtor may attempt to amend its plan, parties have defined when substantial consummation is deemed to occur in the text of the plan itself. This way, there is no question as to when substantial consummation occurs such that a plan may be modified or amended.

· ***Default Remedies.***

Assuming that a plan is determined to be substantially consummated and therefore cannot be amended, if there is a default under the plan, creditors have a few options.

- ***Revocation of Confirmation Orders.*** If the default occurs before six months after the confirmation order is entered, parties can go back into the bankruptcy court and seek a revocation of the confirmation order.[361] The effect of this is to vacate any discharge that was given under the confirmation order and plan, and otherwise puts the parties back to the position they were in before the plan was confirmed and all of the debts substituted by the plan. The only way a confirmation order will be revoked is if the creditor can prove that the order was procured by fraud. Fraud does not mean that the debtor simply miscalculated on its projections, the creditor must show actual fraud on the court. If that happens, the debtor (and presumably its attorneys or anyone else that participated in the fraud) will have bigger problems than the mere revocation of the confirmation order.[362] Revocation of confirmation orders is fairly rare.
- ***Action on the Debt.*** The other possibility for a disgruntled creditor faced with a defaulted plan is to sue the reorganized debtor on the creditor's debt. The debt that is referred to is the debt as set forth in the plan of reorganization and not the debt as it existed prior to confirmation of the plan of reorganization. Accordingly, if a plan provided that the reorganized debtor was going to pay 20 percent of creditors' claims, a creditor that was owed prior to the confirmation $100 could bring a lawsuit to collect $20, not the full $100. Confirmation of the plan terminates the automatic stay that was invoked when the company filed its bankruptcy.[363] As such, a creditor is free to resort to its state law remedies against the reorganized debtor to collect on its debt. A creditor with a lien on assets of the debtor can foreclose on those assets. In addition, disgruntled unsecured creditors could file an involuntary bankruptcy petition against the reorganized debtor as a collection mechanism.[364]

· ***Serial Filings.***

Finally, an option available to a company faced with a failed plan is to file another bankruptcy proceeding. These are called "***serial filings***," and are also known in bankruptcy circles as "***Chapter 22s***" (meaning the second Chapter 11 petition). This happens unfortunately more often than one would hope (see discussion in Chapter Two concerning *The Odds* (*How The Deck Is Stacked*). Oftentimes a second Chapter 11 filing is a controlled liquidation although that is not always the case.

The "Final Decree"

So now the plan is confirmed, and the reorganized debtor goes forth with a clean balance sheet and a court-approved business plan. The bankruptcy case will remain "open" until all postconfirmation litigation (such as claims objections and avoidance actions) is completed. This could take years, but should not interfere with the reorganized debtor's ongoing business operations.[365] When all the postconfirmation litigation is ended, the debtor files a "final report" and a "***final decree***" is entered, officially closing the case.

Congratulations! You have now made it through an arduous process, and will have a lifetime of experiences to regale others with in your golden years. If you're particularly twisted, you may have enjoyed the process so much you become a "turnaround consultant," using your experience to join the ranks of reorganization professionals!

CHAPTER SIX

TEN MYTHS ABOUT REORGANIZATION

"Contemporary man has rationalized the myths, but he has not been able to destroy them."

Octavio Paz
The Labyrinth Of Solitude
[Appendix] (1950)

When people talk about bankruptcy, they will invariably regale one another with stories about its benefits or pitfalls. Like many anecdotal reminiscences, they are usually based on partial information and subject to embellishment (both good and bad).[366] If you read through the previous five chapters, you're now armed with the whole story. If you skipped right to this chapter, you'll be referred back to where you can get the whole story.

There are at least ten "myths" that clients (and sometimes non-bankruptcy attorneys) like to perpetuate. Let's debunk some of those myths. They are, in no particular order of priority, as follows:

"You Can Sell Assets Out from Under Liens!"

The company with assets that are overleveraged by secured creditors understands at least a portion of the concept of sales free and clear of liens. What they generally understand is that property subject to a secured creditor's lien can be sold even if that secured creditor does not consent to the sale. What they fail to understand, however, are the concepts of credit bidding, adequate protection, the inability to give exclusive purchase rights, and liens attaching to sales proceeds. All of these rights of secured creditors and obligations of a debtor-in-possession are restrictions on the general concept of selling assets out from under liens (see discussion in Chapter Four involving *Sales Of Assets*).[367]

"You Can 'Cramdown' a Plan on Your Creditors and Keep the Company!"

The general concept of "cramdown" is understood in that it is generally perceived that a plan can be confirmed over the objecting vote of a creditor or a class of creditors. While the bankruptcy laws are clearly intended to allow the majority in numbers within a particular class (and a supermajority in the amount of claims within a class) to bind plan treatment on creditors that don't accept the plan, the legal remedy of "cramdown" in the plan confirmation process does have its downsides that are generally not understood or fully appreciated. The downsides of cramdown that tend to be glossed over or ignored are the concepts that: (1) a plan proponent must have at least one accepting class of impaired creditors;[368] and (2) the prohibition that prebankruptcy equity may not retain its equity interests in the company without substantial new capital if the plan is being crammed down on unsecured creditors who are not being paid in full (see discussion in Chapter Five on *Cramdown Of Unsecured Creditors—The "Absolute Priority Rule"*).[369] In reorganization proceedings, as in life, there is no free lunch. The price the debtor pays for invoking the Bankruptcy Code's cramdown provisions on unsecured creditors is that old equity does not get to keep its position in the company without paying for it—behold the infamous "absolute priority rule."

"It's Business as Usual During the Case."

This myth, like many urban legends, has some basis in fact. Bankruptcy reorganization is intended to allow a company to stabilize its operations. As such, there is no court-appointed person that takes over the company as in Chapter 7 liquidations, and the existing management remains in control of the company. Unfortunately, there are other aspects of a bankruptcy filing that are decidedly unusual from a business perspective. For example, the company will need to obtain the permission of a lender with a lien on the company's cash flows (such as accounts receivable), or failing that an order of the bankruptcy court, before using cash even for ordinary operations—the concept of "cash collateral" use.[370] In addition, it is not an unusual occurrence if vendors put a company on C.O.D. terms upon the news of the filing, and those same vendors may not agree to extend normal trade terms for at least a little bit into the case.[371] As such, the filing of a bankruptcy reorganization case will not destroy a company's business operations, but management should expect that there will be some reaction by vendors and the marketplace. How severe that reaction is tends to be a function of how well the lines of communication are kept open and how proactive the company is in proceeding with its reorganization.

"Customers Will Never Deal with a Company in Bankruptcy!"

Similar to the discussion above on *"It's business as usual during the case,"* whether customers will deal with a company in bankruptcy is a function of how well the company handles the "spin" of the bankruptcy filing, how competitive of an industry the company is in, and just how crucial customer confidence is in that company.[372] It is also a function of how commonplace bankruptcies are in that industry. For example, reorganization filings in the health care industry are now so commonplace that customers are not likely to pay them too much heed. The same is true in the airline, casino, and retail industries as well. While bankruptcy filings are never good news for anyone, they are also not fatal to a company's ability to continue to deal with its customers. Once again, being proactive in handling the spin is critical.

"The Automatic Stay Protects You Against All Evils!"

It is not unusual for a besieged company to quickly grasp the concept of the automatic stay in bankruptcy because, like a "wonder drug," it automatically stops all litigation that is being brought against the company. It is a blanket injunction that binds all creditors whether they know of the bankruptcy filing or not. Unlike a wonder drug, however, the automatic stay unfortunately does not protect against all evils. For example, the automatic stay will not stop securities fraud and class-action lawsuits against individual directors and officers of a company (although it stops those lawsuits against the company itself). The automatic stay also doesn't stop governmental entities from enforcing their police or regulatory powers, or criminal powers for that matter (which situation arises sometimes where companies are involved in environmental contamination).[373] Finally, the automatic stay might not help a company that is tangling with state governments because of some restrictions on bankruptcy court jurisdiction in these situations.[374]

"All Your Contracts are Renegotiable!"

The concept of being able to get out of your prebankruptcy contracts and leases is an often talked about feature of bankruptcy among business executives. The concept of rejection of executory contracts and unexpired leases[375] is a powerful tool that a company can use to shed contracts and leases that are economically burdensome. However, to the extent that a company files a bankruptcy proceeding primarily to get out of one or two bad contracts, the concept of "bad faith dismissal" has been known to raise its ugly head and thwart a company's desires.[376] In addition, while a company can get out of burdensome contracts or leases, the bankruptcy process does not allow a company to get out of just certain portions of contacts or leases that it finds objectionable, but a company must choose between rejecting an entire contract or assuming the entire contract (with all its benefits and burdens). In other words, a company is not able to rewrite the contracts under the bankruptcy law other than with the consent of the other party to those agreements.

"I'm the DIP—It's My Business Judgment, Dammit, and I'm in Control of the Process!"

The concept of the debtor-in-possession being in full control of the process and exercising business judgment is one of the features of Chapter 11 reorganizations that appeals to many business executives.[377] The powers of a debtor-in-possession to recover prebankruptcy payments made to certain creditors and to void out liens that may have some defects are also nice touches.[378] Not surprisingly, with all of that power comes some responsibilities and headaches.[379] While the bankruptcy laws envision that prebankruptcy management will continue to operate the business and exercise certain powers to preserve and maintain assets, existing management has to change its focus and understand that it now owes duties to parties other than shareholders. The business judgment of management will now be subject to second, third, and in some instances fourth-guessing by numerous parties in the process. While management's business judgment will be given some deference, the bankruptcy process is such that it can and will be called into question by numerous parties that will have a more active say in business decisions as a result of the reorganization process. In addition, while the concept of a debtor-in-possession is intended to give the company, at least initially, control over the process, that control can be taken away by the passage of time or by an order of the bankruptcy court, or frankly, by the negotiating dynamics in the case.[380] If management believes it is in total control of the process and manifests that belief in not dealing with the key constituencies in the case, the company will soon find itself on the outside looking in as the other parties negotiate around the debtor.[381] While the company and its management are the gatekeepers, failure to deal with the key constituencies will be destructive to the process.

"What's Good for the Shareholders is Good for the Company!"

Similar to the discussion above in *"I'm the DIP—It's my business judgment, dammit, and I'm in control of the process,"* the filing of a bankruptcy requires management to make attitudinal and mental adjustments so that it understands that in a company that is financially distressed, its fiduciary obligations go beyond the shareholders and it now owes allegiance to a broader constituency.[382] In a company that is insolvent, what's good for the shareholders is indeed not necessarily good for the company, and the shareholders are the last ones in the pecking order.[383]

"The Discharge Clears All the Company's Debts!"

The "Holy Grail" of the bankruptcy process is the discharge, which cleans up a company's balance sheet and enables it to go forward.[384] The discharge will not deal with some residual liabilities of personal officers and directors (such as pending or future securities fraud lawsuits, personal environmental contamination liabilities, and possible personal liability for unpaid withholding taxes.)[385] A bankruptcy proceeding's ability to deal with personal liabilities of officers and directors is limited and is one of the circumstances where what's good for the company may not be good for the officers and directors personally.

"You'll Never Borrow in This Town Again!"

The concept of a company having to file bankruptcy is anathema to many business executives. They don't wish to be associated with a company that has filed a reorganization proceeding because they may view it as a failed endeavor. They may also have concerns about the ability of the company to ever attract credit in the future. In fact, many companies have gone through Chapter 11 proceedings and have emerged substantially healthier than they were when they went in, having used the bankruptcy reorganization process as a way to obtain a discharge of potentially company-destroying debt loads or liabilities.[386] It is a truism that the debt market has a short memory, and the fact that a company went through a Chapter 11 proceeding is not by any stretch of the imagination a death knell as far as creditworthiness for the company forever into the future. Unlike a bankruptcy filing by an individual, bankruptcies of corporations are seen by some as viable and understandable means by which to deal with potentially catastrophic liabilities.[387] In fact, there are times when lenders will only lend to a company if it files a reorganization proceeding because the lender knows that it will be able to get certain assurances by a court order if it lends to the company in bankruptcy.[388] While bankruptcy filings should never be the first strategy for a financially distressed company, it should also not be viewed as the death sentence for future creditworthiness.

As you can see, there are many half-truths and oversimplifications in some of the common misperceptions about bankruptcy. Knowing that, in bankruptcy as in life, all benefits have some degree of burden associated with them allows you to make reasoned decisions. In *The Iliad*, Homer warns us that "Zeus does not bring all men's plans to fulfillment."[389] Armed with some knowledge, good advisors, some business acumen, and perhaps a little luck, you will be able to wind your way through the reorganization process.

May Zeus smile upon you!

APPENDICES

A. Glossary Of Commonly Used Bankruptcy Terms

B. Hypothetical Reorganization Timeline

C. Sample Press Release

D. Sample Petition and Related Filing Documents

E. Sample "First Day Orders" (*Unison HealthCare Corp.*)

F. Sample Management Severance Agreement (Preconfirmation) (*Unison HealthCare Corp.)*

G. Sample "Chinese Wall" Agreement (*Megafoods Stores, Inc.*)

H. Sample Confidentiality Agreement (*Unison HealthCare Corp.*)

I. Sample Cash Collateral Agreement (*The Rookery Building*)

J. Sample DIP Financing Agreement (*Boston Chicken, Inc.*)

K. Sample Operating Report (McCulloch Corp.)

L. Sample Bar Date Order (*Unison HealthCare Corp.*)

M. Sample "Solicitation Package" (*Stuart Entertainment, Inc.*)

N. Sample Plan and Disclosure Statement—Debt-to-Equity Conversion (*Stuart Entertainment, Inc.*)

O. Sample Plan—Liquidation (*Baptist Foundation of Arizona, Inc.*)

P. Sample Plan—Sale To Third Party (*America West Airlines, Inc.*)

Q. DIP Facility Pricing Study (prepared by ***Houlihan, Lokey, Howard & Zukin***—used with permission)

R. Summary Of Employee Incentive Plans (prepared by ***Houlihan, Lokey, Howard & Zukin***—used with permission)

APPENDIX A

GLOSSARY OF COMMONLY USED BANKRUPTCY TERMS [1]

"2004" Exam

Under Bankruptcy Rule 2004, the examination of any entity under oath is permitted with court approval. It's like a deposition, but with a much broader scope—in fact, it's been called a "fishing expedition." The examination is usually conducted as an oral deposition, but the scope is broad and is not limited to a specific adversary proceeding. Unlike a deposition, a motion and order are required. The order also may provide that the person being examined produce documents. *See* Bankruptcy Rule 2004; Chapter Three, *Life In A Fishbowl.*

"341" Meeting

See ***First Meeting Of Creditors***, below.

Abandonment

The process by which a ***trustee*** or ***Debtor-In-Possession*** designates property in which the estate has no interest. Abandonments must generally be applied for and noticed to creditors. The effect of an abandonment is to lift stays only against the estate's interest in property, and is not inconsistent with the debtor's retention of property under a reaffirmation agreement or redemption. *See* Bankruptcy Code § 554.

Absolute Priority Rule

The requirement that provides that in order to obtain confirmation of a ***plan of reorganization*** using the ***cramdown*** provisions of the Bankruptcy Code, generally speaking classes of unsecured creditors must either be paid in full (with interest), or agree as part of ***class voting*** to accept less than full payment or no junior classes of creditors or interests can receive or retain anything in the confirmed plan as a result of their junior claims or interests. Practically speaking, this means that ***equityholders*** in a company that is not paying its unsecured creditors in full, with interest, may not retain their interests in the ***Reorganized Debtor*** unless the unsecured creditors consent. *See* Bankruptcy Code § 1129(b); Chapter Five, *Step Five: The Plan Confirmation Process. See, also* ***"New Value Exception,"*** below.

---

[1] Words used in ***bold*** in the definitions are defined themselves in this Glossary. Where applicable, reference is made to where in the text the defined term is discussed in more detail.

Abstention

The doctrine under which the District Court or Bankruptcy Court may decide not to hear a matter that it determines is more appropriately heard in another court, usually a state court or tax court. Abstention by the Bankruptcy Court is mandatory in ***"non-core" matters*** that involve only state law and that may be commenced quickly in another forum. Motions for abstention are filed in the Bankruptcy Court.

Ad Hoc Committee

An unofficial committee of creditors or equityholders. Such unofficial committees may participate in a case, and their professionals request to be paid fees as an ***Administrative And Priority Claim*** under the ***Substantial Contribution*** test. *See* Bankruptcy Code § 503(b); Chapter Two, *The Players And Their Roles.*

Adequate Assurance Of Future Performance

A requirement before a debtor may ***assume*** any ***executory contract*** or ***unexpired lease***. Specifically, the debtor must show that not only will it ***cure defaults***, but also that it will be able to perform its future obligations under the contract or lease after assumption. *See* Bankruptcy Code § 365; Chapter Four, *Dealing With Executory Contracts And Unexpired Leases.*

Adequate Protection

A concept developed to ensure that a creditor's interest in property is protected during the pendency of a bankruptcy. Examples include: (1) replacement liens; (2) cash payments; or (3) an ***"indubitable equivalent."*** An ***"equity cushion"*** may also be used as adequate protection. The concept is crucial in ***stay relief***, ***cash collateral,*** and ***asset sale*** proceedings. *See* Bankruptcy Code § 361; Chapter Four, *The Automatic Stay.*

Administrative And Priority Claims

Those claims that are reasonable and necessary expenses of the ***estate*** postpetition, including postpetition wages, taxes, the ***DIP's*** and ***Creditors Committee's*** professionals' fees and costs, and the compensation/reimbursement for a ***Trustee***, an ***Examiner***, or Committee members. These claims must be paid before ***unsecured claims*** may be paid. *See* Bankruptcy Code §§ 503 and 507; Chapter Two, *The "Administrative And Priority Claimants." See also* **Priority Claim**.

Administrative Convenience Claim

A small claim in a Chapter 11 bankruptcy proceeding. Normally the Bankruptcy Code requires that all ***unsecured claims*** be placed together in one class in a ***plan of reorganization***. The Bankruptcy Code makes an exception for administrative convenience claims. This is generally done in a plan where small claims (such as claims of $500 or less, or where creditors are willing to reduce their claims to $500) will be separately classified in a plan, and will be paid a lump-sum cash payment shortly after plan confirmation. *See* Bankruptcy Code § 1122(b); *see generally* Chapter Five, *The Plan Of Reorganization.*

Adversary Proceeding

The type of action defined in Bankruptcy Rule 7001 that must be commenced by the filing of a complaint, requires a filing fee, and must be served with a summons. All normal discovery rules of the Federal Rules of Civil Procedure (as modified by the ***Bankruptcy Rules***) apply in adversary proceedings.

"Affiliate Rule"

The rule that provides that when ***venue*** in a particular bankruptcy court is proper for one entity, other entities that are "affiliates" of the debtor may file in that jurisdiction even if venue would not be proper for those entities when considered by themselves. An example would be a California corporation that had a wholly owned subsidiary that was a Delaware corporation. Even if the Delaware subsidiary had no assets in Delaware, under current bankruptcy law it could file a bankruptcy petition in Delaware. Once that bankruptcy was filed, the California corporation, as an affiliate of the debtor, could also file in Delaware under the affiliate rule. *See* Bankruptcy Code § 101(2); 28 U.S.C. § 1408; Chapter Four, *The Venue Game.*

Allowed Claims

A ***claim*** that is either: (1) listed by the debtor in the ***Schedules*** as being undisputed; (2) filed in the form of a ***Proof Of Claim*** and to which no ***Claims Objection*** is filed; or (3) objected to and ultimately determined by the bankruptcy court to be due and owing by the debtor. *See* Bankruptcy Code § 502; Chapter Five, *Who Is Entitled To Vote?*

Allowed Secured Claim

Under bankruptcy law, a secured claim is "allowed" to the extent of the value of the ***collateral*** securing it. The balance is treated as an unsecured claim. For example, a bank with a $100,000 debt secured by assets with a fair market value of $50,000 at the time of the bankruptcy filing has an allowed secured claim of $50,000 and an ***unsecured claim*** of $50,000. *See* Bankruptcy Code § 506; Chapter Five, *Who Is Entitled To Vote?*

Antecedent Debt

A pre-existing debt or obligation. The phrase is used in connection with ***Preferences***. *See* Bankruptcy Code § 547; Chapter Four, *The Strong Arm" Powers.*

Assume or Assumption

The process whereby a debtor elects to take on all of the responsibilities and benefits of an ***executory contract*** or ***unexpired lease***. This would occur where the debtor is a party to an economically favorable lease or contract and wishes to obtain the benefits of that contract. In order to do that, the debtor must also take all of the burdens of that contract. The debtor must ***cure defaults***, and also provide ***adequate assurance of future performance***. The bankruptcy court must approve any assumption of leases or executory contracts. Under bankruptcy law, certain types of contracts (such as prebankruptcy contracts to make loans to a debtor, or personal service type contracts) may not be assumed. *See* Bankruptcy Code § 365; Chapter Four, *Dealing With Executory Contracts And Unexpired Leases*. *See also* **Reject** or **Rejection**.

Automatic Stay

When the debtor files bankruptcy, creditors everywhere are automatically enjoined (or "stayed") from proceeding in any way to collect their debts from the debtor. The Bankruptcy Code modifies the stay in certain circumstances and awards damages for willful violations of the stay in certain situations. Moreover, the Bankruptcy Code prohibits acts to exercise control over property of the debtor. Certain actions (such as continuation of criminal matters or regulatory actions by governments) are not subject to the automatic stay. *See* Bankruptcy Code § 362; Chapter Four, *The Automatic Stay*.

Avoiding Powers

The debtor's rights to recover money, assets transferred (or the monetary value of such assets), or liens granted under the ***preference, fraudulent conveyance, postpetition transfer,*** and other ***"strong arm"*** provisions of the Bankruptcy Code. *See* Bankruptcy Code §§ 544, 547, 548, 549; Chapter Four, *The "Strong Arm" Powers*.

BAFJA

Bankruptcy Amendments and Federal Judgeship Act of 1984. This act added many new provisions to the Bankruptcy Code.

Ballot Report

The report compiled by the debtor and filed with the bankruptcy court detailing the ***plan ballots*** received either accepting or rejecting the plan of reorganization. The ballot report is necessary in order to determine if the plan is in a ***cramdown*** posture. *See* Chapter Five, *Step Four: The Solicitation Process*.

Bankruptcy

A federal system for collective creditor payment from the assets of the debtor that are not exempt. *See* Chapter One, *Introduction*.

Bankruptcy Appellate Panel (BAP)

The potential first level of appellate review in those circuits in which they exist. A BAP is comprised of seven bankruptcy judges who are appointed to serve by the ***Circuit Court of Appeals***. A panel of three of these judges sits as the first level of appellate review. A decision of the BAP is then appealed to the Circuit Court of Appeals. All appeals are automatically referred to the BAP, but any party may opt out of the BAP, whereupon the first appellate level will be the ***District Court***. *See* 28 U.S.C. §158.

Bankruptcy Code

Provisions passed by Congress in 1978, found in Title 11 of the U.S. Code, which govern the bankruptcy system, its parties, and their rights and duties. The Bankruptcy Code has been amended numerous times since 1978. *See* Chapter Two, *The "Bankruptcy Code."*

Bankruptcy Court

The branch of the federal judicial system that administers bankruptcy law and presides over bankruptcy cases, presently subordinated to the federal ***District Court***. ***BAFJA*** clearly designates the Bankruptcy Court as a unit of the District Court. *See* 28 U.S.C. § 151; Chapter Two, *The Players And Their Roles*.

Bankruptcy Court Jurisdiction

The authority of the ***Bankruptcy Court*** to decide controversies and disputes, as well as the ability to preside over bankruptcy proceedings. *See* 28 U.S.C. § 1334; Chapter Four, *Bankruptcy Court Jurisdiction (And Limitations On That Jurisdiction). See also* ***"Core" Matters, "Non-Core" Matters*** and ***"Non-Core/Non-Related" Matters***, below.

Bankruptcy Rule 2004 Examination

See ***"2004" Exam***, above.

Bankruptcy Rules

The federal rules of bankruptcy procedure that help implement the Bankruptcy Code.

Bar Date

A date set by the court in the ***Bar Date Order*** within which pleadings must be filed. The bar date typically refers to the last day to file a ***Proof Of Claim***. *See* Chapter Five, *Quantifying The Debts—The "Bar Date" Order*.

Bar Date Order

The Order signed by the bankruptcy court setting the ***Bar Date***. The Bar Date Order will then be noticed to all creditors (either by mailing, by some sort of publication such as a newspaper notice, or even in exceptional cases television notice, or some combination of several methods) so that all parties with potential ***claims*** against the debtor will know the deadline to file a ***Proof of Claim***. *See* Chapter Five, *Quantifying The Debts—The "Bar Date" Order*.

"Best Interests of Creditors" Test

The requirement contained in the Bankruptcy Code that before the bankruptcy court may ***confirm*** a plan, to the extent that any individual holder of a claim has voted to reject the plan, the bankruptcy court must be shown that the rejecting creditor will receive at least as much under the plan as it would receive in a liquidation under Chapter 7. This is usually not too difficult to do. *See* Bankruptcy Code § 1129(a)(7); Chapter Five, *Step Five: The Plan Confirmation Process*.

Bona Fide Purchaser

Purchaser of property or interest in property who gives fair value and has no notice of adverse claims against the property. *See* Chapter Four, *The "Strong Arm" Powers*.

Business Judgment Rule

The rule of corporate law that provides that a Board of Directors will not be subject to attack for decisions made provided the decisions were made on a rational and reasonable business basis. In bankruptcy proceedings, the business judgment of the ***Debtor-In-Possession*** is afforded deference until such time as the parties bring matters to the attention of the bankruptcy court that show that the management of a troubled company is not acting in a businesslike and reasonable manner.

Business Reorganization

A ***Chapter 11 Proceeding*** filed by a business entity, although a business reorganization can also be filed by individuals. *See* Chapter Two, *The Reorganization Process*.

"Bust Up" Fees

An amount payable to a bidder that is the first bidder to come forward but is subsequently outbid at the bankruptcy court approval process with respect to a sale. Most sophisticated bidders will insist upon bankruptcy court approval, up front, of a "bust-up" fee (also called a "break-up" fee) because frequently in order to make an initial bid a bidder will have to do some due diligence since it may not be the ultimate purchaser, and it wants to be reimbursed for being a ***"stalking horse."*** Bust-up fees are generally tied to the amount of out-of-pocket expenses of the initial bidder, and are sometimes tied to a percentage of the amount of the transaction. Bankruptcy courts vary widely in their willingness to approve bust-up fees. *See* Chapter Four, *Sale Of Assets*.

"Carveout"

A concession by a lender with a ***lien*** on ***cash collateral*** whereby certain ongoing expenses of a debtor are allowed to be paid from the cash receipts from the business subject to liens. Carveouts are usually put in cash collateral ***stipulations***, and are most often used with respect to a secured lender agreeing that the professional fees of a debtor may be paid during the course of the case from the cash collateral. *See* Chapter Four, *Financing The Preconfirmation Operations.*

Cash Collateral

Collateral for a loan that is cash or a cash equivalent. Examples include accounts receivable, pledged accounts or certificates of deposit, assigned rents, or cash proceeds from the sale of collateral. The debtor is not allowed to use this type of collateral after filing bankruptcy, except by consent or an order of the bankruptcy court. The Bankruptcy Code specifically defines cash collateral as cash proceeds of a secured party's collateral whether the collateral was sold pre- or postpetition. *See* Bankruptcy Code § 363; Chapter Four, *Financing The Preconfirmation Operations.*

"Cause"

Relief from stay, dismissal, and other remedies under the Bankruptcy Code are available on a showing of cause, that is, any ground that justifies the relief sought. Cause in stay relief matters includes a lack of adequate protection, but may also include judicial findings of bad faith or other grounds. *See* Bankruptcy Code § 362(d)(1); Chapter Four, *The Automatic Stay.*

Channeling Injunctions

In cases where companies have substantial actual or potential mass tort liability, the Bankruptcy Code allows for the issuance of an injunction whereby all potential claimants have to look to a trust fund established under a plan of reorganization for recovery. An example would be where a company has substantial personal injury claims from environmental contamination. The debtor and/or the insurance company might fund a trust fund, and a plan of reorganization would provide that all claimants (who would need to file claims by a ***Bar Date***) would look only to the trust fund to be paid. This encourages an insurance company, for example, to fund insurance policy proceeds without worrying about repetitive lawsuits, and helps ensure that all claimants have access to insurance proceeds (not just the first ones to get judgments). Other uses of channeling injunctions include attempting to channel officers and director securities fraud liability into a trust fund (perhaps funded by a D&O insurance coverage and/or the officers and directors), or claims against general partners (which has been used in law firm bankruptcies). *See* Bankruptcy Code § 524(g); Chapter Five, *Step Six: "Going Effective."*

Chapter 7 Proceeding

A type of bankruptcy in which the debtor's assets are liquidated by a court-appointed trustee; often referred to as a straight liquidation or straight bankruptcy. Corporations, partnerships, and individuals may file a Chapter 7 bankruptcy. The Bankruptcy Code provides remedies for "substantial abuses" of Chapter 7. *See* Chapter Two, *The "Bankruptcy Code."*

Chapter 9 Proceeding

A type of bankruptcy in which a municipality or governmental unit, such as a water district, seeks relief under the Bankruptcy Code. *See* Chapter Two, *The "Bankruptcy Code."*

Chapter 11 Proceeding

A type of bankruptcy in which debtors attempt to prepare a plan of reorganization of their debts and assets that must be approved by the bankruptcy court. A trustee is not appointed unless the creditors so convince the court. Corporations, partnerships, and individuals may file a Chapter 11 bankruptcy. This chapter was primarily designed for business reorganizations. *See* Chapter Two, *The "Bankruptcy Code."*

Chapter 12 Proceeding

A form of relief added to the Code by the 1986 bankruptcy legislation. The proceeding provides a hybrid relief for family farmers, adopting protections, rights, and duties from Chapters 11 and 13. The family farmer requirements of Bankruptcy Code § 101(18) and regular income requirements of Bankruptcy Code § 101(19) must be satisfied. The aggregate debts must not exceed $1.5 million on the date of filing. *See* Chapter Two, *The "Bankruptcy Code."*

Chapter 13 Proceeding

A type of bankruptcy in which an individual with "regular income" proposes an arrangement of debts and assets (up to a three- to five-year period); previously called wage earner bankruptcies. Only an individual may file a Chapter 13, and he or she may not owe more than $250,000 in unsecured debts or more than $750,000 in secured debts. A standing trustee serves only as disbursing agent to collect part of the debtor's income and pay it out under the plan. The debt limits were substantially increased in the 1994 Bankruptcy Reform Act (from $100,000 and $350,000, respectively). *See* Chapter Two, *The "Bankruptcy Code."*

"Chapter 22s"

A slang term used for a repeat filing under Chapter 11. This is also known as a ***"serial filing."*** Some companies have to file successive Chapter 11 bankruptcy petitions because of an inability to perform under the terms of a confirmed plan, or a further downturn in the business of the ***Reorganized Debtor***. *See* Chapter Five, *Plan Defaults*. *See also* ***Serial Filings***.

"Chinese Walls"

A slang term for an information-blocking mechanism. It is used most frequently with respect to investment houses that have both direct claims against a company and also hold the company's debt or equity securities for client portfolios. If a representative of that investment house is sitting on a

Creditor's Committee and as a result of that position is receiving confidential and non-public information (usually pursuant to a ***Confidentiality Agreement***), a "Chinese Wall" mechanism is set up to preclude that individual from providing the non-public information to the trading arm of the institution. The phrase Chinese Wall is derived from the fact that the Great Wall of China is the only man-made structure that is visible on the earth from space. As such, the information-blocking mechanism is intended to be as apparent and impenetrable as the "Great Wall of China."

Circuit Court Of Appeals

The federal appellate court that is the second level of appeal from bankruptcy court decisions. In non-bankruptcy federal courts, the Circuit Court of Appeals is the first level of appellate review (and the decisions of the Circuit Court are only appealable to the U.S. Supreme Court). In bankruptcy cases, the first level of appellate review is either the ***District Court*** or the ***Bankruptcy Appellate Panel***, so the Circuit Court of Appeals is really the second level of appellate review. As such, Circuit Court of Appeals decisions in bankruptcy cases take on a little more significance. The courts are called "circuit courts" because the judges on those courts, although they will be based in a particular city, will frequently hear arguments in other cities within the circuit (that is, the cities that are within their particular jurisdiction). Currently there are twelve federal circuits, each (except for the District of Columbia Circuit) encompassing numerous states. The judges are said to "ride the circuit."

Claim

The broad definition of a claim in the Code includes any right to payment, even if the right is in dispute or not fixed in amount, and any right to an equitable remedy for breach of performance. *See* Bankruptcy Code §101(5). *See* Chapter Two, *The "Pecking Order" — Payment Priorities In Reorganization Cases. See also* **Secured Creditor** and **Unsecured Claim**.

Claims Objection

A dispute between the debtor and the holder of a ***claim*** whereby the debtor asserts that it does not owe the amount asserted by the creditor, it does not owe the creditor anything, it has certain ***offsets***, or otherwise objects to a ***lien*** or ***collateral*** claimed by the creditor. The bankruptcy court will determine how much the creditor is owed, even if the creditor's claim is contingent or unliquidated. For plan confirmation purposes, sometimes the bankruptcy court will conduct a ***temporary allowance*** hearing to make an expedited decision on how much a creditor is owed for purposes of voting on a plan. *See* Bankruptcy Code § 502; Chapter Five, *Step Four: The Solicitation Process.*

Class Voting

The mechanism whereby creditors vote on a ***plan of reorganization***.

Under bankruptcy law, creditors with similar claims are put in the same class within a plan. For example, all unsecured creditors are generally put in the same class within a plan and treated the same way. Under bankruptcy law, a class is deemed to accept a plan if the class meets the ***one-half/two-thirds requirement*** for voting purposes. If this test is met, the creditors that voted against the plan will still be bound by the provisions of the plan because the creditors' *class* has voted to accept the plan. *See* Bankruptcy Code § 1126(c); Chapter Five, *Step Four: The Solicitation Process*.

COD Income

"Cancellation of debt" income. Under the tax laws, if creditors forgive a debt or if the debt is otherwise discharged, the taxpayer may recognize taxable income to the extent of some or all of the waived debt. This is known as "COD Income."

Collateral

The assets subject to a ***lien***, which secure repayment of a debt. In business bankruptcies, typical assets serving as collateral are accounts receivable, contract rights, inventory, furniture, fixtures and equipment, general intangibles, and other real property and personal property. *See* Chapter Two, *The "Pecking Order" — Payment Priorities In Reorganization Cases. See also* ***Cash Collateral***.

Complaint

The pleading required to commence an ***Adversary Proceeding***, setting forth the claims against the defendants, the basis for the claims, and a request for relief in a brief fashion.

Confidentiality Agreements

An agreement between a company and a third party whereby confidential, non-public and/or proprietary information will be kept confidential by the person receiving it. In companies with publicly held debt or equity securities, any financial information other than what is put out in appropriate press releases and SEC filings is generally only provided pursuant to an appropriate confidentiality agreement. This prevents people from speculating on securities of a company based on inside information. Moreover, in the event that information is proprietary or trade secret in nature, a confidentiality agreement may also be given as part of due diligence for a prospective purchase or sale of assets of a company. Confidentiality agreements are standard for members of ***Creditors Committees*** and ***Equityholders Committees***. *See* Chapter Three, *Protecting The Franchise: Confidentiality Agreements And "Chinese Walls." See also* ***"Chinese Walls,"*** above.

Confirmation

The process whereby a bankruptcy court approves a plan of reorganization. *See* Bankruptcy Code § 1129; Chapter Five, *Step Five: The Plan Confirmation Process. See also* ***"Cramdown,"*** below.

Confirmation Hearing

The hearing before the bankruptcy court on whether the proposed plan of reorganization in a Chapter 11 case has been accepted by the necessary group or groups of creditors and also meets other statutory restrictions. *See* Chapter Five, *Step Five: The Plan Confirmation Process.*

Consensual Lien

A ***Lien*** created by agreement of the parties, usually by a security agreement on personal property, or a mortgage or deed of trust on real property.

Contested Matter

Essentially, any disputed matter other than an ***Adversary Proceeding***. Relief in a contested matter is sought by motion, generally with no filing fee, and no responses are required unless ordered by the court. Generally, the discovery rules of the Federal Rules of Civil Procedure (as modified by the Bankruptcy Rules) apply in contested matters. *See* Bankruptcy Rule 9014.

Conversion

The process in which a debtor determines (or a creditor moves) to change the chapter under the Bankruptcy Code under which the debtor sought relief. Most commonly, conversion is from Chapter 11 to Chapter 7, after a plan proves to be infeasible.

"Core Business"

An analysis by either a troubled company or its financial advisors to determine whether a troubled business enterprise, once stabilized, has a viable business that produces (or is able to produce) meaningful ***EBITDA*** from which to pay creditors. There have been numerous instances where companies with huge gross revenues do not have any viable core business and produce minimal if any EBITDA even under stabilized circumstances. *See* Chapter Two, *The "Proactive" Versus "Reactive Reorganization Cases*.

"Core" Matters

Those matters before a bankruptcy court directly tied to the bankruptcy case and arising under the Bankruptcy Code. Core proceedings include estate administration matters, allowance or disallowance of claims, use and sale of property, obtaining credit by the debtor/estate, turnover matters, preference litigation, automatic stay litigation, fraudulent conveyance litigation, non-dischargeability litigation, plan confirmation, use of cash collateral litigation, lien validity litigation, and so forth. *See* 28 U.S.C. §157(b)(2)(A)-(O); Chapter Four, *Bankruptcy Court Jurisdiction (And Limitations).*

Cramdown

A slang term referring to the ***confirmation*** of a ***plan of reorganization*** in Chapter 11 over the objection of a creditor. *See* Bankruptcy Code § 1129(b); Chapter Five, *Step Five: The Plan Confirmation Process.*

Cramdown Posture

The situation when, as a result of the ***Ballot Report***, the debtor must use the ***Cramdown*** provisions of the Bankruptcy Code to obtain ***confirmation*** of the ***plan of reorganization***.

Credit Bid Rights

The right of a creditor with a ***perfected lien*** on ***collateral*** to bid in any sale of the collateral without using cash, but rather offsetting against the debt secured by the lien. For example, the creditor is owed $100.00, which debt is secured by a valid lien on a machine. If the debtor wishes to sell that machine for $80.00, the secured creditor can come to the auction sale and "credit bid" up to $100.00 of its debt. Unless another bidder bids more than that, the secured creditor will be the successful bidder and will not have to pay the debtor any cash. Rather, the secured creditor credits the debt. *See* Bankruptcy Code § 363(k); Chapter Four, *Sale Of Assets.*

Creditor

One who holds a ***claim*** against the ***debtor*** or a ***lien*** on property of the ***estate***.

Creditors Committee

See ***Official Committee Of Unsecured Creditors***.

Cure Of Defaults

Before a debtor may ***assume*** an ***executory contract*** or ***unexpired lease***, as a condition to such an assumption the debtor must pay arrearages and other defaults under the contract or lease. This is known as a "cure of defaults." The cure of defaults is not always a lump-sum payment, but it is generally a fairly accelerated payment provision. Under bankruptcy law, the debtor does not need to cure non-monetary defaults such as financial covenant defaults. *See* Bankruptcy Code § 365; Chapter Four, *Dealing With Executory Contracts And Unexpired Leases.*

De Novo

A term meaning "anew," and referring to an appellate court's new look at a record on appeal without being bound by or giving deference to a lower court's prior findings or conclusions.

Deceleration

A debt that became fully due before its natural term may be extended, under certain circumstances, and a new payment schedule proposed.

Debtor

An individual, partnership, or corporation who files a bankruptcy proceeding or has one filed involuntarily against him/her or it. *See* Chapter Two, *The Players And Their Roles.*

Debtor-In-Possession

The official title of the debtor after having filed a Chapter 11 proceeding, sometimes shortened to "DIP." The debtor-in-possession exercises all the power and rights of a trustee in bankruptcy and is similarly charged with all of the duties. For a corporation or business partnership, this means that current management will remain in control after filing Chapter 11. *See* Chapter Two, *The Players And Their Roles.*

Demand Registration Rights

These rights, often found in tandem with piggyback registration rights, are rights that a company grants to a shareholder who has acquired shares from the company in a private placement. In other words, the shareholder holds restricted securities and may not freely trade such shares without doing so pursuant to an effective registration statement. Demand registration rights enable the person who holds these rights to require the company to file a registration statement with the SEC so that such shareholder can freely sell his or her shares in the company. *See* Chapter Five, *Understanding And Appreciating What The Constituents Want And Need.*

Deposition

The procedure for taking oral examination of a witness provided for in the Federal Rules of Civil Procedure and applicable in adversary and contested matters. It differs from a ***2004 Exam*** in that no court order or motion is necessary to notice a deposition, but an adversary proceeding or contested matter must first be pending, and the scope of questioning is somewhat more limited. *See also* ***"2004" Exam***, above.

DIP

See ***Debtor-In-Possession***, above.

DIP Financing

"Debtor-In-Possession" financing. This is the ability of a ***DIP*** to obtain loans once a bankruptcy proceeding is commenced. Under the Bankruptcy Code the bankruptcy court can authorize ***Super priority Financing*** as an incentive for lenders to make loans to debtors in Chapter 11. *See* Bankruptcy Code § 364; Chapter Four, *Financing The Preconfirmation Operations.*

Discharge

The official order of the bankruptcy court that releases the debtor from unsecured debts incurred prior to bankruptcy and bars creditors from future collection efforts on released debts. Secured debts are not discharged, except to the extent that the ***collateral*** is insufficient to cover the amount of the claim. *See* Bankruptcy Code § 1141; Chapter Five, *Step Five: The Plan Confirmation Process.*

Discharge Injunction

An ***order*** of the bankruptcy court, usually provided as part of a confirmed ***plan of reorganization***, which prohibits (or enjoins) any party with a claim dealt with in the confirmed plan from taking any action to collect on the claim other than as provided in the confirmed plan. *See* Bankruptcy Code § 1141; Chapter Five, *Step Six: "Going Effective."*

Disclosure Statement

A document, similar to a stock prospectus, that is sent to the creditors explaining the background of the proposed Chapter 11 plan. The Disclosure Statement must be approved by the bankruptcy court and must be mailed to the creditors with the proposed plan. *See* Bankruptcy Code § 1125; Chapter Five, *Step Three: The Disclosure Statement.*

"Disinterested Person"

A term of art under the Bankruptcy Code, which provides that in order for a professional to be retained by the ***estate***, that person must not have any actual or potential conflicts of interests that would impair his or her objectivity in representing the estate. By definition, a "disinterested person" is a person that is not a ***creditor***; an ***equityholder***; an ***insider***; an investment banker for any securities of the debtor; officer, director or employee of the debtor; or a person who has any other connections that would provide a materially adverse interest to the interests of the debtors. *See* Bankruptcy Code § 101(14); Chapter Two, *The Players And Their Roles.*

Dismissal

The process by which a bankruptcy case or proceeding is terminated. Dismissal of a case terminates all stays and the existence of the estate. *See* Bankruptcy Code § 1112(e).

Distribution

The process under a ***plan of reorganization*** wherein proceeds of the estate are paid to various classes of claimants. *See* Chapter Five, *Step Six: "Going Effective."*

District Court

The Federal District Court that is directly over the bankruptcy court. All bankruptcy courts are deemed to be "units" of a District Court. As such, a bankruptcy court will be denominated as, for example, "The U.S. Bankruptcy Court for The Southern District Of New York." A District Court also acts as the appellate court for bankruptcy court decisions. *See* 28 U.S.C. § 151; Chapter Two, *The Players And Their Roles.*

Docket

The summary of pending legal matters and their times, dates, and places. Law firms often maintain a docket as a calendar system. Court clerks maintain docket sheets as an index to a case file, and to indicate matters pending on the bankruptcy court's calendar.

"Doctrine Of Necessity"

The legal justification used by bankruptcy courts, which allows debtors, usually as part of ***First Day Orders***, to pay certain prebankruptcy claims that would otherwise not be able to be paid other than as part of plan confirmation. *See* Chapter Four, *First Day Orders*.

Drag-Along Rights

These rights are basically the same as tag-along rights, only now the selling shareholder can require that the other shareholders sell their shares along with such shareholder (*i.e.,* drag them along). Major shareholders in a company might require that the other shareholders agree to such a provision so they can effectively sell the other shareholders' interest in the company. An acquirer might not want to have minority shareholders to get in the way. Drag-along rights would most likely have some sort of fair market value requirement with respect to the proposed sale price, as well as the other protections that would ensure that those shareholders who are dragged along are treated "fairly." *See* Chapter Five, *Understanding And Appreciating What The Constituents Want And Need.*

EBITDA

Earnings Before Interest, Taxes, Depreciation, and Amortization. It generally refers to the operational cash flow of a business that's available to pay debt service to creditors.

"Effective Date"

The date when a debtor must perform under the terms of a confirmed ***plan of reorganization***. There are times when a plan will be confirmed, but before the ***Reorganized Debtor*** must perform under that plan, certain events must occur. These conditions might include, for example, finalizing a working-capital line of credit, completion of some important litigation, or other such conditions. The "effective date" is not defined in the Bankruptcy Code, and is therefore usually specified under the terms of the plan of reorganization (along with any conditions that must be fulfilled before the debtor must perform under the plan). Once the Effective Date is reached, the plan has "gone effective" and the debtor must meet its obligations under that confirmed plan. *See* Chapter Five, *Step Six: "Going Effective."*

Encumbrance

See ***Lien***, below.

Equity Cushion

A form of adequate protection wherein the value of property is compared to a claimant's lien interest; junior liens are not considered as deductions from value. *See* Bankruptcy Code § 361; Chapter Four, *Relief From Stay And The Concept Of "Adequate Protection."*

Equityholders

Holders of a company's stock, warrants, options, partnership interests, membership units, or any other indicia of a right to share in the profits of a company. *See* Chapter Two, *The Players And Their Roles.*

Equityholders Committees

See ***Official Committee of Equityholders***, below.

Estate

Upon the filing of a bankruptcy petition, a new entity is created consisting of all of a debtor's legal and equitable rights in and to the debtor's property, which entity is termed the bankruptcy estate. In the Chapter 11 case the representative of the estate is the ***Debtor-In-Possession***. *See* Bankruptcy Code § 541; Chapter Four, *The "Estate" — What Exactly Is It?*

Ex Parte

Without notice to other parties. *Ex parte* relief is granted only in emergency circumstances. Usually ***First Day Orders*** are entered as ***Interim Orders*** by the bankruptcy court on an *ex parte* basis subject to ***negative notice***.

Examiner

A court-appointed investigator authorized to delve into the financial and business affairs of a Chapter 11 debtor-in-possession. Examiners are frequently accounting firms. Examiners generally have limited powers and are compensated as an administrative claim of an estate. Examiner appointments are mandatory in certain circumstances. *See* Bankruptcy Code § 1104(c); Chapter Two, *The Players And Their Roles.*

Exclusivity Period

In Chapter 11 cases, a period of 120 days after the order for relief is entered wherein only the debtor may file a plan of reorganization. If a plan is filed within that time, the debtor has another sixty days to get the plan confirmed. This period may be extended for cause, or be shortened or terminated for cause, or as the result of a Chapter 11 trustee being appointed. *See* Bankruptcy Code § 1121(b); Chapter Five, *Step One: The Negotiation Process And Dynamics.*

Executory Contract

An unexpired contract requiring performance by both parties, which the trustee or debtor may elect to assume and continue or reject. Example: The trustee might elect to keep a valuable lease by paying the back rent and assuming the lease. Special rules apply to collective bargaining agreements, retiree benefit plans, shopping center leases, time-share contracts, and intellectual property licenses. *See* Bankruptcy Code §§ 365, 1113 and 1114; Chapter Four, *Dealing With Executory Contracts And Unexpired Leases. See also* ***Unexpired Leases***, below.

Family Farmer

For the purposes of Chapter 12 proceedings, a family farmer is an individual (and spouse) engaged in farming operations or a corporation that meets the debt limitation of $1.5 million, plus certain other debt and ownership restrictions set forth in Bankruptcy Code § 101(18)(A) and (B). *See* Chapter Two, *The "Bankruptcy Code."*

Feasibility Analysis

The analysis by which the debtor shows to the bankruptcy court that it will be able to make payments required of it under a ***plan of reorganization***. The bankruptcy court can only ***confirm*** a plan of reorganization if it finds that the plan is "feasible." *See* Bankruptcy Code § 1129(a)(11); Chapter Five, *Step Five: The Plan Confirmation Process.*

Feasibility Requirement

The Bankruptcy Code's requirement that before a bankruptcy court can ***confirm*** a ***plan of reorganization*** that it be satisfied that confirmation of the plan is not likely to be followed by a subsequent liquidation or need for further reorganization (unless subsequent liquidation is contemplated under the terms of the plan). The Bankruptcy Court makes this finding pursuant to the ***feasibility analysis*** that must be presented by the debtor as part of the plan confirmation process. *See* Bankruptcy Code § 1129(a)(11); Chapter Five, *Step Five: The Plan Confirmation Process.*

Fiduciary Obligation

The obligation of the ***DIP*** to act in the best interests of the creditors and all other parties in interest. The DIP must act with the highest degree of honesty, similar to a trustee of a trust. When a company is ***insolvent***, it is generally accepted that the DIP owes a fiduciary obligation to the creditors and not the ***equityholders*** of the company. Committees also have fiduciary obligations to their constituents. *See* Chapter Two, *The Players And Their Roles*; Chapter Three, *Making The Transitions — Attitudinal Adjustments."*

Final Decree

An ***order*** entered by the bankruptcy court formally closing a ***Chapter 11 Proceeding*** after confirmation of a ***Plan*** when litigation and other matters have been completed. *See* Chapter Five, *The "Final Decree."*

"First Day" Orders

Orders entered by the bankruptcy court usually within the first few days of a Chapter 11 proceeding, which provide emergency relief to a debtor to allow it to continue to operate its business. First day orders typically include orders allowing the DIP to continue to honor employee wage checks that were issued prebankruptcy, payment of essential trade vendors (usually under the so-called ***"Doctrine Of Necessity"***), and perhaps immediate approvals of ***Cash Collateral Stipulations*** and ***DIP Financing*** arrangements. Most first day orders are entered as ***interim orders***, and sometimes on an ***ex parte*** basis. *See* Chapter Four, *First Day Orders*.

First Meeting Of Creditors

The debtor's first duty to appear and testify under oath and to be questioned by creditors occurs at this meeting, held not less than twenty nor more than forty days after the order for relief. The meeting is presided over by a hearing officer or a trustee, but not a judge. Bankruptcy Code § 341; Rule 2003.

"Flat Puppy Filing"

A slang term originated by Patrick Murphy (a very well-respected lawyer in San Francisco) used to denote a bankruptcy proceeding filed under emergency circumstances with little or no preplanning or preparation. The phrase comes from the vignette of the small child bringing a puppy that has been run over by a car or truck to its parent, handing the mangled animal to the parent with pleading eyes saying "Fix it." In emergency bankruptcy cases with little or no preparation or cash, the odds of successfully restructuring, while not insurmountable, are certainly weighing against the debtor. *See* Chapter Two, *The "Proactive" Versus "Reactive" Reorganization Cases. See also* ***"Free Fall" Bankruptcy***, below.

Foreign Subpoena

A subpoena served outside the jurisdiction in which a bankruptcy case is pending, usually by having another District Court reissue a subpoena obtained locally.

Fraudulent Conveyance

Under both state and federal law, a transfer of property by the debtor for less than the true value of the property during the year (or more) prior to bankruptcy. Example: Debtor transfers real property worth $10,000 to an uncle for $50 during the year prior to the bankruptcy. Such fraudulent conveyances may be voided or the fair value of the asset recovered. This may also be called a "fraudulent transfer." *See* Bankruptcy Code §§ 544 and 548; Chapter Four, *The "Strong Arm" Powers*.

Fraudulent Transfers

See ***Fraudulent Conveyance***, above.

"Free Fall" Bankruptcy

See ***Flat Puppy Filing***, above.

Gap Period

The period between when an ***Involuntary Bankruptcy Petition*** is filed and the time when the ***Order For Relief*** is entered. During this time the debtor may continue to operate its business. *See* Bankruptcy Code § 303; Chapter Two, *Getting The Process Started.*

"Going Effective"

The phrase used to denote when a debtor is obligated to perform under a confirmed plan of reorganization. After the bankruptcy court confirms he plan, there may still be conditions to going effective under that plan. or example, a condition might be that the debtor finalizes documentation and funding of a working-capital exit facility or some other condition. *See* Chapter Five, *Step Six: "Going Effective."*

Impaired Claims

A ***claim*** by a creditor that will have its legal or equitable rights altered under plan of reorganization. The significance of having an impaired claim is that only holders of impaired claims may vote on a plan of reorganization. Generally, any alteration of a creditor's claim will make that claim impaired thereby allowing the creditor to vote on a plan of reorganization. *See* Bankruptcy Code § 1124; Chapter Five, *Step Four: The Solicitation Process*.

Indubitable Equivalent

A form of adequate protection allowing the court or debtor flexibility in fashioning a remedy that protects a creditor's interest in collateral; for example, giving a portion of the collateral back to a lender in partial satisfaction of debt. *See* Bankruptcy Code § 361. *See* Chapter Four, *Relief From Stay And The Concept Of "Adequate Protection."*

Information-Blocking Mechanisms.

See ***"Chinese Walls,"*** above.

Insider

Someone who has a particularly close relationship to the debtor. This can include relatives, partners or partnerships, affiliated companies (parents or subsidiaries), or a "person in control" of the debtor. The danger of being an insider is that it increases one's vulnerability to a preference suit by the trustee. Whereas unsecured creditors are susceptible to preference recoveries for payments made during the ninety days prior to bankruptcy, insiders are vulnerable for payments received within one year prior to bankruptcy. *See* Bankruptcy Code § 101(31).

Insolvent

The general inability to pay debts as they become due, or a financial condition whereby liabilities exceed the value of assets at a fair market value. *See* Bankruptcy Code § 101(32); Chapter Two, *What's This "Insolvency" Thing?*

Interim Orders

An ***order*** issued by a bankruptcy court that is presently effective but will still be subject to a fairly short period when creditors and other parties may object to the terms of the order and have the bankruptcy court reconsider it. Interim orders sometimes, but not always, are entered on an ***ex parte*** basis, and usually ***First Day Orders*** are entered as interim orders. Interim orders are usually entered in circumstances where relief is required immediately (such as in cases where immediate ***DIP financing*** is needed) and there is not sufficient time for parties to be heard before the entry of the interim order. *See* Chapter Four, *First Day Orders.*

Interlocutory

Not final. Regarding judgments and orders of the bankruptcy court, an interlocutory order may not be appealed to the ***Bankruptcy Appellate Panel*** or ***District Court*** without obtaining, by motion, leave of court. A motion for leave to appeal is filed with the notice of appeal.

Involuntary Bankruptcy

A bankruptcy case that is commenced against a company, not by the company, as in the case of a ***voluntary bankruptcy***. For an involuntary petition to be filed, the debtor must generally not be paying debts as they come due. Under current bankruptcy law, if the debtor has more than twelve creditors, then three creditors with claims totaling at least $10,775 are required in order to file an involuntary petition; if there are less than twelve creditors, only one petitioning creditor is necessary if the claim equals or exceeds $10,775. *See* Bankruptcy Code § 303; Chapter Two, *Getting The Process Started.*

Involuntary Petition

A ***petition*** filed by creditors seeking an order for relief against the debtor under Chapters 7 or 11. Creditors are usually seeking to stop an action of another creditor by the imposition of the automatic stay, or control over actions of insiders through protections. *See* Bankruptcy Code § 303; Rules 1003, 1010, 1011, 1013; Official Form 5.

Judicial Lien

A lien (or interest in property) obtained by judgment, levy, sequestration, or other legal or equitable remedy, and includes garnishment liens. *See* Bankruptcy Code § 101(32).

Jurisdiction

The power of a court over persons, property, or the subject matter of dispute. Bankruptcy courts are commonly held to have nationwide jurisdiction over persons. *See also* ***Bankruptcy Court Jurisdiction***.

Leveraged Buyout or "LBO"

A process whereby the equity in a company is acquired and the assets of the acquired company are used to either act as ***collateral*** for the acquisition debt, or where the acquired company itself becomes obligated on the acquisition debt. If the acquired company subsequently gets into financial difficulties, the other creditors of that company may assert that the LBO debt or ***liens*** should be avoided as a ***fraudulent conveyance*** because the company itself received no benefit from the LBO, but rather the selling and purchasing shareholders received the benefit. From a straight balance-sheet perspective, the acquired company became obligated on a debt (or perhaps gave a lien on its assets), but the consideration for the loan flowed to old shareholders who sold their shares. *See* Chapter Two, *The "Proactive" Versus "Reactive" Reorganization Ca*ses.

Lien

A charge against or interest in property (such as a mortgage or security interest) taken to secure payment of a debt or performance of an obligation. Generally, liens are consensual (by agreement), judicial, or statutory. *See* Bankruptcy Code § 101(33).

Lien Priming

See ***Super Priority Financing***, below.

Liquidation Analysis

The analysis performed by the debtor (or its professionals), to show the bankruptcy court as part of the plan confirmation process that creditors will receive more under the plan of reorganization than they would in a liquidation of the company under a ***Chapter 7 Proceeding***. This analysis is necessary in order to meet the ***"Best Interests Of Creditors Test."*** *See* Chapter Five, *Step Five: The Plan Confirmation Process*.

Mortgage

See ***Lien***, above.

Motion

A pleading used to commence contested matters, usually setting forth the factual and legal basis for relief. Any request for a court order that is not an adversary proceeding under Rule 7001 should be commenced by a motion.

Negative Amortization

The phrase used to identify when a plan is capitalizing some or all interests such that it is added to the principal of the debt. For example, a ***plan of reorganization*** may provide that a creditor's claim of $1,000 is to be paid at an interest rate of prime plus 2 percent, but the pay rate will only be at prime with the additional 2 percent being added to the principal of the loan to be paid in the future. This is usually done because the cash-flow projections for the ***Reorganized Debtor*** presented as part of its ***feasibility analysis*** do not support the full payment of all interest. Negative amortization plans are viewed very skeptically by bankruptcy courts because they clearly indicate problems with the ***feasibility requirement*** portion of the Bankruptcy Code for plan confirmation purposes.

Negative Notice

A process whereby a bankruptcy court will enter an ***Interim Order***, and then direct the debtor (or some other party) to provide notice to creditors and parties in interest. The order will be presently effective, but parties will have a period of time to voice their concerns or objections at which time the bankruptcy court may have a hearing and modify the ***Interim Order***. The mechanism of negative notice is essential for emergency situations, and is most often used with ***First Day Orders***. *See* Chapter Four, *First Day Orders*.

"New Value Exception" or ***"New Value Corollary"***

A judicially created exception to the ***Absolute Priority Rule*** that provides, essentially, that old ***equityholders*** may receive or retain their equity in a debtor when unsecured creditors are not being paid in full provided they infuse "new value" into the debtor as part of the plan confirmation process. There is still uncertainty as to whether the so-called "new value exception" to the Absolute Priority Rule survived the enactment of the Bankruptcy Code in 1978, and the U.S. Supreme Court, notwithstanding having this issue squarely before it at least three times since 1988, has yet to issue a definitive ruling on this point. *See* Bankruptcy Code § 1129(b); Chapter Five, *Step Five: The Plan Confirmation Process*.

"Non-Core" Matters

A claim or action that is related to a bankruptcy case but is not a core matter. The bankruptcy court does not have jurisdiction to render a final order on non-core matters absent consent of all parties, which may be implied under certain circumstances. *See* 28 U.S.C. § 157(b); Chapter Four; *Bankruptcy Court Jurisdiction (And Limitations On That Jurisdiction)*.

"Non-Core/Non-Related" Matters

A claim or action that does not arise under the Bankruptcy Code, and also does not have a tangible connection to the bankruptcy case. When a matter is deemed to be "non-core/non-related," the bankruptcy court has no ***jurisdiction*** to render any decisions with respect to such disputes. *See* 28 U.S.C. § 157(b); Chapter Four, *Bankruptcy Court Jurisdiction (And*

Limitations On That Jurisdiction).

Notice

A process whereby creditors and parties in interest are given notice that a debtor (or some other party) is seeking to do something in a bankruptcy proceeding. In the Bankruptcy Rules and Bankruptcy Code, notice requirements are whatever notice is appropriate under the circumstances. Forms of notice may include formal written notice, telephonic notice, or even Internet/e-mail notice, depending on the matter. *See* Bankruptcy Code § 102; Chapter Four, *First Day Orders. See also* ***Notice By Publication***.

Notice By Publication

Giving ***notice*** to creditors and parties in interest through publication of the form of notice in newspapers or, in exceptional circumstances, by television or radio advertisements. This is frequently done, for example, in circumstances where the debtor is not exactly sure which people hold claims against it, such as in potential mass tort cases or other such circumstances. Notice by publication has also been used to provide notice via the Internet, and is frequently used with respect to giving notice of a ***Bar Date***. *See* Bankruptcy Rule 9007. *See also* ***Channeling Injunctions***, above.

Official Committee Of Equityholders

In a Chapter 11 case, a committee appointed by the U.S. Trustee generally comprised of the seven largest holders of the debtor's equity securities willing to serve. Also known as an Equityholders Committee. *See* Bankruptcy Code § 1102; Chapter Two, *The Players And Their Roles. See also* ***Official Committee of Unsecured Creditors***, below.

Official Committee Of Unsecured Creditors

In Chapter 11 cases, a committee appointed by the U.S. Trustee of the seven largest unsecured creditors of the debtor willing to serve. The Unsecured Creditors Committee serves both watchdog and proactive functions in a case, and may hire its own counsel, financial advisors, and so forth. Unsecured Creditors Committees are authorized in Chapter 7 cases, but are rarely used. Also known as a Creditors Committee. The 1994 Bankruptcy Reform Act amended the Code to allow for reimbursement, as an administrative claim, of the reasonable costs of members of the Committee. *See* Bankruptcy Code § 1102; Chapter Two, *The Players And Their Roles.*

Offset

The ability to credit a debt owed to one by the debt owed by that person to you. For example, if a debtor owes a creditor $100, but that creditor also owes the debtor $80, under the principles of offset, the debtor could take the position that it only owes the creditor $20 and not the full $100 because of a credit of the debt owed by the creditor to the debtor. *See* Bankruptcy Code § 553. *See also* ***Setoff***, below.

One-Half/Two-Thirds Requirement

For purposes of ***class voting*** in a ***plan of reorganization***, a class is deemed to accept a plan if more than one-half in numbers of creditors that actually vote on the plan *and* more than two-thirds in the amounts of those claims vote to accept the plan. Under those circumstances, the class will be deemed to accept the plan and even creditors that do not vote to accept the plan will be bound by the terms of that plan. *See* Bankruptcy Code § 1126; Chapter Five, *Step Four: The Solicitation Process.*

Operating Reports

Reports required to be filed periodically (usually monthly) by a ***Debtor-In-Possession***, which set forth operational financial information so that the Bankruptcy Court and all creditors can see how the debtor is doing operationally in its Chapter 11 proceeding. *See* Chapter Four, *Reporting Requirements And Other Annoyances.*

Order

A judicial command or direction. Orders are sought by ***motion***. A judgment generally is broader than an order, determines all rights at issue, and resolves all matters pending in a dispute. A judgment is sought in an ***adversary proceeding***.

Order For Relief

The ***order*** entered by the bankruptcy court upon the filing of a voluntary ***Chapter 11 Proceeding***. Prior to the Bankruptcy Code, the mere filing of a ***voluntary petition*** did not in and of itself result in an order for relief being entered, but rather a hearing was necessary to "adjudicate" the company a bankrupt. Under the Bankruptcy Code (in place since 1978), the filing of a Chapter 11 voluntary petition acts as the order for relief at which time the ***automatic stay*** is in place and the debtor officially becomes a ***Debtor-In-Possession***.

"Ordinary Course Transactions"

Transactions in which a ***DIP*** is allowed to engage in a ***Chapter 11 Proceeding*** without an ***order*** of the bankruptcy court. For example, if a debtor company is in the retail sales business, the debtor can continue to sell to ordinary course customers without bankruptcy court approval or interference. *See* Bankruptcy Code § 1107, Chapter Four, *Stabilizing The Business Operations.*

Overbid Protections

In asset sales in bankruptcy cases, an initial bidder (to prevent itself from becoming a "***stalking horse***"), may require, as a condition to its submitting its initial bid, that it be given certain protections in the bidding process. One of those protections may be an "overbid protection," which would essentially provide that any bid over the initial bid must be a large increment to avoid one- or two-dollar bidding wars. *See* Chapter Four, *Sale Of Assets.*

Party In Interest

A term of art in bankruptcy law that means any party that has the right to stand up and be heard by a bankruptcy court. The term "party in interest" goes beyond a ***creditor***. For example, the Securities and Exchange Commission, while rarely holding a ***claim***, is a party in interest that has the right to be heard in all bankruptcy cases. *See* Bankruptcy Code § 1109.

Perfected Lien

A ***lien*** for which all of the necessary steps for ***perfection*** have been taken. If a secured creditor has a lien that is not perfected under applicable nonbankruptcy law, the DIP may use its ***"strong arm" powers*** to avoid the lien.

Perfection

Steps necessary under the Uniform Commercial Code and other applicable state law to make a lien effective as to third parties and, ultimately, effective against a ***trustee*** in bankruptcy. Forms of perfection usually involve filing of documents in the public records for the county or state in which the property is located.

Petition

The document filed by a debtor that initiates a bankruptcy proceeding. Petitions may be filed voluntarily by the debtor or filed involuntarily. *See* Chapter Two, *Getting The Process Started.*

Petitioning Creditor

A creditor that has filed an ***Involuntary Petition*** against a company.

Plan Ballot

A ballot by which the holder of an ***impaired claim*** votes to accept or reject a ***plan of reorganization***. *See* Chapter Five, *Step Four: The Solicitation Process. See also* **Ballot Report**, above.

Plan Of Reorganization

A document that divides the claims of creditors into groups and restructures their payments and/or collateralization. Some creditors are not affected and are considered "unimpaired." All creditors (other than unimpaired creditors) vote on the plan of reorganization. Each class that is impaired must accept the plan by the ***one-half/two-thirds requirement***. *See* Bankruptcy Code § 1123; Chapter Five, *Step Two: The Plan Of Reorganization.*

Preference

A payment made to an unsecured creditor or, possibly, an undersecured creditor during the ninety days prior to the bankruptcy filing. These payments are voidable and recoverable by the trustee (or even the debtor on behalf of the estate). An unsecured or undersecured creditor who receives new security during the ninety-day period also receives a preferential transfer, and the new collateralization may be voided. The Bankruptcy Code prohibits a trustee from bringing a preference action if the amount to be recovered is less than $600. *See* Bankruptcy Code § 547; Chapter Four, *The "Strong Arm" Powers.*

"Prepackaged" Bankruptcy"

A phrase used to identify a wide range of circumstances, starting from a situation where a debtor has had the opportunity to negotiate the essential terms of a ***plan of reorganization*** with some or all of its creditors (technically called a "prenegotiated" bankruptcy), to where the debtor has not only negotiated the terms of the plan of reorganization, but also solicited ***plan ballots*** from creditors prior to filing a ***Chapter 11 Proceeding***. *See* Chapter Two, *The "Proactive" Versus "Reactive" Reorganization Cases.*

Prima Facie

Presumption that facts are true unless rebutted by opposing party. A proof of claim is *prima facie* proof of the claim amount until a party objects and presents evidence to the contrary.

Priority Claim

Claims that, under bankruptcy law, must be paid before unsecured claims may be paid anything. Examples include certain taxes, wages, consumer deposits, and so forth. Priority claims can also include, as a first priority, all ***administrative claims*** of the ***estate***. *See* Bankruptcy Code § 507; Chapter Two, *The "Pecking Order" — Payment Priorities In Reorganization Cases.*

Pro Hac Vice

Signifies the admission of a member of the bar in one jurisdiction to practice, usually on a limited matter, in another jurisdiction's courts. A member of the bar of the second jurisdiction must generally move for admission *pro hac vice* of the out-of-state attorney.

Pro Rata Basis

A proportionate amount. When applied to a ***claim*** it refers to the ratio of the consideration distributed on the amount of that claim to the amount that the claim bears to all the other claims in a particular class. Simply put, if there are $1,000 of total claims in a class of which one creditor holds $100 (or 10 percent), for every dollar that is payable to the creditors in that class, the creditor with the $100 amount will receive 10¢ (or 10 percent) on a *pro rata* basis.

Pro Se or Pro Per

Without legal representation, or appearing on one's own behalf. Corporations, partnerships, and business entities other than sole proprietorships may not appear without counsel in bankruptcy cases.

Proof Of Claim

A pleading filed with the clerk of the bankruptcy court setting forth the claim's amount, nature and classification (such as, secured, unsecured, administrative, priority and so forth). The supporting documentation is usually attached. *See* Chapter Five, *Quantifying The Debts—The "Bar Date" Order*. *See also* ***Bar Date*** and ***Bar Date Order***.

Purchase-Money Security Interest

Description of ***security interest*** taken by creditor in property that the debtor acquired with funds advanced by the creditor taking the security interest. *See also* ***Lien***.

Reclamation

The ability under certain states' laws to get products back that were sold to a company on credit if the company was insolvent at the time of the sale. This usually affects retail bankruptcies where vendors who supply inventory ship goods, and within a short period of time the company files bankruptcy. Under most states' laws, a claim for reclamation must be made within a short period of time (usually ten days) after delivery of the goods. *See* Chapter Four, *Dealing With The "Special Claims."*

Reject or Rejection

The process whereby a debtor elects to walk away from its responsibilities and benefits under an ***executory contract*** or ***unexpired lease***. Under these circumstances, the other party to the lease or contract will have a ***claim*** for money damages as a result of the rejection, which equates to a breach of the lease or contract. *See* Bankruptcy Code § 365; Chapter Four, *Dealing With Executory Contracts And Unexpired Leases*. *See also* ***Assume or Assumption***.

Relief From The Automatic Stay

A contested matter filed with the bankruptcy court in which the creditor requests that the bankruptcy court modify or lift the stay to allow the creditor to proceed in its actions against the debtor's property. Example: A secured creditor requests the bankruptcy court to lift the automatic stay in order to continue the state foreclosure on the debtor's realty. The creditor normally asserts that the secured position does not have adequate protection, *e.g.*, a $100,000 mortgage on realty worth only $75,000. *See* Bankruptcy Code § 362(d); Chapter Four, *The Automatic Stay*.

Reorganization

The recapitalization of a distressed company through a ***Chapter 11 Proceeding***.

Reorganization Process

The process of negotiating and documenting the restructuring of a company. *See* Chapter Two, ***The Reorganization Process.***

Reorganized Company

The debtor company after it emerges from Chapter 11 pursuant to a confirmed plan of reorganization. *See* Chapter Five, *Step Six: "Going Effective."*

Reorganized Debtor

See ***Reorganized Company***, above.

Sales Free And Clear of Liens

The ability of a ***DIP*** under the Bankruptcy Code to sell assets even if the ***secured creditor*** with a ***lien*** on the asset to be sold does not consent. In such sales, a secured creditor may have ***credit bid rights***. Usually what occurs in these cases is that the bankruptcy court will order the assets sold with the secured lender's lien to "attach to the sales proceeds." Accordingly, a lender with a first lien on a machine in the amount of $100 that is sold for $105 will have its lien on the machine removed as part of the sale, but the lien will attach to the first $100 in sales proceeds. *See* Bankruptcy Code § 363; Chapter Four, *Sales Of Assets*.

Schedules

Schedules of Assets and Liabilities, which all debtors (or the trustee) must file with the court under penalty of perjury. *See* Chapter Four, *Reporting Requirements And Other Annoyances*.

Secured Creditor

A creditor that has a ***perfected lien*** or ***security interest*** on assets of the ***estate***.

Security Agreement

An agreement between a creditor and debtor that creates a consensual lien under the Uniform Commercial Code. *See also* ***Lien***.

Security Interest

The creditor's right in property created in a security agreement. *See also* ***Lien***.

Serial Filings

See ***Chapter 22s***, above.

Setoff

See ***Offset,*** above.

Single-Asset Real Estate Cases

Under the 1994 Bankruptcy Reform Act, this definition was added to the Bankruptcy Code to describe real estate: (1) with a single property or project (other than residential real property with less than four units); (2) which generates substantially all of the debtor's income; and (3) on which no other substantial business is conducted; and (4) with no more than $4 million of secured debt. The consequence of being a single-asset real estate case is expanded rights of creditors with respect to stay relief if the debtor has neither filed a plan within ninety days of the order for relief nor commenced monthly payments to secured creditors. *See* Bankruptcy Code § 101(51B).

Small Business Chapter 11

Under the 1994 Bankruptcy Reform Act, an accelerated (and hopefully less expensive) reorganization proceeding that an individual, partnership, or corporation, if eligible can elect but is not required to do so. The Small Business Chapter 11 provisions of the Code limit exclusivity period extensions, combine the hearing on the Disclosure Statement and the plan, and allow the court not to appoint an unsecured creditors committee. A business is considered a small business if it has total unsecured and secured debt of no more than $2 million. *See* Bankruptcy Code § 101(51C).

Solicitation Package

A package consisting of a Disclosure Statement, plan of reorganization, all of the exhibits to those documents, the bankruptcy court's ***order*** approving the Disclosure Statement, the plan ballot and any other materials that will be sent by a debtor in order to seek acceptances of its plan of reorganization. *See* Chapter Five, *Step Four: The Solicitation Process.*

Solicitation Process

The process whereby the ***solicitation package*** is sent to all holders of ***impaired claims*** to get them to vote on a ***plan of reorganization***. *See* Chapter Five, *Step Four: The Solicitation Process.*

"Stalking Horse"

The term used in asset sales in bankruptcies to describe the disadvantage of being the first bidder willing to come forward on an asset. Since asset sales are always auction sales in bankruptcy proceedings, the first bidder is generally the one that all other bidders are bidding against. The phrase is derived from the old hunting technique where an animal was used to attract game for hunters. Potential bidders usually seek to minimize the downside to being a "stalking horse" by the use of ***Overbid Protections***, ***"Bust Up" Fees***, and ***"Window Shop" Provisions***. *See* Chapter Four, *Sale Of Assets.*

Statement Of Financial Affairs

Document that must be filed by all debtors, under penalty of perjury, listing detailed information as to the whereabouts of financial records, prebankruptcy transfers, prebankruptcy income, and so forth. *See* Chapter Four, *Reporting Requirements And Other Annoyances.*

Statements and Schedules

See ***Schedules*** and ***Statement Of Financial Affairs***, above.

Statutory Lien

A lien created by operation of law, such as a mechanic's or garageman's lien, a stableman's lien or a landlord's lien.

Stay Relief

See ***Relief From Automatic Stay***, above.

Stipulation

A voluntary agreement between the parties resolving a legal dispute or a part thereof. In a bankruptcy proceeding, stipulations often must be noticed to creditors.

"Strong Arm Powers"

The powers of the trustee or DIP to avoid certain liens and bring property into the estate for the benefit of creditors, including ***preference*** and ***fraudulent transfer*** avoidance powers. *See* Bankruptcy Code §§ 544, 547, 548, and 549; Chapter Four, *The "Strong Arm" Powers.*

Sua Sponte

On the court's own motion. Sometimes, particularly in emergency situations, courts enter ***orders*** even when no party has requested they do so.

Subordinated Claims

Claims that takes a junior position in priority to other claims. Claims may be subordinated by agreement or through an adversary proceeding. *See* Bankruptcy Code § 510.

Subpoena

A command of the court for the party to whom it is addressed to appear at a specific place, at a certain time.

Subpoena Duces Tecum

A command of the court for the party to whom it is addressed to appear and produce certain documentary evidence.

Subrogation

The substitution of one party into another party's position. For example, when a guarantor pays the debtor's obligation to a creditor, the guarantor steps into the shoes of the creditor and may pursue the creditor's claim. *See* Bankruptcy Code § 509.

Substantial Contribution

A term of art used in the Bankruptcy Code whereby a creditor can seek to have its professional fees reimbursed as an ***administrative claim*** on the basis that the creditor's actions in the case (for which it incurred professional fees) benefited all of the creditors of the ***estate***. Frequently, ***"Bust Up" Fees*** and the professional fees of ***Ad Hoc Committees*** are sought under the substantial contribution provisions of the Bankruptcy Code. *See* Bankruptcy Code § 503(b).

Substantive Consolidation

The legal theory whereby numerous companies (with their assets and liabilities) are treated as one company. This can either be done pursuant to a ***motion*** filed in a bankruptcy court in a ***Chapter 11 Proceeding***, but is most often done through a confirmed ***plan of reorganization***. *See* Chapter Five, *Step Two: Drafting The Plan Of Reorganization.*

Super Priority Administrative Claim

An ***administrative claim*** that takes seniority over all other administrative claims in a case. *See* Bankruptcy Code § 507; Chapter Four, *Financing The Preconfirmation Operations.*

Super Priority Financing

DIP financing whereby a creditor is given a senior ***lien*** on assets of the ***estate*** even though those assets are already subject to liens. This is also known as "***lien priming***." *See* Bankruptcy Code § 364(d); Chapter Four, *Financing The Preconfirmation Operations.*

Tag-Along Rights

Rights that are triggered when one or more shareholder gives notice to the other parties to a shareholder agreement (*i.e.,* the other shareholders) that such shareholders intends to sell their shares to a third party. Tag-along rights allow the shareholder(s) receiving this notice to include their shares in the sale (hence the term "tag along"), usually on a *pro rata* basis (and thereby carving back the number of shares that the selling shareholder can sell). The provisions granting these rights are typically lengthy and set forth the mechanics for how the rights become operable.

Temporary Allowance

When a ***claim*** has been objected to, it is not an ***allowed claim*** such that it may vote on a plan of reorganization. Accordingly, the ***Bankruptcy Rules*** provide that the bankruptcy court may temporarily allow the claim for voting purposes. This avoids the filing of ***claims objections*** just to disenfranchise a particular creditor. *See* Bankruptcy Rule 3018; Chapter Five, *Step Four: The Solicitation Process.*

Transfer Taxes

Under some states' laws, any transfer of real or personal property may be subject to state taxes, which are usually levied as a percentage of the value of the property being transferred. This may also be known as a "document tax" or "stamp tax." Under the Bankruptcy Code, transfer taxes are not enforceable such that assets transferred under a ***plan of reorganization*** are not collectible. *See* Bankruptcy Code § 1146(c); Chapter Five, *Step Two: The Plan Of Reorganization.*

Trustee

A person appointed by the bankruptcy court to administer the bankruptcy ***estate***. In a ***Chapter 7 Proceeding,*** the trustee's primary function is to be a liquidating and collection agent. If a trustee is appointed in a ***Chapter 11 Proceeding***, he or she is charged with responsibility for proposing a plan of reorganization. In Chapters 12 and 13, a standing trustee exists to administer the plan. *See* Bankruptcy Code § 1104; Chapter Two, *The Players And Their Roles.*

Unexpired Leases

A real or personal property lease under which the debtor is the lessee or lessor, which has not ended under its own terms prebankruptcy, or which has not been terminated prebankruptcy. Only unexpired leases that are in existence as of the date the ***Chapter 11 Proceeding*** is filed may be ***assumed*** by the ***DIP***. *See* Bankruptcy Code § 365; Chapter Four, *Dealing With Executory Contracts And Unexpired Leases. See also* **Executory Contracts**.

Unofficial Committees

See **Ad Hoc Committees**, above.

Unsecured Claims

Those ***claims*** asserted in a bankruptcy proceeding that are not secured by ***lien*** rights in any real property or personal property of the ***estate*** or the debtor. An unsecured claim may have seniority over other claims as an unsecured ***Priority Claim***. *See* Chapter Two, *The "Pecking Order"—Payment Priorities In Reorganization Cases. See also* **Administrative And Priority Claims**, above.

U.S. Trustee

In all districts, a formal Office of the U.S. Trustee exists as an arm of the U.S. Department of Justice. The U.S. Trustee, not the court, appoints trustees from a private panel. The U.S. Trustee program was designed to free the courts from administrative supervision over trustees. *See* Chapter Two, *The Players And Their Roles.*

Venue

A concept determining the proper geographical location for filing a bankruptcy case or other action. Venue is proper if the debtor has resided or has a domicile, place of business, or property in the district 180 days preceding the filing of the petition. More than one venue may be proper in a case. *See* 28 U.S.C. § 1408; Chapter Four, *The Venue Game.*

Voluntary Bankruptcy

When a troubled company voluntarily files a Chapter 11 petition, thereby commencing a ***Chapter 11 Proceeding*** and resulting in an ***Order For Relief***. *See* Bankruptcy Code § 301; Chapter Two, *Getting The Process Started*.

"Window Shop" Provisions

Buyer protection devices usually negotiated in asset sales in bankruptcy cases. Since the ***Debtor-In-Possession*** has a fiduciary duty to maximize values for all assets, generally speaking all asset sale contracts in bankruptcy cases are subject to "higher and better bids" through some sort of an auction process. Potential buyers, to protect themselves from being a ***"stalking horse"*** against whom other bidders will compete, may require that the debtor not actively solicit other offers, but rather may only entertain other offers if bidders come to them. The bankruptcy court must approve any such restrictions in asset purchase and sale agreements in bankruptcy cases. *See* Chapter Four, *Sale Of Assets*.

"Zone Of Insolvency"

An imprecise term that is sometimes used in law review articles and in some judicial decisions. While ***insolvency*** is a balance-sheet test, when a company is in financial distress and may not be technically insolvent but is still clearly on its way there, some courts have imposed special ***fiduciary duties*** on the Board of Directors of such companies because they are in the "zone of insolvency." *See* Chapter Three, *Making The Transitions: Attitudinal Adjustments*.

APPENDIX B

HYPOTHETICAL REORGANIZATION TIMELINE

This is a timeline for a hypothetical Chapter 11 case, and is presented as an illustration only. While this timeline includes generally the events that usually occur in a Chapter 11 case, actual cases may have different issues and timelines for events. Also, some of the events set forth below may be the subject of continuous and recurring negotiations or litigation or both (for example, cash collateral negotiations, reclamation claims, and reestablishment of trade credit).

The events described below are dealt with, in detail, in Chapters Two through Five.

Petition Date to 30 Days

- Filing of Petition.
- Filing of application for retention of professionals.
- Filing of "First Day" Motions (wages, cash management, essential suppliers, etc.).
- Hearing on "First Day" Motions (possible entry of Orders on negative-notice procedures).
- Filing of Schedules of Assets and Liabilities and Statement of Financial Affairs (unless bankruptcy court grants extension of time).
- Filing (and/or negotiation) of cash collateral motions (or stipulations) for debtor's use of cash collateral.
- Hearing on cash collateral motions (or stipulations), and entry of orders regarding cash collateral use (may be on an interim basis and/or subject to negative-notice procedures).
- Negotiation for, and hearing on approval of, debtor-in-possession financing (may be on an interim basis and/or subject to negative-notice procedures).
- Negotiations with utilities regarding security deposits and/or hearings on adequate assurance of payment.
- Negotiations with trade creditors regarding reclamation claims and/or reestablishment of trade terms (this will usually be an ongoing negotiation).

31 Days to 60 Days

- Beginning of business stabilization process (of course, easier said than done; an ongoing process).
- Meeting with U.S. Trustee (also called the "initial debtor interview" in some jurisdictions).
- First meeting of creditors (called the "341 Meeting" in bankruptcy parlance—Bankruptcy Code § 341 requires such meetings).
- Meetings with official Committees and their professionals (to open a dialogue—these meetings may be on a regular basis depending on the case).
- Negotiations with secured creditors regarding "adequate protection" arrangements (may also be dealt with as part of cash collateral discussions) .
- Defense of stay relief motions brought by secured creditors if negotiations are unsuccessful.
- Determination of which unexpired contracts or non-residential real property leases the debtor wishes to assume or reject, and filing of appropriate pleadings (may also include a motion for an extension of this time period).[1]
- Continued discussions and negotiations with creditor constituencies.
- Defense of ancillary litigation that might be brought in case (such as motions for appointment of examiners or trustee).[2]
- Respond to requests for information from the various creditor constituencies (these requests may be maddening but, if properly responded to, can and should lead to less ancillary litigation and a more constructive dynamic between the debtor and its creditor groups).[3]

---

[1]The Bankruptcy Code imposes a sixty-day deadline for assumption or rejection of unexpired non-residential real property leases.

[2]If a Chapter 11 debtor is forthcoming with its creditors, generally this type of ancillary litigation can be minimized. Unfortunately, it is rarely dispensed with entirely as aggressive litigation tactics are frequently employed by certain creditors as a means to obtain concessions from debtors. If a debtor faces this type of litigation from official Committees, it is usually (but not always) a sign that either the debtor or the Committees are not engaged in open dialogues.

[3]If the parties are represented by experienced professionals, they should be able to agree on set reporting formats and timing matters, along with appropriate confidentiality arrangements to protect information. Also, in a well-run Chapter 11 case, financial information can and should flow directly between financial professionals.

- Negotiations or discussions with the SEC regarding potential delisting or suspension (for public debt or equity).
- Negotiations with unions regarding collective bargaining agreements (and, if consensual modifications are not forthcoming, the filing of a motion seeking bankruptcy court approval of modifications to collective bargaining agreements).

61 Days to 120 Days

- Continued discussions and negotiations with creditor constituencies.
- Negotiation and refinement of ultimate exit strategy in the case (for example, formulation of necessary financial modeling for reorganization plan and discussion of exit alternatives).[4]
- Identification of, and negotiation with, any financial or strategic parties that may provide necessary exit funding under the plan of reorganization.
- Evaluation and possible commencement of potential avoidance actions (preferences, fraudulent transfers, etc.).[5]
- Negotiating, drafting, and filing of either: (i) a plan of reorganization and Disclosure Statement; or (ii) a motion to extend the exclusivity period.
- Negotiations or discussions with state and federal governmental entities regarding potential tax or other regulatory claims (such as underfunded pension claims, environmental claims, or other nontraditional types of claims that can adversely affect the reorganization process).
- Entry of "bar date" order (requiring claims to be filed by a certain date—absent such an order, claims are due to be filed by the date

---

[4] This process may (and usually does in all but the simplest cases) take longer than four months. The process should certainly be started sooner rather than later, and how it ultimately comes out is a function of: (a) how long it takes the business to stabilize; (b) the dynamics between the debtor and creditor constituencies; and (c) what consensus is reached (if any) regarding an exit strategy.

[5] Commencement of avoidance actions can (and sometimes does) occur postconfirmation, provided: (a) such potential actions are adequately disclosed in a Disclosure Statement (to avoid waiver arguments); (b) such potential actions are specifically assigned to an appropriate estate representative for pursuit; (c) the plan provides specific retention of bankruptcy court jurisdiction with respect to these actions; and (d) the actions are commenced within a two-year period after the petition is filed.

of the hearing on approval of the Disclosure Statement).[6]

121 Days to Whenever

- Continued plan negotiations.[7]
- Filing of Disclosure Statement and plan.
- Hearing on adequacy of Disclosure Statement and approval of same.
- Solicitation of acceptances (the balloting process).
- Objections to claims for voting purposes (and potential motions for temporary allowance of claims for voting purposes).
- Estimation of contingent claims for feasibility purposes.
- Collection and tabulation of ballots.
- Receipt of and response to plan confirmation objections (if any).
- Plan confirmation hearings.
- Post-confirmation claims objections.[8]
- Post-confirmation performance under the plan.
- Closure of Chapter 11 case.

---

[6] This hypothetical timeline assumes the filing of a plan within the first six months of the case. If this does not happen (which is not unusual in most Chapter 11 cases), the entry of bar date orders may occur later in the case.

[7] In a Chapter 11 case, the filing of a plan (except in so-called "prepackaged" cases) does not necessarily end the discussions, but usually leads to yet more negotiations. It is not unusual for a plan to be amended and/or supplemented once it is filed but before confirmation in order to build a consensus among creditor constituencies.

[8] As with post-confirmation pursuit of avoidance actions, potential objections to claims must be fully disclosed in the Disclosure Statement to avoid waiver arguments. In addition, claims litigation can occur preconfirmation.

APPENDIX C

SAMPLE PRESS RELEASE

A company that has just filed its voluntary Chapter 11 petition will want to set the tone and content of the market discourse about its filing as much as possible. An initial press release—issued simultaneously with the filing of the petition—is not only required for reporting companies with public debt or equity securities, but is also an excellent first step in the company's efforts to stabilize its business and prevent overreaction to the filing by customers, suppliers, landlords, and other parties. Press releases can be and usually are drafted by crisis public relations firms. This sample press release is based on the one issued at the commencement of the ***Stuart Entertainment*** bankruptcy, filed in Delaware in August 1999. Stuart was particularly concerned with assuring its many customers and vendors that the Chapter 11 restructuring was going to strengthen the company's financial position, and a description of the prebankruptcy restructuring agreement Stuart reached with certain of its largest creditors was included to bolster that impression.

STUART ENTERTAINMENT FILES REORGANIZATION PETITION

COUNCIL BLUFFS, Iowa; August 16, 1999 – Stuart Entertainment, Inc. d/b/a Bingo King (OTC Bulletin Board: STUA) ("Stuart" or the "Company") filed a petition for relief under Chapter 11 of the Bankruptcy Code (the "Chapter 11 Case") in the United States Bankruptcy Court for the District of Delaware on August 13, 1999, in order to effect the Restructuring Agreement (the "Agreement"), dated May 21, 1999, between certain holders (the "Noteholders") of its $100 million 12 ½% Senior Subordinated Notes due 2004 (the "Notes") and Stuart. As previously announced, Stuart did not make the May 15 interest payment with respect to the Notes. Under the Agreement, however, the Noteholders have agreed to refrain from taking any action to enforce the Notes or the obligations of Stuart.

Under the Agreement, upon effectiveness of the Plan of Reorganization (the "Plan"), the holders of the Notes will receive, pro-rata, 100% of the common stock to be authorized under Stuart's amended and restated Certificate of Incorporation to be filed with the Delaware Secretary of State after the Bankruptcy Court approves the Plan ("New Common Stock"), subject to dilution of up to approximately 10% on a fully-diluted basis by shares reserved for issuance under options to be issued to Stuart's executive management. The existing equity holders of Stuart will have their shares cancelled and, subject to approval by the Bankruptcy Court, will receive a pro-rata portion of $150,000 in cash.

Joseph M. Valandra, Chairman and Chief Executive Officer of the Company, said: "The filing of the Plan of Reorganization is a crucial next step in the revitalization of the Company. We are confident that with the support of a majority of our Noteholders, we can emerge quickly from Chapter 11. As reorganized, the Company will be financially stronger and will continue to compete vigorously in all of our markets. This process will protect the continuing interests of our customers, suppliers and employees in the viability of the Company's business."

Under the Plan, all persons who hold, together with all affiliates of such persons, $500,000 or less in principal amount of Notes will receive a cash payment equal to 25% of such Noteholder's allowed claim in lieu of New Common Stock, unless such Noteholder elects to receive New Common stock. Stuart may fund up to $3 million of such cash payments ("Company Funding"), with the remainder of the funding to be supplied by the largest holder of the Notes in accordance with a standby funding commitment. Under such commitment, the Noteholder providing the funding will receive, in exchange for any such funding actually provided, an allowed claim as a Noteholder, thereby entitling such holder to an additional pro-rata distribution of New Common Stock under the Plan.

The Agreement also provides for certain key executive officers of Stuart to receive vested options to purchase up to 4% of the outstanding New Common Stock, and performance based incentive options to purchase up to 6% of the outstanding New Common Stock as of the Effective Date of the Plan on a fully diluted basis. These percentages are subject to increase based on the amount of Company Funding, and the accretive effect of such funding, in accordance with a formula set forth in the Plan.

Additionally, under the Agreement, the Noteholders have agreed to support the payment of all trade claims in the ordinary course of Stuart's business. As a result, Stuart's trade creditors will not be impaired or negatively impacted by the contemplated restructuring. As part of the initial hearings in Delaware, the Bankruptcy Court approved a debtor-in-possession senior secured revolving credit facility for Stuart in an amount of $20 million, which will be increased to $30 million upon final approval of the financing facility. The Bankruptcy Court also approved Stuart's request to pay key trade and vendor claims that arose before the bankruptcy petition was filed.

Mr. Valandra went on to say: "We are pleased that the Noteholders have agreed with the Company to support the full payment of our trade creditors under normal credit terms. This allows the Company to continue our business on a normal basis and displays confidence in the ongoing operational and financial performance of the Company."

The Plan is subject to numerous conditions, and no assurance can be given that the consensual restructuring provided for in the Agreement and the Plan or any other consensual restructuring will be finalized or that any completed restructuring will not be on terms materially different from those contained in the Agreement and the Plan.

Stuart is a worldwide leader in the manufacture of bingo paper, pulltabs and related electronic gaming equipment and supplies, with locations in the United States, Canada and Mexico. Its subsidiaries include Bazaar & Novelty, Canada's largest supplier of bingo paper and related supplies, and Video King, a major supplier of fixed base electronic gaming systems.

Information provided herein by Stuart may contain "forward-looking" information, as that term is defined by the Private Securities Litigation Reform Act of 1995 (the "PSLRA"). These cautionary statements are being made in accordance with the provisions of the PSLRA. Stuart cautions investors that any forward-looking statements made by Stuart are not guarantees of future performance and that actual results may differ materially from those in the forward-looking statements as a result of various factors, including but not limited to risks or uncertainties detailed in Stuart's filing with the Securities and Exchange Commission. Stuart undertakes no obligation to publicly update or revise any forward-looking statements.

APPENDIX D

SAMPLE PETITION AND RELATED FILING DOCUMENTS

This sample Voluntary ***Petition*** for Chapter 11 relief was used to commence the ***Unison HealthCare Corporation*** bankruptcy (involving a parent company and thirty-two subsidiaries and affiliates), a large bankruptcy of a nursing home provider filed in May 1998. The form of the Voluntary Petition is uniform throughout all jurisdictions, as it is dictated by Official Form 1 of the ***Bankruptcy Rules***. The Petition is always accompanied by an Exhibit "A," which sets forth basic information (in a summary form) regarding the debtor's assets and liabilities and capital structure, as well as a description of the debtor's business. In the corporate context, the Voluntary Petition must also be accompanied by a resolution of the corporation's board authorizing the filing of the Voluntary Petition. Usually, the Voluntary Petition is also accompanied by a list of the twenty creditors with the largest amount of unsecured debt—usually called the "Top 20 List." A complete sample set of these materials is included in this Appendix . The list of facilities for this debtor is short because the Voluntary Petition for Unison HealthCare was accompanied by separate Voluntary Petitions for all of Unison's subsidiaries and affiliates, most of which owned and operated dozens of nursing homes throughout the country.

All of the information in this Appendix is a matter of public record on file with the U.S. Bankruptcy Court, so no confidences or privileges are breached by this publication.

United States Bankruptcy Court
District of Arizona

VOLUNTARY PETITION

IN RE: (Name of debtor - If individual, enter: Last, First, Middle **Unison Healthcare Corporation**	NAME OF JOINT DEBTOR (Spouse)(Last, First, Middle)
ALL OTHER NAMES used by debtor in the last 6 years (inc. married, maiden, and trade names) **Alliance HealthCare Corp., Sunquest Healthcare Corp., Hillside Health Care and Bonner Health Center**	ALL OTHER NAMES used by joint debtor in the last 6 years (inc. married, maiden, and trade names)
SOC. SEC./TAX I.D. NO. (If more than one, state all) **86-0684011**	SOC. SEC./TAX I.D. NO. (If more than one, state all)
STREET ADDRESS OF DEBTOR (No. and street, city, state and zip code) **8800 N. Gainey Center Drive, Suite 245** **Scottsdale, AZ 85258** COUNTY OF RESIDENCE/BUSINESS: **Maricopa**	STREET ADDRESS OF JOINT DEBTOR (No. and street, city, state and zip code) COUNTY OF RESIDENCE/BUSINESS:
MAILING ADDRESS OF DEBTOR (If different from street address) **Same**	MAILING ADDRESS OF JOINT DEBTOR (If different from street address)
LOCATION OF PRINCIPAL ASSETS OF BUSINESS DEBTOR (if other than street address) **See "List of Facilities" Attached**	VENUE (Check one box) [X] Debtor has been domiciled or has had a residence, principal place of business, or principal assets in this District for 180 days immediately preceding the date of this petition or for a longer part of such 180 days than in any other District. [ ] There is a bankruptcy case concerning debtor's affiliate, general partner, or partnership pending in this District.

INFORMATION REGARDING DEBTOR (Check applicable boxes)

TYPE OF DEBTOR (Check one box [ ] Individual [X] Corporation Publicly Held [ ] Joint (Husband & Wife) [ ] Corporation Not Publicly Held [ ] Partnership [ ] Municipality [ ] Other ________ NATURE OF DEBT (Check one box) [ ] Non-Business/Consumer [X] Business-Complete A&B below A. TYPE OF BUSINESS (Check one box) [ ] Farming [ ] Transportation [ ] Commodity Broker [ ] Professional [ ] Manufacturing/ [ ] Construction [ ] Retail/Wholesale [ ] Mining [ ] Real Estate [ ] Railroad [ ] Stockbroker[X] Other Business	CHAPTER OR SECTION OF BANKRUPTCY CODE FOR PETITION (Check one box) [ ] Chapter 7 [X] Chapter 11 [ ] Chapter 13 [ ] Chapter 9 [ ] Chapter 12 [ ] Sec. 304 SMALL BUSINESS (Chapter 11 only) [ ] Debtor is a small business as defined in 11 U.S.C. ?1 01. [ ] Debtor is and elects to be considered a small business under 11 U.S.C. ?112(e). (opt'l) FILING FEE (Check one box) [X] Filing fee attached [ ] Filing fee to be paid in installments. (Applicable to individuals only.) Must attach signed application for the court's consideration certifying that the debtor is unable to pay fee except in installments. Rule 1006(b); see Official Form No. 3
B. BRIEFLY DESCRIBE NATURE OF BUSINESS **Long term and specialty healthcare services provider**	NAME AND ADDRESS OF LAW FIRM OR ATTORNEY **Squire, Sanders & Dempsey L.L.P.** **40 North Central, Suite 2700** **Phoenix, Arizona 85004** **Telephone No: (602) 528-4000** NAME(S) OF ATTORNEY(S) DESIGNATED TO REPRESENT THE DEBTOR **Thomas J. Salerno (AZ Bar # 007492)** **Craig D. Hansen (AZ Bar # 007405)** **Jordan A. Kroop (AZ Bar #018825)**
STATISTICAL/ADMINISTRATIVE INFORMATION (28 U.S.C. ?604) (Estimates only)(Check applicable boxes)	[ ] Debtor is not represented by an attorney. Telephone No. of Debtor not represented by an attorney:

[X] Debtor estimates that funds will be available for distribution to unsecured creditors.
[ ] Debtor estimates that, after any exempt property is excluded and administrative expenses paid, there will be no funds available for distribution to unsecured creditors.

THIS SPACE FOR COURT USE ONLY

ESTIMATED NUMBER OF CREDITORS

1-15	16-49	50-99	100-199	200-999	1000-over
[ ]	[ ]	[ ]	[ ]	[X]	[ ]

ESTIMATED ASSETS (in thousands of dollars)

Under 50	50-99	100-499	500-999	1,000-9,999	10,000-99,999	100,000-over
[ ]	[ ]	[ ]	[ ]	[ ]	[X]	[ ]

ESTIMATED LIABILITIES (in thousands of dollars)

Under 50	50-99	100-499	500-999	1,000-9,999	10,000-99,999	100,000-over
[ ]	[ ]	[ ]	[ ]	[ ]	[ ]	[X]

EST. NO. OF EMPLOYEES - CH. 11 & 12 ONLY

0	1-19	20-99	100-999	1000-over
[ ]	[ ]	[ ]	[X]	[ ]

EST. NO. OF EQUITY SECURITY HOLDERS - CH. 11 & 12 ONLY

0	1-19	20-99	100-999	1000-over
[ ]	[ ]	[ ]	[ ]	[X]

FORM 1. VOLUNTARY PETITIO - Page 2

Name of Debtor(s): Unison Healthcare Corporation
Case Number:

FILING OF PLAN

For Chapter 9, 11, 12 and 13 cases only. Check appropriate box.
[ ] A copy of debtor's proposed plan dated ____________, is attached.

[X] Debtor intends to file a plan within the time allowed by statute, rule or order of the court.

PRIOR BANKRUPTCY CASE FILED WITHIN LAST 6 YEARS (if more than one, attach additional sheet)

Name of Debtor	Case Number	Date

PENDING BANKRUPTCY CASE FILED BY ANY SPOUSE, PARTNER, OR AFFILIATE OF THE DEBTOR (if more than one, attach additional sheet)

Name of Debtor	Case Number	Date
Britwill Investments-I, Inc. **Britwill Investments-II, Inc.** **Britwill Indiana Partnership**	**98-00173-PHX-GBN** **98-00174-PHX-GBN** **98-00175-PHX-GBN**	**01-07-98**

Relationship	District	Judge
The entities listed are wholly owned subsidiaries of Unison.	**Arizona**	**George B. Nielsen**

REQUEST FOR RELIEF

Debtor is eligible for and requests relief in accordance with the chapter of title 11, United States Code, specified in this petition.

SIGNATURES

ATTORNEY

X________________________________ ______________ Date

Thomas J. Salerno
Craig D. Hansen
Kathleen T. Tobin
Renée Sandler

INDIVIDUAL/JOINT DEBTOR(S)

I declare under penalty of perjury that the information provided in this petition is true and correct.

x**Not Applicable**

____
Date

x**Not Applicable**

____
Date

CORPORATE OR PARTNERSHIP DEBTOR

I declare under penalty of perjury that the information provided in this petition is true and correct and that I have been authorized to file this petition on behalf of the debtor.

x______________________________
Signature of Authorized Individual

Clayton Kloehr
Print or Type Name of Authorized Individual

Senior Vice President
Title of Individual Authorized by Debtor to File this Petition

____________**, 1998**
Date

If the debtor is a corporation filing under chapter 11, Exhibit "A" is attached and made part of this petition.

TO BE COMPLETED BY INDIVIDUAL CHAPTER 7 DEBTOR WITH PRIMARILY CONSUMER DEBTS (See P.L. 98-353 ?322)

I am aware that I may proceed under chapter 7, 11, 12, or 13 of title 11, United States Code, understand the relief available under each such chapter, and choose to proceed under chapter 7 of such title.
If I am represented by an attorney, Exhibit "B" has been completed.

x**Not Applicable**
Signature of Debtor   Date

x**Not Applicable**
Signature of Joint Debtor   Date

EXHIBIT "B"
(To be completed by attorney for individual chapter 7 debtor(s) with primarily consumer debts.)

I, the attorney for the debtor(s) named in the foregoing petition, declare that I have informed the debtor(s) that (he, she, or they) may proceed under chapter 7, 11, 12, or 13 of title 11, United States Code, and have explained the relief available under such chapter.

x**Not Applicable**
Signature of Attorney   Date

CERTIFICATION AND SIGNATURE OF NON-ATTORNEY BANKRUPTCY PETITION PREPARER (See 11 U.S.C. ?110)

I certify that I am a bankruptcy petition preparer as defined in 11 U.S.C. ?110, that I prepared this document for compensation, and that I have provided the debtor with a copy of this document.

Not Applicable
Printed or Typed Name of Bankruptcy Petition Preparer

Not Applicable
Social Security Number

____
____
____
Address

____
Telephone

Name and Social Security number of all other individuals who prepared or assisted in preparing this document:
Not Applicable

If more than one person prepared this document, attach additional signed sheets conforming to the appropriate Official Form for each person.

x**Not Applicable**
Signature of Bankruptcy Petition Preparer

A bankruptcy petition preparer's failure to comply with the provisions of title 11 and the Federal Rules of Bankruptcy Procedure may result in fines or imprisonment or both. 11 U.S.C. ?110; 18 U.S.C. ?156.

LIST OF FACILITIES

1. Home Office
   Unison Healthcare Corporation
   8800 North Gainey Center Dr. #245
   Scottsdale, AZ 85258

2. Bonner Health Center
   520 East Morse Ave.
   Bonner Springs, KS 66012

3. Hillside Care Center (closed)
   510 East Morse Ave.
   Bonner Springs, KS 66012

UNITED STATES BANKRUPTCY COURT
District of Arizona

In re: Unison Healthcare Corporation Case No. ____________
Chapter 11

Exhibit "A" to Voluntary Petition

1.Debtor's employer identification is 86-0684011.

2.If any of debtor's securities are registerd under section 12 of the Securities and Exchange Act of 1934, the SEC file number is 0-27374.

3.The following financial data is the latest available information and refers to debtor's condition on 12/31/97.

a. Total assets	$74,245,879	
b. Total liabilities	$182,032,094	
		Approximate number of holders
Fixed, liquidated secured debt	$25,293,522	32
Contingent secured debt	0	0
Disputed secured claims	0	0
Unliquidated secured debt	0	0
		Approximate number of holders
Fixed, liquidated unsecurd debt	$156,738,572	200[10]
Contingent unsecured debt	0	0
Disputed unsecured claims	0	0
Unliquidated unsecured debt	0	0
Number of shares of preferred stock	0	
Number of shares of common stock	6,422,096	

Comments, if any: The values stated above are Debtor's book values. As indicated in recent public filings and disclosures, Debtor is currently engaged in a comprehensive review of its assets and liabilities. The results of Debtor's internal review may have an impact on the above-referenced figures.

4.Brief description of debtor's business:

Long term and specialty health care services provider.

5.List the name of any person who directly or indirectly owns, controls, or holds, with power to vote, 20% or more of the voting securities of debtor:

David A. Kremser, Director

6.List the names of all corporations with 20% or more of the outstanding voting securities of which are directly or indirectly owned, controlled, or held, with power to vote, by debtor.

None

---

[10]This number represents the Indenture Trustees of two Senior Note Offerings, seven of the largest record holders from such offerings, insider creditors, and several trade creditors.

UNITED STATES BANKRUPTCY COURT
District of Arizona

In re: Unison Healthcare Corporation Case No.

Chapter 11

Statement Regarding Authority To Sign And File Petition

I, Clayton Kloehr, declare under penalty of perjury that I am the Senior Vice President of UNISON HEALTHCARE CORPORATION, a Delaware corporation, and that on ______________________, 1998, a resolution was duly adopted by the Board of Directors of this corporation, a copy of which is attached hereto as Exhibit "1".

Executed on: Signed:

EXHIBIT "1"

CONSENT TO RESOLUTIONS CONSIDERED AT THE MEETING OF THE DIRECTORS OF UNISON HEALTHCARE CORPORATION

The undersigned are all of the members of the Board of Directors of Unison Healthcare Corporation, a Delaware corporation (the "Corporation"). The undersigned consent to and approve of the actions set forth in the following resolutions. The undersigned waive notice of the meeting to consider the matters incorporated in the resolutions.

WHEREAS, the Board of Directors of the Corporation (the "Board") has determined that it is in the best interests of the Corporation to file a voluntary petition in the United States Bankruptcy Court pursuant to Chapter 11 of Title 11 of the United States Code;

NOW, THEREFORE, BE IT RESOLVED, that the President, any Vice President, Secretary and Assistant Secretary of the Corporation (the "Authorized Officers"), and any member of the law firm of Squire, Sanders & Dempsey L.L.P. are hereby authorized and directed to execute and deliver all documents necessary to effect the filing of a Chapter 11 voluntary bankruptcy case on behalf of the Corporation;

RESOLVED FURTHER, that the Authorized Officers are hereby authorized and directed to appear in all bankruptcy proceedings on behalf of the Corporation, and to otherwise do and perform all acts and deeds and to execute and deliver all necessary documents on behalf of the Corporation in connection with such bankruptcy case;

RESOLVED FURTHER, that the Authorized Officers are hereby authorized and directed to employ the law firm of Squire, Sanders & Dempsey L.L.P. and its members and associates to represent the Corporation in such bankruptcy case;

RESOLVED FURTHER, that the officers of the Corporation, or any of them, and other persons appointed to act on the Corporation's behalf in connection with the bankruptcy filing are hereby authorized and empowered by and on behalf of the Corporation and in its name, to execute and deliver all applications, certificates, agreements or any other instruments or documents or any amendments or supplements thereto and to do and to cause any and all other acts and things as they or any of them may deem necessary or appropriate to effectuate the purpose of the foregoing resolutions and the execution by such officer or officers of such documents shall conclusively establish their authority therefore from the Corporation and the approval and ratification by the Corporation of such documents so executed and the actions so taken;

RESOLVED FURTHER, that any such action taken prior to the effective date of this Consent by the officers of the Corporation, or any of them, and other persons appointed to act on the Corporation's behalf in connection with the foregoing resolutions, hereby are ratified, confirmed and approved by the Corporation; and

RESOLVED FURTHER, that this Consent, when executed by the proper signatories hereto, shall be effective as of ____________ ___, 1998.

* * * * * * * *

SPECIAL COMMITTEE OF THE BOARD OF DIRECTORS

/s/ Michael A. Jeffries
Michael A. Jeffries

/s/ John Casey
John Casey

/s/ John Lynch
John Lynch

/s/ Mark White
Mark White

/s/ Tyrell Garth
Tyrell Garth

UNITED STATES BANKRUPTCY COURT
DISTRICT OF ARIZONA

Unison Healthcare Corporation

Case No. ________
Chapter 11

List Of Creditors Holding 20 Largest Unsecured Claims

Name of creditor and complete mailing address including zip code	Name, telephone number and complete mailing address, including zip code, of employee, agent, or dept. of creditor familiar with claim who may be contaded	Nature of claim (trade debt, bank loan, gov- ernment contract, etc.)	Indicate if claim is contingent, unliquidated, disputed or subject to setoff	Amount of claim [if secured also state value of security]
First Bank National Association First Trust Center 180 East Fifth Street, Ste. 200 St. Paul, MN 55101	Frank Leslie First Trust Center 180 East Fifth Street, #200 St. Paul, MN 55101 (612) 244-9721 TEL (612) 244-0711 FAX	12-1/4% Senior Notes due 2006; Debt Offering	See Note[11]	$ 100,000,000[12]
Dean Witter 2 World Trade Center, 72nd Floor New York, NY 10048	Peter Avelar Dean Witter 2 World Trade Center 72nd Floor New York, NY 10048 (212) 392-0409 TEL (212) 392-1648 FAX	Notes	See Note[1]	$ 47,000,000[2]
IBJ Schroder Bank & Trust Co. 1 State Street, 11th Floor New York, NY 10004	Lance Wickel 1 State Street, 11th Floor New York, NY 10004 (212) 858-2203 TEL (212) 858-2156 FAX	13% Senior Notes due 1999; Forbearance Agreement	See Note[1]	$ 20,000,000[2]
Capital Group Companies 333 South Hope Street Los Angeles, CA 90071	Glenn Payne David Daigle Capital Group Companies 333 Soouth Hope Street Los Angeles, CA 90071 (213) 486-9200 TEL (310) 996-6041 FAX	Notes	See Note[1]	$ 16,000,000[2]
UBS Asset Management 1345 Avenue of Americas 48th Floor New York, NY 10105	Victor Consoli Gred Hradsky 1345 Avenue of Americas 48th Floor New York, NY 10105 (212) 821-6452 TEL (212) 821-6299 FAX	Notes	See Note[1]	$ 14,700,000[2]
Baker Nye, L.P. 767 5th Avenue, Suite 2800 New York, NY 10153	Mathew Glass Baker Nye, L.P. 767 5th Avenue, Suite 2800 New York, NY 10153	Notes	See Note[1]	$ 10,000,000[2]
Cargill Financial Services Corp. 6000 Clearwater Drive Minnetonka, MN 55343-9497	Steven M. Adams Cargill Financial Services Corp. 6000 Clearwater Drive Minnetonka, MN 55343-9497 (612) 984-3404 TEL (612) 984-3898 FAX	Notes	See Note[1]	$ 10,000,000[2]
Bank of America Personal Trust 555 S. Flower Street,	Rosa DeLaToore Bank of American Personal Trust	Notes	See Note[1]	$ 7,300,000[2]

---

[11] Debtor is currently examining the status of this creditor's claim and its classification is pending further review.

[12] Debtor is currently examining this creditor's claim, and its amount is subject to amendment.

Bank of Montreal c/o Harris Trust & Savings Bank 111 West Monroe Street, 1150 Chicago, IL 60603	Lacy Watkins Harris Trust & Savings Bank Proxy Operations 111 West Monroe Street 1130 Chicago, IL 60603 (312) 845-2174 TEL (312) 461-7954 FAX	Notes	See Note[13]	$ 6,500,000[14]
CMS Therapies, Inc./RehabWorks 4235 S. Stream Blvd. #400 Charlotte, NC 28217	Ron Pierce CMS Therapies, Inc./RehabWorks 4235 S. Stream Blvd. #300 Charlotte, NC 28217 (800) 477-4002 TEL	Trade Payable	Fixed, Liquidated	$ 1,098,820
Quarles & Brady One East Camelback Road Phoenix, AZ 85012	Robert Moya Quarles & Brady One East Camelback Road Phoenix, AZ 85012 (602) 230-5500 TEL	Trade Payable	Fixed, Liquidated	$ 323,279
Spine Rehabilitation and Physical Therapy Center, Inc. 3635 A Bienville Blvd. Ocean Springs, MS 39564	Spine Rehabilitation and Physical Therapy Center, Inc. Douglas L. Bates 3635 A Bienville Blvd. Ocean Springs, MS 39564 (601) 875-1898 TEL	Trade Payable	Fixed, Liquidated	$ 300,000
Ernst & Young LLP 40 North Central Ave. Phoenix, AZ 85004	Dee Balle Ernst & Young LLP 40 North Central Ave. Phoenix, AZ 85004 (602) 452-8000 TEL	Trade Payable	Fixed, Liquidated	$ 218,896
National Union Fire Insurance 175 Water St. New York, NY 10038	National Union Fire Insurance 175 Water St. New York, NY 10038 (212) 770-7000 TEL	Trade Payable	Fixed, Liquidated	$ 160,597
Spencer Stuart 10900 Wilshire Blvd. Los Angeles, CA 90024	Spencer Stuart 10900 Wilshire Blvd. Los Angeles, CA 90024 (310) 209-0610 TEL	Trade Payable	Fixed, Liquidated	$ 135,215
Gibson, Dunn & Crutcher LLP 1050 Connecticut Ave NW #900 Washington, DC 20036-5306	Gibson, Dunn & Crutcher LLP 1050 Connecticut Ave NW #900 Washington, DC 20036-5306 (202) 955-8500 TEL	Trade Payable	Fixed, Liquidated	$ 71,381
A I Credit Corporation 101 Federal St. Boston, MA 2110	Lura Kiernan A I Credit Corporation 101 Federal St. Boston, MA 02110 (617) 345-6437 TEL	Trade Payable	Fixed, Liquidated	$ 50,155
Vencor Hospital P. O. Box 100877 Atlanta, GA 30384	Vencor Hospital P. O. Box 100877 Atlanta, GA 30384 (404) 873-2871 TEL	Trade Payable	Fixed, Liquidated	$ 44,473
Bowne of Phoenix P. O. Box 29699 Phoenix, AZ 85038	Emily McCormack Bowne of Phoenix P. O. Box 29699 Phoenix, AZ 85038 (602) 223-4455 TEL	Trade Payable	Fixed, Liquidated	$ 40,727
AON Risk Services 99 High Street Boston, MA 2110	AON Risk Services 99 High Street Boston, MA 02110 (617) 589-3625 TEL	Trade Payable	Fixed, Liquidated	$ 34,193
*** Excluding Insider Creditors**				

I, Clayton Kloehr, Senior Vice President of the corporation named as a debtor in this case, declare under penalty of perjury that I have read the foregoing list and that it is true and correct to the best of my information and belief.

Date: ____________ Signature: ________________________

[13] Debtor is currently examining the status of this creditor's claim and its classification is pending further review.

[14] Debtor is currently examining this creditor's claim, and its amount is subject to amendment.

UNITED STATES BANKRUPTCY COURT
District of Arizona

In re: Unison Healthcare Corporation

Case No.___________
Chapter 11

VERIFICATION OF CREDITOR MATRIX

The above named debtor does hereby certify under penalty of perjury that the attached Master Mailing List of creditors, consisting of ___ sheet(s) is complete, correct and consistent with the debtor's schedules pursuant to Local Bankruptcy Rules and I assume all responsibility for errors and omissions.

APPENDIX E

SAMPLE "FIRST DAY ORDERS"

This Appendix contains some selected first day motions and ***First Day Orders*** filed in the Chapter 11 case of ***Unison HealthCare Corporation*** (involving a parent company and 32 subsidiaries and affiliates), a large bankruptcy of a nursing home provider, in May 1998. These particular first day motions involved some administrative and ministerial matters (such as the consolidation of all of the bankruptcy cases in front of one judge and having the Bankruptcy Court set the type of caption and other such logistics) to some more substantive matters (involving payment of prepetition wages and also payments of so-called "critical vendors"). Note that the first day motions were supported by an omnibus affidavit of a senior officer of the debtor, and the orders that were entered were entered as ***Interim Orders*** subject to ***negative notice***.

In addition to the motions that are contained in this Appendix, cash collateral motions and DIP financing motions were also filed as part of the first day motions in those Chapter 11 cases. Those matters would have been addressed by separate pleadings and supporting affidavits. In some jurisdictions, each type of relief sought might be filed as a separate motion or they might be combined as a single motion (as was done in the pleadings in this Appendix from *Unison HealthCare*). The importance of having an accompanying affidavit of an officer of the debtor is that the Bankruptcy Court will have an evidentiary basis upon which to grant the ***ex parte*** relief being requested. The nature, scope and types of first day motions and orders that are sought in a particular case will depend upon the type of business engaged in, and also the types of relief that the bankruptcy judges presiding over the particular bankruptcy case will grant.

All of the information in this Appendix is a matter of public record on file with the United States Bankruptcy Court, so no confidences or privileges are affected by their publication.

Thomas J. Salerno, Esq.
Craig D. Hansen, Esq.
Jordan A. Kroop, Esq.
SQUIRE, SANDERS & DEMPSEY L.L.P.
40 North Central, Suite 2700
Phoenix, Arizona 85004
(602) 528-4000

Attorneys for Debtors

IN THE UNITED STATES BANKRUPTCY COURT
FOR THE DISTRICT OF ARIZONA

In re: UNISON HEALTHCARE CORPORATION, and related proceedings, Federal I.D. No. 86-0684011 Debtors.	In Proceedings Under Chapter 11 Case No. B-98-06583-PHX-GBN (Jointly Administered)

APPLICABLE DEBTOR(S)	(Check)
UNISON HEALTHCARE CORPORATION (Case No. 98-06583-PHX-RGM)	☒
SUNQUEST SPC, INC. (Case No. 98-06584-PHX-SSC)	☒
BRITWILL HEALTHCARE COMPANY (Case No. 98-06585-PHX-SSC)	☒
BRITWILL FUNDING CORPORATION (Case No. 98-06602-PHX-CGC)	☒
MEMPHIS CLINICAL LABORATORY, INC. (Case No. 98-06588-PHX-CGC)	☒
AMERICAN PROFESSIONAL HOLDINGS, INC. (Case No. 98-06587-PHX-GBN)	☒
AMPRO MEDICAL SERVICES, INC. (Case No. 98-06609-PHX-GBN)	☒
GAMMA LABORATORIES, INC. (Case No. 98-06611-PHX-SSC)	☒
SIGNATURE HEALTH CARE CORPORATION (Case No. 98-06591-PHX-SSC)	☒
BROOKSHIRE HOUSE INC. (Case No. 98-06608-PHX-RGM)	☒
CHRISTOPHER NURSING CENTER, INC. (Case No. 98-06596-PHX-JMM)	☒
AMBERWOOD COURT, INC. (Case No. 98-06597-PHX-RGM)	☒
THE ARBORS HEALTH CARE CORPORATION (Case No. 98-06598-PHX-CGC)	☒
LOS ARCOS, INC. (Case No. 98-06603-PHX-RGM)	☒

EX PARTE MOTION FOR ORDER AUTHORIZING JOINT ADMINISTRATION AND UTILIZATION OF A JOINT CREDITORS' COMMITTEE

PUEBLO NORTE, INC. ☒)
(Case No. 98-06604-PHX-RTB))
RIO VERDE NURSING CENTER, Inc. ☒)
(Case No. 98-06606-PHX-CGC))
SIGNATURE MANAGEMENT GROUP, INC. ☒)
(Case No. 98-06605-PHX-GBN))
CORNERSTONE CARE CENTER, INC. ☒)
(Case No. 98-06595-PHX-RTB))
ARKANSAS, INC. ☒)
(Case No. 98-06590-PHX-GBN))
DOUGLAS MANOR, INC. ☒)
(Case No. 98-06589-PHX-CGC))
SAFFORD CARE, INC. ☒)
(Case No. 98-06593-PHX-RTB))
REHABWEST, INC. ☒)
(Case No. 98-06594PHX-CGC))
QUEST PHARMACIES, INC. ☒)
(Case No. 98-06586-PHX-RGM))
SUNBELT THERAPY MANAGEMENT SERVICES, INC.)
(ALABAMA) ☒)
(Case No. 98-06607-PHX-RTB))
DECATUR SPORTS FIT & WELLNESS CENTER,)
INC. ☒)
(Case No. 98-06601-PHX-SSC))
THERAPY HEALTH SYSTEMS, INC. ☒)
(Case No. 98-06600-PHX-GBN))
HENDERSON & ASSOCIATES REHABILITATION,)
INC. ☒)
(Case No. 98-06599-PHX-SSC))
SUNBELT THERAPY MANAGEMENT SERVICES, INC.)
(ARIZONA) ☒)
(Case No. 98-06592-PHX-RGM))
CEDAR CARE, INC. ☒)
(Case No. 98-06612-PHX-GBN))
SHERWOOD HEALTHCARE CORP. ☒)
(Case No. 98-06610-PHX-SSC))
BRITWILL INVESTMENTS-I, INC. ☒)
(Case No. 98-0173-PHX-GBN))
BRITWILL INVESTMENTS-II, INC. ☒)
(Case No. 98-0174-PHX-GBN))
BRITWILL INDIANA PARTNERSHIP ☒)
(Case No. 98-0175-PHX-GBN))

UNISON HEALTHCARE CORPORATION, INC., a Delaware corporation ("Unison" or the "Debtor"), together with all of its wholly owned operating subsidiaries, Debtors and Debtors-In-Possession herein (collectively, the "Debtors"), by and through undersigned counsel, and pursuant to Bankruptcy Rule 1015, respectfully request that this Court enter an Order authorizing: (1) the joint administration of Debtors' estates; and (2) the utilization of a joint creditors' committee.

Three of the above captioned Debtors, Britwill Investments-I, Inc., Britwill Investments II, Inc. and Britwill Indiana Partnership (collectively, the "Britwill Entities"), filed petitions for relief under Chapter 11 or Title 11 of the United States Code (the "Bankruptcy Code") on January 7, 1998. On January 8, 1998, this Court entered an order authorizing and directing joint administration of the Britwill Entities before the Honorable George N. Nielsen. On January 28, 1998, pursuant to Sections 1102(a) and 1102(b) of the Bankruptcy Code, the Office of the United States Trustee appointed six creditors to serve as members of the Official Committee of Unsecured Creditors (the "Britwill Committee"). Shortly thereafter, the Britwill Committee retained the services of Milbank, Tweed, Hadley & mccloy ("Milbank Tweed") as counsel for the Britwill Committee. Since then, Milbank Tweed has spent a considerable amount of time reviewing and analyzing the relevant facts and issues and has been actively involved in the Britwill Entities' Chapter 11 cases.

On the petition date, Unison and substantially all of its other wholly owned subsidiaries (the "Unison Entities") filed petitions for relief under Chapter 11 of the Bankruptcy Code. The Unison Entities and the Britwill Entities are affiliates as that term is defined in Section 101(2) of the Bankruptcy Code. Specifically, all of the entities are subsidiaries of Unison, a company which is engaged in the business of providing long-term and specialty healthcare services. Accordingly, the Debtors respectfully request that the court enter an Order authorizing joint administration of the Debtors' estates before the Honorable George B. Nielsen in accordance with Bankruptcy Rule 1015, applicable herein and utilization of a joint creditors' committee in the Debtors' cases. Judge Nielsen has been presiding over the Britwill Entities' Chapter 11 cases and is familiar with much of the procedural and historical background of the Debtors' businesses.

Joint administration and utilization of a joint committee will not result in any prejudice of the creditors in these cases. In fact, utilization of a joint committee and joint administration is in the best interest of these bankruptcy estates since the issues in each of the above captioned proceedings pertain to common ownership, creditor and management interests. Furthermore, many of the motions, hearings and orders in these cases will affect each of the Debtors. In addition, the vast majority of unsecured debt in the Debtors' cases is held by the same bondholders who are listed on every individual Debtors' petition. As these bondholders are well represented on the Britwill Committee, the Britwill Committee is representative of all of the Debtors' unsecured creditors. With respect to the representation of trade creditors, those creditors currently appointed to the Britwill Committee are representative of the trade creditors holding claims against the Unison Entities. Consequently, joint administration and utilization of a joint committee will facilitate the administration process, as well as ease the burden and expense of administering these estates.

CONCLUSION AND RELIEF REQUESTED.

Debtors respectfully pray for entry of an Order authorizing joint administration of these estates before the Honorable George G. Nielsen and utilization of a joint committee, such joint committee to consist of either: (1) all of the members of the current Britwill Committee; or (2) an expanded version of the Britwill Committee, which will include all of the members of the current Britwill Committee with the addition of a few new members off of the Unison Entities' list of top twenty unsecured creditors.

RESPECTFULLY SUBMITTED this 28th day of May, 1998.

SQUIRE, SANDERS & DEMPSEY L.L.P.
Two Renaissance Square
40 North Central Avenue, Suite 2700
Phoenix, Arizona 85004-4441

By: ***/s/ Thomas J. Salerno***
Thomas J. Salerno, Esq.
Craig D. Hansen, Esq.
Jordan A. Kroop, Esq.

Attorneys for Debtors

Thomas J. Salerno, Esq.
Craig D. Hansen, Esq.
Jordan A. Kroop, Esq.
SQUIRE, SANDERS & DEMPSEY L.L.P.
40 North Central, Suite 2700
Phoenix, Arizona 85004
(602) 528-4000

Attorneys for Debtors

IN THE UNITED STATES BANKRUPTCY COURT
FOR THE DISTRICT OF ARIZONA

In re: UNISON HEALTHCARE CORPORATION, and related proceedings, Federal I.D. No. 86-0684011 Debtors.	In Proceedings Under Chapter 11 Case No. B-98-06583-PHX-GBN (Jointly Administered)

APPLICABLE DEBTOR(S)	(Check)
UNISON HEALTHCARE CORPORATION (Case No. 98-06583-PHX-RGM)	☒
SUNQUEST SPC, INC. (Case No. 98-06584-PHX-SSC)	☒
BRITWILL HEALTHCARE COMPANY (Case No. 98-06585-PHX-SSC)	☒
BRITWILL FUNDING CORPORATION (Case No. 98-06602-PHX-CGC)	☒
MEMPHIS CLINICAL LABORATORY, INC. (Case No. 98-06588-PHX-CGC)	☒
AMERICAN PROFESSIONAL HOLDINGS, INC. (Case No. 98-06587-PHX-GBN)	☒
AMPRO MEDICAL SERVICES, INC. (Case No. 98-06609-PHX-GBN)	☒
GAMMA LABORATORIES, INC. (Case No. 98-06611-PHX-SSC)	☒
SIGNATURE HEALTH CARE CORPORATION (Case No. 98-06591-PHX-SSC)	☒

ORDER DIRECTING JOINT ADMINISTRATION OF A JOINT CREDITORS' COMMITTEE

BROOKSHIRE HOUSE INC. ☒)
(Case No. 98-06608-PHX-RGM))
CHRISTOPHER NURSING CENTER, INC. ☒)
(Case No. 98-06596-PHX-JMM))
AMBERWOOD COURT, INC. ☒)
(Case No. 98-06597-PHX-RGM))
THE ARBORS HEALTH CARE CORPORATION ☒)
(Case No. 98-06598-PHX-CGC))
LOS ARCOS, INC. ☒)
(Case No. 98-06603-PHX-RGM))
PUEBLO NORTE, INC. ☒)
(Case No. 98-06604-PHX-RTB))
RIO VERDE NURSING CENTER, Inc. ☒)
(Case No. 98-06606-PHX-CGC))
SIGNATURE MANAGEMENT GROUP, INC. ☒)
(Case No. 98-06605-PHX-GBN))
CORNERSTONE CARE CENTER, INC. ☒)
(Case No. 98-06595-PHX-RTB))
ARKANSAS, INC. ☒)
(Case No. 98-06590-PHX-GBN))
DOUGLAS MANOR, INC. ☒)
(Case No. 98-06589-PHX-CGC))
SAFFORD CARE, INC. ☒)
(Case No. 98-06593-PHX-RTB))
REHABWEST, INC. ☒)
(Case No. 98-06594PHX-CGC))
QUEST PHARMACIES, INC. ☒)
(Case No. 98-06586-PHX-RGM))
SUNBELT THERAPY MANAGEMENT SERVICES, INC.)
(ALABAMA) ☒)
(Case No. 98-06607-PHX-RTB))
DECATUR SPORTS FIT & WELLNESS CENTER,)
INC. ☒)
(Case No. 98-06601-PHX-SSC))
THERAPY HEALTH SYSTEMS, INC. ☒)
(Case No. 98-06600-PHX-GBN))
HENDERSON & ASSOCIATES REHABILITATION,)
INC. ☒)
(Case No. 98-06599-PHX-SSC))
SUNBELT THERAPY MANAGEMENT SERVICES, INC)
(ARIZONA) ☒)
(Case No. 98-06592-PHX-RGM))
CEDAR CARE, INC. ☒)
(Case No. 98-06612-PHX-GBN))
SHERWOOD HEALTHCARE CORP. ☒)
(Case No. 98-06610-PHX-SSC))
BRITWILL INVESTMENTS-I, INC. ☒)
(Case No. 98-0173-PHX-GBN))
BRITWILL INVESTMENTS-II, INC. ☒)
(Case No. 98-0174-PHX-GBN))
BRITWILL INDIANA PARTNERSHIP ☒)
(Case No. 98-0175-PHX-GBN))
)
______________________________________)

This matter came before the Court pursuant to the "Ex Parte Motion for Order Directing Joint Administration" (the "Motion") filed on May 28, 1998 by the Debtors.[1] In light of the foregoing, and good cause appearing therefor,

IT IS HEREBY ORDERED, that the above captioned cases shall be, and hereby are, authorized to utilize a joint creditors committee, such joint committee to consist of either: (1) all of the members of the current Britwill Committee; or (2) an expanded version of the Britwill Committee, which will include all of the members of the current Britwill Committee with the addition of a few new members off of the Unison Entities' list of top twenty unsecured creditors.

IT IS FURTHER ORDERED, that the above captioned cases shall be, and hereby are, consolidated, for procedural purposes only, and shall be administered jointly before the Honorable George B. Nielsen, Jr. (collectively the "Consolidated Cases") under the name of *In re Unison Healthcare Corporation*, Case Number 98-06583-PHX-GBN as set forth above and in accordance with the provisions of Rule 1015 of the Federal Rules of Bankruptcy Procedure. The caption of the consolidated cases shall read as follows:

A. If the filing relates to all Consolidated Cases:

In re: UNISON HEALTHCARE CORPORATION and Related proceedings, Debtors.	In Proceedings Under Chapter 11 Case Nos. B-98-0173- through 6612-PHX-GBN

B. If the filing relates to only a specific debtor:

In re: UNISON HEALTHCARE CORPORATION, and related proceedings, Federal I.D. No. 86-0684011 Debtors.		In Proceedings Under Chapter 11 Case No. B-98-06583- through 6612-PHX-GBN (Jointly Administered)
APPLICABLE DEBTOR(S)	(Check)	
UNISON HEALTHCARE CORPORATION (Case No. 98-06583-PHX-RGM)	☐	
SUNQUEST SPC, INC. (Case No. 98-06584-PHX-SSC)	☐	

[1] All terms not otherwise defined herein shall have the meanings set forth in the Motion.

BRITWILL HEALTHCARE COMPANY ☐
(Case No. 98-06585-PHX-SSC)
BRITWILL FUNDING CORPORATION ☐
(Case No. 98-06602-PHX-CGC)
MEMPHIS CLINICAL LABORATORY , INC. ☐
(Case No. 98-06588-PHX-CGC)
AMERICAN PROFESSIONAL HOLDINGS, INC. ☐
(Case No. 98-06587-PHX-GBN)
AMPRO MEDICAL SERVICES, INC. ☐
(Case No. 98-06609-PHX-GBN)
GAMMA LABORATORIES, INC. ☐
(Case No. 98-06611-PHX-SSC)
SIGNATURE HEALTH CARE CORPORATION ☐
(Case No. 98-06591-PHX-SSC)
BROOKSHIRE HOUSE INC. ☐
(Case No. 98-06608-PHX-RGM)
CHRISTOPHER NURSING CENTER, INC. ☐
(Case No. 98-06596-PHX-JMM)
AMBERWOOD COURT, INC. ☐
(Case No. 98-06597-PHX-RGM)
THE ARBORS HEALTH CARE CORPORATION ☐
(Case No. 98-06598-PHX-CGC)
LOS ARCOS, INC. ☐
(Case No. 98-06603-PHX-RGM)
PUEBLO NORTE, INC. ☐
(Case No. 98-06604-PHX-RTB)
RIO VERDE NURSING CENTER, Inc. ☐
(Case No. 98-06606-PHX-CGC)
SIGNATURE MANAGEMENT GROUP, INC. ☐
(Case No. 98-06605-PHX-GBN)
CORNERSTONE CARE CENTER, INC. ☐
(Case No. 98-06595-PHX-RTB)
ARKANSAS, INC. ☐
(Case No. 98-06590-PHX-GBN)
DOUGLAS MANOR, INC. ☐
(Case No. 98-06589-PHX-CGC)
SAFFORD CARE, INC. ☐
(Case No. 98-06593-PHX-RTB)
REHABWEST, INC. ☐
(Case No. 98-06594PHX-CGC)
QUEST PHARMACIES, INC. ☐
(Case No. 98-06586-PHX-RGM)
SUNBELT THERAPY MANAGEMENT SERVICES, INC. (ALABAMA) ☐
(Case No. 98-06607-PHX-RTB)
DECATUR SPORTS FIT & WELLNESS CENTER, INC. ☐
(Case No. 98-06601-PHX-SSC)
THERAPY HEALTH SYSTEMS, INC. ☐
(Case No. 98-06600-PHX-GBN)
HENDERSON & ASSOCIATES REHABILITATION, INC. ☐
(Case No. 98-06599-PHX-SSC)
SUNBELT THERAPY MANAGEMENT SERVICES, INC (ARIZONA) ☐
(Case No. 98-06592-PHX-RGM)
CEDAR CARE, INC. ☐
(Case No. 98-06612-PHX-GBN)
SHERWOOD HEALTHCARE CORP. ☐
(Case No. 98-06610-PHX-SSC)
BRITWILL INVESTMENTS-I, INC. ☐
(Case No. 98-0173-PHX-GBN)
BRITWILL INVESTMENTS-II, INC. ☐
(Case No. 98-0174-PHX-GBN)
BRITWILL INDIANA PARTNERSHIP ☐
(Case No. 98-0175-PHX-GBN)

IT IS FURTHER ORDERED, that all original docket entries shall be made on the docket of *In re Unison Healthcare Corporation*, Case Number 98-006583-PHX-GBN, and a docket entry shall be made on the dockets of Case Nos. 98-06583 through 98-06612 and Case Nos. 98-0173 through 98-0175 substantially as follows: "An order has been entered consolidating this case for procedural purposes only and providing for its joint administration with *In re Unison Healthcare Corporation*, Case No. 98-06583-PHX-GBN."

IT IS FURTHER ORDERED, that Debtors shall immediately serve this Order on the United States Trustee, the unsecured creditors' committee for the Britwill Entities, the twenty (20) largest unsecured creditors of each Unison Entity and any other party requesting special notice. Any party objecting to this Order shall do so in writing, to be timely filed with the court within twenty (20) days of service of this Order, and to be served on counsel for Debtors as follows:

Thomas J. Salerno, Esq.
Craig D. Hansen, Esq.
Jordan A. Kroop, Esq.
Squire, Sanders & Dempsey L.L.P.
40 North Central, Suite 2700
Phoenix, Arizona 85004

If no objections are timely filed, this Order shall become final.

Dated: May 28, 1998

/s/ ***George B. Nielsen, Jr.***
HON. GEORGE B. NIELSEN, JR.
CHIEF JUDGE, UNITED STATES
BANKRUPTCY COURT

Thomas J. Salerno, Esq.
Craig D. Hansen, Esq.
Jordan A. Kroop, Esq.
Squire, Sanders & Dempsey L.L.P.
Two Renaissance Square
40 North Central Avenue, Suite 2700
Phoenix, Arizona 85004-4441
(602) 528-4000

Attorney for Debtors

IN THE UNITED STATES BANKRUPTCY COURT
FOR THE DISTRICT OF ARIZONA

In re:	) In Proceedings Under Chapter 11
UNISON HEALTHCARE CORPORATION, a Delaware corporation, and its affiliated and related entities,	) Case Nos. B-98-0173 through B-98-6612-PHX-GBN
Debtors.	) **EX PARTE MOTION FOR AUTHORITY TO: (1) MAINTAIN DEBTORS' EXISTING ACCOUNTS, CASH MANAGEMENT SYSTEM AND BUSINESS FORMS; (2) PAY WAGES, SALARIES, EMPLOYMENT TAXES, EMPLOYEE BENEFITS AND WORKERS' COMPENSATION PAYMENTS; AND (3) PAY CERTAIN PREPETITION CLAIMS OF ESSENTIAL VENDORS AND SUPPLIERS**

UNISON HEALTHCARE CORPORATION, INC., a Delaware corporation, ("Unison" or the "Debtor"), together with the wholly owned operating subsidiaries indicated above (collectively, the "Debtors"), Debtors and Debtors-in-Possession herein, by and through undersigned counsel, respectfully submit this Ex Parte Motion seeking authority: (1) for maintenance of the Debtors' Bank accounts, cash management system, and business forms (the "Cash Management Protocol"); (2) to pay wages, salaries, employment taxes, employee benefit payments and workers' compensation payments (the "Payroll And Benefits Protocol"); and (3) to pay certain prepetition claims of essential vendors and supplies (the "Essential Vendor Protocol") (collectively the "First Day Motion").

This First Day Motion is supported by the accompanying Memorandum of Points and Authorities, the "Affidavit of Clayton Kloehr" filed contemporaneously herewith, and the record herein.

RESPECTFULLY SUBMITTED this 28th day of May, 1998.

SQUIRE, SANDERS & DEMPSEY L.L.P.
Two Renaissance Square
40 North Central Avenue, Suite 2700
Phoenix, Arizona 85004-4441

By: *<u>/s/ Thomas J. Salerno, Esq.</u>*
Thomas J. Salerno
Craig D. Hansen, Esq.
Jordan A. Kroop, Esq.

Attorneys for Debtors

MEMORANDUM OF POINTS AND AUTHORITIES

I. FACTUAL AND PROCEDURAL BACKGROUND.

1.1. Voluntary Petitions. Debtors commenced these cases on May 28, 1998 by filing voluntary petitions for relief under Chapter 11 of Title 11 of the United States Code (the "Bankruptcy Code").

1.2. Healthcare Entities. Debtors are primarily engaged in the business of providing comprehensive long-term and specialty healthcare services. The majority of Debtors' operating entities are dedicated to providing healthcare facilities (the "Healthcare Entities"). The Healthcare Entities currently operate approximately 30 skilled nursing facilities (collectively, the "Healthcare Facilities") located in Arizona, Alabama, Colorado, Indiana, Idaho, Kansas, Mississippi, Nevada, Pennsylvania, Texas, and Washington. The Healthcare Facilities contain approximately 2,579 licensed beds. Attached hereto as Exhibit "1" is a list of the 30 Healthcare Facilities operated by the Debtors.

1.3. Ancillary Entities. In addition, Debtors operate entities which act as suppliers of certain laboratory, pharmacy, and therapy services (the "Ancillary Entities"). The Ancillary Entities supply their products and services to the Debtors' Healthcare Facilities as well as to other, non-affiliated facilities. Attached hereto as Exhibit "2" is a list of the eleven Ancillary Entities operated by the Debtors. Combined, the Healthcare Entities and the Ancillary Entities employ approximately 2,812 individuals.

1.4. Debtor-In-Possession Status. Debtors are operating their businesses and managing their assets as Debtors-in-Possession in accordance with Sections 1107 and 1108 of the Bankruptcy Code. No examiner, trustee, or unsecured creditors committee has been appointed in these cases.

1.5. Jurisdiction and Venue. This Court has jurisdiction over these cases pursuant to 28 U.S.C. § 1334. The subject matter of this Motion is a "core proceeding" pursuant to 28 U.S.C. § 157 (b)(2)(A) and (M). Venue is proper pursuant to 28 U.S.C. § 1408.

1.6. Notice. Notice of this First Day Motion has been given to the U. S. Trustee and any additional parties listed on the official service list.

II. CASH MANAGEMENT PROTOCOL

Existing Cash Management System

2.1. Cash Management System. The primary sources of cash collections for nursing services for all Healthcare Entities operating nursing home facilities include private pay, Medicare, Medicaid and commercial insurance revenue. The cash management function for nursing home facilities operated by the Healthcare Entities is centralized at the corporate headquarters located in Scottsdale, Arizona. Attached hereto as Exhibit "3" is a flow chart illustrating the Debtors' current cash management system.

Individual Facility Depository Accounts

2.2. Existing Bank Accounts. Each nursing facility maintains two bank accounts: a local depository account and a patient trust account.

2.3. Local Depository Account. A bank account exists for each nursing facility at a local bank near the facility (the "Local Account"). Deposits to the Local Accounts include payments from private pay residents, commercial insurance payors, and miscellaneous revenue (vending machine revenue, etc.). Revenues generated by a number of facilities are included as part of the collateral base under a secured revolving line of credit (the "Revolving Line") provided by Healthcare Financial Partners ("HCFP") to Unison and a number of its subsidiaries.[1] Under the terms of the Revolving Line, the Local Accounts are swept by wire transfer each Wednesday and Friday into a lockbox account (No. 1180-3511) maintained at Bank One Arizona.

2.4. Patient Trust Accounts. Each facility operated by a Healthcare Entity also maintains as trustee a local depository account for certain of the residents' personal funds. The Administrator and Director of Nursing of each facility are typically the authorized signers on the accounts. The facility business office manager reconciles the accounts and maintains a separate ledger for each resident. The accounts are interest bearing as required by federal regulation and the interest is allocated to each resident's balance at the end of the month. The maintenance of the patient trust accounts is done strictly at the individual facility level and the funds are not available for use by the facility or any Healthcare Entity.

Operating Accounts

2.5. Bank One Lockbox Account. In addition to the deposits made to the Local Accounts, which are swept into the Bank One lockbox (the "Lockbox") twice weekly, all Medicare and Medicaid revenues generated at each Healthcare Entity facility covered under the HCFP Revolving Line are directly deposited into the Lockbox in accordance with the terms of the Revolving Line. The Lockbox is then swept daily HCFP.

2.6. Wells Fargo General Account. Based upon availability under the Revolving Line, advances are made by HCFP into an account maintained by Unison at Wells Fargo Bank ("Wells Fargo"). The Wells Fargo account acts as a general operating account for Unison and the various

---

[1] Signature Health Care Corporation and its subsidiaries (the "Signature Entities") are not borrowers under the Revolving Line. The nursing home facilities operated by the Signature Entities maintain separate local depository and trust accounts. Revenues generated by the facilities and deposited into the local depository accounts are then transferred to the Fleet Bank Concentration Account.

Healthcare Entities. Deposits to the account include miscellaneous cash receipts from the corporate office and other related entities as well as advances from the HCFP Revolving Line. Disbursements from this account include wire transfers to the Fleet Bank concentration account to cover daily presentments, obligations to certain lease and mortgage holders, obligations to affiliate companies for intercompany advances, and various other disbursements as needed. Also, the lease payment to Care Computer, which is the provider of the accounts receivable software for all nursing facilities operated by the various Healthcare Entities, is automatically withdrawn each month.

2.7. Fleet Bank Concentration Account. The Fleet Bank concentration account's primary purpose is to automatically fund the checks presented on the controlled disbursement accounts and to fund drawdowns initiated by Ceridian Employer Services ("Ceridian"), which provides third-party administrative services for processing payroll for all Healthcare Entities. Payroll taxes for all nursing home facilities are withdrawn from the account one day before the pay date of each facility payroll. Amounts to be debited are determined by notifications faxed to the Unison treasury department from Ceridian, usually 2-3 days before the drawdown date. Deposits into this account include wire transfers from the Wells Fargo general account.

2.8. Zero Balance Accounts. Unison maintains three Zero Balance Accounts (ZBA), currently at Fleet Bank, from which it disburses payments for accounts payable, payroll, and health insurance claims for all nursing home facilities. The bank notifies Unison of check presentment totals and funding requirements by 9:15 a.m. ET through the on-line balance reporting system. The presentments are funded by the concentration account at Fleet Bank.

2.9. Accounts Payable. Accounts Payable for all Healthcare Entities are handled at the Scottsdale corporate office. An expenditure budget for all Healthcare Entities is compiled weekly. On a daily basis, cash requirement reports that itemize the invoices to be paid are approved for payment by the Unison treasurer or assistant treasurer before the checks are actually issued. The accounts payable department for Healthcare Entities consists of six clerks who report to the accounts payable manager. Five of the clerks are responsible for the processing of invoices for each facility within the five operating regions of Unison, while one is responsible for all home office invoices.

2.10. Payroll. The Payroll department prepares a summary of all payroll and tax liabilities by facility and date. The Unison treasury department uses the total payroll amounts to forecast check presentments for the period around the payroll date. Payroll tax amounts are used to verify that Ceridian is debiting the Fleet Bank concentration account for the correct tax amount. The payroll department consists of six clerks who report to the payroll manager. Five of the clerks are responsible for processing the payrolls for each facility within the five operating regions, while one is responsible for processing all garnishments for all facilities.

2.11. Health Insurance Claims. Unison currently uses a third party, United HealthCare, to administer claims for partially self-funded health insurance plan for all employees of nursing facilities operated by Healthcare Entities. United HealthCare submits a cash requirement report to the Unison Human Resources department for reconciliation on a weekly basis. Once reconciled, the Treasurer will sign off on the itemized claims and United HealthCare will write checks on Unison's behalf from the Fleet Bank Health Insurance Claims account to each of the payees.

2.12. Ancillary Entities' Accounts. The Ancillary Entities maintain several local bank accounts used for all deposits and all payroll and accounts payable disbursements. Most of these accounts are integrated into the overall cash management system, with all accounts payable and payroll for certain of the Ancillary Entities being processed through an operating account. Because these Ancillary Entities supply products and services to the Debtors' healthcare facilities as well as to other, non-affiliated facilities, the individual local bank accounts maintained by these Ancillary Entities are integrated into the overall cash management system to the extent necessary to facilitate the ongoing relationship between the Debtors and the Ancillary Entities.

MAINTENANCE OF THE CASH MANAGEMENT SYSTEM

2.13. Need for Cash Management System. It is essential to the Debtors' successful transition to Debtors-in-Possession and to ensure essential services to facility residents are not disrupted that the Debtors minimize any alteration to the present cash management system until such time as the Debtors can evaluate the system and establish and implement any necessary changes in accounting procedures by which the Debtors can more accurately maintain and track cash disbursements and income for each of the Debtors' facilities. The Debtors do not believe, however, in their best business judgment, that any changes are warranted, since cash flow is adequately documented for each facility by the current system.

2.14. Cash Management Protocol Proposal. The Debtors propose the following:

(a) The Debtors will maintain the existing cash management system and continue to utilize the system during the pendency of these cases, altering those procedures only to the extent necessary to address individual Debtor issues that may arise.

(b) The Debtors will maintain the existing Local Accounts and local patient trust accounts as they existed prepetition without reference to the Debtors' status as Debtors-in-Possession. Debtors submit that closing the existing Local Accounts offers no benefit to these estates while presenting Debtors with numerous undue and un necessary burdens.

(c) To the extent it becomes necessary, the Debtors will establish and implement as quickly as possible any necessary account procedures to allow personnel to better track cash revenues, accounts receivables and accounts payable generated by each Debtor.

2.15. Business Forms Maintenance. The Debtors further request, in light of the complex intercompany structure of the Debtors' operations and the sheer number of facilities operated by the Healthcare Entities, that the Debtors be authorized to maintain and utilize correspondence and business forms existing prepetition without reference to their status and Debtors-in-Possession.

2.16. Benefits of Cash Management Protocol. The Debtors believe that the above-described procedures will avoid interruptions of their existing business operations, will assist in a smooth and orderly post petition transition and is in the best interests of all parties in interest, including employees and creditors to these estates.

III. PAYROLL AND BENEFITS PROTOCOL.

Wages and Salaries

3.1. Employees. As of the petition date, the Debtors employed approximately 2,813 people. Specifically, the Healthcare Entities employed approximately 1,989 people, and the Ancillary Entities employed approximately 824 people. A table providing a complete breakdown of the number of employees employed by each Debtor entity, along with their corresponding monthly wages and benefits is attached hereto as Exhibit "4".

3.2. Third Party Administration. The Healthcare Entities utilize the services of Ceridian Employer Services ("Ceridian"), a third party administrator company, in order to perform services attendant to payroll distribution. The Healthcare Entities, through Ceridian, pay its employees on a biweekly basis in arrears. Thus, on each payday approximately 1,989 of the Debtors' work force receives payment for the period ending the preceding two weeks.

3.3 Healthcare Entities' Prepetition Payroll. On May 18, 20, 22, and 25, 1998, in accordance with the Healthcare Entities' customary practice, payroll checks in the amount of approximately $905,694 were distributed to the Healthcare Entities' employees. (The wages and salaries owed to the Healthcare Entities' employees referred to as the "Healthcare Entities' Prepetition Payroll").

3.4. Ancillary Entities. The Ancillary Entities do not utilize the services of Ceridian, and pay their employees directly on a bi-weekly basis in arrears. Thus, on each payday, approximately 824 of the Debtors' work force receives payment for the period ending the preceding two weeks.

3.5. Ancillary Entities' Prepetition Payroll. On May 22 and 26, 1998, in accordance with the Ancillary Entities' customary practice, payroll checks in the amount of approximately $1,030,000 were distributed to the Ancillary Entities employees. (The wages and salaries owed to the Ancillary Entities employees referred to as the "Ancillary Entities Prepetition Payroll").

3.6. Postpetition Payroll. As the Debtors' payroll obligations are spread out over a two week time frame, the Debtors have additional payroll days arising in the immediate future. In accordance with the Healthcare Entities' customary practice, the Healthcare Entities intend to distribute, via Ceridian, payroll checks on May 29, 1998 and June 1, 5 and 8, 1998, in the aggregate amount of approximately $905,694. Similarly, in accordance with the Ancillary Entities' customary practice, the Ancillary Entities intend to distribute payroll checks on June 5 and 9, 1998, in the aggregate amount of $1,030,000. (These wages and salaries are referred to collectively as the "Debtors' Postpetition Payroll".)

3.7. Request For Authority. As discussed in Section II, above, as part of the Cash Management Protocol, Debtors are requesting authority to: (a) continue to use the unified cash management system established by Unison; (b) maintain certain prepetition bank accounts; and (c) continue to use existing business forms and checks. Absent the preceding measures, Debtors believe that payroll checks previously issued to certain employees *i.e.*, the Healthcare Entities Prepetition Payroll and the Ancillary Entities Prepetition Payroll) may be dishonored by the banks upon which such checks were drawn due to the commencement of these proceedings and the creation of the new bank accounts. In order to ensure the payment of the individual employees, Debtors wish to maintain their current bank accounts to ensure that all Prepetition Payroll checks are honored in the ordinary course.

3.8. Honoring of Prepetition Payroll. In addition, due to potential time delays in opening the new bank accounts, Debtors believe that payroll checks to be issued in the immediate future (*i.e.*, the Debtors' Postpetition Payroll) may be dishonored. In this regard, Debtors wish to maintain their current bank accounts to ensure that the Debtors' Postpetition Payroll checks are honored in the ordinary course.

3.9 Priority Expenses. With respect to the majority of employees receiving wages and salaries in accordance with this Motion, amounts received do not exceed the amount which such employees would be entitled to as a priority payment in accordance with Section 507(a)(3) of the Bankruptcy Code. Based upon Debtors' payroll records, approximately 271 employees out of in excess of 2,812 employees (less than 1 % of Debtors' employees) have payroll checks above the statutory limitation of $4,000. Debtors submit that such excess amount is *de minimis* in the context of Debtors' Chapter 11 cases.

Employment Taxes

3.10. Fleet Bank Account. Necessarily attendant to the payment of the Debtors' Pre and Postpetition Payroll is the Debtors' obligation to pay federal and state withholding taxes. Debtors' concentration account maintained at Fleet Bank (the "Fleet Bank Account") provides funds for drawdowns initiated by Ceridian to pay these employment taxes for the employees to the Healthcare Entities. The Healthcare Entities' employment taxes are withdrawn from the Fleet Bank Account one (1) day prior to the pay date of each facility payroll. Amounts to be debited are determined by notifications faxed to Ceridian, usually 2-3 days prior to the drawdown date. The Healthcare Entities are current on all employment taxes, and wish to maintain their current method of payment through Ceridian in the ordinary course.

3.11. Ancillary Entities' Employment Taxes. As mentioned above, the Ancillary Entities do not use a third party payroll service such as Ceridian. Instead, the Ancillary Entities distribute payroll and pay withholding taxes directly. The Ancillary Entities utilize six (6) separate banks, each local to the individual Ancillary Entity, for the purpose of distributing payroll and paying payroll taxes. A list of the banks is as follows: (a) Gilmer National Bank, Gilmer, Texas; (b) Bloomfield State Bank, Bloomfield, Indiana; (c) Austin Bank, Whitehouse, Texas; (d) Colonial Bank, Birmingham, Alabama; (e) Bank One, Dallas, Texas; and (f) Mercantile Bank, Poplar Bluff, Missouri. The Ancillary Entities are current on all employment taxes, and wish to maintain their current method of payment in the ordinary course.

3.12. Employee Benefit Payments. In the ordinary course of business and as is customary with most companies, the Debtors have established various employee benefit plans and policies that provide present and former employees with health, life, disability and retirement benefits (the "Employee Benefits"). Some of the Debtors' payments for Employee Benefits (the "Employee Benefit Payments") are made to Debtors' insurers or other third parties; others are paid directly to employees. Debtors are current on all Employee Benefit Payments, and wish to maintain their current procedures for making the Employee Benefit Payments in the ordinary course.

3.13. Workers' Compensation Payments. Debtors maintain various policies and programs for workers' compensation, as required by law. These policies and programs generally fall into two categories: (a) self-insurance programs where the Debtors pay workers' compensation claims with respect to their employees on a regular basis, and (b) conventional insurance where the Debtors obtain coverage from third party insurers with respect to workers' compensation. In many instances where the Debtors act as a self-insurer, in order to comply with various state regulations, the Debtors provide the state with a bond, letter of credit or other type of assurance to secure their obligation as self-insurers.

3.14. Related Payments. In the ordinary course of business, Debtors: (a) process and pay all workers compensation claims related to Debtors existing and former employees (including all judgements and settlements related thereto) (collectively, the "Workers' Compensation Claims") in those instances where the Debtors are self-insurers, (b) pay all insurance premiums (the "Workers' Compensation Premiums") for insurance policies with various insurance companies with respect to workers' compensation; and (c) pay all administrative expenses (the "Workers' Compensation Administrative Expenses") associated with the maintenance of workers' compensation programs, including all expenses associated with processing of workers' compensation claims submitted, maintenance of insurance coverage, and action as is necessary to process workers' compensation claims covered by third party insurance policies.

IV. ESSENTIAL VENDOR PROTOCOL.

4.1. Essential Vendors and Suppliers. As described above, the Debtors, through the various Healthcare Entities, currently operate approximately 30 skilled nursing facilities servicing nearly 2,600 patients. In providing such healthcare services, the Debtors maintain ongoing relationships with dozens of vendors and suppliers that provide the Debtors with the necessary goods and services required for ongoing patient care. The goods and services purchased from certain of these vendors and suppliers (the "Essential Vendors and Suppliers") are so critical to patient care that any cessation in the provision of those goods and services would not only gravely compromise the Debtors' businesses, but would also virtually preclude the Debtors from meeting daily obligations to their patients.

4.2. Critical Nature of Goods and Services. These Essential Vendors and Suppliers provide the Debtors with such critical goods and services as goods, pharmaceuticals, laboratory supplies, respiratory therapy, physical therapy, linens, and medical forms. Certain of these Essential Vendors and Suppliers provide medical advisory services required by state and federal law, without which the Debtor would be unable to operate their healthcare facilities in compliance with such law. In addition, one Essential Vendor provides critical dietary consultation with respect to all the Debtors' healthcare facilities throughout the country. A list of the Essential Vendors and Suppliers subject to this Motion is attached as Exhibit "5."

4.3. Need For Retention of Critical Vendors. Because these Essential Vendors and Suppliers enable the Debtors to feed, medicate, and otherwise provide ongoing skilled nursing care to the Debtors' nearly 2,600 patients, it is essential that the Debtors retain vendors and suppliers in whom the Debtors have confidence and with whom the Debtors maintain good relations. Many such Essential Vendors and Suppliers service all the Debtors' healthcare facilities throughout the country, and it is likely that in many instances the Debtors' operations constitute a significant percentage of such Essential Vendors and Suppliers' businesses.

4.4. Competitive Arrangements with Critical Vendors. Based on their substantial experience with these Essential Vendors and Suppliers, the Debtors have confidence in the quality and reliability of their goods and services, and the Debtors believe that their contracts with them are at very competitive rates and on terms favorable to the Debtors.

4.5. Need to Avoid Compromise of Patient Care. The filing of the Debtors' petitions obviously cannot be permitted to effect ongoing services to the Debtors' patients. In light of the Debtors' critical obligations to their patients, and in light of the indispensable nature of the goods and services provided by the Essential Vendors and Suppliers, the Debtors must be able to maintain their strong relationships with such Essential Vendors and Suppliers throughout the pendency of these Chapter 11 cases. Maintaining such relationships, in fact, may be one of the most important steps during the beginning stages of these Chapter 11 cases in ensuring that the patient care is not compromised at any of the Debtors' facilities.

V. LEGAL ARGUMENT.

1. CASH MANAGEMENT AND PROTOCOL.

Given the substantial size and complexity of the Debtors' operations, the prospects for a successful reorganization of the Debtors' businesses, as well as the preservation and enhancement of the Debtors' respective values as going concerns, necessarily would be threatened by any disruption in the Debtors' ordinary and usual cash management proceeds. It is essential, therefore, that the Debtors be permitted to continue to consolidate the management of their cash and transfer monies from entity to entity, as necessary and in the ordinary course of business, including the Ancillary Entities, in amounts necessary to continue the efficient operation of the Debtors' businesses.

The basic transactions incident to the cash management system described above have been utilized by the Debtors with only minor modifications for several years, and constitute ordinary, usual and essential business practices. The cash management system is similar to those commonly employed by corporate enterprises comparable to the Debtors in size and complexity. The widespread use of such systems, moreover, is attributable to the numerous benefits they provide, including the ability to tightly control corporate funds, invest idle cash, insure cash availability, and reduce administrative expense by facilitating the movement of funds and the development of timely and accurate account balance and presentment information.

In addition, given the corporate and financial structure of the Debtors, it would be difficult, if not impossible, for the Debtors quickly and efficiently to establish a new system of accounts and a new cash management and disbursement system. For instance, the Debtors maintain their cash management system by means of a sophisticated computer system. If certain Debtors were to withdraw from this system, or if all Debtors were required to dismantle the cash management system, such Debtors would need to generate the information maintained on the central computer system and monitor and control the flow of cash manually at substantial additional costs to those Debtors' estates and creditors. Thus, under the circumstances, maintenance of the existing cash management system without disruption is not only essential, but also in the best interest of the Debtors' respective estates and creditors. Further, preserving a "business as usual" atmosphere and avoiding the unnecessary distractions that would inevitably be associated with any disruption in the Debtors' existing cash management system will facilitate the Debtors' ongoing efforts to emerge from Chapter 11 as quickly as possible.

A. *The Debtors' Continued Use of their Centralized Cash Management System is Consistent with Applicable Provisions of the Bankruptcy Code.*

Bankruptcy Courts routinely grant Chapter 11 debtors authority to continue utilizing existing cash management systems, treating requests for such authority as a relatively "simple matter." *In re Baldwin-United Corp.*, 79 B.R. 321, 327 (Bankr. S.D. Ohio 1987). This is particularly true where, as here, a Chapter 11 case involves affiliated entities with complex financial affairs. In *In re The Charter Co.*, 778 F.2d 617, 620 (11th Cir. 1985), for example, the bankruptcy court entered an order authorizing the debtor and 43 of its subsidiaries "to continue to consolidate the management of their cash as has been usual and customary in the past and to transfer monies from affiliated entity to entity, including operating entities that are not debtors." The Court of Appeals then affirmed a subsequent District Court decision denying a creditors motion for leave to appeal the bankruptcy court's cash management order, holding that authorizing the debtors to utilize their prepetition "routine cash management system" was "entirely consistent" with applicable provisions of the Bankruptcy Code. *Id. a*t 621.

Likewise, in another context, the Bankruptcy Court in the *Columbia Gas* Chapter 11 cases explained that a centralized cash management system "allows sufficient utilization of cash resources and recognizes the impracticalities of maintaining separate cash accounts for the many different purposes that require cash." *In re Columbia Gas Systems. Inc.*, 136 B.R. 930, 934 (Bankr. D. Del.) (examining validity of certain customer refund claims to funds maintained in debtors' centralized cash management system); *aff'd in part and rev'd in part*, 1992 U.S. Dist. LEXIS 9460 (D. Del. 1992), *aff'd in part and rev'd in part*, 997 F.2d 1039 (3rd Cir. 1993); *cert.*

denied sub nom, Official Committee of Unsecured Creditors v. Columbia Gas Transmission Com., 114 S. Ct. 1050 (1994).

The continued use of case management systems employed in the ordinary course of a debtors' prepetition business has also been approved as a routine matter at the outset of many large and complex Chapter 11 cases.[2]

B. Use of Existing Bank Accounts and Business Forms

It is also critical that, to avoid substantial disruption to the normal operation of their businesses and to preserve a "business as usual" atmosphere, the Debtors be permitted to use their existing bank accounts and business forms. Only if these accounts and forms are maintained with the same account numbers can the Debtors accomplish a smooth transition to operations in Chapter 11.

To protect against the possible inadvertent payment of prepetition claims, all banks with which the Debtors hold accounts will be advised immediately not to honor checks issued before the Petition Date, except as otherwise ordered by this Court.[3] The Debtors, moreover, have the capacity to distinguish clearly between pre- and postpetition obligations and payments without closing existing accounts and opening new ones.

The Debtors, and their estates and creditors, would be subject to tremendous administrative burdens and expenses if they were required to close and reopen accounts and create an entirely manual system for issuing checks and paying postpetition obligations. Accordingly, in order to avoid these burdens and expenses, the Debtors request authority to continue to utilize their prepetition bank accounts and business forms under existing account numbers.

Bankruptcy Courts routinely permit debtors to utilize their existing bank accounts, finding that such relief is entirely consistent with applicable provisions of the Bankruptcy Code. *See, e.g., In re New York City Shoes, Inc.*, 78 B.R. 426, 427 (Bankr. E.D. Pa. 1987); *In re Grant Broadcasting, Inc.*, 75 B.R. 819, 820 (E.D. Pa. 1987). In addition, Bankruptcy Courts

---

[2] *See, e.g., In re HSSI, Inc.*, 176 B.R. 809 (N.D. Ill. 1995); *In re Interco., Inc.*, 130 B.R. 301 (E.D. Mo. 1991); *In re FRG, Inc.*, 107 B.R. 461, 465 (Bankr. S.D.N.Y. 1989); *In re Family Health Services, Inc.*, 104 B.R. 279, 281 (Bankr. C.D. Cal. 1989), *rev'd on other grounds and remanded*, 143 B.R. 232 (C.D. Cal. 1992).

[3] For example, the Debtors have already filed motions requesting authority to pay, in the ordinary course of their business, certain prepetition wages, salaries, employee benefits, trade claims and other similar items for or on behalf of certain employees and vendors. If the Court grants the relief requested in these motions, the Debtors will immediately notify all appropriate banks that the checks relating to such items, as identified by the Debtors on a case-by-case basis, should continue to be honored.

routinely grant debtors in large and complex Chapter 11 cases authority to continue using existing checks, business forms, and other similar instruments without altering such instruments to include the legend "Debtor-in-Possession" or a so-called "Debtor-in-Possession number." *See, e.g., In re Johnson*, 106 R.R. 623, 624 (Bankr. D. Neb. 1989) (debtors not required to obtain new checks imprinted with "Debtor-in-Possession" legend).

2. *PAYROLL AND BENEFITS PROTOCOL.*

The Debtors seek authority to pay, in the ordinary course of business,amounts owing as of the Petition Date and to maintain on an uninterrupted basis all policies and programs with respect to: (a) wages and salaries; (b) employment taxes; (c) employee benefit payments; and (d) Workers' Compensation Administrative Expenses.

The payment of employees is an ordinary course transaction which is vital to the Debtors continued existence and viability. Failure to allow Debtors to honor these ordinary course payroll checks would greatly hinder Debtors' ability to effectively maintain the core group of employees necessary to effectuate the Debtors' successful restructuring.

Several courts have recognized the necessity for reorganization debtors to pay prepetition claims where such payment is essential to the debtor's continued operation. *See In re Ionosphere Clubs*, 98 B.R. 174 (Bankr. S.D.N.Y. 1989). The *Ionosphere Clubs* court observed that the doctrine of necessity permits "immediate payment of claims of creditors where those creditors will not supply services or materials essential to the conduct of the business until their prereorganization claims shall have been paid." *Id.* at 176. The doctrine of necessity as also recognized by the Ninth Circuit Court of Appeals in *In re Adams Apple, Inc.*, 829 F.2d 1484, 1490 (9th Cir. 1987). In *Adams Apple*, the Ninth Circuit espouses the concept that unequal treatment of the prepetition claims is allowed when necessary for the rehabilitation of a debtor. The court identified payments to "providers of unique and irreplaceable supplies" as being necessary, and stated that the policy of equal treatment of creditors may be superseded when it conflicts with the policy of rehabilitation of a debtors. *Id.* at 1490. *See also In re Sharon Steel Corp.*, 159 B.R. 730, 737 (authorizing payment of prepetition wage claim because it was "necessary to avert a serious threat to the Chapter 11 process"); *In re NVR L.P.*, 147 B.R. 126, 128 (Bankr. E.D. Va. 1992) (necessity of payment doctrine provides an exception to the rule prohibiting such payments where the payment is necessary to permit the effectuation of the rehabilitative purposes of the Bankruptcy Code). Courts have particularly recognized the importance of employees to the reorganization process. *See In re Lehigh and New England Railway Co.*, 657 F.2d 570, 581 (3rd Cir. 1981) (payment of employee wages benefits all interested parties and should be approved).

It is essential to the continued operation of Debtors' healthcare facilities and to this Chapter 11 proceeding that the services of the Debtors' employees be retained and that the morale of such persons be maintained. A significant deterioration in employee morale at this critical time undoubtedly will have a substantial adverse impact on Debtors, the level of care provided to facility residents, the value of Debtors' assets and business activities, as well as any meaningful post-petition efforts to preserve and maximize value for all creditors and other parties in interest. Debtors submit that the total amount to be paid is *de minimis* compared to the size of these estates and the importance of these employees to a successful Chapter 11 proceeding.

Failure to pay the amounts sought herein will work substantial personal hardships on Debtors employees, and increase the Debtors' operating costs. Debtors submit that the relief herein will help maintain the continuity of the Debtors' businesses in a manner beneficial to all parties in interest and will enhance the value of the Debtors' Estates.

3. ESSENTIAL VENDOR PROTOCOL.

Debtors seek authority to pay, in the ordinary course of business, amounts due to the Essential Vendors and Suppliers as of the Petition Date to the extent necessary to maintain all contracts and ongoing relationships with such Essential Vendors and Suppliers. Additionally, Debtors request that the Court's Order granting the requested relief be without prejudice to the Debtors' right to include additional essential vendors or suppliers as necessary within the Debtors' business judgment within the relief granted in the Order without additional motion to the Court, on notice to the Creditors Committee and the U.S. Trustee.

For the reasons set forth below, it is essential to the Debtors' successful reorganization and to patient care that this Court enter an order authorizing the Debtors to pay the invoices submitted by the Essential Vendors and Suppliers for prepetition goods and services delivered to the Debtors. Without the authority to pay such entities the amounts requested in this Motion, it is, in the Debtors' best business judgment, unlikely that the Essential Vendors and Suppliers will continue to provide the goods and services so essential to the Debtors' patients and ongoing maintenance of the Debtors' businesses, and the Debtors could potentially be forced into premature liquidation, with thousands of patients left without critical care. Like any other business entity, each of the Essential Vendors and Suppliers is reluctant to provide goods or services to businesses that do not pay their bills. Authorizing the Debtors to maintain strong credit relationships with these Essential Vendors and Suppliers by allowing the Debtors to pay prepetition invoices is the only way to protect the Debtors' businesses and the paramount interests of the Debtors' patients.

Furthermore, if forced to look elsewhere for such essential goods and services, the efficient operation of the Debtors' businesses will undoubtedly be interrupted, with attendant shortcomings in patient care. In addition, such replacement contracts would likely not be on terms even reasonably as favorable to the Debtors as those in place with the Essential Vendors and Suppliers, thereby exposing the Debtors' estates and creditors to unnecessary expense. Even if such replacement contracts could be negotiated, the Debtors' inexperience with such replacement vendors and suppliers would make it difficult for the Debtors to ensure that the quality of the goods and services rendered by such replacement vendors and suppliers matches that of the Debtors' current vendors and suppliers, thus possibly exposing patients to diminished quality of care. Moreover, such replacement vendors and suppliers would inevitably charge a premium in light of the perceived risk of doing business with the Debtors during the pendency of these Chapter 11 cases. Accordingly, this Court should ensure the Debtors' ability to maintain their critical relationships with these Essential Vendors and Suppliers by authorizing the Debtors to pay their prepetition invoices.

Federal and state Medicare and Medicaid regulations also require that the Essential Vendors and Suppliers be paid on their prepetition invoices. Under such regulations, health care providers such as the Debtors must enter into provider agreements with state and federal agencies responsible for Medicaid and Medicare programs to be eligible for prospective reimbursement of "allowable costs." Under this arrangement, the various state and federal agencies implementing Medicare and Medicaid (often through private insurance companies acting as fiscal intermediaries authorized under relevant federal regulations) estimate reimbursement amounts to be paid monthly to providers based on, among other things and according to set formulae (which differ from state to state under Medicaid), the provider's actual costs for "allowable costs" for the provider's previous fiscal year. After the end of the provider's fiscal year, the provider is required to submit a "Final Cost Report" to serve as the basis for reconciliation between the actual, allowable costs incurred at the interim reimbursement payments advanced throughout that fiscal year. If interim reimbursements exceed actual costs incurred, the provider is required to remit the difference. Likewise, if interim reimbursements were less than actual costs incurred, the intermediary remits the difference to the provider. After such reconciliation, adjustments to future interim payment levels are made.

Such a system would likely present a problem for the Debtors during the pendency of these Chapter 11 cases, since the Debtors could be faced with the loss of their right to reimbursement, and since future interim payments (which essentially provide the Debtors with working capital throughout the fiscal year for operations at the individual facilities) would be reduced if prepetition invoices from the Essential Vendors and Suppliers are not paid. Medicare and Medicaid regulations provide that any invoice or debt for an allowable cost that is not liquidated (*i.e.*, paid) within twelve (12) months becomes no longer reimbursable. Thus, if the Essential Vendors and Suppliers are not paid now in the ordinary course of business but rather are paid only a discounted *pro rata* distribution at the end of these cases (which, given the size and complexity of these Chapter 11 cases, is not likely to occur within the next 12 months), the Debtors will have lost their valuable right to receive reimbursement for such expenses. This would, in turn, greatly reduce the historical reimbursement levels used to determine future interim payments and result in insufficient interim payments throughout the next fiscal year, further hampering the Debtors Operation.

A. *Debtors should be Authorized to Pay these Prepetition Invoices Under 11 U.S.C. § 105.*

The Court may authorize the Debtors to honor their prepetition obligations to these Essential Vendors and Suppliers under Section 105(a) of the Bankruptcy Code. Because the Debtors' continued viability depends in large part on their ability to honor such obligations, it is both proper and appropriate for the Court to exercise its discretion in these cases under the authority granted to the Court under Section 105(a).

It is well established that under the "doctrine of necessity" a Bankruptcy Court may authorize the postpetition payment by a debtor-in-possession of prepetition obligations where necessary to preserve or enhance the value of the estate for the benefit of its creditors. (*See, e.g., Miltenberger v. Logansport Ry.*, 106 U.S. 286 (1882) (payment of pre-receivership claim before completion of reorganization permitted to prevent "stoppage of . . . [crucial] business relations"); *In re Ionosphere Clubs*, 98 B.R. 174, 176 (Bankr. S.D.N.Y. 1989) (doctrine of necessity permits "immediate payment of claims of creditors where those creditors will not supply services or materials essential to the conduct of the business until their pre-reorganization claims shall have been paid"). The doctrine of necessity was also recognized by the Ninth Circuit Court of Appeals in *In re Adams Apple, Inc.*, 829 F.2d 1484, 1490 (9th Cir. 1987), where the court held that unequal treatment of prepetition claims is permissible "when necessary for rehabilitation, in such context as . . . debts to providers of unique and irreplaceable supplies" and stated that the policy of equal treatment of creditors may be superseded when it conflicts with the debtor's rehabilitation. *See also In re Leighy and New England Ry. Co.*, 657 F2d 570, 581 (3rd Cir. 1981) (doctrine of necessity permits "immediate payment of claims of creditors where those creditors will not supply services or material essential to the conduct of the business until their pre-reorganization claims shall have been paid"); *In re NVR L.P.,* 147 B.R. 126, 128 (Bankr. E.D. Va. 1992) (necessity of payment doctrine provides an exception to the rule prohibiting payments to prepetition creditors when the payment is necessary to effectuate the rehabilitative purposes of the Bankruptcy Code).

Here, the payment of these prepetition invoices to Essential Vendors and Suppliers is clearly appropriate under these authorities and under Section 105 of the Bankruptcy Code. As shown above, the Debtors believe in their best business judgment that the goods and services of these Essential Vendors and Suppliers will become unavailable in the postpetition period if certain invoices are not paid. In that event, the Debtors would face unreasonable delay and substantial increased costs in their ongoing businesses, concerns regarding quality and reputation, and perhaps irreversible cessation of operations, with the resulting interruption of critical patient care. Conversely, the payments of these invoices will permit the Debtors to maintain patient services at a quality level that these patients and their families have come to expect from the Debtors, and help ensure the continued business of the Debtors for the benefit of their estates and creditors.

Such invoices aggregate less than $1,800,000. Moreover, more than half of these invoices are less than 60 days old. Given what would likely be astronomical costs associated with finding replacement vendors and suppliers and the deleterious effect that non-payment of these essential invoices would have on the Debtors' goodwill and ongoing business interests (not to mention patient care), payment of these invoices will not prejudice the Debtors' estates or creditors. In the Debtors' best judgment, such payments can only enhance Debtors' potential for reorganization and successful completion of these Chapter 11 cases.

VI. CONCLUSION AND RELIEF REQUESTED.

For all the foregoing reasons, the Debtor respectfully requests a Court Order as follows:

A. Authorizing Debtors to maintain their currently existing Cash Management System (including maintenance of existing bank accounts, cash management systems, and business forms);

B. Authorizing Debtors to pay, in the ordinary course of business, amounts due related to prepetition wages, salaries, employment taxes, employee benefit payments and workers' compensation pay ments;

C. Authorizing Debtors to pay, in the ordinary course of business, amounts due to the Essential Vendors and Suppliers on account of prepetition invoices, such Order to be without prejudice to the Debt ors' right to include additional essential vendors or suppliers as necessary within the Debtors' business judgment within the relief granted in the Order without additional motion to the Court on notice to the Creditors Committee and the U.S. Trustee; and

D. Granting such other and further relief as is appropriate under the facts and circumstances of this case.

RESPECTFULLY SUBMITTED this 28th day of May, 1998.

SQUIRE, SANDERS & DEMPSEY L.L.P.
Two Renaissance Square
40 North Central Avenue, Suite 2700
Phoenix, Arizona 85004-4441

By: <u>*/s/ Thomas J. Salerno*</u>
Thomas J. Salerno, Esq.
Craig D. Hansen, Esq.
Jordan A. Kroop, Esq.

Attorneys for Debtors

Copy of the foregoing
sent via hand-delivery/
fax/overnight mail this
28th day of May, 1998 to
the parties on the Official
Service List

<u>*/s/ Barbara D. Clapper*</u>

EXHIBIT "1"

LIST OF HEALTHCARE FACILITIES

1. Enumclaw Healthcare & Rehab
2. Henry Clay Villa
3. Oswega Manor Care Center
4. Marshall Manor
5. Mountainside Care Center Inc.
6. Mountain Vista
7. Nightengale West
8. Oaks at Boise
9. Oaks at Home Health
10. Oaks Hospice
11. Quest Supply
12. Suncrest
13. Ridgewood Care
14. Terrace Lake Village
15. Walla Walla Healthcare Center
16. White Pine
17. Arkansas Manor Nursing Home
18. Cornerstone
19. Douglas Manor
20. Village Catered,
21. Peppertree Catered
22. Safford Care Center
23. Bonner Health Center
24. Brookshire House
25. Christopher House
26. Amberwood Court Care Center
27. Los Arcos Health Center
28.Pueblo Norte Nursing Center
29. Rio Verde Nursing Center
30. The Arbors Healthcare Center

EXHIBIT "2"

LIST OF ANCILLARY ENTITIES

1. Gamma Laboratories
2. Ampro Medical Services, Inc.
3. American Professional Holdings, Inc.
4. Memphis Clinical Laboratory, Inc.
5. Quest Pharmacies, Inc. *d/b/a* Indiana Prescription Laboratory, and Quest Total Care Pharmacy
6. Sunbelt Therapy Management Services, Inc. (Alabama)
7. Henderson & Associates Rehabilitation, Inc.
8. Therapy Health Systems, Inc.
9. Decatur Sports Fit & Wellness Center, Inc.
10. Sunbelt Therapy Management Services, Inc. (Arizona)
11. Rehab West, Inc. *d/b/a* Therapy West Inc.

EXHIBIT "3"

CASH MANAGEMENT SYSTEM

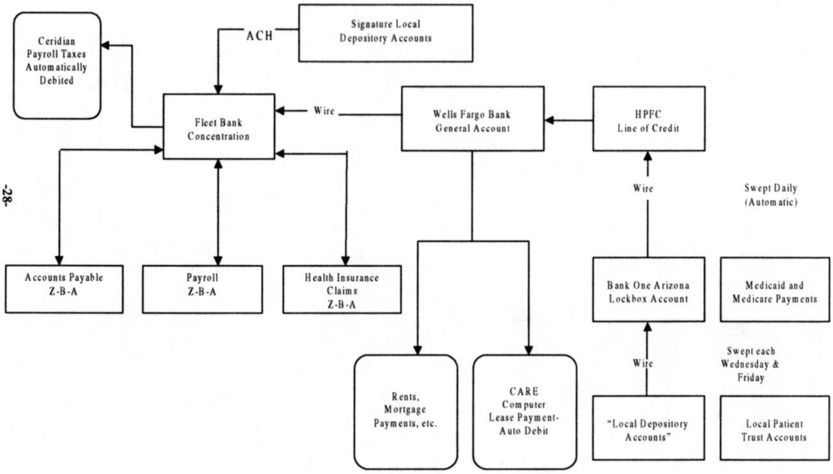

-28-

EXHIBIT "4"

PAYROLL OBLIGATIONS

	Number of Employees	Employee Breakdown	Aggregate Amount of Payroll Each Pay Period	Tax Obligations Each Pay Period	Number of Employees with Monthly Pay Greater than $4,000	401K Payment	Employee Benefit Payments, i.e., Health, Life, Dental	Payroll Dates
Unison	93	15 management 78 staff 6 admin. support 22 office & staff 33 patient care	$176,189	$96,757	41	$8,500	28,500/month due Dec. 1, 1997	Semi-monthly in arrears, on the 5th and 20th via Ceridian
Sunquest SPC	987	65 general support 140 admin. & office 1016 patient care	$533,964	$212,487	17	$18,000	See Unison	Bi-weekly in arrears, cutoff days vary by facility (Sat., Sun., Wed., Tues.) via Ceridian
Britwill Healthcare Company	0	N/A	0	0	0	0	0	N/A
Quest Pharmacies	94	3 management 55 patient care 36 staff	$63,000	$20,000	9	0	$7,210	Bi-weekly in arrears, paid directly
Sunbelt Therapy Mgmt. Services	0	N/A	0	0	0	0	0	N/A
Safford Care	109	3 general support 15 admin. & office 120 patient care	$52,176	$17,332	1	0	See Unison	Bi-weekly in arrears, via Ceridian
Rehab West	0	N/A	0	0	0	0	0	N/A
Cornerstone Care	117	4 general staff 10 admin. & office 123 patient care	$65,094	$21,349	1	$600		Bi-weekly in arrears, via Ceridian
Signature Health Care Corporation	0	N/A	0	0	0	0	0	N/A
Arkansas	98	5 general support 9 admin. & office 89 patient care	$51,568	$15,274	1	$2,200	See Unison	Bi-weekly in arrears, via Ceridian
Douglas Manor	53	6 general support 7 admin. & office 52 patient care	$23,215	$8,301	1	$1,000	See Unison	Bi-weekly in arrears, via Ceridian
Memphis Clinical Laboratory	18	1 office staff 1 management 16 patient care	$13,000	$3,300	1	0	$771.53	Bi-weekly in arrears, paid directly

	Number of Employees	Employee Breakdown	Aggregate Amount of Payroll Each Pay Period	Tax Obligations Each Pay Period	Number of Employees with Monthly Pay Greater than $4,000	401K Payment	Employee Benefit Payments, i.e., Health, Life, Dental	Payroll Dates
American Professional Holding	0	N/A	0	0	0	0	0	N/A
Britwill Funding Corporation	0	N/A	0	0	0	0	0	N/A
Decatur Sportsfit & Wellness Center	0	N/A	0	0	0	0	0	N/A
Therapy Health Systems	0	N/A	0	0	0	0	0	N/A
Henderson & Associates Rehabilitation	0	N/A	0	0	0	0	0	N/A
Sunbelt Therapy Mgmt. Services (Alabama)	600	50 clerical 100 management 450 patient care	$850,000	$275,000	191	$63,000	$26,700	Bi-weekly in arrears, by company directly
Brookshire House	59	3 general support 5 admin. & support 55 patient care	$34,679	$12,935	0	$1,500	See Unison	Bi-weekly in arrears, via Ceridian
Christopher Nursing Center	73	5 general support 6 admin. & office 73 patient care	$39,301	$15,308	0	$4,500	See Unison	Bi-weekly in arrears, via Ceridian
Amberwood Court	65	4 general support 5 admin. & office 75 patient care	$37,381	$15,094	1	$800	See Unison	Bi-weekly in arrears, via Ceridian
The Arbors	90	10 general support 8 admin. & office 105 patient care	$57,037	$20,335	1	$1,700	See Unison	Bi-weekly in arrears, via Ceridian
Los Arcos	88	4 general support 8 admin. & office 97 patient care	$41,228	$13,340	1	$500	See Unison	Bi-weekly in arrears, via Ceridian
Pueblo Norte	80	3 general support 8 admin. & office 78 patient care	$44,378	$16,017	1	$1,500	See Unison	Bi-weekly in arrears, via Ceridian

Exhibit "4"
- 31 -

	Number of Employees	Employee Breakdown	Aggregate Amount of Payroll Each Pay Period	Tax Obligations Each Pay Period	Number of Employees with Monthly Pay Greater than $4,000	401K Payment	Employee Benefit Payments, i.e., Health, Life, Dental	Payroll Dates
Rio Verde	76	1 general support 10 admin. & office 84 patient care	$37,506	$13,386	0	$1,700	See Unison	Bi-weekly in arrears, via Ceridian
Signature Mgmt.	0	N/A	0	0	0	0	0	N/A
Ampro Medical Services	67	5 management 7 technical 18 office/building 37 field	$62,000	$16,500	3	0	Health $7,905 Dental $357	Bi-weekly in arrears, by company directly
Gamma Laboratories	46	1 management 12 clerical 33 technical	$42,000	$9,000	1	0	0	Bi-weekly by company directly
Emory	0	N/A	0	0	0	0	0	N/A
TOTAL	2,813		$2,223,716	$810,715	271	$105,000		

Exhibit "4"
- 32 -

EXHIBIT "5"
ESSENTIAL VENDORS AND SUPPLIERS

Allegiance Healthcare	Direct Laboratory Supplies
Baxter Scientific	Direct Laboratory Supplies
Biomerieux Vitek, Inc.	Direct Laboratory Supplies
Chiron Diagnostics	Direct Laboratory Supplies
Dade Chemistry Systems	Direct Laboratory Supplies
Federal Express	Emergency Pharmaceutical Shipping
UPS	Emergency Pharmaceutical Shipping
Ultra Care	Intravenous Supply
HCI	Intravenous Supply
McGaw	Intravenous Supply
C&S Textiles	Linen
Alfred Nickles Bakery	Local Food (Bread) Vendor
Earthgrains Baking	Local Food (Bread) Vendor
Flower's Baking	Local Food (Bread) Vendor
Gai's Seattle French Baking	Local Food (Bread) Vendor
Hardins Bakery	Local Food (Bread) Vendor
Holsum Bakery	Local Food (Bread) Vendor
Klosterman Baking	Local Food (Bread) Vendor
Kremo Bakers	Local Food (Bread) Vendor
Mrs. Baird's Bakery	Local Food (Bread) Vendor
Snyder's Bakery	Local Food (Bread) Vendor
Blue Bell Creameries	Local Food (Dairy) Vendor
Handy's Milk & Ice Cream	Local Food (Dairy) Vendor
Barber Pure Milk	Local Food (Dairy) Vendor
Barber Ice Cream	Local Food (Dairy) Vendor
Fike's Dairy	Local Food (Dairy) Vendor
Ideal American Dairy	Local Food (Dairy) Vendor
Inland NW Dairies	Local Food (Dairy) Vendor
Instant Whip Foods	Local Food (Dairy) Vendor
Melody Farms	Local Food (Dairy) Vendor
Oak Farms Dairy	Local Food (Dairy) Vendor
Praire Farms Dairy	Local Food (Dairy) Vendor
Pure Sealed Dairy	Local Food (Dairy) Vendor
Robinson's Dairy	Local Food (Dairy) Vendor
Schepp's Dairy	Local Food (Dairy) Vendor
JP Foodservice	Local Food Vendor
Anderson's Foodtown	Local Food Vendor
Bashas	Local Food Vendor
Brookshire Bros. #28	Local Food Vendor
Dave's Hometown Market	Local Food Vendor
Emerald Distributors	Local Food Vendor
Gordon Food Service	Local Food Vendor
Harold's	Local Food Vendor
Rykoff-Sexton	Local Food Vendor
Shamrock Foods	Local Food Vendor
Wood Fruiticher	Local Food Vendor
Ben E. Keith	Local Food Vendor
U.S. Food Supply	Local Food Vendor
Goodwin Street Pharmacy	Local Support Pharmacy
Apothecary Pharmacy	Local Support Pharmacy
Gatti Pharmacy	Local Support Pharmacy

Rite Aid Pharmacy	Local Support Pharmacy
Pioneer Pharmacy	Local Support Pharmacy
Medicap Pharmacy	Local Support Pharmacy
Bridgeport Pharmacy	Local Support Pharmacy
Northside Pharmacy TX	Local Support Pharmacy
Northside Pharmacy IN	Local Support Pharmacy
Walgreens Pharmacy	Local Support Pharmacy
Cornerstone Pharmacy	Local Support Pharmacy
TeamCare IN	Local Support Pharmacy
VitaLink/TeamCare MI	Local Support Pharmacy
Flagstaff Pharmacy	Local Support Pharmacy
Pharmasource	Local Support Pharmacy
Rx Associates	Local Support Pharmacy
David Shillington	Medical Advisory Services (required by law)
Michael Riehl	Medical Advisory Services (required by law)
A.R. Hudson	Medical Advisory Services (required by law)
Athan Siddiqui	Medical Advisory Services (required by law)
Dale J. Smith	Medical Advisory Services (required by law)
Gerimed of America	Medical Advisory Services (required by law)
Michael J. Flores	Medical Advisory Services (required by law)
Alexander Jacobs	Medical Advisory Services (required by law)
Aaron Bornstein	Medical Advisory Services (required by law)
Charles Welly	Medical Advisory Services (required by law)
Andrew March	Medical Advisory Services (required by law)
Pinal Mountain Medical	Medical Advisory Services (required by law)
Mari Rowe	Medical Advisory Services (required by law)
Wonder Bread / Hostess	National Bread Vendor
Ecolab	National Contract – Linen/Dietary Chemicals
Direct Supply	National Contract – Maintenance Equip.
Briggs	National Contract – Medical Forms
Redline Healthcare	National Contract – Medical Supplies
Airborne Express	National Contract – Overnight Mail
Crandall & Associates	National Dietary Consultant
Borden	National Milk Vendor
Meadow Gold Dairies	National Milk Vendor
Kinetic Concepts	National Therapy Product provider
Anda Generics	Pharmaceutical (Generic) Supply
McKesson Corp.	Pharmaceutical Wholesale Supply
Morris & Dickson	Pharmaceutical Wholesale Supply
Amerisource	Pharmaceutical Wholesale Supply
Specialized Pharmacy Service	Pharmacy
Walgreen Advanced Care	Pharmacy
APS/Lahr Pharmacy	Pharmacy
Quest Pharmacies	Pharmacy
Sunbelt Therapy	Physical Therapy
Sundance Rehabilitation	Physical Therapy
Labcorp	Reference Laboratory
Vencor Hospital	Respiratory Therapy
Heritage Hospital	Respiratory Therapy
Hospital Therapy Service	Respiratory Therapy
Subacute Respiratory Therapy	Respiratory Therapy
Lutheran Medical Center	Respiratory Therapy
Marcus J. Lawrence Hospital	Respiratory Therapy

Thomas J. Salerno, Esq.
Craig D. Hansen, Esq.
Jordan A. Kroop, Esq.
SQUIRE, SANDERS & DEMPSEY L.L.P.
Two Renaissance Square
40 North Central Avenue, Suite 2700
Phoenix, Arizona 85004-4441
(602) 528-4000

Attorney for Debtors

IN THE UNITED STATES BANKRUPTCY COURT FOR THE DISTRICT OF ARIZONA

In re:	)	In Proceedings Under Chapter 11
	)	
UNISON HEALTHCARE CORPORATION, a Delaware corporation, and its affiliated and related entities,	))	Case Nos. B-98-0173 through B-98-6612-PHX-GBN
	)	
Debtors.	))	**AFFIDAVIT OF CLAYTON KLOEHR IN SUPPORT OF ALL FIRST DAY MOTIONS**
	))	

STATE OF ARIZONA	)	
	)	ss.
COUNTY OF MARICOPA	)	

I, Clayton Kloehr, having been first duly sworn upon my oath, depose and state as follows:

1. I am the Senior Vice President of Unison Healthcare Corporation ("Unison"), as well as each of the related debtors in these Chapter 11 cases (collectively, the "Debtors" or the "Companies"). I am responsible for overseeing the financial operations of the Companies. I have served in this capacity since July 1997.

2. I make this affidavit on personal knowledge in support of the following motions submitted contemporaneously with this affidavit:

(a) Ex Parte Motion for Order Approving Debtor's Maintenance of Certain Bank Accounts, Cash Management System, and Business Forms;

(b) Ex Parte Motion for Authority to Pay Certain Prepetition Claims of Essential Vendors and Suppliers;

(c) Ex Parte Motion for Authority to Pay Wages, Salaries, Employment Taxes, Employee Benefit Payments, and Workers' Compensation Payments;

(d) Motion for Enlargement of Time to File Statements and Schedules;*

(e) Ex Parte Motion for an Order Establishing Noticing Requirements with Respect to All Proceedings Herein;*

3. Debtors commenced these cases by filing voluntary petitions for relief under Chapter 11 of Title 11 of the United States Code (the "Bankruptcy Code").

4. Debtors are primarily engaged in the business of providing comprehensive long-term and specialty healthcare services through several operating entities (the "Healthcare Entities"). The Healthcare Entities currently operate approximately 30 skilled nursing facilities (collectively, the "Healthcare Facilities") located in Arizona, Alabama, Colorado, Indiana, Idaho, Kansas, Mississippi, Nevada, Pennsylvania, Texas and Washington. The Healthcare Facilities contain approximately 2,579 licensed beds.

5. In addition, Debtors operate entities which act as suppliers of certain laboratory, pharmacy, and therapy services (the "Ancillary Entities"). The Ancillary Entities supply their products and services to the Debtors' Healthcare Facilities as well as to other, non-affiliated facilities. Combined, the Healthcare Entities and the Ancillary Entities employ approximately 2,812 individuals.

MAINTENANCE OF CERTAIN BANK ACCOUNTS CASH MANAGEMENT SYSTEM AND BUSINESS FORMS

Existing Cash Management System

6. The primary sources of cash collections for nursing services for all Healthcare Entities operating nursing home facilities include private pay, Medicare, Medicaid and commercial insurance revenue. The cash management function for nursing home facilities operated by the Healthcare Entities is centralized at the corporate headquarters located in Scottsdale, Arizona.

Individual Facility Depository Accounts

7. Each nursing facility maintains two bank accounts: a local depository account and a patient trust account.

8. Local Depository Account. A bank accounts exists for each nursing facility at a local bank near the facility (the "Local Account"). Deposits to

---

****Author's Note:*** Not all of the ***First Day Motions*** to which this Affidavit applied were reprinted in the Appendix.

the Local Accounts include payments from private pay residents, commercial insurance payors, and miscellaneous revenue (vending machine revenue, etc.). Revenues generated by a number of facilities are included as part of the collateral base under a secured revolving line of credit (the "Revolving Line") provided by Healthcare Financial Partners ("HCFP") to Unison and a number of its subsidiaries.[1] Under the terms of the Revolving Line, the Local Accounts are swept by wire transfer each Wednesday and Friday into a lockbox account (No. 1180-3511) maintained at Bank One Arizona.

9. Patient Trust Accounts. Each facility operated by a Healthcare Entity also maintains as trustee a local depository account for certain of the residents' personal funds. The Administrator and Director of Nursing of each facility are typically the authorized signers on the accounts. The facility business office manager reconciles the accounts and maintains a separate ledger for each resident. The accounts are interest bearing as required by federal regulation and the interest is allocated to each resident's balance at the end of the month. The maintenance of the patient trust accounts is done strictly at the individual facility level and the funds are not available for use by the facility or any Healthcare Entity.

Operating Accounts

10. Bank One Lockbox Account. In addition to the deposits made to the Local Accounts, which are swept into the Bank One lockbox (the "Lockbox") twice weekly, all Medicare and Medicaid revenues generated at each Healthcare Entity facility covered under the HCFP Revolving Line are directly deposited into the Lockbox in accordance with the terms of the Revolving Line. The Lockbox is then swept daily by HCFP.

11. Wells Fargo General Account. Based upon availability under the Revolving Line, advances are made by HCFP into an account maintained by Unison at Wells Fargo Bank ("Wells Fargo"). The Wells Fargo account acts as a general operating account for Unison and the various Healthcare Entities. Deposits to the account include miscellaneous cash receipts from the corporate office and other related entities as well as advances from the HCFP Revolving Line. Disbursements from this account include wire transfers to the Fleet Bank concentration account to cover daily presentments, obligations to certain lease and mortgage holders, obligations to affiliate companies for intercompany advances, and various other disbursements as needed. Also, the lease payment to Care Computer, which

---

[1] Signature Health Care Corporation and its subsidiaries (the "Signature Entities") are not borrowers under the Revolving Line. The nursing home facilities operated by the Signature Entities maintain separate local depository and trust accounts. Revenues generated by the facilities. Revenues generated by the facilities and deposited into the local depository accounts are then transferred to the First Bank Concentration Account.

is the provider of the accounts receivable software for all nursing facilities operated by the various Healthcare Entities, is automatically withdrawn each month.

12. Fleet Bank Concentration Account. The Fleet Bank concentration account's primary purpose is to automatically fund the checks presented on the controlled disbursement accounts and to fund drawdowns initiated by Ceridian Employer Services ("Ceridian"), which provides third-party administrative services for processing payroll for all Healthcare Entities. Payroll taxes for all nursing home facilities are withdrawn from the account one day before the pay date of each facility payroll. Amounts to be debited are determined by notifications faxed to the Unison treasury department from Ceridian, usually 2-3 days before the drawdown date. Deposits into this account include wire transfers from the Wells Fargo general account.

13. Zero Balance Accounts. Unison maintains three Zero Balance Accounts (ZBA), currently at Fleet Bank, from which it disburses payments for accounts payable, payroll, and health insurance claims for all nursing home facilities. The bank notifies Unison of check presentment totals and funding requirements by 9:15 a.m. ET through the on-line balance reporting system. The presentments are funded by the concentration account at Fleet Bank.

14. Accounts Payable. Accounts Payable for all Healthcare Entities are handled at the Scottsdale corporate office. An expenditure budget for all Healthcare Entities is compiled weekly. On a daily basis, cash requirement reports that itemize the invoices to be paid are approved for payment by the Unison Treasurer or Assistant Treasurer before the checks are actually issued. The accounts payable department for Healthcare Entities consists of six clerks who report to the accounts payable manager. Five of the clerks are responsible for the processing of invoices for each facility within the five operating regions of Unison, while one is responsible for all home office invoices.

15. Payroll. The Payroll department prepares a summary of all payroll and tax liabilities by facility and date. The Unison treasury department uses the total payroll amounts to forecast check presentments for the period around the payroll date. Payroll tax amounts are used to verify that Ceridian is debiting the Fleet Bank concentration account for the correct tax amount. The payroll department consists of six clerks who report to the payroll manager. Five of the clerks are responsible for processing the payrolls for each facility within the five operating regions, while one is responsible for processing all garnishments for all facilities.

16. Health Insurance Claims. Unison currently uses a third party, United HealthCare, to administer claims for a partially self-funded health insurance plan for all employees of nursing facilities operated by Healthcare Entities. United HealthCare submits a cash requirement report to the Unison Human

Resources department for reconciliation on a weekly basis. Once reconciled, the Treasurer will sign off on the itemized claims and United HealthCare will write checks on Unison's behalf from the Fleet Bank Health Insurance Claims account to each of the payees.

Ancillary Entities' Accounts

17. The eleven Ancillary Entities maintain several local bank accounts used for all deposits and all payroll and accounts payable disbursements. Most of these accounts are integrated into the overall cash management system, with all accounts payable and payroll for certain of the Ancillary Entities being processed through an operating account. Because these Ancillary Entities supply products and services to the Debtors' healthcare facilities as well as to other, non-affiliated facilities, the individual local bank accounts maintained by these Ancillary Entities are integrated into the overall cash management system to the extent necessary to facilitate the ongoing relationship between the Debtors and the Ancillary Entities.

Maintenance Of The Cash Management System

18. It is essential to the Debtors' successful transition to Debtors-in-Possession and to ensure essential services to facilitate residents are not disrupted that the Debtors minimize any alteration to the present cash management system until such time as the Debtors can evaluate the system and establish and implement any necessary changes in accounting procedures by which the Debtors can more accurately maintain and track cash disbursements and income for each of the Debtors' facilities. The Debtors do not believe, however, in their best business judgment, that any changes are warranted, since cash flow is adequately documented for each facility by the current system.

19. Given the substantial size and complexity of the Debtors' operations, the prospects for a successful reorganization of the Debtors' business, as well as the preservation and enhancement of the Debtors' respective values as going concerns, necessarily would be threatened by any disruption in the Debtors' ordinary and usual cash management proceeds. It is essential, therefore, that the Debtors be permitted to continue to consolidate the management of their cash and transfer monies from entity to entity, as necessary and in the ordinary course of business in amounts necessary to continue the efficient operation of the Debtors' businesses,

20. The basic transactions incident to the cash management system described above have been utilized by the Debtors with only minor modifications for several years, and constitute ordinary, usual and essential business practices. The cash management system is similar to those commonly employed by corporate enterprises comparable to the Debtors in size and complexity. The widespread use of such systems, moreover, is attributable to the numerous benefits they provide, including the ability to tightly control corporate funds, invest idle cash, insure cash availability, and reduce administrative expense

by facilitating the movement of funds and the development of timely and accurate account balance and presentment information.

21. In addition, given the corporate and financial structure of the Debtors, it would be difficult, if not impossible, for the Debtors quickly and efficiently to establish a new system of accounts and a new cash management and disbursement system. For instance, the Debtors maintain their cash management system by means of a sophisticated computer system. If certain Debtors were to withdraw from this system, or if all Debtors were required to dismantle the cash management system, such Debtors would need to generate the information maintained on the central computer system and monitor and control the flow of cash manually at substantial additional costs to those Debtors' estates and creditors. Thus, under the circumstances, maintenance of the existing cash management system without disruption is not only essential, but also in the best interest of the Debtors' respective estates and creditors. Further, preserving a "business as usual" atmosphere and avoiding the unnecessary distractions that would inevitably be associated with any disruption in the Debtors' existing cash management system will facilitate the Debtors ongoing efforts to emerge from Chapter 11 as quickly as possible.

22. It is also critical that, to avoid substantial disruption to the normal operation of their businesses and to preserve a "business as usual" atmosphere, the Debtors be permitted to use their existing bank accounts and business forms. Only if these accounts and forms are maintained with the same account numbers can the Debtors accomplish a smooth transition to operations in Chapter 11.

23. The Debtors, moreover, have the capacity to distinguish clearly between pre- and postpetition obligations and payments without closing existing accounts and opening new ones. The Debtors, and their estates and creditors, would be subject to tremendous administrative burdens and expenses if they were required to close and reopen accounts and create an entirely manual system for issuing checks and paying postpetition obligations.

PAYMENT OF CERTAIN PREPETITION CLAIMS OF ESSENTIAL VENDORS AND SUPPLIERS

24. The Debtors, through the various Healthcare Entities, currently operate approximately 30 skilled nursing facilities servicing nearly 2,600 patients. In providing such healthcare services, the Debtors maintain ongoing relationships with dozens of vendors and suppliers that provide the Debtors with the necessary goods and services required for ongoing patient care. The goods and services purchased from certain of these vendors and suppliers (the "Essential Vendors and Suppliers") are so critical to patient care that any cessation in the provision of those goods and services would not only gravely compromise the Debtors' businesses, but would also virtually preclude the Debtors from meeting daily obligations to their patients.

25. These Essential Vendors and Suppliers provide the Debtors with such critical goods and services as food, pharmaceuticals, respiratory therapy, physical therapy, linens, and medical forms. Certain of these Essential Vendors and Suppliers provide medical advisory services required by state and federal law, without which the Debtor would be unable to operate their healthcare facilities in compliance with such law. In addition, one Essential Vendor provides critical dietary consultation with respect to all the Debtors' healthcare facilities throughout the country.

26. Because these Essential Vendors and Suppliers enable the Debtors to feed, medicate, and otherwise provide ongoing skilled nursing care to the Debtors' nearly 2,600 patients, it is essential that the Debtors retain vendors and suppliers in whom the Debtors have confidence and with whom the Debtors maintain good relations. Many such Essential Vendors and Suppliers service all the Debtors' healthcare facilities through the country, and it is likely that in many instances the Debtors' operations constitute a significant percentage of such Essential Vendors and Suppliers businesses.

27. Based on their substantial experience with these Essential Vendors and Suppliers, the Debtors have confidence in the quality and reliability of their goods and services, and the Debtors believe that their contracts with them are at very competitive rates and on terms favorable to the Debtors.

28. The filing of the Debtors' petitions obviously cannot be permitted to effect ongoing services to the Debtors' patients. In light of the Debtors' critical obligations to their patients, and in light of the indispensable nature of the goods and services provided by the Essential Vendors and Suppliers, the Debtors must be able to maintain their strong relationships with such Essential Vendors and Suppliers throughout the pendency of these Chapter 11 cases. Maintaining such relationships, in fact, maybe one of the most important steps during the beginning stages of these Chapter 11 cases in ensuring that patient care is not compromised at any of the Debtors' facilities.

29. Without paying such entities, it is, in the Debtors' best business judgment, unlikely that the Essential Vendors and Suppliers will continue to provide the goods and services so essential to the Debtors' patients and ongoing maintenance of the Debtors' businesses, and the Debtors could potentially be forced into premature liquidation, without thousands of patients left without critical care. Like any other business entity, each of the Essential Vendors and Suppliers is reluctant to provide goods or services to businesses that do not pay their bills. Authorizing the Debtors to maintain strong credit relationships with these Essential Vendors and Suppliers by allowing the Debtors to pay prepetition invoices is the only way to protect the Debtors' businesses and the paramount interests of the Debtors' patients.

30. Furthermore, if forced to look elsewhere for such essential goods and services, the efficient operation of the Debtors' businesses will undoubtedly be interrupted, with attendant shortcomings in patient care. In addition,

such replacement contracts would likely not be on terms even reasonably as favorable to the Debtors as those in place with the Essential Vendors and Suppliers, thereby exposing the Debtors' estates and creditors to unnecessary expense. Even if such replacement contracts could be negotiated, the Debtors' inexperience with such replacement vendors and suppliers would make it difficult for the Debtors to ensure that the quality of the goods and services rendered by such replacement vendors and suppliers matches that of the Debtors' current vendors and suppliers, thus possibly exposing patients to diminished quality of care. Moreover, such replacement vendors and suppliers would inevitably charge a premium in light of the perceived risk of doing business with the Debtors during the pendency of these Chapter 11 cases.

31. Federal and state Medicare and Medicaid regulations also require that the Essential Vendors and Suppliers be paid on their prepetition invoices. Under such regulations, health care providers such as the Debtors must enter into provider agreements with state and federal agencies responsible for Medicaid and Medicare programs to be eligible for prospective reimbursement of "allowable costs." Under this arrangement, the various state and federal agencies implementing Medicare and Medicaid (often through private insurance companies acting as fiscal intermediaries authorized under relevant federal regulations) estimate reimbursement amounts to be paid monthly to providers based on, among other things and according to set formulae (which differ from state to state under Medicaid), the provider's actual costs for "allowable costs"[2] for the provider's previous fiscal year. After the end of the provider's fiscal year, the provider is required to submit a "Final Cost Report" to serve as the basis for reconciliation between the actual, allowable costs incurred at the interim reimbursement payments advanced through the fiscal year. If interim reimbursements exceed actual costs incurred, the provider is required to remit the difference. Likewise, if interim reimbursements were less than actual costs incurred, the intermediary remits the difference to the provider. After such reconciliation, adjustments to future interim payment levels are made.

32. Such a system would likely present a problem for the Debtors during the pendency of these Chapter 11 cases, since the Debtors could be faced with the loss of their right to reimbursement, and since future interim payments (which essentially provide the Debtors with working capital throughout the fiscal year for operations at the individual facilities) would be reduced if

[2] Virtually all expenditures for goods and services at each of the Debtors' facilities fall within the bounds of "allowable costs," and all goods and services supplied by the Essential Vendors and Suppliers and reflected in the invoices sought to be paid under authority from this Motion, are "allowable costs" under Medicaid and Medicare.

prepetition invoices from the Essential Vendors and Suppliers are not paid. Medicare and Medicaid regulations provide that any invoice or debt for an allowable cost that is not liquidated (i.e., paid) within twelve (12) months becomes no longer reimbursable. Thus, if the Essential Vendors and Suppliers are not paid now in the ordinary course of business but rather are paid only a discounted pro rata distribution at the end of these cases (which, given the size and complexity of these Chapter 11 cases, is not likely to occur within the next 12 months), the Debtors will have lost their valuable right to receive reimbursement for such expenses. This would, in turn, greatly reduce the historical reimbursement levels used to determine future interim payments and result in insufficient interim payments throughout the next fiscal year, further hampering the Debtors' operations.

PAYMENT OF WAGES, SALARIES, EMPLOYMENT TAXES, EMPLOYEE BENEFITS AND WORKERS COMPENSATION

Wages and Salaries

33. As of the Petition Date, the Debtors employed approximately 2,813 people. Specifically, the Healthcare Entities employed approximately 1,989 people, and the Ancillary Entities employed approximately 824 people.

34. The Healthcare Entities utilize the services of Ceridian Employer Services ("Ceridian"), a third party administrator company, in order to perform services attendant to payroll distribution.

35. The Healthcare Entities, through Ceridian, pay its employees on a bi-weekly basis in arrears. Thus, on each payday, approximately 1,989 of the Debtors' work force receives payment for the period ending the preceding two weeks.

36. On May 18, 20, 22, and 25, 1998, in accordance with the Healthcare Entities' customary practice, payroll checks in the amount of approximately $905,694 were distributed to the Healthcare Entities' employees. (The wages and salaries owed to the Healthcare Entities' employees referred to as the "Healthcare Entities' Prepetition Payroll").

37. The Ancillary Entities do not utilize the services of Ceridian, and pay their employees directly on a bi-weekly basis in arrears. Thus, on each payday, approximately 824 of the Debtors' work force receives payment for the period ending the preceding two weeks.

38. On May 22 and 26, 1998, in accordance with the Ancillary Entities' customary practice, payroll checks in the amount of approximately $1,030,000 were distributed to the Ancillary Entities employees. (The wages and salaries owed to the Ancillary Entities employees referred to as the "Ancillary Entities Prepetition Payroll").

39. As the Debtors' payroll obligations are spread out over a two week time frame, the Debtors have additional payroll days arising in the immediate

future. In accordance with the Healthcare Entities' customary practice, the Healthcare Entities intend to distribute, via Ceridian, payroll checks on May 29, 1998, and June 1, 5 and 8, 1998, in the aggregate amount of approximately $905,694. Similarly, in accordance with the Ancillary entities' customary practice, the Ancillary Entities intend to distribute payroll checks on June 5 and 9, 1998, in the aggregate amount of $1,030,000. (These wages and salaries are referred to collectively as the "Debtors' Postpetition Payroll.")

40. As discussed above, Debtors are requesting authority to continue to participate in the unified cash management system established by Unison Healthcare Corporation and maintain certain prepetition bank accounts. Absent these measures, Debtors believe that payroll checks previously issued to certain employees, i.e., the Healthcare Entities Prepetition Payroll and the Ancillary Entities Prepetition Payroll, may be dishonored by the banks upon which such checks were drawn due to the commencement of these proceedings.

Employment Taxes

41. Necessarily attendant to the payment of the Debtors' Pre and Postpetition Payroll is the Debtors' obligation to pay federal and state withholding taxes. Debtors' concentration account maintained at Fleet Bank (the "Fleet Bank Account") provides funds for drawdowns initiated by Ceridian to pay these employment taxes for the employees of the Healthcare Entities. The Healthcare Entities' employment taxes are withdrawn from the Fleet Bank Account 1 day prior to the pay date of each facility payroll. Amounts to be debited are determined by notifications faxed to Ceridian, usually 22 days prior to the drawdown date. The Healthcare Entities are current on all employment taxes, and with to maintain their current method of payment through Ceridian in the ordinary course.

42. As mentioned above, the Ancillary Entities do not use a third party payroll service such as Ceridian, and instead, they distribute payroll and pay withholding taxes directly. The Ancillary Entities utilize five separate banks, each local to the individual Ancillary Entity, for the purpose of distributing payroll and paying payroll taxes. A list of the banks is as follows: (1) Gilmer National Bank, Gilmer, Texas; (2) Bloomfield State Bank, Bloomfield, Indiana; (3) Austin Bank, Whitehouse, Texas; (4) Colonial Bank, Birmingham, Alabama; (5) Bank One, Dallas, Texas; and (6) Mercantile Bank, Poplar Bluff, Missouri. The Ancillary Entities are current on all employment taxes, and wish to maintain their current method of payment in the ordinary course.

Employee Benefit Payments

43. In the ordinary course of business and as is customary with most companies, the Debtors have established various employee benefit plans and policies that provide present and former employees with health, life, disability and retirement benefits (the "Employee Benefits"). Some of the

Debtors' payments for Employee Benefits (the "Employee Benefit Payments") are made to Debtors' insurers or other third parties; others are paid directly to employees. Debtors are current on all Employee Benefit Payments, and wish to maintain their current procedures for making the Employee Benefit Payments in the ordinary course.

Workers' Compensation Payments

44. Debtors maintain various policies and programs for workers' compensation, as required by law. These policies and programs generally fall into two categories: (i) self-insurance programs where the Debtors pay workers' compensation claims with respect to their employees on a regular basis, and (ii) conventional insurance where the Debtors obtain coverage from third party insurers with respect to workers' compensation. In many instances where the Debtors act as a self-insurer, in order to comply with various state regulations, the Debtors provide the state with a bond, letter of credit or other type of assurance to secure their obligation as self-insurers.

45. In the ordinary course of business, Debtors (i) process and pay all workers compensation claims related to Debtors existing and former employees (including all judgements and settlements related thereto) (collectively, the "Workers' Compensation Claims") in those instances where the Debtors are self-insurers, (ii) pay all insurance premiums (the "Workers' Compensation Premiums") for insurance policies with various insurance companies with respect to workers' compensation; and (iii) pay all administrative expenses (the "Workers' Compensation Administrative Expenses") associated with the maintenance of workers' compensation programs, including all expenses associated with processing of workers' compensation claims submitted, maintenance of insurance coverage, and such action as is necessary to process workers' compensation claims covered by third party insurance policies.

It is essential to the continued operation of Debtors' healthcare facilities and this Chapter 11 proceeding that the services of the Debtors' employees be retained and that the morale of such persons be maintained. A significant deterioration in employee morale at this critical time undoubtedly will have a substantial adverse impact on Debtors, the level of care provided to facility residents, the value of Debtors' assets and business activities, as well as any meaningful post-petition efforts to preserve and maximize value for all creditors and other parties in interest. The total amount to be paid is de minimis compared to the size of these estates and the importance of these employees to a successful Chapter 11 proceeding.

Failure to pay the amounts sought herein will work substantial personal hardships on Debtors employees, and increase the Debtors' operating costs. The relief herein will help maintain the continuity of the Debtors' businesses in a manner beneficial to all parties in interest and will enhance the value of the Debtors' Estates.

ENLARGEMENT OF TIME TO FILE STATEMENTS AND SCHEDULES

46. Under the unified cash management system of the Debtors, Unison (the parent company), is responsible for all business office services for the Debtors, including, billing and accounts receivable management, accounts payable, accounting and finance, quality assurance, and regulatory compliance at each facility. All of these services are performed at the corporate offices of Unison, located in Scottsdale, Arizona. Due to this unified cash management program, a great deal of time and effort is required to separate and prepare the Statements and Schedules for each Debtor.

47. Additionally, the Debtors have been required to devote a significant amount o time and effort in connection with, inter alia, cash collateral matters and other proceedings which have interfered with Debtors' ability to compile and analyze the information needed to complete the Statements and Schedules by June 12, 1998.

DATED this 28th day of May, 1998.

/s/ Clayton Kloehr
CLAYTON KLOEHR

SUBSCRIBED AND SWORN to before me this 28th day of May, 1998.

/s/ Barbara D. Clapper
Notary Public

My Commission Expires:
June 13, 2000

IN THE UNITED STATES BANKRUPTCY COURT FOR THE DISTRICT OF ARIZONA

In re:	) In Proceedings Under Chapter 11
	)
UNISON HEALTHCARE CORPORATION, a Delaware corporation, and its affiliated and related entities,	) Case Nos. B-98-0173 through B-98-6612-PHX-GBN
	)
Debtors.	) **ORDER APPROVING MOTION TO: (1) MAINTAIN DEBTORS' EXISTING ACCOUNTS, CASH MANAGEMENT SYSTEM AND BUSINESS FORMS; (2) PAY WAGES, SALARIES, EMPLOYMENT TAXES, EMPLOYMENT BENEFITS AND WORKERS' COMPENSATION PAYMENTS; AND (3) PAY CERTAIN PREPETITION CLAIMS OF ESSENTIAL VENDORS AND SUPPLIERS**
	)

This matter came before the Court pursuant to the "Ex Parte Motion For Authority To: (1) Maintain Debtors' Existing Accounts, Cash Management System And Business Forms; (2) Pay Wages, Salaries, Employment Taxes, Employee Benefits And Workers' Compensation Payments; And (3) Pay Certain Prepetition Claims Of Essential Vendors And Suppliers" (the Motion"), filed by the debtors and debtors-in-possession identified above (collectively, "Debtors") on May 28, 1998. In light of the foregoing, and good cause appearing therefor,

THE COURT FINDS as follows:

1. This Court has jurisdiction over the Motion pursuant to 28 U.S.C. §§ 157 and 1334. The Motion presents a "core" proceeding with respect to which the Court may enter a binding Order pursuant to 28 U.S.C. § 157(b). The Motion may be granted under the statutory predicates within 11 U.S.C. §§ 105, 1107 and 1108.

2. This Court has authority to grant relief on an *ex parte* basis without general notice to creditors under 11 U.S.C. §§ 105(a) and 102(1), and Bankruptcy Rule 9006, and based upon the immediacy of the Motion.

3. This Court may grant the Motion to preserve Debtors' going concern values and normal business relationships. In granting this Motion, the Court considered the broad aims and purposes of the U .S. Trustee's Operating Guidelines, and has determined that for the limited purposes of this case, the estates and interested parties can be better served by the conservation of Debtors' already scarce financial resources.

4. The granting of the Motion as to payments of prepetition essential vendors and suppliers will enhance the Debtors' ability to efficiently operate their businesses and will benefit the interests of the Debtors' estates and creditors.

ACCORDINGLY, IT IS HEREBY ORDERED as follows:

A. The Motion shall be, and hereby is, GRANTED;

B. The Debtors are hereby authorized to continue to participate in the unified cash management system as described in the Motion;

C. The Debtors are hereby authorized to maintain certain prepetition bank accounts identified in the Motion as Local Accounts* and Patient Trust accounts;

D. The Debtors are hereby authorized to continue to utilize correspondence and business forms existing as of the Petition Date for each facility operated by the Debtors without reference to their status as debtors-in-possession;

E. The Debtors are hereby authorized to pay, in the ordinary course of business, amounts due related to prepetition wages, salaries, employment taxes, employee benefits and workers' compensation payments;

F. The Debtors are hereby authorized to pay, in the ordinary course of business, those prepetition claims asserted by the Essential Vendors and Suppliers for good sand services provided to the Debtors in the ordinary course of the Debtors' businesses;

G. The Debtors may include additional essential vendors or suppliers as necessary within Debtors' business judgment within the relief granted in this Order without additional motion to this Court, on notice to the Creditors Committee and the U .S. Trustee.

H. The Debtors shall immediately serve this Order on the United States Trustee, the twenty (20) largest unsecured creditors of each Debtor, and any other party specifically affected by the relief granted herein. Any party objecting to this Order shall do so in writing, to be timely filed with the Court within twenty (20) days of service of this Order, and to be served on counsel for Debtors as follows:

Thomas J. Salerno, Esq.
Craig D. Hansen, Esq.
Jordan A. Kroop, Esq.
SQUIRE, SANDERS & DEMPSEY L.L.P.
2600 North Central Avenue
Phoenix, Arizona 85004

If no objections are timely filed, this Order shall become final.

DATED: May 28, 1998

/s/ George B. Nielsen, Jr.
HON. GEORGE B. NIELSEN, JR.
CHIEF JUDGE
UNITED STATES BANKRUPTCY COURT

*All capitalized terms not otherwise defined herein shall have the meanings set forth in the Motion.

APPENDIX F

SAMPLE MANAGEMENT SEVERANCE AGREEMENT *(PRECONFIRMATION)*

This Appendix includes a motion to approve severance agreements for members of a debtor's senior and mid-level management, a form of the severance agreement, and a bankruptcy court order approving those agreements. The severance terms are representative of the types of severance terms ordinarily given to management personnel in order to ensure their continued dedication to the debtor during a Chapter 11 restructuring. The specific terms of particular severance agreements in particular cases will almost always depend on the applicable pre-bankruptcy severance arrangements already in place, creditor confidence in the debtor's management, and what can be lengthy negotiations among the debtor and creditor constituencies. This sample is taken from the 1998 ***Unison Healthcare Corp.*** reorganization in Phoenix involving a nationwide nursing home operator, and was used primarily to retain the services of Unison's senior-most executives, but also included lower-level management. This agreement was negotiated with an Unsecured Creditors' Committee as well as an Ad Hoc Committee of Bondholders.

Thomas J. Salerno, Esq.
Jordan A. Kroop, Esq.
SQUIRE, SANDERS & DEMPSEY, L.L.P.
40 North Central Avenue, Suite 2700
Phoenix, Arizona 85004
(602) 528-4000

Attorneys for Debtors

IN THE UNITED STATES BANKRUPTCY COURT
FOR THE DISTRICT OF ARIZONA

In re: UNISON HEALTHCARE CORPORATION, and related proceedings, Federal I.D. No. 86-0684011	In Proceedings Under Chapter 11 Case No. B-98-06583-PHX-GBN (Jointly Administered) **DEBTORS' MOTION FOR ORDER APPROVING MANAGEMENT SEVERANCE PACKAGES AND GRANTING RELATED RELIEF**

UNISON HEALTHCARE CORPORATION ("Unison"), and its affiliated Debtors and Debtors-In-Possession in the above-captioned Chapter 11 Cases (the "Debtors"), by and through their undersigned counsel, move the Court for an Order under sections 105(a), 363(b), and 365(a) of Title 11 of the United States Code (the "Bankruptcy Code") authorizing the Debtors to adopt and implement certain severance benefit packages for certain of its senior and mid-level management as a necessary inducement for continued service during the pendency of these Chapter 11 cases and authorizing the Debtors to assume certain executory employment contracts.

Background

On January 7, 1998 (the "Britwill Petition Date"), Debtors Britwill Investments-I, Inc., Britwill Investments-II, Inc., and Britwill Indiana Partnership (the "Britwill Debtors") filed their respective petitions for relief under Chapter 11 of the Bankruptcy Code. The Britwill Debtors continue to operate their businesses and manage their properties as debtors-in-possession under Bankruptcy Code §§ 1107(a) and 1108.

On May 28, 1998 (the "Unison Petition Date"), the Debtors filed their respective petitions for relief under Chapter 11 of the Bankruptcy Code. The Debtors continue to operate their businesses and manage their properties as debtors-in-possession under Bankruptcy Code §§ 1107(a) and 1108.

The Debtors are primarily engaged in the business of providing comprehensive long-term and specialty healthcare services. The majority of the Debtors' operating entities are dedicated to operating approximately 32 skilled nursing facilities located in five states clustered in the Midwest, Southwest, and Southeast. In addition, certain Debtors operate entities which act as suppliers of certain laboratory, pharmacy, and rehabilitation, respiratory, and therapy services, supplying products and services to the Debtors' healthcare facilities as well as to other, non-affiliated facilities.

Since well before the Unison Petition Date, the Debtors have been engaged in extensive restructuring negotiations with their largest creditors. The Debtors' senior management played a critical role in these prepetition negotiations, which led ultimately to the completion, shortly after the Unison Petition Date, of a consensual "term sheet," setting forth the basic terms of a plan of reorganization in these cases. While the eventual plan or plans of reorganization to be filed in these cases will undoubtedly depart from certain items set forth in the term sheet, the term sheet has remained the critical operative document driving continued negotiations of what the Debtors desire to be a fully consensual plan process. Without the tireless, expert assistance of the Debtors' senior management, these cases would not have enjoyed anything close to the progress achieved to this point.

In order to continue working toward the formulation and confirmation of a plan or plans of reorganization in these cases, the Debtors will require the continued efforts and expertise of its senior management. Moreover, in order to maintain operation of the Debtors' businesses and preserve and enhance the Debtors' estates in anticipation of plan confirmation, the Debtors must avoid to the fullest extent possible any disruption in the midlevel management ranks.

Severance Packages

Therefore, in order to induce senior and midlevel management employees to remain in the Debtors' employ and to continue to serve the creditors' interests during the pendency of these cases, the Debtors seek this Court's authorization to adopt and implement severance benefit packages (the "Severance Packages") for their key management personnel.

The management employees eligible for one of the Severance Packages are set forth on the attached Exhibit A. The identities of these employees are subject to minor change pending final approval of this Motion by the Court.

Senior Severance Packages. The Debtors propose that the five senior management employees identified as "Group 1" on Exhibit A ("Senior Management") receive, subject to the conditions below, a Senior Severance Package comprised of one year's salary payable in the event of an involuntary termination without cause on or before three months after the effective date of a plan or plans of reorganization in these cases (the

"Effective Date"):

1. The board of directors of reorganized Unison (or a committee appointed by the board), as it exists after the Effective Date, will evaluate the Senior Management within three months after the Effective Date to determine:

a) which members of Senior Management will be given employment contracts ("New Contracts") after the Effective Date, which must be in substantially the same form as the existing employment contracts between the Debtors and Senior Management, at substantially similar compensation terms as currently existing, and contain not less than twelve months severance (specifically excluding any terms or provisions contained in the executive severance agreements dated as of April 30, 1998 (the "Severance Agreements"), the Court's approval for which is sought in this Motion;

b) the terms of those New Contracts; and

c) the terms of participation in certain options and cash bonuses arising under the terms of an eventual plan of reorganization;

2. If any member of Senior Management declines to accept an offered New Contract, that member may be terminated without a Severance Package;

3. On the Court's approval of the Senior Severance Packages, each member of Senior Management will have waived and released all other claims for severance or other termination payments as may have existed before the Unison Petition Date or the Britwill Petition Date, as applicable, other than the Closing Costs Reimbursement, and the terms of the Senior Severance Packages as set forth here supersede and replace, in their entirety, any prepetition severance or termination agreements or arrangements.

Mid-Level Severance Packages. The Debtors propose that the individuals identified on Exhibit A as "Group 2" (the "Mid-Level Management") receive, subject to the following modifications and provided they agree to remain through the Interim Period, the one-year's salary severance payment provided in their existing employment contracts, which will remain in full force and effect in accordance with their assumption under Bankruptcy Code § 365(a) by the Debtors (authorization for which is also sought in this Motion):

1. A sale of Quest Pharmacies, Inc. ("Quest") will not constitute an involuntary termination for purposes of entitlement to Mid-Level Severance Package benefits for Mr. Wayne Oberfield or Mr. Dan Roberts.

2. No severance payments will be made, and any severance rights will expire:

a) for Mr. Robert Oberfield, on Unison's purchase of the 25% interest in Quest from Mr. Robert Oberfield; and

b) for Mr. Paul Henderson and Mr. Paige Plash, on the sale of Sunbelt Therapy Management Services, Inc.

3. On the Court's approval of the Mid-Level Severance Packages, each member of Mid-Level Management will have waived and released all other claims for severance or any other termination payments (whether contained in employment contracts or otherwise) as may have existed before the Unison Petition Date or the Britwill Petition Date, as applicable, and the terms of the Mid-Level Severance Packages supersede and replace, in their entirety, any prepetition severance or termination agreements or arrangements.

Other Management. The Debtors propose that the individuals identified on Exhibit A as "Group 3" through "Group 6" (the "Other Management") receive, provided they agree to remain through the Interim Period, the severance rights set forth on Exhibit A.

Maintenance Of Status Quo. Other than the revisions to severance rights as set forth above, the basic terms of employment of Senior Management, Mid-Level Management and Other Management (such as compensation, insurance and other benefits, etc.) will remain in full force and effect throughout the Interim Period (specifically excluding the Severance Agreements).

Severance Agreements. The Severance Packages described above are incorporated and constitute the terms of the Severance Agreements, a form of which is attached as Exhibit B, and as a means of adoption and implementation of the Severance Packages, the Debtors seek authority to execute and enter into the Severance Agreements.

Severance Packages are Necessary and Appropriate

Without the immediate adoption of the Severance Packages as a necessary incentive, the Debtors believe, in their best business judgment, that certain of these critical management employees will refuse to remain with the Debtors during the difficult period between now and the confirmation of a plan or plans of reorganization (the "Interim Period") still ahead in these cases. If a large number of management employees were to resign before the Debtors are able to fully implement the restructuring of their operations, the Debtor's efforts to successfully reorganize would be severely undermined.

Moreover, the implementation of the Severance Packages is essential in helping to alleviate the natural anxiety of the Debtors' management employees attendant to these cases and the potentially different management agendas of creditor groups engaged in plan negotiations with the Debtors. Only if these key employees realize that the Debtors will continue to value their contributions in the post-petition period will those employees continue to dispatch their responsibilities with the same dedication and commitment as they did before the Petition Date. Accordingly, authorizing the Debtors to adopt the Severance Packages for management-level employees will enable all of the Debtors' employees to focus their attention on performing their duties during the pendency of these cases without the worry that the Debtors' management employees will resign, creating organizational lapses and inefficiencies.

Assumption of Mid-Level Management Contracts

As indicated above, the Debtors also seek authorization under Bankruptcy Code § 365(a) to assume the executory employment contracts of the members of Mid-Level Management. It is settled law that the decision to assume or reject an executory contract or unexpired lease under Bankruptcy Code § 365(a) is within the debtor's reasonable business judgment, a test that requires a showing that either assumption or rejection of the executory contract at issue will benefit the debtor's estate. *NLRB v. Bildisco & Bildisco*, 465 U.S. 513 (1984).

The Debtors submit that assumption of the Mid-Level Management employment contracts, which govern the terms and conditions of employment for members of Mid-Level Management, as well as their severance and termination benefits, represents the sound exercise of the Debtors' best business judgment. The continued service and dedication of Mid-Level Management is critical to the ongoing operation of the Debtors' businesses, which ultimately inures to the benefit of all creditors. Without the ability to maintain the status quo with respect to the employment terms of these employees, the Debtors will be unable to induce these employees to remain with the Debtors during the difficult stage ahead before the Effective Date. Assumption of these employment contracts indicates to these employees that the Debtors do not intend this reorganization to imperil their continued employment, allowing the employees to focus their attention solely on their responsibilities to continuing operations. Moreover, because the Debtors believe that certain members of Mid-Level Management have at very most minor prepetition claims for compensation, any cure payments arising from the assumption of the employment contracts will be insignificant when compared to the benefit to ongoing operations and the Debtors' estates and creditors. Accordingly, the Debtors request that the Court authorize the assumption of the Mid-Level Management employment contracts.

Conclusion and Relief Requested

Accordingly, the Debtors respectfully request that the Court:

1) Enter the proposed "Order Approving Management Severance Packages and Granting Related Relief," attached as Exhibit C; and

2) Grant any additional relief as the Court deems just and proper.

RESPECTFULLY SUBMITTED this 10th day of August, 1998.

SQUIRE, SANDERS & DEMPSEY, L.L.P.

By: ***/s/ Thomas J. Salerno***
Thomas J. Salerno, Esq.
Jordan A. Kroop, Esq.
40 North Central Avenue, Suite 2700
Phoenix, Arizona 85004
(602) 528-4000

Attorneys for Debtors

EXHIBIT A

Name/Position	Annual Salary	Svrnc. Period (mos.)	Severance Amount
Group 1			
Mike Jeffries/CEO			
Nir Margalit/EX VP CLC			
Clayton Kloehr/Sr VP Treas			
Jimmy Fields/CFO			
Terry Troxell/Sr. VP Clinical			
TOTAL			
Group 2			
Bob Oberfield/VP Pharmacy			
Lisa Buechel/VP Fin. Reporting			
Helen Johnson/Asst. Tres			
Shelley Greget/VP Radm			
Warren Jerrems/VP Contr.			
Debbie Montoya/VP Field Acct			
Wayne Oberfield/Pharmacy			
Dan Roberts/Pharmacy			
Pat Schriebat/Dir. HR			
Paul Henderson/VP Sunbelt			
Paige Plash/VP Sunbelt			
TOTAL			
Group 4			
Tracy Lesson/Dir. Risk mgmt			
Gary Potts/Dir MIS			
Jeff Glaser/Asst. Cont			
Lisa Turner/Ast. Sec			
Petra Dodd/Dir. Reimbursa			
TOTAL			
Group 6			
All other clerical (30 people)			
TOTAL			

Name/Position	Annual Salary	Svrnc. Period (mos.)	Severance Amount
Group 5			
Mike Longnecker/Mgr Fac.			
Colleen Duffy/Mgr. Fin Reprodn			
Rob Gardner/Mgr MIS			
Derek Beacham/Mgr Purch			
Matt Ericson/Mgr AP			
Sandy Ravel/Mgr Legal			
Annet's Durham/Mgr Payroll			
Cindy Cheattle/Mgr AR			
Lori Tolan/Mgr Marketing			
TOTAL			
Group 3			
Mike Little/RDO			
Randy Dains/RDO			
John Sword/RDO			
Hector Ampana/Reg Controls			
Beth Blankenship/Reg Cont			
Bryan Cashman/Reg Cont			
Mark Farrainolo/Acct			
Chris Monorid/Reg Cont			
Christine Nelson/Acct			
Georgia Morens/Clin			
Lori Nelson/Field Acct			
Amy Richmond/Fld Mrk			
Shirley Shockley/Clin			
Vicki Adams/Clin			
Yvonne Allen/Fld Acct			
Andrea Anderson/Fld Markt			
Nancy Cozed/Clin			
Kathy Crouch/Fld Mark			
Wendy Gould/Clin			
Susan Hoffman/Fld Acct			
Elizabeth Holt/Clin			
Melody Lee/Acct			
TOTAL			
GRAND TOTAL			

EXHIBIT B

EXECUTIVE SEVERANCE AGREEMENT

THIS EXECUTIVE SEVERANCE AGREEMENT ("Agreement") is made and entered into as of April 30, 1998, by and among UNISON HEALTHCARE CORPORATION, a Delaware corporation (the "Company"), and **[NAME]** ("Executive").

WHEREAS, the Company desires to retain Executive, and Executive desires to continue to serve, as an officer and employee of the Company, on the terms and conditions hereinafter set forth;

NOW, THEREFORE, in consideration of the mutual covenants contained herein and other valuable consideration, the receipt, adequacy and sufficiency of which is hereby acknowledged, the parties agree as follows:

1.Definitions. For purposes of this Agreement, the following terms are defined:

(a) "Company" means and includes the Company and any subsidiary thereof and any successor or assign unless the context indicates otherwise.

(b) "Effective Date" means the last to occur of:

(i) the first business day that is at least eleven (11) days after the date on which the United States Bankruptcy Court enters an order (the "Confirmation Order") confirming a plan or reorganization (the "Plan") in the Company's Chapter 11 case and on which no stay of the Confirmation Order is in effect; and

(ii) the business day on which all conditions to confirmation and effectiveness of the Plan have been satisfied or waived.

(c) "Cause" means:

(i) the Executive has been convicted of (or pleads guilty to) a felony; or

(ii) the Executive has engaged in willful misconduct or gross negligence in the performance of his employment duties to the Company.

(d) "Good Reason" means any of the following:

(i) The Company's failure to elect or reelect, or to appoint or reappoint, Executive to offices or positions involving duties, responsibilities, authority and dignity of a scope comparable to those of Executive's most significant offices or positions held at any time during the 90-day period immediately preceding the Effective Date;

(ii) Material change by the Company in the Executive's function, duties or responsibilities (including reporting responsibilities) to a scope less than that associated with Executive's most significant position with the Company during the 90-day period immediately preceding the Effective Date;

(iii) Executive's base salary is reduced by the Company;

(iv) Relocation of the Company's corporate headquarters or Executive's principal place of employment to a place located outside of the greater Phoenix metropolitan area; provided that required travel on the Company's business shall not be deemed a relocation so long as Executive is not required to be outside of the greater Phoenix metropolitan area for a period of time that is greater than the period of time he was required to be outside of the greater Phoenix metropolitan area for the twelve month period immediately preceding the Effective Date.

(e) Unless specifically stated to the contrary, all references to "days" and "months" mean calendar days and calendar months, respectively.

(f) "Board" means the Board of Directors of the Company, or a Committee of the Board designated by the Board to fulfill one or more of the Board's responsibilities under this Agreement.

2. <u>Termination by the Company for Cause.</u>

(a) The Company retains the right to terminate Executive's employment for Cause on or before three (3) months after the Effective Date. If Executive's employment is terminated for Cause, Executive will not be entitled to the Severance Benefits described in Paragraph 5 of this Agreement and the Company will have no further liability or obligation to Executive except for amounts earned or accrued under Company sponsored benefit plans before such termination.

(b) No later than three (3) months after the Effective Date, the post-Effective Date Board, if it wishes to continue Executive employment, must present Executive with a new employment contract (the "New Contract"), substantially in the same form and with substantially similar compensation terms (including not less than twelve (12) months severance benefits but specifically excluding any terms or provisions contained in this Agreement) as Executive's then-existing employment contract. If Executive refuses to accept an offered New Contract, the Company retains the right to terminate Executive's employment at any time after Executive's refusal of the New Contract and Executive waives the right to receive the Severance Benefits described in Paragraph 5 of this Agreement.

3. Termination by the Company Without Cause. The Company retains the right to terminate Executive's employment on or before three (3) months after the Effective Date without Cause upon written notice to Executive. In such event, Executive will be entitled to the Severance Benefits described in Paragraph 5 of this Agreement.

4. Termination By Executive for Good Reason.

(a) If Executive does not receive a new contract of employment on or before three (3) months after the Effective Date, Executive will have the right to terminate his employment with the Company at any time after three (3) months after the Effective Date and such termination will be deemed a termination for Good Reason, entitling Executive to receive Severance Benefits described in Paragraph 5 of this Agreement as if the Company had terminated Executive without Cause.

(b) Executive retains the right to terminate his employment with the Company at any time on or before three (3) months after the Effective Date for Good Reason. In such event, subject to the provisions set forth in subparagraph (c) of this paragraph, Executive will receive Severance Benefits described in Paragraph 5 of this Agreement as if the Company had terminated Executive without Cause.

(c) Any termination by the Company without Cause or by the Executive for Good Reason must be communicated by written notice (the "Notice of Termination") to the other party. The Executive's Termination Date will be the date specified in the Notice of Termination where required or in any other case the date upon which the Executive ceases to perform services for the Company; provided that if within thirty days after any Notice of Termination is given, the party receiving such Notice of Termination notifies the other party that a dispute exists concerning the termination, the Termination Date will be the date finally determined to be the Termination Date, either by mutual written agreement of the parties or by binding arbitration in the manner provided in Paragraph 5 below; provided further that the Termination Date will be extended by a notice of dispute only if such notice is given in good faith and the party giving such notice pursues the resolution of such dispute with reasonable diligence. Notwithstanding the pendency of any such dispute, the Company will continue to pay the Executive his full compensation in effect when the notice giving rise to the dispute was given and continue the Executive as a participant in all compensation, benefit and insurance plans in which he was participating when the notice giving rise to the dispute was given, until the dispute is finally resolved in accordance with this subparagraph. Amounts paid under this subparagraph are in addition to all other amounts due under this Agreement and are not to be offset against or used to reduce any other amounts due under this Agreement. However, if the arbitrator determines that the Executive did not terminate for Good Reason or that the Company terminated the Executive for Cause, the Executive must repay the Company the amount of compensation paid to the Executive pursuant to this subparagraph from the Termination Date specified in the Notice of Termination, plus interest thereon at the applicable federal rate provided for in Section 1274(d) of the Internal Revenue Code of 1986, as amended (the "Code") or any successor provision thereof, for an obligation with a term equal to the period from the date of payment to the date of repayment pursuant to this subparagraph.

5. Post-Termination Severance Benefits.

(a) If Executive terminates his employment for Good Reason under Paragraph 4 above, or if the Company terminates Executive's employment without Cause under Paragraph 3 above, the Company must pay to Executive "Severance Benefits," constituting liquidated damages, comprised of:

(i) A lump sum amount equal to twelve (12) months of base salary at the Executive's salary rate in effect as of the Termination Date (as defined below). In addition, the Company must pay to Executive all compensation that Executive earned but remains unpaid as of the Termination Date. All such amounts are to be paid in one lump sum on the Termination Date;

(ii) The Company must maintain in full force and effect for the Executive's continued benefit and the benefit of his eligible beneficiaries, for a period of twelve (12) months following the Termination Date, the employee benefits under the Company's health plan(s) that he or they were eligible to receive immediately before the Termination Date, subject to the terms and conditions of such plan(s); provided that his continued participation or the participation of such eligible dependents or beneficiaries is possible under the general terms and provisions of such plan(s). In the event that the Executive's participation or the participation of such eligible dependents or beneficiaries in any such plan(s) is barred, the Company must arrange to provide him or such eligible dependents or beneficiaries for such period with health benefits substantially similar to those that the Executive and such eligible dependents or beneficiaries are entitled to receive under such plan(s) as of the Termination Date;

(iii) Executive will have the right to exercise, for a period of twelve (12) months following the Termination Date, all vested unexercised stock options and any restricted stock awards outstanding at the Termination Date. Such exercise will be limited by and in accordance with the terms of the plans and agreements pursuant to which such options were issued; and

(iv) If at the Termination Date Executive holds stock options and/or restricted stock awards not then vested or exercisable, all such options and restricted stock awards will immediately vest and become exercisable in accordance with their terms for a period of twelve (12) months from the Termination Date.

6. No Right of Set-Off; No Obligation to Mitigate; Indemnification.

(a) The Company's obligation to make the payments provided for in this Agreement and otherwise to perform its obligations under this Agreement are not to be affected by any set-off, counterclaim, recoupment, defense or other claim, right, or action which the Company may have against the Executive or others. In no event will the Executive be obligated to seek other employment or take any other action by way of mitigation of the amounts payable to the Executive under any of the provisions of the Agreement and such amounts are not to be reduced whether or not the Executive obtains other employment.

(b) The Company intends that Executive should not be required to incur the expenses associated with the enforcement of his rights under this Agreement because the such expenses would substantially detract from the benefits intended to be extended to him under this Agreement, nor be bound to negotiate any settlement of his rights under this Agreement under threat of incurring all of such expenses. Accordingly, if the Company fails to comply with any of its obligations under this Agreement or in the event that the Company or any other person takes any action to declare this Agreement void or unenforceable, the Company must indemnify Executive for all legal costs and fees (including without limitation, attorneys' fees, retainers, arbitration costs, charges for transcripts, fees of experts, witness fees, travel expenses, duplicating costs, printing and binding costs, telephone charges, postage and delivery service fees, and all other disbursements or out-of-pocket expenses) that Executive incurs by asserting or defending his rights under this Agreement. The Company will be obligated to reimburse Executive for the fees and expenses of his chosen counsel on a regular, periodic basis upon presentment by him of a statement or statements prepared by such counsel in accordance with its customary practices, but in no event later than 45 days after such presentment. If such fees and expenses are not reimbursed within 45 days of presentment, the Company must pay Executive interest running from the date of such presentment at the applicable federal rate provided for in Section 1274(d) of the Code, or any successor provision thereof, for an obligation with a term equal to the length of such delay.

7. Arbitration. Any dispute or controversy arising under or in connection with this Agreement must be settled exclusively by arbitration in Phoenix, Arizona in accordance with the rules of the American Arbitration Association then in effect. Judgment may be entered on the arbitrator's award in any court having jurisdiction; provided, however, that the Executive is entitled to seek specific performance of his right to be paid during the pendency of any dispute or controversy arising under or in connection with this Agreement pursuant to Paragraph 4(c) above.

8. Miscellaneous.

(a) This Agreement and all rights provided for under this Agreement are personal to Executive and may not be assigned by him. Any purported assignment is null and void and not binding on the Company. This Agreement is binding upon, and inures to the benefit of, Executive and the Company and their respective successors and assigns.

(b) Except as required by law, no right to receive payments under this Agreement is subject to anticipation, commutation, alienation, sale, assignment, encumbrance, charge, pledge, or hypothecation or to execution, attachment, levy, or similar process or assignment by operation of law, and any attempt, voluntary or involuntary, to effect such action is null, void, and of no effect.

(c) This Agreement may not be modified or amended except by an instrument in writing signed by the parties hereto. No term or condition of this Agreement is to be deemed to have been waived, nor is there to be any estoppel against the enforcement of any provision of this Agreement, except by written instrument of the party charged with such waiver or estoppel. No such written waiver is to be deemed a continuing waiver unless specifically stated therein, and each such waiver will operate only as to the specific term or condition waived and will not constitute a waiver of such term or condition for the future or as to any act other than specifically waived. This Agreement represents the entire agreement of the parties with respect to the subject matter contained herein.

9. Severability. If for any reason any provision of this Agreement is held invalid, such invalidity does not affect any other provision of this Agreement

not held so invalid, and each such other provision will, to the full extent consistent with law, continue in full force and effect. If any provision of this Agreement is held invalid in part, such invalidity will in no way affect the rest of such provision not held so invalid, and the rest of such provision, together with all other provisions of this Agreement, will, to the full extent consistent with law, continue in full force and effect. The parties desire and intend that, if any provision in this Agreement is adjudicated to be invalid or unenforceable by reason of its scope in terms of area, length of time or otherwise, but may be enforceable by limitations thereon, a reviewing court is authorized and empowered by the parties to re-write any such provision to make it enforceable to the maximum extent permissible under law.

10. Notices. All notices, requests, demands and other communications that are required or may be given pursuant to this Agreement must be in writing and will be deemed to have been duly given if delivered personally or sent by certified mail, postage prepaid, as follows:

(a) If to the Company:

UNISON HEALTHCARE CORPORATION
8800 North Gainey Center Drive, Suite 245
Scottsdale, Arizona 85258

(b) If to Executive, to him at:

____

____

____

or such other address as any party hereto designates by notice in writing to the other party. All such notices, requests, demands and communications are to be deemed to have been given on the date of delivery, or, if given by certified mail, on the second business day after mailing.

11. Amendment of Prior Agreements. All prior agreements between the Company and Executive relating to Executive's employment are amended to the extent necessary to be consistent with the terms and conditions of this Agreement, with the terms and conditions of this Agreement controlling in the event of any inconsistency.

12. Headings. The headings of paragraphs herein are included solely for convenience of reference and do not control the meaning or interpretation of any provision of this Agreement.

13. Governing Law. This Agreement has been executed and delivered in the State of Arizona, and its validity, interpretation, performance, and enforcement are governed by the internal laws of Arizona.

IN WITNESS WHEREOF, the Company has caused this Agreement to be executed by its duly authorized officers, and Executive has signed this Agreement, all as of the day and year first written above.

COMPANY:

UNISON HEALTHCARE CORPORATION, a Delaware corporation

By

____

Its ___________________________________

EXECUTIVE:

____
(Signature)

____
(Printed Name)

EXHIBIT C

IN THE UNITED STATES BANKRUPTCY COURT FOR THE DISTRICT OF ARIZONA

In re: UNISON HEALTHCARE CORPORATION, and related proceedings, Federal I.D. No. 86-0684011	In Proceedings Under Chapter 11 Case No. B-98-06583-PHX-GBN (Jointly Administered) **ORDER APPROVING MANAGEMENT SEVERANCE PACKAGES AND GRANTING RELATED RELIEF**

This matter is before the Court on the "Motion For Order Approving Management Severance Packages And Granting Related Relief" of UNISON HEALTHCARE CORPORATION ("Unison"), and its affiliated Debtors and Debtors-In-Possession indicated above (the "Debtors"), dated August 10, 1998 (the "Motion"); the Court having reviewed the Motion; the Court being apprised of the "Kremser Group Response to Motion for Order Approving Management Severance Packages," dated August 28, 1998 (the "Kremser Objection"), the sole objection filed to the Motion; the Kremser Objection having been withdrawn at a hearing before the Court on October 8, 1998; the Court being satisfied that the relief requested in the Motion is necessary and appropriate under the circumstances and under Bankruptcy Code §§ 105(a), 363(b) and 365(a); and after due consideration and reasonable cause appearing therefor,

THE COURT FINDS as follows:

A. The Motion and relief requested therein constitute a "core proceedings" in which this Court may enter final and dispositive orders under 28 U.S.C. §§ 1334 and 157(b)(2)(A) and (O) and Bankruptcy Code §§ 105, 363 and 365.

B. Assumption of the employment contracts for the Debtors' Mid-Level Management employees, as described more fully in the Motion, is a valid exercise of the Debtors' reasonable business judgment and is in the best interests of the Debtors' estates and creditors.

C. Adoption and implementation of the Severance Packages described in the Motion and set forth in the Severance Agreements, the form of which is attached to the Motion as Exhibit B, constitute a valid exercise of the Debtors' reasonable business judgment and is essential to the continued operation of the Debtors' businesses, thereby inuring to the benefit of the Debtors' estates and creditors.

ACCORDINGLY, IT IS HEREBY ORDERED as follows:

1. The Motion is granted in all respects.

2. The Debtors are authorized to adopt and implement the Severance Packages for the individuals identified on Exhibit A to this Order by executing and entering into the Severance Agreements, the form of which, attached as Exhibit B to the Motion, is approved.

3. The Debtors are authorized to assume the employment contracts applicable to all Mid-Level Management employees listed in "Group 2" on Exhibit A to the Motion.

DATED: October 28, 1998

/s/ George B. Nielsen, Jr.

HON. GEORGE B. NIELSEN, JR.
CHIEF UNITED STATES BANKRUPTCY JUDGE

APPENDIX G

SAMPLE "CHINESE WALL" AGREEMENT

The following ***"Chinese Wall"*** procedures (otherwise referred to as "*Information-Blocking Procedures*") were instituted in the ***Megafoods Stores*** Chapter 11 proceedings in 1994. The debtor was the operator of a large regional chain of supermarkets. Certain members of the Unsecured Creditors' Committee were current holders of the debtor's bonds. The blocking procedures were established to ensure that the bondholders' activities as members of the Committee would be insulated and separated from those members' trading desks with respect to the debtor's bonds. The concern in this case is present in many cases: the bondholder member of a Committee will become privy to extensive non-public, confidential information regarding the debtor and its operations and finances. Trading on such information would create many legal and fiduciary problems, so the bondholder will erect a "Chinese Wall" to separate its trading desk from its workout and reorganization desk.

THOMAS J. SALERNO
CRAIG D. HANSEN
JORDAN A. KROOP
SQUIRE, SANDERS & DEMPSEY L.L.P.
40 North Central Avenue, Suite 2700
Phoenix, Arizona 85004
(602) 528-4000
Counsel For The Debtors

PAUL S. ARONZON
VALERIE A. LONGMIRE
MILBANK, TWEED, HADLEY & McCLOY
601 South Figueroa, 32nd Floor
Los Angeles, California 90017
(213) 892-4000
Counsel for the Official Committee
of Unsecured Creditors

IN THE UNITED STATES BANKRUPTCY COURT FOR THE DISTRICT DISTRICT OF ARIZONA

In re MEGAFOODS STORES, INC., a Nevada corporation; HANDY ANDY, INC., a Delaware corporation; MEGAFOODS REAL ESTATE, INC., a Nevada corporation; TEXAS NATIONAL FOOD STORE LEASING CO., a Texas corporation; Debtors.	Case Nos.: B-94-7410 through 94-7413 (Jointly Administered) Chapter 11 **JOINT MOTION OF THE DEBTORS AND THE OFFICIAL COMMITTEE OF UNSECURED CREDITORS, OF PAINEWEBBER INCORPORATED, AND OF ALLIANCE CORPORATE FINANCE GROUP INCORPORATED (ON BEHALF OF THE EQUITABLE LIFE ASSURANCE SOCIETY OF THE UNITED STATES) FOR AN ORDER APPROVING SPECIFIED INFORMATION BLOCKING PROCEDURES AND PERMITTING SECURITIES TRADING IN CERTAIN CIRCUMSTANCES**

Megafoods Stores, Inc. (the "Debtor") and the Official Committee (the "Committee") of Unsecured Creditors of Megafoods Stores, Inc., Handy Andy, Inc., Megafoods Real Estate, Inc. and Texas National Food Store Leasing, Inc. (collectively, the "Debtors"), appointed by the United States Trustee (the "Trustee") on August 18, 1994, of PaineWebber Incorporated ("PaineWebber"), and of Alliance Corporate Finance Group Incorporated ("Alliance") (acting on behalf of The Equitable Life Assurance Society of the United States ("Equitable") (collectively, PaineWebber and Alliance are referred to herein as the "Bondholders"), as individual members of the Committee, hereby jointly bring this Motion for an Order Approving Specified Information Blocking Procedures And Permitting Securities Trading In Certain Circumstances" (the "Motion").

By this Motion, the Debtors, the Committee and the Bondholders (collectively, the "Movants") respectfully request that the Court enter an order determining that the Bondholders will not be violating their respective duties as members of the Committee (and accordingly will not be subjecting their claims to possible disallowance, subordination or other adverse treatment) by trading in the Debtors' securities, during the pendency of the Debtors' chapter 11 case. To that end, the Bondholders will establish and maintain certain specified information blocking procedures to insulate the Bondholders' trading activities from their activities as members of the Committee.

The Motion is made on the grounds that the Bondholders' continued membership on the Committee is vital to the reorganization process and the protection of the interests of their investor constituents. Additionally, both the courts and the Securities and Exchange Commission (the "SEC") have favored such bondholder committee membership subject to information blocking devices similar to the ones proposed herein.

The Motion is filed pursuant to chapter 11 of Title 11 of the United States Code (the "Bankruptcy Code"), the Memorandum of Points and Authorities, exhibits, and Declarations of Paul H. Phaneuf and Kate Kutasi filed concurrently herewith, the files, records and other pleadings in these cases, as well as all matters of which this court properly may take judicial notice.

The Movants further move this Court for an order setting a hearing only upon the objection and a request for a hearing. Any such objection and request for a hearing must be in writing and must set forth with particularity the grounds for objection to the Motion. Any objection must be filed and served not later than fifteen (15) days from the date of the "Notice of Filing of Motion of the Official Committee of Unsecured Creditors, of PaineWebber Incorporated, and of Alliance Corporate Finance Group

Incorporated (On Behalf of the Equitable Life Assurance Society of the United States) for an Order Approving Specified Information Blocking Procedures and Permitting Securities Trading in Certain Circumstances." Failure to file and serve an objection may be deemed by the Court to be consent to the granting of the relief requested.

Dated: October 3, 1994 RESPECTFULLY SUBMITTED,

SQUIRE SANDERS & DEMPSEY LLP

By: ***/s/ Thomas J. Salerno***
Thomas J. Salerno
Craig D. Hansen
Jordan A. Kroop
Attorneys For The Debtors

MILBANK, TWEED, HADLEY & McCLOY

By: ***/s/ Paul S. Aronzon***
Paul S. Aronzon
Valerie S. Longmire
Attorneys for Official Committee of Unsecured Creditors

MEMORANDUM OF POINTS AND AUTHORITIES

INTRODUCTION

The Official Committee (the "Committee") of Unsecured Creditors of Megafoods Stores, Inc., Handy Andy, Inc., Megafoods Real Estate, Inc. and Texas National Food Store Leasing, Inc. (collectively, the "Debtors"), appointed by the United States Trustee (the "Trustee") on August 18, 1994, of PaineWebber Incorporated ("PaineWebber"), and of Alliance Corporate Finance Group Incorporated ("Alliance") (acting on behalf of The Equitable Life Assurance Society of the United States ("Equitable")) (collectively, PaineWebber and Alliance are referred to herein as the "Bondholders"), as individual members of the Committee, submit this "Memorandum of Points and Authorities in Support of the Motion of the Official Committee of Unsecured Creditors, of PaineWebber Incorporated, and of Alliance Corporate Finance Group Incorporated (on behalf of Equitable Life Assurance Society of the United States), for an Order Approving Specified Information Blocking Procedures And Permitting Securities Trading In Certain Circumstances" (the "Motion").

The Debtors.

The Debtors commenced their reorganization case on August 17, 1994, by filing a voluntary petition under the Bankruptcy Code. Megafoods Stores, Inc. filed a motion with this Court to jointly administer its case with that of Megafoods Real Estate, Inc., Handy Andy, Inc., and Texas National Food Store Leasing Co. The administrative consolidation motion was granted by this Court on September 7, 1994. The Debtors have continued to operate their businesses as debtors-in-possession pursuant to Bankruptcy Code §§ 1107(a) and 1108.

Pursuant to Bankruptcy Code § 1102(a)(1), the United States Trustee for the District of Arizona appointed the Committee on August 18, 1994, to represent the interests of the Debtors' unsecured creditors. A copy of the United States Trustee's Appointment of Committee of Unsecured Creditors is attached hereto as Exhibit 1. Paul Phaneuf, First Vice President of the High Yield Capital Markets Division of PaineWebber ("Phaneuf"), was appointed to represent PaineWebber on the Committee. *See* Declaration of Phaneuf (the "Phaneuf Declaration"), ¶ 3, attached hereto. Kate Kutasi, an investment officer of Equitable and a Managing Director of Alliance "Kutasi"), was appointed to represent Equitable on the Committee. *See* Declaration of Kutasi (the "Kutasi Declaration"), ¶ 3, attached hereto.

The Information Blocking Procedures.

Alliance.

Alliance proposes that the information blocking procedures ("IBP") that it has established and maintained, be continued as a condition precedent to its trading in the securities. These internal procedures include: (i) written acknowledgment by relevant Alliance personnel that they have received, reviewed and are in full compliance with the firm's IBP's and guidelines; (ii) a prohibition against employees engaged in transactional activities, sharing, discussing or exchanging any written or oral non-public information, whether or not material, with employees performing investment management activities; (iii) a prohibition against disclosing written or oral material non-public information to employees engaged in investment management activities and limiting access to such information to employees engaged in transactional activities (and to directors and senior executives of Alliance who are not actually involved in investment management decisions, compliance officers, and certain identified accountants, lawyers or other outside professional advisors); (iv) restrictions to help assure the confidentiality of material non-public information including limiting access to office areas where inside information may be discussed, securing confidential documents in locked cabinets or other secure locations; (v) where necessary, prohibitions against any employee engaged in investment management activities who has access to material non-public information from buying, selling, trading or recommending the securities, or participating in any decisions to do so; and (vi) an internal compliance review process to assure that any trades of securities by Alliance were made in compliance with the IBP's. As discussed more fully below, other courts and the SEC commonly approve such IBP's in similar circumstances.

PaineWebber.

PaineWebber proposes that the IBP's that PaineWebber has established and maintained, be continued as a condition precedent to its trading in the securities. These internal procedures include: (i) written acknowledgement by PaineWebber personnel that they have received, reviewed and are in full compliance with the firm's IBP's and guidelines; (ii) a prohibition against investment banking personnel (including employees who serve on creditor's committee) sharing, discussing or exchanging any material non-public information with employees engaged in research, sales, trading, portfolio management and administrative activities; (iii) a prohibition against disclosing material non-public information to any other person except firm personnel or persons outside the firm (such as the firm's outside counsel or accountants) who have a valid business reason for receiving such information, *i.e.,* who have a "need to know" the information to serve the business purposes of the firm or clients; (iv) restrictions to help assure the confidentiality of material non-public information including limiting access to office areas where inside information may be discussed, securing confidential documents in locked file cabinets or other secure locations and, where appropriate, physically segregating various business units of the firm; (v) prohibitions against any investment banking personnel who have access to material non-public information from buying, selling, trading or recommending the securities, or participating in any decisions to do so; and (vi) internal compliance restrictions and reviews to assure that any trades of securities by PaineWebber are made in compliance with the IBP's. As discussed more fully below, other courts and the SEC commonly approve such IBP's in similar circumstances.

ARGUMENT

The Policy Underlying the Appointment of Committees, the Securities Trading Regulations, and the Securities and Exchange Commission Support the Use of Information Blocking Procedures as a Means of Allowing Committee Members to Trade in the Debtors' Securities.

Compelling policy reasons exist in favor of allowing trading bondholders to serve on a committee. Robert C. Pozer and Judy K. Mencher, "Chinese Walls For Creditors' Committee", 48 *Bus. Law.* 747 (1993).

The Bondholders are obligated to maximize returns for their investors through the trading of securities. But, as members of the Committee, the Bondholders' representatives may have access to confidential information regarding the Debtors and, thus, owe a fiduciary duty to other holders of the securities not to profit from their status as insiders. The result is that the Bondholders may be prevented from trading in the Debtors' securities during the pendency of the Debtors' chapter 11 case because of their duties to others as a member of the Committee.

If the Bondholders are barred from trading in the securities during the pendency of the Debtors' case because of their fiduciary duties to other creditors, they face a dilemma: they can remain members of the Committee and risk the loss of beneficial investment opportunities for their investors, or resign from the Committee and possibly compromise their shareholders' existing positions in the securities by not contributing to the reorganization process as a member of the Committee. Moreover, for the Committee, the unpleasant alternatives are either to lose the services of a potentially valuable member, or to risk damage to the Committee's role in the reorganization process from allegations that one of its members violated its fiduciary duties as a Committee member.

The solution to this dilemma is to allow the Bondholders to serve on the Committee and to trade in the securities on terms that protect the interests of others. Therefore, the Movants seek an order of this Court holding that the Bondholders will not be violating their fiduciary duties as members of the Committee (and, therefore, will not be subjecting their claims to possible disallowance, subordination or other adverse treatment) by trading in the securities during the pendency of the Debtors' chapter 11 case. Such an order should be granted provided that they use IBP's to insulate their trading activities from their activities as a member of the Committee. Such IBP's are common throughout the securities trading industry as a means for financial institutions to provide different types of financial services to their customers without violating the federal securities laws. The Movants submit that just as IBP's are an accepted means under the federal securities law for permitting financing institutions to trade without misusing "inside information," so too will the IBP's in the instant situation ensure that the Bondholders' trading in the securities will not constitute an abuse of their Committee position or a violation of their fiduciary duties as members of the Committee.

The Securities and Exchange Commission and the Courts Have Supported the Use of Information Blocking Procedures in Similar Situations

The order that the Movants seek is identical to orders entered in at least five other Chapter 11 cases. *In re Federated Departments Stores, Inc.*, 1991 Bankr. LEXIS 288, No. 1-900130, slip. op. (Bankr. S.D. Ohio, entered March 7, 1991) (bondholder may sit on creditors' committee when it employs the appropriate information blocking devices); *In re Harvard Industries, Inc.*, Nos. 91-404, 91-479 to 91-487, slip op. (Bankr. D. Del., entered July 15, 1991) (same); *In re Farley, Inc.*, No. 91-B-15610 (Bankr. N.D. Ill., entered November 8, 1991) (same); *In re Days Inn of America, Inc.*, Nos. 91-978 through 91-986 inclusive (Bankr. D. Del., entered January 31, 1992) (same); and, *In re Interco, Inc.*, No. 91-40442-172-BKC-JJB (Bankr. E.D. Mo., entered February 7, 1992) (same). Copies of the foregoing orders are annexed hereto as Exhibits 2, 3, 4, 5 and 6, respectively. The order entered in each of these cases provides that a committee member will not violate its fiduciary duties as a committee member if it trades in the debtors' securities in accordance with information blocking procedures set forth therein and approved in advance by those courts. Under those orders, the courts reserved the right to take appropriate action if an actual breach of fiduciary duty occurs because the IBP's are not followed or for any other unrelated reason.

The SEC filed a memorandum supporting the entry of an order instituting information blocking procedures in the *Federated Department Stores* case.[1] As the SEC explained in its memorandum, neither the federal securities laws nor the Bankruptcy Code precludes a court from granting relief of this kind:

[1]The SEC memorandum contains a thorough analysis of the relevant law and is often cited as the seminal piece of IBPs for creditors' committees. In lieu of preparing and filing an additional memorandum of law on the identical subject with substantially the same arguments, the Committee adopts the legal analysis in the SEC's memorandum and annexes a copy as Exhibit 7 in support of the Motion.

> [C]onsistent with the requirements of the federal securities laws and the bankruptcy laws, an entity that is engaged in the trading of securities as a regular part of its business and that has implemented procedures reasonably designed to prevent the transmission to its trading personnel of information obtained through service on an official committee is not precluded from serving on the committee and, at the same time, trading in the debtor's securities.

SEC Memorandum at p. 3; *see also* Alan R. Bromberg & Lewis D. Lowenfels, *Securities Fraud &_Commodities Fraud*, § 7.5 (312) (1993).

The result urged by the SEC is consistent with good corporate practice regardless of the existence of a bankruptcy case. The use of IBP's, such as those suggested here, have become a common method by which firms such as the Bondholders guard against the misuse of non-public information. *See SEC Memorandum* at p. 3; 48 *Bus. Law.* at 754-757. In fact, such devices are mandated under the Insider Trading Securities Fraud Enforcement Act of 1988 for broker-dealers and investment advisers and provide a defense to actions brought under the anti-fraud provisions of the securities laws. *See* 15 U.S.C. §78(o)f and 15 U.S.C. §80b-4a. There is no reason why the same techniques should not be employed in a bankruptcy reorganization case, particularly when (i) the same danger – trading on insider information – is to be protected against; (ii) nothing in the Bankruptcy Code or Bankruptcy Rules would prohibit such trading; and (iii) strong bankruptcy policies that encourage participation on creditors' committees militate towards such a result. 48 *Bus. Law.* at 756-757.

The SEC also observed that large institutional creditors may be among a debtor's largest creditors and "have skills and expertise that are likely to be extremely valuable to the committee," and concluded that there should be no "legal impediment to permitting the service of such entities on official committees." *SEC Memorandum* at p. 3. The Bankruptcy Courts in *Federal Department Stores, Harvard Industries, Farley, Days Inn, and Interco* concurred. *See* Exhibits 2, 3, 4, 5 and 6, respectively.

Allowing the Debtors' Largest Creditors to Serve on the Committee Constitutes Sound Bankruptcy Policy

The Bondholders rank among the Debtors' largest security holders and creditors. As such, they have a great incentive to pursue Committee work diligently toward the goal of confirming a plan of reorganization. Moreover, as a matter of sound bankruptcy policy, the largest creditors of a debtor, who often have substantial expertise and experience in reorganizations, should not be deterred from serving on a committee. *See SEC Memorandum* at p. 3; 48 *Bus. Law*. at 747-749. This result would be contrary to the expressed intent of the Bankruptcy Code, which states in pertinent part that an appointed committee "shall ordinarily consist of the persons, willing to serve, that hold the . . . largest claims against the debtor of the kinds represented on such committee." Bankruptcy Code § 1102(b)(1).

The Movants submit that in light of the present financial environment, trading by committee members in a debtor's securities makes even more sense. During the past several years, high yield securities have coma to represent a significant portion of the unsecured claims against financially distressed companies. Unlike traditional bank loans, most high yield securities are actively traded and the largest investors in them place great importance on the liquidity of the securities in which they invest. Further, many of the large holders of such securities, as are the Bondholders in this case, are financial managers or other fiduciaries investing on behalf of their clients. A financial manager's decision to sell and buy securities is generally driven by the decisions of its clients as they increase or withdraw their investments.

The Bondholders should not be precluded from trading in the Securities during the pendency of the Debtors' chapter 11 cases. The Bondholders, by establishing IBP's have complied with such procedures, and have the experience to make their presence on the Committee particularly valuable. *See SEC Memorandum* at p. 3.

Approval of the motion without a Hearing is Appropriate.

It is appropriate that the Court consider the Motion without a hearing if none is specifically requested under the circumstances of this case. Given the size of this case and the need to begin active committee participation in the bankruptcy case, an order based on notice and opportunity to request a hearing is appropriate for this Motion.

CONCLUSION

WHEREFORE, the Movants respectfully request that this Court enter an order in the form attached as Exhibit 8 (i) determining that the Bondholders will not be violating their fiduciary duties as members of the Committee (and accordingly will not be subjecting their claims to possible disallowance, subordination, or other adverse treatment) by trading in the securities of the Debtors during the pendency of the Debtors' chapter 11 cases, provided that the Bondholders use their IBP's to insulate their trading activities from their activities as members of the Committee: (ii) approving the order attached as Exhibit 8 without a hearing unless one is specifically requested; and (iii) granting such other and further relief as the Court may consider appropriate.

Dated: October 3, 1994 RESPECTFULLY SUBMITTED,

SQUIRE SANDERS & DEMPSEY LLP

By: ***/s/ Thomas J. Salerno***
Thomas J. Salerno
Craig d. Hansen
Jordan A. Kroop
Attorneys For The Debtors

MILBANK, TWEED, HADLEY & McCLOY

By: ***/s/ Paul S. Aronzon***
Paul S. Aronzon
Valerie S. Longmire
Attorneys for Official Committee of Unsecured Creditors

DECLARATION OF PAUL R. PHANEUF

I, Paul H. Phaneuf, hereby declare:

1. I have personal knowledge of each of the facts stated in this Declaration, except for those facts stated on information and belief and, as to those facts, I am informed and believe them to be true. I am submitting this Declaration in support of the "Memorandum of Points and Authorities in Support of Motion of the Debtor And The Official Committee of Unsecured Creditors, of PaineWebber Incorporated, and of Alliance Corporate Finance Group Incorporated (on behalf of The Equitable Life Assurance Society of the United States) for an order Approving Specified Information Blocking Procedures and Permitting Securities Trading in Certain Circumstances" (the "Motion"). Capitalized terms not defined herein are used as defined in the Motion.

2. I am a First Vice President of the High Yield Capital Markets Division of PaineWebber, one of the bondholders that hold securites in the Debtors' cases. In that capacity, I am the representative for such finds that serve on committees in out-of-court restructurings and chapter 11 reorganization cases. In addition to being PaineWebber's representative on the Committee in this case, I currently am representing or in the past have represented other Bondholders on committees in such cases as Kash 'n Karry, Inc. In each of those cases the information blocking procedures described in Paragraph 5 below have been in place, and I have complied with they fully.

3. Pursuant to Bankruptcy Code § 1102(a)(1), the United States Trustee for the District of Arizona appointed the Committee on August 18, 1994, to represent the interests of the Debtors' unsecured creditors. I was appointed by the United States Trustee to represent PaineWebber on the Committee.

4. I have read the Motion and, to the best of my knowledge, the statements set forth therein, and the exhibits attached thereto, are true and correct.

5. On behalf of PaineWebber, I propose that information blocking procedures ("IBP") that PaineWebber has established and maintained, be continued as a condition precedent to its trading in the securities. These internal procedures include: (i) written acknowledgment by PaineWebber personnel that they have received, reviewed and are in full compliance with the firm's IBP's and guidelines: (ii) a prohibition against investment banking personnel (including employees who serve on creditor's committees) sharing, discussing or exchanging any material non-public information with employees engaged in research, sales, trading, portfolio management and administrative activities: (iii) a prohibition against disclosing material nonpublic information to any other person except firm personnel or persons outside the firm (such as the firm's outside counsel or accountants) who have a valid business reason for receiving such, information, *i.e.*, who have a "need to know" the information

to serve the business purposes of the firm or clients; (iv) restrictions to help assure the confidentiality of material nonpublic information including limiting access to office areas where inside information may be discussed, securing confidential documents in locker file cabinets or other secure locations and, where inside information may be discussed, securing confidential documents in locked file cabinets or other secure locations and, where appropriate, physically segregating various business units of the firm: (v) prohibitions against any investment banking personnel who have access to material nonpublic information from buying, selling, trading or recommending the securities, or participating in any decisions to do so; and (vi) internal compliance restrictions and reviews to assure that any trades of securities by PaineWebber are made in compliance with the IBP's.

6. Since my appointment to the Committee I have complied with the information blocking procedures set forth above with respect to the securities.

I declare under penalty of perjury that the foregoing is true and correct.

Executed this 28th day of September 1994, at New York, New York.

By: ***/s/ Paul H. Phaneuf***
Paul H. Phaneuf

DECLARATION OF KATE KUTASI

I, Kate Kutasi, hereby declare:

1. I have personal knowledge of each of the facts stated in this Declaration, except for those facts stated on information and belief and, as to those facts, I am informed and believe them to be true. I am submitting this Declaration in support of the "Memorandum of Points and Authorities in Support of Motion the Debtors And The Official Committee of Unsecured Creditors, of PaineWebber Incorporated, and of Alliance Corporate Finance Group Incorporated ("Alliance") (on behalf of The Equitable Life Assurance Society of the United States "Equitable"), for an Order Approving Specified Information Blocking Procedures and Permitting Securities Trading in Certain Circumstances" (the "Motion"). Capitalized terms not defined herein are used as defined in the Motion.

2. I am a Managing Director at Alliance and an investment officer at Equitable, a holder of securities in the Debtors' cases. In that capacity, I am the representative for such funds that saws on committees in out-of-court restructurings and chapter 11 reorganization cases.

3. Pursuant to Bankruptcy Code § 1102(a)(1), the United States Trustee for the District of Arizona appointed the Committee on August 18, 1994, to represent the interests of the Debtors' unsecured creditors. I was appointed by the United States Trustee to represent Equitable on the Committee.

4. I have read the Motion and, to the best of my knowledge, the statements set forth therein, and the exhibits attached thereto, are true and correct.

5. On behalf of Equitable, I propose that information blocking procedures ("IBP") that Alliance has established and maintained, be continued as a condition precedent to its trading in the securities. These internal procedures include: (i) written acknowledgment by relevant personnel that they have received, reviewed and are in full compliance with the firm's IBP's and guidelines; (ii) a prohibition against employees engaged in transactional activities, sharing, discussing or exchanging any written or oral non-public information, whether or not material, with employees performing investment management activities; (iii) a prohibition against disclosing written or oral material nonpublic information to employees engaged in investment management activities and limiting access to such information to employees engaged in transactional activities (and to directors and senior executives of Alliance who are not actually involved in investment management decisions, compliance officers, and certain identified accountants, lawyers or other outsides professional advisors); (iv) restrictions to help assure the confidentiality of material nonpublic information including limiting access to office areas where inside information may be discussed, securing confidential documents in locked cabinets or other secures locations; (v) where necessary, prohibitions against any employees engaged in investment management activities who has access to material nonpublic information from buying,

selling, trading or recommending the securities, or participating in any decisions to do so; and (vi) an internal compliance review process to assure that any trades of securities by Alliance were made in compliance with the IBP's.

6. Since my appointment to the Committee I have complied with the information blocking procedures set forth above with respect to the securities.

I declare under penalty of perjury that the foregoing is true and correct.

Executed this 27th day of September 1994, at New York, New York.

By: ***/s/ Kate Kutasi***
Kate Kutasi

IN THE UNITED STATES BANKRUPTCY COURT FOR THE DISTRICT OF ARIZONA

In re

MEGAFOODS STORES, INC., a Nevada corporation; HANDY ANDY, INC., a Delaware corporation; MEGAFOODS REAL ESTATE, INC., a Nevada corporation; TEXAS NATIONAL FOOD STORE LEASING CO., a Texas corporation;
Debtors.

Case Nos.: B-94-7410 through 94-7413

(Jointly Administered)

Chapter 11

ORDER APPROVING SPECIFIED INFORMATION BLOCKING PROCEDURES AND PERMITTING SECURITIES TRADING IN CERTAIN CIRCUMSTANCES

The Court, having considered the "Motion of the Debtors And The Official Committee of Unsecured Creditors, of PaineWebber Incorporated, and of Alliance Corporate Finance Group Incorporated (on behalf of the Equitable Life Assurance Society of the United States) for an Order Approving Specified Information Blocking Procedures and Permitting Securities Trading in Certain Circumstances" (the "Motion") dated October 3, 1994, the Memorandum of Points and Authorities and Declarations of Paul H. Phaneuf and Kate Kutasi in support thereof and the Exhibits attached thereto, and that the Motion received no opposition to the relief requested therein, finds that (a) the notice of the Motion was sufficient; (b) no objection to the Motion having been filed and no request for hearing having been made; (c) the relief requested in the Motion is appropriate; (d) good and sufficient cause exists therefore; and, accordingly,

IT IS HEREBY ORDERED THAT:

1. PaineWebber Incorporated and Alliance Corporate Finance Group (acting on behalf of the Equitable Life Assurance Society of the United States) (the "Bondholders") will not be violating their fiduciary duties as members of the Committee and, accordingly, will not be subjecting their claims to possible disallowance, subordination, or other adverse treatment, by trading in the debt securities of Megafoods Stores Inc. *et al.* ("Megafoods"), during the pendency of the Megafoods' Chapter 11 case, provided that, the Bondholders have satisfied and effectively implemented appropriate information blocking procedures.

DATED: October 20, 1994

Hon. Redfield T. Baum
Hon. Redfield T. Baum
UNITED STATES BANKRUPTCY JUDGE

APPENDIX H

SAMPLE CONFIDENTIALITY AGREEMENT

To encourage the free flow of information between a debtor and members of official committees, or prospective asset purchasers, or even potential DIP lenders, a debtor will often (and usually should) insist on an agreement with the recipient of such information that the information will remain confidential, undisclosed, and immune from inappropriate use (such as a basis for trading in the debtor's securities). These protections are especially necessary when the information to be disclosed concerns proprietary, nonpublic financial information, operations data, and internal analyses of liabilities. With an active committee (and certainly with a potential acquiror), there is little information that the debtor can reasonably withhold, particularly when the recipient executes an appropriate confidentiality agreement such as the one included here, which was derived from the confidentiality agreement in the ***Unison HealthCare Corporation*** Chapter 11 case.

CONFIDENTIALITY AGREEMENT

This Confidentiality Agreement is dated as of March __, 1998 (the "Agreement") by and among ***Unison HealthCare Corporation*** and its subsidiaries and affiliates, debtors and debtors in possession in their pending Chapter 11 cases (collectively, the "Company") and ______________________, a member of the Committee of Unsecured Creditors appointed pursuant to 11 U.S.C. § 1102 (the "Committee").

WITNESSETH

WHEREAS, the Company is currently undergoing a reorganization proceedings under Chapter 11 of the Federal Bankruptcy Code (the "Restructuring");

WHEREAS, you have agreed to serve as a member of the Committee; and

WHEREAS, during the course of any discussions and negotiations regarding the Restructuring, the Company will provide to you and the Committee certain Information (as defined below).

AGREEMENT

NOW THEREFORE, in consideration of the foregoing and for good and valuable consideration, the receipt and adequacy which are hereby acknowledged, the parties hereto agree as follows:

1. Confidential Information. As used herein, the term "Information" means any and all information concerning the Company (whether prepared by the Company, its advisors or otherwise and irrespective of the form of communication) that is furnished to you or any of your agents or advisors (collectively, "Representatives") now or in the future by or on behalf of the Company. In addition, "Information" shall be deemed to include all notes, analyses, compilations, studies, interpretations and other documents prepared by you, the Committee or any of your respective Representatives which contain, reflect or are based upon, in whole or in part, the information furnished to you or any of your Representatives pursuant to this Agreement. The term "Information" does not include information which: (i) is or becomes available to the public generally (other than as a result of a disclosure by you, the Committee or any of your respective Representatives); (ii) becomes available to you on a non-confidential basis from a source other than the Company, provided that such source is not, to the best of your knowledge, bound by a confidentiality agreement with, or any contractual, legal or fiduciary obligation of confidentiality to, the Company or any other person with respect to such information; (iii) has been independently acquired or developed by you or any of your Representatives without violating any of the obligations under this Agreement; or (iv) was within the possession of you or any of your Representatives prior to being furnished by or on behalf of the Company, whether pursuant to this Agreement or otherwise.

2. Accuracy of Information. Although the Company will provide such Information as it believes to be relevant to the Restructuring, neither the Company nor any of its officers, directors, employees or agents makes any representation or warranty, express or implied, as to the accuracy or completeness of any of the Information. You agree that neither the Company nor any of its officers, directors, employees or agents shall have any liability to you or to any of your Representatives relating to or resulting from the use of the Information or any errors therein or omissions therefrom.

3. Use of Information and Confidentiality.

A. As a condition to the furnishing of the Information to you and your Representatives, you agree that all Information furnished to you, whether prior to or after your acceptance of this letter, by the Company or any of the Company's Representatives or by the Committee or any of its Representatives, will be kept strictly confidential; provided, however, that you may disclose Information: (i) to your Representatives who have a need to know such Information for the sole purpose of evaluating the Restructuring (it being understood that such Representatives shall be informed by you of the substance of this Agreement and that, by receiving such Information, such Representatives shall agree to be bound by the terms and conditions hereof); and (ii) in all other cases, to the extent that the Company gives its prior written consent to such disclosure. You agree to take all reasonable measures to keep the Information confidential and to take all reasonable measures to restrain your Representatives from prohibited or unauthorized disclosure or use of the Information.

B. In the event that you or any of your Representatives are requested or required (by oral questions, interrogatories, requests for information or documents in legal proceedings, subpoena, civil investigative demand or other similar process) to disclose any of the Information, you shall provide the Company with written notice as promptly as reasonably practicable of any such request or requirement so that the Company may seek a protective order or other appropriate remedy or waive compliance with the provisions of this Agreement. If the Company waives compliance with the provisions of this Agreement with respect to a specific request or requirement, you and your Representatives shall disclose only that portion of the Information that is covered by such waiver and which is necessary to disclose in order to comply with such request or requirement. If, in the absence of a protective order or other remedy or a waiver by the Company, you or any of your Representatives is nonetheless, as set forth in a written opinion of independent legal counsel, legally compelled to disclose any Information, you or such Representative may, without liability hereunder, disclose only that portion of the Information which such counsel opines is legally required to be disclosed. Notwithstanding the foregoing, in the event that you or any of your Representatives discloses Information under the terms of this subsection, you and/or such Representative shall take all reasonable measures to preserve the confidentiality of the Information, including, without limitation, by cooperating with the Company to obtain an appropriate protective order or other reliable assurance that confidential treatment will be accorded the Information.

C. At such time as (i) the Company notifies you in writing (it being understood that the Company may make such request in its discretion and without providing any reason therefor), (ii) you notify the Company in writing that you do not wish to receive any further Information, or (iii) you notify the Company in writing that you do not wish to pursue the Restructuring or you cease to be a member of the Committee, you shall deliver promptly to the Company all Information furnished to you or any of your Representatives by or on behalf of the Company or the Committee, together with all copies of such Information in your possession or control or in the possession or control of any of your Representatives. In such event, you agree to destroy any and all other Information prepared by you or any of your Representatives or in your possession or control or in the possession or control of any of your Representatives, together with all copies thereof (including, without limitation, electronic copies). Notwithstanding the return or destruction of the Information, you and your Representatives will continue to be bound by your respective obligations of confidentiality hereunder.

D. You hereby acknowledge that you are aware (and that any person to whom you disclose Information has been, or upon receiving such information will be, advised) of the restrictions imposed by federal and state securities laws on a person possessing material nonpublic information about a company, including certain Information.

4. Access to and Solicitation of Employees. You agree to submit or direct to the Company or its designee all: (a) communications with the Company regarding the Restructuring; (b) requests for additional information from the Company; (c) requests for facility tours or management meetings; and (d) discussions or questions regarding procedures. You agree that, for a period of three (3) years from the date hereof, you will not solicit for employment any individual currently serving as director, officer, employee or agent of the Company without obtaining the prior written consent of the Company.

5. Remedies. It is understood and agreed that money damages would not be a sufficient remedy for any breach of this Agreement by you or any of your Representatives and that the Company shall be entitled to equitable relief, including injunction and specific performance, as a remedy for such breach. Such remedies shall not be deemed to be the exclusive remedies for a breach by you of this Agreement, but shall be in addition to all other remedies available at law or equity to the Company. In the event of litigation relating to this Agreement, if a court of competent jurisdiction determines that you or any of your Representatives has breached this Agreement, you shall be liable for and pay to the Company on demand the legal fees and expenses incurred by the Company in connection with such litigation, including any appeal therefrom.

6. Waiver and Amendments. No failure or delay by any party in exercising any right, power or privilege hereunder shall operate as a waiver thereof, nor shall any single or partial exercise thereof preclude any other or future exercise thereof or the exercise of any other right, power or privilege hereunder. No provisions of this Agreement can be amended without the specific written consent of each of the parties hereto.

7. Counterparts. For the convenience of the parties, any number of counterparts of this Agreement may be executed by the parties hereto. Each such counterpart shall be, and shall be deemed to be, an original instrument, but all such counterparts taken together shall constitute one and the same agreement.

8. Governing Law. This agreement shall be governed by and construed in accordance with the laws of the State of Arizona without giving effect to the conflicts of laws principles thereof.

If the foregoing correctly sets forth our agreement with respect to the matters contained herein, please so indicate by signing a copy of this agreement and returning a copy to the undersigned, whereupon this Agreement shall constitute our binding agreement with respect to the matters set forth herein.

UNISON HEALTHCARE CORPORATION

By: ______________________________
Name: ____________________________

By: ______________________________
Member of the Committee

APPENDIX I

SAMPLE CASH COLLATERAL AGREEMENT

To avoid litigation over the value of the secured lender's collateral and to avoid damage to the debtor's business operation from lack of cash, the debtor and its secured lender will often enter into an agreement for continued use of the secured lender's cash collateral (that is, the cash generated by the debtor's business operations). The debtor's use of cash collateral during the bankruptcy case is typically conditioned on giving the secured lender "adequate protection" of its secured position. In the case from which this sample is taken—the reorganization of the historic office building in Chicago, the ***Rookery Building***—adequate protection was given by granting the lender "replacement liens" on new cash generated during the bankruptcy case by the debtor's building and periodic payments of interest. Usually the Stipulated Order will contain an extensive description of the secured lender's loan documents and security instruments. Note that the Stipulated Order contains a budget, by expense categories, as an attached exhibit. In this case, the operating budget is done quarterly, although it can be done monthly or, in extreme cases, weekly. Finally, this order was entered as an ***interim order*** on ***negative notice.***

UNITED STATES BANKRUPTCY COURT
NORTHERN DISTRICT OF ILLINOIS
EASTERN DIVISION

In re	A Voluntary Case Under Chapter 11 of the Bankruptcy Code
THE ROOKERY, L.L.C., an Illinois limited liability company,	Case No. 98 B 31861
Debtor.	The Hon. Susan Pierson Sonderby

STIPULATED FINAL ORDER AUTHORIZING DEBTOR'S USE OF CASH COLLATERAL

This Stipulated Final Order Authorizing Debtor's Use of Cash Collateral (the "Stipulated Order") is agreed to by ING Bank N.V. ("ING Bank"), formerly known as NMB Postbank Groep N.V. ("Postbank"), on its own behalf and that of certain of its branches, subsidiaries, and affiliates, including NMB Vastgoedprojekt I B.V. ("Vastgoedprojekt"), as secured creditors and parties-in-interest, (collectively, the "ING Group"), and THE Rookery, l.l.C., above-captioned debtor and debtor-in-possession (the "Debtor"), in response to the Debtor's Motion to Approve Stipulated Interim Order Authorizing Debtor's Use of Cash Collateral, dated October 9, 1998 (the "Motion"). Attached as Exhibit A to the Motion was a proposed Stipulated Interim Order Authorizing Debtor's Use of Cash Collateral (the "Interim Order"). In light of the foregoing, and good cause appearing therefor,

THIS COURT FINDS AND CONCLUDES only with respect to paragraphs A, B, C, D, E, F, G, H, I, K, M, and Q, R, S, U, V, and it is hereby stipulated only between the Debtor and ING Group as follows:

A. The Chapter 11 Case. On October 8, 1998 (the "Petition Date"), the Debtor filed its voluntary petition for relief under Chapter 11 of 11 U.S.C. §§ 101-1330 (the "Bankruptcy Code"). The Debtor continues to operate its business and manage its properties as debtor-in-possession under Bankruptcy Code sections 1107 and 1108. No official committee of unsecured creditors has yet been appointed, nor any trustee appointed.

B. Jurisdiction. This Court has jurisdiction over this case and these parties under 28 U.S.C. §§ 157 and 1334. This is a core proceeding under 28 U.S.C. §157(b) and Bankruptcy Code sections 363(c) and (e).

C. Need for Cash Collateral Use. The Debtor has an immediate need for funds in this Chapter 11 case in order to pay operating expenses, continue operations, and maintain and preserve the Debtor's sole significant asset, the Rookery Building, located at 209 S. LaSalle Street, Chicago, Illinois (the "Building"). Without the Court's immediate and ongoing authorization to use cash collateral, the Debtor's existing and future business operations will be jeopardized, resulting in immediate and irreparable harm to the Debtor, the Debtor's bankruptcy estate and creditors.

D. Debtor's Submission. In support of the Motion, the Debtor filed an Appendix of Exhibits concurrently with the Motion and a Supplemental Appendix on October 13, 1998 (collectively, the "Appendices"). The Appendices contain a number of loan documents held by the ING Group, including certified copies of certain of the loan documents which had been recorded with the Cook County Recorder of Deeds, various financing statements, and a Title Report for the Building issued in December, 1997.

E. Initial Hearing and Entry of Stipulated Interim Order. The Court conducted an initial hearing on the Motion on October 14, 1998 (the "Initial Hearing"). At the Initial Hearing, the Court heard and considered statements of counsel present. As a result of statements name by various counsel, including Steve Wolfe from the Office of the United States Trustee, and concerns raised by the Court at the Initial Hearing, subsequent thereto counsel for the Debtor revised the Interim Order (the "Revised Interim Order"). The Revised Interim Order was circulated to counsel present at the Initial Hearing. The Revised Interim Order was thereafter executed and submitted to the Court for entry on October 22, 1998. The Court entered the Revised Interim Order or October 28, 1998. The Revised Interim Order scheduled a final hearing on the Motion for November 3, 1998 at 10:30 a.m. before this Court (the "Final Hearing").

F. Notice of Final Hearing. The Revised Interim Order directed the Debtor to send notice of the Final Hearing to the Debtor's twenty largest unsecured creditors, all secured creditors, the United States Trustee, and counsel for any official committee of unsecured creditors appoint in this case by no later than October 22, 1998. The Debtor sent notice of the Final Hearing to the parties directed by the Court on October 22, 1998 as evidenced by that certain Certificate of Service filed on October 23, 1998. The Debtor filed an additional Certificate of Service on October 27, 1998.

G. Stipulated Final Order. On October 30, 1998, counsel for the Debtor circulated a proposed Stipulated Final Order Authorizing the Debtor's Use of Cash Collateral to counsel present at the Final Hearing (the "Final Order"). The Debtor filed the Final Order with the Court on November 2, 1998.

H. LSREH Objection. On Objection 30, 1998, LaSalle Street Real Estate Holdings, Inc. ("LSREH") filed an objection to the Final Order (the "LSREH Objection"). The Debtor disputes the matters raised in the LSREH Objection.

I. Final Hearing. At the Final Hearing, the Court heard and considered statements of counsel present. The Court also considered the offer of proof of Jordan Kroop, counsel for the ING Group, who summarized the outstanding indebtedness under the ING Bank Senior Loan and the Vastgoedprojekt Junior Loan. Mr. Kroop advised the Court that the source of the figures was Cormack McKenna for the ING Bank Senior Loan and Robert Blair for the Vastgoedprojekt Junior Loan. The Court directed Mr. Kroop to file affidavits from Mr. McKenna and Mr. Blair in further support of the amounts claimed. The Court also reviewed the following documents contained in the Appendices and more fully described in paragraph L of this Stipulated Order.

1. Promissory Note, dated January 7, 1991 (App. #2);
2. Construction Loan Mortgage and Security Agreement, dated as of January 7, 1991 (App. #3);
3. Assignment of Leases and Rent, dated as of January 7, 1991(App. #4);
4. Loan Agreement, dated September 27, 1991 (the "Vastgoedprojekt Junior Loan, (App. #15);
5. Mortgage, dated September 27, 1991 (App. #16);
6. Initial Loan Promissory Note, dated September 27, 1991 (App. #17);
7. Primary Project Expense Note, dated September 27, 1991 (App. #18);
8. Assignment of Leases, dated September 27, 1991 (App. #20).

Counsel for the Debtor and the ING Group requested that the Court take judicial notice of the Illinois Conveyance Act 765 ILCS 5/1 *et seq.* in connection with the recordation of certain of the loan documents identified above as evidencing the perfection of the first lien asserted by ING Group on the Building and the rents and income generated thereby and the second lien asserted by Vastgoedprojekt on the Building and the rents and income generated by the leases for the Building.

J. Necessity for Stipulation. This Stipulated Order is necessary because the ING Group retains a senior secured interest in the Building and the rents and other icome generated by the Building, which constitutes "cash collateral," as defined in Bankruptcy Code Section 363(a) (the "Cash Collateral") and asserts a senior secured interest in nearly all other assets derived from or related to the Building.

K. The ING Group Debt. The Debtor acknowledges that it remains indebted to the ING Group under two separate loan facilities, which the Debtor further acknowledges are both currently in default, as set forth below:

1. **ING Bank Senior Loan** – the Debtor's current obligations under the ING Bank Senior Loan (more specifically defined below) are com-

prised of outstanding principal of $77,000,000, accrued interest as of July 31, 1998 of approximately $16,345,589.24, exclusive of attorneys' fees and costs due under the ING Bank Senior Loan. As of the Petition Date, the Debtor continued to incur liability for accrued interest at a rate of approximately $46,649.47 per day, plus accrued and accruing attorneys' fees and costs. The ING Bank Senior Loan is secured by, *inter alia*, a first, valid, perfected and enforceable lien on, and security interest in, the Building and all improvements, furniture, fixtures, equipment, easements, rents, income, leases, intangible assets, and all after acquired property located in or on or used or intended to be used in connection with the Building, as set forth with specificity in the loan and security documents described in paragraph L, below. The ING Bank Senior Loan is fully matured, due and payable at this time.

2. **Vastgoedprojekt Junior Loan** – the Debtor's current obligations under separate notes issued under the Vastgoedprojekt Junior Loan (more specifically defined below) are comprised of outstanding aggregate principal of $18,458,642, aggregate accrued interest as of July 31, 1998 of $14,161,088, exclusive of attorneys' fees and costs due under the Vastgoedprojekt Junior Loan. As of the Petition Date, the Debtor continued to accrue interest at a rate of approximately $8,537.88 per day, plus accrued and accruing attorneys' fees and costs. The Vastgoedprojekt Junior Loan is secured by, *inter alia*, a valid, perfected and enforceable lien on, and security interest in, the Building and all improvements, furniture, fixtures, equipment, easements, rents, income, leases, intangible assets, and all after acquired property located in or on or used or intended to be used in connection with the Building, as set forth in the loan and security documents described in paragraph L, below, which lien is junior only to the ING Bank Senior Loan set forth above. The Vastgoedprojekt Junior Loan is fully matured, due and payable at this time.

L. The Loan and Security Documents. The ING Group asserts that the Debtor's obligations to the ING Group are governed by the following loan instruments (the "Prepetition Loan Documents"), the validity and enforceability of which the Debtor does not dispute:[1]

[1] The Prepetition Loan Documents governing the Debtor's obligations to the ING Group and the various forms of collateral pledged to secure those obligations appear in the separately-bound Appendix to the Revised Interim Order (the "Appendix") (references to which are "App. #__"), all such instruments being incorporated into this Stipulated Order by this reference. The Appendix was filed simultaneously with the Motion. A Supplemental Appendix was also filed on October 13, 1998. Due to their volume, the Appendix and Supplemental Appendix were not circulated to the Service List, but were made available upon request.

ING BANK SENIOR LOAN

1. Building Loan Agreement, dated as of January 7, 1991 (the "ING Bank Senior Loan," App. #1), by and among Postbank,[2] the Debtor and LaSalle National Trust, N.A. (the "LaSalle Trustee"), as successor Trustee to LaSalle National Bank, under the Trust Agreement, dated December 12, 1988 (the "LaSalle Trust");

2. Promissory Note, dated January 7, 1991 (the "ING Bank Senior Note," App. #2), in the amount of $77,000,000, made by the Debtor and the LaSalle Trustee payable to Postbank, which provides for, among other things, the applicable interest rates on outstanding principal advanced under the ING Bank Senior Loan;

3. Construction Loan Mortgage and Security Agreement, dated as of January 7, 1991 (the "First Mortgage," App. #3), given in the Building (including the land at 209 S. LaSalle Street, all improvements, easements, rents, leases, profits, and other rights appurtenant to the Building, collectively, the "Mortgaged Property") by the Debtor and the LaSalle Trustee to Postbank;

4. Assignment of Leases and Rents, dated as of January 7, 1991 (the "First Assignment of Leases," App. #4), granted as security for the ING Bank Senior Note by the Debtor and the LaSalle Trustee to Postbank, covering all present and future leases in the Building and all rents and profits arising under such leases;

5. Assignment of Contracts, Warranties and Permits, dated as of January 7, 1997 (the "First Assignment of Contracts," App. #5), granted as security for the ING Bank Senior Note by the Debtor and the LaSalle Trustee to Postbank, covering all contracts, warranties and permits affecting or relating to the Building or relating to the operation, management, maintenance, construction or sale of the Building;

6. Collateral Assignment of Partnership Interest, dated as of January 7, 1991 (the "First Assignment of Interest," App. #6), granted to Postbank a continuing first priority security interest in all present and future right, title and interest of T. Baldwin Development Co. and Baldwin Real Estate Holdings, Inc. (two of the general partners in the Debtor as of the date of the ING Bank Senior Loan)[3] as security for the ING Bank Senior Note;

---

[2] ING Bank has succeeded to the interests of Postbank with respect to all relevant transactions. Descriptions of the various loan documents in this Stipulated Order will continue to refer to Postbank for the sake of clarity.

[3] Both T. Baldwin Development Co. and Baldwin Real Estate Holdings, Inc. were controlled by L. Thomas Baldwin, III ("Baldwin"). As part of the Debtor's debt restructuring in September 1991, T. Baldwin Development Co. withdrew from the Debtor as general partner, and Baldwin Real Estate Holdings, Inc., of which Baldwin is the sole shareholder, changed its name to LaSalle Street Real Estate Holdings, Inc. ("LSREH").

7. Collateral Assignment of Beneficial Interest, dated as of January 7, 1991 (the "First Assignment of Beneficial Interest," App. #7), granting to Postbank all beneficial rights held by the Debtor in the LaSalle Trust and all property held by the LaSalle Trust as security for the ING Bank Senior Note;

8. Development Cost Overrun Guaranty Agreement, dated January 7, 1991 (the "Baldwin Guaranty," App. #8), providing, among other things, that Baldwin guarantees the payment by the original general partners of the Debtor of all "Development Cost Overruns" pertaining to the "Guaranteed Development Cost Budget Line Items Schedule," as those terms are defined in the ING Bank Senior Loan;

9. Second Amendment to Building Loan Agreement, dated as of August 16, 1993 (App. #9), providing for, among other things, the extension of the maturity date of the loans extended under the ING Bank Senior Loan to December 31, 1997 and incorporating a new Operating Budget for the Building;

10. Commitment Letter from ING Fonds to the Debtor dated August 16, 1993 (the "Standby Commitment," App. #10), under which ING Fonds provides to the Debtor a standby credit facility for all outstanding principal, interest, expenses and other amounts under the ING Bank Senior Note, for the purpose of financing the repayment of the Debtor's debt obligations to Postbank (by then, ING Bank) under the ING Bank Senior Loan, to be drawn on only if Postbank (now ING Bank) were to refuse to extend the maturity date of the loans under the ING Bank Senior Note beyond December 31, 1997, provided that none such loans were in default;

11. First Note Modification and Extension Agreement, dated as of August 16, 1993 (App. #11), amending the ING Bank Senior Note to reflect the new December 31, 1997 maturity date of loans made under the ING Bank Senior Loan and adjusting certain definitions and formulae used to calculate interest and additional financial terms in the ING Bank Senior Note;

12. First Amendment to Construction Loan Mortgage and Security Agreement, dated as of August 16, 1993 (App. #12), amending the non-financial terms of the First Mortgage to reflect the amended and modified loan documents also executed as of August 16, 1993 listed above;

13. Amendment to Assignment of Leases and Rents and Other Loan Documents, dated as of August 16, 1993 (App. #13), amending certain non-financial terms of the Assignment of Leases and related loan documents listed above to reflect the amended and modified loan documents also executed as of August 16, 1993 listed above;

14. Subordination and Standstill Agreement, dated as of August 16, 1993 (the "Second Subordination Agreement," App. #14), providing that, among

other things, all debt obligations of the Debtor to LaSalle Street Real Estate Holdings, Inc. are continually subordinated to all debt obligations of the Debtor to ING Bank (successor to Postbank) under the ING Bank Senior Loan;

VASTGOEDPROJEKT JUNIOR LOAN

15. Loan Agreement, dated September 27, 1991 (the "Vastgoedprojekt Junior Loan," App. #15), between the Debtor and the LaSalle Trustee as borrower and Vastgoedprojekt as lender, providing for, among other things, loans advanced from time to time up to a total of $25,000,000 to fund 70% of certain cost overruns, operating deficits, and other costs arising from the Debtor's rehabilitation and operation of the Building, the other 30% of such expenses coming from subordinated, parallel loans from Baldwin;

16. Mortgage, dated September 27, 1991 (the "Second Mortgage," App. #16), granting Vastgoedprojekt a mortgage and security interest in the Mortgaged Property, subordinate only to the interest retained by Postbank (later ING Bank) under the First Mortgage, as security for all obligations under the Vastgoedprojekt Junior Loan;

17. Initial Loan Promissory Note, dated September 27, 1991 (the "Vastgoedprojekt Junior Note," App. #17), made by the Debtor and the LaSalle Trustee payable to Vastgoedprojekt in accordance with the Second Loan Agreement, in the principal sum of $9,800,000, payable on September 27, 2016, unless called on in the event of default;

18. Primary Project Expense Note, dated September 27, 1991 (App. #18), made by the Debtor and the LaSalle Trustee payable to Vastgoedprojekt in accordance with the Vastgoedprojekt Junior Loan, in the principal sum of $4,258,025, payable on September 27, 2016, unless called on in the event of default;

19. Assignment of Contracts, dated September 27, 1991 (the "Second Assignment of Contracts," App. #19), granting Vastgoedprojekt virtually the same rights as those granted to Postbank in the First Assignment of Contracts, except in a secondary position, as security for the obligations under the Vastgoedprojekt Junior Loan;

20. Assignment of Leases, dated September 27, 1991 (the "Second Assignment of Leases," App. #20), granting Vastgoedprojekt essentially the same rights as those granted to Postbank in the First Assignment of Leases, except in a secondary position, as security for the obligations under the Vastgoedprojekt Junior Loan;

21. Collateral Assignment of Beneficial Interest, dated September 27, 1991 (the "Second Assignment of Beneficial Interest," App. #21), granting Vastgoedprojekt essentially the same rights as those granted to Postbank in the First Assignment of Interest, except in a secondary position, as security for the obligations under the Vastgoedprojekt Junior Loan;

22. Collateral Assignment of Notes, dated as of September 27, 1991 (the "Assignment of Notes," App. #22), assigning Vastgoedprojekt's interest in the Primary Project Expense Note, as well as LSREH's interest in a separate note in the principal amount of $1,824,868, to Postbank;

23. LaSalle Street Real Estate Holdings, Inc. Partnership Interest Pledge Agreement, dated September 27, 1991 (the "Pledge Agreement," App. #23), under which LSREH, the sole general partner in the Debtor, pledges its partnership interest in the Debtor to Vastgoedprojekt as security for the obligations under the Vastgoedprojekt Junior Loan;

24. First Amendment to Building Loan Agreement and Other Loan Documents, dated as of September 27, 1991 (App. #24), amending certain provisions of the ING Bank Senior Loan and related loan documents to reflect and accommodate changes in the ownership structure of the Debtor and setting forth Postbank's consent to the Third Amended and Restated Partnership Agreement governing the Debtor (which provided that Projekt' had withdrawn as limited partner in the Debtor and that Chevron Corp. remained sole limited partner);

25. Foreclosure Subordination Agreement, dated as of September 27, 1991 (the "Subordination Agreement," App. #25), affirming the arms-length nature of the loan transactions between Vastgoedprojekt and the Debtor and establishing that Vastgoedprojekt retains all rights to distribution of assets from a sale of its collateral senior to any rights of the Debtor or LSREH in such collateral;

26. Subordination and Standstill Agreement, dated as of September 27, 1991 (the "First Subordination Agreement," App. #26), providing that, among other things, the Debtor's debt obligations to Vastgoedprojekt with respect to the Vastgoedprojekt Junior Loan are subordinated to the Debtor's debt obligations to Postbank with respect to the ING Bank Senior Loan.

M. Perfection of Liens. All liens in the Building, and the rents and income generated thereby created by the Prepetition Loan Documents have been and remain duly perfected in the State of Illinois.

N. Default by Debtor. The ING Group has met all its obligations under the Prepetition Loan Documents, and has delivered to the Debtor sufficient notices of default (App. #27 and #28) under both the ING Bank Senior Loan and the Vastgoedprojekt Junior Loan, including sufficient notice of the maturity of all obligations under the Prepetition Loan Documents under their own terms. The Debtor remains in default under the Prepetition Loan Documents and has to date made no attempt to cure such defaults, nor is the Debtor able to effect such cure.

O. Unpaid Real Property Taxes. The Debtor acknowledges there are unpaid real property taxes, which, including accrued penalties as of the Petition Date, total approximately $2,698,571.

P. Lack of Equity. The Debtor acknowledges that for purposes of the proposed use of Cash Collateral and the accompanying adequate protection being provided to the ING Group, the Debtor has no equity in any of the property constituting the collateral securing the ING Groups loans to the Debtor, including the Building, the Cash Collateral, all rents collected from the Building's tenants, the income and profits generated by the Building, the Debtor's contracts with third parties, and the balance of the assets assigned to the ING Group under the Prepetition Loan Documents to secure the Debtor's obligations under the Prepetition Loan Documents.

Q. Need for Adequate Protection. Absent an order of this Court, and given the necessities attending a Chapter 11 proceeding, the Debtor's use and disposition of some or all of the collateral may result in the diminution in value of the ING Group's interests in the Debtor's property.

R. Inability to Obtain Postpetition Financing. As a result of the Debtor's current financial condition, the Debtor is unable, in the ordinary course of business or otherwise, to obtain significant unsecured credit in accordance with Bankruptcy Code sections 364(a) or (b), as allowable under Bankruptcy Code section 503(b)(1) as an administrative expense.

S. Consent to Use of Cash Collateral. The ING Group consents to the use of cash collateral in accordance with Bankruptcy Code section 363, but only subject to the terms and conditions set forth below.

T. Arms' Length Negotiations. The terms and conditions of this Stipulated Order were negotiated at arms' length and in good faith, with all parties represented by counsel, are fair and reasonable under the circumstances, and reflect the Debtor's prudent business judgment consistent with its fiduciary duties.

U. Notice. Notice of the Motion has provided to all secured creditors, the Debtor's twenty largest unsecured creditors, and the United States Trustee. Such notice constitutes due and sufficient notice of the hearing to consider the Motion and this Stipulated Order.

V. Good Cause Shown. In consideration of the foregoing and all relevant evidence in the record before the Court, good cause has been shown for the relief granted in this Stipulated Order.

ACCORDINGLY, IT IS HEREBY ORDERED as follows:

1. Motion Granted. The Motion shall be, and hereby is, GRANTED in all respects in accordance with the restrictions and conditions set forth below.

2. Use of Cash Collateral. The Debtor shall be, and hereby is, authorized to use Cash Collateral on an interim basis in accordance with the following restrictions, terms, and conditions:

a) All expenditures of cash (or cash equivalents) in any amount during the pendency of this Chapter 11 case must conform in every respect to the most recently-approved Operating Budget (the "Budget"), annexed to this Stipulated Order as Exhibit A;

b) Any proposed expenditure of cash (or its equivalent) in excess of $500 not within the guidelines set forth in the Budget must be approved in writing by an authorized officer of ING Bank before the Debtor makes such expenditure, ING Bank being entitled to withhold its approval of such expenditure unilaterally, with or without cause;

c) The Debtor may not sell, lease, or otherwise dispose of any collateral unless expressly provided for in the Budget;

d) Any sale, lease, or other disposition of any collateral with a value in excess of $500 not within the guidelines set forth in the Budget must be approved in writing by an authorized officer of ING Bank before the Debtor makes such expenditure, ING Bank being entitled to withhold its approval of such expenditure unilaterally, with or without cause;

e) The Debtor may not enter into any new tenant lease or terminate any current tenant lease without the ING Group's advance written approval (of both the financial terms of the lease and the form of such lease) or an order of this Court obtained after express notice to the ING Group;

f) The John Buck Company (the "Independent Manager") appointed receiver of the Building pursuant to the Order appointing receiver entered by the United States District Court for the Northern District of Illinois in matter 98 C 2570 on May 28, 1998, or a successor approved in writing by the ING Group in advance, must remain as manager of the Building for the duration of the Chapter 11 case;

g) Absent additional written agreement between the ING Group and the Debtor or further Order of the Court, interim use of Cash Collateral, and the relief granted in this Stipulated Order, expires at the earliest of:

    (1) the close of business on November 30, 1998;

    (2) the occurrence of a change in the identity of the managing member of the Debtor;

    (3) the appointment of a trustee or examiner in this case;

    (4) confirmation of a plan of reorganization under Bankruptcy Code section 1129; and

    (5) the granting of a lien on any property of the Debtor constituting all or part of the ING Group's collateral either senior to, junior to, or *pari passu* with, the ING Group's interest in such collateral.

3. Breaches of Stipulated Order. If, for any reason, the Debtor initiates any action prohibited, or fails to perform any act required, under the restrictions and conditions set forth in paragraph 2(a) through (g) above, the Debtor's authority to use any Cash Collateral in accordance with this Stipulated Order will immediately cease without further Order of the Court, **provided,** however, that nothing in this Stipulated Order precludes the Debtor from seeking leave of the Court to use cash collateral under Bankruptcy Code section 363(c)(2)(A). By way of example and not limitation, if for any reason: (a) the Independent Manager is removed as manager of the Building during this Chapter 11 case, or (b) there is a change in the identity of the managing member of the Debtor during this Chapter 11 case, then the Debtor's authority to use any Cash Collateral in accordance with this Stipulated Order will immediately cease without further Order of the Court, **provided,** however, that nothing in this Stipulated Order precludes the Debtor from seeking leave of the Court to use cash collateral under Bankruptcy Code section 363(c)(2)(A).

4. Adequate Protection – Replacement Liens. In addition to the restrictions set forth in paragraph 2, above, as replacement security and adequate protection for the Debtor's use of the ING Group's Cash Collateral, the ING Group is granted: (a) a first priority lien and replacement lien on all assets (including all rents, issues, profits, and proceeds of such assets) of the Debtor and its estate existing on the Petition Date or arising thereafter to the same extent and with the same priority as was held by the ING Group immediately before the Petition Date subject only to the valid, perfected, and unavoidable security interests and liens existing as of the Petition Date, if any, held by parties other than the ING Group; and (b) with respect to assets that are subject to superior prepetition liens, a junior priority lien in such assets subject only to those superior prepetition liens (so long as and to the extent that such liens are and remain outstanding) to the extent of any diminution in the ING Group's prepetition secured interest resulting from the Debtor's use of cash collateral in accordance with this Stipulated Order (collectively, the "Postpetition Liens"). Notwithstanding the foregoing, neither this Stipulated Order nor any of its provisions are to be deemed an adjudication that the ING Group is adequately protected for purposes other than for purposes of the use of Cash Collateral under the express terms and provisions of this Stipulated Order (including the restrictions set forth in paragraph 2, above).

5. Adequate Protection – Periodic Payments. As further adequate protection of the ING Group's interest in the cash collateral, the Debtor must make monthly payments to the ING Group equal to the net cash flow generated by the Building after payment of all authorized expenditures in accordance with the Budget annexed as Exhibit A, up to the amount of the monthly principal, interest, and fees otherwise due under the Prepetition Loan Documents.

6. Perfection of Postpetition Liens. The Postpetition Liens are valid, enforceable, attached, and perfected as of the Petition Date without any further act and without regard to any other federal, state, or local requirement or law requiring notice, filing, registration, recording, or possession of the Postpetition Collateral or other act. If the ING Group elects for any reason to file, record, or otherwise perform any act to perfect the Postpetition Liens, such act is deemed to have been accomplished as of the Petition Date, notwithstanding the actual date and time performed. A filing or recording of a certified copy of this Stipulated Order is tantamount to an act of perfection. Should the ING Group elect to file, record or perform an act of perfection, no defect or failure in connection with such act in any way limits, waives, or alters the validity, enforceability, attachment, or perfection of the Postpetition Liens.

7. Seniority of Postpetition Liens. Except for the subordination to administrative expenses specifically delineated in paragraph 8, below, the Postpetition Liens will remain senior to, and may not be subordinated or made equal to any lien, security interest, mortgage, or any other interest in favor of any party other than the ING Group by any order of the Court unless: (a) the ING Group has given its express prior written consent, which may not be implied from any other action, inaction, or acquiescence by the ING Group; or (b) the order providing for such lien, interest, or subordination is conditioned on prior full satisfaction of the Postpetition Liens and all obligations arising under the Prepetition Loan Documents, provided however, nothing contained in this paragraph 7 shall be deemed a waiver or release of the rights of any person under Section 506(c) of the Bankruptcy Code.

8. Carveout. All obligations under the Postpetition Liens, the ING Bank Senior Loan and the Vastgoedprojekt Junior Loan have the superpriority in payment afforded by Bankruptcy Code section 507(b), except for: (a) statutory fees payable to the United States Trustee under 28 U.S.C. § 1930; and (b) aggregate fees and expenses of $75,000 actually and reasonably incurred by counsel for the Debtor retained by order of the Court under Bankruptcy Code section 327(a).

9. Limited Stay Relief. Without further notice, motion, application, hearing, or order, all stays and injunctions, including without limitation, the automatic stay under Bankruptcy Code section 362 or any injunction imposed under Bankruptcy Code section 105, Bankruptcy Rule 7065, or otherwise, existing now or arising at any time in the future, are lifted and absolved in favor of the ING Group to permit the ING Group: (a) to implement the terms of this Stipulated Order; and (b) if relief from the automatic stay is granted in favor of a party other than the ING Group with respect to all or a portion of the assets comprising the ING Group's collateral, to exercise all rights with respect to such collateral.

10. Consent to Expedited Consideration of Emergency Motions. If, for any reason, the Debtor initiates any action prohibited, or fails to perform any act required, by the terms and conditions of this Stipulated Order, the ING Group will be entitled in its sole discretion to move this Court for an order lifting or modifying the automatic stay under Bankruptcy Code section 362(d) with respect to some or all of the ING Group's collateral. Should the ING Group so move, the Debtor consents to this Court's expedited consideration of such motion to the fullest extent that the Court's calendar and rules permit.

11. Reporting. At all times during the pendency of this case, the Debtor, the Independent Manager, or any trustee or examiner appointed in this case must grant the ING Group access to all books, records, electronic data, or any other information relevant or related to the Debtor's operation or the Building upon twenty four (24) hours notice, during regular business hours. The ING Group's availing itself of such access to any extent and at any time will not constitute a violation of the automatic stay under Bankruptcy Code section 362.

12. Additional Documents. The Debtor is authorized and instructed to execute any additional documents necessary to perfect any of the ING Group's interests created by, or set forth in, this Stipulated Order.

13. Mootness. No order of any court reversing or modifying the relief granted in this Stipulated Order will impair or diminish the validity of any priority, liens, or other relief granted in the ING Group's favor under the terms of this Stipulated Order.

14. Effective Date. Except with respect to the stipulations between the Debtor and the ING Group and except as hereinafter provided, all provisions of this Stipulated Order and all relief granted in this Stipulated Order are deemed effective and binding on all parties.

15. Right to Contest. Neither the stipulations of the Debtor, not the provisions of this Order shall constitute a waiver of, or prejudice to the rights of, any claimant, interest holder or other party in interest in this estate (excluding only the Debtor to the extent of the stipulations contained herein) or committee of creditors appointed in this case, to the extent permitted by the Bankruptcy Code and applicable law, to contest or object to the validity, perfection or enforceability of any liens, security interests or encumbrances of ING Group provided, however, that any claimant or committee of creditors appointed in this case must assert by applicable pleading such objection on or before December 15, 1998, with five (5) business days written notice to the ING Group, or be forever barred.

16. Preservation of Rights and Withdrawal of LSREH Objection. The entry of this Stipulated Order shall be without prejudice to the right of LSREH to raise the matters set forth in the LSREH Objection, and the Debtor's right to contest such matters, in a subsequent proceeding before this Court. All such rights are expressly preserved. Based upon the preservation of rights as provided herein, the LSREH Objection is hereby withdrawn.

DATED: December 7, 1998

/s/ Susan Pierson Sonderby
UNITED STATES BANKRUPTCY JUDGE

AGREED AND CONSENTED TO:

SQUIRE SANDERS & DEMPSEY, L.L.P.
1201 Pennsylvania Avenue, N.W.
Washington, D.C. 20044

SQUIRE SANDERS & DEMPSEY, L.L.P.
Two Renaissance Square
40 North Central Avenue, Suite 2700
Phoenix, Arizona 85004

By: ***/s/ Thomas J. Salerno***
Thomas J. Salerno
Jordan A. Kroop

GREENBERG TRAURIG
227 West Monroe Street, 35th Floor
Chicago, Illinois 60606

By: ***/s/ Keith J. Shapiro***

Attorneys for ING Group

ADELMAN, GETTLEMEN, MERENS, BERISH & CARTER, LTD.
53 West Jackson Boulevard
Suite 1050
Chicago, Illinois 60604

By: ***/s/ Howard L. Adelman***
Howard L. Adelman

Attorneys for Debtor

APPENDIX J

SAMPLE DIP FINANCING AGREEMENT

This final order authorizing the debtors to obtain postpetition secured financing was entered at the beginning of the ***Boston Chicken, Inc.,*** Chapter 11 in 1998. This order is representative of DIP financing orders entered in larger cases, and incorporates a fairly standard form of loan agreement and security agreement (which is voluminous and not included here), and includes a ***Carve out*** arrangement for the estate's professionals. The DIP facility was essentially a continuation of a prebankruptcy loan facility by prebankruptcy lenders, converted into a postpetition working-capital facility. Because the Boston Market restaurant chain's working-capital needs were so large, the DIP financing was provided by a group of participating lenders, with GE Capital Corporation and Bank of America serving as Administrative Agent and Collateral Agent, respectively, for the entire group of lenders. The case did not turn out well for anyone—McDonald's agreed to purchase most of the assets of the Boston Market chain, but for a price that afforded only cents on the dollar to senior secured debt and left junior secured debt, as well as all unsecured debt, completely out of the money.

LEWIS AND ROCA, LLP
40 North Central Avenue
Phoenix, Arizona 85004
(602) 262-5311

Randolph J. Haines (AZ Bar #005440)

SQUIRE, SANDERS & DEMPSEY, LLP
40 North Central Avenue
Phoenix, Arizona 85004
Facsimile (602) 253-8129
Telephone (602) 528-4000

Thomas J. Salerno (AZ Bar #007492)
Craig D. Hansen (AZ Bar #007493)
Jordan A. Kroop (AZ Bar #018825)

AKIN, GUMP, STRAUSS, HAUER & FELD, LLP
1900 Pennzoil Place - South Tower
111 Louisiana
Houston, Texas 77002
(713) 220-5800

H. Rey Stroube, III (TX Bar #19422000)
Attorneys for Debtor BCE West, L.P., *et al*

MURPHY, SHENEMAN, JULIAN & ROGERS
2049 Century Park East, Suite 2100
Los Angeles, California 94111
(310) 788-3700

Jean B. LeBlanc (CA Bar #130907)

Attorneys for GE Capital Corporation

IN THE UNITED STATES BANKRUPTCY COURT FOR THE DISTRICT OF ARIZONA

In re

BCE WEST, L.P., *et al.*,

Debtors.

In Proceedings Under Chapter 11
Case Nos. 98-12547-ECF-CGC through 98-12570-ECF-CGC
(Jointly Administered)

FINAL ORDER APPROVING POSTPETITION FINANCING AND GRANTING LIENS AND SUPER-ADMINISTRATIVE PRIORITY PURSUANT TO 11 U.S.C. §§ 364(c) and (d) AND MODIFYING THE AUTOMATIC STAY

The Motion for Authority to Obtain Credit and Incur Debt Secured by Senior Liens (the "Motion") filed by the above-referenced debtors and debtors in possession (each a "Debtor," and collectively "Debtors") in the above-captioned respective bankruptcy cases (each a "Chapter 11_Case," and collectively the "Chapter 11 Cases"), duly came on (1) for preliminary hearing (the "Interim Hearing") before the undersigned United States Bankruptcy Judge on October 5, 1998 and (2) for final hearing (the "Final Hearing") before the undersigned United States Bankruptcy Judge on October 26, 1998. At each such hearing, appearances were made as noted in the record of such hearing.

Pursuant to the Motion and subject in all respects to the terms and conditions hereof, Debtors sought authority: (1) to obtain secured postpetition financing from General Electric Capital Corporation ("GE Capital"), Bank of America National Trust and Savings Association ("BofA"), and certain other lenders (collectively with GE Capital and BofA, "Lenders") in an aggregate principal amount not to exceed $70,000,000 pursuant to (A) that certain Debtor in Possession Credit Agreement dated as of October 5,

1998 (the "Credit Agreement"),[1] by and between each Debtor, GE Capital, as administrative agent (in such capacity, "Administrative Agent") and as a lender, BofA, as collateral agent (in such capacity, "Collateral Agent," Administrative Agent and Collateral Agent being referred to collectively as "Agents") and as a lender, and the other Lenders signatory thereto from time to time, in substantially the form annexed to the Motion, and (B) the other Loan Documents; (2) to grant to Collateral Agent, for the benefit of Agents and Lenders, pursuant to Sections 364(c)(2), (c)(3) and (d) of the Bankruptcy Code,[2] as security for the payment and performance of the Obligations, Liens upon all of the Collateral, including all of Debtors' Accounts, books and records, Chattel Paper, Contracts, Documents, Equipment, Fixtures, General Intangibles, Goods, Instruments, Inventory, Investment Property, Real Estate, money, cash and cash equivalents, whether now existing or hereafter arising, wherever located, and all Proceeds of the foregoing; (3) to grant administrative priority to the Obligations pursuant to Section 364(c)(1); and (4) to modify the automatic stay in certain respects in connection with such postpetition financing.

Having reviewed and considered the Motion, all papers filed in connection with the Motion, and the record made by the Debtors at the Interim Hearing, and appropriate notice of the Motion and the Interim Hearing under the circumstances having been given pursuant to Rule 4001(c) , this Court entered its Interim and Proposed Final Order Approving Postpetition Financing and Granting Liens and Super Administrative Priority Pursuant to 11 U.S.C. §§ 364(c) and (d) and Modifying the Automatic Stay (the "Interim Order") and scheduled the Final Hearing to consider entering the Interim Order as a final order (as set forth herein, this "Final Order").

Having reviewed and considered the Motion again, all papers (including objections, if any) filed in connection with the Motion, and the record made by the Debtors at the Interim Hearing and the Final Hearing, and appropriate notice of the Final Hearing having been given pursuant to Rule 4001(c), based upon the foregoing and other good cause appearing therefor,

THE COURT HEREBY FINDS AND CONCLUDES AS FOLLOWS:

A. On October 5, 1998 (the "Petition Date"), each Debtor commenced its Chapter 11 Case by filing a voluntary petition for relief under Chapter 11

---

[1]Unless otherwise defined herein, capitalized terms or matters of construction defined or established in the Credit Agreement shall be applied herein as defined or established therein; capitalized terms that are not defined herein or in the Credit Agreement shall be as defined in the Security Agreement (as defined in the Credit Agreement).

[2]Unless otherwise provided herein, all references herein to (1) "Sections" shall refer to sections of the Bankruptcy Code and (2) "Rules" shall refer to rules of the Bankruptcy Rules.

of the Bankruptcy Code in the United States Bankruptcy Court for the District of Arizona. Pursuant to Sections 1107 and 1108, each Debtor continues to operate its business and manage its properties as a debtor and debtor in possession.

B. Consideration of the Motion by this Court constitutes a core proceeding within the meaning of 28 U.S.C. § 157(b)(2). Accordingly, this Court has jurisdiction over these proceedings and the parties and property affected hereby pursuant to Section 364 and 28 U.S.C. § 157(b)(1).

C. Debtors represent that, prior to the Petition Date:

(1) Pursuant to the Master Lease Agreement dated as of September 27, 1995 (the "1995 Master Lease"), Citizens Bank of Rhode Island, as successor in interest to GE Capital, for itself and as agent for certain participants (in both such capacities, "1995 Lessor"), made loans, in the form of a lease, to Debtor Boston Chicken, Inc. ("BCI") that were used by BCI to purchase certain equipment referred to as the "Lease Assets" in the 1995 Master Lease. BCI retained certain of such Lease Assets for its own use, and subleased the balance thereof to, among others, certain of its subsidiaries who are also Debtors and assigned such subleases to 1995 Lessor (such Lease Assets, together with all underlying subleases and the related obligations of the sublessees thereunder, are referred to herein as the "1995 Master Lease Collateral"). As of the Petition Date, BCI was indebted to 1995 Lessor under the 1995 Master Lease for obligations totaling not less than $55 million, plus accrued interest, fees and costs, including professional fees and costs (collectively, the "1995 Lease Obligations"). As security for the 1995 Lease Obligations, BCI granted to 1995 Lessor a security interest in all of the 1995 Master Lease Collateral.

(2) (a) On December 9, 1996:

(i) BCI and GE Capital, for itself and as agent for certain participants (in both such capacities, "1996 Lessor"), entered into that certain Master Lease Agreement No. 2 dated as of December 9, 1996 (such agreement, as amended by Amendment No. 1 to Master Lease Agreement No. 2 dated as of February 28, 1997, Amendment No. 2 to Master Lease Agreement dated as of March 18, 1997, and Amendment No. 2 [sic] to Master Lease Agreement No. 2 dated as of July 15, 1998 (including all schedules thereto), the "1996 Master Lease"), pursuant to which 1996 Lessor made loans, in the form of a lease, to BCI that were used by BCI to purchase certain equipment and real property, which equipment and real property are referred to as the "Lease Assets" in the 1996 Master Lease. BCI retained certain of such Lease Assets for its own use, and subleased the balance thereof to, among others, certain of its subsidiaries who are also Debtors and assigned such subleases to 1996 Lessor (such Lease Assets, together with all underlying subleases and the related obligations of the sublessees thereunder, are referred to herein as the "1996 Master Lease Collateral"). As of the Petition Date, BCI was indebted to 1996 Lessor under the 1996 Master Lease for obligations totaling not less than $166 million, plus accrued interest, fees and costs, including professional fees and costs (collectively, the "1996 Lease Obligations"); and

(ii) BCI, BofA, as loan agent (in such capacity, "Prepetition Revolver Agent") and as a lender, and certain other lenders (collectively with BofA, "Prepetition Revolver Lenders"), entered into that certain Secured Revolving Credit Agreement dated as of December 9, 1996 (such agreement, as amended by the First Amendment and Consent to Secured Revolving Credit Agreement dated as of October 24, 1997 and the Second Amendment and Consent to Secured Revolving Credit Agreement (the "Second Revolver Amendment") dated as of July 15, 1998 (collectively, the "Prepetition Revolving Loan Agreement"), pursuant to which the Prepetition Revolver Lenders have made revolving credit loans to, and incurred letter of credit obligations for the benefit of, BCI. As of the Petition Date, BCI was indebted to Prepetition Revolver Agent and Prepetition Revolver Lenders for obligations totaling not less than $92 million, plus accrued interest, fees and costs, including professional fees and costs (collectively, the "Prepetition Revolver Obligations").

(b) As security for the 1996 Lease Obligations and the Prepetition Revolver Obligations (collectively, the "1996 Obligations"), BCI granted to (i) 1996 Lessor a security interest in the 1996 Master Lease Collateral and (ii) to BofA, as common collateral agent (in such capacity, "Common Collateral Agent"), a security interest in substantially all of its assets other than the 1995 Master Lease Collateral. In addition, certain of BCI's subsidiaries who are also Debtors guaranteed the payment and performance of the 1996 Obligations and pledged substantially all of their assets (excluding any 1995 Master Lease Collateral) as security therefor. All of the collateral described in the preceding two sentences shall be referred to collectively as the "Common 1996 Collateral." The 1996 Lease Obligations and the Prepetition

Revolver Obligations are *pari passu* with each other.

(3) Pursuant to the Second Revolver Amendment, BofA and GE Capital, as co-agents (collectively, in such capacities, "Prepetition Liquidity Agent") and as lenders, and certain other lenders (collectively with BofA and GE Capital, "Prepetition Liquidity Lenders") made the "Liquidity Loans" as defined therein to BCI during the period from and after July 15, 1998 until the Petition Date. As of the Petition Date, BCI was indebted to Prepetition Liquidity Agent and Prepetition Liquidity Lenders with respect to such Liquidity Loans for obligations totaling not less than $35 million, plus accrued interest, fees and costs, including professional fees and costs (collectively, the "Prepetition Liquidity Obligations"). The Prepetition Liquidity Obligations are guaranteed by the guaranties described in clause (2)(b) of this paragraph (C), and are secured by the Common 1996 Collateral. The 1996 Lessor (and all of the participants in the 1996 Master Lease), the Prepetition Revolver Agent and the Prepetition Revolver Lenders agreed to subordinate their right to payment with respect to the 1996 Lease Obligations and the Prepetition Revolver Obligations, respectively, to the prior payment in full of the Prepetition Liquidity Obligations.

(4) Pursuant to certain agreements and arrangements more fully described in Exhibit A to the Second Amended and Restated Intercreditor Agreement dated as of July 15, 1998, with respect to BCI and certain of its subsidiaries who are also Debtors (the "Intercreditor Agreement"), certain institutions (collectively the "Cash Management Banks") agreed to provide continuing cash management services critical to the continuing operations of BCI and such subsidiaries. In addition, BCI is obligated with respect to certain "Other Obligations" owing to the "Other Creditors" (as both such terms are defined in the Intercreditor Agreement). Certain of BCI's subsidiaries who are also Debtors have guaranteed the payment and performance of the foregoing obligations owing to such Cash Management Banks and Other Creditors. All of such obligations are secured by a junior security interest in favor of the Common Collateral Agent, for the benefit of such Cash Management Banks and Other Creditors, in substantially all of the Common 1996 Collateral.

D. Pursuant to Rule 4001(c) and in accordance with the Interim Order, the Debtors have provided notice of the time, place, and nature of the Final Hearing on the Motion and opportunity to object to the entry of this Final Order to counsel to the Prepetition Revolver Lenders, counsel for the Official Committee of Unsecured Creditors (the "Official Committee"), the United States Trustee for the District of Arizona, (4) the participants under the 1995 Master Lease, (5) all other persons entitled to notice in accordance with paragraph 18 of the Interim Order and (6) any other parties entitled to notice under Bankruptcy Rule 4001(b). The foregoing notice is adequate and sufficient.

E. Debtors have requested that Lenders extend, and Lenders have agreed on the terms set forth in the Loan Documents to extend, certain financial accommodations to Debtors on a postpetition, secured, superpriority basis. Debtors, Agents and Lenders have conducted good faith negotiations for the extension of such financial accommodations, such negotiations were at arms length, and the proposed terms and conditions of such financial accommodations are fair and reasonable.

F. Debtors have represented that they have discussed with other potential lenders the possibility of extending postpetition credit to Debtors. Debtors are unable to obtain postpetition financing in the form of unsecured credit allowable as an administrative expense under Section 503(b)(1) , unsecured credit allowable under Sections 364(a) or 364(b) , or secured credit pursuant to Section 364(c) or (d) on terms and conditions more favorable to their respective estates than those offered by Agents and Lenders, as evidenced by this Final Order and the other Loan Documents.

G. Lenders have represented that they are not willing to extend postpetition financial accommodations unless each Debtor grants to Collateral Agent, for the benefit of Agents and Lenders, perfected Liens upon all of the Collateral with the priorities set forth herein.

H. The financial accommodations contemplated in the Interim Order and by the Credit Agreement and the other Loan Documents were necessary on an interim basis to avoid immediate and irreparable harm to each Debtor, its estate, and its creditors. The financing approved by the Interim Order on an interim basis was limited to an amount necessary to avoid immediate and irreparable harm pending the Final Hearing.

I. The Debtors have represented that, without continuing adequate financing, each Debtor will be unable to maintain its operations, preserve and maximize the value of its estate, and reorganize its business. Permitting each Debtor to obtain financial accommodations from Agents and Lenders will minimize disruption of such Debtor's business as a going concern, enable such Debtor to preserve and maintain its assets, and increase the possibility of a successful reorganization of such Debtor's business. Accordingly, good cause exists for approval of the Motion and entry of this Final Order, which is in the best interest of each Debtor, its creditors, and its estate. The terms of the postpetition financing and granting of Liens and super administrative expense priority authorized hereby are fair and equitable under the circumstances.

J. Based upon the record presented to the Court by the Debtors at the Interim Hearing and the Final Hearing, it appears that the terms and conditions to which Debtors, Agents and Lenders have agreed pursuant to the Loan Documents constitute a part of this Court's authorization under Section 364 and are, therefore, subject to the protections contained in Section 364(e).

IN ACCORDANCE WITH THE FOREGOING, IT IS HEREBY ORDERED, ADJUDGED AND DECREED AS FOLLOWS:

1. The Motion was granted on an interim basis as set forth in the Interim Order. Subject to the terms hereof, this Final Order is valid immediately, is fully effective upon its entry, and replaces and supersedes the Interim Order in all respects.

2. Each Debtor is authorized and directed to enter into and perform under and in accordance with the terms and conditions of the Loan Documents and to execute and deliver to Agents such additional documents, instruments, and agreements as may be required by Agents to implement the terms, or effectuate the purposes, of this Final Order or any other Loan Document. The terms and conditions of the Loan Documents are hereby approved; *provided, that* the "Budget" attached to the Credit Agreement as Schedule 3.4(b) thereto shall be replaced and superseded by the Budget that was entered into evidence during the Final Hearing. The failure to reference or discuss any particular provision of any Loan Document in this Final Order shall not affect the validity or enforceability of any such provision. However, notwithstanding the foregoing or anything in the Loan Documents to the contrary, to the extent there is a conflict between the terms and provisions of this Final Order (without regard to any amendments or modifications hereof) and the terms and provisions of any of the Loan Documents, the terms and provisions of this Final Order shall control in all respects and the underlying Loan Documents shall be deemed to be, and hereby are, amended to reflect the foregoing.

3. BCI, on behalf of itself or any Debtor, is authorized to request and receive Revolving Credit Advances from Lenders and to request that Lenders incur L/C Obligations for the benefit of the relevant Debtor on the terms and conditions set forth in the Loan Documents in an aggregate outstanding principal amount not to exceed $70,000,000 on a final basis, which amount is inclusive of, and not in addition to, the $41,900,000 in financial accommodations authorized in the Interim Order. Each Debtor is authorized and directed to use proceeds of the Revolving Credit Advances for the purposes set forth in the Credit Agreement, including, without limitation, the satisfaction in full of the Prepetition Liquidity Obligations from the proceeds of the initial advance under the Credit Agreement.

4. Each Debtor has stipulated and is hereby deemed: (a) to release and discharge Prepetition Liquidity Agent and Prepetition Liquidity Lenders, in their respective capacities as such, together with their respective agents, attorneys, employees, heirs, executors, administrators, officers, directors,

successors and assigns, from any and all claims, causes of action and remedies (whether under the Bankruptcy Code or other applicable law) arising out of, based upon or related to the Prepetition Liquidity Obligations or the Common 1996 Collateral securing such obligations; and (b) to waive any and all defenses (including, without limitation, offsets and counterclaims of any nature or kind) as to the validity, perfection, priority, enforceability, and nonavoidability (under the Bankruptcy Code or otherwise) of the Prepetition Liquidity Obligations and the security interests in and liens upon the Common 1996 Collateral securing such obligations. The releases and waivers set forth in this paragraph are deemed effective upon the date of entry of the Interim Order, but are binding only on the Debtors and their respective estates and not on any other party in interest, with all rights, claims, causes of action, remedies, challenges, objections, defenses and other matters referred to above that the Debtors' estates have, or may (but for the provisions this decretal paragraph 4) have, being expressly reserved to and preserved for the benefit of such parties in interest.

5. Each Debtor is authorized to grant to Collateral Agent, for the benefit of Agents and Lenders, and Collateral Agent is hereby granted, pursuant to Sections 364(c)(2), (c)(3) and (d), valid, perfected, and enforceable Liens upon the Collateral (including the 1995 Master Lease Collateral and the Common 1996 Collateral) subject only to (a) Permitted Senior Encumbrances that would be prior to such Liens as a matter of law, (b) 1995 Lessor's interest in the 1995 Master Lease Collateral, and (c) the Carve-Out (as defined below). Subject to the Carve-Out, such Liens shall at all times be senior to the rights of any successor trustee or estate representative in any Chapter 11 Case or any subsequent case commenced upon the conversion of any Chapter 11 Case to a case under Chapter 7 of the Bankruptcy Code.

6. Each of 1996 Lessor, each participant in the 1996 Master Lease, Prepetition Revolver Agent, each Prepetition Revolver Lender, each Cash Management Bank, and each Other Creditor has consented to the grant to Collateral Agent, for the benefit of Agents and Lenders, pursuant to Section 364(d), of a valid, perfected, and enforceable first priority Lien upon the Common 1996 Collateral pursuant to (i) an acknowledgment of the Request for Participants' Consent dated as of September 23, 1998 and/or (ii) the Consent to Modification of Second Amended and Restated Intercreditor Agreement dated as of September 24, 1998.

7. The Obligations shall have administrative priority under Section 364(c)(1). Subject to the Carve-Out, such administrative expenses shall have priority over all other costs and expenses of the kinds specified in, or ordered pursuant to, Sections 326, 330, 331, 503(b), 507(a) or 507(b), and shall at all times be senior to the rights of each Debtor, its estate, and any successor trustee or estate representative in its Chapter 11 Case.

8. Nothing contained in this Final Order or otherwise, and no action or

inaction of the Collateral Agent, the Agents or the Lenders, shall be deemed to be a consent by any of them to any charge, lien, assessment or claim against the Collateral under section 506(c) of the Code or otherwise. The Debtors and the Official Committee, on their own behalf but not on behalf of any other party-in-interest, hereby waive any rights they may have to seek to impose any charge, lien, assessment or claim against the Collateral under section 506(c) of the Code or otherwise. Except as set forth in paragraph 9 hereof with respect to the Carve-Out, no costs or expenses of administration that have been or may be incurred in these proceedings are or will be prior to or on a parity with the claims of the Collateral Agent, the Agents or the Lenders against the Debtors or any successor debtor-in-possession or Chapter 11 trustee or with the security interests, liens, and mortgages of the Collateral Agent, the Agents or the Lenders upon the Collateral.

9. Collateral Agent's Liens upon the Collateral and the super administrative priority granted to Agents and Lenders under Section 364(c)(1) shall be subject only to unpaid professional fees and expenses incurred by Debtors, the Official Committee, and any other statutory committee appointed by the U.S. Trustee in the Chapter 11 Cases (any such committee, an "Other Committee"), but only if such Other Committee's fees are, pursuant to an order of the Bankruptcy Court, required to be paid by the Debtors (which expenses described in this clause (a) shall include the allowed out-of-pocket expenses of Official Committee and (if applicable) Other Committee members) as and when allowed on a final basis pursuant to Section 330, and fees payable to the United States Trustee and to the Clerk of the Bankruptcy Court pursuant to 28 U.S.C. § 1930 in the Chapter 11 Cases, in an aggregate amount under the foregoing clauses (a) and (b) not to exceed $3,500,000 (such fees and expenses referred to in clauses (a) and (b) of this paragraph 9 being collectively referred to as the "Carve-Out"); *provided, that* the Carve-Out (i) shall only apply after the termination of the Revolving Loan facility under Section 8.2(i) of the Credit Agreement (the "Facility Termination Date"), (ii) shall only include unpaid professional fees and expenses accrued as of the Facility Termination Date and professional fees and expenses incurred after the Facility Termination Date, and shall neither include nor be reduced by any professional fees and expenses that were allowed by this Court under any interim compensation orders pursuant to Sections 330 or 331 and paid by the Debtors prior to the Facility Termination Date, (iii) shall not be paid from amounts on deposit in the Cash Collateral Account, (iv) shall not include any professional fees or expenses arising after the conversion of any Chapter 11 Case to a case under Chapter 7 of the Bankruptcy Code, (v) shall not apply to the extent there is equity in encumbered assets or there are unencumbered assets of any Debtor's estate that may be used to satisfy the fees and expenses included in the Carve-Out, and (vi) shall be payable only after the Facility Termination Date.

10. The Liens granted to Collateral Agent pursuant to this Order and the other Loan Documents shall be perfected by operation of law upon execution of this Order by this Court. Neither any Agent nor any Lender shall be required to file or record any financing statements, mortgages or other documents in any jurisdiction, to give any notices to, to receive acknowledgments or consents from any Person, or to take any other action to validate or perfect the Liens granted hereunder. This Order shall be deemed sufficient and conclusive evidence of the validity and perfection of the Liens granted hereunder. If Collateral Agent shall, in its sole discretion or upon the request of Administrative Agent, choose to file financing statements or record mortgages or other documents, or otherwise confirm perfection of such Liens, Collateral Agent is hereby authorized to effect such filings and recordations (and all such financing statements, mortgages, and similar documents shall be deemed to have been filed, recorded or made on the date of entry of the Interim Order); *provided*, that if the Debtors have filed or recorded a copy of this Final Order and/or evidence of the pendency of the Chapter 11 Cases in all applicable jurisdictions, the aggregate amount of fees and expenses (including without limitation professional fees and recording costs) that may be charged to the Debtors (either directly or as part of the fees and expenses otherwise contractually payable by the Debtors) in connection with filings and recordings by the Collateral Agent shall not exceed $10,000.

11. Reasonable fees and expenses due to Agents and Lenders under and in connection with the Loan Documents shall be charged and promptly paid as required by the Credit Agreement and the other Loan Documents. The Agents consent to, and this Court hereby directs, the provision of copies of all invoices relating to such fees and expenses (which invoices shall be in sufficient detail to enable the parties to review the tasks performed, the individuals performing such tasks, and the hourly rates being charged with respect to each such individual), by the Debtors as and when received to counsel for the Official Committee, counsel for any Other Committee, and the United States Trustee. Nothing in this Final Order or in the Loan Documents shall be construed as waiving or limiting the rights of the Debtors, the Official Committee, any Other Committee, the United States Trustee or any other party-in-interest to seek judicial review of the reasonableness of the fees and expenses being charged.

12. Except as specifically permitted under the Loan Documents, the Adequate Protection Order applicable to the 1996 Obligations, or consented to by each Agent in writing, as long as any Obligations remain outstanding under the Loan Documents, the occurrence of either of the following events shall constitute an Event of Default entitling the Agents to take action as described in decretal paragraph 13 of this Final Order: (a) this Court granting or imposing, under Section 364 or otherwise, (i) super administrative priority status senior or equal to that granted to Agents and Lenders here-

under or (ii) postpetition Liens upon any of the Collateral, or (b) this Court permitting any Debtor to use Agents' and Lenders' Cash Collateral.

13. The automatic stay of Section 362 is hereby modified to the extent necessary to permit Agents and Lenders to perform in accordance with, and exercise their respective rights and remedies pursuant to, this Final Order and the other Loan Documents. Upon the occurrence of and during the continuation of an Event of Default, and without application or motion to, or further order from, this Court or any other court, Agents and Lenders are hereby authorized, *inter alia,* (a) to cease making Revolving Credit Advances, incurring L/C Obligations, or otherwise extending any other financial accommodations under the Loan Documents, (b) to declare all principal of, and accrued interest on, the Obligations to be immediately due and payable and require that the L/C Obligations be cash collateralized, (c) to revoke each Debtor's right to use Cash Collateral in which Agents and Lenders have an interest, and (d) upon five Business Days' prior written notice to (i) BCI, (ii) the United States Trustee, and (iii) counsel for the Official Committee and counsel for any Other Committee, exercise any and all other rights and remedies provided for under this Final Order, any Loan Document, or applicable law, including the right to sell or otherwise dispose of all or any part of the Collateral in a commercially reasonable manner.

14. Upon entry of this Final Order, the Debtors shall not have any right to contest the enforcement of the remedies set forth in the Credit Agreement on any basis other than the fact that an Event of Default has not occurred, and, except with respect to an objection to the existence of an Event of Default, the Debtors shall not have the right to seek injunctive relief against such enforcement under Section 105 or otherwise, or to seek injunctive relief in conflict with the provisions of this Final Order or any other Loan Document. The foregoing restrictions on the Debtors' rights shall not in any way be construed or deemed to constitute a restriction as to any such rights that the Official Committee, any Other Committee, and any other party-in-interest may have.

15. If any provisions of this Final Order or any Loan Document are hereafter modified, vacated, reversed, limited or stayed by subsequent order of this Court, an appellate court, or any other court, such modification, vacation, reversal, limitation or stay shall not affect the validity or priority of any Obligations incurred prior thereto, or the validity, enforceability or priority of any Lien. Notwithstanding any such modification, vacation, reversal, limitation or stay, any Obligation of any Debtor pursuant to this Final Order or under any Loan Document arising prior thereto shall be governed in all respects by the original provisions of this Final Order and the Loan Documents, and Agents and Lenders shall be entitled to all of the rights, privileges, and benefits granted hereunder and thereunder with respect to all such Obligations.

16. No order dismissing any Chapter 11 Case under Section 1112 or providing for the sale of any Debtor or substantially all of such Debtor's assets under Section 363 or otherwise shall be entered unless the Obligations have first been paid in full in cash, or would be paid in full in cash upon the consummation of any such sale.

17. This Order shall not be construed in any way as a waiver or relinquishment of any rights that any Agent or Lender may have (i) to be heard on any matter brought before this Court or (ii) to bring any matter before this Court, including seeking the appointment of a trustee, examiner, or other representative for any Debtor's estate under Section 1104, converting any Chapter 11 Case to a case under Chapter 7 pursuant to Section 1112, or opposing extension of the exclusivity periods of Section 1121. The rights and remedies of Agents and Lenders specified herein are cumulative and not exclusive of any rights or remedies that they may have under this Final Order, any other Loan Documents, or otherwise.

18. The Agents consent to the provision by the Debtors, and this Court hereby directs the Debtors to provide, to counsel for the Official Committee and counsel for any Other Committee copies of all financial reports and notices delivered as required in, or in connection with, the Loan Documents.

19. Nothing contained in this Final Order or in the Loan Documents shall constitute a finding or determination by the Court concerning the amount, validity, perfection, priority, enforceability or non-avoidability of the obligations incurred or the liens and security interests granted by one or more of the Debtors to any of the 1996 Lessor, the 1995 Lessor, the Prepetition Revolver Agent, the Prepetition Revolver Lenders, the Common Collateral Agent or the Prepetition Liquidity Agent prior to the Petition Date.

20. This Final Order and, subject to the final sentence of decretal paragraph 2 hereof, each other Loan Document shall be binding upon each Debtor and its respective estate, each Agent, each Lender, and their respective successors and assigns, including any trustee or other estate representative hereafter appointed or elected for the estate of any Debtor in its Chapter 11 Case or any subsequent Chapter 7 case. This Final Order and each other Loan Document shall inure to the benefit of each Debtor, each Agent, each Lender, and their respective successors and assigns, but not to any trustee or other estate representative hereafter appointed for the estate of any Debtor in proceedings under Chapter 7 or Chapter 11 of the Bankruptcy Code. Except as otherwise explicitly set forth in this Final Order, no third parties are intended to be or shall be deemed to be third party beneficiaries of the provisions of this Final Order or any other Loan Document.

21. Except to such matters as are expressly waived or limited herein, nothing in this Final Order shall be deemed to confer standing on, or deny

standing to, any party-in-interest in the Chapter 11 Cases.

Dated: October 29, 1998

By: ***/s/ Charles G. Case II***
Hon. Charles G. Case II
UNITED STATES BANKRUPTCY JUDGE

APPENDIX K

SAMPLE OPERATING REPORT

This sample ***Operating Report*** is from the Chapter 11 case of ***McCulloch Corporation***. ***McCulloch*** was originally involved in the manufacture and distribution of chainsaws and other lawn and garden devices, with manufacturing and assembling facilities in Arizona and Mexico. The ***Operating Report*** is a standard format used in most jurisdictions, although in certain instances the U.S. Trustee's Office and Bankruptcy Court will allow some deviation based on a company's existing accounting systems.

All of the information in this Appendix is a matter of public record on file with the U.S. Bankruptcy Court, so no confidences or privileges are breached by this publication.

IN THE UNITED STATES BANKRUPTCY COURT FOR THE DISTRICT OF ARIZONA

In re:	)	CASE NO. B-99-00074-TUC-JMM
	)	**BUSINESS AND INDUSTRY**
McCulloch North America, Inc.	)	**MONTHLY OPERATING REPORT**
	)	
and	)	for McCulloch North America, Inc.
	)	
McCulloch Corporation	)	MONTH OF September 1999
	)	
(99-00097-TUC-JMM)	)	DATE PETITION FILED: January 12, 1999
	)	
(Jointly Administered Case)	)	TAX PAYER ID NO. 95-3832942

Nature of Debtor's Business: Manufacture of outdoor power equipment and lawn and garden equipment

DATE DISCLOSURE STATEMENT:	FILED	August 5, 1999	TO BE FILED:	
DATE PLAN OF REORGANIZATION:	FILED	August 5, 1999	TO BE FILED:	

I CERTIFY UNDER PENALTY OF PERJURY THAT THE FOLLOWING MONTHLY OPERATING REPORT AND THE ACCOMPANYING ATTACHMENTS ARE TRUE AND CORRECT TO THE BEST OF MY KNOWLEDGE.

RESPONSIBLE PARTY:

	President and Chief Executive Officer
ORIGINAL SIGNATURE OF RESPONSIBLE PARTY	TITLE
/s/ Michael R. D'Appolonia	President and Chief Executive Officer
PRINTED NAME OF RESPONSIBLE PARTY	TITLE

PREPARER:

	President and Chief Executive Officer
ORIGINAL SIGNATURE OF PREPARER	TITLE
Michael R. D'Appolonia	President and Chief Executive Officer
PRINTED NAME OF RESPONSIBLE PARTY	TITLE

PERSON TO CONTACT REGARDING THIS REPORT: Michael R. D'Appolonia

PHONE NUMBER: (520) 574-4148

ADDRESS: 6085 S. McCulloch Drive.
Tucson, AZ 85706

ORIGINAL REPORT IS FILED WITH THE COURT. COPY IS FILED WITH U.S. TRUSTEE'S OFFICE

Case Number: B-99-00074-TUC-JMM

9/30/99

CURRENT MONTH'S
RECEIPTS AND DISBURSEMENTS

	BANK ACCOUNTS							
	OPERATING #2072-0179	PAYROLL #6025-8221	PAYROLL #0625-8205	RETENTION #2967-2767	DREYFUSS #321289	HOLDBACK #0752-4552	JD MILLIGAN #3341-3012	TOTAL
CASH AND BANK BALANCE - BEGINNING OF MONTH	$ 850,302	$ 14,402	$ -	$ -	$ 3,837,234	$ -	$ 195,240	$ 4,896,878
RECEIPTS								
CASH SALES	$ 45,300							$ 45,300
ACCOUNTS RECEIVABLE - PREPETITION	$ 80,748						$ 6,939	$ 87,687
ACCOUNTS RECEIVABLE - POSTPETITION	$ 9,078							$ 9,078
LOANS AND ADVANCES	$ -			$ -	$ -	$ -	$ -	$ -
SALE OF ASSETS	$ 59,440							$ 59,440
TRANSFERS IN FROM OTHER ACCOUNTS	$ 514,463	$ 306,318	$ -	$ -	$ -	$ -		$ 820,781
DIVIDENDS & INTEREST	$ -	$ -	$ -	$ -	$ 14,463	$ -	$ -	$ 14,463
OTHER (ATTACH LIST)	$ 1,140	$ 62						$ 1,201
		refund of tax overpayment						$ -
TOTAL RECEIPTS	$ 710,168	$ 306,380	$ -	$ -	$ 14,463	$ -	$ 6,939	$ 1,037,949
DISBURSEMENTS								
BUSINESS – ORDINARY OPERATIONS	$ 810,452	$ 182,301	$ -	$ -		$ -	$ 202,180	$ 1,194,932
CAPITAL IMPROVEMENTS	$ -							$ -
PRE-PETITION DEBT	$ 191,982							$ 191,982
TRANSFERS TO OTHER DIP ACCOUNTS	$ 306,318	$ -	$ -	$ -	$ 514,463	$ -	$ -	$ 820,781
OTHER (ATTACH LIST)	$ -							$ -
								$ -
REORGANIZATION EXPENSES:								$ -
ATTORNEY FEES	$ -							$ -
ACCOUNTANT FEES	$ 47,473							$ 47,473
OTHER PROFESSIONAL FEES	$ -							$ +-
U.S. TRUSTEE QUARTERLY FEES	$ -							$ -
COURT COSTS	$ -							$ -
								$
TOTAL DISBURSEMENTS	$ 1,356,226	$ 182,301	$ -	$ -	$ 514,463	$ -	$ 202,180	$ 2,255,169
CASH BANK BALANCE - END OF MONTH	$ 204,243	$ 138,181	$ -	$ -	$ 3,337,234	$ -	$ -	$ 3,679,658

DISBURSEMENTS FOR CALCULATING QUARTERLY FEES:		
TOTAL DISBURSEMENTS FROM ABOVE:		
LESS: TRANSFERS OUT TO OTHER DIP ACCOUNTS		
TOTAL DISBURSEMENTS FOR CALCULATING QUARTERLY FEES:		

McCulloch North America, Inc.
99-00074-TUC-JMM

Deposits

Post Petition A/R

Date	Bank Amount	Control	A/R	Sales (rent)	Ins/Cobra	Interco. Transfers	Loans/ Advances	Asset Sales	Interest	Other	Notes
September 1999											
9/1/99	14,462.53					14,462.53					
9/3/99	1,620.00	-			1,620.00						
9/3/99	2,543.77	-			2,543.77						
9/3/99	60,000.00	-	60,000.00								WJ Connell Settlement
9/9/99	52,580.80	-	6,972.80	45,300.00						308.00	Sterilite Rent (45k); McCulloch shirts (308)
9/13/99	5,079.87	-	4,820.75							259.12	Swift – refund on freight overpayment
9/15/99	54,910.01	-						54,910.01			Norman Levy
9/17/99	4,250.00	-						4,250.00			
9/24/99	1,550.00	-			1,550.00						
9/24/99	3,053.99	-			3,053.99						
9/28/99	500,000.00	-				500,000.00					Move from Dreyfus Account
9/30/99	310.00	-			310.00						
9/30/99	9,806.61	-	8,954.11					280.00		572.5	Reimbursement for trade show shirts from OEI
	710,167.58	-	80,747.66	45,300.00	9,077.76	514,462.53	-	59,440.01	-	1,139.62	710,167.58

McCulloch North America
Balance Sheet
For Period Ending **9/30/99**
All Figures are in 000's

	Mexico	Canada	US	Sub-Total	Consolidation Entries	Domestic
Assets						
Current Assets						
Cash	38	-	2,929	2,967		2,967
Notes Receivable	-	-	-	-		-
Accounts Receivable						
Pre Petition Trade A/R	-	-	5,474	5,474		5,474
Other	124	-	507	631	-	631
Reserve for Bad Debts	-	-	(1,626)	(1,626)		(1,626)
Net Accounts Receivable	124	-	4,355	4,479	-	4,479
Total Current Assets	162	-	7,284	7,446	-	7,446
Land	3,004	-	4,497	7,501		7,501
Buildings	8,968	-	5,543	14,511		14,511
Accumulated Depreciation	(523)	-	(707)	(1,230)		(1,230)
Fixed Assets, Net	11,449	-	9,333	20,782	-	20,782
Other Assets	-	-	1,329	1,329		1,329
Trademarks	-	-	9,559	9,559		9,559
Equity in International Subsidiaries	-	-	7,861	7,861	(7,861) c	-

Total Assets	11,611	-	35,366	46,977	(7,861)		39,116
Liabilities and Net Worth							
Current Liabilities							
Debt Obligations	-	-	19,565	19,565			19,565
Capitalized Leases	-	-	216	216			216
Accounts Payable Trade Suppliers	181	-	33,011	33,192			33,192
Accrued Expense							
Accrued Interest Expense	-	-	536	536			536
Accrued Post September Expenses	-	-	1,611	1,611			1,611
Worker's Comp	-	-	167	167			167
Product Liability	-	-	150	150			150
	181	-	55,256	55,437	-		55,437
Reserves:							
Environmental	-	-	1,309	1,309			1,309
Pension	-	-	1,853	1,853			1,853
Retiree Benefits	-	-	2,400	2,400			2,400
	-	-	5,562	5,562	-		5,562
Shareholders' Equity							
Common Stock	-	-	42	42			42
Paid in Capital	9,860	(15,418)	61,012	55,454	5,529	c	60,983
Foreign Translation Adjustment	64	(396)	-	(332)			(332)
Accum Earnings Prior Year	1,455	15,822	(84,742)	(67,465)	(13,390)	c	(80,855)
Accum Earnings This Year	51	(8)	(1,764)	(1,721)	-		(1,721)
	11,430	-	(25,452)	(14,022)	(7,861)		(21,883)
Total Liabilities and Net Worth	11,611	-	35,366	46,977	(7,861)		39,116

McCulloch North America
Monthly Income Statement – Post Petition
For Period Ending 9/30/99
All Figures are in 000's

	Mexico	Canada	US	Sub-Total	Consolidation Entries		Domestic
Gross Sales - Domestic	-	-	-	-			-
- International	-	-	-	-			-
- Intercompany	-	-	-	-		e	-
Return Allowance	-	-	3	3			3
Sales Commissions	-	-	-	-			-
Cash Discounts	-	-	-	-			-
Net Sales	-	-	(3)	(3)	-		(3)
Standard Cost Margin %	#DIV/0!			#DIV/0!	#DIV/0!		
Std Cos- Domestic	-	-	-	-		e	-
- International	-	-	-	-			-
- Intercompany	(94)	-	-	(94)	94	e	-
Manufacturing variances	-	-	116	116	(94)	e	22
Total Cost of Sales	(94)	-	116	22	-		22
Gross Profit Margin	94	-	(119)	(25)	-		(25)
Operations							
- Research & Development	-	-	-	-			-
- Purchasing / Logistics	-	-	-	-			-
- Quality Assurance	-	-	-	-			-
- Manufacturing Management	-	-	-	-			-
Total Operations	-	-	-	-			-
Sales & Marketing							

- Sales Administration	-	-	-	-		-
- Salesmen	-	-	-	-		-
- Marketing & Advertising	-	-	34	34		34
- Co-op Advertising	-	-	-	-		-
- Media Advertising	-	-	-	-		-
- Product Distribution	-	-	24	24		24
- Product Services	-	-	-	-		-
- Customer Service	-	-	-	-		-
- Transportation	-	-	-	-		-
Total Sales & Marketing	-	-	58	58	-	58
Administration						
- Accounting/Finance	-	-	51	51		51
- MIS	-	-	1	1		1
- Human Resources	-	-	244	244		244
- Legal	-	-	-	-		-
- Executive	-	-	140	140		140
Total Administration	-	-	436	436	-	436
Total Selling, General & Admin	-	-	494	494	-	494
Earnings Before Interest/Taxes	94	-	(613)	(519)	-	(519)
Professional Fees	-	-	15	15		15
Exchange (Gain) or Loss	-	-	-	-		-
Interest Expense	-	-	192	192		192
Interest Income	-	-	90	90		90
Other (Income) Expense	-	-	(68)	(68)		(68)
(Gain) or Loss Property Disposal	-	-	-	-		-
Amortization Expense	-	-	-	-		-
Earnings Before Taxes	94	-	(842)	(748)	-	(748)
Extraordinary (Gain) Loss	-	-	(59)	(59)		(59)
Taxes	-	-	-	-		-
Net Earnings	94	-	(783)	(689)	-	(689)

McCulloch North America
YTD Income Statement – Pre Petition
For Period Ending 1/12/99 as of 9/30/99
All Figures are in 000's

	Mexico	Canada	US	Sub-Total	Consolidation Entries	Domestic
Gross Sales - Domestic	-	30	10,081	10,111		10,111
- International	-	-	965	965		965
- Intercompany	1,683	-	1,787	3,470	(1,683) e	1,787
Return Allowance	-	-	(4,380)	(4,380)		(4,380)
Sales Commissions	-	-	37	37		37
Cash Discounts	-	-	185	185		185
Net Sales	1,683	30	16,991	18,704	(1,683)	17,021
Standard Cost Margin %	0		36.61%	31.60%		37.28%
Std Cos- Domestic	-	-	7,147	7,147	(24) e	7,123
- International	-	-	748	748		748
- Intercompany	1,649	-	1,499	3,158	(1,659) e	1,499
Manufacturing variances	-	-	1,842	1,842		1,842
Total Cost of Sales	1,659	-	11,236	12,895	(1,683)	11,212
Gross Profit Margin	24	30	5,755	5,809	-	5,809
	0	100%	34%	31.1%	-	34.1%
Operations						
- Research & Development	-	-	213	213		213
- Purchasing / Logistics	-	-	148	148		148
- Quality Assurance	-	-	54	54		54
- Manufacturing Management	-	-	64	64		64
Total Operations	-	-	479	479	-	479
Sales & Marketing						
- Sales Administration	-	-	-	-		-
- Salesmen	-	15	408	423		423
- Marketing & Advertising	-	-	206	206		206
- Co-op Advertising	-	-	(933)	(933)		(933)
- Media Advertising	-	-	15	15		15
- Product Distribution	-	-	502	502		502
- Product Services	-	-	91	91		91
- Customer Service	-	-	200	200		200
- Transportation	-	5	561	566		566
Total Sales & Marketing	-	20	1,050	1,070	-	1,070
Administration						
- Accounting/Finance	-	-	238	238		238
- MIS	-	-	189	189		189
- Human Resources	-	-	140	140		140
- Legal	-	-	151	151		151
- Executive	-	-	46	46		46
Total Administration	-	-	764	764	-	764
Total Selling, General & Admin	-	20	2,293	2,313	-	2,313
Earnings Before Interest/Taxes	24	10	3,462	3,496	-	3,496
Professional Fees	-	-	660	660		660
Exchange (Gain) or Loss	1	-	4	5	-	5
Interest Expense	-	-	1,222	1,222		1,222
Interest Income	(7)	-	(36)	(43)		(43)
Other (Income) Expense	3	-	(7)	(4)		(4)
Amortization Expense	-	-	98	98		98
Earnings Before Taxes	27	10	1,521	1,558	-	1,558
Extraordinary (Gain) Loss	-	-	(7,588)	(7,588)		(7,588)
Taxes	-	-	-	-		-
Net Earnings	27	10	9,109	9,146	-	9,146

McCulloch North America
Year to Date – Post Petition
For Period Ending **as of 9/30/99**
All Figures are in 000's

	Mexico	Canada	US	Sub-Total	Consolidation Entries	Domestic
Gross Sales - Domestic	-	21	9,763	9,784	-	9,784
- International	-	-	1,806	1,806	-	1,806
- Intercompany	3,898	-	2,424	6,322	(3,451) e	2,871
Return Allowance	-	-	2,808	2,808	-	2,808
Sales Commissions	-	-	37	37	-	37
Cash Discounts	-	-	61	61	-	61
Net Sales	3,898	21	11,087	15,006	(3,451)	11,555
Std Cos - Domestic	-	-	17,969	17,969	(203) e	17,766
- International	-	-	1,684	1,684	-	1,684
- Intercompany	3,970	-	2,809	6,779	(3,154) e	3,625
Manufacturing variances	-	-	5,672	5,672	(94)	5,578
Total Cost of Sales	3,970	-	28,134	32,104	(3,451)	28,652
Gross Profit Margin	(72)	21	(17,047)	(17,098)	-	(17,098)
Operations						
- Research & Development	-	-	150	150	-	150
- Purchasing / Logistics	-	-	291	291	-	291
- Quality Assurance	-	-	137	137	-	137
- Manufacturing Management	-	-	104	104	-	140
Total Operations	-	-	718	718	-	718
Sales & Marketing						
- Sales Administration	-	-	-	-	-	-
- Salesmen	-	35	252	287	-	287
- Marketing & Advertising	-	-	492	492	-	492
- Co-op Advertising	-	-	172	172	-	172
- Media Advertising	-	-	-	-	-	-
- Product Distribution	-	-	565	565	-	564
- Product Services	-	-	204	204	-	204
- Customer Service	-	-	199	199	-	199
- Transportation	-	4	831	835	-	835
Total Sales & Marketing	-	39	2,715	2,754	-	2,754
Administration						
- Accounting/Finance	-	-	511	511	-	511
- MIS	-	-	156	156	-	156
- Human Resources	-	-	1,430	1,430	-	1,430
- Legal	-	-	412	412	-	412
- Executive	-	-	214	214	-	214
Total Administration	-	-	2,723	2,723	-	2,723
Total Selling, General & Admin	-	39	6,156	6,195	-	6,195
Earnings Before Interest/Taxes	(72)	(18)	(23,203)	(23,293)	-	(23,293)
Professional Fees	-	-	3,369	3,369	-	3,369
Exchange (Gain) or Loss	1	-	-	-	-	-
Interest Expense	1	-	2,469	2,470	-	2,470
Interest Income	(173)	-	28	(145)	-	(145)
Other (Income) Expense	-	-	(237)	(237)	-	(237)
(Gain) or Loss Property Disposal	74	-	(825)	(751)	-	(751)
Amortization Expense	-	-	343	343	-	343
Earnings Before Taxes	25	(18)	(28,350)	(28,343)	-	(28,343)
Extraordinary (Gain) Loss	-	-	(17,477)	(17,477)	-	(17,477)
Taxes	-	-	-	-	-	-
Net Earnings	25	(18)	(10,873)	(10,866)	-	(10,866)

McCulloch North America
Year to Date Income Statement Total
For Period Ending **as of 9/30/99**
All Figures are in 000's

	Mexico	Canada	US	Sub-Total	Consolidation Entries	Domestic
Gross Sales - Domestic	-	51	19,844	19,895		19,895
- International	-	-	2,771	2,771		2,771
- Intercompany	5,581	-	4,211	9,792	(5,134) e	4,658
Return Allowance	-	-	(1,572)	(1,572)		(1,572)
Sales Commissions	-	-	74	74		74
Cash Discounts	-	-	246	246	-	246
Net Sales	5,581	51	28,078	33,710	(5,134)	28,576
Std Cos - Domestic	-	-	25,116	25,116	(227) e	24,889
- International	-	-	2,432	2,432	-	2,432
- Intercompany	5,629	-	4,308	9,937	(4,813) e	5,124
Manufacturing variances	-	-	7,514	7,514	(94)	7,420
Total Cost of Sales	5,629	-	39,370	44,999	(5,134)	39,865
Gross Profit Margin	(48)	51	(11,292)	(11,289)	-	(11,289)
Operations						
- Research & Development	-	-	363	363	-	363
- Purchasing / Logistics	-	-	439	439	-	439
- Quality Assurance	-	-	191	191	-	191
- Manufacturing Management	-	-	204	204	-	204
Total Operations	-	-	1,197	1,197	-	1,197
Sales & Marketing						
- Sales Administration	-	-	-	-	-	-
- Salesmen	-	50	660	710	-	710
- Marketing & Advertising	-	-	698	698	-	698
- Co-op Advertising	-	-	(761)	(761)	-	(761)
- Media Advertising	-	-	15	15	-	15
- Product Distribution	-	-	1,067	1,067	-	1,067
- Product Services	-	-	295	295	-	295
- Customer Service	-	-	399	399	-	399
- Transportation	-	9	1,392	1,401	-	1,401
Total Sales & Marketing	-	59	3,765	3,824	-	3,824
Administration						
- Accounting/Finance	-	-	749	749	-	749
- MIS	-	-	345	345	-	345
- Human Resources	-	-	1,570	1,570	-	1,570
- Legal	-	-	563	563	-	563
- Executive	-	-	260	260	-	260
Total Administration	-	-	3,487	3,487	-	3,487
Total Selling, General & Admin	-	59	8,449	8,508	-	8,508
Earnings Before Interest/Taxes	(48)	(8)	(19,741)	(19,797)	-	(19,797)
Professional Fees	-	-	4,029	4,029	-	4,029
Exchange (Gain) or Loss	2	-	4	6	-	6
Interest Expense	2	-	3,691	3,693	-	3,693
Interest Income	(180)	-	(8)	(188)	-	(188)
Other (Income) Expense	3	-	(241)	(241)	-	(241)
(Gain) or Loss Property Disposal	74	-	(825)	(751)		(751)
Amortization Expense	-	-	441	441	-	441
Earnings Before Taxes	51	(8)	(26,829)	(26,786)	-	(26,786)
Extraordinary (Gain) Loss	-	-	(25,065)	(25,065)	-	(25,065)
Taxes	-	-	-	-	-	-
Net Earnings	51	(8)	(1,764)	(1,721)	-	(1,721)

Case Number: B - 99-00074-TUC-JMM

Status of Assets

9/30/99

ACCOUNTS RECEIVABLE	Total	0 - 30 Days	31 - 60 Days	60 + Days
Total Accounts Receivable	5,773,560			5,773,560
Less Amount Considered Uncollectible	(1,626,426)	-	-	(1,626,426)
Accounts Receivable (Net)	4,147,124	-	-	4,147,124

DUE FROM INSIDERS	
Scheduled Amount	$ -
Plus: Amount Extended Since Date of Filing	-
Less: Amount Collected Since Date of Filing	-
Less: Amount Considered Uncollectible	-
Total Due From Insiders	$ -

INVENTORY	
Beginning Inventory	$ -
ADD: PURCHASES	-
LESS: COST OF GOODS SOLD (COST BASIS)	-
Ending Inventory	$ -

DATE THE LAST PHYSICAL INVENTORY WAS TAKEN: October-98

FIXED ASSETS - (in thousands)	SCHEDULED AMOUNT	ADDITIONS	DELETIONS	CURRENT AMOUNT
REAL PROPERTY	4,497	-	-	4,497
BUILDINGS/PLANT	5,543		-	5,543
ACCUM. DEPREC.	(719)	(12)	-	(731)
NET BUILDINGS/PLANT	(4,424	(12)	-	4,812
EQUIPMENT	-	-	-	-
ACCUM. DEPREC.	-	-	-	-
NET EQUIPMENT	-	-	-	-
AUTOS & VEHICLES	-	-	-	-
ACCUM. DEPREC.	-	-	-	-
NET AUTOS	-	-	-	-

Please provide a description of fixed asset additions and deletions that occurred during the reporting period including date court order signed authorizing same.

B&I-5 11/1/96

Case Number: B - 99-00074-TUC-JMM

9/30/99

STATUS OF LIABILITIES
AND SENSITIVE PAYMENTS

POSTPETITION UNPAID OBLIGATIONS	TOTAL	0-30	31-60	61-90	91+
ACCOUNTS PAYABLE	$ 1,782	$ 1,170	$ -	$ -	$ 612
TAXES PAYABLE	$ -	$ -	$ -	$ -	$ -
NOTES PAYABLE	$ -	$ -	$ -	$ -	$ -
PROFESSIONAL FEES	$ -	$ -	$ -	$ -	$ -
SECURED DEBT	$ -	$ -	$ -	$ -	$ -
OTHER (ATTACH LIST)	$ -	$ -	$ -	$ -	$ -
TOTAL POST-PETITION LIABILITIES	$ 1,782	$ 1,170	$ -	$ -	$ 612

*DEBTORS MUST ATTACH AN AGED LISTING OF ACCOUNTS PAYABLE

PAYMENTS TO INSIDERS AND PROFESSIONALS

INSIDERS				
NAME		REASON FOR PAYMENT	AMOUNT PAID THIS MONTH	TOTAL PAID TO DATE
NONE				
TOTAL PAYMENTS TO INSIDERS				

PROFESSIONALS					
NAME		AMOUNT APPROVED	AMOUNT PAID	TOTAL PAID TO DATE	TOTAL INCURRED AND UNPAID
Streich Lang	Legal	$ -	$ -	$ 657,210	$ -
Weil, Gotshal & Manges	Legal	$ -	$ -	$ 284,999	$ -
Marshall, O'Tolle, Gerstein	Legal	$ -	$ -	$ 94,240	$ -
Bosley & Hutzelman	Legal	$ -	$ -	$ 22,242	$ -
Baker & McKenzie	Legal	$ -	$ -	$ 17,489	$ -
Nightengale	Accounting	$ -	$ -	$ 556,353	$ -
Squire, Sanders & Dempsey	Legal	$ -	$ -	$ 82,031	$ -
Earnst & Young	Accounting	$ -	$ 47,473	$ 72,139	$ -
TOTAL PAYMENTS TO PROFESSIONALS		$ -	$ 47,473	$ 1,766,703	$ -

Case Number: B - 99-00074-TUC-JMM

CASE STATUS

QUESTIONNAIRE

	YES	NO
HAVE ANY FUNDS BEEN DISBURSED FROM ANY ACCOUNT OTHER THAN A DEBTOR IN POSSESSION ACCOUNT?		X
ARE ANY POSTPETITION RECEIVABLES (ACCOUNTS, NOTES OR LOANS) DUE FROM RELATED PARTIES?		X
ARE ANY WAGE PAYMENTS PAST DUE?		X
ARE ANY U.S. TRUSTEE QUARTERLY FEES DELINQUENT?		X

IF THE ANSWER TO ANY OF THE ABOVE QUESTIONS ID "YES," PROVIDE A DETAILED EXPLANATION OF EACH ITEM. (ATTACH ADDITIONAL SHEETS IF NECESSARY).

CURRENT NUMBER OF EMPLOYEES: 23

INSURANCE

TYPE OF POLICY	CARRIER AND POLICY NUMBER	PERIOD COVERED	EXPIRATION DATE	PAYMENT AMOUNT & FREQUENCY
	SEE ATTACHED SCHEDULE			

WHAT STEPS HAVE BEEN TAKEN TO REMEDY ANY OF THE PROBLEMS THAT BROUGHT ABOUT THE CHAPTER 11 FILING?

The Company has determined that reorganizing itself under the current configuration/structure is not feasible and is taking steps towards an orderly liquidation.

LIST ANY MATTERS THAT ARE DELAYING THE FILING OF A PLAN OF REORGANIZATION.

McCulloch Corporation
North America
Insurance Premium and Financing Analysis
Fiscal 1999

Insurer	Policy Number	Type of Coverage
National Union	857-26-14	Director, Officers and Corporate Liability Insurance
National Union	857-26-22	Commercial Crime Insurance
National Union	857-26-25	Pension Trust Liability Insurance
		Total
Arkwright Mutua	6020478	Domestic All Risk Property/Boiler & Machinery
Seguros Commercial (Arkwright)	6888046	Mexico All Risk Property/Boiler & Machinery
CIGNA	CXC 035724	Internation Liability
J&H Marsh & McLennan Placement Fee	N/A	J&Y Marsh & McLennan Placement Fee
		Total
Reliance National Indemnity Co.	NKA 0125692-03	Automobile Liability
Reliance National Indemnity Co.	NGB 0125691-03	Commercial General Liability
Reliance National Indemnity Co.	NGB 0125691-03	Commercial General Liability
Reliance National Indemnity Co.	NWA 0125690-03	Workers' Compensation and Employers' Liability
Chubb & Sons – Federal Insurance Co.	7969-86-76	Commercial Umbrella Liability
AIG – National Union	BE 357 21 25	Commercial Umbrella Liability
		Total
Royal Insurance Company of America	POC102310	Inland Transit – Europe excluding Italy (4)
Royal Insurance Company of America	POC1012310	Marine Cargo (Worldwide)
		Total

March USA, Inc.
Richard F. Landy
Senior Vice President
1166 Avenue of the Americas
New York, New York 10036+2774
212/345-3545
RichardF.Landy@marshmc.com

McCulloch North America, Inc. **99-00074-TUC-JMM**

Outstanding Accounts Payables as of 9/30/99

Vendor	Description	Open-Amt	Current	30 DAYS	60-Days	90 & Over
PN506436	MCCARTHY, JIM	1,019.95	1,019.95	-	-	-
PN521772	IOS CAPITAL	561.76	-	-	-	561.76
PN522114	HERITAGE ENVIRONMENTAL	150.00	150.00	-	-	-
PT093486	CON-WAY WESTERN EXPRESS	50.00	-	-	-	50.00
		1,781.71	1,169.95	-	-	611.76

McCulloch North America 99-00074-TUC-JMM
Accounts Receivable Aging as of 9/30/99
U.S. Dollar Customers

CUST #.	CUSTOMER NAME	Payments September	9/30/99 Total Open
11200	CALDOR CORP.		353,513.85
11201	CALDOR CORP. D.I.P.		(33,181.84)
11250	AMES DEPARTMENT STORES		(439.10)
11260	HILL'S STORES, CO.		7,530.10
11275	PERGAMENT		887.59
11415	SPAG'S SUPPLY INC.		(5,081.07)
11450	B.J.'S WHOLESALE CLUB		(256.75)
11500	KMART CORPORATION		2,142,611.45
11510	KMART CORPORATION		1,627.59
11630	MENARDS		191,460.40
11650	TARGET CENTRAL PROCESSING		38,316.34
11700	VENTURE STORES, INC.		(1,427.95)
11701	VENTURE STORES, INC.		(2,758.20)
11900	BI-MART CO.		8,492.40
12375	PAMIDA, INC.		28,574.96
12500	GRANDPA'S		(795.25)
12800	DISTRIBUTION AMERICA		(673.79)
12801	EMERY-WATERHOUSE CO.		4,842.63
12805	KRUSE HARDWARE CO.		(55.00)
12807	ORGILL BROTHERS & CO. INC.		4,466.34
12809	HOUSE-HASSON HARDWARE CO.		(750.48)
12811	JENSEN DIST. SERVICES		(19.37)
12819	FREDERICK TRADING COMPANY		(1,291.81)
12830	SMITH HARDWARE COMPANY		(501.68)
12833	MONROE HARDWARE CO., INC.		(392.00)
12900	BLISH-MIZE COMPANY		(662.26)
12901	WALLACE HARDWARE CO, INC.		(1,066.00)
12902	YAKIMA HARDWARE COMPANY		(685.94)
12908	BOSTWICK-BRAUN CO.		(971.00)
12919	MOORE-HANDLEY INC		(3,803.51)
12922	WATTERS & MARTIN, INC.		(829.25)
12931	GALBRAITH STEEL & SUPPLY		(563.40)
13002	MONTGOMERY WARD		(2,900.50)
13012	MONTGOMERY WARD		(375,408.76)
13013	MONTGOMERY WARD		3,183.52
13025	MONTGOMERY WARD		(356.81)
13800	L.G. COOK DISTRIBUTOR, INC.		47,078.04
13900	AMARILLO/CALIFORNIA		(3,652.63)
13911	HDW, INC. - GREENWOOD		(780.50)

CUST #.	CUSTOMER NAME	Payments September	9/30/99 Total Open

CASH DISBURS EMENTS CHECK #..	CK.DATE..	PAYEE	Purpose	CK.AMT...
522322	9/2/99	RODNEY J. GOLD	Employee Benefits	60.00
522323	9/2/99	TRI-DENT DENTAL PC	Employee Benefits	180.00
522324	9/2/99	ROGER ANDERSON, DMD	Employee Benefits	91.00
522325	9/2/99	HAVASU VALLEY DENTAL	Employee Benefits	244.50
522326	9/2/99	VIP RUBBER CO	Tooling Prep	1,200.00
522327	9/2/99	ERNST & YOUNG LLP	Professional Services	47,473.00
522328	9/2/99	AFFODABLE PLUMBING	Building Maintenance	250.00
522329	9/2/99	SUNSTATE EQUIPMENT C	Equipment Rental	1,438.08
522330	9/2/99	BARICH INC.	JF Tooling	6,250.00
522336	9/3/99	MICHAEL CANAL & SONS	Warranty	226.81
522337	9/3/99	STREICH LANG	Reimbursement for Service	14,534.81
522338	9/3/99	ACCOUNTEMPS	Hired Labor	648.74
522339	9/3/99	ARNOLD'S LAWN & GARD	Warranty	119.43
522340	9/3/99	GREVER MOWER MARINE	Warranty	53.75
522341	9/3/99	F M PILE HARDWARE CO.	Warranty	29.83
522342	9/3/99	SIERRA SAW SALES & S	Warranty	36.74
522343	9/3/99	G & H DISTRIBUTORS	Warranty	48.00
522344	9/3/99	FULWIDER OUTDOOR PWR	Warranty	70.72
522345	9/3/99	R G & SONS	Warranty	100.10
522346	9/3/99	GEORGE SANDERS SALES	Warranty	50.07
522347	9/3/99	TED'S QUALITY SERVICE	Warranty	118.39
522348	9/3/99	OUTBACK LAWN & SNOW	Warranty	54.87
522349	9/3/99	BOONVILLE LAWN & GAR	Warranty	30.32
522350	9/3/99	ZIMMER'S LAWN & GARD	Warranty	36.00
522351	9/3/99	PAUL'S MCCULLOCH SAL	Warranty	48.34
522352	9/3/99	R J DANIELS FUEL & T	Warranty	93.60
522353	9/3/99	DAVE FRANCISS LAWN E	Warranty	34.31
522354	9/3/99	BEEGLES WELDING & SM	Warranty	24.30
522355	9/3/99	USGAARD & SMITH INC.	Warranty	73.89
522356	9/3/99	OMAR'S STIHL	Warranty	56.59
522357	9/3/99	J & M REPAIR	Warranty	17.06
522358	9/3/99	ABSHIRE'S RENTALS, I	Warranty	50.16
522359	9/3/99	101 MOWER MART	Warranty	61.75
522360	9/3/99	PARROTT, INC.	Warranty	68.63
522361	9/3/99	TROY'S SAW & MOWER	Warranty	20.61
522362	9/3/99	MR. QUICK FIX	Warranty	105.00
522363	9/3/99	HALL AIRCOOLED ENGINE	Warranty	28.14
522364	9/3/99	ALOHA POWER EQUIPMENT	Warranty	492.18
522365	9/3/99	BILLS SERVICE CER	Warranty	21.68
522366	9/3/99	PROVENZANO'S KINGS P	Warranty	72.94
522367	9/3/99	J & M MOWER SERVICE	Warranty	67.22
522368	9/3/99	FOXBORO LAWN & POWER	Warranty	34.96
522369	9/3/99	MOWER DOCTOR CORP	Warranty	59.07

APPENDIX L

SAMPLE BAR DATE ORDER

This ***Bar Date Order*** was entered in the ***Unison Healthcare*** Chapter 11 case. Much of this Bar Date Order—which is itself a form of notice to be given to all creditors regarding the bar date—is standard for most Chapter 11 cases, but certain additional provisions addressed specific features of the *Unison Healthcare* case, including the ability of the indenture trustee for each of the notes issued to file a master proof of claim on behalf of all noteholders. The special proof of claim form attached to the Bar Date Order allowed creditors to indicate which of the thirty-three debtors (or which of the debtor's many nursing homes) the claim was asserted against. Ultimately, the thirty-three debtors' estates were substantively consolidated for purposes of distributions on claims, but at the time this Bar Date Order was issued, the debts of each individual debtor were kept separate. The form of this Bar Date Order was not only mailed to all creditors, but also published in *The Wall Street Journal (National Edition)* and newspapers where *Unison* operated its nursing homes.

IN THE UNITED STATES BANKRUPTCY COURT
FOR THE DISTRICT OF ARIZONA

In re: UNISON HEALTHCARE CORPORATION, and related proceedings, Federal I.D. No. 86-0684011 Debtors.	In Proceedings Under Chapter 11 Case No. B-98-06583-PHX-GBN (Jointly Administered) NOTICE AND Order Setting Bar Date And Establishing Notice Procedures **BAR DATE: SEPTEMBER 21, 1998**

This matter is before the Court on the "Ex Parte Motion For Order Fixing Time Within Which Proofs of Claim Must Be Filed" of UNISON HEALTHCARE CORPORATION ("Unison"), and its affiliated Debtors and Debtors-In-Possession indicated above (the "Debtors"), dated July 30, 1998 (the "Motion"); the Court having reviewed the Motion and the Memorandum of Points and Authorities submitted in support of the Motion; the Court having conducted a hearing on August 14, 1998 (the "Hearing") to consider the objections of certain parties to the relief requested in the Motion; the Court being satisfied that the relief requested in the Motion is appropriate under the circumstances; after due consideration and reasonable cause appearing therefor,

THE COURT FINDS as follows:

D. The Motion and relief requested therein constitute "core proceedings" in which this Court may enter final and dispositive orders under 28 U.S.C. §§ 1334 and 157(b)(2)(A) and (O) and Bankruptcy Code § 105.

E. The provisions of this Order adequately addresses certain of the objections voiced at the Hearing, and with respect to those objections not addressed in this Order, such objections are overruled. Furthermore, with respect to the securities plaintiffs' speaking motion requesting a class proof of claim, the Court finds that this issue is not properly before the Court at this time.

F. The form of "Proof of Claim," attached as Exhibit 1 to this Order, is appropriate for use by creditors in asserting claims against the Debtors in these cases and appropriate for providing suitable notice to creditors of the deadline and procedures for filing proofs of claim.

ACCORDINGLY, IT IS HEREBY ORDERED as follows:

4. The Motion is GRANTED as set forth below:

5. **BAR DATE:** The deadline for filing proofs of claim in these cases is fixed as **September 21, 1998** (the "Bar Date"). Except as otherwise specifically provided in this Order, the Bar Date applies to any "claim," as such term is defined in Bankruptcy Code § 101(5), against any of the Debt-

ors arising from any event occurring during the Debtors' operation of their businesses before and until the applicable Debtors' Petition Date including, without limitation: (a) personal injury claims, including such claims that have been asserted in litigation where the plaintiffs have sued or joined as co-defendants present or former directors, officers, or employees of the Debtors, or other individuals or entities, who may have indemnification claims or contribution claims against the Debtors, or who may expose the Debtors to vicarious liability under various principles or provisions of applicable state law; (b) any worker's compensation claims; (c) any administrative agency claims or similar kinds of private enforcement claims, including, but not limited to, wage and hour claims, wrongful termination and discharge claims, loss of benefits claims, harassment claims, employment discrimination claims, and other employment related claims; and (d) claims (including class action claims, if applicable) of any person (including but not limited to holders of the 12¼% Senior Notes, maturing in 2006 (the "Notes"), the 13% Senior Notes, maturing in 1999 (the "Senior Notes"), or common stock) against the Debtors for alleged violations of federal or state securities laws and regulations.

6. **NOTICE OF THIS BAR DATE ORDER:** The Debtors must serve notice of the Bar Date as follows: (a) mailed notice of a conformed copy of this Order, no later than August 19, 1998, to all creditors and parties in interest on the master mailing matrix as maintained by the Debtors; (b) one publication in the national edition of the *Wall Street Journal*; and (c) one publication in a newspaper of general circulation in each county in Alabama, Arizona, Colorado, Indiana, Kansas, Michigan, and Texas where the Debtors currently maintain or previously maintained operations. The form of "Proof of Claim" attached as Exhibit 1 to this Order (the "Proof of Claim Form") is approved in all respects. Notice of the Bar Date as provided in this Order is deemed adequate and proper under Bankruptcy Rules 2002 and 3003.

7. **ADDRESS FOR FILING OF PROOFS OF CLAIM:** Except as otherwise specifically provided in this Order, all persons or entities wishing to assert a claim against any of the Debtors must file such claim, using the Proof of Claim Form, so that it is **received** no later than 4:00 p.m., Mountain Time, on the Bar Date, by PricewaterhouseCoopers, L.L.P., the Claims Agent, at:

Proofs of claim will be treated as filed only when actually received by the Claims Agent. Creditors are advised not to file or send copies of proofs of claim to the Debtors, counsel for the Debtors, the Creditors' Committee or counsel for the Creditors' Committee. If a creditor wishes to receive an acknowledgement of receipt of its proof of claim, the creditor must provide the Claims Agent with an additional copy of the proof of claim with a self-addressed, postage-paid return envelope, unless such proof of claim is filed by facsimile, in which case a facsimile confirmation will be sent by first-class mail to the creditor's address indicated on the proof of claim.

8. **<u>REVIEW OF SCHEDULES</u>:** The Debtors have filed their Schedules of Assets and Liabilities with the Clerk of the Bankruptcy Court, setting forth claim amounts for all creditors as they appear on the Debtors' books and records. **All creditors are advised to review the Schedules, which are available at the Office of the Clerk, United States Bankruptcy Court, 2929 N. Central Avenue, 10th Floor, Phoenix, Arizona 85012, during regular business hours. A copy of the Schedules may also be requested by contacting Quick & Confidential, 352 E. Camelback Road, Suite 200, Phoenix, Arizona 85012, telephone (602) 277-4474, facsimile (602) 277-4556.**

9. **<u>WHO NEED NOT FILE A PROOF OF CLAIM</u>:** Creditors need not file a proof of claim if: (a) they have previously filed a proof of claim in these cases, properly indicating the specific Debtor or Debtors against whom the claim is asserted; or (b) they agree in all respects with the information contained in the Schedules regarding the amount of their claim and the Debtor or Debtors against whom their claim is listed **and** such claim is **not** listed as contingent, unliquidated, or disputed. **If a creditor is unsure whether its claim has been accurately allocated to the proper Debtor or Debtors in the Schedules, the creditor must file a proof of claim by the Bar Date. If a creditor's claim is listed as contingent, unliquidated, or disputed in the Schedules, the creditor MUST file a proof of claim by the Bar Date, using the Proof of Claim Form. If a creditor is unsure whether its claim is listed as contingent, unliquidated, or disputed, the creditor must file a proof of claim by the Bar Date. If a creditor disagrees in any respect with the information contained in the Schedules, the creditor must file a proof of claim by the Bar Date, using the Proof of Claim Form.**

10. **<u>HOLDERS OF NOTES AND SENIOR NOTES</u>:** Creditors need not file a proof of claim if their claims are limited exclusively to claims for the repayment by the Debtors of the principal and accrued interest (including any premiums) on the Notes or the Senior Notes. The filing of an aggregate proof of claim by the indenture trustees for the Senior Notes and the Notes obviates the filing of proofs of claim by individual holders of the Notes or the Senior Notes. Notwithstanding the foregoing, any Note or Senior Note holder who has, may have, or may assert any claim against any of the Debtors with respect to any violations of federal or state securities laws must file a proof of claim by the Bar Date.

11. **<u>EXECUTORY CONTRACT AND UNEXPIRED LEASE CLAIMS</u>:** Any claims arising out of, or otherwise related to, the Debtors' rejection of executory contracts and unexpired nonresidential leases under Bankruptcy Code § 365 as of July 31, 1998 must be filed on or before the Bar Date. Any claims arising out of, or otherwise related to, the Debtors'

rejection of additional executory contracts or unexpired nonresidential leases after July 31, 1998 must be filed on or before the earlier of: (a) thirty (30) days following the entry of the order of the Court approving such rejection, provided the effectiveness of such order has not been stayed; and (b) thirty (30) days following the effective date of any plan or plans or reorganization confirmed by the Bankruptcy Court in the Debtors' Chapter 11 cases.

12. **EQUITY INTERESTS:** Holders of the Debtors' equity securities, including holders of common stock, warrants, and stock options issued by the Debtors, need not file proofs of interest with respect to the interests represented by such equity securities. However, any equity security holder who has, may have, or may assert any claim against any of the Debtors with respect to such equity security (including, without limitation, any claim for violation of federal or state securities laws and any claim for unpaid dividends), must file a proof of claim on or before the Bar Date.

13. **STOCKBROKERS AND OTHER AGENTS:** Stockbrokers or other agents of noteholders, stockholders or optionholders (including record holders or depository agents) that hold debt or equity securities of the Debtors as trustee or nominee, in street name or otherwise, should immediately transmit a copy of this notice to each beneficial holder of any such security. Beneficial holders of debt or equity securities have the right under the Federal Rules of Bankruptcy Procedure to file a statement setting forth facts that entitle them to be treated as record holders.

14. **REQUIREMENT OF PROOF OF CLAIM FORM:** In filing their proofs of claim, all creditors must use the Proof of Claim Form or another form containing comparable information to permit designation of the Debtor or Debtors to which each claim relates. **If a creditor wishes to assert multiple claims against different Debtors, such creditor should file a separate Proof of Claim Form for each such claim.**

15. **FAILURE TO FILE PROOF OF CLAIM: Any holder of a claim that fails to file a proof of claim on or before the Bar Date as required by this Order is forever barred, estopped and enjoined from (a) asserting any such claim against any of the Debtors or their respective successors and assigns and (b) voting on or receiving any distribution under any plan or reorganization for any of the Debtors on account of such claim, except as ordered by the Court upon the filing of a motion and opportunity for a hearing.**

16. **EXTENSION OF BAR DATE:** Notwithstanding the Bar Date set in this Order, the following parties will have until 4:00 p.m. on October 1, 1998 to file their respective proofs of claim, if any: (a) David A. Kremser, Bernice E. Kremser, Michael P. Kremser, Stanley A. Kremser, Holly M. Kremser, and Elk Meadows Investments, L.L.C.; (b) BritWill Investments Company, Ltd. and UNHC Real Estate Holdings, Inc.; (c) Prime Leasing, Inc.; (d) John Filkoski, Michael Filkoski, Lisa Filkoski, and David Filkoski.;

and (e) the representative plaintiffs and the putative class of plaintiffs in Grossman et. al. v. Unison.

17. **NOTICE OF AMENDMENTS TO SCHEDULES:** If the Debtors elect to amend the Schedules previously filed in order to more accurately reflect known claims against their estates, the Debtors must provide appropriate notice of such amendment to affected creditors, who will have thirty (30) days from the date of such service to file a proof of claim, if necessary.

18. **RESERVATION OF RIGHTS:** Nothing in this Order is to be deemed to limit or prejudice, in any way, any party's right to object to, dispute or assert defenses or offsets to any claim filed or deemed filed in these cases.

19. **NOTICE BY DEBTORS:** Counsel for the Debtors are directed to provide a conformed copy of this Order to creditors and parties in interest in accordance with the terms and provisions of this Order, and file an appropriate Certificate of Service with the Court.

DATED: August 30, 1998

By: ***/s/ George B. Nielsen, Jr.***
HON. GEORGE B. NIELSEN, JR.
APPENDIX M

APPENDIX M

SAMPLE "SOLICITATION PACKAGE"

In order to solicit creditors' votes on the plan of reorganization in the ***Stuart Entertainment*** Chapter 11 case in Wilmington, Delaware, a package of materials was sent to all creditors entitled to vote. This package included a copy of the bankruptcy court's order approving the Disclosure Statement, notice of the confirmation hearing and the deadline to cast votes, a letter from the debtor's CEO recommending that creditors vote to accept the plan, and several ballot forms to be used by various creditors in different classes under the plan. The types of ballots used in the *Stuart* case are fairly common in cases in which the debtor has issued public debt, public equity, or both. When soliciting the votes of holders of publicly issued securities, it is customary to solicit the recordholders (or the "street names" by which investors hold their securities) with instructions to solicit the votes of individual beneficial holders, the identities of which the debtor rarely knows. This package contains such ballots for *Stuart's* publicly traded notes and publicly traded common stock.

IN THE UNITED STATES BANKRUPTCY COURT
FOR THE DISTRICT OF DELAWARE

In re

Case No. 99-2847 (MFW)

STUART ENTERTAINMENT, INC.,

Chapter 11

Debtor.

ORDER APPROVING DISCLOSURE STATEMENT UNDER 11 U.S.C. § 1125

THIS MATTER is before the Court on the Debtor's Motion for Order Approving Disclosure Statement Under 11 U.S.C. § 1125 (the "Motion"), dated October 12, 1999, seeking approval of the Disclosure Statement In Support of First Amended Plan of Reorganization, dated October 11, 1999 (the "Disclosure Statement"). It appearing that notice of the motion was adequate and sufficient under the circumstances, that the Debtor, the Committee of Unsecured Creditors, the Indenture Trustee for the Notes, and Contrarian Capital Management LLC have agreed to certain revisions to the Disclosure Statement and its various exhibits described at a hearing held before the Court on October 27, 1999, that the Disclosure Statement, as amended, contains "adequate information" within the meaning of 11 U.S.C. § 1125 regarding the Debtor's First Amended Plan of Reorganization (the "Plan"), and that sufficient cause exists for granting the relief requested in the Motion, it is

ORDERED that the Motion is granted; and it is further

ORDERED that the Disclosure Statement is approved for use in soliciting acceptances and rejections of the Plan from creditors and interest holders in accordance with the Court's "Order (A) Setting Date For Hearing To Consider Approval Of Disclosure Statement; (B) Establishing Procedures For Soliciting And Tabulating Votes On Joint Plan Of Reorganization; (C) Approving Form Of Ballots; (D) Approving Notice And Publication Procedures; And (E) Scheduling A Hearing On Confirmation Of Plan Of Reorganization" (the "Solicitation and Voting Order") previously entered in this Chapter 11 case; and it is further

ORDERED that the Debtor is authorized and required to commence solicitation of votes to accept or reject the Plan in accordance with the procedures set forth in the Solicitation and Voting Order no later than November 12, 1999.

Dated: Wilmington, Delaware
October 10, 1999

By: ***/s/ Mary F. Walrath***
UNITED STATES BANKRUPTCY JUDGE

IN THE UNITED STATES BANKRUPTCY COURT
FOR THE DISTRICT OF DELAWARE

In re

STUART ENTERTAINMENT, INC.,

Debtor.

Case No. 99-2847 (MFW)

Chapter 11

NOTICE OF DEADLINE FOR CASTING VOTES TO ACCEPT OR REJECT PLAN OF REORGANIZATION AND CONFIRMATION HEARING

On October 12, 1999, STUART ENTERTAINMENT, INC., (the "Debtor") filed its First Amended Plan of Reorganization (the "Plan") and a related Disclosure Statement (the "Disclosure Statement") under Bankruptcy Code § 1125. After a hearing (the "Disclosure Statement Hearing") held on October 27, 1999, the Court entered an Order approving the Disclosure Statement (the "Disclosure Statement Order"), in accordance with which you are receiving the copy of the Disclosure Statement and the Plan and certain materials (including a Ballot) relating to the solicitation of votes to accept or reject the Plan. You are not receiving a copy of the Plan Supplement, which is voluminous. If you wish to obtain a copy of the Plan Supplement, contact IKON Document Services, 901 North Market Street, Suite 718, Wilmington, Delaware 19801; Tel. (302) 777-4500, Fax. (302) 777-5155.

A hearing (the "Confirmation Hearing") to consider the confirmation of the Plan will be held before the Honorable Mary F. Walrath in the United States Bankruptcy Court, 824 Market Street, 5th Floor, Wilmington, Delaware at **2:00 p.m. EST** on **December 14, 1999.**

If you are the owner of a claim against, or equity interest in, the Debtor as of October 27, 1999, the Record Date as established in the Disclosure Statement Order, you have received with this Notice a Ballot form containing voting instructions appropriate for your claim or interest. In order for your vote to accept or reject the Plan to be counted, you must complete all required information on the Ballot, execute the Ballot, and return the completed Ballot to the address indicated on the Ballot by **4:00 p.m. EST** on **November 26, 1999**. Any failure to follow the voting instructions included with the Ballot may disqualify your Ballot and your vote.

Objections, if any, to the confirmation of the Plan must: (a) be in writing; (b) state the name and address of the objecting party and the nature of the claim or interest of such party; (c) state with particularity the basis and nature of any objection or proposed modification; and (d) be filed, together with proof of service, with the Court (with a copy to chambers) and served so that they are received by chambers, co-counsel for the Debtor indicated below, counsel for the Committee of Unsecured Creditors (Adelman Lavine

Gold & Levin P.C., Two Penn Center Plaza, Suite 1900, Philadelphia, Pennsylvania 19102, Attn: Gary Schildhorn, Esq.), and counsel for Contrarian Capital Management LLC (Milbank, Tweed, Hadley & McCloy, LLP, 601 South Figueroa Street, 30th Floor, Los Angeles, California 90017, Attn: Paul S. Aronzon, Esq.) no later than **4:00 p.m. EST** on **November 26, 1999**.

The Confirmation Hearing may be continued from time to time without further notice other than the announcement of the adjourned date(s) at the Confirmation Hearing or any continued hearing.

Dated: November 12, 1999

Craig D. Hansen, Esq.
Thomas J. Salerno, Esq.
Jordan A. Kroop, Esq.
SQUIRE, SANDERS & DEMPSEY, L.L.P.
40 North Central Avenue, Suite 2700
Phoenix, Arizona 85004
(602) 528-4000

Norman L. Pernick, Esq.
J. Kate Stickles, Esq.
SAUL, EWING, REMICK & SAUL
P.O. Box 1266
222 Delaware Avenue, Suite 1200
Wilmington, Delaware 19899
(302) 421-6800

Co-Counsel to the Debtor

STUART ENTERTAINMENT, INC.

November 12, 1999

TO ALL CREDITORS OF AND HOLDERS OF EQUITY INTERESTS IN STUART ENTERTAINMENT, INC.:

Attached to this letter is the *Disclosure Statement In Support of First Amended Plan of Reorganization*, which contains as an attachment the *First Amended Plan of Reorganization* (the "Plan"). Stuart Entertainment, Inc. ("Stuart") has proposed the Plan as the blueprint for Stuart's reorganization and emergence from Chapter 11 bankruptcy.

Before filing its petition for relief commencing its Chapter 11 case on August 13, 1999, Stuart began actively pursuing restructuring alternatives in an attempt to address the viability of Stuart's highly leveraged capital structure. On May 21, 1999, Stuart announced that it had reached an agreement (the "Restructuring Agreement") with certain holders of an ad hoc committee of holders of Stuart's 12½% Senior Subordinated Notes due November 15, 2004 (the "Notes"). The Restructuring Agreement provided for, among other things, a full conversion of the Notes into 100% of the equity in the reorganized company and a corresponding cancellation of existing equity. The basic terms of the Restructuring Agreement became the basis for Stuart's first plan of reorganization, which was filed with the Bankruptcy Court on August 13, 1999. Despite having filed that first plan, Stuart continued to negotiate with its creditor constituencies.

The Plan reflects the results of those negotiations and Stuart's efforts to propose a plan of reorganization that met with the approval of all Stuart's creditor groups. The Plan, if confirmed by the Bankruptcy Court, will substantially deleverage Stuart since the holders of Notes will receive 100% of the equity in Reorganized Stuart, unless such holders elect to receive cash in lieu of stock. All other unsecured creditors will receive a cash payment on account of their claims.

Stuart's management, the Board of Directors, and I believe very strongly that the Plan not only represents the most viable basis for emerging from bankruptcy but provides the greatest possible recovery to creditors. **The Plan is supported by the Official Committee of Unsecured Creditors and by the Indenture Trustee for the Notes, both of whom recommend that unsecured creditors (including holders of Notes) vote in favor of the Plan.**

It is our sincere belief that the Plan is in the best interests of Stuart and its creditors. We further believe that the Plan represents the most expeditious resolution of the financial difficulties facing Stuart. In the competitive and highly regulated business environment in which Stuart operates, time is of the essence in finalizing this restructuring. Therefore, while no restructuring will completely satisfy all creditor groups, it is Stuart's belief that the Plan is fair to all creditors and preserves Stuart's going concern value. Stuart believes that absent an expeditious restructuring, it will not be able to compete in its industry effectively. Preserving Stuart's enterprise value is critical to maximizing recovery for all creditors and creating the greatest potential for future success. **I respectfully urge all creditors and equity interest holders to vote to accept the Plan.** The Stuart management team is dedicated to Stuart's successful and prompt emergence from Chapter 11 for the benefit of Stuart's creditors, employees, suppliers, and customers.

Thank you for your support.

Very truly yours,

By: ***/s/ Joseph M. Valandra***

Joseph M. Valandra
Chief Executive Officer and Chairman of the Board
STUART ENTERTAINMENT, INC.

IN THE UNITED STATES BANKRUPTCY COURT
FOR THE DISTRICT OF DELAWARE

In re: STUART ENTERTAINMENT, INC., Debtor.	Case No. 99-2847 (MFW) **BALLOT FOR ACCEPTING OR REJECTING PLAN OF REORGANIZATION** **BALLOT A**

CLASS 3A: ELLIOTT TRUST SECURED CLAIM

THE VOTING DEADLINE TO ACCEPT OR REJECT THE PLAN IS 4:00 PM, EASTERN TIME, NOVEMBER 26, 1999

Stuart Entertainment, Inc. (the "Debtor") filed its Plan of Reorganization on October 12, 1999 (the "Plan"). The Bankruptcy Court has approved a disclosure statement with respect to the Plan (the "Disclosure Statement"). The Disclosure Statement provides information to assist you in deciding how to vote your Ballot. You should have received a copy of the Disclosure Statement with this Ballot, but if you do not have a Disclosure Statement, you may obtain a copy from IKON Document Services, 901 North Market Street, Suite 718, Wilmington, Delaware 19801, Telephone (302) 777-4500, Fax (302) 777-5155. Court approval of the Disclosure Statement does not indicate approval of the Plan by the Court.

You should review the Disclosure Statement and the Plan before you vote. You may wish to seek legal advice concerning the Plan and your classification and treatment under the Plan. If you hold claims or equity interests in more than one class, you should use appropriate Ballots for each class in which you are entitled to vote.

If your Ballot is not received by your record holder from whom you received this Ballot, your vote will not count as either an acceptance or rejection of the Plan. If the Plan is confirmed by the Bankruptcy Court it will be binding on you whether or not you vote.

ACCEPTANCE OR REJECTION OF THE PLAN

The undersigned, the holder of a Claim in Class 3A, votes to:
(Check one box only)

☐ **Accept** the Plan ☐ **Reject** the Plan

Date: ______________________

Print or type name: ______________________

Signature: ______________________

Title: ______________________

Address: ______________________

PLEASE MAIL OR FAX YOUR BALLOT TO THE FOLLOWING VOTING AGENT PROMPTLY!

Send by U.S. Mail, Overnight Delivery, or Courier to → or **Fax to (602) 286-2199**	**U.S. Mail:** **Stuart Plan Voting** **c/o Arthur Andersen LLP / Josh Skevington** **P.O. Box 60725** **Phoenix, Arizona 85082**	**Overnight Delivery or Courier:** **Stuart Plan Voting** **c/o Arthur Andersen LLP / Josh Skevington** **501 N. 44th Street** **Phoenix, Arizona 85008**

Questions regarding this Ballot or the voting procedures should be directed to Josh Skevington at (602) 286-1841

IN THE UNITED STATES BANKRUPTCY COURT
FOR THE DISTRICT OF DELAWARE

In re:	Case No. 99-2847 (MFW)
STUART ENTERTAINMENT, INC.,	**BALLOT FOR ACCEPTING OR REJECTING PLAN OF REORGANIZATION**
Debtor.	**GREEN MASTER BALLOT B-1**

CLASS 4: NOTES CLAIMS

THE VOTING DEADLINE TO ACCEPT OR REJECT THE PLAN IS 4:00 PM, EASTERN TIME, NOVEMBER 26, 1999

Stuart Entertainment, Inc. (the "Debtor") filed its Joint Plan of Reorganization on October 12, 1999 (the "Plan"). The Bankruptcy Court has approved a disclosure statement with respect to the Plan (the "Disclosure Statement"). The Disclosure Statement provides information to assist you in deciding how to vote your Ballot. You should have received a copy of the Disclosure Statement with this Ballot, but if you do not have a Disclosure Statement, you may obtain a copy from IKON Document Services, 901 N. Market Street, Suite 718, Wilmington, DE 19801, Phone (302) 777-4500, Fax (302) 777-5155. Court approval of the Disclosure Statement does not indicate approval of the Plan by the Court.

You should review the Disclosure Statement and the Plan before you vote. You may wish to seek legal advice concerning the Plan and your classification and treatment under the Plan. If you hold claims or equity interests in more than one class, you should use appropriate Ballots for each class in which you are entitled to vote.

If your Ballot is not received by the Voting Agent at the address below on or before 4:00 p.m. Eastern time on November 26, 1999, and such deadline is not extended by order of the Bankruptcy Court, your vote will not count as either an acceptance or rejection of the Plan. If the Plan is confirmed by the Bankruptcy Court it will be binding on you whether or not you vote.

This Master Ballot is being sent to, and should be used by, banks, brokers, authorized agents, or other nominees of beneficial owners of the Notes (as defined in the Plan). This Green Master Ballot B-1 should only be used if you are solely the holder of record of Notes and NOT the beneficial owner. If you are BOTH the record owner and beneficial owner of Notes, you should use the Blue Ballot B-3. If you are solely the beneficial owner of Notes, but not a record owner, you should use the Yellow Ballot B-2 and return it to your record owner, NOT the Voting Agent.

By signing this Master Ballot, the undersigned certifies that it is the record or registered owner as of October 27, 1999 of $ ________________ in principal amount of Notes, for which voting instructions have been received from the beneficial owners, for whom the undersigned owns Notes in its name as listed below. The undersigned certifies that the following beneficial owners of Notes, as identified by their respective customer account numbers or the respective sequence numbers set forth below, have delivered to the undersigned Ballots casting votes, and that the undersigned has accurately transcribed the information below from each such Ballot. (Indicate the aggregate amount of Notes for each respective account under the appropriate column and use additional sheets of paper if necessary):

Customer Name and/or Account Number for each Beneficial Owner	Certificate Numbers	Amount of Notes to **ACCEPT** the Plan	Amount of Notes to **REJECT** the Plan	Noteholder Election (Cash or Stock)
1.		$	$	
2.		$	$	
3.		$	$	
4.		$	$	
5.		$	$	
6.		$	$	
7.		$	$	
8.		$	$	
9.		$	$	
10.		$	$	

NOTE: Beneficial owners of Notes may not split their votes on the Plan. Thus, if you are submitting a vote with respect to any Notes that are beneficially owned, such beneficial owner MUST vote all of its Notes in the same manner (*i.e.,* all "accept" or all "reject"). You must indicate the Small Noteholder Election from each Yellow Ballot B-2 on the chart above. If no Noteholder Election is indicated on a Yellow Ballot B-2, insert "Cash" in the Noteholder Election column and row corresponding to that beneficial holder.

This Master Ballot is **not** a letter of transmittal and may **not** be used for any purpose other than to vote to accept or reject the Plan. Accordingly, no certificates representing Notes should be surrendered at this time.

YOU MUST DELIVER A YELLOW BALLOT B-2 TO EACH BENEFICIAL OWNER OF NOTES AND TAKE ANY ACTION REQUIRED TO ENABLE EACH SUCH BENEFICIAL OWNER TO VOTE ITS AGGREGATE AMOUNT OF ITS NOTES TO ACCEPT OR REJECT THE PLAN. WITH REGARD TO EACH YELLOW BALLOT B-2 RETURNED TO YOU, YOU MUST (A) RETAIN SUCH YELLOW BALLOT B-2 IN YOUR FILES AND TRANSFER THE REQUESTED INFORMATION FROM SUCH BALLOT ONTO THIS GREEN MASTER BALLOT B-1, (B) EXECUTE THE GREEN MASTER BALLOT B-1, AND (C) ARRANGE FOR DELIVERY OF SUCH GREEN MASTER BALLOT B-1 TO THE

VOTING AGENT INDICATED BELOW.

No fees, commissions, or other remuneration will be payable to any broker, dealer, or other person for soliciting Ballots from beneficial owners. Nothing in this Ballot or in the enclosed documents constitutes an appointment of you or any other person as the agent of the Debtor, or authorizes you or any other person to use any document or make any statement on behalf of any of the Debtor with respect to the Plan, except for the statements contained in the enclosed documents themselves.

Date: ______________________________

Print or type name: ______________________________

Signature: ______________________________

Title: ______________________________

Address: ______________________________

____

PLEASE MAIL OR FAX YOUR BALLOT TO THE FOLLOWING VOTING AGENT PROMPTLY!

Send by U.S. Mail, Overnight Delivery, or Courier to → or **Fax to (602) 286-2199**	**U.S. Mail:** **Stuart Plan Voting** **c/o Arthur Andersen LLP / Josh Skevington** **P.O. Box 60725** **Phoenix, Arizona 85082**	**Overnight Delivery or Courier:** **Stuart Plan Voting** **c/o Arthur Andersen LLP / Josh Skevington** **501 N. 44th Street** **Phoenix, Arizona 85008**

Questions regarding this Ballot or the voting procedures should be directed to Josh Skevington at (602) 286-1841

IN THE UNITED STATES BANKRUPTCY COURT FOR THE DISTRICT OF DELAWARE

In re:	Case No. 99-2847 (MFW)
STUART ENTERTAINMENT, INC.,	BALLOT FOR ACCEPTING OR REJECTING PLAN OF REORGANIZATION
Debtor.	YELLOW BALLOT B-2

CLASS 4: NOTES CLAIMS

THE VOTING DEADLINE TO ACCEPT OR REJECT THE PLAN IS 4:00 PM, EASTERN TIME, NOVEMBER 26, 1999

Stuart Entertainment, Inc. (the "Debtor") filed its Plan of Reorganization on October 12, 1999 (the "Plan"). The Bankruptcy Court has approved a disclosure statement with respect to the Plan (the "Disclosure Statement"). The Disclosure Statement provides information to assist you in deciding how to vote your Ballot. You should have received a copy of the Disclosure Statement with this Ballot, but if you do not have a Disclosure Statement, you may obtain a copy from IKON Document Services, 901 N. Market Street, Suite 718, Wilmington, DE 19801, Phone (302) 777-4500, Fax (302) 777-5155. Court approval of the Disclosure Statement does not indicate approval of the Plan by the Court.

You should review the Disclosure Statement and the Plan before you vote. You may wish to seek legal advice concerning the Plan and your classification and treatment under the Plan. If you hold claims or equity interests in more than one class, you should use appropriate Ballots for each class in which you are entitled to vote.

If your Ballot is not received by your record holder from whom you received this Ballot, your vote will not count as either an acceptance or rejection of the Plan. If the Plan is confirmed by the Bankruptcy Court it will be binding on you whether or not you vote.

Use this Yellow Ballot B-2 ONLY if you are SOLELY the beneficial owner of Notes (as defined in the Plan) and not the record owner of Notes. Once fully completed, RETURN THIS YELLOW BALLOT B-2 TO YOUR RECORD OWNER FROM WHOM YOU RECEIVED IT. If you are BOTH the record owner AND the beneficial owner of Notes, use the Blue Ballot B-3. If you are SOLELY the record owner and NOT the beneficial owner of Notes, use the Green Master Ballot B-1.

Indicate your Noteholder Election below. A Noteholder Election is an election by a holder of a claim in Class 4 (a claim based on ownership of Notes) to receive a cash payment on account of such claim (the "Cash Payment Option" under the Plan) rather than to receive a distribution of New Common Stock. If you do not indicate a Noteholder Election on this Ballot, you will be deemed to have accepted the Cash Payment Option.

ACCEPTANCE OR REJECTION OF THE PLAN

The undersigned, the beneficial owner of Notes:

☐ **Accepts** the Plan ☐ **Rejects** the Plan

☐ **Elects** the Cash Payment Option ☐ **Declines** the Cash Payment Option

By signing this Ballot, the undersigned certified that it is the beneficial owner of Notes as of October 27, 1999.

Name of Owner: ____________________

Taxpayer I.D. No.: ____________________

Certificate No.(s): ____________________

Unpaid Principal Amount: ____________________

NOTE: Beneficial owners of Notes may not split their votes on the Plan. Thus, if you are submitting a vote with respect to any Note, you must vote **all** of the Notes in the same manner (*i.e.*, all "accept" or all "reject").

Date: ____________________

Print or type name: ____________________

Signature: ____________________

Title: ____________________

Address: ____________________

____

PLEASE MAIL OR FAX YOUR BALLOT TO YOUR RECORD OWNER PROMPTLY!

Questions regarding this Ballot or the voting procedures should be directed to your record owner.

IN THE UNITED STATES BANKRUPTCY COURT FOR THE DISTRICT OF DELAWARE

In re:

STUART ENTERTAINMENT, INC.,

Debtor.

Case No. 99-2847 (MFW)

BALLOT FOR ACCEPTING OR REJECTING PLAN OF REORGANIZATION

BLUE BALLOT B-3

CLASS 4: NOTES CLAIMS

THE VOTING DEADLINE TO ACCEPT OR REJECT THE PLAN IS 4:00 PM, EASTERN TIME, NOVEMBER 26, 1999

Stuart Entertainment, Inc. (the "Debtor") filed its Plan of Reorganization on October 12, 1999 (the "Plan"). The Bankruptcy Court has approved a disclosure statement with respect to the Plan (the "Disclosure Statement"). The Disclosure Statement provides information to assist you in deciding how to vote your Ballot. You should have received a copy of the Disclosure Statement with this Ballot, but if you do not have a Disclosure Statement, you may obtain a copy from IKON Document Services, 901 N. Market Street, Suite 718, Wilmington, DE 19801, Phone (302) 777-4500, Fax (302) 777-5155. Court approval of the Disclosure Statement does not indicate approval of the Plan by the Court.

You should review the Disclosure Statement and the Plan before you vote. You may wish to seek legal advice concerning the Plan and your classification and treatment under the Plan. If you hold claims or equity interests in more than one class, you should use appropriate Ballots for each class in which you are entitled to vote.

If your Ballot is not received by the VOTING AGENT below on or before 4:00 p.m. Eastern time on November 26, 1999, and such deadline is not extended by order of the Bankruptcy Court, your vote will not count as either an acceptance or rejection of the Plan. If the Plan is confirmed by the Bankruptcy Court it will be binding on you whether or not you vote.

Use this Blue Ballot B-3 ONLY if you are BOTH the beneficial owner AND record owner of Notes (as defined in the Plan). If you are ONLY the beneficial owner and NOT the record owner of Notes, use the Yellow Ballot B-2 and RETURN IT TO YOUR RECORD OWNER. If you are SOLELY the record owner and NOT the beneficial owner of Notes, use the Green Master Ballot B-1.

Indicate your Noteholder Election below. A Noteholder Election is an election by a holder of a claim in Class 4 (a claim based on ownership of Notes) to receive a cash payment on account of such claim (the "Cash Payment Option" under the Plan) rather than to receive a distribution of New Common Stock. If you do not indicate a Noteholder Election on this Ballot, you will be deemed to have accepted the Cash Payment Option.

ACCEPTANCE OR REJECTION OF THE PLAN

The undersigned, the beneficial owner of Notes:

☐ **Accepts** the Plan ☐ **Rejects** the Plan

☐ **Elects** the Cash Payment Option ☐ **Declines** the Cash Payment Option

By signing this Ballot, the undersigned certified that it is the beneficial owner of Notes as of October 27, 1999.

Name of Owner: ____________________

Taxpayer I.D. No.: ____________________

Certificate No.(s): ____________________

Unpaid Principal Amount: ____________________

NOTE: Beneficial owners of Notes may not split their votes on the Plan. Thus, if you are submitting a vote with respect to any Note, you must vote **all** of the Notes in the same manner (*i.e.*, all "accept" or all "reject").

Date: ____________________

Print or type name: ____________________

Signature: ____________________

Title: ____________________

Address: ____________________

____

Telephone: ____________________

PLEASE MAIL OR FAX YOUR BALLOT TO YOUR RECORD OWNER PROMPTLY!

Send by U.S. Mail, Overnight Delivery, or Courier to → or **Fax to (602) 286-2199**	**U.S. Mail:** **Stuart Plan Voting** **c/o Arthur Andersen LLP / Josh Skevington** **P.O. Box 60725** **Phoenix, Arizona 85082**	**Overnight Delivery or Courier:** **Stuart Plan Voting** **c/o Arthur Andersen LLP / Josh Skevington** **501 N. 44th Street** **Phoenix, Arizona 85008**

Questions regarding this Ballot or the voting procedures should be directed to Josh Skevington at (602) 286-1841

IN THE UNITED STATES BANKRUPTCY COURT
FOR THE DISTRICT OF DELAWARE

In re:

STUART ENTERTAINMENT, INC.,

Debtor.

Case No. 99-2847 (MFW)

BALLOT FOR ACCEPTING OR REJECTING PLAN OF REORGANIZATION

BALLOT C

CLASS 5: GENERAL UNSECURED CLAIMS

THE VOTING DEADLINE TO ACCEPT OR REJECT THE PLAN IS 4:00 PM, EASTERN TIME, NOVEMBER 26, 1999

Stuart Entertainment, Inc. (the "Debtor") filed its Plan of Reorganization on October 12, 1999 (the "Plan"). The Bankruptcy Court has approved a disclosure statement with respect to the Plan (the "Disclosure Statement"). The Disclosure Statement provides information to assist you in deciding how to vote your Ballot. You should have received a copy of the Disclosure Statement with this Ballot, but if you do not have a Disclosure Statement, you may obtain a copy from IKON Document Services, 901 N. Market Street, Suite 718, Wilmington, DE 19801, Phone (302) 777-4500, Fax (302) 777-5155. Court approval of the Disclosure Statement does not indicate approval of the Plan by the Court.

You should review the Disclosure Statement and the Plan before you vote. You may wish to seek legal advice concerning the Plan and your classification and treatment under the Plan. If you hold claims or equity interests in more than one class, you should use appropriate Ballots for each class in which you are entitled to vote.

If your Ballot is not received by the VOTING AGENT below on or before 4:00 p.m. Eastern time on November 26, 1999, and such deadline is not extended by order of the Bankruptcy Court, your vote will not count as either an acceptance or rejection of the Plan. If the Plan is confirmed by the Bankruptcy Court it will be binding on you whether or not you vote.

You must vote all of your Claims within a single Class under the Plan to either accept or reject the Plan. You may not vote certain of your Claims to accept the Plan and other of your Claims to reject the Plan. A Ballot that partially rejects and partially accepts the Plan will be counted as an acceptance for all Claims represented by the Ballot.

ACCEPTANCE OR REJECTION OF THE PLAN

The undersigned, the holder of Class 6 Claims against the Debtor in the unpaid aggregate amount of $ ____________ ____________ :

(Check one box only)

☐ **Accept** the Plan ☐ **Reject** the Plan

Date: ____________________

Print or type name: ____________________

Signature: ____________________

Title: ____________________

Address: ____________________

____

PLEASE MAIL OR FAX YOUR BALLOT TO THE FOLLOWING VOTING AGENT PROMPTLY!

Send by U.S. Mail, Overnight Delivery, or Courier to → or **Fax to (602) 286-2199**	**U.S. Mail:** **Stuart Plan Voting** **c/o Arthur Andersen LLP / Josh Skevington** **P.O. Box 60725** **Phoenix, Arizona 85082**	**Overnight Delivery or Courier:** **Stuart Plan Voting** **c/o Arthur Andersen LLP / Josh Skevington** **501 N. 44th Street** **Phoenix, Arizona 85008**

Questions regarding this Ballot or the voting procedures should be directed to Josh Skevington at (602) 286-1841

IN THE UNITED STATES BANKRUPTCY COURT FOR THE DISTRICT OF DELAWARE

In re:	Case No. 99-2847 (MFW)
STUART ENTERTAINMENT, INC.,	**BALLOT FOR ACCEPTING OR REJECTING PLAN OF REORGANIZATION**
Debtor.	**BALLOT D**

CLASS 6: SUBSIDIARY CLAIMS

THE VOTING DEADLINE TO ACCEPT OR REJECT THE PLAN IS 4:00 PM, EASTERN TIME, NOVEMBER 26, 1999

Stuart Entertainment, Inc. (the "Debtor") filed its Plan of Reorganization on October 12, 1999 (the "Plan"). The Bankruptcy Court has approved a disclosure statement with respect to the Plan (the "Disclosure Statement"). The Disclosure Statement provides information to assist you in deciding how to vote your Ballot. You should have received a copy of the Disclosure Statement with this Ballot, but if you do not have a Disclosure Statement, you may obtain a copy from IKON Document Services, 901 N. Market Street, Suite 718, Wilmington, DE 19801, Phone (302) 777-4500, Fax (302) 777-5155. Court approval of the Disclosure Statement does not indicate approval of the Plan by the Court.

You should review the Disclosure Statement and the Plan before you vote. You may wish to seek legal advice concerning the Plan and your classification and treatment under the Plan. If you hold claims or equity interests in more than one class, you should use appropriate Ballots for each class in which you are entitled to vote.

If your Ballot is not received by the VOTING AGENT below on or before 4:00 p.m. Eastern time on November 26, 1999, and such deadline is not extended by order of the Bankruptcy Court, your vote will not count as either an acceptance or rejection of the Plan. If the Plan is confirmed by the Bankruptcy Court it will be binding on you whether or not you vote.

You must vote all of your Claims within a single Class under the Plan to either accept or reject the Plan. You may not vote certain of your Claims to accept the Plan and other of your Claims to reject the Plan. A Ballot that partially rejects and partially accepts the Plan will be counted as an acceptance for all Claims represented by the Ballot.

ACCEPTANCE OR REJECTION OF THE PLAN

The undersigned, the holder of Class 6 Claims against the Debtor in the unpaid aggregate amount of $ ______________ ______________ :

(Check one box only)

☐ **Accept** the Plan ☐ **Reject** the Plan

Date: ______________

Print or type name: ______________

Signature: ______________

Title: ______________

Address: ______________

____

PLEASE MAIL OR FAX YOUR BALLOT TO THE FOLLOWING VOTING AGENT PROMPTLY!

Send by U.S. Mail, Overnight Delivery, or Courier to → or **Fax to (602) 286-2199**	**U.S. Mail:** **Stuart Plan Voting** **c/o Arthur Andersen LLP / Josh Skevington** **P.O. Box 60725** **Phoenix, Arizona 85082**	**Overnight Delivery or Courier:** **Stuart Plan Voting** **c/o Arthur Andersen LLP / Josh Skevington** **501 N. 44th Street** **Phoenix, Arizona 85008**

Questions regarding this Ballot or the voting procedures should be directed to Josh Skevington at (602) 286-1841

IN THE UNITED STATES BANKRUPTCY COURT
FOR THE DISTRICT OF DELAWARE

In re:	Case No. 99-2847 (MFW)
STUART ENTERTAINMENT, INC.,	BALLOT FOR ACCEPTING OR REJECTING PLAN OF REORGANIZATION
Debtor.	WHITE MASTER BALLOT E-1

CLASS 7: EQUITY INTERESTS

THE VOTING DEADLINE TO ACCEPT OR REJECT THE PLAN IS 4:00 PM, EASTERN TIME, NOVEMBER 26, 1999

Stuart Entertainment, Inc. (the "Debtor") filed its Plan of Reorganization on October 12, 1999 (the "Plan"). The Bankruptcy Court has approved a disclosure statement with respect to the Plan (the "Disclosure Statement"). The Disclosure Statement provides information to assist you in deciding how to vote your Ballot. You should have received a copy of the Disclosure Statement with this Ballot, but if you do not have a Disclosure Statement, you may obtain a copy from IKON Document Services, 901 N. Market Street, Suite 718, Wilmington, DE 19801, Phone (302) 777-4500, Fax (302) 777-5155. Court approval of the Disclosure Statement does not indicate approval of the Plan by the Court.

You should review the Disclosure Statement and the Plan before you vote. You may wish to seek legal advice concerning the Plan and your classification and treatment under the Plan. If you hold claims or equity interests in more than one class, you should use appropriate Ballots for each class in which you are entitled to vote.

If your Ballot is not received by the Voting Agent on or before 4:00 p.m. Eastern time on November 26, 1999, and such deadline is not extended by order of the Bankruptcy Court, your vote will not count as either an acceptance or rejection of the Plan. If the Plan is confirmed by the Bankruptcy Court it will be binding on you whether or not you vote.

This White Master Ballot is being sent to, and should be used by, banks, brokers, authorized agents, or other nominees of beneficial owners of Equity Interests (as defined in the Plan). **This White Master Ballot E-1 should only be used if you are solely the holder of record of Equity Interests and NOT the beneficial owner. If you are BOTH the record owner and beneficial owner of Equity Interests, you should use the Orange Ballot E-3. If you are solely the beneficial owner of Equity Interests, but not a record owner, you should use the Pink Ballot E-2 and return it to your record owner, NOT the VOTING AGENT.**

By signing this White Master Ballot, the undersigned certifies that it is the record or registered owner as of October 27, 1999 of ______________ shares of Old Common Stock, for which voting instructions have been received from the beneficial owners, for whom the undersigned owns Equity Interests in its name as listed below. The undersigned certifies that the following beneficial owners of Equity Interests, as identified by their respective customer account numbers or the respective sequence numbers set forth below, have delivered to the undersigned Ballots casting votes, and that the undersigned has accurately transcribed the information below from each such Ballot. (Indicate the aggregate amount of shares for each respective account under the appropriate column and use additional sheets of paper if necessary):

Customer Name and/or Account Number for each Beneficial Owner	Certificate Numbers	Amount of Shares to **ACCEPT** the Plan	Amount of Shares to **REJECT** the Plan
1.			
2.			
3.			
4.			
5.			
6.			
7.			
8.			
9.			
10.			

NOTE: Beneficial owners of Equity Interests may not split their votes on the Plan. Thus, if you are submitting a vote with respect to any shares that are beneficially owned, such beneficial owner MUST vote all of its shares in the same manner (*i.e.,* all "accept" or all "reject").

This White Master Ballot is **not** a letter of transmittal and may **not** be used for any purpose other than to vote to accept or reject the Plan. Accordingly, no certificates representing Equity Interests should be surrendered at this time.

YOU MUST DELIVER A PINK BALLOT E-2 TO EACH BENEFICIAL OWNER OF EQUITY INTERESTS AND TAKE ANY ACTION REQUIRED TO ENABLE EACH SUCH BENEFICIAL OWNER TO VOTE ITS AGGREGATE SHARES TO ACCEPT OR REJECT THE PLAN. WITH REGARD TO EACH PINK BALLOT E-2 RETURNED TO YOU, YOU MUST (A) RETAIN SUCH PINK BALLOT E-2 IN YOUR FILES AND TRANSFER THE REQUESTED INFORMATION FROM SUCH BALLOT ONTO THIS WHITE MASTER BALLOT E-1, (B) EXECUTE THE WHITE MASTER BALLOT E-1, AND (C) ARRANGE FOR DELIVERY OF SUCH WHITE MASTER BALLOT E-1 TO THE VOTING AGENT INDICATED BELOW.

No fees, commissions, or other remuneration will be payable to any broker, dealer, or other person for soliciting Ballots from beneficial owners. Nothing in this Ballot or in the enclosed documents constitutes an appointment of you or any other person as the agent of the Debtor, or authorizes you or any other person to use any document or make any statement on behalf of any of the Debtor with respect to the Plan, except for the statements contained in the enclosed documents themselves.

Date: ______________________

Print or type name: ______________________

Signature: ______________________

Title: ______________________

Address: ______________________

____

Telephone: ______________________

PLEASE MAIL OR FAX YOUR BALLOT TO YOUR RECORD OWNER PROMPTLY!

Send by U.S. Mail, Overnight Delivery, or Courier to → or **Fax to (602) 286-2199**	**U.S. Mail:** **Stuart Plan Voting** **c/o Arthur Andersen LLP / Josh Skevington** **P.O. Box 60725** **Phoenix, Arizona 85082**	**Overnight Delivery or Courier:** **Stuart Plan Voting** **c/o Arthur Andersen LLP / Josh Skevington** **501 N. 44th Street** **Phoenix, Arizona 85008**

Questions regarding this Ballot or the voting procedures should be directed to Josh Skevington at (602) 286-1841

IN THE UNITED STATES BANKRUPTCY COURT FOR THE DISTRICT OF DELAWARE

In re:	Case No. 99-2847 (MFW)
STUART ENTERTAINMENT, INC.,	BALLOT FOR ACCEPTING OR REJECTING PLAN OF REORGANIZATION
Debtor.	PINK BALLOT E-2

CLASS 7: EQUITY INTERESTS

THE VOTING DEADLINE TO ACCEPT OR REJECT THE PLAN IS 4:00 PM, EASTERN TIME, NOVEMBER 26, 1999

Stuart Entertainment, Inc. (the "Debtor") filed its Plan of Reorganization on October 12, 1999 (the "Plan"). The Bankruptcy Court has approved a disclosure statement with respect to the Plan (the "Disclosure Statement"). The Disclosure Statement provides information to assist you in deciding how to vote your Ballot. You should have received a copy of the Disclosure Statement with this Ballot, but if you do not have a Disclosure Statement, you may obtain a copy from IKON Document Services, 901 N. Market Street, Suite 718, Wilmington, DE 19801, Phone (302) 777-4500, Fax (302) 777-5155. Court approval of the Disclosure Statement does not indicate approval of the Plan by the Court.

You should review the Disclosure Statement and the Plan before you vote. You may wish to seek legal advice concerning the Plan and your classification and treatment under the Plan. If you hold claims or equity interests in more than one class, you should use appropriate Ballots for each class in which you are entitled to vote.

If your Ballot is not received by your record holder from whom you received this Ballot, your vote will not count as either an acceptance or rejection of the Plan. If the Plan is confirmed by the Bankruptcy Court it will be binding on you whether or not you vote.

Use this Pink Ballot E-2 ONLY if you are SOLELY the beneficial owner of Equity Interests (as defined in the Plan) and not the record owner of Equity Interests. Once fully completed, RETURN THIS PINK BALLOT E-2 TO YOUR RECORD OWNER FROM WHOM YOU RECEIVED IT. If you are BOTH the record owner AND the beneficial owner of Equity Interests, use the Orange Ballot E-3. If you are SOLELY the record owner and NOT the beneficial owner of Notes, use the White Master Ballot E-1.

ACCEPTANCE OR REJECTION OF THE PLAN

The undersigned, the beneficial owner of Notes:

☐ **Accepts** the Plan ☐ **Rejects** the Plan

By signing this Ballot, the undersigned certified that it is solely the beneficial owner of Equity Interests as of October 27, 1999. Please fill in the following information:

Name of Owner: ______________________

Taxpayer I.D. No.: ______________________

Certificate No.(s): ______________________

Unpaid Principal Amount: ______________________

NOTE: Beneficial owners of Notes may not split their votes on the Plan. Thus, if you are submitting a vote with respect to any Note, you must vote **all** of the Notes in the same manner (*i.e.*, all "accept" or all "reject").

Date: ______________________

Print or type name: ______________________

Signature: ______________________

Title: ______________________

Address: ______________________

____

PLEASE MAIL OR FAX YOUR BALLOT TO YOUR RECORD OWNER PROMPTLY!
Questions regarding this Ballot or the voting procedures should be directed to your record owner.

IN THE UNITED STATES BANKRUPTCY COURT
FOR THE DISTRICT OF DELAWARE

In re:

STUART ENTERTAINMENT, INC.,

Debtor.

Case No. 99-2847 (MFW)

BALLOT FOR ACCEPTING OR REJECTING PLAN OF REORGANIZATION

ORANGE BALLOT E-3

CLASS 7: EQUITY INTERESTS

THE VOTING DEADLINE TO ACCEPT OR REJECT THE PLAN IS 4:00 PM, EASTERN TIME, NOVEMBER 26, 1999

Stuart Entertainment, Inc. (the "Debtor") filed its Plan of Reorganization on October 12, 1999 (the "Plan"). The Bankruptcy Court has approved a disclosure statement with respect to the Plan (the "Disclosure Statement"). The Disclosure Statement provides information to assist you in deciding how to vote your Ballot. You should have received a copy of the Disclosure Statement with this Ballot, but if you do not have a Disclosure Statement, you may obtain a copy from IKON Document Services, 901 N. Market Street, Suite 718, Wilmington, DE 19801, Phone (302) 777-4500, Fax (302) 777-5155. Court approval of the Disclosure Statement does not indicate approval of the Plan by the Court.

You should review the Disclosure Statement and the Plan before you vote. You may wish to seek legal advice concerning the Plan and your classification and treatment under the Plan. If you hold claims or equity interests in more than one class, you should use appropriate Ballots for each class in which you are entitled to vote.

If your Ballot is not received by the Voting Agent below on or before 4:00 p.m. Eastern time on November 26, 1999, and such deadline is not extended by order of the Bankruptcy Court, your vote will not count as either an acceptance or rejection of the Plan. If the Plan is confirmed by the Bankruptcy Court it will be binding on you whether or not you vote.

Use this Orange Ballot E-3 ONLY if you are BOTH the beneficial owner AND record owner of Equity Interests (as defined in the Plan). If you are ONLY the beneficial owner and NOT the record owner of Equity Interests, use the Pink Ballot E-2 and RETURN IT TO YOUR RECORD OWNER. If you are SOLELY the record owner and NOT the beneficial owner, use the White Master Ballot E-1.

ACCEPTANCE OR REJECTION OF THE PLAN

The undersigned, the beneficial and record owner of Equity Interests (check one box only):

☐ **Accept** the Plan ☐ **Reject** the Plan

By signing this Ballot, the undersigned certified that it is the beneficial owner and record owner of Equity Interests as of October 27, 1999.

Name of Owner: ______________________

Taxpayer I.D. No.: ______________________

Certificate No.(s): ______________________

Unpaid Principal Amount: ______________________

NOTE: Beneficial owners of Notes may not split their votes on the Plan. Thus, if you are submitting a vote with respect to any Note, you must vote **all** of the Notes in the same manner (*i.e.*, all "accept" or all "reject").

Date: ______________________

Print or type name: ______________________

Signature: ______________________

Title: ______________________

Address: ______________________

____

Telephone: ______________________

PLEASE MAIL OR FAX YOUR BALLOT TO YOUR RECORD OWNER PROMPTLY!

Send by U.S. Mail, Overnight Delivery, or Courier to → or **Fax to (602) 286-2199**	**U.S. Mail:** **Stuart Plan Voting** **c/o Arthur Andersen LLP / Josh Skevington** **P.O. Box 60725** **Phoenix, Arizona 85082**	**Overnight Delivery or Courier:** **Stuart Plan Voting** **c/o Arthur Andersen LLP / Josh Skevington** **501 N. 44th Street** **Phoenix, Arizona 85008**

Questions regarding this Ballot or the voting procedures should be directed to Josh Skevington at (602) 286-1841

IN THE UNITED STATES BANKRUPTCY COURT
FOR THE DISTRICT OF DELAWARE

In re:

STUART ENTERTAINMENT, INC.,

Debtor.

Case No. 99-2847 (MFW)

BALLOT FOR ACCEPTING OR REJECTING PLAN OF REORGANIZATION

BALLOT E-4

CLASS 7: EQUITY RELATED CLAIMS

THE VOTING DEADLINE TO ACCEPT OR REJECT THE PLAN IS 4:00 PM, EASTERN TIME, NOVEMBER 26 1999

Stuart Entertainment, Inc. (the "Debtor") filed its Plan of Reorganization on October 12, 1999 (the "Plan"). The Bankruptcy Court has approved a disclosure statement with respect to the Plan (the "Disclosure Statement"). The Disclosure Statement provides information to assist you in deciding how to vote your Ballot. You should have received a copy of the Disclosure Statement with this Ballot, but if you do not have a Disclosure Statement, you may obtain a copy from IKON Document Services, 901 N. Market Street, Suite 718, Wilmington, DE 19801, Phone (302) 777-4500, Fax (302) 777-5155. Court approval of the Disclosure Statement does not indicate approval of the Plan by the Court.

You should review the Disclosure Statement and the Plan before you vote. You may wish to seek legal advice concerning the Plan and your classification and treatment under the Plan. If you hold claims or equity interests in more than one class, you should use appropriate Ballots for each class in which you are entitled to vote.

If your Ballot is not received by the Voting Agent below on or before 4:00 p.m. Eastern time on November 26, 1999, and such deadline is not extended by order of the Bankruptcy Court, your vote will not count as either an acceptance or rejection of the Plan. If the Plan is confirmed by the Bankruptcy Court it will be binding on you whether or not you vote.

You must vote all of your Claims within a single Class under the Plan to either accept or reject the Plan. You may not vote certain of your Claims to accept the Plan and other of your Claims to reject the Plan. A Ballot that partially rejects and partially accepts the Plan will be counted as an acceptance for all Claims represented by the Ballot.

ACCEPTANCE OR REJECTION OF THE PLAN

The undersigned, the holder of Class 7 Claims against the Debtor in the unpaid aggregate amount of $ ____________________ ____________ :

(Check one box only)

☐ **Accept** the Plan ☐ **Reject** the Plan

Date: ______________________________

Print or type name: ______________________________

Signature: ______________________________

Title: ______________________________

Address: ______________________________

____

PLEASE MAIL OR FAX YOUR BALLOT TO THE FOLLOWING VOTING AGENT PROMPTLY!

Send by U.S. Mail, Overnight Delivery, or Courier to → or **Fax to (602) 286-2199**	**<u>U.S. Mail:</u>** **Stuart Plan Voting** **c/o Arthur Andersen LLP / Josh Skevington** **P.O. Box 60725** **Phoenix, Arizona 85082**	**<u>Overnight Delivery or Courier:</u>** **Stuart Plan Voting** **c/o Arthur Andersen LLP / Josh Skevington** **501 N. 44th Street** **Phoenix, Arizona 85008**

Questions regarding this Ballot or the voting procedures should be directed to Josh Skevington at (602) 286-1841

APPENDIX N

SAMPLE PLAN AND DISCLOSURE STATEMENT – DEBT TO EQUITY CONVERSION

This Disclosure Statement and Plan of Reorganization were the culmination of the 1999 Chapter 11 reorganization of ***Stuart Entertainment, Inc.***, a leading manufacturer and distributor of bingo and bingo-related gaming supplies. The reorganization was pre-negotiated with a majority of Stuart's debt holders before the petition was filed, and was structured around a "conversion" of Stuart's $100 million of unsecured bonds into all the equity of the reorganized company. Old equity was cancelled, and the holders of old common shares received a small cash distribution under the Plan. While the Plan provided that general unsecured claims received 25¢ on the dollar on account of their claims, most general unsecured creditors were trade vendors and suppliers, who had already been paid in full in accordance with an order issued by the Delaware bankruptcy court at the beginning of the case. This version of the Disclosure Statement has been edited and excerpted for publication purposes.

IN THE UNITED STATES BANKRUPTCY COURT FOR THE DISTRICT OF DELAWARE

In re

STUART ENTERTAINMENT, INC.,
a Delaware corporation,

Debtor.

Case No. 99-2847 (MFW)

Chapter 11

DISCLOSURE STATEMENT IN SUPPORT OF FIRST AMENDED PLAN OF REORGANIZATION

SQUIRE, SANDERS & DEMPSEY L.L.P.
Two Renaissance Square
40 North Central Avenue, Suite 2700
Phoenix, Arizona 85004
(602) 528-4000

Attorneys: Craig D. Hansen
Thomas J. Salerno
Jordan A. Kroop

Co-Counsel to Stuart Entertainment, Inc.,
Debtor-In-Possession

SAUL, EWING, REMICK & SAUL L.L.P.
P.O. Box 1266
222 Delaware Avenue, Suite 1200
Wilmington, Delaware 19899
(302) 421-6800

Attorneys: Norman L. Pernick
J. Kate Stickles

Co-Counsel to Stuart Entertainment, Inc.,
Debtor-In-Possession

TABLE OF CONTENTS

EXHIBITS:

QUESTIONS AND ANSWERS ABOUT THE STUART REORGANIZATION

The following is a brief summary of certain basic questions and answers pertinent to Stuart's reorganization. This summary is not intended to be a complete discussion of the matters raised in this summary. You should refer to the remainder of the Disclosure Statement and the Plan for a detailed description of Stuart's reorganization.

Q: Why is Stuart reorganizing?

A: Over the past several years Stuart has incurred significant indebtedness in connection with the operation of its business, as well as increased competition in its industry. As a result, Stuart has no ability to service or otherwise satisfy its existing obligations to its Noteholders. Stuart believes that the restructuring contemplated by the attached Plan will enable its Creditors to recover more than if Stuart were to seek other restructuring alternatives or a liquidation under Chapter 7 of the Bankruptcy Code.

Q: What is a Chapter 11 proceeding?

A: Chapter 11 is the principal reorganization chapter of the United States Bankruptcy Code. Under Chapter 11, a debtor such as Stuart may reorganize its business for the benefit of itself and its creditors and shareholders. Bankruptcy Court confirmation of a plan of reorganization is the principal objective of a Chapter 11 case.

Q: How are parties that have a relationship with Stuart treated in a Chapter 11 proceeding?

A: It depends on what sort of claim you have against Stuart and how that claim is classified under the Plan of Reorganization. In general, the Chapter 11 Plan divides claims and equity interests that individuals and entities have against Stuart into separate classes. The Plan specifies the property of Stuart that each class is to receive and contains other provisions necessary to the reorganization of Stuart. Depending on how your claim is classified, and assuming you have an allowed claim, you may receive cash, equity securities in Stuart, the preservation of your relationship with Stuart, or nothing at all. You should review this Disclosure Statement to more fully understand what your rights are under the Plan.

Q: What is the process for approving Stuart's Chapter 11 reorganization?

A: Generally under the Bankruptcy Code, every class of claims that is "impaired" under the Plan must vote in favor of the Plan in order for it to be confirmed by the Bankruptcy Court. A class of claims in impaired if claims in that class are paid less than the full value of the claims under the Plan. Holders of claims constituting at least two-thirds in dollar amount and more than one-half in number of allowed claims within each class must vote to accept the Plan for that class to be deemed to have accepted the Plan. Holders of at least two-thirds in the amount of allowed equity interests in each impaired class of equity interests must vote to accept the Plan in order for that class to be deemed to have accepted the Plan.

If a class of claims will be paid in full under the Plan, or reinstated, or their legal, equitable and contractual rights are to remain unchanged by the reorganization, such classes will be deemed to be unimpaired and to have accepted the Plan. Accordingly, holders of such claims will not be entitled to vote on the Plan.

Q: Can the Plan be approved if one or more of the impaired classes doesn't receive the requisite vote to accept the Plan?

A: Yes. Chapter 11 of the Bankruptcy Code permits a plan of reorganization to be confirmed if at least one class of impaired claims vote in favor of the plan. However, if not all impaired classes vote to accept the plan, the Bankruptcy Court must find that the plan meets a number of statutory tests before it may confirm, or approve, the plan. Many of these tests are designed to protect the interests of holders of claims or equity interests who do not vote to accept the plan but who will nonetheless be bound by its provisions if confirmed by the Bankruptcy Court.

Q: What do I, as a holder of a claim against Stuart, need to do to ensure that I have an Allowed Claim under the Plan?

A: You should read carefully this Disclosure Statement and ensure that you follow the instructions contained in it for asserting your claim and that you meet the appropriate deadlines. You also should ensure that you vote timely on the Plan by promptly returning your Ballot. You may wish to consult legal counsel with respect to your rights.

Q: As a current holder of Stuart common stock, what will I receive if the Plan is confirmed by the Bankruptcy Court?

A: If the Plan is confirmed by the Bankruptcy Court, you will receive a pro rata share of $150,000 and nothing else. For example, if you own ten percent (10%) of the outstanding shares of Common Stock of Stuart on the applicable voting record date, you would be entitled to ten percent (10%) of the $150,000, or $15,000. This also means that, following confirmation of the Plan, you will no longer be a shareholder of Stuart and will have no other rights against Stuart.

Q: As a current holder of 12-1/2% Senior Subordinated Notes due 2004 (the "Notes") of Stuart, what will I receive if the Plan is approved by the Bankruptcy Court?

A: If the Plan is confirmed by the Bankruptcy Court, Stuart will issue one hundred percent (100%) of the shares of its New Common Stock to holders of the Notes. Accordingly, subject to the discussion below, you will receive your pro rata share of the New Common Stock issued by Stuart. For example, if you own ten percent (10%) of the Notes, you will be entitled to receive ten percent (10%) of the shares of New Common Stock then issued by Stuart.

Q: Is the percentage of New Common Stock that I receive under the Plan subject to decrease in any way?

A: Yes. The Plan contemplates that the executive management of Stuart will receive options to purchase New Common Stock upon confirmation of the Plan. If exercised, these options (which are referred to under the Plan as the Executive Options and the Equity Incentive Options) will result in the issuance of additional shares of New Common Stock, which will result in a decrease in the percentage of shares of New Common Stock held by you. This concept is commonly referred to as dilution.

Q: As a holder of Notes, may I elect to receive cash in lieu of shares of New Common Stock?

A: Yes. You may elect to receive cash in lieu of shares of New Common Stock by selecting the appropriate box on your Ballot. By making such an election, you will be entitled to receive a cash payment equal to twenty five percent (25%) of your Allowed Claim based on your ownership of Notes. For example, if you have an Allowed Notes Claim of $800,000 and you elect on your Ballot to receive cash, you would be entitled to receive $200,000 in cash in full satisfaction of your Claim.

Q: What do I need to do now?

A: If you are the holder of a Claim or Equity Interest in Classes 3A, 4, 5, 6, or 7, you should review this Disclosure Statement and the Plan, and fill out a Ballot to accept or reject the Plan. All Ballots must be actually received by the Voting Agent, Arthur Andersen LLP, Attn: Josh Skevington, P.O. Box 60725, Phoenix, Arizona 85082, Tel. (602) 286-1841, Fax (602) 286-2199, by 4:00 p.m., Eastern time, on **November 26, 1999**, unless the Bankruptcy Court extends that deadline.

If you are the holder of a Claim in Classes 1, 2, or 3, your Class is unimpaired and is therefore deemed to have accepted the Plan. Accordingly, you are not entitled to vote.

Q: When is Stuart expected to complete its reorganization?

A: A hearing before the Bankruptcy Court to consider confirmation of the Plan is currently set for December 14, 1999. Assuming that hearing occurs as scheduled, and is completed as Stuart intends and anticipates, the Plan will become effective, and Stuart's reorganization will be complete, by December 31, 1999.

Q: Who should I contact if I have questions concerning the plan?

A: If you have additional questions concerning the Plan, please contact:

Craig D. Hansen

Thomas J. Salerno

Jordan A. Kroop

SQUIRE, SANDERS & DEMPSEY L.L.P.

40 North Central Avenue, Suite 2700

Phoenix, Arizona 85004

Telephone: (602) 528-4000

Facsimile: (602) 253-8129

INTRODUCTION AND SUMMARY

Overview

On August 13, 1999, STUART ENTERTAINMENT, INC., a Delaware corporation ("Stuart"), filed its petition for relief under Chapter 11 of Title 11 of the United States Code (the "Bankruptcy Code") with the United States Bankruptcy Court for the District of Delaware (the "Bankruptcy Court"). That same day, Stuart filed with the Bankruptcy Court its Plan of Reorganization. On August 23, 1999, Stuart filed a Disclosure Statement with respect to the August 13, 1999 Plan of Reorganization. On October 11, 1999, Stuart filed its First Amended Plan of Reorganization (the "Plan") and this Disclosure Statement. With this Disclosure Statement, Stuart has filed with the Bankruptcy Court the First Amended Supplement to the Plan of Reorganization (the "Plan Supplement"), which contains, among other things, certain documentation necessary to implement the Plan. For purposes of this Disclosure Statement, the Plan and the Plan Supplement will be collectively referred to as the Plan, unless otherwise noted.

The purpose of this Disclosure Statement is to provide Stuart's Creditors and holders of Equity Interests with adequate information to make an informed judgment about the Plan. This information includes, among other matters, a brief history of Stuart, a summary of its Chapter 11 Case, a description of Stuart's assets and liabilities, a description of the terms under which Stuart's business will be reorganized and restructured in accordance with the Plan, and an explanation of how the Plan will function.

It is important that Creditors and holders of Equity Interests read and carefully consider this Disclosure Statement and the Plan, and that such Creditors and holders of Equity Interests vote promptly on the acceptance of the Plan. Stuart's current capital structure is over-leveraged and, as a result, Stuart has no ability to service or otherwise satisfy its obligations to holders of the 12½% Senior Subordinated Notes due November 15, 2004 (the "Notes"). Stuart believes that the restructuring contemplated by the Plan will yield a recovery to Creditors greater than the return that could be achieved through other restructuring alternatives or a liquidation under Chapter 7 of the Bankruptcy Code.

YOU SHOULD READ THIS DISCLOSURE STATEMENT IN ITS ENTIRETY BEFORE VOTING ON THE PLAN. THIS DISCLOSURE STATEMENT SUMMARIZES CERTAIN TERMS OF THE PLAN, BUT THE PLAN ITSELF IS THE GOVERNING DOCUMENT. IF ANY INCONSISTENCY EXISTS BETWEEN THE PLAN AND THE DISCLOSURE STATEMENT, THE TERMS OF THE PLAN CONTROL.

If you have any questions concerning the procedures for voting, please contact Donald E. Tanguilig, Squire, Sanders & Dempsey L.L.P., Two Renaissance Square, 40 North Central Avenue, Suite

2700, Phoenix, Arizona 85004, telephone number (602) 528-4000, facsimile number (602) 253-8129.

If you have questions concerning your treatment under the Plan, please contact legal counsel to Stuart, Craig D. Hansen and Jordan A. Kroop, Squire, Sanders & Dempsey L.L.P., Two Renaissance Square, 40 North Central Avenue, Suite 2700, Phoenix, Arizona 85004, telephone number (602) 528-4000, facsimile number (602) 253-8129.

A SUMMARY DESCRIPTION OF THE CLASSIFICATION OF YOUR CLAIM OR EQUITY INTEREST AND THE TREATMENT PROPOSED UNDER THE PLAN ARE CONTAINED IN "OVERVIEW OF THE PLAN – Treatment of Claims and Equity Interests Under the Plan" BELOW. EXHIBIT 1 TO THIS DISCLOSURE STATEMENT IS A COMPLETE COPY OF THE PLAN.

Stuart reserves the right to amend, modify, or supplement the Plan at any time before the confirmation of the Plan, provided that such amendments or modifications do not materially alter the treatment of, or distributions to, Creditors and holders of Equity Interests under the Plan.

SECURITIES ARE TO BE ISSUED BY REORGANIZED STUART IN ACCORDANCE WITH THE PLAN. STUART BELIEVES THAT SUCH SECURITIES ARE BEING OFFERED AND ISSUED UNDER EXEMPTIONS PROVIDED IN SECTION 1145 OF THE BANKRUPTCY CODE AND CERTAIN RULES AND REGULATIONS PROMULGATED UNDER THAT SECTION. WHILE THESE SECURITIES MAY BE TRANSFERRED AND RESOLD WITHOUT REGISTRATION UNDER THE UNITED STATES SECURITIES ACT OF 1933, AS AMENDED, THE PLAN MAY IMPOSE CERTAIN RESTRICTIONS ON THE TRANSFERABILITY OF SUCH SECURITIES. THE SECURITIES AND EXCHANGE COMMISSION HAS NOT TAKEN A POSITION WITH RESPECT TO THE SECURITIES TO BE ISSUED IN ACCORDANCE WITH THE PLAN.

THE FINANCIAL PROJECTIONS CONTAINED IN THIS DISCLOSURE STATEMENT REPRESENT STUART'S ESTIMATES OF FUTURE EVENTS BASED ON CERTAIN ASSUMPTIONS MORE FULLY DESCRIBED BELOW, SOME OR ALL OF WHICH MAY NOT BE REALIZED. NONE OF THE FINANCIAL ANALYSES CONTAINED IN THIS DISCLOSURE STATEMENT IS CONSIDERED TO BE A "FORECAST" OR "PROJECTION" AS TECHNICALLY DEFINED BY THE AMERICAN INSTITUTE OF CERTIFIED PUBLIC ACCOUNTANTS. THE USE OF THE WORDS "FORECAST," "PROJECT," OR "PROJECTION" WITHIN THIS DISCLOSURE STATEMENT RELATE TO THE BROAD EXPECTATIONS OF FUTURE EVENTS OR MARKET CONDITIONS AND

QUANTIFICATIONS OF THE POTENTIAL RESULTS OF OPERATIONS UNDER THOSE CONDITIONS.

ALL FINANCIAL INFORMATION PRESENTED IN THIS DISCLOSURE STATEMENT WAS PREPARED BY STUART. reference IS MADE TO EXHIBIT 2 OF THE DISCLOSURE STATEMENT, WHICH IS STUART'S ANNUAL REPORT ON FORM 10-K FOR THE FISCAL YEAR ENDED DECEMBER 31, 1998, AS AMENDED ("FORM 10-K/A"). REFERENCE IS ALSO MADE TO STUART'S QUARTERLY REPORT ON FORM 10-Q FOR QUARTERLY PERIOD ENDED JUNE 30, 1999 ("FORM 10-Q"), LOCATED AT EXHIBIT 3. EACH CREDITOR AND EQUITY INTEREST HOLDER IS URGED TO REVIEW THE PLAN IN FULL BEFORE VOTING ON THE PLAN TO ENSURE A COMPLETE UNDERSTANDING OF THE PLAN AND THIS DISCLOSURE STATEMENT.

Certain statements, projections of future operating results, valuation estimates and the like contained in this Disclosure Statement and elsewhere are statements that Stuart believes constitute "forward-looking statements" within the meaning of the Private Securities Litigation Reform Act of 1995. Such forward-looking statements involve known and unknown risks, uncertainties and other important factors that could cause the actual results, performance or achievements of Reorganized Stuart, or industry results, to differ materially from any future results, performance or achievements expressed or implied by such forward-looking statements. Such risks, uncertainties and other important factors include, among others: general economic and business conditions; competition; loss of any significant customers; changes in business strategy or development plans; availability, terms and deployment of capital; adverse uninsured determinations in any existing or future litigation or regulatory proceedings and any other factors referenced in this Disclosure Statement or otherwise. See "RISK FACTORS." These forward-looking statements speak only as of the date of this Disclosure Statement, and Stuart expressly disclaims any obligation or undertaking to disseminate any updates or revisions to any forward-looking statement contained in this Disclosure Statement to reflect any change in Stuart's or Reorganized Stuart's expectations with regard to such statements or any change in events, conditions or circumstances on which any such statement is based.

THIS DISCLOSURE STATEMENT IS INTENDED FOR THE SOLE USE OF CREDITORS AND OTHER PARTIES IN INTEREST, AND FOR THE SOLE PURPOSE OF ASSISTING THEM IN MAKING AN INFORMED DECISION ABOUT THE PLAN. NO PERSON HAS BEEN AUTHORIZED TO GIVE ANY INFORMATION OR MAKE ANY REPRESENTATIONS IN CONJUNCTION WITH THE SOLICITATION OF VOTES TO ACCEPT OR REJECT THE PLAN OTHER THAN THE INFORMATION AND REPRESENTATIONS

CONTAINED IN THIS DISCLOSURE STATEMENT OR IN THE BALLOTS. IF GIVEN OR MADE, ANY SUCH INFORMATION OR REPRESENTATIONS MUST NOT BE RELIED UPON AS HAVING BEEN AUTHORIZED BY STUART.

THIS DISCLOSURE STATEMENT HAS BEEN APPROVED BY THE BANKRUPTCY COURT AS CONTAINING ADEQUATE INFORMATION TO PERMIT A CREDITOR TO VOTE ON THE PLAN.

CAPITALIZED TERMS USED BUT NOT DEFINED IN THIS DISCLOSURE STATEMENT HAVE THE DEFINITIONS GIVEN TO THEM IN THE PLAN.

STUART STRONGLY URGES ACCEPTANCE OF THE PLAN, THE TERMS OF WHICH IT NEGOTIATED WITH CONTRARIAN CAPITAL MANAGEMENT, L.L.C., WHO ALSO STRONGLY URGES ACCEPTANCE OF THE PLAN.

Summary of Classification and Treatment Under the Plan [1]

As described more fully in this Disclosure Statement, the Plan enables a restructuring of Stuart's prepetition indebtedness and operations. Among other things, the Plan provides for the exchange of Notes for New Common Stock, provided that certain holders of Notes may elect to receive a cash distribution in lieu of New Common Stock. Holders of General Unsecured Claims, to the extent not otherwise previously satisfied, will receive in satisfaction of their Claims a cash payment equivalent to twenty-five percent (25%) of the value of their Allowed General Unsecured Claim. Holders of Old Common Stock, and other holders of Equity Interests and Equity Related Claims will receive a Pro Rata portion of $150,000 in Cash, subject to certain conditions. Set forth in the following section is a summary of the classification and treatment of Claims and Equity Interests under the Plan.

The Plan divides the Claims of known Creditors and Equity Interests into Classes and sets forth the treatment afforded to each Class. The classification of Claims and the distributions to be made under such classification takes into account the relative priorities of Claims, Equity Interests, and Equity Related Claims. Stuart believes that it has classified all Claims, Equity Interests, and Equity Related Claims in compliance with the provisions of Section 1122 of the Bankruptcy Code.

If the Plan is confirmed by the Bankruptcy Court, each holder of an Allowed Claim will receive the same treatment as all holders of other Allowed Claims in the same Class, regardless of whether a particular holder voted to accept the Plan. Moreover, upon confirmation, the Plan will be binding on all Creditors and Equity Interests regardless of whether such Creditors or Equity Interests voted to accept the Plan.

The Plan creates various Classes of Claims against, and Equity Interests in, Stuart. The table below sets forth the specific classification and treatment under the Plan of each of the Classes.

---

[1] This summary contains only a brief and simplified description of the classification and treatment of Claims and Equity Interests under the Plan. This summary does not describe every provision of the Plan. Accordingly, you should refer to the entire Disclosure Statement (including exhibits), the Plan, and the Plan Supplement for a complete description of the classification and treatment of Claims and Equity Interests.

Class	Type of Claim or Interest	Treatment
Unclassified	Allowed Administrative Expense Claims	Paid in full in Cash (or otherwise satisfied in accordance with its terms) on the latest of: (a) the Effective Date, or as soon thereafter as practicable; (b) such date as may be fixed by the Bankruptcy Court, or as soon thereafter as practicable; (c) the tenth Business Day after such Claim is Allowed, or as soon thereafter as practicable; and (d) such date as the holder of such Claim and Reorganized Stuart agree.
Unclassified	Preserved Ordinary Course Administrative Claims	Paid by Reorganized Stuart in accordance with either: (a) the terms and conditions under which such Claim arose; or (b) in the ordinary course of Reorganized Stuart's business. Such payments are to be made by Reorganized Stuart without further action by the holder of such Claim.
Unclassified	Allowed Priority Tax Claims	Paid in full in Cash on the Effective Date; *provided, however,* that Reorganized Stuart may elect to pay such Claims through deferred Cash payments over a period not exceeding six (6) years after the date of assessment of such Claim, of a value as of the Effective Date, equal to the Allowed amount of such Claim. In that event, such payments are to be made in equal annual installments of principal, plus interest accruing from the Effective Date at the rate on the unpaid portion of Allowed Priority Tax Claim set forth in the Internal Revenue Code of 1986, as amended, Sections 6621 and 6622.The first such payment is to be made payable on the latest of: (a) the Effective Date, or as soon thereafter as practicable; (b) the tenth Business Day after the date on which an order allowing such Claim becomes a Final Order, or as soon thereafter as practicable; and (c) such other time as is agreed upon by the holder of such Claim and Reorganized Stuart;*provided, however,*that Reorganized Stuart retains the right to prepay and such Allowed Priority Tax Claim, or any remaining balance of such Claim, in full or in part, at any time on or after the Effective Date without premium or penalty.
Unclassified	Allowed Reclamation Claims	Paid in full in Cash upon the latest of: (a) the Effective Date, or as soon thereafter as practicable; (b) such date as may be fixed by the Bankruptcy Court, or as soon thereafter as practicable; (c) the tenth Business Day after the date on which an order allowing such Claim becomes a Final Order, or as soon thereafter as practicable; and (d) such other time as is agreed upon by the holder of such Claim and Reorganized Stuart.
Unclassified	Allowed Claims of DIP Lender	Simultaneously with the closing of the Exit Financing Facility, all the Debtor's obligations to the DIP Lender under the DIP Facility and the DIP Loan Documents are to be fully and finally satisfied in accordance with their terms using proceeds derived from, among other things, the Exit Financing Facility and/or Cash held by Reorganized Stuart.
1	Priority Claims	**Unimpaired.** Each holder of an Allowed Priority Claim is to receive Cash in an amount equal to such Allowed Priority Claim on the later of: (a) the Effective Date, or as soon thereafter as practicable; and (b) ten Business Days after the date such Priority Claim becomes an Allowed Priority Claim, or as soon thereafter as practicable, unless the holder of such Allowed Priority Claim and Reorganized Stuart agree otherwise.

Class	Type of Claim or Interest	Treatment
2	Secured Tax Claims	**Unimpaired.** Paid in full in Cash upon the latest of: (a) the Effective Date, or as soon thereafter as practicable; (b) such date as may be fixed by the Bankruptcy Court, or as soon thereafter as practicable; (c) the tenth Business Day after such Claim is Allowed, or as soon thereafter as practicable; (d) the date on which such Secured Tax Claim is scheduled to be paid in the ordinary course of business under applicable law or regulation; and (e) such date as the holder of such Claim and Reorganized Stuart agree.
3	Miscellaneous Secured Claims	**Unimpaired.** Paid in full in Cash upon the latest of: (a) the Effective Date, or as soon thereafter as practicable; (b) such date as may be fixed by the Bankruptcy Court, or as soon thereafter as practicable; (c) the tenth Business Day after such Claim is Allowed, or as soon thereafter as practicable; (d) the date on which such Miscellaneous Secured Claim is scheduled to be paid in the ordinary course of business under applicable law or regulation; and (e) such date as the holder of such Claim and Reorganized Stuart agree.
3A	Elliott Trust Secured Claim	**Impaired.**In full and final satisfaction of the Elliott Trust Secured Claim, the Elliott Trust shall be paid in full in Cash as follows: (a) eight (8) equal quarterly payments of $111,736.53, commencing on October 1, 1999 and continuing on each subsequent January 1, April 1, July 1, and October 1, with the last installment to be paid, rather than on July 1, 2001, no later than August 1, 2001; (b) except with respect to the foregoing payment schedule, Reorganized Stuart shall meet all its obligations to the Elliott Trust under the Elliot Trust Promissory Note, which, except to the extent altered by the foregoing payment schedule, shall remain in full force and affect in accordance with its own terms from and after the Effective Date.
4	Notes Claims	**Impaired.** On the Effective Date, or as soon thereafter as practicable, each holder of an Allowed Notes Claim is to receive, in full and final satisfaction of such Allowed Notes Claim, a Pro Rata portion of a number of shares of New Common Stock equivalent to approximately one hundred percent (100%) of the New Common Stock on a Fully Diluted Basis. A Holder of an Allowed Notes Claim may make a Noteholder Election to receive in full satisfaction of such Claim a distribution of Cash in an amount of twenty-five percent (25%) of its Allowed Notes Claim in full satisfaction of such Claim. *Additional conditions apply to this treatment; see* ***Error! Reference source not found. Error! Reference source not found.Error! Reference source not found.***
5	General Unsecured Claims	**Impaired.** On the latest of: (a) the Effective Date, or as soon thereafter as practicable; (b) such date as may be fixed by the Bankruptcy Court, or as soon thereafter as practicable; (c) the tenth Business Day after such Claim is Allowed, or as soon thereafter as practicable; and (d) such date as the holder of such Claim and Reorganized Stuart agree, each Allowed Claim in Class 5 shall receive in full and final satisfaction of such Claim
6	Subsidiary Claims	**Impaired.**The holders of Subsidiary Claims will receive no distributions under the Plan, and all such Claims are discharged as of the Effective Date under the Plan.
7	Equity Interests and	**Impaired.** Subject to the provisions of Section 4.8.6 of the Plan, on the Effective Date, or as soon thereafter as practicable, each holder of an Allowed Equity Interest and Allowed Equity Related Claim is to receive its Pro Rata portion of $150,000 in Cash.

Voting and Confirmation Procedures

This Disclosure Statement is accompanied by copies of the following: (a) the Plan, attached as Exhibit 1 to this Disclosure Statement; (b) an Order of the Bankruptcy Court approving this Disclosure Statement under Section 1125 of the Bankruptcy Code; (c) an Order of the Bankruptcy Court approving the forms of Ballots to be used for voting on the Plan, and approving the notice of, and fixing the time for, submitting Ballots and the Confirmation Hearing; and (d) a Ballot to accept or reject the Plan.

The appropriate form of Ballots are to be used by holders of Claims and Equity Interests in Classes 3A, 4, 5, 6, and 7. Holders of Claims in Classes 1, 2, and 3 are unimpaired under the Plan and are deemed to have accepted the Plan without voting. With respect to holders of Notes and Equity Interests, Ballots are being furnished to record holders of such Notes and Equity Interests as of the Voting Record Date, with instructions requiring that all such record holders distribute Ballots to their respective beneficial holders, collect such beneficial holders' Ballots, and complete and submit a master Ballot summarizing the Ballots received from beneficial holders.

Who May Vote. Under the Bankruptcy Code, impaired classes of Claims or Equity Interests are entitled to vote on a plan of reorganization. A Class that is not impaired under a plan is deemed to have accepted a Plan and does not vote. A Class is "impaired" under the Bankruptcy Code unless the legal, equitable, and contractual rights of the holders of Claims or Equity Interests in that Class are not modified or altered. For purposes of the Plan, holders of Claims and Equity Interests in Classes 3A, 4, 5, 6, and 7 are impaired and entitled to vote on the Plan.

Voting Instructions. All votes to accept or reject the Plan must be cast by using the appropriate form of Ballot enclosed with this Disclosure Statement. No votes other than ones using such Ballots will be counted, except to the extent the Bankruptcy Court orders otherwise. The Bankruptcy Court has set October 27, 1999 as the Voting Record Date under the Plan. The Voting Record Date is the date for the determination of record holders of Claims entitled to receive a copy of this Disclosure Statement and vote, using appropriate Ballots, to accept or reject the Plan. All Ballots (including master Ballots for record holders of Notes and Equity Interests as described above) must be actually received by Arthur Andersen LLP, Attn: Josh Skevington, P.O. Box 60725, Phoenix, Arizona 85082, Tel. (602) 286-1841, Fax (602) 286-2199 (the "Voting Agent"), by 4:00 p.m., Eastern time, on **November 26, 1999** (the "Voting Deadline"), unless the Bankruptcy Court extends such date before such time.

For your vote to count, your Ballot must be properly completed according to the voting instructions on the Ballot and received no later than the Voting Deadline by the Voting Agent. Any Ballot not indicating an acceptance or rejection will be deemed an acceptance of the Plan. If you are a beneficial holder of a security held by a nominee or record holder, your Ballot must be returned to your nominee or record holder in time for the nominee or record holder to include a summary of your Ballot on the Master Ballot to be submitted to the Voting Agent by the Voting Deadline.

For questions about voting procedures, the amount of your Claim, or the packet that you received, please contact:

Donald E. Tanguilig
Squire, Sanders & Dempsey L.L.P.
40 North Central Avenue, Suite 2700
Phoenix, Arizona 85004
Telephone: (602) 528-4000
Facsimile: (602) 253-8129

If you have any questions concerning the restructuring or the Plan, please contact:

Craig D. Hansen
Thomas J. Salerno
Jordan A. Kroop
SQUIRE, SANDERS & DEMPSEY L.L.P.
40 North Central Avenue, Suite 2700
Phoenix, Arizona 85004
Telephone: (602) 528-4000
Facsimile: (602) 253-8129

<u>Acceptance or Rejection of the Plan</u>

Under the Bankruptcy Code, a voting Class of Claims is deemed to have accepted the Plan if it is accepted by creditors in such Class who, of those voting on the Plan, hold at least two-thirds in amount and more than one-half in number of the Allowed Claims of such Class. A voting Class of Equity Interests is deemed to have accepted the Plan if it is accepted by holders of Equity Interests who hold at least two-thirds in amount of the Equity Interests of such Class that have actually voted on the Plan.

If the Plan is not accepted by all impaired Classes of Allowed Claims, the Plan may still be confirmed by the Bankruptcy Court under Section

1129(b) of the Bankruptcy Code if: (a) the Plan has been accepted by at least one impaired Class of Claims; and (b) the Bankruptcy Court determines, among other things, that the Plan "does not discriminate unfairly" and is "fair and equitable" with respect to each non-accepting impaired Class (the "Cramdown Provisions"). If the Plan is not accepted by all impaired Classes of Allowed Claims or Equity Interests, Stuart reserves the right to ask the Bankruptcy Court to confirm the Plan under the Cramdown Provisions.

Confirmation Hearing, Objections

Section 1128(a) of the Bankruptcy Code requires the Bankruptcy Court, after notice, to hold a Confirmation Hearing. Section 1128(b) of the Bankruptcy Code provides that any party-in-interest may object to Confirmation of the Plan. Under Section 1128 of the Bankruptcy Code and Rule 3017(c) of the Bankruptcy Rules, the Bankruptcy Court has scheduled the Confirmation Hearing before the Honorable Mary F. Walrath, United States Bankruptcy Judge, at the United States Bankruptcy Court, District of Delaware, 824 Market Street, 5th Floor, Wilmington, Delaware for **December 14, 1999** at **2:00 p.m.** A notice (the "Confirmation Hearing Notice") setting forth the time and date of the Confirmation Hearing has been included along with this Disclosure Statement. The Confirmation Hearing may be adjourned from time to time by the Bankruptcy Court without further notice, except for an announcement of such adjourned hearing date by the Bankruptcy Court in open court at such hearing.

Any objection to Confirmation of the Plan must be in writing, must comply with the Bankruptcy Rules and the Local Rules of the Bankruptcy Court, and must be filed and served as required in the Confirmation Hearing Notice.

BACKGROUND AND EVENTS PRECIPITATING THE CHAPTER 11 FILING

Overview of the Debtor and Its Business Operations

Stuart, formerly known as Bingo King Company, Inc. and currently doing business as Bingo King (in conjunction with several non-debtor subsidiaries), is a leading manufacturer of a full line of bingo and bingo-related products, including disposable bingo paper, pulltab tickets, ink dabbers, electronic bingo systems and related equipment and supplies. Stuart enjoys a broad reputation for innovation and new product development and has been a leader in the bingo industry for approximately 50 years, having helped to popularize many important breakthroughs in bingo, such as disposable bingo paper and electronic bingo systems.

Bingo is one of North America's most popular forms of gaming and entertainment. Many nonprofit organizations sponsor bingo games for fundraising purposes, while commercial entities, Indian gaming enterprises, casinos and government sponsored entities operate bingo games for profit. Stuart sells or leases its products to this diverse group of end-users through more than 300 distributors, its direct sales force and Stuart-owned distribution outlets.

Stuart believes that it derives a competitive advantage in the bingo industry by offering a wider array of bingo and bingo-related products than its competitors. Stuart supplies bingo halls with all the products and equipment necessary to operate a bingo game of any size, including bingo paper, fixed-base or hand-held electronic bingo systems, ink dabbers, pulltab tickets, bingo ball blowers, public address systems, television monitors, multi-media flashboards, computerized verification systems, tables, chairs, concession equipment, and party supplies.

Stuart was reincorporated in Delaware in 1986, and is a successor, by merger effective as of January 21, 1987, to a business formed in 1948. Stuart's principal executive office is currently located at 3211 Nebraska Avenue, Council Bluffs, Iowa 51501. Its telephone number is (712) 323-1488.

Relationship of Debtor With Its Subsidiaries

Stuart is the operating parent company of a family of subsidiary companies, certain of which maintain ongoing operations relating either to certain areas of Stuart's business or certain geographical areas. Additionally, certain subsidiaries do not maintain ongoing operations, but rather hold various gaming licenses necessary to enable Stuart and its operating subsidiaries to maintain business operations in compliance with applicable law and gaming regulations. Stuart and its subsidiaries are organized as follows:

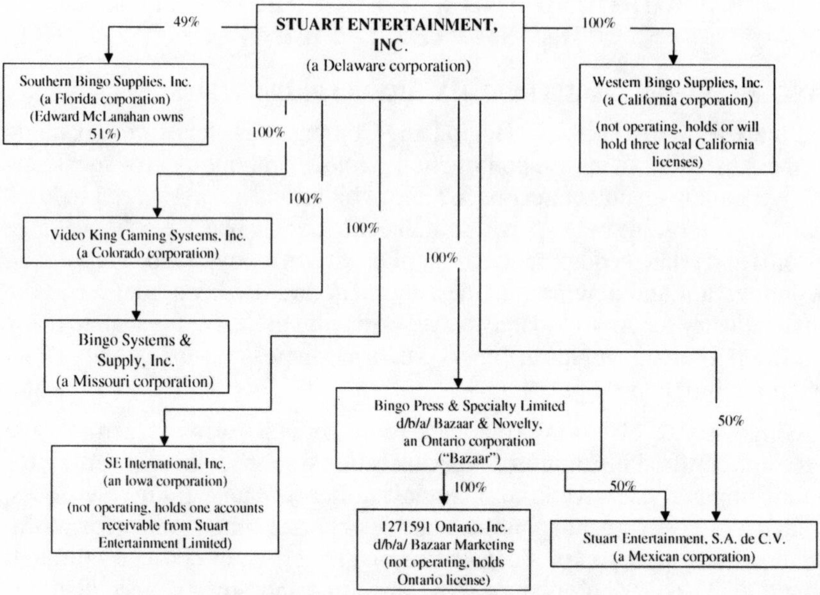

As reflected in the chart above, Stuart's significant operating subsidiaries are as follows:

Video King Gaming Systems, Inc. Video King Gaming Systems, Inc., a wholly owned subsidiary of Stuart ("Video King"), was formed in 1992 to develop a line of electronic gaming equipment, primarily for Stuart's bingo markets. Video King began manufacturing and shipping selected products in 1993. Video King continues to focus its sales efforts within the Company's established bingo markets. The traditional domestic and international for profit gaming markets may be a future market, but Video King has no current plans for such markets.

Stuart Entertainment, S.A. de C.V. Stuart Entertainment, S.A. de C.V., a Mexican corporation and a wholly owned subsidiary of Stuart ("Stuart Entertainment Mexico") was formed in 1991 by Stuart and Bingo Press & Specialty Limited for the purpose of printing and finishing bingo paper exclusively for their respective needs. During 1998, 1997 and 1996 all of the bingo paper manufactured by Stuart Entertainment Mexico was sold to Stuart.

Bingo Press & Specialty Limited. Bingo Press & Specialty Limited, an Ontario, Canada corporation and a wholly owned subsidiary of Stuart ("Bazaar"), operates under the trade name Bazaar & Novelty and was acquired by Stuart in December 1994. Bazaar manufactures and distributes a complete line of bingo cards, pulltab tickets, ink dabbers, supplies and accessories in Canada. Bazaar's products are sold primarily to distributors, who resell them to fraternal, charitable, religious and social organizations, lodges, hospitals, nursing homes, PTA groups, legions, and other similar not-for-profit organizations that use such products to raise money and provide entertainment. To a lesser extent, Bazaar's products are sold to charitable and commercial bingo halls, governmental lottery agencies, and through Stuart-owned distribution outlets.

Bingo Systems and Supply, Inc. Bingo Systems and Supply, Inc. ("Bingo Systems") became a wholly owned subsidiary of Stuart by virtue of an acquisition effective on November 1, 1998. Bingo Systems finishes bingo paper manufactured by Stuart and distributes bingo paper, ink dabbers, bingo equipment, pulltabs tickets, and other related products to fraternal, charitable, religious and social organizations, lodges, hospitals, nursing homes, PTA groups, legions, and other similar not-for-profit organizations that use such products to raise money and provide entertainment.

Previous Acquisitions

Acquisition of Bingo Systems & Supply, Inc. On November 1, 1998, Stuart completed the acquisition of all the outstanding capital stock of Bingo Systems for aggregate consideration of $2,200,000, consisting of $1,000,000 in cash and a $1,200,000 promissory note, made payable to the Elliott Trust and providing the basis for the Elliott Trust Secured Claim.

Acquisition of Alberta Bingo Supply, Inc. On June 1, 1998, Bazaar purchased certain assets related to the bingo business formerly conducted by one of its distributors, Alberta Bingo Supply, Inc. ("ABS"). Under the terms of the agreement, Bazaar paid C$1,000,000 for the goodwill of the acquired business and C$410,000 for certain equipment and fixtures. Bazaar agreed to sell the ABS existing inventory relating to its bingo business, as an agent for ABS, for a period of six months ending December 1, 1998. Bazaar agreed to pay to ABS the difference between C$1,404,113 and the amount of such inventory (valued at cost) sold during the six-month period. As of December 31, 1998, Bazaar paid or has been credited C$1,354,113 for the inventory and has withheld C$50,000 pending a minor dispute concerning inventory valuation.

Acquisition of Power Bingo Corp. On July 1, 1997, Stuart completed the acquisition of substantially all the assets of Power Bingo Corp., a market leader in hand-held electronic bingo units for a purchase price of $1.2 million, consisting of $1.1 million in cash and forgiveness of a note receivable plus future payments of approximately $2.7 million that was based on the market performance of the hand-held electronic bingo units. All payments have been made.

Industry Overview

Bingo Industry. The National Association of Fundraising Ticket Manufacturers' 1996 Charity Gaming in North America Report (the "NAFTM

Report") estimated that over 60,000 organizations have licenses to operate bingo games in the United States and Canada. According to industry reports compiled by the Bingo Bugle, which is a series of regional newspapers aimed at bingo players, bingo players visit bingo halls in the United States and Canada an estimated 1.2 billion times a year. Stuart believes that significant amounts are wagered on bingo in the United States and Canada, and that electronic bingo systems may be a positive factor in encouraging additional players to visit bingo halls. Over each of the last few years, more states have begun to permit electronic bingo and Stuart is finding increased player acceptance of electronic bingo systems as the products are introduced into different markets.

Regulations governing traditional paper bingo and electronic bingo systems vary by jurisdiction. In the United States, traditional paper bingo is legal in all states except Arkansas, Hawaii, Tennessee and Utah. Electronic bingo systems are currently legal in 29 states in some form and in Indian gaming halls in compliance with the Indian Gaming Regulatory Act ("IGRA"). In Canada, traditional paper bingo is legal in all ten provinces and two territories. Fixed-base electronic bingo systems, however, may only be used in halls owned or authorized by the provincial governments. Currently, fixed-base electronic gaming systems are permitted only in British Columbia and Manitoba, while hand-held electronic bingo systems are legal only in Ontario and must be used in conjunction with bingo paper.

The bingo industry in the United States is highly fragmented among numerous bingo game operators. The majority of bingo games in the United States are operated by small nonprofit organizations for fundraising purposes. Such organizations include religious, fraternal, social, military, and civic organizations. A smaller percentage of bingo games in the United States are operated for profit in large bingo halls by casinos, Indian gaming enterprises, and commercial operators. For example, Foxwoods Resort and Casino in Connecticut, the Seminole Indian Casino in Florida, the Potawatomi Bingo Casino in Wisconsin, and Win River Casino Bingo in California all feature large-scale modern bingo halls with seating capacities ranging in size from approximately 1,000 to 3,000 seats.

In Canada, bingo is generally highly centralized under the administration of government-sponsored entities or licensed commercial operators, which own and operate large bingo halls, with average session attendance in excess of 175 players. These government sponsored entities and commercial operators run games on behalf of various charitable organizations, often playing several sessions per day.

Satellite-linked bingo games have been introduced in recent years in the Canadian Provinces of Alberta, British Columbia, Quebec, and Ontario. The British Columbia, Quebec, and Ontario satellite bingo systems are government operated. These satellite-linked bingo games pool the prize money available among commercial bingo halls thus offering higher jackpots.

Satellite-linked games have been approved in the state of Washington, but have not been introduced.

Pulltab Industry. In the United States and Canada, pulltab tickets generally are sold at charitable bingo halls as an additional source of fundraising. In several states and the Province of Ontario, pulltab tickets are approved for sale in third party retail locations, including bars and taverns. Eleven states also use pulltab tickets, in addition to scratch-off tickets, in their instant lottery ticket sales. Stuart believes that significant amounts of money are wagered on pulltab tickets in the United States and Canada, and that these amounts may increase if additional jurisdictions permit the sale of pulltab tickets and if jurisdictions that currently permit the use of pulltab tickets expand the permitted point of sale locations to include third party retail locations.

In the United States, pulltab tickets are currently legal (either through state lotteries or through other outlets) in approximately 40 states. Each state has developed specific regulations that affect the style of play in its market by regulating the point of sale, price per ticket, game themes and payouts.

In Canada, seven provincial lotteries use pulltab tickets in their instant lottery ticket sales. Ontario allows the sale of pulltab tickets at charitable bingo halls and under charity license at third party retail locations such as bars, restaurants, concessionaires, gas stations, hotels, mall kiosks, supermarkets, convenience stores and bowling alleys. Currently there are approximately 9,500 such third party retail locations in Ontario.

In November 1997, Stuart was awarded a five-year contract by the Ontario Gaming Control Commission ("OGC") to be the sole supplier of pulltab tickets to all charity licensed retail locations in the Province of Ontario (see "Government Regulations"). Stuart's position in Ontario, which is, according to the 1997 NAFTM Report, North America's largest charity marketplace, has been solidified with the five-year contract with possible extensions. In September 1997, the OGC announced the list of the final proponents for operation and ownership of the 44 charity gaming clubs that were to replace the system of roving Monte Carlo casinos. In 1998, the OGC withdrew its approval of such clubs and assumed ownership and operation of the five clubs then operating. The OGC also authorized the use of slot machines at seventeen racetracks in Ontario. Stuart is currently unable to anticipate whether the clubs or slot machines will have a material impact on the bingo and pulltab markets in Ontario.

Competition

The markets in which Stuart's products compete are extremely competitive. The principal competitive factors in the bingo paper and pulltab ticket markets are quality, service, and price. Stuart's major competitor in the bingo paper and pulltab markets is Arrow International. Stuart's electronic bingo systems, System 12Ô and Power Bingo KingÔ, compete with a number of other manufacturers of electronic bingo systems, none of whom manufacture a full line of bingo and bingo-related products. Stuart also competes with other forms of entertainment such as lotteries, on-line gaming products and the continued expansion of the legalization by the United States, Canada, and other foreign jurisdictions of casino gaming. While there can be no assurances that Stuart will continue to remain competitive in these or other areas, Stuart believes that through its strong distribution network, manufacturing facilities, and technology it will be able to maintain its unique position as a manufacturer of a full line of both consumable and electronic bingo and bingo-related products.

Stuart's Business

Products

Stuart offers a wide array of bingo and bingo-related products. Stuart is capable of supplying a bingo hall with all the products and equipment necessary to operate a bingo game of any size, including bingo paper, fixed-base or hand-held electronic bingo systems, ink dabbers, pulltab tickets, bingo ball blowers, public address systems, television monitors, multi-media flashboards, computerized verification systems, tables, chairs, concession equipment and party supplies. Stuart is organized on a global product line basis under three reportable segments.

Consumable Bingo Products

Bingo Paper. Stuart sells a complete line of bingo paper, which is generally sold in booklet form and is available in a variety of sizes, styles and colors, Stuart's bingo paper line includes a number of specialty bingo games under proprietary trademarks or licenses such as Bonanza Bingo®, Bonus Line®, Double Action™, Wildcard Bingo™, Triangle Bingo™, three styles of 90-number bingo games and other specialty bingo games that can be played as variations on or concurrently with the standard 75-number bingo game. Stuart also sells a line of disposable cards designed for play on tour buses, cruise ships and other environments with limited space for play.

Stuart's bingo card configurations are developed in-house by a mathematician using sophisticated algorithmic models, which are validated through computer simulation in which in excess of 1,000,000 simulated games are played on a given pattern in order to determine the probability of a winner occurring when a specific number of cards are in play and a specific number of balls are called. Stuart has a number of unique series of cards. These different series types range in size from a series of 9,000 unique cards to a series in excess of 3,000,000 unique cards. These card series are stored electronically in Stuart's verification system, which allows the sponsoring organization to verify and display winning cards electronically. Stuart believes that this seamless integration of several paper bingo card series and electronic verification is matched by only one other competitor in the industry.

Ink Dabbers. Stuart manufactures ink dabbers, used to mark called numbers on paper bingo sheets, and ink refills for such dabbers. Stuart sells a varied line of ink colors, bottle styles and sizes, including its successful line of gift packs, which are 3, 4, or 5 bottles packaged together in a decorative gift box using different themes such as movies, comedy and seasonal holidays. Stuart pioneered the use of decorative and innovative labels on ink dabbers, for seasonal items like Christmas and Halloween and for customized labels for bingo halls and distributors. Stuart also developed a labeling process that allows distributors to directly customize labels on-site for their bingo halls. Stuart launched its new 3 and 4 ounce ergonomically designed bottles in 1998. Stuart has applied for a utility patent relating to this new marker. Stuart has been sued by a competitor, alleging that the marker infringes that competitor's patent. Stuart believes the new bottle may have a positive impact on sales of its ink dabbers.

General Merchandise. Stuart distributes other supplies and equipment used by bingo hall operators, such as tables, chairs, public address systems and concession supplies. Stuart purchases for resale bingo accessories such as key chains, lighters, marker holders, coffee mugs and other advertising products, many of which can be customized. Party supplies, flags, balloons and bar and concession equipment for use at fundraising events and bazaars are also sold by Stuart both through Stuart-owned distribution outlets in Canada and through Stuart's distributor network.

Pulltab And Lottery Products

Pulltab Tickets. Stuart manufactures and sells pulltab tickets, which are also referred to as break open tickets, lucky seven tickets, instant bingo and Nevada tickets. Stuart also manufactures scratch off tickets and instant lottery tickets. Stuart currently has a library of over 800 different designs and denominations for pulltab tickets. Stuart has contracted to provide pulltab lottery tickets in four states and five Canadian provinces. A typical pulltab ticket consists of two thin sheets of cardboard, one of which is opaque, printed with colorful designs and laminated together. The player pulls open from one to five perforated windows to reveal hidden combinations of symbols to determine whether the card is a winner, and if so, the amount of the prize. Each set of tickets sold contains a predetermined number of winning tickets. A typical pulltab ticket has a prize structure that varies from approximately 60% to 85% of the gross receipts being paid out as prizes to the players. The remaining percentage of the gross receipts is used to cover the cost of the product and expenses and to provide fundraising dollars or revenue to the sponsoring organization.

Electronic Bingo Products

Electronic Bingo Systems. Stuart believes that electronic bingo systems will be the next major evolutionary step in the industry, and that it is well positioned to capitalize on the opportunity provided by electronic bingo. The popularity of electronic bingo systems is growing rapidly because electronic bingo systems provide the player with additional entertainment value and permit simultaneous play on many more cards than is possible in a typical paper game. The ability to play more cards leads to greater sums wagered per player and, thus, higher profits per bingo session for the bingo hall operator. Stuart's strategy is to be a leading producer of electronic bingo systems. As part of this strategy, Stuart currently manufactures two electronic bingo systems: (i) System 12™ and (ii) Power Bingo King™.

System 12™ is a fixed-base cashless electronic bingo and multi-game system that integrates computer technology with player interactive touch-screen terminals and live bingo. System 12™ is based on a local area network in which terminals for bingo players are connected to a host computer. The host computer allows players to play up to 255 electronic cards per game. Bingo players also have the opportunity to play a bingo game electronically on touch-screen terminals while simultaneously playing traditional paper bingo with other players. System 12™ provides the player access to a stand-alone bingo game and to other games such as video keno, video poker, video slots and video pulltab tickets, where permitted by law. System 12™ enables hall management to control all game functions, track player trends and generate sales reports. Stuart had more than 2,300 System 12™ fixed-base units in place at December 31, 1998 which includes systems sold in prior years.

Power Bingo King™, a hand-held electronic bingo system, allows players to play up to 200 electronic bingo cards simultaneously per game. Each Power Bingo King™ unit is completely portable and has the capability to show the electronic bingo card closest to winning at any given point in time. The system also automatically notifies a player of a winning card. Stuart derived revenues from more than 31,000 Power Bingo King™ hand-held units at December 31, 1998.

Bingo Hall Equipment. Stuart manufactures and sells an extensive line of electronic bingo hall equipment traditionally used in bingo establishments. The electronic bingo hall equipment line includes: (a) electronic blowers that select numbers for bingo games by ejecting numbered balls one at a time; (b) electronic flash boards, measuring up to five feet high and 22 feet wide, which display to the bingo players the numbers selected from the electronic blowers; (c) electronic systems that allow quicker verification of winning bingo cards and (d) electronic pulltab ticket dispensing machines.

Marketing And Sales

Stuart sells its bingo and bingo-related products to a diverse set of end-user groups through more than 300 independent distributors, 11 Stuart-owned distribution outlets in Canada, Stuart's direct sales force and mail order catalogs. Stuart believes that its ability to act as a full-service provider of bingo and bingo-related products and services and its sale of well-known brand names provide it with a significant marketing advantage.

Stuart maintains strong relationships with its distributors, many of whom received assistance from Stuart in the development of their businesses. Distributors are supported by Stuart-sponsored seminars designed to assist the distributors in developing and refining sales and marketing programs and to introduce new products. Stuart believes that the seminars have enhanced customer relations and generated incremental sales.

Relationships with distributors are important because the distributors maintain close contact with bingo halls and are attuned to changing preferences among bingo players. These relationships have resulted in new product ideas and opportunities for Stuart. Stuart has historically been able to capitalize on these opportunities through utilizing its existing distributor network.

Catalogs represent another form of marketing for Stuart. Stuart utilizes catalogs to support distributors, some of which are customized with the distributor's name. Catalogs are also used in direct mail campaigns to end-users. Additionally, customers can order product support information through an automated ordering system.

Stuart also markets its products through advertising in gaming publications and through participation in national, regional and local gaming tradeshows and in distributor tradeshows. For example, in 1998 Stuart was a prominent exhibitor and seminar participant at the Bingo World Expo and at the World Gaming Congress and Exposition, large trade shows that have attracted over 20,000 participants.

During 1998, Stuart continued to direct its marketing efforts toward strengthening relations with its existing distributors and adding new distributors. Stuart plans to focus marketing efforts during 1999 on further developing its distributor network with an emphasis on its electronic bingo products. Stuart has also sponsored group seminars designed to assist distributors and other customers in developing and refining sales and marketing programs and to introduce new products. Stuart believes the seminars have been well received by its distributor network and have been successful in enhancing customer relations and generating incremental sales. Stuart sales personnel also conduct seminars with individual distributors designed to assist them in developing sales and marketing programs, to educate distributors in ways of improving the success of their customers' fund-raising efforts and to provide management assistance to certain distributors. Stuart makes available to distributors catalogs of Stuart's full product line on which distributors may imprint their names and which they may give to their customers.

Stuart markets the bingo hall equipment, as well as the fixed-base and hand-held electronic bingo systems through Stuart's distributor network, by submitting proposals to bid tenders by governmental entities, principally in the United States and Canada, by soliciting for-profit gaming markets, and by submitting proposals directly to Native American gaming facilities. Solicitation of charitable and for-profit gaming markets is performed primarily by Stuart's existing sales staff. Stuart also markets its equipment at selected trade shows and exhibitions.

Bazaar's bingo products are marketed principally through Stuart-owned locations, independent distributors and government agencies. The independent distributors are located in the Canadian provinces of British Columbia, Newfoundland, Ontario, Quebec, and Saskatchewan. Government agencies distribute bingo paper products exclusively in the provinces of British Columbia and Manitoba. Stuart-owned distribution outlets operate in the provinces of Alberta, Manitoba, New Brunswick, Nova Scotia, and Ontario.

Foreign And Export Sales

To date, Stuart has not had a significant volume of export sales. During 1998, approximately 69% of sales were to the United States, 30% to Canada, with the balance representing sales to other foreign countries.

Seasonality And Backlog

Stuart's business is somewhat seasonal as its sales are traditionally stronger during the first half of the year than during the second half of the year. As of December 31, 1998 and 1997, the dollar amount of backlog orders believed to be firm amounted to $2,924,000 and $1,425,000, respectively.

Manufacturing Process

Stuart utilizes technologically advanced equipment to manufacture its products. Manufacturing personnel take an active part in the research and development process to ensure that continual improvements in cost control, quality and technology are achieved. Stuart has undertaken a project to implement perpetual inventory and material resource planning programs at all manufacturing locations via networking on a main frame computer. Stuart has implemented this project at certain of its locations and plans to implement the project at all principal locations by the end of 1999.

On November 13, 1996, Stuart acquired substantially all the assets and assumed certain liabilities of Trade Products, Inc. ("Trade Products"). Stuart's domestic pulltab ticket production is consolidated at Trade Products' manufacturing facility in Lynnwood, Washington. Stuart began to consolidate Stuart's domestic production of bingo paper and ink dabbers is consolidated at its Texas border facilities. Stuart has recently engaged an independent consulting firm to determine if other consolidation efforts would be beneficial to Stuart.

Bingo Paper. Stuart manufactures bingo cards on a number of specialized high-speed web presses capable of printing a variety of different game cards in configurations of 24, 30, 36 and 48 cards per sheet. The bingo cards are produced for inventory and then sold unfinished or are cut and packaged to meet customer specifications.

The introduction of a new sophisticated laser printer in fiscal year 1997 has enabled Stuart to manufacture in excess of 3,000,000 unique bingo cards for use primarily in satellite and high stakes games. Stuart as a result, is actively servicing those markets.

Ink Dabbers. Stuart fills ink dabbers and refills through automated liquid filling lines. Stuart has the ability to customize ink dabbers by applying unique and distinct labels. A number of ink formulas have been developed specifically for use in the bingo industry, but the ink markers have also been sold to a variety of other markets.

Pulltab Tickets. In manufacturing pulltab tickets, Stuart utilizes a number of high speed, multicolor offset presses and a variety of other equipment, including laminators, collators, die-cutters and serial numbering machinery.

Suppliers

The components for Stuart's bingo equipment and the paper and other materials used in printing bingo sheets and pulltab tickets, are generally available from various suppliers at competitive prices. As a result, Stuart is generally not dependent on any single supplier. Stuart experienced stable prices in paper products during 1997. During 1998, the price of paper products increased slightly. The equipment, accessories and supplies which Stuart distributes are standard items and are available from other manufacturers.

Research And Development Activities

Stuart maintains a continuous product development program intended to enhance Stuart's product lines and, thus, increase Stuart's market penetration. Product development efforts in the bingo paper and pulltab ticket product lines are directed toward new product development, as well as, improvement of the graphic design of its current lines. The market for pulltab tickets, in particular, is ever-changing, requiring the continual introduction of new pulltab tickets in response to changing consumer preferences of design and color.

Stuart has substantially increased its commitment to the growing importance of electronic bingo systems in Stuart's overall product mix by increasing the resources for development of its electronic bingo products. Stuart believes that as a result of this increased commitment, Stuart's electronic bingo systems have innovations unique in the industry and that the features offered in its electronic bingo systems are as comprehensive as any found in the market place. Stuart is currently developing the next generation of Stuart's fixed-based and hand-held electronic bingo products. These products were introduced at the Bingo World Expo in the first quarter of 1999.

Stuart continually updates and redesigns its bingo hall equipment products in an effort to maximize the utility, ease of use and reliability of these products. A significant effort is being devoted to the diversification of products within the electrical equipment product line in response to the trend within the bingo and gaming industries toward the adaptation of electrical and mechanical devices. In particular, in 1998 Stuart introduced a new PC-based bingo blower and desk that offers increased video capabilities and a touch screen user interface during the fourth quarter of 1998.

Government Regulation

Overview. Stuart is subject to regulation in most jurisdictions in which its bingo, bingo-related products (including pulltabs) and electronic gaming systems are sold or used by persons or entities licensed to conduct gaming activities. The gaming regulatory requirements vary from jurisdiction to jurisdiction and licensing, other approval or finding of suitability processes with respect to Stuart, its personnel, and its products can be lengthy and expensive. Many jurisdictions have comprehensive licensing, reporting, and operating requirements with respect to the sale and manufacture of bingo and bingo-related products, including bingo paper, pulltab tickets, and electronic bingo equipment. These licensing requirements have a direct impact on the conduct of Stuart's day-to-day operations. Generally, gaming regulatory authorities may deny applications for licenses, other approvals or findings of suitability for any cause they deem reasonable. There can be no assurance that Stuart, its products, or its personnel will receive or be able to maintain any necessary gaming licenses, other approvals or findings of suitability. The loss of a license in a particular jurisdiction will prohibit Stuart from selling products in that jurisdiction and may prohibit Stuart from selling its products in other jurisdictions. The loss of one or more licenses held by Stuart could have a material adverse effect on Stuart's business.

Native American Gaming. Gaming on Native American lands, including the terms and conditions under which gaming equipment can be sold or leased to Native American tribes, is or may be subject to regulation under the laws of the tribes, the laws of the host state and the IGRA. Under the IGRA, gaming activities are classified as Class I, II, or III. Class II gaming includes bingo and, if played at the same location as bingo, pulltab tickets. Class III gaming includes slot machines, video lottery terminals, and casino style games. Native American tribes may conduct Class II gaming under the IGRA without entering into a written compact with the state in which gaming is conducted if such state permits Class II gaming, but must enter into a separate written compact with the state in which they are located in order to conduct Class III gaming activities. Tribal-state compacts vary from state to state. Many compacts require that equipment suppliers meet ongoing registration and licensing requirements of the state and/or the tribe, some establish equipment standards that may limit or prohibit the placement of electronic gaming systems on Indian lands, and some impose background check requirements on the officers, directors and shareholders of gaming equipment suppliers. Under the IGRA, tribes are required to regulate all gaming under ordinances approved by the Chairman of the National Indian

Gaming Commission ("NIGC"). Such ordinances may impose standards and technical requirements on gaming hardware and software, and may impose registration, licensing and background check requirements on gaming equipment suppliers and their officers, directors and shareholders.

Regulation of Traditional Bingo Products and Pulltab Tickets. Traditional paper bingo is legal in all states in the United States except Arkansas, Hawaii, Tennessee and Utah, and is legal in all provinces and territories in Canada. Pulltab tickets currently are legal for sale (either through state lotteries or through other outlets) in approximately 40 states. Each state has developed regulations that impact the style of play for its market. In several states, including Alaska, Minnesota, Nebraska, North Dakota, Ohio, and Washington, it is legal for bars and taverns to sell pulltab tickets on their premises. In Minnesota, Ohio, and North Dakota, pulltab tickets are sold by licensed nonprofit organizations in taverns, while in Alaska and Nebraska, taverns sell pulltab tickets as sales agents of licensed nonprofit organizations. In Washington, taverns sell pulltab tickets directly to their customers.

At present, Alaska, Colorado, Idaho, Illinois, Indiana, Iowa, Kansas, Kentucky, Louisiana, Maine, Michigan, Minnesota, Mississippi, Missouri, Nebraska, New Hampshire, New Jersey, New York, North Dakota, Oklahoma, Pennsylvania, South Carolina, South Dakota, Texas, Vermont, Virginia, Washington, West Virginia, and Wisconsin require bingo and/or charitable gaming manufacturers and/or suppliers to be licensed. Stuart is currently licensed in each of these jurisdictions, except for Maine and Virginia. Stuart has not applied for a license in Maine and Virginia and does not conduct activities that it believes are subject to licensing in those states. Stuart is permitted to and does ship products to licensed distributors in Maine and Virginia. Stuart also holds a Bingo Suppliers License in Los Angeles, California and in Anne Arundel County, Maryland and licenses from several Native American tribes that require licensing through their own tribal gaming commissions. Stuart is registered in the Provinces of Ontario, Manitoba, New Brunswick, and Nova Scotia, which require the registration of manufacturers.

In Canada, the Canadian National Gaming Law gives provincial governments the ultimate authority to conduct and manage all lottery schemes, including pulltabs and bingo. Ontario allows the sale of pulltab tickets at third-party retail locations under charity license. In November 1997, Stuart was awarded a five-year provincial contract by the OGC to be the sole supplier of pulltab tickets to charity licensed retail locations in the Province of Ontario. The Provinces of British Columbia and Manitoba also have contracts with manufacturers to supply pulltab tickets and bingo paper. There is nothing to prevent any of the other Provinces from issuing requests for proposals for bingo paper, pulltab tickets or any other device utilized in legalized gaming. There can be no assurance that Stuart would be successful if additional contracts were tendered for these types of products.

Because not all Stuart's products are legally allowed to be sold in every locality to which Stuart ships products, Stuart routinely contacts state agencies to determine the existence and nature of any state and local restrictions applicable to its products in order to comply with such restrictions.

Regulation of Electronic Gaming Systems. Stuart's electronic products, including System 12™ and Power Bingo King™, are more heavily regulated than traditional paper bingo, and federal, state, provincial, tribal and local regulations vary by jurisdiction.

IGRA defines Class II gaming to include "the game of chance commonly known as bingo, whether or not electronic, computer or other technologic aids are used in connection therewith," and defines Class III gaming to include "electronic or electromechanical facsimiles of any game of chance or slot machines of any kind." Stuart believes that both its System 12™ and Power Bingo King™ are Class II games. In the event that either System 12™ or Power Bingo King™ is classified as a Class III device, such a designation would either (a) reduce the potential market for the devices, because only Indian gaming halls that had entered into a tribal-state compact that permits Class III electronic gaming systems would be permitted to use the device, or (b) require Stuart to modify System 12™ or Power Bingo King™ to have it reclassified as a Class II game. If programmed to play video poker, video keno, video bingo, video slots, or video pulltab tickets, System 12™ is properly classified as a Class III gaming system subject to the full range of regulations applicable to such systems.

Electronic bingo is less widely permitted than paper bingo. Electronic bingo is currently operated at locations in over 25 states. Because many state laws and regulations are silent with respect to electronic bingo, changes in regulatory and enforcement policies could impact the continued operation of electronic bingo in these states.

Some jurisdictions require the inspection, approval or modification of electronic bingo systems before sale in those states. In February 1998, Stuart announced that the Texas Lottery Commission had approved Stuart's application to enter the Texas market with its fixed-base product System 12™. Stuart has submitted System 12™ for approval in Mississippi but has not yet submitted, nor received, approval for System 12™ in any other charitable gaming jurisdiction in the United States (other than various tribal locations). Stuart is licensed by the Colorado Limited Gaming Commission to manufacture and sell slot machines in Colorado. This license will permit Stuart to market System 12™ in Colorado once the system is tested and approved by the Commission. Stuart has received written approvals for its Power Bingo King™ system in at least ten states. Written approvals is not required in certain jurisdictions.

Although Canadian federal law prohibits the playing of games of chance on or through slot machines, computer or video devices, this law excepts playing such games in halls operated or authorized by the provincial governments. The Manitoba Lottery Corporation has installed System 12™ in its government-owned bingo halls. Stuart is currently marketing System 12™ to the other provincial governments. Ontario is currently the only province that permits the use of hand-held bingo systems, and such systems are only permitted to be used in conjunction with paper bingo.

General Regulation of Stockholders and Other Security Holders of Publicly Traded Corporations. In certain jurisdictions, any beneficial owner of the Old Common Stock or New Common Stock may be subject on a discretionary basis to being required to file applications with gaming regulatory authorities, to being investigated and found suitable or to being qualified. The gaming laws and regulations of some jurisdictions provide that beneficial owners of more than 5% of the common stock and, potentially, holders of the debt securities of a company may be subject to certain reporting procedures and may be required to be investigated and licensed, qualified or found suitable. Stuart's Certificate of Incorporation authorizes Stuart under certain circumstances to redeem, at the lesser of the holder's original investment in Stuart or the current market price, the Old Common Stock held by any person whose status as a shareholder may jeopardize Stuart's gaming licenses or approvals. Likewise, the Plan provides for certain restrictions on distribution of New Common Stock to comply with the Gaming Regulations. See "ADDITIONAL IMPLEMENTION OF THE PLAN – Description of Gaming Regulations."

Federal Regulation. The Federal Gambling Devices Act of 1962 (the "Federal Act") makes it unlawful for a person to transport in interstate or foreign commerce or receive from interstate or foreign commerce any gambling device or component thereof, unless the person is registered with the Attorney General of the United States. Stuart has registered and must renew its registration annually. In addition, various record keeping and equipment identification requirements are imposed by the Federal Act. Violation of the Federal Act is a criminal act and penalties may include seizure and forfeiture of the equipment as well as other penalties.

Application of Future or Additional Regulatory Requirements. In the future, Stuart intends to seek the necessary licenses, approvals, and findings of suitability for Stuart, its products, and its personnel in all jurisdictions throughout the world where significant sales are anticipated to be made. However, there can be no assurance that such licenses, approvals, or findings of suitability will be obtained, that they will not be revoked, suspended, or conditioned or that they will be obtained in a timely manner. If a license, approval, or finding of suitability is required by a regulatory authority and Stuart fails to seek, does not receive the necessary approved license or finding of suitability, or the necessary license approval or finding of suitability is revoked, Stuart may be prohibited from selling its products for use in the respective jurisdiction or may be required to sell its products through other licensed entities at a reduced profit to Stuart.

Employees

As of December 31, 1998, Stuart and its Subsidiaries had approximately 1,740 full-time employees in the United States, Canada and Mexico. Approximately 250 employees of Stuart Entertainment Mexico are members of a union subject to a collective bargaining agreement. The collective bargaining agreement does not place any significant financial or operational burdens on Stuart. A group of approximately 300 employees in the St. Catherines, Ontario plant recently voted to organize and be represented by the United Steelworkers of America. Stuart considers relations with its employees to be good. Stuart's employee benefits include medical insurance, long-term disability insurance, and life insurance. Stuart also offers a 401(K) retirement plan to all eligible employees.

Facilities

Stuart's corporate offices are currently located in Council Bluffs, Iowa. Stuart intends to relocate its corporate offices to the Minneapolis/St. Paul, Minnesota area. The following table sets forth Stuart's principal properties as of the Petition Date:

as a director of Stuart.

Location	Business Segment	Owned or Leased	Expiration Date	Square Feet
Council Bluffs, Iowa	Corporate Office	Leased	12/31/1999(1)	25,000
McAllen, Texas	Bingo paper Ink dabbers General Merchandise	Leased	03/31/2008(2)	157,600
Reynosa, Mexico	Bingo paper	Leased	12/31/2009(3)	130,132
St. Catharines, Ontario	Bingo paper Pulltab tickets Ink dabbers	Leased	08/31/2000(4)	158,000
St. Catharines, Ontario	General merchandise	Leased	08/31/2000(4)	24,057
Littleton, Colorado	Video King gaming systems Bingo hall equipment	Leased	08/31/2001(4)	20,000
Lynnwood, Washington	Pulltab tickets Bingo paper	Leased	11/13/2006(5)	165,000

(1) Stuart amended the lease agreement on June 30, 1998. Pursuant to this amendment, Stuart has the option to renew the lease for one additional nine month period. Stuart plans to relocate its corporate headquarters to the Minneapolis, Minnesota but may decide to keep the Council Bluffs location open for a certain period, which may require Stuart to exercise its option to renew the lease.

(2) Stuart has the option to renew this lease for one additional five-year period. Stuart has rejected the lease for the McAllen, Texas facility and will vacate that facility by November 15, 1999.

(3) Stuart Entertainment S.A. de C.V., Stuart's wholly-owned Mexican subsidiary, is the lessee under this lease, and Stuart is guarantor. Stuart has obtained the Bankruptcy Court's authority to assume its obligations as guarantor under the lease.

(4) Stuart has the option to renew this lease for two additional five-year periods.

(5) Stuart has the option to renew this lease for one additional ten-year period.

Substantially all Stuart's property and equipment are subject to liens to secure borrowings by Stuart under the DIP Facility (or other financing agreements). In general, Stuart's properties and equipment are in good condition and are considered to be adequate for their present use.

Current Directors and Executive Officers

Directors. The following table sets forth the name and age of each director of Stuart, his principal occupation and business experience during the past five years, and the year of commencement of his term as a director of Stuart.

Name and Age	Principal Occupation or Employment During the Past Five Years; Other Directorships	Director Since
Ernie Marchand (41)	**Executive Vice President and Chief Operating Officer since November 1998; Director of Special Projects for Greg Thompson Production from April 1993 to November 1998.**	1999
Lawrence X. Taylor, III (34)	Executive Vice President and Chief Financial Officer since October 1998; Director of Financial Planning & Analysis for Grand Casinos, Inc. from June 1998 to October 1998; Director of Investor Relations for Grand Casinos., Inc. from 1996 to June 1998; Regional Manager – Financial Planning & Analysis for Grand Casinos Resorts, Inc. from 1994-1996.	1999
Jock Patton (53)	Private investor since 1997, Mr. Patton also served as president of StockVal, Inc. from November 1993 to June 1997. Mr. Patton also serves as a director of Hypercom Corporation and JDA Software Group, Inc. and is a trustee of the Pilgrim Mutual Funds, a group of eight mutual funds. Mr. Patton was appointed to the board of directors effective February 3, 1999.	1999
Ira Starr (39)	Managing Director of Long Point Capital, Inc. since January 1998; vice president of Morgan, Lewis, Githens & Ahn, an investment banking firm, from 1988 to 1993 and a managing director from 1994 to December 1997.	1994
Joseph M. Valandra (43)	Chairman of the Board, Chief Executive Officer and President since October 1998. Vice President of Grand Casinos, Inc. from November 1993 to October 1998.	1998

Executive Officers. The following table sets forth the name and age of each executive officer of Stuart, his principal occupation and business experience during the past five years, and the year of commencement of his term as an executive officer of Stuart.

Name and Age	Present Executive Officers	Executive Officer Since
Joseph M. Valandra (43)	**Chairman of the Board, Chief Executive Officer and President since October 1998. Vice President of Grand Casinos, Inc. from November 1993 to October 1998.**	1998
Ernie Marchand (41)	**Executive Vice President and Chief Operating Officer since November 1998; Director of Special Projects for Greg Thompson Production from April 1993 to November 1998.**	1998
Lawrence X. Taylor, III (34)	Executive Vice President and Chief Financial Officer since October 1998; Director of Financial Planning & Analysis for Grand Casinos, Inc. from June 1998 to October 1998; Director of Investor Relations for Grand Casinos., Inc. from 1996 to June 1998; Regional Manager - Financial Planning & Analysis for Grand Casinos Resorts, Inc. from 1994-1996.	1998
Paul Curtin (40)	Senior Vice President – Compliance and Regulatory Affairs since February 1999. General Manager – Texas/Mexico from February 1998 to February 1999; General Manager – Mexico since prior to April 1994 to February 1998.	1999
Jimmy D. Helton (50)	Senior Vice President – Strategic Planning since February 1999. Director of Strategic Planning & Analysis from October 1998 to February 1999; Construction Controller at Grand Casinos Resorts, Inc. from prior to April 1994 to April 1998.	1999
Clement F. Chantiam (39)	Senior Vice President – New Business & Special Projects since February 1999. Executive Vice President from November 1992 to February 1999, and Vice President – Manufacturing from March 1989 to November 1992.	1989
Leslie A. Lombardi (44)	Senior Vice President – Information Systems since February 1999; Vice President Information Systems from July 1997 to February 1999; Manager of Information Technology at Ohmed, Inc. from September 1986 to July 1997.	1999
Lori McLaughlin (44)	Senior Vice President – Bingo Paper, Ink and General Merchandise since February 1999. Divisional Vice President - Tabs Manufacturing November 1996 to February 1999; Vice President Manufacturing for Trade Products, Inc. from prior to April 1994 to November 1996.	1999
Douglas W. Rye (33)	Senior Vice President – Gaming Ticket Division since February 1999; Division Vice President – Canadian Sales from November 1996 to February 1999; General Manager of Operations of Bazaar & Novelty from October 1995 to November 1996; Controller of Bazaar & Novelty from June 1991 to October 1995.	1999
Michael A.Schalk (51)	Senior Vice President, General Counsel and Corporate Secretary since February 1999Corporate Secretary and Resident Counsel from January 1991 to February 1999.	1999

Prepetition Debt Structure

The Notes

On November 16, 1996, Stuart raised \$100 million by issuing \$100 million aggregate principal amount of 12½% Senior Subordinated Notes due November 15, 2004 (the "Notes"). The Notes were issued in a private placement in reliance upon Rule 144A under the Securities Act of 1933, as amended. Interest on the Notes is payable semi-annually in arrears on May 15 and November 15. Stuart did not make the May 15, 1999 interest payment on the Notes and approximately $9,097,221 in unpaid interest has accrued as of the Petition Date. The grace period with respect to such payment expired on June 15, 1999, thereby resulting in an "Event of Default" under the Indenture governing the terms of the Notes (the "Indenture"). HSBC Bank USA, formerly known as Marine Midland Bank, is the Indenture Trustee for the Notes. The Notes mature on November 15, 2004. The Indenture imposes certain limitations on Stuart's ability to, among other things, incur additional indebtedness, pay dividends or make certain other restricted payments, and consummate certain asset sales.

Stuart used the net proceeds from the Notes (i) to repay in full existing revolving credit and term facilities, at which time such facilities were cancelled, and certain other outstanding debt instruments, and (ii) to acquire substantially all of the assets and assume certain liabilities of Trade Products, as described in the Asset Purchase Agreement, dated August 6, 1996, and amended on October 10, 1996, between Stuart, Trade Products, and Harry Poll, Ronald G. Rudy and Harry Wirth as the shareholders of Trade Products (collectively, the "Shareholders"). Stuart purchased the Assets on November 13, 1996, for a total purchase price of $37.2 million, subject to certain post-closing adjustments, plus the issuance of warrants to purchase 300,000 shares of Stuart's Old Common Stock. Neither Trade Products nor the Shareholders were affiliated with Stuart.

Prepetition Working Capital Facility

In November 1997, Stuart entered into a credit facility consisting of two loan and security agreements, one between Stuart and Congress Financial Corporation ("Congress") (Central) (the "U.S. Facility") and one between Bingo Press & Specialty Limited, a wholly owned subsidiary of Stuart ("Bazaar"), and Congress Financial Corporation (Canada) (the "Canadian Facility" and collectively with the U.S. Facility, the "Credit Facility"). The Credit Facility provided for maximum borrowings of up to $30 million, of which up to $20 million could be borrowed under the U.S. Facility and up to US$10 million could be borrowed under the Canadian Facility. The Credit Facility provided for a three-year term and expires in November 2000. The Credit Facility was secured by substantially all of Stuart's operating assets.

The Credit Facility imposed certain covenants and other requirements on Stuart and Bazaar (the "Borrowers"), including the requirement that the Borrowers maintain a certain minimum level of net worth. As of the Petition Date, the Borrowers were not compliance with many of these covenants. The Credit Facility also contained cross-default provisions with any other agreement, document, or instrument relating to indebtedness for borrowed money in an amount in excess of $50,000 owing to any person other than Congress. These cross-default provisions provided that, if Stuart were in default under any other applicable indebtedness, Stuart also would be in default under the Credit Facility. Accordingly, Stuart's default under the Notes was an "Event of Default" under the Credit Facility. As of the Petition Date, Stuart had not obtained a waiver of these defaults. Congress had not, however, indicated any intention to declare Stuart in default. Congress did not exercise its remedies under the Credit Facility, so the obligations outstanding under the Credit Facility were not accelerated and payable in full as of the Petition Date. Rather, Congress agreed to extend the U.S. Facility into the postpetition period to provide Stuart with interim debtor-in-possession financing in accordance with an order of the Bankruptcy Court entered on the Petition Date.

In accordance with a subsequent order of the Bankruptcy Court, Stuart entered into a replacement $30 million revolving credit facility with Foothill Capital Corporation (the "Foothill Facility") for debtor-in-possession financing throughout the Chapter 11 Case. Obligations under the Foothill Facility are secured by substantially all Stuart's operating assets, with certain assets of certain of Stuart's subsidiaries provided additional borrowing base for revolving loans. Certain proceeds of the Foothill Facility were required to be used to satisfy all outstanding obligations under the Credit Facility with Congress. Simultaneously with the closing of the Foothill Facility, all Stuart's and Bazaar's obligations to Congress under the Credit Facility were satisfied in full. All obligations under the Foothill Facility are to be satisfied in accordance with Section 2.7 of the Plan.

Prepetition Capital Structure

General

Stuart is a Delaware corporation and its affairs are governed by its Amended and Restated Certificate of Incorporation and Amended and Restated Bylaws and the Delaware General Corporation Law.

The authorized capital stock of Stuart consists of 30,000,000 shares of Old Common Stock, par value $0.01 per share. As of the Petition Date, there were 6,946,211 shares of Old Common Stock issued and outstanding, held of record by approximately 1,500 stockholders.

Common Stock

Holders of shares of Old Common Stock are entitled to one vote per share on all matters to be voted on by stockholders and do not have cumulative voting rights. The holders of Old Common Stock are entitled to share ratably in dividends, if any, as may be declared from time to time by the Board of Directors of Stuart in its discretion from funds legally available therefor. In the event of liquidation, dissolution, or winding up of Stuart, the holders of Old Common Stock are entitled to share ratably in all assets available for distribution to the stockholders after payment of Stuart's liabilities. The Old Common Stock has no preemptive or other subscription rights, and there are no conversion rights or redemption or sinking fund provisions with respect to such shares. All of the outstanding shares of Old Common Stock are fully paid and nonassessable.

Anti-Takeover Provisions of Delaware Law

Stuart is subject to the provisions of Section 203 of the Delaware General Corporation Law. In general, the statute prohibits a publicly held Delaware corporation from engaging in a "business combination" with an "interested stockholder" for a period of three years after the date that the person became an interested stockholder unless (with certain exceptions) the business combination or the transaction in which the person became an interested stockholder is approved in a prescribed manner. Generally, a "business combination" includes a merger, asset or stock sale or other transaction resulting in a financial benefit to the stockholder, and an "interested stockholder" is a person who, together with affiliates and associates, owns (or within three years prior, did own) fifteen percent (15%) or more of the corporation's outstanding voting stock. This provision may have the effect of delaying, deferring or preventing a change in control of Stuart without further action by the stockholders.

Delisting from NASDAQ SmallCap Market

On February 26, 1998, NASDAQ notified Stuart that Stuart was not in compliance with the new net tangible assets/market capitalization/net income maintenance requirements that became effective on February 23, 1998. On July 20, 1998, NASDAQ notified Stuart that, effective July 28, 1998, the Old Common Stock was scheduled for delisting from the NASDAQ SmallCap Market. On July 28, 1998, the Common Stock was delisted from the NASDAQ SmallCap Market and is currently quoted on the OTC Electronic Bulletin Board under the symbol "STUA." As a result, an investor may now find it more difficult to dispose of, and to obtain accurate quotations as to the value of, the Old Common Stock.

If the trading price of the Old Common Stock is less than $5.00 per share at a time when Stuart's net tangible assets total less than $5,000,000, trading in the Old Common Stock will also be subject to the requirements of Rule 15g-9 promulgated under the Securities Exchange Act of 1934, as amended. Under such rule, broker/dealers who recommend such low-priced securities to persons other than established customers and accredited investors must satisfy special sales practice requirements, including a requirement that they make an individualized written suitability determination for the purchaser and receive the purchaser's written consent before the transaction. The Securities Enforcement Remedies and Penny Stock Reform Act of 1990 also requires additional disclosure in connection with any trades involving a stock defined as a "penny stock" (generally, according to recent regulations adopted by the Securities and Exchange Commission, any equity security not traded on an exchange or quoted on the NASDAQ SmallCap Market that has a market price of less than $5.00 per share, subject to certain exceptions), including the delivery, before any penny stock transaction, of a disclosure schedule explaining the penny stock market and the risks associated with such stock. Such requirements could have the effect of severely limiting the market liquidity of the Old Common Stock.

Events Precipitating Chapter 11 Filing

Stuart's operating margins have suffered recent declines in part because of increased competition, including competition from companies offering new forms of gaming that are outside the traditional consumable bingo and pulltab markets that Stuart supplies. Stuart has attempted to offset this increase in competition by developing electronic bingo and pulltab systems and by consolidating manufacturing operations. Additionally, Stuart has been pursuing an aggressive acquisition program in an effort to quickly broaden its product offerings. In order to finance these acquisitions, Stuart took on substantial debt, including the Notes.

Stuart also implemented a number of initiatives in an effort to improve operations and reduce costs. Specifically, Stuart announced plans to relocate its headquarters to the Minneapolis/St. Paul, Minnesota area and to close certain of its production facilities, including a manufacturing and distribution facility in McAllen, Texas, whose operations could be combined with and moved to other existing Stuart facilities.

Despite recent improvements in operations, the benefits from Stuart's initiatives have not completely offset the effects of declining margins caused by increased competition and the apparent decline in the popularity of traditional forms of bingo and pulltabs. Furthermore, Stuart's declining margins and its inability to generate profits as projected resulted in cash flow levels insufficient to service Stuart's current debt, resulting in defaults under the Indenture and the Credit Facility as described above.

In an effort to address the viability of Stuart's highly leveraged capital structure and explore opportunities to restructure its debt, Stuart engaged the assistance of Wasserstein Perella & Co. ("Wasserstein"), as its financial advisor, and Squire, Sanders & Dempsey, L.L.P ("SS&D") as its restructuring counsel, in January 1999. Stuart, Wasserstein and SS&D contacted holders of Notes to facilitate the formation of an ad hoc committee of holders of the Notes to discuss restructuring alternatives ahead of the May 15, 1999 interest payment on the Notes.

The Restructuring Agreement

Negotiations regarding a restructuring of Stuart's debt and equity commenced with members of the ad hoc committee. On May 21, 1999, Stuart announced that it had reached an agreement with certain members the ad hoc committee regarding a restructuring of Stuart's debt and equity (the "Restructuring Agreement"). Before the completion of the negotiations that culminated in the Restructuring Agreement, Contrarian Capital Management, L.L.C., ("Contrarian"), a member of the ad hoc committee, purchased all Notes held by another member of the ad hoc committee who had engaged in those negotiations. As of May 24, 1999, Contrarian and Salomon Smith Barney had executed the Restructuring Agreement, which provided for a full conversion of the Notes into 100% of the equity in the reorganized company and a corresponding cancellation of existing equity. In July 1999, after Salomon Smith Barney executed the Restructuring Agreement, Contrarian purchased all the Notes held by Salomon Smith Barney such that Contrarian currently holds in excess of 50% of the Notes.

Stuart did not make the May 15, 1999 interest payment to holders of the Notes. In accordance with the Restructuring Agreement, however, Contrarian has agreed to refrain from taking any action to enforce the Notes or the obligations of Stuart under the Indenture for a period of time designed to accommodate the Chapter 11 process and confirmation of the Plan.

Under the Restructuring Agreement, upon the effectiveness of the Plan, the holders of the Notes will receive one hundred percent (100%) of the common stock issued and outstanding on that date, subject to dilution by shares reserved for issuance under the Executive Management Options and the Equity Incentive Options. See "OVERVIEW OF THE PLAN – Description of Transactions to be Implemented in Connection with the Plan" for a detailed description of the Executive Management Options and the Equity Incentive Options. The Restructuring Agreement originally contemplated that the Old Common Stock would be canceled and that holders of Old Common Stock would receive warrants to obtain shares of New Common Stock. Because Stuart intends to become a private company after the Effective Date of the Plan (*see* "OVERVIEW OF THE PLAN – Description of Transactions to be Implemented in Connection with the Plan – Private Company Status."), Contrarian consented to changing this treatment for purposes of the Plan such that, subject to numerous conditions, including approval by the Bankruptcy Court in the Chapter 11 Case, holders of Old Common Stock will, rather than warrants, receive a Pro Rata share of $150,000 in Cash under the Plan. The Restructuring Agreement also provides that the Credit Facility in the principal amount of $30 million will be restructured or satisfied under a new senior secured working capital facility. See "SIGNIFICANT EVENTS DURING THE CHAPTER 11 CASE – Post-Petition Financing." Further, under the Restructuring Agreement, Contrarian has agreed to support the payment of all trade claims in the ordinary course of Stuart's business.

Efforts to Solicit an Alternative Transaction

In view of this full conversion of the Notes, the ad hoc committee and Stuart agreed to solicit third party offers for an outright sale that might generate a better recovery to creditors than the debt conversion contemplated by the Restructuring Agreement. Wasserstein directed the solicitation process and initially identified 13 prospects and ultimately received two non-binding offers — including one from an entity that was not one of the original 13 prospects. In close consultation with Wasserstein and members of the ad hoc committee, Stuart considered the two proposals, and determined that neither would provide a greater potential recovery to creditors than the debt conversion under the Restructuring Agreement. Accordingly, Stuart rejected the proposals and filed its Chapter 11 petition in order to propose the restructuring contemplated by the Restructuring Agreement, which Stuart believes will provide the greatest potential recovery for creditors with the greatest likelihood of being consummated.

Closure of McAllen, Texas Plant

In addition to operations maintained in facilities located in Ontario, Colorado, California, and Washington, Stuart also maintains certain manufacturing and distribution operations at two facilities in McAllen, Texas and Reynosa, Mexico. Stuart has determined that it is in the best interests of creditors and its ongoing business operations to close the McAllen facility and migrate all operations conducted there to the Reynosa facility and possibly other current facilities. Stuart believes that such changes will enhance its manufacturing and operational efficiencies and relieve it of the significant financial burdens arising under the McAllen lease. As of the Petition Date, Stuart was negotiating with the landlord for both the McAllen and Reynosa facilities, ProLogis Trust, regarding the date Stuart will vacate the McAllen facility and the terms and conditions of an amendment to the lease covering the Reynosa facility. Stuart has obtained the Bankruptcy Court's authority to reject the lease covering the McAllen facility, and Stuart expects to vacate that facility by no later than November 15, 1999.

SIGNIFICANT EVENTS DURING THE CHAPTER 11 CASE

Commencement of the Chapter 11 Case

On August 13, 1999 (the "Petition Date"), in furtherance of its restructuring efforts, Stuart filed its voluntary petition for relief under Chapter 11 of the Bankruptcy Code. The Chapter 11 Case was assigned to the Honorable Mary F. Walrath, United States Bankruptcy Judge for the District of Delaware. Since the Petition Date, Stuart has continued to operate its businesses and manage its properties as debtor-in-possession under Sections 1107(a) and 1108 of the Bankruptcy Code. No trustee or official committee of unsecured creditors has been appointed in the Chapter 11 Case.

First Day Orders

On or shortly after the Petition Date, the Bankruptcy Court entered several orders authorizing Stuart to pay various prepetition claims and granting other relief necessary to help Stuart stabilize its day-to-day business operations. These orders were designed to allow Stuart to continue business operations with minimum disruptions and dislocations, and to ease the strain on Stuart's relationships with its employees and other parties. Included among the orders entered by the Bankruptcy Court were orders authorizing

Stuart to: (a) pay wages, salaries, employment taxes, employee benefit payments, and workers compensation payments; (b) pay certain trade creditors; (c) maintain certain bank accounts, cash management systems and business forms; and (d) ensure continued utility service.

Post-Petition Financing

Before the Petition Date, Stuart and certain of its operating subsidiaries negotiated with Foothill Capital Corporation ("Foothill"), the DIP Lender, to provide approximately $30 million in debtor-in-possession financing to Stuart (along with post-petition financing to certain of Stuart's non-debtor operating Subsidiaries), of which $8 million is a term loan and a maximum of $22 million is a revolving credit line. Upon final approval by the Bankruptcy Court, the post-petition financing provided by Foothill satisfied all outstanding debt to Stuart's prepetition working capital lender, Congress Financial Corporation. The Foothill financing is secured by senior liens on significant portions of the assets of Stuart and its operating Subsidiaries and entitled to satisfaction as a super-priority administrative expense claim (subject to a carveout for fees to the U.S. trustee and specific professionals). A final hearing on approval of the DIP Facility was held on September 14, 1999, at which time the Bankruptcy Court entered the DIP Financing Order, approving the DIP Facility. The DIP Financing Order terminates, unless extended, on the earliest of: (1) August 31, 2000; (2) the appointment of a Chapter 11 trustee; (3) the effective date of a confirmed plan of reorganization; (4) conversion of the Chapter 11 Case to one under Chapter 7; (5) dismissal of the Chapter 11 Case; and (6) the appointment of an examiner with power to manage or operate the financial affairs of the Debtor.

Retention of Professionals

On or shortly after the Petition Date, the Bankruptcy Court entered orders authorizing Stuart to retain, among others: (a) Squire, Sanders & Dempsey L.L.P., 40 North Central Avenue, Suite 2700, Phoenix, Arizona 85004, as bankruptcy and reorganization counsel; (b) Saul, Ewing, Remick & Saul, 222 Delaware Avenue, Suite 1200, Wilmington, Delaware 19899, as local bankruptcy and reorganization counsel; (c) Wasserstein Perella & Co., 32 West 52nd Street, New York, New York 10019, as financial advisors; (d) Arthur Andersen LLP, 501 North 44th Street, Suite 300, Phoenix, Arizona 85008, as accountants and as the Voting Agent; and (e) Deloitte & Touche LLP, 2000 First National Center, Omaha, Nebraska, as independent auditors and accounting and tax consultants.

OVERVIEW OF THE PLAN

A copy of the Plan accompanies this Disclosure Statement as Exhibit 1. The following summary of the material provisions of the Plan is qualified in its entirety by the specific provisions of the Plan, including the Plan's definitions of certain terms used below.

Brief Explanation of Chapter 11 Reorganization

Chapter 11 of the Bankruptcy Code is the principal reorganization chapter of the Bankruptcy Code. Under Chapter 11, a debtor is authorized to reorganize its business for the benefit of itself and its creditors and shareholders. Confirmation of a plan of reorganization is the principal objective of a Chapter 11 case.

In general, a Chapter 11 plan of reorganization (a) divides claims and equity interests into separate classes, (b) specifies the property that each class is to receive under the plan, and (c) contains other provisions necessary to the reorganization of the debtor. A Chapter 11 plan may specify that certain classes of claims or equity interests are either to be paid in full upon the effective date of the plan, reinstated, or their legal, equitable and contractual rights are to remain unchanged by the reorganization effectuated by the plan. Such classes are referred to under the Bankruptcy Code as "unimpaired" and, because of such favorable treatment, are deemed to accept the plan. Accordingly, it is not necessary to solicit votes from the holders of claims or equity interest in such classes. A Chapter 11 plan also may specify that certain classes will not receive any distribution of property. Such classes are deemed to reject the plan.

All other classes of claims and equity interests contain "impaired" claims and equity interests entitled to vote on the plan. As a condition to confirmation, the Bankruptcy Code generally requires that each impaired class of claims or equity interests votes to accept a plan. Acceptances must be received (a) from the holders of claims constituting at least two-thirds in dollar amount and more than one-half in number of the allowed claims in each impaired class of claims that have voted to accept or reject the plan, and (b) from the holders of at least two-thirds in amount of the allowed equity interests in each impaired class of equity interest that have voted to accept or reject the plan. If any class or classes of claims or equity interests entitled to vote with respect to the plan rejects the plan, upon request of the plan proponents, the Bankruptcy Court may nevertheless confirm the plan if certain minimum treatment standards are met with respect to such class or classes.

Chapter 11 of the Bankruptcy Code does not require each holder of a claim or equity interest to vote in favor of a plan of reorganization in order for the bankruptcy court to confirm the plan. However, the Bankruptcy Court must find that the plan of reorganization meets a number of statutory tests (other than the voting requirements described in this section) before it may confirm, or approve, the plan of reorganization. Many of these tests are designed to protect the interest of holders of claims or equity interest who do not vote to accept the plan of reorganization but who will nonetheless be bound by the plan's provisions if it is confirmed by the Bankruptcy Court.

Solicitation of Acceptances of the Plan

Stuart is seeking acceptances of the Plan from holders of Allowed Claims classified in Classes 3A, 4, 5, 6, and 7 under the Plan, which are the only Classes entitled to vote under the Plan. If the requisite acceptances are received, Stuart will use the acceptances as evidenced by Ballots solicited in accordance with this Disclosure Statement and the Disclosure Statement Approval Order to seek confirmation of the Plan under Chapter 11 of the Bankruptcy Code.

If any impaired Class is determined to have rejected the Plan in accordance with Section 1126 of the Bankruptcy Code, Stuart may use the provisions of Section 1129(b) of the Bankruptcy Code to satisfy the requirements for confirmation of the Plan. See "ACCEPTANCE AND CONFIRMATION OF THE PLAN – Confirmation – Confirmation Without Acceptance by All Impaired Classes."

Stuart believes that this Disclosure Statement complies with applicable bankruptcy and non-bankruptcy law. This Disclosure Statement and the Plan (along with the Plan Supplement) are being transmitted to all known holders of impaired Claims and Equity Interests. Stuart believes that this Disclosure Statement contains adequate information for all holders of impaired Claims and Equity Interests to cast an informed vote to accept or reject the Plan. Furthermore, Stuart believes that holders of impaired Claims and Equity Interests will obtain a greater recovery under the Plan than they would otherwise obtain if Stuart's assets were liquidated under Chapter 7 of the Bankruptcy Code and that the Plan will enable Stuart to emerge from Chapter 11 as a viable and competitive enterprise, enhancing Stuart's ability to return to profitability.

If the Plan is confirmed by the Bankruptcy Court, each holder of an impaired Claim will receive the same pro rata consideration as other holders of Claims in the same Class, whether or not such holder voted to accept the Plan. Moreover, upon Confirmation, the Plan will bind all creditors and equity interest holders regardless of whether or not such creditors and equity interest holders voted to accept the Plan.

Unimpaired Classes

The following Classes of Claims are not impaired under the Plan, and under Section 1126(f) of the Bankruptcy Code, are conclusively deemed to accept the Plan, and are not entitled to vote on the Plan:

Class 1	Priority Claims
Class 2	Secured Tax Claims
Class 3	Miscellaneous Secured Claims

Classification of Claims and Equity Interests

Section 1123 of the Bankruptcy Code provides that a plan of reorganization must classify claims against a debtor. Under Section 1122 of the Bankruptcy Code, a plan must classify claims and equity interests into classes that contain substantially similar claims and interests. The Plan divides the Claims of known Creditors and the Equity Interests into Classes and sets forth the treatment offered each Class. Stuart believes it has classified all Claims and Equity Interests in compliance with the provisions of Section 1122 of the Bankruptcy Code, but it is possible that a Creditor or Equity Interest holder may challenge such classification of Claims and Equity Interests and that the Bankruptcy Court may find that a different classification is required for the Plan to be confirmed. If so, Stuart intends, to the extent permitted by the Bankruptcy Code and the provisions of the Plan, to amend or revoke the Plan and file an amended or different Plan that would make modifications to the classification of Claims or Equity Interests required by the Bankruptcy Court for confirmation.

The Classes under the Plan take into account the differing nature and priority of Claims against Stuart. Section 101(5) of the Bankruptcy Code defines "claim" as a "right to payment, whether or not such right is reduced to judgment, liquidated, fixed, contingent, matured, unmatured, disputed, undisputed, legal, equitable, secured, or unsecured; or a "right to an equitable remedy for breach of performance if such breach gives rise to a right to payment whether or not such right to an equitable remedy is reduced to judgment, fixed, contingent, matured, unmatured, disputed, undisputed, secured, or unsecured." A "claim" against Stuart also includes a Claim against Stuart's property as provided in Section 102(2) of the Bankruptcy Code. An "interest" is an equity interest in a debtor.

Because Stuart believes that the New Common Stock to be issued to holders of Class 4 Claims will have limited liquidity and because potentially all holders of New Common Stock must comply with the Gaming Requirements (*see* "ADDITIONAL IMPLEMENTION OF THE PLAN – Description of Gaming Regulations"), with which individual investors may be unable or unwilling to comply, the Plan provides for a means by which holders of Notes may receive a Cash payment rather than shares of New Common Stock. Receipt of a Cash payment in lieu of New Common Stock is strictly voluntary under the Plan, and any holder of Notes may make a Noteholder Election, by so indicating on its Ballot, to have its Claim treated with a Cash payment, or treated with a distribution of New Common Stock. For a complete description of the Noteholder Election and the Cash Payment Option, *see* "OVERVIEW OF THE PLAN – Treatment of Claims and Equity Interests Under the Plan – Classified Claims."

For the holder of a Claim to participate in a reorganization plan and receive the treatment offered to the class in which it is classified, its Claim must be Allowed. Under the Plan, an Allowed Claim is defined as a Claim: (a) proof of which, requests for payment of which, or application for allowance of which, was filed or deemed filed on or before the Bar Date,

Administrative Claim Bar Date, or the Professional Fee Bar Date, as applicable, for filing proofs of claim or requests for payment for Claims of such type against the Debtor; (b) if no proof of claim is filed, which has been or is ever listed by the Debtor in the Schedules as liquidated in amount and not disputed or contingent; or (c) a Claim that is allowed in any contract, instrument, indenture, or other agreement entered into in connection with the Plan and, in any case, a Claim as to which no objection to its allowance has been interposed within the applicable period of limitation fixed by the Plan, the Bankruptcy Code, the Bankruptcy Rules, or the Bankruptcy Court.

Treatment of Claims and Equity Interests Under the Plan

The following describes the Plan's classification of Claims against and Equity Interests and the treatment the holders of Allowed Claims and Allowed Equity Interests would receive under the Plan. The treatment of Claims set forth below is consistent with the requirements of Section 1129(a)(9)(A) of the Bankruptcy Code.

Unclassified Claims. In accordance with Section 1123(a)(1) of the Bankruptcy Code, the following Claims are designated as unclassified under Article 3 of the Plan.

Administrative Claims. Administrative Claims are generally any Claims that arise after the Petition Date in conjunction with the administration of the Chapter 11 Case and allowed under Section 503(b), Section 507(b) or Section 546(c)(2) of the Bankruptcy Code and entitled to priority under Section 507(a)(1) of the Bankruptcy Code. To the extent that a Claim is Allowed as an Administrative Claim under Section 365(d)(3) of the Bankruptcy Code, such Claim will also be treated as an Administrative Claim under the Plan. Administrative Claims include, for example, quarterly fees to the U.S. Trustee payable under Section 1930 of Title 28 of the United States Code, Claims for the payment of Professional Fees, actual and necessary costs and expenses incurred in the ordinary course of Stuart's business or of preserving Stuart's Estate, Reclamation Claims, and Preserved Ordinary Course Administrative Claims.

Professional Fees. Claims for Professional Fees are Claims of professionals providing service to parties involved in the Chapter 11 Case. Stuart estimates that Professional Fees for the entire Chapter 11 Case will aggregate approximately $2,200,000.

Reclamation Claims. These are Claims by Creditors arising out of the sale of goods to Stuart, in the ordinary course of the Creditor's business, provided that such Creditor has otherwise satisfied the requirements of Section 546(c) of the Bankruptcy Code and applicable provisions of the Uniform Commercial Code. Stuart does not anticipate any Reclamation Claims as of the Effective Date.

Preserved Ordinary Course Administrative Claims. These are generally Claims for liabilities incurred by Stuart in the ordinary course of its business during the Chapter 11 Case relating to the purchase, lease, or use of goods and services, including services provided by Stuart's employees. Stuart does not anticipate any Preserved Ordinary Course Administrative Claims as of the Effective Date.

Priority Tax Claims. These are Claims of a governmental unity for taxes entitled to priority under Section 507(a)(8) of the Bankruptcy Code. Stuart estimates that Priority Tax Claims will not aggregate in excess of approximately $40,000.

Treatment.

Generally. Each Allowed Administrative Expense Claim, other than Preserved Ordinary Course Administrative Claims and Reclamation Claims, is to be paid in full in Cash (or otherwise satisfied in accordance with its terms) on the latest of: (a) the Effective Date, or as soon thereafter as practicable; (b) such date as may be fixed by the Bankruptcy Court, or as soon thereafter as practicable; (c) the tenth Business Day after such Claim is Allowed, or as soon thereafter as practicable; and (d) such date as the holder of such Claim and Reorganized Stuart agree.

Preserved Ordinary Course Administrative Claims. Each Allowed Preserved Ordinary Course Administrative Claim is to be paid by Reorganized Stuart in accordance with either: (a) the terms and conditions under which such Claim arose; or (b) in the ordinary course of Reorganized Stuart's business. Such payments are to be made by Reorganized Stuart without further action by the holder of such Claim.

Priority Tax Claims. Any Allowed Priority Tax Claim is to be paid in full in Cash on the Effective Date; *provided, however,* that Reorganized Stuart may elect to pay such Claims through deferred Cash payments over a period not exceeding six years after the date of assessment of such Claim, of a value as of the Effective Date, equal to the Allowed amount of such Claim. In that event, such payments are to be made in equal annual installments of principal, plus interest accruing from the Effective Date at the rate on the unpaid portion of Allowed Priority Tax Claim set forth in Internal Revenue Code Sections 6621 and 6622. The first such payment is to be made payable on the latest of: (a) the Effective Date, or as soon thereafter as practicable; (b) the tenth Business Day after the date on which an order allowing such Claim becomes a Final Order, or as soon thereafter as practicable; and (c) such other time as is agreed upon by the holder of such Claim and Reorganized Stuart; *provided, however,* that Reorganized Stuart retains the right to prepay and such Allowed Priority Tax Claim, or any remaining balance of such Claim, in full or in part, at any time on or after the Effective Date without premium or penalty.

Reclamation Claims. All requests for payment of Reclamation Claims must be filed by the Bar Date or the holders of such Claims are forever barred from asserting such Reclamation Claims against the Debtor and Reorganized Stuart. Each Allowed Reclamation Claim is to be satisfied, at Reorganized Stuart's sole option, by either: (a) the return of the goods subject to the Reclamation Claim; or (b) payment in full in Cash upon the latest of: (i) the Effective Date, or as soon thereafter as practicable; (ii) such date as may be fixed by the Bankruptcy Court, or as soon thereafter as practicable; (iii) the tenth Business Day after the date on which an order allowing such Claim becomes a Final Order, or as soon thereafter as practicable; and (iv) such other time as is agreed upon by the holder of such Claim and Reorganized Stuart.

Claims for Professional Fees. Each Person seeking an award by the Bankruptcy Court of Professional Fees: (a) must file its final application for allowance of compensation for services rendered and reimbursement of expenses incurred through the Confirmation Date within thirty days after the Confirmation Date; and (b) if the Bankruptcy Court grants such an award, each such Person must be paid in full in Cash in such amounts as are allowed by the Bankruptcy Court (i) on the later of the Effective Date or the date such Claim becomes an Allowed Administrative Expense Claim, or as soon thereafter as practicable, (ii) upon such other terms as may be mutually agreed upon between the holder of such Allowed Administrative Expense Claim and the Debtor or Reorganized Stuart, or (iii) in accordance with the terms of any applicable administrative procedures order entered by the Bankruptcy Court. All Professional Fees for services rendered in connection with the Chapter 11 Case and the Plan after the Confirmation Date including, without limitation, those relating to the occurrence of the Effective Date, the prosecution of Causes of Action preserved under the Plan, and the resolution of Disputed Claim, are to be paid by Reorganized Stuart upon receipt of an invoice for such services, or on such other terms as Reorganized Stuart may agree to, without the need for further Bankruptcy Court authorization or entry of a Final Order. If Reorganized Stuart and any Professional cannot agree on the amount of post-Confirmation Date fees and expenses to be paid to such Professional, such amount is to be determined by the Bankruptcy Court.

Claims of the DIP Lender. Simultaneously with the closing of the Exit Financing Facility, all the Debtor's obligations to the DIP Lender under the DIP Facility and the DIP Loan Documents are to be fully and finally satisfied in accordance with their terms using proceeds derived from, among other things, the Exit Financing Facility and/or Cash held by Reorganized Stuart.

Fees and Expenses of Indenture Trustee. The Indenture Trustee shall be compensated by Reorganized Stuart for services rendered during the period up to but not including the Effective Date, including the reasonable compensation, disbursements, and expenses of the agents and legal counsel of the Indenture Trustee in connection with the performance of their duties under the Indenture and under the Plan upon presentation of invoices without application by or on behalf of the Indenture Trustee to the Bankruptcy Court and without notice and a hearing unless specifically requested by a party in interest.

Indenture Trustee's Lien. Upon payment in full of the Allowed fees and expenses of the Indenture Trustee and its agents and counsel, the Indenture Trustee's liens on the distributions to the holders of the Notes shall be released and extinguished. If Reorganized Stuart and the Indenture Trustee cannot agree upon the amount of fees and expenses to be paid, such fees and expenses shall be determined by the Bankruptcy Court.

Classified Claims. As additionally described below, the treatment of classified Claims and the provisions governing distributions on account of Allowed Claims is set forth in Articles 4 and 5 of the Plan. You should refer to the Plan itself for the complete provisions governing the treatment of your particular Claim.

Class 1 – Priority Claims. Class 1 is unimpaired by the Plan; consequently, all holders of Allowed Claims in Class 1 are deemed to have accepted the Plan and are not entitled to vote on the Plan. Each holder of an Allowed Priority Claim is to receive Cash in an amount equal to such Allowed Priority Claim on the later of: (a) the Effective Date, or as soon thereafter as practicable; and (b) ten Business Days after the date such Priority Claim becomes an Allowed Priority Claim, or as soon thereafter as practicable, unless the holder of such Allowed Priority Claim and Reorganized Stuart agree otherwise. Stuart estimates that as of the Petition Date, Priority Claims aggregated approximately $178,000.

Class 2 – Secured Tax Claims. Class 2 is unimpaired by the Plan; consequently, all holders of Allowed Claims in Class 2 are deemed to have accepted the Plan and are not entitled to vote on the Plan. Each Allowed Secured Tax Claim is to be paid in full in Cash upon the latest of: (a) the Effective Date, or as soon thereafter as practicable; (b) such date as may be fixed by the Bankruptcy Court, or as soon thereafter as practicable; (c) the tenth Business Day after such Claim is Allowed, or as soon thereafter as practicable; (d) the date on which such Secured Tax Claim is scheduled to be paid in the ordinary course of business under applicable law or regulation; and (e) such date as the holder of such Claim and Reorganized Stuart agree. Stuart is not aware of any Secured Tax Claims.

Class 3 – Miscellaneous Secured Claims. Class 3 is unimpaired by the Plan; consequently, all holders of Allowed Claims in Class 3 are deemed to have accepted the Plan and are not entitled to vote on the Plan. Each Allowed Miscellaneous Secured Claim is to be paid in full in Cash upon the latest of: (a) the Effective Date, or as soon thereafter as practicable; (b) such date as may be fixed by the Bankruptcy Court, or as soon thereafter as practicable; (c) the tenth Business Day after such Claim is Allowed, or as soon thereafter as practicable; (d) the date on which such Miscellaneous Secured Claim is scheduled to be paid in the ordinary course of business under applicable law or regulation; and (e) such date as the holder of such Claim and Reorganized Stuart agree. Excluding the Claims of the DIP Lender and of the Elliott Trust, Stuart estimates that Miscellaneous Secured Claims do not exceed approximately $500,000.

Class 3A – Elliott Trust Secured Claim. Class 3A is impaired by the Plan; consequently, the holder of the Elliott Trust Secured Claim is entitled to vote on the Plan. The Elliott Trust is The Robert and Jeannette Elliott Trust U/T/A dated August 13, 1997, with Robert Elliott and Jeannette Elliott as trustees, and was the former owner of all outstanding shares in Bingo Systems, now a Subsidiary of Stuart. In accordance with a Stock Purchase Agreement by and among the Elliott Trust, Stuart, and Bingo Systems, dated August 12, 1998, Stuart acquired all outstanding shares of Bingo Systems from the Elliott Trust and, among other consideration including a payment of cash, Stuart made a promissory note (the "Elliott Trust Promissory Note"), in the principal amount of $1,200,000, payable to the Elliott Trust. The Elliott Trust Secured Claim is in the principal amount of $800,000, as of the Petition Date, arising under the Elliott Trust Promissory Note, which is Secured by, among other things, a $600,000 irrevocable letter of credit granted to the Elliott Trust by Stuart and a second mortgage on certain real property owned by Bingo Systems. In full and final satisfaction of the Elliott Trust Secured Claim, the Elliott Trust is to be paid in full in Cash as follows: (a) eight (8) equal quarterly payments of $111,736.53, commencing on October 1, 1999 and continuing on each subsequent January 1, April 1, July 1, and October 1, with the last installment to be paid, rather than on July 1, 2001, no later than August 1, 2001; (b) except with respect to the foregoing payment schedule, Reorganized Stuart shall meet all its obligations to the Elliott Trust under the Elliot Trust Promissory Note, which, except to the extent altered by the foregoing payment schedule, shall remain in full force an affect in accordance with its own terms from and after the Effective Date.

Class 4 – Notes. Class 4 is impaired by the Plan; consequently, all holders of Allowed Notes Claims and Allowed Notes Securities Claims are entitled to vote on the Plan. On the Confirmation Date, all Notes Claims are deemed Allowed in the aggregate amount of $100,000,000 plus accrued and unpaid interest relating to the period up to but not including the Petition Date. On the Effective Date, or as soon thereafter as practicable, each holder of an Allowed Notes Claim shall receive, subject to such holder's surrender of its Debt Instrument(s) evidencing its Allowed Notes Claim in accordance with Section 4.5.9 of the Plan, in full and final satisfaction of such Allowed Notes Claim, a Pro Rata portion of a number of shares of New Common Stock equivalent to one-hundred percent (100%) of the New Common Stock, subject to dilution by the Adjusted Management Shares of New Common Stock issuable upon the exercise of the Equity Incentive

Options and the Executive Options (see "OVERVIEW OF THE PLAN – Description of Transactions to be Implemented in Connection with the Plan – New Incentive Stock Option Plan."). As of the Petition Date, the aggregate amount of Allowed Notes Claims (including accrued, unpaid interest up to but not including the Petition Date) was approximately $109,100,000. Stuart is unaware of any Notes Securities Claims.

Cash Payment Option. Any holder of an Allowed Notes Claim may make a Noteholder Election, by so indicating on its Ballot, to receive Cash in lieu of New Common Stock in full satisfaction of its Allowed Notes Claim. On the latest of: (a) the Effective Date, or as soon thereafter as practicable; (b) such date as may be fixed by the Bankruptcy Court, or as soon thereafter as practicable; (c) the tenth Business Day after such Claim is Allowed, or as soon thereafter as practicable; and (d) such date as the holder of such Claim and Reorganized Stuart agree, each holder of an Allowed Claim in Class 4 who makes a Noteholder Election to participate in the Cash Payment Option shall receive in full and final satisfaction of such Claim twenty-five percent (25%) of the Allowed Notes Claim in Cash, subject to such holder's surrender of its Debt Instrument(s) evidencing its Allowed Notes Claim in accordance with Section 4.5.9 of the Plan. Distributions pursuant to the Cash Payment Option shall be funded in accordance with the Company Funding Commitment and the Standby Funding Commitment. Any holder of an Allowed Claim in Class 4 who either does not submit a Ballot or does not indicate its Noteholder Election on its Ballot shall be deemed to have elected the Cash Payment Option.

Gaming Requirements. Any holder of an Allowed Notes Claim who is to receive more than five percent (5%) of the shares of New Common Stock issued to holders of Class 4 Claims must comply at all times with the Gaming Requirements as described in "ADDITIONAL IMPLEMENTION OF THE PLAN – Description of Gaming Regulations" below. If at any time (the "Disqualification Date") any holder of New Common Stock refuses to comply with the Gaming Requirements, or if the Gaming Authorities of any jurisdiction in which Reorganized Stuart maintains a gaming license find that any holder of New Common Stock is not qualified or otherwise suitable to hold such New Common Stock in Reorganized Stuart, such holder shall either: (a) divest itself of its New Common Stock within 60 days after the Disqualification Date or such shorter period as directed by any Gaming Authorities; or (b) accept, within 60 days after the Disqualification Date or such shorter period as directed by any Gaming Authorities, the redemption of its New Common Stock by Reorganized Stuart for an amount in Cash equal to the lesser of the current market value of such New Common Stock and such holder's original cost basis in such New Common Stock determined as of the Effective Date. If such holder has not divested itself of its New Common Stock or accepted redemption of its New Common Stock within such period or periods, Reorganized Stuart shall have the option, but not the obligation, to cancel such New Common Stock.

Cancellation of Notes. As of the Effective Date, except to the extent provided otherwise in the Plan, all Notes, and all agreements, instruments, and other documents evidencing the Notes and the rights of the holders of Notes, shall be automatically canceled, extinguished, and deemed void (all without further action by any Person), and all obligations of any Person, including the Debtor, under such instruments and agreements shall be deemed fully and finally satisfied, released, and discharged.

Cancellation of Indenture. On the Effective Date, except to the extent provided otherwise in the Plan, the Indenture shall be deemed to be canceled, and the obligations of the Debtor thereunder, except for the obligation to indemnify the Indenture Trustee, shall be discharged; provided, however, that the Indenture or other agreement that governs the rights of the holders of Notes and that is administered by the Indenture Trustee, an agent or services, shall continue in effect solely for the purposes of (a) allowing such Indenture Trustee, as Disbursing Agent, to make distributions to holders of Notes under the Plan and (b) permitting such Indenture Trustee to maintain any rights or liens it may have for fees, costs, and expenses under such Indenture or other agreement.

Notes Securities Claims. In full and final satisfaction of all Notes Securities Claims, and in consideration of the distributions to the holders of Allowed Notes Claims, each holder of an Allowed Notes Securities Claim shall retain any proceeds derived from or relating to any litigation instituted or judgment obtained by any such holder or on his behalf payable by either: (a) any entity other than the Debtor, Reorganized Stuart, or any of their respective Subsidiaries; or (b) proceeds of insurance policies maintained by the Debtor. Aside from the above treatment, the holders of Notes Securities Claims shall receive no distributions under the Plan.

Class 5 – General Unsecured Claims. Class 5 is impaired by the Plan; consequently, all holders of Allowed General Unsecured Claims are entitled to vote on the Plan. On the latest of: (a) the Effective Date, or as soon thereafter as practicable; (b) such date as may be fixed by the Bankruptcy Court, or as soon thereafter as practicable; (c) the tenth Business Day after such Claim is Allowed, or as soon thereafter as practicable; and (d) such date as the holder of such Claim and Reorganized Stuart agree, each Allowed General Unsecured Claim, in full and final satisfaction of such Allowed General Unsecured Claim, shall be paid an amount in Cash equivalent to twenty-five percent (25%) of the amount of such Allowed General Unsecured Claim. Stuart obtained authority from the Bankruptcy Court on the Petition Date to pay the prepetition claims of its various vendors, suppliers, and other trade creditors in the ordinary course of business. As such, few, if any, Unsecured Claims of trade creditors will remain for treatment as Class 5 Claims under the Plan. Accordingly, Stuart estimates that Class 5 General Unsecured Claims will aggregate less than $500,000.

Class 6 – Subsidiary Claims. Class 6 is impaired by the Plan; consequently, all holders of Allowed Claims in Class 6 are entitled to vote on the Plan. The holders of Subsidiary Claims will receive no distributions under the Plan, and all such Claims are discharged under the Plan in accordance with Section 12.2 of the Plan.

Class 7 – Equity Interests and Equity Related Claims. Class 7 is impaired by the Plan; consequently, all holders of Allowed Equity Interests and Equity Related Claims are entitled to vote on the Plan. No securities litigation is currently pending against Stuart or its officers and directors; accordingly, Stuart is unaware of any Equity Related Claims. Allowed Equity Interests and Allowed Equity Related Claims are to be satisfied as follows:

Distributions. In full and final satisfaction of all Allowed Equity Interests and Allowed Equity Related Claims, subject to the provisions of Section 4.8.6 of the Plan (see "Alternative Treatment," immediately below), on the Effective Date, or as soon thereafter as practicable, each holder of an Allowed Equity Interest and Allowed Equity Related Claim shall receive its Pro Rata portion of $150,000 in Cash. Only those holders of Equity Related Claims whose Claims are Allowed as of the Effective Date shall be entitled to receive a distribution on account of such Claims. No distribution shall be made on account of any Equity Related Claims not Allowed as of the Effective Date.

Alternative Treatment. If: (a) the Bankruptcy Court determines that the treatment of, and distributions to, Class 7 under the Plan violates the provisions of Section 1129(b) of the Bankruptcy Code (to the extent such provisions apply); or (b) Class 7 does not vote to accept the Plan; then all Equity Interests are to be canceled and extinguished on the Confirmation Date without further action under any applicable agreement, law, regulation, order, or rule, and the holders of Equity Interests will not receive or retain any rights, property, or distributions on account of their Equity Interests.

Description of Transactions to be Implemented in Connection with the Plan

New Common Stock.

As stated above, holders of Allowed Claims in Class 4 are to receive shares of New Common Stock under the Plan. The following describes the New Common Stock and the rights and restrictions associated with it.

The Reorganized Stuart Certificate authorizes the issuance of 10,000,000 shares of New Common Stock and 5,000,000 of preferred stock. On the Effective Date, or as soon thereafter as practicable, Reorganized Stuart will issue approximately 1,000,000 shares of such New Common Stock, which will represent one hundred percent (100%) of the then-outstanding equity in Reorganized Stuart, subject to dilution by the shares of New Common Stock issuable upon the exercise of the Executive Options and the Equity Incentive Options (see "OVERVIEW OF THE PLAN – Description of Transactions to be Implemented in Connection with the Plan – New Incentive Stock Option Plan."). The aggregate number of share underlying the Executive Options and the Equity Incentive Options (the "Adjusted Management Shares") is calculated using the following Accretion Calculation:

$$\frac{\text{Actual Company Funding Amount} \times 4}{\text{Allowed Notes Claims as of Petition Date}} = \text{Reduced Notes Percentage (RNP)}$$

$$\text{Initial Management Percentage (IMP)} + (\text{IMP} \times \text{RNP}) = \textbf{Adjusted Management Percentage} \text{ (AMP)}$$

$$(1{,}000{,}000 \div (100\% - \text{AMP})) - 1{,}000{,}000 = \textbf{Adjusted Management Shares}$$

The Actual Company Funding Amount is the amount of Cash that Reorganized Stuart pays to holders of Allowed Class 4 Claims who elect the Cash Payment Option under the Company Funding Commitment (*see* "OVERVIEW OF THE PLAN – Description of Transactions to be Implemented in Connection with the Plan – Effect of Standby Funding Commitment."). The Initial Management Percentage is ten percent (10%), derived through negotiations with the Executive Management Group and Contrarian. The Adjusted Management Percentage is the percentage of the issued and outstanding shares of New Common Stock issuable to members of the Executive Management Group, on a Fully Diluted Basis, upon exercise of the Equity Incentive Options and the Executive Management Options, resulting from the above Accretion Calculation. The Adjusted Management Shares is the aggregate number of shares of New Common Stock issuable to members of the Executive Management Group upon exercise of the Executive Options and the Equity Incentive Options, as calculated using the above Accretion Calculation. The purpose of the Accretion Calculation is to determine the accretive effect of Reorganized Stuart's Cash payments to those holders of Claims electing the Cash Payment Option under the Company Funding Commitment on the percentage of total outstanding New Common Stock purchasable by members of the Executive Management Group upon exercise of the Equity Incentive Options and the Executive Options. For example, if the Actual Company Funding Amount is $3,000,000, the Allowed Notes Claims total is $109,097,221, and the Initial Management Percentage is 10% (which is the sum of the 4% and 6% of outstanding shares of New Common Stock to be issued upon the exercise of the Executive Options and the Equity Incentive Options, respectively), the Accretion Calculation would be as follows:

$\$3{,}000{,}000 \times 4 / \$109{,}097{,}221 = 10.99\%$

$10\% + (10\% \times 10.99\%) = 11.1\%$ = Adjusted Management Percentage

$(1{,}000{,}000 \div (100\% - 11.1\%)) - 1{,}000{,}000 = 124{,}859$ = Adjusted Management Shares

All shares of New Common Stock to be issued in accordance with the Plan (including, without limitation, those shares issued upon the exercise of the Executive Options, and the Equity Incentive Options), will, at issuance, be duly authorized, fully paid and non-assessable. The holders of such shares will have no preemptive or other rights to subscribe for additional shares. The New Common Stock will have a par value of $0.001 per share.

Divestiture. If at any time (the "Disqualification Date") any holder of New Common Stock refuses to comply with the Gaming Requirements, or if Gaming Authorities of any jurisdiction in which Reorganized Stuart maintains a gaming license find that any holder of New Common Stock is not qualified or otherwise suitable to hold such New Common Stock in Reorganized Stuart, such holder shall be required either: (a) to divest itself of its New Common Stock within 60 days after the Disqualification Date or such shorter period as directed by any Gaming Authorities; or (b) to accept, within 60 days after the Disqualification Date or such other period as directed by any Gaming Authorities, the redemption of its New Common Stock by Reorganized Stuart for an amount in Cash equal to the lesser of: (i) the current market value of such New Common Stock; and (ii) such holder's original per-share cost basis in such New Common Stock, which shall be determined by dividing the number of shares of New Common Stock issued as of the Effective Date by the aggregate reorganized equity value of Reorganized Stuart as determined by the Bankruptcy Court. If such holder has not divested itself of its New Common Stock or accepted redemption of its New Common Stock within such period or periods, Reorganized Stuart shall have the option, but not the obligation, to cancel such New Common Stock.

Effect of Standby Funding Commitment.

Stuart and certain holders of Notes have entered into, or will enter into, the "Standby Funding Commitment," an agreement under which both Reorganized Stuart and such holders are obligated, under certain circumstances, to fund Cash payments on account of Allowed Claims in Class 4 under the Cash Payment Option. Reorganized Stuart's funding obligation, the "Company Funding Commitment," is the obligation of Reorganized Stuart to provide funding of up to $3,000,000 for Cash payments to Allowed Claims in Class 4 under the Cash Payment Option. The Standby Funding Commitment also provides that upon satisfaction by Reorganized Stuart of its obligations under the Company Funding Commitment, those holders of Notes executing the Standby Funding Commitment shall provide any additional funding of Cash payments to Allowed Claims in Class 4 in accordance with the terms of the Standby Funding Commitment. Pursuant to the Standby Funding Commitment and the Plan, each holder of Notes contributing to the funding of Cash Payments to Allowed Class 4 Claims shall receive, in exchange for any such funding provided to satisfy Allowed Claims in Class 4, an Allowed Claim in Class 4 in an amount equivalent to the Allowed Notes Claims such holder satisfies pursuant to the Standby Funding Commitment, and shall receive distributions of New Common Stock in accordance with Section 4.5.5 of the Plan on account of such Allowed Class 4 Claim.

New Incentive Stock Option Plan.

Exhibit D to the Plan Supplement contains the New Incentive Stock Option Plan, which provides for the granting to certain Stuart employees options to purchase New Common Stock. The Incentive Stock Option Plan is intended to facilitate the granting of the Equity Incentive Options and the Executive Options to members of the Executive Management Group, entitling such members, if such options are exercised, to receive an aggregate number of shares of New Common Stock equivalent to the Adjusted Management Percentage of the outstanding New Common Stock on a Fully Diluted Basis. The Executive Options and the Equity Incentive Options are described below.

Executive Options.

As of the Effective Date, Reorganized Stuart shall issue to the Executive Management Group the Executive Options, entitling such members to acquire an aggregate number of shares of New Common Stock equivalent to four percent (4%) of the outstanding New Common Stock as of the Effective Date on a Fully Diluted Basis, subject to the Adjusted Management Percentage. Such shares, when issued, shall dilute all shares of New Common Stock issued and outstanding at the time of issuance on a Pro Rata basis. The Executive Options shall be exercisable and shall be governed by the terms and conditions set forth in the New Incentive Stock Option Plan and the applicable Employment Agreement, and shall be allocated among the Executive Management Group in a manner and in an amount as determined by Mr. Valandra on or before the Effective Date. The number of shares of New Common Stock subject to the Executive Options shall be adjusted in the event of stock splits, stock dividends, mergers, and similar events.

Equity Incentive Options.

As of the Effective Date, members of the Executive Management Group shall receive the Equity Incentive Options, entitling the holders of such options to acquire an aggregate number of shares of New Common Stock equivalent to six percent (6%) of the outstanding New Common Stock as of the Effective Date on a Fully Diluted Basis, subject to the Adjusted Management Percentage.

Exercise Price. The Equity Incentive Options have an exercise price per share equal to the fair market value per share of New Common Stock as of the Effective Date.

Vesting. The Equity Incentive Options vest and become exercisable if Reorganized Stuart meets the following EBITDA[2] targets during the first three full fiscal years following the Confirmation Date in accordance with the vesting schedule set forth below:

Fiscal Year	EBITDA ($ in millions)	Vesting
1	$12	1/3
2	$14	1/3
3	$16	1/3

Notwithstanding the foregoing, the EBITDA targets set forth above are cumulative and the Equity Incentive Options may vest earlier or later than as set forth in the vesting schedule. For example, if Reorganized Stuart fails to meet the total EBITDA target for the first two fiscal years, but meets the EBITDA target in the third fiscal year, and the aggregate EBITDA for all three fiscal years exceeds $42 million, the Equity Incentive Options will vest in full. Similarly, if Reorganized Stuart meets the EBITDA target established for any fiscal year during an earlier fiscal year, the Equity Incentive Options that would have vested based on achieving such EBITDA target in the later fiscal year will vest in full. The Equity Incentive Options are to be governed by the terms and conditions set forth in the New Incentive Stock Option Plan. Such options are to be allocated among the Executive Management Group in a manner and in an amount as determined by Mr. Valandra before the Effective Date. The number of shares and exercise price of the Equity Incentive Options are to be adjusted in the event of stock splits, stock dividends, mergers, and similar events.

Employment Contracts.

As of the Effective Date, all employment contracts of existing employees

[2]"EBITDA" is defined in Section 1.48 of the Plan: During each applicable fiscal year, for Reorganized Stuart and its Subsidiaries on a consolidated basis, determined in accordance with consistently applied generally accepted accounting principals, the Net Income for such period, plus, to the extent reflected in the statement of Net Income for such period , the sum of (a) Income Tax, (b) Interest Expense, (c) Depreciation Expense, and (d) Amortization (each as defined in the Plan).

of the Debtor are deemed rejected, canceled, and terminated, *except that* the Employment Contracts, substantially in the forms contained in Exhibit F to the Plan Supplement, will be assumed and will remain effective from and after the Effective Date of the Plan. The Employment Contracts will be between Reorganized Stuart and the members of the Executive Management Group: Joseph M. Valandra, Lawrence X. Taylor, III, Ernest M. Marchand, Jimmy D. Helton, and Clement F. Chantiam, in their respective capacities for Reorganized Stuart as set forth in "BACKGROUND AND EVENTS PRECIPITATING THE CHAPTER 11 FILING – Current Directors and Executive Officers."

The principal terms of the Employment Contracts are as follows:

- Term – Each Employment Contract provides for an initial term expiring on December 31, 2002.
- Base Salary – The annual base salary of each Executive is as follows:

Executive	Base Salary
Joseph M. Valandra	$250,000
Ernest M. Marchand	$150,000
Jimmy D. Helton	$140,000
Lawrence X. Taylor	$165,000
Clement F. Chantiam	$160,000

- General Perquisites - The Executives are entitled to participate with all other senior executive officers of Reorganized Stuart in bonus and incentive compensation programs and in Company 401(k), health and welfare benefit plans, each as adopted by Reorganized Stuart from time to time.
- Incentive Compensation –

  Restructuring Bonus. Upon the successful consummation of either an exchange offer in which the Notes are exchanged for equity in Stuart, or the entry of a final non-appealable order confirming a Chapter 11 plan of reorganization (a "Conversion Event"), the Executives (as a group) will receive a restructuring bonus of options entitling the Executives to receive equity equal to four percent (4%) of the equity in the entity resulting from such Conversion Event, on a Fully Diluted Basis. Each Executive has been allocated a share of the four percent (4%) by Mr. Valandra. Under the Plan, this Restructuring Bonus is satisfied by virtue of the Executive Options (*see* "OVERVIEW OF THE PLAN – Description of Transactions to be Implemented in Connection with the Plan – Executive Options.").

  Equity Incentive Options. The Executives (as a group) also are entitled to receive the Equity Incentive Options, described in

"OVERVIEW OF THE PLAN – Description of Transactions to be Implemented in Connection with the Plan – Equity Incentive Options."

- Severance Benefits – Under the terms of the Employment Contracts, Reorganized Stuart may terminate an Executive's employment at any time for cause, and in such event, all of such Executive's rights to compensation would cease upon his termination. If the termination is Without Cause or for Good Reason (as such terms are defined in the Employment Agreements), Reorganized Stuart must pay to the applicable Executive, in addition to amounts accrued in respective periods prior to the termination, a cash lump sum in an amount determined as follows: (A) prior to the effective date of any Conversion Event, his base salary (as in effect at the time of such termination) for a period of 18 months; and (B) from and after the effective date of any Conversion Event, an amount equal to his base salary for a period equal to the greater of 12 months or the number of months remaining until the expiration of the term of the applicable Agreement. Reorganized Stuart is also required to continue benefits of the Executive and his eligible beneficiaries for a period of 12 months following the termination date, and permit the Executive to exercise in full all outstanding vested stock options and restricted stock awards for such period. The Executive would also be entitled to exercise any equity incentive options that subsequently vest at the end of the fiscal year in which the Executive is terminated and at the end of the next succeeding fiscal year. The latter right also applies in the event an Executive is terminated due to death or disability.

- Put Rights – If an Executive terminates his employment for Good Reason or Reorganized Stuart terminates an Executive Without Cause, the Executive will have the right to put any securities he beneficially owns to Reorganized Stuart at price to be determined at the time such put right is exercised.

- Non-compete – Each Executive is subject to a two year non-compete that commences on the date of termination. The non-compete is not operative in the event Reorganized Stuart elects not to extend the term of the applicable Employment Agreement.

Severance and Retention Bonus Program.

Stuart has determined that it is in the best interests of its ongoing operations to (i) close its McAllen, Texas plant and migrate all its operations to certain of Stuart's other manufacturing facilities, and (ii) relocate its corporate headquarters from Council Bluffs, Iowa to the Minneapolis/St. Paul metropolitan area. In order to provide employees affected by the closure of these two facilities with some degree of comfort in the stability of their jobs through these closures, thereby ensuring their continued employment and assistance during the pendency of the Chapter 11 Case, Stuart believed it was necessary to adopt a comprehensive severance and retention program.

The approximately 200 employees affected by the McAllen plant closure and headquarters relocation will receive, provided they agree to remain through a specified date determined by Stuart, a severance payment equal to one (1) week's pay for each year of employment with Stuart. Should all 200 employees participate in the severance program, the aggregate cost of the severance program to Stuart will be approximately $233,843.

Furthermore, on December 31, 1999, each employee listed on Exhibit H to the Plan Supplement will be entitled to receive a Retention Bonus consisting of Cash in an amount equal to ten percent (10%) of that employee's annual base salary in effect on the Petition Date, *provided* that such employee remains an employee of Reorganized Stuart through December 31, 1999, unless such requirement is waived by Reorganized Stuart in its sole discretion. Should all employees listed in Exhibit H to the Plan Supplement become eligible for Retention Bonuses, the aggregate cost of such bonuses will be approximately $767,400.

Exit Financing Facility.

On or before the Effective Date, the Debtor or Reorganized Stuart, as the case may be, shall execute the Exit Financing Documents, which shall have been approved by separate, prior Final Order of the Bankruptcy Court. The Exit Financing Facility, among other things, shall (a) be effective on the Effective Date, (b) be a senior secured facility, and (c) contain terms and conditions in form and substance acceptable to the Debtor and/or Reorganized Stuart.

Reorganized Stuart Certificate of Incorporation and By-Laws.

As of the Effective Date and without any further action by the stockholders or directors of the Debtor or Reorganized Stuart, the Debtor's certificate of incorporation and by-laws will be amended and restated substantially in the forms of the Reorganized Stuart Certificate and Reorganized Stuart By-Laws contained in the Plan Supplement, which provide for, among other things, the authorization of all acts necessary to implement the Plan including, without limitation, the issuance of the New Common Stock. Such restated certificate of incorporation and by-laws will also prohibit (to the extent required by Section 1123(a) and (b) of the Bankruptcy Code) the issuance of non-voting equity securities. The initial members of the board of directors of Reorganized Stuart are to serve until such directors, or their successors, are elected at a properly noticed and constituted stockholders meeting of Reorganized Stuart. After the Effective Date, Reorganized Stuart may amend and restate its certificate of incorporation and by-laws as permitted by such documents and applicable state law.

Stock Transfer Restriction.

Following the Effective Date, no Person holding shares of New Common Stock shall transfer, and Reorganized Stuart shall not register the transfer of, such shares of New Common Stock, whether by sale, assignment, gift, bequest, appointment or otherwise (collectively, a "Transfer"), if such Transfer would cause the aggregate number of outstanding shares of New Common Stock to be held of record by five hundred (500) or more Persons. Any purported Transfer of shares of New Common Stock in violation of this provision shall be null and void, and the purported transferee, with respect to the shares transferred, shall have no rights as a stockholder of Reorganized Stuart and no other rights against or with respect to Reorganized Stuart.

Private Company Status.

Stuart is currently a public company, registered under Section 12 of the Exchange Act, and its Old Common Stock is presently quoted on the OTC Electronic Bulletin Board under the symbol "STUA." Following the Effective Date of the Plan, Reorganized Stuart intends to terminate its registration under the Exchange Act such that Reorganized Stuart will no longer file reports with the SEC or otherwise be subject to the reporting requirements under the Exchange Act and the New Common Stock will not be traded on any recognized stock exchange or over-the-counter securities market. Reorganized Stuart will file necessary forms, including a Form 15, with the Securities and Exchange Commission to effect the termination of reporting requirements.

Registration Rights.

As soon as practicable following the Effective Date, Reorganized Stuart and any holder of 10% or more of the New Common Stock to be issued to holders of Allowed Class 4 Claims in accordance with the Plan shall enter into registration rights agreement(s) substantially in the form of the Registration Rights Agreement included as Exhibit K to the Plan Supplement. The Registration Rights Agreement provides, among other things, that if Reorganized Stuart registers any of its New Common Stock either for its own account or for the account of other holders of New Common Stock, any holder of New Common Stock (irrespective of its percentage holdings) shall be entitled to include its shares of New Common Stock in such registration, subject to the ability of the underwriters to limit the number of shares included in the offering. Within thirty (30) days following the Effective Date, Reorganized Stuart shall file appropriate shelf registration documents as required in the Registration Rights Agreement.

Shareholder Agreement.

As of the Effective Date, Reorganized Stuart will enter into a Shareholder Agreement with certain holders of New Common Stock and members of the Executive Management Group. Under the terms of the Shareholder

Agreement, the parties thereto have agreed to grant each other a right of first refusal with respect to the sale of such party's shares of New Common Stock, subject to certain conditions. Similarly, a party who has agreed to sell its shares of New Common Stock to a third party, subject to the right of first refusal, must provide the other parties the right to include their shares in such sale (*i.e.,* tag-along rights). Under Section 1.5 of the Shareholder Agreement, those persons who beneficially ten percent (10%) or more of the outstanding New Common Stock as of the Effective Date also will be entitled to the tag-along rights granted in that Section.

Cancellation and Surrender of Securities and Instruments.

As of the Effective Date, all Notes and Equity Interests, and all agreements, instruments, and other documents evidencing the Notes and Equity Interests and the rights of the holders of Notes and Equity Interests are canceled, extinguished, and deemed void (all without further action by any Person), and all obligations of any Person under such instruments and agreements is deemed fully and finally satisfied and released. On or before the Distribution Date, or as soon thereafter as practicable, each holder of a Debt Instrument evidencing an Allowed Notes Claim or a security evidencing an Allowed Equity Interest must surrender or cause to be surrendered such Debt Instrument or security to the Disbursing Agent. No distribution of property under the Plan is to be made to or on behalf of any such holder unless and until such Debt Instrument or security is received by the Disbursing Agent, or the unavailability of such Debt Instrument or security is reasonably established to the Disbursing Agent's satisfaction. If any holder of an Allowed Notes Claim or Allowed Equity Interest seeks to establish the unavailability of the Debt Instrument or security evidencing such Claim or Interest, the Disbursing Agent must, within the first Business Day thirty days after receipt of the holder's evidence of unavailability and statement of indemnity of Reorganized Stuart and the Disbursing Agent: (a) provide the holder, in writing, with a detailed description regarding the unacceptability of such evidence and statement of indemnity, if any; or (b) (in the case of holders of Notes) deliver to Indenture Trustee and Reorganized Stuart a notice of compliance and distribute to such holder its Pro Rata portion of the New Common Stock. Any such holder who fails to surrender or cause to be surrendered such Debt Instrument or security or fails to execute and deliver an affidavit of loss and indemnity reasonably satisfactory to the Disbursing Agent and Reorganized Stuart before the first anniversary of the Effective Date will be deemed to have forfeited all rights, Claims, and Interests in respect of such Debt Instrument or security and may not participate in any distribution under the Plan, and all property in respect of such forfeited distribution, including interests accrued on such distribution, will revert to Reorganized Stuart notwithstanding any federal or state escheat laws to the contrary.

Asset Transfer.

On or before December 31, 1999, Stuart intends to transfer all or substantially all of its business operating assets including, but not limited to, property, plant, and equipment, inventory, accounts receivable, and goodwill associated therewith, to one or more of its Subsidiaries as a capital contribution to such Subsidiaries. It is anticipated that the employees of Stuart associated with the transferred businesses will also be transferred to the applicable Subsidiary. The proposed transfer of assets will facilitate the ability of the management team associated with each Subsidiary to focus on the operations of the business transferred to such Subsidiary. In addition, the transfer of such assets will insulate the assets of one Subsidiary from the business risks associated with each other Subsidiary.

ADDITIONAL IMPLEMENTION OF THE PLAN

Description of Gaming Regulations

Stuart is subject to regulation in most jurisdictions in which its bingo, bingo-related products (including pulltabs) and electronic gaming systems are sold or used by persons or entities licensed to conduct gaming activities. The gaming regulatory requirements vary from jurisdiction to jurisdiction and licensing, other approval or finding of suitability processes with respect to Stuart, its personnel and its products, can be lengthy and expensive. Many jurisdictions have comprehensive licensing, reporting and operating requirements with respect to the sale and manufacture of bingo and bingo-related products, including bingo paper, pulltab tickets and electronic bingo equipment. These licensing requirements have a direct impact on the conduct of Stuart's day-to-day operations. Generally, gaming regulatory authorities may deny applications for licenses, other approvals or findings of suitability for any cause they may deem reasonable. There can be no assurance that Stuart, its products or its personnel will receive or be able to maintain any necessary gaming licenses, other approvals or findings of suitability. The loss of a license in a particular jurisdiction will prohibit Stuart from selling products in that jurisdiction and may prohibit Stuart from selling its products in other jurisdictions. The loss of one or more licenses held by Stuart could have a material adverse effect on Stuart's business, results of operations, and financial condition.

In certain jurisdictions, any beneficial owner of Stuart's common stock may, at gaming authorities' discretion, be required to file applications with gaming regulatory authorities so that such authorities may investigate such shareholder and determine whether such shareholder is suitable or qualified to hold stock in Stuart. The gaming laws and regulations of some jurisdictions provide that beneficial owners of more than five percent (5%) of the common stock and, potentially, holders of the debt securities of Stuart may be subject to certain reporting procedures and may be required to be investigated and licensed, qualified, or found suitable. The Reorganized Stuart Certificate of

Incorporation authorizes Reorganized Stuart, under certain circumstances, to redeem, at the lesser of the holder's original basis or the current market price, the New Common Stock held by any person whose status as a shareholder may jeopardize Stuart's gaming licenses or approvals. See "OVERVIEW OF THE PLAN – Description of Transactions to be Implemented in Connection with the Plan – New Common Stock."

Generally, those individuals and entities required to comply with Gaming Requirements of any of the approximately 30 jurisdictions in which Stuart currently holds a gaming license may run afoul of such requirements by either: (1) failure to make full and adequate disclosure; and (2) a finding of unsuitability by gaming authorities. There are no bright line tests for suitability and criteria vary often substantially by jurisdiction. Typically, however, authorities could find a person or entity unsuitable if there were evidence of convictions or arrests relating to crimes of moral turpitude, violation of gambling laws, association with undesirable characters, an intentional failure to adequately disclose requested information, or misrepresentation or fraud in such disclosure.

Attached as Exhibit 6 to this Disclosure Statement is a grid briefly cataloguing shareholder disclosure requirements for the jurisdictions in which Stuart is currently licensed. **This grid should be considered a guideline only and is not intended to be a complete analysis of applicable Gaming Requirements in any jurisdiction.** Required disclosure for individuals typically involves information regarding such items as personal background, criminal history, and personal net worth, and may include requirements for the submission of certain documentation including income statements and/or tax returns, photographs, fingerprint cards (including spouse), and investigative waivers.

If the disclosing shareholder is a corporate entity or investment fund, principals with voting and investment discretion may be required to make similar disclosures. Gaming authorities (and investigative agencies working on their behalf) may, at their discretion, require disclosure of fund participants even if those participants do not have voting rights. Investigations may take up to two years or more and could include interviewing neighbors and former employers.

Gaming authorities typically do not have uniform standards for unsuitability. Stuart is aware of the following instances that did not, by themselves, lead to a finding of unsuitability: (1) a 15-year-old conviction of Obstruction of a Police Officer relating to a tavern altercation; and (2) an arrest for drug possession (no conviction) more than 20 years ago. Stuart is aware of the following instances that would, on the other hand, be more likely to result in a finding of unsuitability: (1) failure to completely disclose personal history (for instance, a previous marriage and divorce); (2) participation in the dealing of gray market gaming machines on Native

American reservations; (3) failure to disclose actual ownership of an applicant or any of its significant shareholders. Stuart believes that that convictions for violation of gambling laws and convictions relating to fraudulent conduct would also result in a finding of unsuitability.

THE FOREGOING DESCRIPTION OF GAMING REQUIREMENTS IS INTENDED ONLY TO PROVIDE HOLDERS OF CLAIMS AND EQUITY INTERESTS WITH SOME GUIDANCE REGARDING THE TYPES OF ISSUES THAT MAY ARISE IN COMPLYING WITH THE GAMING REQUIREMENTS FOR PURPOSES OF RECEIVING SHARES OF NEW COMMON STOCK UNDER THE PLAN. IT IS IMPRACTICAL FOR STUART TO ADEQUATELY DESCRIBE EVERY STATUTE AND REGULATION RELATING TO GAMING COMPLIANCE IN EVERY JURISDICTION IN WHICH STUART OR REORGANIZED STUART IS LICENSED OR MAY BECOME LICENSED IN THE FUTURE. INDIVIDUAL HOLDERS OF CLAIMS AND EQUITY INTERESTS CONCERNED ABOUT GAMING REQUIREMENTS ARE STRONGLY CAUTIONED TO CONSULT WITH COUNSEL IN CONNECTION WITH THE RECEIPT OF SHARES OF NEW COMMON STOCK UNDER THE PLAN.

Funding for the Plan

Funds to be used to make Cash payments under the Plan have been or will be generated from, among other things, the operation of Stuart's business, certain asset dispositions, the Standby Funding Commitment, and borrowing under the Exit Financing Facility.

Post-Confirmation Officers and Directors

Initial Board of Directors.

The initial board of directors of Reorganized Stuart following the Confirmation Date will be comprised of five directors as follows: (i) Joseph M. Valandra, as director and Chairman of the Board; (ii) Jock Patton; (iii) three members selected by Contrarian.

Initial Officers.

Reorganized Stuart's officers immediately before the Effective Date (as set forth in "Current Directors and Executive Officers" above) will serve as the initial officers of Reorganized Stuart on and after the Effective Date. Post-Effective Date base salaries for Reorganized Stuart's officers are as follows:

Officer	Base Salary
Joseph M. Valandra - Chief Executive Officer, President	$250,000
Lawrence X. Taylor - Chief Financial Officer, Executive Vice President	$165,000
Ernest Marchand - Chief Operating Officer	$150,000
Jimmy D. Helton - Senior Vice President-Strategic Development	$140,000
Clement F. Chantiam - Senior Vice President-Special Projects	$160,000

Description of Other Provisions of the Plan

Disputed Claims.

The Plan provides that with respect to any Disputed Claims and Equity Interests, for the purposes of effectuating the provisions of the Plan and the distributions to holders of Allowed Claims and Equity Interests, the Bankruptcy Court, on or before the Effective Date or another date the Bankruptcy Court may set, may fix or liquidate the amount of such Disputed Claims and Equity Interests under Section 502(c) of the Bankruptcy Code, in which event the amounts so fixed or liquidated will be deemed the maximum amounts of the Disputed Claims and Equity Interests under Section 502(c) of the Bankruptcy Code for purposes of distributions under the Plan.

When a Disputed Claim or Equity Interest becomes an Allowed Claim or Allowed Equity Interest, Reorganized Stuart will distribute to the holder of such Allowed Claim or Allowed Equity Interest the property to be distributed under the applicable provisions of the Plan.

Disputed Payments.

The Plan provides that if any dispute between and among holders of Claims or Equity Interests or holders of a Disputed Claim or Equity Interest as to the right of any Person to receive or retain any payment or distribution to be made to such Person under the Plan, Reorganized Stuart may, in lieu of making such payment or distribution to such Person, instead hold such payment or distribution, without interest, until the Bankruptcy Court or other court with appropriate jurisdiction issues a Final Order resolving such dispute.

Unclaimed Property.

Any distributions under the Plan that remain unclaimed for a period of one year after the Effective Date will revert and revest in Reorganized Stuart, with any entitlement of any holder of any Claim or Equity Interest to such distributions forever forfeited, extinguished, and barred.

Issuance of New Securities.

Shares of New Common Stock will be issued to holders of Allowed Claims in Class 4, as well as upon the exercise of the Executive Options and the

Equity Incentive Options. For a complete description of these securities, see "OVERVIEW OF THE PLAN – Description of Transactions to be Implemented in Connection with the Plan – New Common Stock."

Discharge.

Except as provided in the Plan or the Confirmation Order, the rights afforded under the Plan and the treatment of Claims and Equity Interests under the Plan are in exchange for and in complete satisfaction, discharge, and release of, all Claims including any interest accrued on General Unsecured Claims from the Petition Date and termination of all Equity Interests. Except as provided in the Plan or the Confirmation Order, Confirmation: (a) discharges the Debtor and Reorganized Stuart from all Claims or other debts that arose before the Confirmation Date, and all debts of the kind specified in Sections 502(g), 502(h) or 502(i) of the Bankruptcy Code, whether or not: (i) a proof of claim based on such debt is filed or deemed filed under Section 501 of the Bankruptcy Code; (ii) a Claim based on such debt is Allowed under Section 502 of the Bankruptcy Code; or (iii) the holder of a Claim based on such debt has accepted the Plan; and (b) terminates all Equity Interests and other rights of Equity Interests in the Debtor except as expressly provided in the Plan. Notwithstanding the foregoing, no Allowed Class 6 Subsidiary Claims are discharged until the later of: (x) the Effective Date; (y) the closing of the Exit Financing Facility; and (z) the payment and satisfaction in full of the Claims of the DIP Lender under the DIP Facility and the DIP Loan Documents in accordance with Section 2.7 of the Plan.

Termination of Subordination Rights.

The classification and manner of satisfying all Claims and Equity Interests under the Plan take into consideration all contractual, legal, and equitable subordination rights, whether arising under general principles of equitable subordination, Sections 510(b) and (c) of the Bankruptcy Code or otherwise, that a holder of a Claim or Equity Interest may have against other Claim or Equity Interest holders with respect to any distribution made in accordance with the Plan. As of the Effective Date, all contractual, legal, or equitable subordination rights that a holder of a Claim or Equity Interest may have with respect to any distribution to be made in accordance with the Plan is discharged and terminated, and all actions related to the enforcement of such subordination rights are permanently enjoined and distributions under the Plan are not subject to payment to a beneficiaries of such terminated subordination rights, or to levy, garnishment, attachment, or other legal process by any beneficiary of such terminated subordination rights. Under Bankruptcy Rule 9019 and in consideration of the distributions and other benefits provided under the Plan, the provisions of Section 5.15 of the Plan constitute a good faith compromise and settlement of all claims or controversies relating to the termination of all contractual, legal, and equitable subordination rights that a holder of a Claim or Equity Interest may have with respect to any

Allowed Claim or Allowed Equity Interest, or any distribution to be made on account of an Allowed Claim or an Allowed Equity Interest. The entry of the Confirmation Order constitutes the Bankruptcy Court's approval of the compromise and settlement of all such claims and controversies, and the Bankruptcy Court's finding that such compromise or settlement is in the best interests of the Debtor, Reorganized Stuart, and their respective property and holders of Claims and Equity Interests and is fair, equitable, and reasonable.

Injunctions.

Except as provided in the Plan or the Confirmation Order, as of the Confirmation Date, all entities that have held, currently hold or may hold a Claim or other debt or liability that is discharged or an Equity Interest, Equity Related Claim, or other right of an equity security holder that is terminated under the Plan are permanently enjoined from taking any of the following actions on account of any such discharged Claims, debts, liabilities, or terminated Equity Interests or rights: (a) commencing or continuing in any manner any action or other proceeding against Stuart or Reorganized Stuart (including any officer or director acting as a representative of Stuart or Reorganized Stuart); (b) enforcing, attaching, collecting or recovering in any manner any judgment, award, decree, or order against Stuart, Reorganized Stuart, or their respective property; (c) creating, perfecting, or enforcing any lien or encumbrance against Stuart, Reorganized Stuart, or their respective property; (d) asserting a setoff, right of subrogation or recoupment of any kind against any debt, liability, or obligation due to Stuart, Reorganized Stuart, or their respective property; and (e) commencing or continuing any action, in any manner, in any place, that does not comply with or is inconsistent with the provisions of the Plan or the Bankruptcy Code.

Exculpation.

None of the Debtor, Reorganized Stuart, the Indenture Trustee, or Contrarian, or any of their respective officers, directors, employees, advisors, attorneys, or agents, have or may incur any liability to any holder of a Claim or Equity Interest, including the holder of any Equity Related Claim, or any other party in interest, or any of their respective members or former members, agents, employees, representatives, financial advisors, attorneys, or affiliates, or any of their successors or assigns, for any act or omission in connection with, relating to, or arising out of, the Chapter 11 Case, the negotiation and execution of the prepetition Restructuring Agreement, the negotiation and pursuit of Confirmation of the Plan, or the consummation of the Plan, or the administration of the Plan *except for* their acts or omissions constituting willful misconduct, as finally determined by a court of competent jurisdiction and in all respects are entitled to reasonably rely upon the advice of counsel with respect to their duties and responsibilities under the Plan or in the context of the Chapter 11 Case. No holder of a Claim, Equity Interest, or

Equity Related Claim, or any other party in interest, including their respective agents, employees, representatives, financial advisors, attorneys, or affiliates, have any right of action against the Debtor, Reorganized Stuart, the Indenture Trustee, Contrarian, or any of their respective officers, directors, employees, advisors, attorneys, or agents, for any act or omission in connection with, relating to, or arising out of, the Chapter 11 Case, the negotiation and execution of the prepetition Restructuring Agreement, the negotiation and pursuit of Confirmation of the Plan, the consummation of the Plan, or the administration of the Plan, *except for* their acts or omissions constituting willful misconduct as finally determined by a court of competent jurisdiction. In addition, as of the Effective Date, the Debtor shall be deemed to have released its current and prior directors and officers from any claims or causes of action the Debtor may have against such parties, unless such claims or causes of action arise out of acts or omissions by such parties constituting willful misconduct.

Section 1146 Exemption.

In accordance with Section 1146(c) of the Bankruptcy Code: (a) the issuance, distribution, transfer, or exchange of the New Common Stock or other Estate property; (b) the creation, modification, consolidation, or recording of any deed of trust or other security interest, the securing of additional indebtedness by such means or by other means in furtherance of, or connection with, this Plan or the Confirmation Order; (c) the making, assignment, modification, or recording of any lease or sublease; or (d) the making, delivery, or recording of a deed or other instrument of transfer under, in furtherance of, or in connection with, this Plan, the Confirmation Order, or any transaction contemplated above, or any transactions arising out of, contemplated by, or in any way related to, the foregoing are not subject to any document recording tax, stamp tax, conveyance fee, intangibles or similar tax, mortgage tax, stamp act or real estate transfer tax, mortgage recording tax or other similar tax or governmental assessment and the appropriate state or local government officials or agents are directed to forego the collection of any such tax or assessment and to accept for filing or recordation any of the foregoing instruments or other documents without the payment of any such tax or assessment.

Full and Final Satisfaction.

In accordance with the Plan, all payments and all distributions are in full and final satisfaction, settlement, release, and discharge or all Claims and Equity Interests, except as otherwise provided in the Plan.

Cramdown.

If any impaired Class entitled to vote does not accept the Plan by the requisite majorities provided in Section 1126(c) or 1126(d) of the Bankruptcy Code as applicable (see "Acceptance or Rejection of the Plan" above), or if any impaired Class is deemed to have rejected the Plan, Stuart reserves the right to undertake to have the Bankruptcy Court confirm the Plan under Section 1129(b) of the Bankruptcy Code (see "ACCEPTANCE AND CONFIRMATION OF THE PLAN" below) and to amend the Plan, in accordance with the applicable provisions of the Plan governing amendments or modifications, to the extent necessary to obtain entry of the Confirmation Order.

Disbursement of Funds and Delivery of Distribution.

Subject to Bankruptcy Rule 9010, all distributions under the Plan are to be made by Reorganized Stuart or the Disbursing Agent to the holder of each Allowed Claim at the address of such holder as listed on the Schedules as of the Distribution Record Date, unless Stuart or Reorganized Stuart has been notified in writing of a change of address, including without limitation, by the filing of a proof of claim or notice of transfer of claim filed by such holder that provides an address for such holder different from the address reflected on the Schedules.

Any payment of Cash made by Reorganized Stuart or the Disbursing Agent under the Plan will be made by check drawn on a domestic bank. Any payment or distribution required to be made under the Plan on a day other than a Business Day will be made on the next succeeding Business Day.

Whenever any payment of a fraction of a cent would otherwise be required, the actual payment will reflect a rounding of such fraction to the nearest whole cent (rounding down for any amount less than one-half of one cent and rounding up for any amount one-half or more of one cent). No fractional shares of New Common Stock will be distributed under the Plan. Factional interests will be combined into as many whole shares of New Common Stock as possible and will be redistributed to holders of Claims and Equity Interests (as applicable) with fractional interests, in descending order, until all such whole shares of New Common Stock are distributed.

At the close of business on the Distribution Record Date, the claims register (for Claims) and the transfer ledgers (for Equity Interests) will be closed, and there will be no further changes in the record holders of any Claims or Equity Interests. Stuart, Reorganized Stuart, and the Indenture Trustee will have no obligation to recognize any transfer of any Claim or Equity Interest occurring after the close of business on the Distribution Record Date, and will instead by entitled to recognize and deal for all purposes under the Plan (except as to voting on the Plan) with only those holders of record as of the close of business on the Distribution Record Date.

Except as to applications for allowances of compensation and reimbursement of expenses under Sections 330 and 503 of the Bankruptcy Code, Stuart or Reorganized Stuart has the exclusive right to make and file objections to Administrative Expense Claims, Claims, and Equity Interests after the Confirmation Date. All objections will be litigated to Final Order, *provided, however,* that Reorganized Stuart retains the authority to compromise, settle, otherwise resolve, or withdraw any objections without authority of the Bankruptcy Court.

Retention of Jurisdiction.

Notwithstanding the entry of the Confirmation Order and the occurrence of the Effective Date, the Bankruptcy Court will, under the Plan, retain such jurisdiction over the Chapter 11 Case after the Effective Date as is legally permissible including, without limitation, jurisdiction to:

- Allow, disallow, determine, liquidate, classify, estimate, or establish the priority or secured or unsecured status of any Claim, including the resolution of any request for payment of any Administrative Claim and the resolution of any and all objections to the allowance or priority of Claims;
- Grant or deny any applications for allowance of compensation or reimbursement of expenses authorized under the Bankruptcy Code or the Plan;
- Resolve any matters related to the assumption, assumption and assignment, or rejection of any executory contract or unexpired lease to which the Debtor is a party and to hear, determine and, if necessary, liquidate, any Claims arising from, or cure amounts related to, such assumption or rejection;
- Ensure that distributions to holders of Allowed Claims are accomplished in accordance with the Plan;
- Decide or resolve any motions, adversary proceedings, contested or litigated matters, and any other matters and grant or deny any applications or motions involving the Debtor that may be pending on the Effective Date;
- Enter such orders as may be necessary or appropriate to implement or consummate the provisions of the Plan and all contracts, instruments, releases, and other agreements or documents created in connection with the Plan or the Disclosure Statement, except as otherwise provided in the Plan;
- Resolve any cases, controversies, suits or disputes that may arise in connection with the consummation, interpretation or enforcement of the Plan or any Person's obligations incurred in connection with the Plan;
- Modify the Plan before or after the Effective Date under Section 1127 of the Bankruptcy Code or modify the Disclosure Statement or any contract, instrument, release, or other agreement or document created in connection with the Plan or the Disclosure Statement; or remedy

any defect or omission or reconcile any inconsistency in any Bankruptcy Court order, the Plan, the Disclosure Statement, the Plan Supplement, or any contract, instrument, release, or other agreement or document created in connection with the Plan, the Disclosure Statement, or the Plan Supplement, in such manner as may be necessary or appropriate to consummate the Plan, to the extent authorized by the Bankruptcy Code;

- Issue injunctions, enter and implement other orders, or take such other actions as may be necessary or appropriate to restrain interference by any entity with consummation or enforcement of the Plan, except as otherwise provided in the Plan;
- Enter and implement such orders as are necessary or appropriate if the Confirmation Order is for any reason modified, stayed, reversed, revoked, or vacated;
- Determine any other matters that may arise in connection with or relate to the Plan, the Disclosure Statement, the Confirmation Order or any contract, instrument, release, or other agreement or document created in connection with the Plan, the Disclosure Statement or the Confirmation Order except as otherwise provided in the Plan;
- Enter an order closing the Chapter 11 Case; and
- Adjudicate the Avoidance Actions, the Litigation Claims (including those to be initiated and prosecuted by Reorganized Stuart as the Estate's representative under Section 1123(b)(3)(B) of the Bankruptcy Code), and any other cause of action or claims of the Debtor.

Executory Contracts and Unexpired Leases; Bar Date.

All executory contracts and unexpired leases that exist between the Debtors and any Person and are *either* set forth on the schedule of rejected executory contracts and unexpired leases filed with the Bankruptcy Court as part of the Plan Supplement, *or* which do not appear in the Plan Supplement shall be deemed rejected as of the Effective Date, *except for* any executory contract or unexpired lease that has been assumed or rejected pursuant to an order of the Bankruptcy Court entered prior to the Confirmation Date.

Entry of the Confirmation Order constitutes: (a) the approval under Section 365(a) of the Bankruptcy Code of the assumption of the executory contracts and unexpired leases assumed under the Plan or otherwise during the Chapter 11 Case; and (b) the approval under Section 365(a) of the Bankruptcy Code of the rejection of the executory contracts and unexpired leases rejected under the Plan or otherwise during the Chapter 11 Cases. Notwithstanding anything contained in this section to the contrary, as part of the Plan Supplement, the Debtor retains the right to add to, or delete from, the list of rejected executory contracts and unexpired leases any executory contract or unexpired lease that is initially an assumed executory contract or an assumed unexpired lease on the Schedules.

On the Effective Date or as soon thereafter as practicable, Reorganized Stuart will Cure any defaults under any executory contract or unexpired lease assumed under this Plan in accordance with Section 365(b)(1) of the Bankruptcy Code.

Executory contracts and unexpired leases entered into, and other obligations incurred, after the Petition Date by the Debtor, will be performed by the Debtor or Reorganized Stuart, as applicable, in the ordinary course of business.

All proofs of claims relating to Claims arising from the rejection of any executory contract or unexpired lease under the Plan must be filed with the Bankruptcy Court no later than thirty (30) days after the Confirmation Date. Any such Claim not filed within that time is forever barred. With respect to any executory contract or unexpired lease rejected by the Debtor before the Confirmation Date, the deadline for filing such Claims will be as set forth in the Bar Date Order.

Indemnification Claims.

Any obligations of the Debtor to indemnify any Person serving as a fiduciary of any employee benefit plan or employee benefit program of the Debtor, under charter, by-laws, contract, or applicable state law is deemed to be, and will be treated as, an executory contract and assumed by Reorganized Stuart on the Confirmation Date. Any obligation of the Debtor to indemnify, reimburse, or limit the liability of any Person, including but not limited to any officer or director of the Debtor or any of its Subsidiaries, or any agent, professional, financial advisor, or underwriter of any securities issued by the Debtor related to any acts or omissions occurring before the Petition Date: (a) are rejected, canceled, and discharged under the Plan as of the Confirmation Date; and (b) any and all Claims resulting from such obligations are disallowed under Section 502(e) of the Bankruptcy Code. Notwithstanding any of the foregoing, nothing contained in the Plan impacts, impairs or prejudices the rights of any Person covered by any applicable D&O Policy with respect to such policy or policies. Moreover, Reorganized Stuart will maintain in force for a period of three years following the Effective Date appropriate D&O Policies covering pre-Effective Date directors and officers of the Debtor and containing substantially the same provisions and limits of coverage as the policies that were in force on the Petition Date, and Reorganized Stuart will also be responsible for paying the deductible or retention amounts under such policies for such three-year period. No securities litigation is currently pending against Stuart or its present or past officers or directors.

Retiree Benefits.

Payment of any Retiree Benefits are to be continued solely to the extent, and for the duration of the period, Stuart is contractually or legally obligated to provide such benefits, subject to any rights Stuart has under applicable law.

Fees and Expenses of Indenture Trustee and Contrarian.

All unpaid reasonable fees, costs, charges, and any other expenses incurred under the Indenture or by Contrarian from and after the Petition Date, including any reasonable fees and expenses of Professionals retained by the Indenture Trustee or Contrarian as of the Effective Date, shall be paid by Reorganized Stuart as administrative expenses under Bankruptcy Code § 503(b)(3)(D). After the Effective Date, all reasonable fees, costs, charges and expenses payable to the Indenture Trustee or Contrarian (if any) including any such items incurred by the Indenture Trustee in its capacity as Disbursing Agent under the Plan, shall be paid by Reorganized Stuart without further Bankruptcy Court approval. The Indenture Trustee shall be compensated by Reorganized Stuart for services rendered during the period up to, but not including, the Effective Date, including the reasonable compensation, disbursements, and expenses of the agents and legal counsel of the Indenture Trustee in connection with the performance of their duties under the Indenture and under the Plan upon presentation of invoices without application by or on behalf of the Indenture Trustee to the Bankruptcy Court and without notice and hearing unless specifically requested by a party in interest. The Debtor and Reorganized Stuart shall indemnify the Indenture Trustee for any loss, liability, or expense incurred by the Indenture Trustee in connection with the performance of such duties to the same extent and in the same manner as provided in the Indenture. Upon payment in full of the fees and expenses of the Indenture Trustee, the Indenture Trustee's liens on the distributions to the holders of the Notes shall be released and extinguished. If Reorganized Stuart or the Indenture Trustee cannot agree upon the amount of fees and expenses to be paid, such fees and expenses shall be determined by the Bankruptcy Court.

Post-Confirmation Fees; Final Decree.

Reorganized Stuart will be responsible for the payment of any post-Confirmation fees due to the U.S. Trustee under 28 U.S.C. § 1930(a)(6) and the filing of post-Confirmation reports, until a final decree is entered. A final decree will be entered as soon as practicable after distributions have commenced under the Plan.

Revesting of Assets.

Subject to the provisions of the Plan, the property of the Estate vests in Reorganized Stuart on the Effective Date. As of the Effective Date, all such property is free and clear of all liens, Claims, and Equity Interests, except as otherwise provided in the Plan. From and after the Effective Date, Reorganized Stuart may operate its business, and may use, acquire, and dispose of its property free of any restrictions of the Bankruptcy Code, including the employment of, and payment to, Professionals, except as otherwise provided in the Plan or the Confirmation Order.

Limited Releases.

Except as otherwise specifically provided in the Plan, for good and valuable consideration, including without limitation the Indenture Trustee's facilitating the expeditious reorganization of the Debtor and implementation of the Plan, the Indenture Trustee, on and after the Effective Date, is released by the Debtor and Reorganized Stuart from any and all claims (as defined in Section 101(5) of the Bankruptcy Code), obligations, rights, suits, damages, causes of action, remedies, and liabilities whatsoever, whether known or unknown, foreseen or unforeseen, existing or hereafter arising, in law, equity, or otherwise, that the Debtor would have been legally entitled to assert in its own right or on behalf of the holder of any Claim or Equity Interest or other Person, based in whole or in part upon any act or omission, transaction, agreement, event or other occurrences taking place on or before the Effective Date.

General Release of Liens.

Except as otherwise provided in the Plan in connection with the Exit Financing Facility, or in any contract, instrument, indenture, or other agreement or document created in connection with the Plan, on the Effective Date, all mortgages, deeds of trust, liens, or other security interests against property of the Estate are released and extinguished, and all the right, title, and interest of any holder of such mortgages, deeds of trust, liens, or other security interests will revert to Reorganized Stuart and its successors and assigns.

Conditions to Confirmation and Effective Date.

Conditions To Confirmation. The following are conditions precedent to confirmation of the Plan:

(a) The Bankruptcy Court enters a Final Order approving the Disclosure Statement with respect to this Plan;

(b) The Confirmation Order has been entered in form and substance reasonably acceptable to the Debtor. If the Debtor is unable to reach an agreement with regard to the form and substance of the Confirmation Order, the Bankruptcy Court will resolve all such disputes between the parties;

(c) The Confirmation Order contains the following:

- The provisions of the Confirmation Order are nonseverable and mutually dependent;
- All executory contracts or unexpired leases assumed by Reorganized Stuart during the Chapter 11 Cases or under this Plan will remain in full force and effect for the benefit of Reorganized Stuart notwithstanding any provision in such contract or

lease (including those described in Sections 365(b)(2) and (f) of the Bankruptcy Code) that prohibits such assignment or transfer or that enables, permits or requires termination of such contract or lease;

- Except as expressly provided in this Plan, the Debtor is discharged as of the Confirmation Date from all Claims and any "debt" (as that term in defined in Section 101(12) of the Bankruptcy Code) that arose on or before the Confirmation Date, and the Debtor's liability in respect of such Claims and debts is extinguished completely, whether reduced to judgment or not, liquidated or unliquidated, contingent or noncontingent, asserted or unasserted, fixed or unfixed, matured or unmatured, disputed or undisputed, legal or equitable, or known or unknown, or that arose from any agreement of the Debtor that has either been assumed or rejected in the Chapter 11 Cases or under this Plan, or obligation of the Debtor incurred before the Confirmation Date, or from the Debtor's conduct before the Confirmation Date, or that otherwise arose before the Confirmation Date including, without limitation, all interest, if any, on any such debts, whether such interest accrued before or after the Petition Date;
- The Plan does not provide for the liquidation of all or substantially all of the Debtor's property and Confirmation is not likely to be followed by the liquidation of Reorganized Stuart or the need for further financial reorganizations; and
- The Confirmation Order, in accordance with Section 1123(b)(3)(B) of the Bankruptcy Code, specifically appoints Reorganized Stuart as a representative and agent of the Debtor to prosecute, compromise, or abandon the Litigation Claims in accordance with the Plan.

(d) The Bankruptcy Court enters a Final Order approving the Standby Funding Commitment.

Conditions To Effectiveness. The following are conditions precedent to the occurrence of the Effective Date:

(a) The Confirmation Date has occurred;

(b) The Confirmation Order is a Final Order, *except that* the Debtor reserves the right to cause the Effective Date to occur notwithstanding the pendency of an appeal of the Confirmation Order, under circumstances that would moot such appeal;

(c) No request for revocation of the Confirmation Order under Section 1144 of the Bankruptcy Code has been made, or, if made, remains pending;

(d) The Bankruptcy Court in the Confirmation Order has approved the retention of jurisdiction provisions in Article 13 of the Plan;

(e) All documents necessary to implement the transactions contemplated by this Plan are made in form and substance reasonably acceptable to the Debtor and the Committee;

(f) Reorganized Stuart retains sufficient Cash on the Effective Date to make required distributions to holders of Allowed Claims on the Distribution Date; and

(g) Reorganized Stuart receives all regulatory approvals including, without limitation, all approvals by applicable gaming authorities, which have become final and nonappealable or any period of objection by regulatory authorities has expired, as applicable, and all other material approvals, permits, authorization, consents, licenses, and agreements from other third parties necessary or appropriate to permit the transactions contemplated by the Plan and any related agreements and to permit Reorganized Stuart to carry on its business after the Effective Date in a manner consistent in all material respects with the manner in which it was carried on before the Effective Date (collectively, the "Approvals"). The Approvals must not contain any condition or restriction that materially impairs Reorganized Stuart's ability to carry on its business in a manner consistent in all respects with the manner as proposed to be carried on by Reorganized Stuart under the Plan.

Waiver Of Conditions. The conditions to Confirmation and the Effective Date may be waived in whole or in part by the Debtor at any time without notice, an order of the Bankruptcy Court, or any further action other than proceeding to Confirmation and consummation of the Plan.

ACCEPTANCE AND CONFIRMATION OF THE PLAN

The following is a brief summary of the provisions of the Bankruptcy Code relevant to acceptance and confirmation of a plan of reorganization. Holders of Claims and Equity Interests are encouraged to review the relevant provisions of the Bankruptcy Code with their own attorneys.

Acceptance of the Plan

This Disclosure Statement is provided in connection with the solicitation of acceptances of the Plan. The Bankruptcy Code defines acceptance of a plan of reorganization by a class of Claims as acceptance by holders of a least two-thirds in dollar amount, and more than one-half in number, of the Allowed Claims of that Class that have actually voted or are deemed to have voted to accept or reject a plan. The Bankruptcy Code defines acceptance of a plan of reorganization by a class of interests as acceptance by at least two-thirds in amount of the allowed interests of that class that have actually voted or are deemed to have voted to accept or reject a plan.

If one or more impaired Classes rejects the Plan, Stuart may, in its discretion, nevertheless seek confirmation of the Plan if Stuart believes that it will be able to meet the requirements of Section 1129(b) of the Bankruptcy Code for Confirmation of the Plan (which are summarized below), despite the lack of acceptance by all Impaired Classes.

Confirmation

Confirmation Hearing.

Section 1128(a) of the Bankruptcy Code requires the Bankruptcy Court, after notice, to hold a hearing on confirmation of a plan. Notice of the Confirmation Hearing regarding the Plan has been provided to all known holders of Claims and Equity Interests or their respective representatives along with this Disclosure Statement. The Confirmation Hearing may be adjourned from time to time by the Bankruptcy Court without further notice except for an announcement of the adjourned date made at the Confirmation Hearing or any subsequent adjourned Confirmation Hearing.

Section 1128(b) of the Bankruptcy Code provides that any party in interest may object to confirmation of a plan. Any objection to Confirmation of the Plan must be in writing, must conform with the Bankruptcy Rules and the Local Rules of the Bankruptcy Court, must set forth the name of the objecting party, the nature and amount of Claims or Equity Interests held or asserted by that party against Stuart's Estate or property, and the specific basis for the objection. Such objection must be filed with the Bankruptcy Court, with a copy forwarded directly to the chambers of the Honorable Mary F. Walrath, together with a proof of service, and served on all parties and by the date set forth on the notice of the Confirmation Hearing.

Statutory Requirements for Confirmation of the Plan.

At the Confirmation Hearing, Stuart will request that the Bankruptcy Court determine that the Plan satisfies the requirements of Section 1129 of the Bankruptcy Code. If the Bankruptcy Court so determines, the Bankruptcy Court will enter an order confirming the Plan. The applicable requirements of Section 1129 of the Bankruptcy Code are as follows:

(a) The Plan must comply with the applicable provisions of the Bankruptcy Code;

(b) Stuart must have complied with the applicable provisions of the Bankruptcy Code;

(c) The Plan must have been proposed in good faith and not by any means forbidden by law;

(d) Any payment made or promised to be made by Stuart under thePlan for services or for costs and expenses in, or in connection with, the Chapter 11 Case, or in connection with the Plan, must have been disclosed to the Bankruptcy Court, and any such payment made before Confirmation of the Plan must be reasonable, or if such payment is to be fixed after Confirmation of the Plan, such payment must be subject to the approval of the Bankruptcy Court as reasonable;

(e) Stuart must have disclosed the identity and affiliates of any indvidual proposed to serve, after Confirmation of the Plan, as a director, officer, or voting trustee of Stuart under the Plan. Moreover, the appointment to, or continuance in, such office of such individual, must be consistent with the interests of holders of Claimsand Equity Interests and with public policy, and Stuart must have disclosed the identity of any insider that Reorganized Stuart will employ or retain, and the nature of any compensation for such insider;

(f) *Best Interests of Creditors Test:* With respect to each Class of Impaired Claims or Equity Interests, either each holder of a Claim or Equity Interest of such Class must have accepted the Plan, or must receive or retain under the Plan on account of such Claim or Equity Interest, property of a value, as of the Effective Date of the Plan, that is not less than the amount that such holder would receive or retain if Stuart were liquidated on such date under Chapter 7 of the Bankruptcy Code. In a Chapter 7 liquidation, creditors and interest holders of a debtor are paid from available assets generally in the following order, with no lower class receiving any payments until all amounts due to senior classes have either been paid in full or payment in full is provided for: (i) first to secured creditors (to the extent of the value of their collateral), (ii) next to priority creditors, (iii) next to unsecured creditors, (iv) next to debt expressly subordinated by its terms or by order of the Bankruptcy Court, and (v) last to holder of equity interests. Attached as Exhibit 4 to this Disclosure Statement is a liquidation analysis prepared by Stuart, which indicates that, in light of the foregoing priority scheme, if the Chapter 11 Case were converted to a Chapter 7 liquidation, holders of Allowed Claims and Equity Interests would receive less than they will receive under the Plan;

(g) Each Class of Claims or Equity Interests must have either accepted the Plan or not be Impaired under the Plan;

(h) Except to the extent that the holder of a particular Claim has agreed to a different treatment of such Claim, the Plan provides that Allowed Administrative and Priority Claims (other than Allowed Priority Tax Claims) will be paid in full on the Effective Date and that Allowed Priority Tax Claims will receive on account of such Claims deferred Cash payment, over a period not exceeding six years after the date of assessment of such Claim, of a value, as of the Effective Date, equal to the Allowed amount of such Claim;

(i) At lease one impaired Class of Claim must have accepted the Plan, determined without including any acceptance of the Plan by any insider holding a Claim of such Class;

(j) *Feasibility:* Confirmation of the Plan must not be likely followed by the liquidation, or the need for further financial reorganization of Stuart or any successor to Stuart under the Plan. Attached as Exhibit 5 to this Disclosure Statement are projections for approximately 30 months following Confirmation and a *pro forma* balance sheet as of the Effective Date that demonstrates that, given estimated expenses and income, and taking into account cash reserves, Reorganized Stuart will be able to satisfy its obligations under the Plan, as well as its obligations arising in connection with its ongoing business operations.

Confirmation Without Acceptance by All Impaired Classes. Section 1129(b) of the Bankruptcy Code allows a Bankruptcy Court to confirm a plan, even if such plan has not been accepted by all impaired classes entitled to vote on such plan, provided that such plan has been accepted by at least one impaired class. If any impaired classes reject or are deemed to have rejected the Plan, Stuart reserves its right to seek the application of the requirements set forth in Section 1129(b) of the Bankruptcy Code for Confirmation of the Plan despite the lack of acceptance by all impaired classes.

Section 1129(b) of the Bankruptcy Code provides that notwithstanding the failure of an impaired class to accept a plan or reorganization, the plan must be confirmed, on request of the plan proponent, in a procedure commonly known as "cramdown," so long as the plan does not "discriminate unfairly" and is "fair and equitable" with respect to each class of impaired Claims or Interests that has not accepted the plan.

The condition that a plan by "fair and equitable" with respect to a rejecting class of secured Claims includes the requirements that (a) the holders of such secured Claims retain the liens securing such Claims to the extent of the allowed amount of the Claims, whether the property subject to the liens is retained by the debtor or transferred to another entity under the plan, and (b) each holder of a secured Claim in the class receives deferred cash payments totaling at least the allowed amount of such Claim with a present value, as of the effective date of the plan, at lease equivalent to the value of the secured claimant's interest in the debtor's property subject to the liens.

The condition that a plan be "fair and equitable" with respect to a rejecting class of unsecured Claims includes the requirement that either (a) such class receive or retain under the plan property of a value as of the effective date of the plan equal to the allowed amount of such Claim or (b) if the class does not receive such amount, no class junior to the non-accepting class will receive a distribution under the plan.

The condition that a plan by "fair and equitable" with respect to a rejecting class of equity interests includes the requirements that either (a) the plan provides that each holder of an equity interest in such class receive or retain under the plan, on account of such equity interest, property of a value, as of the effective date of the plan, equal to the greater of (i) the allowed amount of any fixed liquidation preference to which such holder is entitled, (ii) any fixed redemption price to which such holder is entitled, or (iii) the value of such equity interest, or (b) if the class does not receive such amount, no class of equity interests junior to the rejecting class will receive a distribution under the plan.

VALUATION AND FEASIBILITY

Section 1129(a)(11) of the Bankruptcy Code requires that, in order for the Court to confirm a plan of reorganization, the Court must determine that the plan is feasible – that is, that confirmation of the plan in not likely to be followed by liquidation or by the need for further financial structuring, unless such is specifically provided for in the plan. For purposes of determining whether the Plan meets this requirement, Stuart has analyzed Reorganized Stuart's future prospects and its ability to meet its obligations under the Plan.

Included as part of Exhibit 5 to this Disclosure Statement are: (a) a projected balance sheet as of the Effective Date of the Plan (assumed to be December 31, 1999) (Exhibit 5-A); (b) a valuation analysis (Exhibit 5-B); and (c) a projected cash flow and EBITDA statement (Exhibit 5-C). These projections were prepared by Stuart and include projections of the expected results of operations of Reorganized Stuart.

Based on the projected results of operations, cash flows, and income, Stuart believes that the Plan complies with the financial feasibility standards for confirmation of the Plan set forth in Section 1129(a)(11) of the Bankruptcy Code. Stuart believes that the assumptions set forth in the various projections are reasonable, that the projections are attainable by Reorganized Stuart on an operational basis, and that Reorganized Stuart will have sufficient funds available to meet its obligations under the Plan.

THE PROJECTIONS AND ANALYSES CONTAINED IN THIS DISCLOSURE STATEMENT SHOULD NOT BE REGARDED AS A REPRESENTATION OR WARRANTY BY STUART, REORGANIZED STUART, OR ANY OTHER PERSON, INCLUDING ANY PROFESSIONAL EMPLOYED BY, OR ANY OFFICERS, DIRECTORS, EMPLOYEES, OR OTHER REPRESENTATIVES OF, SUCH PARTIES, THAT ANY PROJECTED RESULTS OF OPERATIONS OR RECOVERIES WILL BE REALIZED. ACTUAL RESULTS ACHIEVED BY REORGANIZED STUART MAY VARY MATERIALLY FROM THE PROJECTED RESULTS. HOLDERS OF CLAIMS AND EQUITY INTERESTS MUST MAKE THEIR OWN DETERMINATION AS TO THE REASONABLENESS OF THE ASSUMPTIONS UNDERLYING THE PROJECTIONS IN REACHING THEIR DECISIONS TO ACCEPT

OR REJECT THE PLAN.

Key Assumptions Underlying the Projections

The projections set forth in Exhibit 5 to this Disclosure Statement assume: (a) an Effective Date of the Plan of December 31, 1999; and (b) from and after the Effective Date, Reorganized Stuart will operate its businesses in substantially the same manner as immediately before the Effective Date and described in this Disclosure Statement. Any other assumptions underlying particular projections are set forth in Exhibit 5 to this Disclosure Statement.

CERTAIN FEDERAL INCOME TAX CONSEQUENCES OF THE PLAN

The following discussion sets forth the material federal income tax consequences of the Plan to Reorganized Stuart and certain holders of Claims. This discussion is based on the provisions of the Internal Revenue Code of 1986, as amended (the "Tax Code"), final, temporary, and proposed Treasury regulations thereunder, and administrative and judicial interpretations thereof, all as in effect as of this Disclosure Statement. There can be no assurance that the Internal Revenue Service (the "Service") will not take a contrary view, and no ruling from the Service or opinion of counsel has been or will be sought as to the federal income tax consequences of the Plan.

The description that follows does not include all matters that may be relevant to any particular holder and could be affected by the specific facts and circumstances pertaining to such holder. Certain holders, including financial institutions, broker-dealers, tax-exempt entities, insurance companies, and foreign persons may be subject to special rules not discussed below.

ALL HOLDERS ARE URGED TO CONSULT WITH THEIR OWN TAX ADVISERS AS TO THEIR PARTICULAR TAX CONSEQUENCES ASSOCIATED WITH THE PLAN, INCLUDING THE APPLICABILITY AND EFFECT OF ANY STATE, LOCAL, OR FOREIGN TAX LAWS, OR ANY PROPOSED LEGISLATION. FURTHER, THERE CAN BE NO ASSURANCE THAT THE TAX CONSEQUENCES TO REORGANIZED STUART WILL BE AS DISCUSSED, SINCE SUCH TAX CONSEQUENCES WILL BE SUBJECT TO FUTURE EVENTS THAT CANNOT BE PREDICTED WITH CERTAINTY.

Consequences to Holders of Certain Claims

Importance of Whether Certain Debt Instruments Constitute "Securities."

As discussed below, the federal income tax consequences to the Claim holders of the exchanges provided for by the Plan will depend, in part, on whether such exchanges qualify as a recapitalization or other "reorganization" as defined in the Tax Code. This, in turn, will depend, in part, on whether the Notes constitute "securities" for federal income tax purposes ("Securities" or "Security"). The term "security" is not defined in the Tax Code or in the regulations, and has not been clearly defined in court decisions. Although there are a number of factors that may affect the determination of whether a debt instrument is a Security, one of the most important factors is the original term of the instrument, *i.e.*, the length of time between the issuance of the instrument and its maturity. In general, instruments with an original term of more than ten (10) years are likely to be treated as Securities and instruments with a term of less than five (5) years are likely not to be treated as Securities. Stuart is not rendering federal income tax advice as to whether the Notes are, or are not, Securities. **ACCORDINGLY, STUART RECOMMENDS THAT THE CLAIM HOLDERS CONSULT WITH THEIR TAX ADVISORS AS TO THE PROPER TREATMENT OF THEIR RESPECTIVE DEBT INSTRUMENTS.**

Class 4 – Allowed Notes Claims

Under the Plan, holders of Allowed Notes Claims will receive New Common Stock. Gain or loss will be realized to the extent that the fair market value of the New Common Stock (other than any portion of consideration allocable to accrued but unpaid interest) received by the Claim holder exceeds (or is less than) the adjusted basis of the Notes (other than any portion of the basis in such Claim allocable to accrued but unpaid interest). However, the amount of gain recognized, if any, for federal income tax purposes depends (in part) on whether the Notes constitute Securities.

If the holder's Note constitutes a Security, then the exchange of such Note for New Common Stock should constitute a "recapitalization," which is a tax-free reorganization exchange under Sections 354(a) and 368(a) of the Tax Code. If so, the holder will not recognize gain or loss on the exchange. If the Note is not a Security, then the holder of such Note will recognize gain or loss on the exchange of such Note for New Common Stock equal to the amount of gain or loss realized.

Class 5 – General Unsecured Claims

Under the Plan, holders of Allowed General Unsecured Claims will receive Cash in full satisfaction of their claims. Gain or loss generally will be recognized to such holder in an amount equal to the difference between the amount of Cash received and the holder's adjusted basis in their Claim.

Class 7 – Equity Interests and Equity Related Claims

Under the Plan, the holders of Old Common Stock will receive Cash in exchange for the Old Common Stock. Gain or loss generally will be recognized to such holder in an amount equal to the difference between the amount of Cash received and the holder's adjusted basis in the Old Common Stock.

Character of Gain, Basis, and Holding Period.

The character of the potential gain or loss described above as long-term or short-term capital gain or loss or as ordinary income or loss will be determined by a number of factors. These factors include whether the particular Claim constitutes a capital asset in the hands of the Claim holder, whether the Claim has been held for more than one year, whether the Claim was purchased at a discount, and whether and to what extent the Claim holder has previously claimed a bad debt deduction with respect to such Claim.

In general, any recognized gain will be treated as capital gain and will be long-term capital gain if the holder held the Note or Old Common Stock as a capital asset, and if such holder held the Note or Old Common Stock for more than 12 months. In the case of a Note holder, if the holder purchased the Note at a market discount within the meaning of section 1278 of the Tax Code, any gain recognized will be treated as ordinary income to the extent of the accrued market discount on the Note.

In the case of any exchange described above that constitutes a reorganization, the Claim holder's basis in the New Common Stock received will equal the Note holder's adjusted tax basis in the Note surrendered. The Note holder's holding period for the stock received will include the Note holder's holding period for the Note surrendered, provided such Note was held as a capital asset.

In the case of any exchange described above that does not constitute a reorganization, the Note holder's basis in the stock received will be equal to the fair market value of such stock. The Note holder's holding period of such stock will begin on the day after receipt thereof.

Treatment of Accrued But Unpaid Interest.

Holders of Notes that have not previously included in their taxable income accrued but unpaid interest on a Note may be treated as receiving taxable interest to the extent any consideration they receive under the Plan is allocable to such accrued but unpaid interest. Holders of Notes that have previously included in their taxable income accrued but unpaid interest on a Note may be entitled to recognize a deductible loss to the extent such accrued but unpaid interest is not satisfied under the Plan. The proper allocation between principal and interest of amounts received in exchange for a Note is unclear and may be affected by, among other things, the rules in the Tax Code relating to imputed interest, original issue discount, market discount, and bond issuance premium. Thus, it is possible that the Service may take the position that a pro rata portion of the consideration received by a holder of a Note must be allocated to interest, or that consideration must be allocated first to accrued but unpaid interest and then to principal. In this regard, holders of Notes should consult their own tax advisors.

Backup Withholding.

All distributions under the Plan are subject to applicable withholding. Under the Tax Code, interest, dividends and other reportable payments may, under certain circumstances, be subject to backup withholding at a 31% rate. Backup withholding generally applies if the holder (a) fails to furnish its social security number or other taxpayer identification number ("TIN"), (b) furnishes an incorrect TIN, (c) fails properly to report interest or dividends, or (d) under certain circumstances, fails to provide a certified statement, signed under penalty of perjury, that the TIN is provided its correct number and that it is not subject to backup withholding. Backup withholding is not an additional tax but merely an advance payment, which may be refunded to the extent it results in an overpayment of tax. Certain persons are exempt from backup withholding, including corporations and financial institutions.

Consequences to Debtors

Discharge of Indebtedness and Reduction of Tax Attributes.

The principal amount of Stuart's aggregate outstanding indebtedness will be substantially reduced under the Plan. Generally, the cancellation or other discharge of indebtedness triggers ordinary income to a debtor unless payment of the liability would have given rise to a deduction. The amount of such discharge of indebtedness income generally will be equal to the excess of the principal amount (as determined for federal income tax purposes) of the indebtedness discharged over the aggregate value of cash and other property (including stock of Stuart) transferred in satisfaction of the debt. If debt is discharged in a case under the Bankruptcy Code, however, no ordinary income to the debtor generally results. Instead, certain tax attributes otherwise available to the debtor are reduced, in most cases by the amount that would otherwise be included as ordinary income.

Tax attributes are subject to reduction generally in the following order: (i) net operating losses ("NOLs") from prior taxable years or from the year in which the discharge occurs; (ii) general business credit carryovers; (iii) minimum tax credits; (iv) capital losses and capital loss carryovers; (v) the tax basis of the debtor's depreciable and non-depreciable assets, including inventory; (vi) passive activity loss and credit carryovers; and (vii) foreign tax credit carryovers. Attribute reduction is calculated only after the tax for the year of discharge has been determined, and asset basis reduction applies to property held by the debtor at the beginning of the taxable year following the taxable year in which the discharge occurs. Asset basis reduction is generally not required in an amount greater than the excess of the aggregate tax bases of the property held by the debtor immediately after the discharge over the aggregate of the debtor's liabilities immediately after the discharge. In very general terms, the basis of property other than inventory and notes and accounts receivable is reduced before the basis of inventory and notes and accounts receivable.

Stuart believes that the amount of the discharge of indebtedness income realized as a result of the Plan will result in a substantial reduction of Stuart's tax attributes. It is anticipated that Stuart's NOLs will be eliminated and that Stuart will be required to reduce the basis in its assets to a significant extent. These attribute reductions may have the effect of subjecting Stuart to greater federal income tax liabilities in taxable years subsequent to the year in which the discharge occurs than would occur absent the attribute reductions.

Limitation on Use of NOLs.

Stuart will very likely experience an "ownership change" for purposes of Section 382 of the Tax Code upon consummation of the Plan. In general, a corporation experiences an ownership change if the percentage of stock of the corporation owned by one or more stockholders that each own at least five percent of the stock of such corporation (or certain specified groups of stockholders) increases by more than 50 percentage points within a prescribed time period. In general, after a corporation experiences an ownership change, the amount of NOLs (and "built-in losses," if any, as defined for this purpose) arising before the ownership change that the corporation is permitted to use each year after the ownership change may not exceed a specified amount, referred to as the "Section 382 Limitation" and described below.

Assuming that Stuart experiences an ownership change, it may qualify for the so-called "Bankruptcy Exception" from the Section 382 Limitation under Tax Code Section 382(1)(5); however, the effect on the NOLs required under the Bankruptcy Exception may impose a greater tax burden on Stuart than the alternative of being subject to the Section 382 Limitation. This might be the case, for example, if, within two years after the ownership change resulting from consummation of the Plan, Stuart experiences another ownership change. If the Bankruptcy Exception is utilized and another ownership change occurs within the two-year period referred to above, then Stuart's Section 382 Limitation for any year thereafter would be zero and Stuart would not be permitted to reduce otherwise taxable income by any NOLs attributable to pre-ownership change years.

If Stuart anticipates that the Bankruptcy Exception will impose a tax burden on it greater than that resulting from application of the Section 382 Limitation, Stuart will likely elect not to have the Bankruptcy Exception apply. Stuart would then be subject to the Section 382 Limitation, which, pursuant to Tax Code Section 382(1)(6), would be calculated by multiplying the ""long-term tax-exempt rate" (which is a rate announced monthly by the Service and is 5.18% for the month of August 1999) by the sum of (i) the value of the outstanding stock of the Stuart immediately before consummation of the Plan plus (ii) the increase in the value of Stuart resulting from the discharge of creditor claims pursuant to the Plan.

As indicated above, it is anticipated that Stuart's NOLs attributable to the pre-ownership change years will be eliminated as a result of Stuart's realization of discharge of indebtedness income. In that case, Stuart's NOLs attributable to pre-ownership change years will not be impacted by the ownership change rules of Tax Code Section 382.

RISK FACTORS

The restructuring of Stuart involves a degree of risk, and this Disclosure Statement and certain of its Exhibits contain forward-looking statements that involve risks and uncertainty. Reorganized Stuart's actual results could differ materially from those anticipated in such forward-looking statements as a result of a variety of factors, including those set forth in the following risk factors and elsewhere in this Disclosure Statement. **HOLDERS OF CLAIMS AND EQUITY INTERESTS SHOULD CONSIDER CAREFULLY THE FOLLOWING FACTORS, IN ADDITION TO THE OTHER INFORMATION CONTAINED IN THIS DISCLOSURE STATEMENT, BEFORE SUBMITTING A VOTE TO ACCEPT OR REJECT THE PLAN.**

Leverage

Although the Plan will restructure a significant amount of Stuart's indebtedness, Reorganized Stuart will remain leveraged, particularly with respect to the Exit Financing Facility. See "OVERVIEW OF THE PLAN – Description of Transactions to be Implemented in Connection with the Plan – Exit Financing Facility." The level of Reorganized Stuart's indebtedness could have important consequences to stockholders, including: (a) a substantial portion of Reorganized Stuart's cash flow from operations must be dedicated to debt service and will not be available for other purposes; (b) Reorganized Stuart's ability to obtain additional debt financing in the future for working capital, capital expenditures, or acquisitions may be limited; and (c) Reorganized Stuart's level of indebtedness could limit its flexibility in reacting to changes in the industry and economic conditions generally. Reorganized Stuart's ability to satisfy its debt obligations will depend upon its future operating performance, which will be affected by prevailing economic conditions and financial, business, and other factors, certain of which are beyond its control. Reorganized Stuart believes that cash flow from operations, together with its other available sources of liquidity, will be adequate to make required payments of principal and interest on its indebtedness, to fund anticipated capital expenditures, and to meet working capital requirements, although there is no assurance that this will be the case. To the extent that cash flow from operations is insufficient to satisfy Reorganized Stuart's cash requirements, Reorganized Stuart will seek to raise additional cash through debt or equity financing. No assurance can be given that any such financing will be available to Reorganized Stuart, if at all, at the time or times needed or on terms acceptable to Reorganized Stuart, if at all.

Dependence on Key Personnel

Reorganized Stuart's operations depend to a great extent on the efforts of its officers and other key personnel, including Joseph M. Valandra, Lawrence X. Taylor, III, Jimmy D. Helton, Clement Chantiam, and Ernest Marchand, and on Reorganized Stuart's ability to attract new key personnel and retain existing key personnel in the future. There can be no assurance that Reorganized Stuart will be successful in attracting and retaining such personnel, or that it will not incur increased costs in order to do so. Reorganized Stuart's failure to attract additional qualified employees or to retain the services of key personnel could have a material adverse effect on Reorganized Stuart's business, financial condition, and results of operations.

Dependence and Relationships with Customers and Suppliers

The loss of sales to any of Stuart's largest customers would cause a substantial decrease in business and would have a material adverse effect on Reorganized Stuart. Furthermore, the principal raw material used in Stuart's business is paper, which is subject to pricing cycles. Stuart generally does not have written contracts with its suppliers. The cyclical nature of paper pricing may have a material adverse effect on Reorganized Stuart's business. For certain of its electronic products, Reorganized Stuart will continue to depend on suppliers to provide Reorganized Stuart with parts and components in adequate amounts and on a timely basis. The failure of one or more suppliers to meet Reorganized Stuart's performance specifications, quality standards, or delivery schedules could have a material adverse effect on Reorganized Stuart's business, financial condition, and results of operations.

Competition

The markets in which Stuart's products compete are extremely competitive. The principal competitive factors in the bingo paper and pulltab ticket markets are quality, service, and price. Stuart's major competitor in the bingo paper and pulltab markets is Arrow International. Stuart's electronic bingo systems, System 12™ and Power Bingo King™, compete with a number of other manufacturers of electronic bingo systems, none of whom manufacture a full line of bingo and bingo-related products. Stuart also competes with other forms of entertainment such as lotteries, on-line gaming products and the continued expansion of the legalization by the United States, Canada and other foreign jurisdictions of casino gaming. While there can be no assurances that Reorganized Stuart will continue to remain competitive in these or other areas, Stuart believes that through its strong distribution network, manufacturing facilities and technology, Reorganized Stuart will be able to maintain a unique position as a manufacturer of a full line of both consumable and electronic bingo and bingo-related products.

Risks Relating to Intellectual Property

Stuart regards its products as proprietary and relies on a combination of trademark, copyright and trade secret laws and employee and third-party nondisclosure agreements to protect its proprietary rights. Defense of intellectual property rights can be difficult and costly, and there can be no assurance that Reorganized Stuart will be able effectively to protect its technology from competitors. In addition, the protections offered by trademark, copyright and trade secret laws may not prevent a competitor from designing games having an appearance and function that closely resemble Reorganized Stuart's games. As the number of electronic gaming products in the industry increases, and the uses and functions of these products further overlap, electronic gaming developers may increasingly become subject to infringement claims. Stuart is currently a defendant in two patent infringement cases. Stuart or Reorganized Stuart may also become subject to additional infringement claims. Any such claims or litigation could be costly and could result in a diversion of management's attention, which could have a material adverse effect on Reorganized Stuart's business and financial condition. Any settlement of such claims or adverse determinations in such litigation could also have a material adverse effect on Reorganized Stuart's business, financial condition, and results of operations.

Projected Financial Information

Stuart failed to operate profitably for some time preceding the Chapter 11 filing. The financial projections annexed as Exhibit 5 to this Disclosure Statement depend on the successful implementation of the business plan and the validity of the other assumptions contained in it and in the Plan. These projections reflect numerous assumptions, including Confirmation of the Plan, and consummation of the Plan in accordance with its terms, the anticipated future performance of Reorganized Stuart, industry performance, certain assumptions with respect to Stuart's competitors, general business and economic conditions, and other matters, many of which are beyond Reorganized Stuart's control. In addition, unanticipated events and circumstances occurring after the preparation of the projections may affect the actual financial results ultimately achieved. Although Stuart believes that the projections are reasonably attainable, variations between the actual financial results and those projected may occur and be material.

Lack of Market for Securities Issued Under the Plan

There is currently no existing market for the New Common Stock and there can be no assurances with respect to the development of an active trading market or the degree of price volatility in any such particular market. Accordingly, no assurances can be given with respect to a security holder's ability to sell such securities in the future or the price at which any such sale may occur. If such a market were to exist, the liquidity of the market for such securities and the prices at which such securities trade will depend on many factors, including the number of holders, investor expectations for Reorganized Stuart, and other factors beyond Reorganized Stuart's control.

Reliance On Bingo Industry

The future profitability and growth of Reorganized Stuart's business is substantially dependent upon factors beyond Reorganized Stuart's control including, among other things, the continued popularity of bingo as a leisure activity and as a means of charitable fundraising. The bingo industry is a mature industry and there can be no assurance that it will not decline in the future due to an increase in competing forms of entertainment such as lotteries, on-line gaming products, and the continued expansion of the legalization by United States and foreign jurisdictions of casino gaming. In addition, the growth of the use of electronic bingo products could encroach upon the use of pulltabs, bingo paper and ink products, which currently constitute Stuart's core business. There can be no assurance that Reorganized Stuart will be able successfully to adapt its core business to such a change in the bingo industry. As a result of such factors, no assurance can be given of Reorganized Stuart's continued growth or profitability.

Relationships With Distributors

Stuart has enjoyed a history of cooperative relationships with most distributors of its products. Stuart generally does not have written contracts with its distributors. The failure to maintain these relationships on a widespread basis may have a material adverse effect on Reorganized Stuart's business, financial condition, and results of operations.

Government Regulation

Stuart is subject to regulation by authorities in most jurisdictions in which its bingo, bingo-related products and electronic gaming systems are sold or used by persons or entities licensed to conduct gaming activities. The gaming regulatory requirements vary from jurisdiction to jurisdiction, and licensing, other approval or finding of suitability processes with respect to Stuart, its personnel and its products can be lengthy and expensive. Many jurisdictions have comprehensive licensing, reporting and operating requirements with respect to the sale and manufacture of bingo and bingo-related products, including bingo paper and electronic bingo hall equipment. These licensing requirements have a direct impact on the conduct of Stuart's day-to-day operations. Generally, gaming regulatory authorities may deny applications for licenses, other approvals or findings of suitability for any cause they may deem reasonable. There can be no assurance that Reorganized Stuart, its products or its personnel will receive or be able to maintain any necessary gaming licenses, other approvals or findings of suitability. The loss of a license in a particular jurisdiction will prohibit Reorganized Stuart from selling products in that jurisdiction. The loss of one or more licenses held by Reorganized Stuart could have an adverse effect on Reorganized Stuart's business. Loss of one or more licenses for an extended period may have a material adverse effect on Reorganized Stuart's business, and the loss of one license could result in the loss of other licenses by Reorganized Stuart. The IGRA defines Class II gaming to include "the game of chance commonly known as bingo, whether or not electronic, computer or other technologic aids are used in connection therewith," and defines Class II gaming devices to include "electronic or electromechanical facsimiles of any game of chance or slot machines of any kind." Stuart believes that Power Bingo King™ and System 12™, which are designed to be played in conjunction with traditional paper bingo products, should properly be classified as Class II games, and has obtained a legal opinion to the effect that System 12™ is a Class II game. Stuart has applied for an advisory opinion from the National Indian Gaming Commission (the "NIGC") that System 12™ is a Class II game, as defined by IGRA, but has not yet received such designation. Stuart has not applied for or received any advisory opinion by the NIGC that Power Bingo King™ is a Class II game. It is possible that one or more regulatory authorities could take the position that Power Bingo King™ or System 12™ should be classified as Class II devices. If either of Reorganized Stuart's electronic gaming systems were classified as Class II devices, these products could not be sold to Indian casinos that did not meet the requirements of IGRA and their host state for carrying Class II devices. Such a result would have a material adverse effect on Reorganized Stuart's sale of its electronic bingo products.

Additionally, state and local laws in the United States, and provincial laws in Canada, which govern the sale and use of gaming products, are widely disparate and continually changing due to legislative and administrative actions and court interpretations. Changes in gaming laws through statutory enactment or amendment, court interpretation or administrative action, so as to restrict the manufacture, distribution or use of some or all of Reorganized Stuart's products could have a material adverse effect on Reorganized Stuart's business, financial condition, and results of operations.

New Product Development; Risk of Obsolescence

The market for certain of Reorganized Stuart's products, particularly for its electronic bingo hall equipment and for Video King products, is characterized by changing technology, new legislation, evolving industry standards and product innovations and enhancements. The introduction of products embodying new technology, the adoption of new legislation, or the emergence of new industry standards could render existing products obsolete or unmarketable. Reorganized Stuart's continued ability to anticipate such changes and to develop and introduce or obtain the rights to technological advancements and new products that will gain customer acceptance may be a significant factor in Reorganized Stuart's ability to expand, remain competitive or attract and retain customers. Reorganized Stuart's business may be adversely affected if Reorganized Stuart incurs delays in developing new products or enhancements or if such products or enhancements do not gain market acceptance. In addition, there can be no assurance that products or technologies developed by others will not render Reorganized Stuart's products or technologies noncompetitive or obsolete.

Risk of International Operations

Stuart derived approximately 31.29% and 29.67% of its revenues in the year ended December 31, 1998 and the six months ended June 30, 1999, respectively, from sales occurring in Canada. These revenues are subject to risks normally associated with international operations, including currency conversion risks, slower and more difficult accounts receivable collection, greater difficulty and expense in administering business abroad and complying with foreign laws. Stuart also operates a manufacturing facility in Mexico and is subject to local conditions, including union activities. Reorganized Stuart's success in dealing with these risks will affect the overall success of Reorganized Stuart's operations.

Reorganization Factors

As with any plan of reorganization or other financial transaction, there are certain risk factors that must be considered. All risk factors cannot be anticipated, some events will develop in ways that were not foreseen, and many or all of the assumptions that have been used in connection with this Disclosure Statement and the Plan will not be realized exactly as assumed. Some or all of such variations may be material. While efforts have been made to be reasonable in this regard, there can be no assurance that subsequent events will bear out the analyses set forth in this Disclosure Statement. Holders of Claims and Equity Interests should be aware of some of the principal risks associated with the contemplated reorganized:

- There is a risk that one of more of the required conditions or obligations under the Plan will not occur, be satisfied or waived, as the case may be, resulting in the inability to confirm the Plan.
- The total amount of all Claims filed in the Chapter 11 Case may be materially in excess of the estimated amounts of Allowed Claims assumed in the development of the Plan and in the valuation estimates provided above. The actual amount of all Allowed Claims in any Class may differ significantly from the estimates provided in this Disclosure Statement. Accordingly, the amount and timing of the distributions that will ultimately be received by any particular holder of an Allowed Claim in any Class may be materially and adversely affected should the estimates be exceeded as to any Class.
- A number of other uncertainties may adversely impact Reorganized Stuart's future operations including, without limitation, economic recession, increased competition, adverse regulatory agency actions, acts of God, or similar circumstances. Many of these factors will be

substantially beyond Reorganized Stuart's control, and a change in any factor or combination of factors could have a material adverse effect on Reorganized Stuart's financial condition, cash flows, and results of operations.

- There can be no assurance that Reorganized Stuart will be able to continue to generate sufficient funds to meet its obligations and necessary capital expenditures, notwithstanding the significant improvements in Reorganized Stuart's operations and financial condition. Although Reorganized Stuart's financial projections assume that Reorganized Stuart will generate sufficient funds to meet its working capital needs for the foreseeable future, its ability to gain access to additional capital, if needed, cannot be assured, particularly in view of possible competitive factors and industry conditions.

Certain Bankruptcy-Related Considerations

Risk of Non-Confirmation of the Plan.

Although Stuart believes that the Plan will satisfy all requirements necessary for Confirmation by the Bankruptcy Court, there can be no assurance that the Bankruptcy Court will reach the same conclusion. There can also be no assurance that modifications of the Plan will not be required for Confirmation, that such negotiations would not adversely affect the holders of Allowed Claims and Equity Interests, or that such modifications would not necessitate the re-solicitation of votes.

Nonconsensual Confirmation.

If any impaired class of claims or equity interests does not accept a plan of reorganization, a bankruptcy court may nevertheless confirm such a plan of reorganization at the proponent's request if at least one impaired class has accepted the plan of reorganization (without including the acceptance of any "insider" in such class) and, as to each impaired class that has not accepted the plan of reorganization, the bankruptcy court determines that the plan of reorganization "does not discriminate unfairly" and is "fair and equitable" with respect to rejecting impaired classes. If any Impaired Class of Claims or Equity Interests fails to accept the Plan in accordance with Section 1129(a)(8) of the Bankruptcy Code, Stuart reserves the right to request nonconsensual Confirmation of the Plan in accordance with Section 1129(b) of the Bankruptcy Code.

Dividends

Reorganized Stuart will be precluded from paying Cash dividends to holders of New Common Stock under the Exit Financing Facility. Reorganized Stuart intends, therefore, to retain earnings, if any, for working capital and to fund capital expenditures. There is no intention to pay Cash dividends on any shares of New Common Stock.

EXEMPTION FROM SECURITIES ACT REGISTRATION

The Plan contemplates the issuance of certain securities to holders of Allowed Claims and Allowed Equity Interests. Section 1145 of the Bankruptcy Code creates certain exemptions from the registration and licensing requirements of federal and state securities laws with respect to the issuance and distribution of securities by a debtor under a plan or reorganization to holders of claims or interests wholly or principally in exchange for those claims or interests.

Issuance of New Securities Under the Plan

With respect to the New Common Stock to be issued on the Effective Date, Stuart intends to rely on the exemption from the registration requirements of the Securities Act (and the equivalent state securities of "blue sky" laws) provided by Section 1145(a)(1) of the Bankruptcy Code. Generally, Section 1145(a)(1) of the Bankruptcy Code exempts the issuance of securities from the requirements of the Securities Act and the equivalent state securities and "blue sky" laws if the following conditions are satisfied: (a) the securities are issued by a debtor, an affiliate participating in a joint plan of reorganization with the debtor, or a successor of the debtor under a plan of reorganization; (b) the recipients of the securities hold a claim against, an interest in, or a claim for an administrative expense against, the debtor; and (iii) the securities are issued entirely in exchange for the recipient's claim against or interest in the debtor, or are issued "principally" in such exchange and "partly" for Cash or property. Stuart believes that the issuance of securities contemplated by the Plan will satisfy the aforementioned requirements and therefore is exempt from federal and state securities laws, although as discussed below, under certain circumstances, subsequent transfers of such securities may be subject to registration requirements under such securities laws.

Subsequent Transfer of Securities Issued Under the Plan

The securities issued pursuant to the Plan may be resold by the holders of such securities without restriction unless, as more fully described below, any such holder is deemed to be an "underwriter" with respect to such securities, as defined in Section 1145(b)(1) of the Bankruptcy Code. Generally, Section 1145(b)(1) of the Bankruptcy Code defines an "underwriter" as any person who (a) purchases a claim against, or interest in, a bankruptcy case, with a view towards the distribution of any security to be received in exchange for such claim or interest, (b) offers to sell securities issued under a bankruptcy plan on behalf of the holders of such securities, (c) offers to buy securities issued under a bankruptcy plan from persons receiving such securities, if the offer to buy is made with a view towards distribution of such securities, or (d) is an issuer as contemplated by Section 2(11) of the Securities Act. Although the definition of the term "issuer" appears in Section 2(4) of the Securities Act, the reference contained in

Section 1145(b)(1) of the Bankruptcy Code to Section 2(11) of the Securities Act purports to include as "underwriters" all persons who, directly or indirectly, through one or more intermediaries, control, are controlled by, or are under common control with, an issuer of securities. "Control" (as such term is defined in Rule 405 of Regulation C under the Securities Act) means the possession, direct or indirect, of the power to direct or cause the direction of the policies of a person, whether through the ownership of voting securities, by contract or otherwise. Accordingly, an officer or director of a reorganized debtor (or its successor) under a plan of reorganization may be deemed to be a "control person," particularly if such management position is coupled with the ownership of a significant percentage of the debtor's (or successor's) voting securities. Moreover, the legislative history of Section 1145 of the Bankruptcy Code suggests that a creditor who owns at least 10% of the voting securities of a reorganized debtor may be presumed to be a "control person."

The foregoing summary discussion is general in nature and has been included in this Disclosure Statement solely for informational purposes. Stuart makes no representations concerning, and does not provide any opinion or advice with respect to, the securities law and bankruptcy law matters described above. In light of the complex and subjectively interpretive nature of whether a particular recipient or securities under the Plan may be deemed to be an "underwriter" within the meaning of Section 1145(b)(1) of the Bankruptcy Code or an "affiliate" or "control person" under applicable federal and state securities laws and, consequently, the uncertainty concerning the availability of exemptions from the registration requirements of the Securities Act and equivalent state securities and "blue sky" laws, Stuart encourages potential recipients of New Common Stock to consider carefully and consult with its own attorneys with respect to these (and related) matters.

ALTERNATIVES TO THE PLAN AND CONSEQUENCES OF REJECTION

Among the possible consequences if the Plan is rejected or if the Bankruptcy Court refuses to confirm the Plan are the following: (1) an alternative plan could be proposed or confirmed; or (2) the Chapter 11 Case could be converted to a liquidation case under Chapter 7 of the Bankruptcy Code.

Alternative Plans

As previously mentioned, with respect to an alternative plan, Stuart and its professional advisors have explored various alternative scenarios and believe that the Plan enables the holders of Claims and Equity Interests to realize the maximum recovery under the circumstances. Stuart believes that the Plan is the best plan that can be proposed and served the best interests of Stuart and other parties in interest.

Chapter 7 Liquidation

For a discussion of a Chapter 7 liquidation, see "ACCEPTANCE AND CONFIRMATION OF THE PLAN – Confirmation – **Error! Reference source not found.**"

RECOMMENDATION AND CONCLUSION

Stuart and its professional advisors have analyzed different scenarios and believe that the Plan will provide for a larger distribution to holders of Claims and Equity Interests than would otherwise result if an alternative restructuring plan were proposed or Stuart's assets were liquidated. In addition, any alternative other than Confirmation of the Plan could result in extensive delays and increased administrative expenses resulting in potentially smaller distributions to the holders of Claims and Equity Interests. Accordingly, Stuart recommends confirmation of the Plan and urges all holders of Impaired Claims and Equity Interests to vote to accept the Plan, and to indicate acceptance by returning their Ballots so as to be received by no later than the Voting Deadline.

Date: Wilmington, Delaware
October 11, 1999

STUART ENTERTAINMENT, INC.

By: *_/s/ Joseph M. Valandra_*
Joseph M. Valandra
Chairman, Chief Executive Officer,
and President

SQUIRE, SANDERS & DEMPSEY L.L.P.
40 North Central Avenue, Suite 2700
Phoenix, Arizona 85004
(602) 528-4000

By: *_/s/ Craig D. Hansen_*
Craig D. Hansen
Thomas J. Salerno
Jordan A. Kroop

SAUL, EWING, REMICK & SAUL LLP
P.O. Box 1266
222 Delaware Avenue, Suite 1200
Wilmington, Delaware 19899
(302) 421-6800

By: *<u>/s/ Norman L. Pernick</u>*
Norman L. Pernick
J. Kate Stickles

Co-Counsel to Debtor

Exhibit 1
Plan of Reorganization
(omitted)

Exhibit 2
Form 10-K
(omitted)

Exhibit 3
Form 10-Q
(omitted)

Exhibit 4
Liquidation Analysis
(omitted)

Exhibit 5
Financial Projections
(omitted)

Exhibit 6
Gaming Requirements
(omitted)

APPENDIX O

SAMPLE PLAN—LIQUIDATION

The following plan is, as of the time of publication, currently proposed for confirmation in the ***Baptist Foundation of Arizona*** bankruptcy in Phoenix, Arizona. With combined debts of over $800 million, the case is the largest bankruptcy of a charitable organization in U.S. history. The Baptist Foundation's failure derives from what is known as "affinity fraud" — using victims' unquestioning faith in a religious or charitable organization to encourage investment in speculative and undercapitalized ventures. The Baptist Foundation's not-for-profit status made it exempt from securities laws and able to sell its securities without disclosing the speculative nature of the Baptist Foundation's investments. In the Chapter 11 case, to realize at least a significant return to the security-holders (many of whom are elderly pensioners and some of whom had invested most of their net worth), the plan of reorganization effects a "controlled liquidation" of the Baptist Foundation, distributing to creditors beneficial shares in a liquidating trust and certificates in two asset pools (held by newly-created entities) that will be held for a term of years to allow those assets to mature and produce income to creditors. The Baptist Foundation of Arizona will, shortly after confirmation, be dissolved. The plan also involves the ***substantive consolidation*** of the 90 plus estates of the debtor entities.

IN THE UNITED STATES BANKRUPTCY COURT FOR THE DISTRICT OF ARIZONA

In re:	) In Proceedings Under Chapter 11
	)
BAPTIST FOUNDATION OF ARIZONA, an Arizona nonprofit corporation; ARIZONA SOUTHERN BAPTIST NEW CHURCH VENTURES, INC., an Arizona nonprofit corporation; A.L.O., INC., an Arizona corporation; E.V.I.G., INC., an Arizona corporation, et al.,	) Case Nos. 99-13275-ECF-GBN through) 99-13364-ECF-RTB)) All Cases Jointly Administered Under Case) No. 99-13275-ECF-GBN)) (Substantive Consolidation Pending)
Debtors.	)))

JOINT LIQUIDATING PLAN OF REORGANIZATION OF THE DEBTORS UNDER CHAPTER 11 OF THE BANKRUPTCY CODE

SQUIRE, SANDERS & DEMPSEY L.L.P.
40 North Central Avenue, Suite 2700
Phoenix, Arizona 85004
Telephone: (602) 528-4000
Attorneys: Craig D. Hansen
Thomas J. Salerno
Larry Watson

Counsel to BAPTIST FOUNDATION OF ARIZONA, et al., Debtors

GALLAGHER & KENNEDY, P.C.
2700 North Central Avenue, Suite
Phoenix, Arizona
Telephone: (602) 530-8000
Attorneys: Charles R. Sterbach
Ed Zachary

Counsel to ARIZONA SOUTHERN BAPTIST NEW CHURCH VENTURES, INC., et al., Debtors

HENDRICKSON & ASSOCIATES
4411 S. Rural Road
Suite 201
Tempe, Arizona 85282
Telephone: (480) 345-7500
Attorneys: Brian W. Hendrickson

Counsel to ALO, INC. and E.V.I.G., INC., et al. Debtors

Dated: February 18, 2000
Phoenix, Arizona

TABLE OF CONTENTS

EXHIBITS

[*ACTUAL EXHIBITS NOT INCLUDED*]

INTRODUCTION

Baptist Foundation of Arizona ("BFA"), Arizona Southern Baptist New Church Ventures, Inc. ("NCV"), ALO, Inc. ("ALO"), E.V.I.G., Inc. ("EVIG"), and their subsidiaries and affiliates that are Chapter 11 debtors ("Chapter 11 Affiliates" and, together with BFA, NCV, ALO and EVIG, the "Debtors") propose the following joint plan of reorganization (the "Plan") for the resolution of their outstanding Claims including, without limitation, all Investor Claims and Equity Interests. All Creditors and other parties-in-interest should refer to the Disclosure Statement Summary and the Disclosure Statement contemporaneously filed with the Plan, for a discussion of the Debtors' history, business, properties, results of operations, risk factors, a summary and analysis of the Plan, and other related matters. The Debtors are the proponents of the Plan within the meaning of Section 1129 of the Bankruptcy Code.

All holders of claims against the Debtors are encouraged to read the Plan, the Disclosure Statement Summary, the Disclosure Statement and the related solicitation materials in their entirety before voting to accept or reject the Plan.

The Plan provides for the orderly sale over time of the assets of the Debtors and the Non-Debtor Affiliates (as defined below). To facilitate the orderly sale of such assets, a Liquidating Trust will be created. To minimize administrative costs and preserve certain favorable tax advantages, including a net operating loss carryforward of approximately $150,000,000, the Liquidating Trust will hold all of the capital stock in the New Residential Real Estate Subsidiary and the sole membership interest in the New Asset Subsidiary, LLC (as both terms are defined below). All of the assets of the Debtors and the Non-Debtor Affiliates will be transferred to either the New Residential Real Estate Subsidiary or the New Asset Subsidiary, LLC , subject to any valid and enforceable Liens, except as otherwise provided in the Plan.

In addition, under the Plan, the Debtors and the Non-Debtor Affiliates will transfer and assign any and all claims and causes of action of any kind that they may have to the Liquidating Trust. The Liquidating Trust will be governed and administered by the Liquidating Trustee, and all periodic cash distributions to the holders of Allowed Claims under the Plan will be made by the Liquidating Trust.

Following the Effective Date, the Debtors and the Non-Debtor Affiliates will no longer conduct their business. This Plan also provides for the dissolution of the Debtors and the Non-Debtor Affiliates following the Effective Date.

Subject to the restrictions on modifications set forth in Section 1127 of the Bankruptcy Code and Bankruptcy Rule 3019, and those restrictions on modification set forth in the Plan, the Debtors reserve the right to alter, amend, modify, revoke or withdraw this Plan prior to its substantial consummation.

Article 1. DEFINITIONS, RULES OF INTERPRETATION, AND COMPUTATION OF TIME

Definitions; Rules of Construction. For purposes of this Plan, except as expressly provided or unless the context otherwise requires, all capitalized terms not otherwise defined shall have the meaning ascribed to them in the Plan. Any term used in the Plan that is not defined in the Plan but is defined in the Bankruptcy Code or the Bankruptcy Rules retains the meaning ascribed to such term in the Bankruptcy Code or the Bankruptcy Rules. Whenever the context requires, such terms shall include the plural as well as the singular, the masculine gender includes the feminine gender, and the feminine gender includes the masculine gender.

Rules of Interpretation. For purposes of the Plan: (a) any reference in the Plan to a contract, instrument, release, indenture, or other agreement or document being in particular form or on particular terms and conditions; (b) any reference in the Plan to an existing document or exhibit filed or to be filed means such document or exhibit as it may have been or may be amended, modified, or supplemented; (c) unless otherwise specified, all references in the Plan to Sections, Articles, Appendices, Schedules, and Exhibits are references to Sections, Articles, Schedules, Appendices and Exhibits of or to the Plan; (d) the words "herein" and "hereto" refer to the Plan in its entirety rather than to a particular portion of the Plan; (e) captions and headings to Articles and Sections are inserted for convenience of reference only and are not intended to be a part of or affect the interpretation of the Plan; and (f) the rules of construction set forth in Section 102 of the Bankruptcy Code and in the Bankruptcy Rules shall apply.

Computation Of Time. In computing any period of time prescribed or allowed by the Plan, the provisions of Bankruptcy Rule 9006(a) shall apply.

Specific Definitions. As used in this Plan, the following terms have the following meanings specified below:

1.1 Administrative Claim. A Claim for any cost or expense of administration of the Chapter 11 Cases allowed under Sections 503(b), 507(b) or 546(c)(2) of the Bankruptcy Code and entitled to priority under Section 507(a)(1) of the Bankruptcy Code, including, without limitation: (a) fees payable under 28 U.S.C. § 1930; (b) actual and necessary costs and expenses incurred in the ordinary course of the Debtors' Estate or administering the Chapter 11 Cases; and (c) all Professional Fees to the extent Allowed by Final Order under Sections 330, 331, or 503 of the Bankruptcy Code.

1.2 Administrative Claim Bar Date. The date or dates established by the Bankruptcy Court for the filing of Administrative Claims, *except*

Claims for Professional Fees and Preserved Ordinary Course Administrative Claims.

1.3 Affiliate. With respect to any specified Person, any other Person directly or indirectly controlling or controlled by or under direct or indirect common control with such Person and, with respect to any specified natural Person, any other Person having a relationship by blood, marriage, or adoption not more remote than first cousins with such natural person. For purposes of this definition, "control" (including, with correlative meanings, the terms "controlled by" and "under common control with"), as used with regards to any Person, means the possession, directly or indirectly, of the power to direct or cause the direction of the management or policies of such Person, whether through the ownership of voting securities, by agreement, or otherwise.

1.4 Allowed. With respect to any Claim against, or Equity Interest in, the Debtors: (a) proof of which, requests for payment of which, or application for allowance of which, was filed or deemed filed on or before the Bar Date, Administrative Claim Bar Date, or the Professional Fee Bar Date, as applicable, for filing proofs of claim or equity interest or requests for payment for Claims of such type against the Debtors; (b) if no proof of claim or equity interest is filed, which has been or is ever listed by the Debtors in the Schedules as liquidated in amount and not disputed or contingent; or (c) a Claim or Equity Interest that is allowed in any contract, instrument, indenture, or other agreement entered into in connection with the Plan and, in any case, a Claim as to which no objection to its allowance has been interposed within the applicable period of limitation fixed by the Plan, the Bankruptcy Code, the Bankruptcy Rules or the Bankruptcy Court. The term "Allowed," when used to modify a reference in the Plan to any Claim, Equity Interest, Class of Claims, or Class of Equity Interests, means a Claim or Equity Interest (or any Claim or Equity Interest in any such Class) that is so allowed, *e.g.*, an "Allowed Secured Claim" is a Claim that has been allowed to the extent of the value, as determined by the Bankruptcy Court under Section 506(a) of the Bankruptcy Code, of any interest in property of the Estate securing such Claim.

1.5 ALO. ALO, Inc., an Arizona corporation, and one of the debtors and debtors in possession in the Chapter 11 Cases.

1.6 Assets. Collectively, each and every item of property and interests of the Debtors and the Non-Debtor Affiliates as of the Effective Date, whether tangible or intangible, legal or equitable, liquidated or unliquidated, including, without limitation: (a) Cash; (b) any amounts owed to one or more of the Debtors and the Non-Debtor Affiliates, including accounts receivable and contract rights; (c) all of the Debtors' and Non-Debtor Affiliates' books and records; and (c) all contracts, agreements, licenses and leases of the Debtors and Non-Debtor Affiliates. Assets shall not include Avoidance Actions and Litigation Claims.

1.7 Avoidance Actions. All statutory causes of actions preserved for the Estate under Sections 510, 542, 543, 544, 547, 548, 549, 550 and 1123(b)of the Bankruptcy Code.

1.8 Ballot. The form of ballot or ballots distributed with the Disclosure Statement Summary and the Disclosure Statement to holders of Claims and Equity Interests entitled to vote on the Plan on which an acceptance or rejection of the Plan and the election of the Preference Settlement Option is to be indicated.

1.9 Bankruptcy Code. Title 11 of the United States Code, 11 U.S.C. §§ 101-1330, as amended from time to time and as applicable to the Chapter 11 Cases.

1.10 Bankruptcy Court. The United States District Court for the District of Arizona having jurisdiction over the Chapter 11 Cases and, to the extent of any reference under 28 U.S.C. § 157, the unit of such District Court under 28 U.S.C. § 151.

1.11 Bankruptcy Rules. Collectively, the Federal Rules of Bankruptcy Procedure as promulgated under 28 U.S.C. § 2075 and any Local Rules of the Bankruptcy Court, as applicable to the Chapter 11 Cases.

1.12 Bar Date. The date or dates fixed by the Bankruptcy Court by which Persons asserting a Claim against the Debtors (*except* Administrative Claims, Preserved Ordinary Course Administrative Claims, and Claims for Professional Fees) must file a proof of claim or be forever barred from asserting a Claim against the Debtors or their property, from voting on the Plan, and sharing in distributions under the Plan.

1.13 BFA. Baptist Foundation of Arizona,, an Arizona non-profit corporation, and one of the debtors and debtors in possession in the Chapter 11 Cases.

1.14 BFA Series D Agreements. The debt securities issued by BFA pursuant to that certain offering of $200 million in aggregate principal amount of Accel-A-Rate Investment Agreements—Series D (Offering Circular dated June 1, 1999).

1.15 BFA Series D Notes. The debt securities issued by BFA pursuant to that certain offering of $100 million in aggregate principal amount of Maximum Value Performance Notes—Series D (Offering Circular dated June 1, 1999).

1.16 Business Day. Any day other than a Saturday, Sunday, or legal holiday (as defined in Bankruptcy Rule 9006).

1.17 Cash. Currency, checks drawn on a bank insured by the Federal Deposit Insurance Corporation, certified checks, money orders, negotiable instruments, and wire transfers of immediately available funds.

1.18 CFP. Christian Financial Partners, Inc., an Arizona non-profit corporation, and one of the debtors and debtors-in-possession in the Chapter 11 Cases.

1.19 CFP Series D Notes. The debt securities issued by CFP pursuant to that certain offering of $50 million in aggregate principal amount of Maximum Value Performance Notes—Series D (Offering Circular dated as of February 15, 1999).

1.20 Chapter 11 Affiliates. The entities set forth on Exhibit 1 to the Plan that are Chapter 11 debtors in the Chapter 11 Cases.

1.21 Chapter 11 Cases. Collectively, the cases under Chapter 11 of the Bankruptcy Code in which the Debtors are the debtors and debtors-in-possession, pending before the Bankruptcy Court.

1.22 Claim. A claim against a Person or its property as defined in Section 101(5) of the Bankruptcy Code, including, without limitation: (a) any right to payment, whether or not such right is reduced to judgment, liquidated, unliquidated, fixed, contingent, mature, unmatured, disputed, undisputed, legal, equitable, secured, or unsecured arising at any time before the Effective Date; or (b) any right to an equitable remedy for breach of performance if such breach gives rise to a right to payment, whether or not such right to an equitable remedy is reduced to judgment, fixed, contingent, matured, unmatured, disputed, undisputed, secured, or unsecured.

1.23 Class. A category of holders of Claims or Equity Interests which are substantially similar in nature to the Claims or Equity Interests of other holders placed in such category, as designated in ARTICLE 4 of this Plan.

1.24 Collateral. Any property or interest in property of the Estate, subject to a Lien to secure the payment or performance of a Claim, the Lien not being subject to avoidance under the Bankruptcy Code, otherwise invalid under the Bankruptcy Code or applicable state law, or invalidated pursuant to the Plea or the Substantive Consolidation Motion.

1.25 Confirmation Date. The date on which the Bankruptcy Court enters the Confirmation Order.

1.26 Confirmation Hearing. The duly noticed hearing held by the Bankruptcy Court concerning confirmation of the Plan pursuant to Section 1128 of the Bankruptcy Code. The Confirmation Hearing may be adjourned by the Bankruptcy Court from time to time without further notice other than the announcement of the adjourned date at the Confirmation Hearing.

1.27 Confirmation Order. The order of the Bankruptcy Court confirming the Plan in accordance with the Bankruptcy Code.

1.28 Consolidated Estates. The Estates of the Debtors, as substantively consolidated in accordance with and pursuant to 0 of the Plan.

1.29 Contingent Claim. Any Claim for which a proof of claim has been filed with the Bankruptcy Court: (a) which was not filed in a sum certain, or which has not accrued and is dependent on a future event that has not occurred and may never occur; and (b) which has not been Allowed on or before the Confirmation Date.

1.30 Creditor. Any holder of a Claim, whether or not such Claim in an Allowed Claim, encompassed within the statutory definition set forth in Section 101(10) of the Bankruptcy Code.

1.31 Creditors' Committee. The official committee of unsecured creditors appointed by the United States Trustee in the Chapter 11 Cases in accordance with Section 1102(a)(1) of the Bankruptcy Code.

1.32 Cure. The distribution on the Initial Distribution Date (or as soon thereafter as practicable) of Cash, or such other property as may be agreed on by the parties or ordered by the Bankruptcy Court, with respect to the assumption of an executory contract or unexpired lease of nonresidential real property, in accordance with Section 365(b) of the Bankruptcy Code, in an amount equal to all unpaid monetary obligations, without interest, or such other amount as may be agreed on by the parties or ordered by the Bankruptcy Court, under such executory contract or unexpired lease, to the extent such obligations are enforceable under the Bankruptcy Code and applicable state law.

1.33 D&O Policy. Any directors and officers liability insurance policy, any errors and omissions policy applicable to directors and officers of any of the Debtors or any of the Non-Debtor Affiliates and any other insurance policy in which the Debtors or any of the Non-Debtor Affiliates are beneficiaries.

1.34 Debt Instrument. A debenture, bond, promissory note, note or other transferable instrument or document evidencing any payment obligation.

1.35 Debt Securities Claim. Any Securities Claim arising directly or indirectly from an Investor Debt Security.

1.36 Debtors. Collectively, BFA, NCV, ALO, EVIG, and the Chapter 11 Affiliates, as debtors and debtors-in-possession in the Chapter 11 Cases, in accordance with Sections 1107 and 1108 of the Bankruptcy Code.

1.37 Disbursing Agent. The Liquidating Trust, or such other Person as may be retained by the Liquidating Trust to make distributions to Allowed Claims under the Plan.

1.38 Disclosure Statement. The written disclosure statement relating to the Plan including, without limitation, all exhibits and schedules to such disclosure statement, in the form approved by the Bankruptcy Court under Section 1125 of the Bankruptcy Code and Bankruptcy Rule 3017.

1.39 Disclosure Statement Summary. The written summary of the Disclosure Statement, in the form approved by the Bankruptcy Court under Section 1125 of the Bankruptcy Code and Bankruptcy Rule 3017.

1.40 Disputed. With respect to Claims or Equity Interests, any Claim or Equity Interest: (a) that is listed in the Schedules as unliquidated, disputed, or contingent; (b) as to which the Debtors or any other party-in-interest has interposed a timely objection or request for estimation, or has sought to equitably subordinate or otherwise limit recovery in accordance with the Bankruptcy Code and the Bankruptcy Rules, or which is otherwise disputed by the Debtors in accordance with applicable law, and such objection, request for estimation, action to limit recovery or dispute has not been withdrawn or determined by a Final Order; or (c) that is a Contingent Claim.

1.41 Distribution Date. The date on which distributions are made to holders of Allowed Claims from time to time under the Plan by the Liquidating Trust.

1.42 Distribution Record Date. The date or dates established by the Bankruptcy Court by which holders of Claims and Equity Interests are determined for purposes of such holders' entitlement to receive distributions under the Plan on the Initial Distribution Date.

1.43 Distribution Reserve. The reserve, if any, established and maintained by the Liquidating Trust, into which the Liquidating Trustee shall deposit, or shall cause to be deposited, the amount of Cash that would have been distributed from time to time to holders of: (a) Disputed Claims; (b) Contingent Claims; and (c) unliquidated Claims, if such Claims had been liquidated on the Initial Distribution Date, such amount to be estimated by the Bankruptcy Court or agreed upon by the Liquidating Trust and the holders of such Claims, or sufficient to satisfy such unliquidated Claims upon such Claims' (x) allowance, (y) estimation for purposes of allowance, or (z) liquidation, pending the occurrence of such estimation or liquidation.

1.44 Easy Access Agreements. The debt securities issued by BFA pursuant to that certain offering of $100 million in aggregate principal amount of Easy Access Investment Agreements (Offering Circular dated June 1, 1999).

1.45 Education Investment Agreements. The debt securities issued by CFP pursuant to that certain offering of $10 million in aggregate principal amount of Education Investment Agreements—Series C (Offering Circular dated February 15, 1999).

1.46 Effective Date. The later of: (a) the first Business Day that is at least eleven days after the Confirmation Date and on which no stay of the Confirmation Order is in effect; and (b) the Business Day on which all of the conditions set forth in Section 0 of the Plan have been satisfied or waived.

1.47 Equity Interest. Any interest in BFA, NCV, ALO, or EVIG represented by any class or series of common or preferred stock before the Effective Date, and any warrants, options, or rights to purchase any such common or preferred stock.

1.48 Equity Securities Claim. Any Securities Claim arising directly or indirectly from an Equity Interest.

1.49 Estate. Collectively, the substantively consolidated estate of the Debtors created in the Chapter 11 Cases in accordance with Section 541 of the Bankruptcy Code and 0 of the Plan.

1.50 EVIG. E.V.I.G., Inc., an Arizona corporation, and one of the debtors and debtors in possession in the Chapter 11 Cases.

1.51 Exchange Act. The Securities Exchange Act of 1934, as amended, and the regulations promulgated under such Act.

1.52 Excise Tax Claims. All Claims against the Debtors for: (a) taxes on prohibited transactions under Section 4975 of the Revenue Code assessed against any disqualified person (as defined in Section 4975(e)(2) of the Revenue Code), participating in a prohibited transaction (as defined in Section 4975(c) of the Revenue Code); and (b) excise taxes imposed pursuant to Sections 4941 through 4945 of the Revenue Code.

1.53 FAS. Foundation Administrative Services Inc., an Arizona corporation, and one of the debtors and debtors in possession in the Chapter 11 Cases.

1.54 Final Order. Any order or judgment of the Bankruptcy Court: (a) as to which the time to appeal, petition for certiorari, or motion for reargument or rehearing has expired; or (b) as to which no appeal, petition for certiorari, or other proceedings for reargument or rehearing is pending; or (c) as to which any right to appeal, petition for certiorari, reargument, or rehearing has been waived in writing in form and substance satisfactory to the Debtors and the Liquidating Trust; or (d) if an appeal, writ of certiorari, or reargument or rehearing has been sought, as to which the highest court to which such order was appealed, or certiorari, reargument or rehearing has determined such appeal, writ of certiorari, reargument, or rehearing, or has denied such appeal, writ of certiorari, reargument, or rehearing, and the time to take any further appeal, petition for certiorari, or move for reargument or rehearing has expired; *provided, however,* that the possibility that a motion under Rule 59 or Rule 60 of the Federal Rules of Civil Procedure, or any analogous rule under the Bankruptcy Rules, may be filed with respect to such order does not prevent such order from being a Final Order.

1.55 GAAP. The generally accepted accounting principles set forth in the opinions and pronouncements of the Accounting Principles Board of the American Institute of Certified Public Accountants and statements and pronouncements of the Financial Accounting Standards Board or in such other statements by such other entity as have been approved by a significant segment of the accounting profession.

1.56 General Litigation Certificate. The Litigation Certificate, substantially in the form of Exhibit 2 to the Plan, to be issued by the Liquidating

Trust to all holders of Allowed Investor Claims, entitling such holder to receive recoveries on account of all Litigation Claims, except recoveries arising from: (a) those claims based on breach of fiduciary duties arising out of or related to the IRA and trust activities of the Debtors prior to the Petition Date; and (b) recoveries from Avoidance Actions.

1.57 General Unsecured Claim. Any Claim, including an Unsecured Deficiency Claim, against any of the Debtors as of the Petition Date not secured by a charge against, Lien upon or interest in property of the Estate, excluding: (a) Secured Claims; (b) Administrative Claims; (c) Preserved Ordinary Course Administrative Claims; (d) Priority Tax Claims; (e) Priority Claims; (f) Claims for Professional Fees; (g) Investor Claims; and (h) Securities Claims.

1.58 General Unsecured Claim Distribution Percentage. The percentage recovery of each holder of an Allowed Unsecured Claim as set forth in the General Unsecured Claim Recovery Schedule.

1.59 General Unsecured Claim Recovery Schedule. The Schedule filed with the Bankruptcy Court by the Debtors pursuant to Section 0 of the Plan, setting forth the Debtors' estimate of the expected recovery under the Plan of each holder of an Allowed General Unsecured Claim notwithstanding the substantive consolidation of the Debtors' Estate pursuant to 0 of the Plan.

1.60 GEF. Group Endowment Fund, and its successors and assigns.

1.61 GIF. Group Investment Fund II, and its successors and assigns.

1.62 GUC-Net Distributable Cash Payment. Net Distributable Cash for any calendar quarter, commencing on the first full calendar quarter following the Effective Date, multiplied by ten percent (10%), except that, in no event, shall the aggregate of all GUC-Net Distributable Cash Payments to the holder of an Allowed General Unsecured Claim exceed the amount to be paid to such holder as set forth on the General Unsecured Claim Recovery Schedule.

1.63 Initial Distribution Date. The first business day after the Effective Date or as soon thereafter as is practical on which distributions are made to holders of Allowed Claims under the Plan.

1.64 Indemnification Claims. Any Claim of any Person arising from or related to obligations for contribution, indemnification and exculpation by the Debtors arising under applicable laws or agreement or as provided in any of the Debtors' or Non-Debtor Affiliates' certificate of incorporation, bylaws, or policies in effect before or as of the Confirmation Date, excluding any Claims of any member of the Restructuring Committee arising under the Restructuring Committee By-Laws.

1.65 Intercompany Claim. The Claim of any Debtor or Non-Debtor Affiliate against any other Debtor or Non-Debtor Affiliate, including any

Claim that is a Subsidiary Claim.

1.66 Investor Advisory Committee. The three Person committee comprised of those individuals selected by the Creditors' Committee, subject to the approval of the Bankruptcy Court, who are holders of Allowed Investor Claims.

1.67 Investor Claims. Any Claim arising out of or related to, directly or indirectly, an Investor Debt Security and Related Investor Claim including accrued and unpaid interest at the non-default rate up to but not including the Petition Date, except those Claims that are Securities Claims.

1.68 Investor Debt Securities. Collectively, the Mortgage Backed Notes (CFP), Mortgage Backed Notes (Series A-E), Series C Shares, Series D Agreements (CFP), 18-Month Series D Agreements, Education Investment Agreements, CFP Series D Notes, Easy Access Agreements, BFA Series D Notes, Series I Agreements, BFA Series D Agreements, Peak Performance Notes, Peak Performance Notes – Series B, Series E Agreements and Mortgage Backed Notes (NCV), and any other debt security issued by BFA, NCV or CFP prior to the Petition Date.

1.69 IRA. Individual Retirement Account.

1.70 IRS. The Internal Revenue Service.

1.71 Lien. A lien as defined in Section 101(37) of the Bankruptcy Code, except a lien that has been avoided in accordance with Sections 544, 545, 546, 547, 548, or 549 of the Bankruptcy Code.

1.72 Liquidating Trust. The trust established pursuant to the Plan and the Liquidating Trust Agreement.

1.73 Liquidating Trust Agreement. The Liquidating Trust Agreement that will, subject to the terms of the Plan, govern the orderly sale of assets of the Debtors and Non-Debtor Affiliates and the distributions to Creditors as provided in the Plan. The Liquidating Trust Agreement shall be substantially in the form contained in Exhibit 3 to the Plan

1.74 Liquidating Trust Board. The three Person board to be selected by the Creditors' Committee and the Restructuring Committee prior to the Confirmation Hearing, subject to the approval of the Bankruptcy Court.

1.75 Liquidating Trustee. The Person to be designated as the "Liquidating Trustee" pursuant to the Plan and the Liquidating Trust Agreement at or prior to the Confirmation Hearing.

1.76 Liquidation Certificate. The certificate to be issued by the Liquidating Trust pursuant to the Plan and the Liquidating Trust Agreement, to the holders of Allowed Investor Claims, entitling them to receive the Cash distributions on the Initial Distribution Date and additional distributions of Net Distributable Cash. The Liquidation Certificate will be substantially in the form of Exhibit 4 to the Plan.

1.77 Litigation Claims. All rights, claims, torts, liens, liabilities, obligations, actions, causes of action, avoiding powers, proceedings, debts, contracts, judgments, offsets, damages and demands whatsoever in law or in equity, whether known or unknown, contingent or otherwise, that the Debtors or their Estates may have against any Person including, without limitation, those listed on Exhibit 5 to the Plan. Litigation Claims shall not include Avoidance Actions. Failure to list a Litigation Claim in the Plan or the Disclosure Statement does not constitute a waiver or release by the Debtors or the Liquidating Trust of such Litigation Claim.

1.78 Mortgage Backed Notes (CFP). The debt securities issued by CFP pursuant to that certain offering of $50 million in aggregate principal amount of Mortgage Backed Notes (Offering Circular dated December 11, 1996).

1.79 Mortgage Backed Notes (NCV). The debt securities issued by NCV pursuant to those certain Offering Circulars dated as of September 1, 1993 (Series B), September 1, 1994 (Series C), September 1, 1995 (Series D), and July 1, 1996 (Series E).

1.80 Mortgage Backed Notes (Series A-E). The debt securities issued by BFA pursuant to those Offering Circulars dated as of September 1, 1992 (Series A), September 1, 1993 (Series B), September 1, 1994 (Series C), September 1, 1995 (Series D) and September 1, 1996 (Series E).

1.81 NCV. Arizona Southern New Church Ventures, Inc., an Arizona non-profit corporation, and one of the debtors and debtors-in-possession in the Chapter 11 Cases.

1.82 Net Avoidance Action Recovery. All recoveries on account of Avoidance Actions (excluding any Litigation Claims and any litigation claims arising under or related to any IRA or trust activities conducted by the Debtors prior to the Petition Date) assigned by the Debtors and the Non-Debtor Affiliates to the Liquidating Trust, minus all Professional Fees and other expenses accrued and paid in conjunction with the prosecution of such Avoidance Actions.

1.83 Net Distributable Cash. All Cash of the Liquidating Trust and the Platform Subsidiaries, including the Net Avoidance Action Recovery, at the end of each calendar quarter, commencing at the end of the first full calendar quarter following the Effective Date, minus the sum of: (a) any accrued and unpaid expenses of the Liquidating Trust and the Platform Subsidiaries for such quarterly period; (b) a capital reserve amount (i.e., for working capital, required capital expenditures and payments reserved for holders of Claims in Class 1, Class 2 and Class 4) as determined, in good faith, by the Liquidating Trustee and approved by the majority of the Liquidating Trust Board; (c) any unpaid obligations (whether interest or principal), arising out of debt, sinking funds or capital lease obligations due during such quarterly period; (d) any reserves for payments to be made pursuant to the Plan as determined, in good faith, by the Liquidating Trustee and approved by the majority of the Liquidating Trust Board; (e) any Distribution Reserve; (f) any unpaid Professional Fees and necessary reserves for pursuing Litigation Claims, as determined in good faith by the Liquidating Trustee, and approved by the majority of the Liquidating Trust Board, in conjunction with the prosecution of Litigation Claims; and (g) the Net Litigation Recovery.

1.84 Net Litigation Recovery. All recoveries on account of Litigation Claims (except for any litigation claims arising under or related to any IRA or trust activities conducted by the Debtors prior to the Petition Date) assigned by the Debtors and the Non-Debtor Affiliates to the Liquidating Trust, minus all Professional Fees and other expenses accrued and paid in conjunction with the prosecution of such Litigation Claims.

1.85 New Asset Subsidiary, LLC. The Arizona limited liability company to be formed pursuant to the Plan which, following the Effective Date, will hold title to, or ownership interests in, certain assets of the Debtors and Non-Debtor Affiliates.

1.86 New Asset Subsidiary, LLC Articles of Organization. The Articles of Organization of the New Asset Subsidiary, LLC , which will be an Arizona limited liability company formed on or before the Effective Date and whose sole member shall be the Liquidating Trust. The Articles of Organization of the New Asset Subsidiary, LLC shall be substantially in the form of Exhibit 7 to the Plan.

1.87 New Asset Subsidiary, LLC Operating Agreement. The Operating Agreement of the New Asset Subsidiary, LLC , which will be an Arizona limited liability company formed on or before the Effective Date and whose sole member shall be the Liquidating Trust. The Operating Agreement of the New Asset Subsidiary, LLC shall be substantially in the form of Exhibit 6 to the Plan.

1.88 New Residential Real Estate Subsidiary. Foundation Administrative Services, Inc., as reorganized and reconstituted pursuant to the Plan which, following the Effective Date, will hold title to, or ownership interests in, certain real estate assets and the net operating loss carryforward of the Debtors and Non-Debtor Affiliates.

1.89 Non-Debtor Affiliates. The entities set forth on Exhibit 8 to the Plan that are owned by or under the common control of the Debtors.

1.90 Peak Performance Notes. The debt securities issued by BFA pursuant to that certain offering of $100 million in aggregate principal amount of Peak Performance Collateral Notes (Offering Circular dated November 1, 1994).

1.91 Peak Performance Notes – Series B. The debt securities issued by BFA pursuant to that certain offering of $100 million in aggregate principal amount of Peak Performance Collateral Notes (Offering Circular dated November 1, 1995).

1.92 Person. Any individual, corporation, partnership, joint venture, association, joint-stock company, trust, unincorporated association or organization, governmental agency or associated political subdivision.

1.93 Petition Date. November 9, 1999, the date on which the Debtors filed their voluntary petitions commencing the Chapter 11 Cases.

1.94 Plan. The Plan of Reorganization, either in its present form or as it may be amended, supplemented or modified from time to time, including all its annexed exhibits and schedules.

1.95 Platform Subsidiaries. Collectively, the New Residential Real Estate Subsidiary and the New Asset Subsidiary, LLC .

1.96 Preference Equalization Credit. The credit against distributions to be made under the Liquidation Certificate and the Cash distribution on the Initial Distribution Date to the holders of Allowed Investor Claims that received Cash payments within the Preference Period and have elected the Preference Settlement Option pursuant to Section 0 of the Plan.

1.97 Preference Period. With respect to any Investor Claims, the period from August 11, 1999 to November 9, 1999.

1.98 Preference Settlement Option. An election, made by so indicating on the Ballot, to receive the Preference Equalization Credit, by the holder of an Allowed Investor Claim that received Cash payments during the Preference Period.

1.99 Preserved Ordinary Course Administrative Claim. Administrative Claims that are based on liabilities incurred by the Debtors in the purchase, lease, or use of goods and services in the ordinary course of their business including, without limitation, Administrative Claims on account of services provided to the Debtors after the Petition Date by their employees.

1.100 Priority Claim. Any Claim (or portions of such Claim) entitled to priority under Section 507(a) of the Bankruptcy Code, other than Priority Tax Claims, Administrative Claims, Preserved Ordinary Course Administrative Claims and Claims for Professional Fees.

1.101 Priority Tax Claim. Any Claim of a governmental unit entitled to priority under Section 507(a)(8) of the Bankruptcy Code, excluding any Excise Tax Claim.

1.102 Professionals. Those Persons: (a) employed in accordance with an order of the Bankruptcy Court under Sections 327 or 1103 of the Bankruptcy Code and to be compensated for services under Sections 327, 328, 329, 330, and 331 of the Bankruptcy Code, or (b) for which compensation and reimbursement has been Allowed by the Bankruptcy Court under Section 503(b) of the Bankruptcy Code.

1.103 Professional Fee Bar Date. The date, as set by order of the Bankruptcy Court, by which all applications for compensation or expense reimbursement, including Professional Fees, must be filed with the Bankruptcy Court.

1.104 Professional Fees. The Administrative Claims for compensation and reimbursement of expenses submitted in accordance with Sections 330, 331, or 503(b) of the Bankruptcy Code of Professionals not otherwise satisfied in accordance with other provisions of the Plan.

1.105 Pro Rata. The ratio of an Allowed Claim in a particular Class under the Plan to the aggregate amount of all such Allowed Claims in such Class.

1.106 Reclamation Claims. Any Claim against the Debtors by any Person arising out of the sale of goods to the Debtors in the ordinary course of such Person's business, *provided that* such Person has otherwise satisfied the requirements of Section 546(c) of the Bankruptcy Code and the Uniform Commercial Code, as applicable.

1.107 Related Investor Claims. Collectively, all of the following: (a) all Claims of trusts in which the assets are invested in GIF or GEF, which, in turn, hold debt instruments issued by ALO, NCV or CFP or any subsidiaries or affiliates thereof; (b) all Claims of trusts that have invested in and currently hold Investor Debt Securities; (c) all Claims of trusts that hold promissory notes issued by Valley Real Estate Opportunities, Inc., NCV, FMC Holding Corp. and West Phoenix Estates; and (d) the Claims of any holder of any annuity contract in which the assets of the annuity are invested in GIF or GEF which, in turn, are invested in debt instruments issued by ALO, NCV or CFP or any subsidiaries or affiliates thereof.

1.108 Restated New Residential Real Estate Subsidiary By-Laws. The Amended and Restated By-Laws of FAS, as reorganized and reconstituted pursuant to the Plan, substantially in the form included as Exhibit 9 to the Plan.

1.109 Restated New Residential Real Estate Subsidiary Certificate. The Amended and Restated Certificate of Incorporation of FAS, as reconstituted and reorganized pursuant to the Plan, substantially in the form of Exhibit 10 to the Plan.

1.110 Restructuring Committee. The five Person committee responsible for the operation of the Debtors and the Non-Debtor Affiliates during the pendency of the Chapter 11 Cases, pursuant to the Order of the Bankruptcy Court dated November 9, 1999.

1.111 Restructuring Committee By-Laws. The By-Laws governing the duties and responsibilities of the Restructuring Committee of the Debtors as approved by the Bankruptcy Court.

1.112 Retiree Benefits. Payments to any Person, pursuant to Section

1114 of the Bankruptcy Code, for the purpose of providing or reimbursing payments for retired employees of the Debtors and of any other entities as to which the Debtors are obligated to provide retiree benefits and the eligible spouses and eligible dependents of such retired employees, for medical, surgical, or hospital care benefits, or in the event of death of a retiree under any plan, fund, or program (through the purchase of insurance or otherwise) maintained or established by the Debtors before the Petition Date, as such plan, fund, or program was then in effect or as later amended.

1.113 Revenue Code. The Internal Revenue Code of 1986, as amended from time to time.

1.114 Schedules. The schedules of assets and liabilities, the list of holders of interests, and the statements of financial affairs filed by the Debtors under Section 521 of the Bankruptcy Code and Bankruptcy Rule 1007, as such schedules, lists, and statements may have been or may be supplemented or amended from time to time.

1.115 SEC. The United States Securities and Exchange Commission.

1.116 Secured Claims. Any Claim, excepting therefrom any Investor Claim, to the extent reflected in the Schedules or a proof of claim as a Secured Claim, which is secured by a Lien on Collateral to the extent of the value of such Collateral, as determined in accordance with Section 506(a) of the Bankruptcy Code, or, if such Claim is subject to setoff under Section 553 of the Bankruptcy Code, to the extent of such setoff.

1.117 Secured Tax Claim. Any Claim of any state or local governmental unit or associated political subdivision that is secured by a Lien on property of the Estate by operation of applicable law including, without limitation, every Claim for unpaid real, personal property, or *ad valorem* taxes.

1.118 Securities Act. The Securities Act of 1933, as amended, and the regulations promulgated under such Act.

1.119 Securities Claim. Any Claim arising from the rescission of a purchase or sale of any Equity Interest, Investor Debt Security or Related Investor Claim issued by any of the Debtors, for damages arising from the purchase or sale of such securities or other damages alleged to arise under federal or state securities laws or regulations or under any contract related to any such sale or purchase, or for reimbursement, contribution or indemnification allowed under Section 502 of the Bankruptcy Code on account of such Claim, including, without limitation, any Indemnification Claims and any Claim with respect to any action pending or threatened against the Debtors and/or their current or former officers and directors.

1.120 Series C Shares. The debt securities issued by CFP pursuant to that certain offering of $20 million in aggregate principal amount of Cash Investment Fund—Series C shares (Offering Circular dated as of February 15, 1999).

1.121 Series D Agreements (CFP). The debt securities issued by CFP pursuant to that certain offering of $50 million in aggregate principal amount of Investment Agreements—Series D (Offering Circular dated February 15, 1999).

1.122 Series E Agreements. The debt securities issued by NCV pursuant to the following Offering Circulars: September 1, 1993 ($50,000,000), September 1, 1994 ($50,000,000), September 1, 1995 ($50,000,000), September 1, 1996 ($50,000,000) and September 1, 1997 ($50,000,000).

1.123 Series I Agreements. The debt securities issued by BFA pursuant to that certain offering of $200 million in aggregate principal amount of Investment Agreements—Series I (Offering Circular dated as of June 1, 1999).

1.124 Setoff Claims. All Claims, if any, against the Debtors, by a holder that has a valid right of setoff with respect to such Claims, which right is enforceable under Section 553 of the Bankruptcy Code as determined by a Final Order, or as otherwise agreed in writing by the Debtors or the Liquidating Trust, to the extent of the amount subject to such right of setoff.

1.125 Share. With respect to the Trust/IRA Litigation Certificate, the ratio of a holder's Claim based on the IRA and trust activities of the Debtors to the aggregate of all Claims based on the IRA and trust activities of the Debtors.

1.126 Subsidiary. Any entity of which all or a majority of the outstanding capital stock entitled to vote for the election of directors is owned or controlled, directly or indirectly, by the Debtors, by one or more subsidiaries of the Debtors, or by a Debtor and one or more of its other Subsidiaries.

1.127 Subsidiary Claim. Any Claim of a Subsidiary on account of any debt owed by one or more of the Debtors to any Subsidiary arising at any time before the Confirmation Date.

1.128 Substantive Consolidation Motion. The Motion to Substantively Consolidate the Debtors' Estates filed with the Bankruptcy Court by the Debtors on November 9, 1999, as may be amended or modified from time to time.

1.129 Summary Disclosure Statement. The short form summary of the Plan and Disclosure Statement in the form approved by the Bankruptcy Court under Section 1125 of the Bankruptcy Code and Bankruptcy Rule 3017.

1.130 Trust/IRA Litigation Certificate. The Litigation Certificate, substantially in the form of Exhibit 11 to the Plan, to be issued by the Liquidating Trust to certain holders of Allowed Investor Claims entitling such holders to receive recoveries on account of claims based on breach of fiduciary duty arising out of, or related to, the IRA and trust activities of the

Debtors prior to the Petition Date.

1.131 Unsecured Deficiency Claims. Any Claim by a Secured Creditor to the extent the value of such Creditor's Collateral, as determined in accordance with Section 506(a) of the Bankruptcy Code, exceeds the Allowed Amount of such Creditor's Claims as of the Petition Date, after taking into account any elections made pursuant to Section 1111(b) of the Bankruptcy Code.

1.132 Voting Record Date. The date established by the Bankruptcy Court by which holders of Allowed Claims and Equity Interests are determined for purposes of such holders' right to submit Ballots.

1.133 18-Month Series D Agreements. The debt securities issued by CFP pursuant to that certain offering of $20 million in aggregate principal amount of 18-Month Investment Agreements—Series D (Offering Circular dated as of February 15, 1999).

Article 2. SUBSTANTIVE CONSOLIDATION OF THE DEBTORS' ESTATES FOR CERTAIN DISTRIBUTION PURPOSES

2.1 Request For Substantive Consolidation. The Plan will be considered in connection with the Substantive Consolidation Motion. Approval of the Substantive Consolidation Motion is a condition precedent to the confirmation of the Plan. The Confirmation Order must contain findings supporting, and conclusions providing for, substantive consolidation of the Debtors' Estates for purposes of distributions on the terms set forth in this 0 of the Plan.

2.2 Effect Of Substantive Consolidation. Except as expressly set forth in Section 0 of the Plan, as a result of the substantive consolidation of the Assets and liabilities of the Debtors: (a) the Chapter 11 Cases shall be consolidated into the case of BFA as a single consolidated case; (b) all property of the Estate of each of the Debtors shall be deemed to be property of the Consolidated Estates; (c) all Claims against each Estate shall be deemed to be Allowed Claims against the Consolidated Estates, any proof of claim filed against one or more of the Debtors shall be deemed to be a single Claim filed against the Consolidated Estates, and all duplicate proofs of Claim for the same Claim filed against more than one Debtor shall be deemed expunged; (d) unless otherwise provided in the Plan, all Equity Interests in any Debtors shall be deemed extinguished for purposes of distributions under this Plan, and no distributions under this Plan shall be made on account of any such Equity Interests; (e) all Intercompany Claims by and against any of the Debtors or Non-Debtor Affiliates shall be eliminated, and no distributions under this Plan shall be made on account of Claims based upon such Intercompany Claims, except that the substantive consolidation shall not preclude the use of the Intercompany Claims as consolidation for the transfer of Assets to the Platform Subsidiaries; (f) except as specifically provided herein, all guarantees by one Debtor in favor of any other Debtor shall be eliminated, and no distributions under this Plan shall be made on account of Claims based upon such guarantees; and (g) for purposes of determining the availability of the right of setoff under Section 553 of the Bankruptcy Code, the Debtors shall be treated as one consolidated entity so that, subject to the other provisions of Section 553 of the Bankruptcy Code, debts due to any Debtor may be set off against the debts of any other Debtor.

2.3 Exceptions to Substantive Consolidation. The Substantive Consolidation Motion, and the consolidation that will occur pursuant to the Plan, shall be subject to the exceptions set forth in this Section.

No Impact on Secured Claims. Substantive consolidation shall have no effect upon valid, enforceable and unavoidable Liens, except for Liens that allegedly secure Investor Claims that are eliminated by virtue of substantive consolidation and Liens against Collateral that are extinguished by virtue of substantive consolidation. Substantive consolidation shall not have the effect of creating a Claim in a Class different from the Class in which a Claim would have been placed under the Plan in the absence of substantive consolidation. The substantive consolidation contemplated herein shall not effect any applicable date(s) for purposes of pursuing any Avoidance Actions.

No Impact on General Unsecured Claims. Substantive consolidation shall have no effect on Allowed General Unsecured Claims, which shall be treated in accordance with the terms of the Plan.

No Impact On Claims Against Non-Debtor Affiliates. Substantive consolidation shall not impact or otherwise affect any Claims against any of the Non-Debtor Affiliates, except Intercompany Claims.

Generally. Substantive consolidation shall not impact or otherwise affect provisions in this Plan which provide that specific entities comprising the Debtors or Non-Debtor Affiliates shall be liable on specific obligations under this Plan.

Article 3. TREATMENT OF UNCLASSIFIED CLAIMS

3.1 Unclassified Claims. As provided in Section 1123(a)(1) of the Bankruptcy Code, Administrative Claims, Preserved Ordinary Course Administrative Claims, Priority Tax Claims, and Reclamation Claims against the Debtors are not classified for purposes of voting on, or receiving distributions under, the Plan. Holders of such Claims are not entitled to vote on the Plan. All such Claims are instead treated separately in accordance with this 0 and in accordance with the requirements set forth in Section 1129(a)(9)(A) of the Bankruptcy Code.

3.2 Administrative Claims.

Generally. Each Allowed Administrative Claim, other than

Preserved Ordinary Course Administrative Claims and Reclamation Claims, is to be paid in full in Cash (or otherwise satisfied in accordance with its terms) on the latest of: (a) the Effective Date, or as soon thereafter as practicable; (b) such date as may be fixed by the Bankruptcy Court, or as soon thereafter as practicable; (c) the tenth Business Day after such Claim is Allowed, or as soon thereafter as practicable; and (d) such date as the holder of such Claim and the Debtors or the Liquidating Trust (as applicable) agree.

Included Expenses. Administrative Claims include costs incurred in the operation of the Debtors' businesses after the Petition Date, fees and expenses of Professionals retained by the Debtors and the Creditors' Committee appointed under Section 1102 of the Bankruptcy Code, and the fees due to the United States Trustee under 28 U.S.C. § 1930.

3.3 Preserved Ordinary Course Administrative Claims. Each Allowed Preserved Ordinary Course Administrative Claim is to be paid by the Liquidating Trust or the Platform Subsidiaries (as applicable) in accordance with either: (a) the terms and conditions under which such Claim arose; or (b) in the ordinary course of the Debtors' business. Such payments are to be made by the Liquidating Trust without further action by the holder of such Claim.

3.4 Priority Tax Claims. Any Allowed Priority Tax Claim is to be paid in full in Cash on the Effective Date by the Liquidating Trust; *provided, however,* that the Liquidating Trust may elect to pay any such Claims through deferred Cash payments over a period not exceeding 6 years after the date of assessment of such Claim, of a value as of the Effective Date, equal to the Allowed amount of such Claim. In that event, such payments are to be made in equal annual installments of principal, plus interest accruing from the Effective Date at the rate on the unpaid portion of Allowed Priority Tax Claim set forth in Revenue Code Sections 6621 and 6622. The first such payment is to be made payable on the latest of: (a) the Initial Distribution Date, or as soon thereafter as practicable; (b) the tenth Business Day after the date on which an order allowing such Claim becomes a Final Order, or as soon thereafter as practicable; and (c) such other time as is agreed upon by the holder of such Claim and the Liquidating Trust; *provided, however,* that the Liquidating Trust retains the right to prepay any such Allowed Priority Tax Claim, or any remaining balance of such Claim, in full or in part, at any time on or after the Effective Date without premium or penalty.

3.5 Reclamation Claims. All requests for payment of Reclamation Claims must be filed by the Bar Date. Any holder of a Reclamation Claim that has not filed a request for payment by the Bar Date shall be forever barred from asserting such Reclamation Claims against the Debtors, the Liquidating Trust and the Platform Subsidiaries. Each Allowed Reclamation Claim is to be satisfied, at the Liquidating Trust's sole option, by either: (a) the return of the goods subject to the Reclamation Claim; or (b) payment in full in Cash upon the latest of (i) the Initial Distribution Date, or as soon thereafter as practicable; (ii) such date as may be fixed by the Bankruptcy Court, or as soon thereafter as practicable; (iii) the tenth Business Day after the date on which an order allowing such Claim becomes a Final Order, or as soon thereafter as practicable; and (iv) such other time as is agreed upon by the holder of such Claim and the Liquidating Trust.

3.6 Claims for Professional Fees. Each Person seeking an award by the Bankruptcy Court of Professional Fees: (a) must file its final application for allowance of compensation for services rendered and reimbursement of expenses incurred through the Confirmation Date within 30 days after the Confirmation Date; and (b) if the Bankruptcy Court grants such an award, each such Person must be paid in full in Cash such amounts as are allowed by the Bankruptcy Court (i) on the later of the Initial Distribution Date or the date such Claim becomes an Allowed Administrative Claim, or as soon thereafter as practicable, (ii) upon such other terms as may be mutually agreed upon between the holder of such Allowed Administrative Claim and the Debtors or the Liquidating Trust, or (iii) in accordance with the terms of any applicable administrative procedures order entered by the Bankruptcy Court.

Post-Confirmation Professional Fees. All Professional Fees for services rendered in connection with the Chapter 11 Cases and the Plan after the Confirmation Date including, without limitation, those relating to the occurrence of the Effective Date, the prosecution of Avoidance Actions preserved under the Plan, and the resolution of Disputed Claims, are to be paid by the Liquidating Trust upon receipt of an invoice for such services, or on such other terms as the Liquidating Trust may agree to, without the need for application, further Bankruptcy Court authorization or entry of a Final Order. If the Liquidating Trust and any Professional cannot agree on the amount of post-Confirmation Date fees and expenses to be paid to such Professional, such amount is to be determined by the Bankruptcy Court.

Article 4. CLASSIFICATION OF CLAIMS AND EQUITY INTERESTS

4.1 Summary of Classification. In accordance with Section 1123(a)(1) of the Bankruptcy Code, all Claims of Creditors and holders of Equity Interests (except those Claims receiving treatment as set forth in 0) are placed in the Classes described below for all purposes, including voting on, confirmation of, and distributions under, the Plan.

Summary Chart

Class 1:	Priority Claims.	Class 1 consists of all Priority Claims – **Unimpaired**.
Class 2:	Secured Tax Claims.	Class 2 consists of all Tax Claims that are Secured – **Unimpaired**.
Class 3:	Investor Claims.	Class 3 consists of all Investor Claims other than Securities Claims – **Impaired**.
Class 4:	Miscellaneous Secured Claims.	Class 4 consists of all Secured Claims other than Secured Tax Claims and Investor Claims – **Impaired**.
Class 5:	General Unsecured Claims.	Class 5 consists of all General Unsecured Claims other than Investor Claims – **Impaired**.
Class 6:	Excise Tax Claims.	Class 6 consists of all Excise Tax Claims of the IRS – **Impaired**.
Class 7:	Debt Securities Claims.	Class 7 consists of all Debt Securities Claims subordinated pursuant to 11 U.S.C. §510 and the Plan – **Impaired**.
Class 8:	Equity Interests and Equity Securities Claims.	Class 8 consists of all Equity Interests and Equity Securities Claims subordinated pursuant to 11 U.S.C. §510 and the Plan – **Impaired**.

4.2 Specific Classification.

Class 1 – Priority Claims. Class 1 consists of all Claims entitled to priority under Section 507(a) of the Bankruptcy Code.

Class 2 – Secured Tax Claims. Class 2 consists of all Secured Tax Claims. Each holder of a Secured Tax Claim is considered to be in its own separate subclass within Class 2, and each such subclass is deemed to be a separate Class for purposes of the Plan.

Class 3 – Investor Claims. Class 3 consists of all Investors Claims other than Securities Claims.

Class 4 – Miscellaneous Secured Claims. Class 4 consists of all Secured Claims, other than the Secured Tax Claims in Class 2 and Investor Claims in Class 3. Each holder of a Secured Claim in Class 4 is considered to be in its own separate subclass within Class 4, and each such subclass is deemed to be a separate Class for purposes of the Plan.

Class 5 – General Unsecured Claims. Class 5 consists of all General Unsecured Claims, other than Investor Claims contained in Class 3.

Class 6 – Excise Tax Claims. Class 6 consists of all Excise Tax Claims of the IRS.

Class 7 – Debt Securities Claims. Class 7 consists of all Debt Securities Claims.

Class 8 – Equity Interests and Equity Securities Claims. Class 8 consists of all Claims and other rights arising out of or related to Equity Interests, including any Equity Securities Claims.

Article 5. TREATMENT OF CLAIMS AND EQUITY INTERESTS

Class 1 – Priority Claims

Impairment and Voting. Class 1 is unimpaired by the Plan; consequently, all holders of Allowed Claims in Class 1 are deemed to have accepted the Plan and are not entitled to vote on the Plan.

Distributions. Each holder of an Allowed Priority Claim shall receive Cash in an amount equal to such Allowed Priority Claim on the later of: (a) the Initial Distribution Date, or as soon thereafter as practicable; (b) the tenth Business Day after the date such Priority Claim becomes an Allowed Priority Claim, or as soon thereafter as practicable; and (c) such other dates as the holder of such Claims and the Liquidating Trust may agree.

Class 2 – Secured Tax Claims

Impairment and Voting. Class 2 is unimpaired by the Plan; consequently, all holders of Allowed Claims in Class 2 are deemed to have accepted the Plan and are not entitled to vote on the Plan.

Distributions. Each Allowed Secured Tax Claim shall be paid in full in Cash upon the later of: (a) the Initial Distribution Date, or as soon thereafter as practicable; (b) such date as may be fixed by the Bankruptcy Court, or as soon thereafter as practicable; (c) the tenth Business Day after such Claim is Allowed, or as soon thereafter as practicable; (d) the date on which such Secured Tax Claim is scheduled to be paid in the ordinary course of business under applicable law or regulation; and (e) such date as the holder of such Claim and the Liquidating Trust may agree.

Class 3 – Investor Claims

Impairment and Voting. Class 3 is impaired by the Plan; consequently, all holders of Allowed Investor Claims are entitled to vote on the Plan.

Allowance of Investor Claims. On the Confirmation Date, all Investor Claims, *except* those Investor Claims held by Persons that received cash payments during the Preference Period and failed to elect the Preference Settlement Option, are deemed to be Allowed in the amount of the unpaid principal plus the sum of: (a) accrued but unpaid interest on such Investor Claims at the non-default contract rate up to but not including the Petition Date; and (b) the amount of Cash, if any, actually received by the holder of an Investor Claim during the Preference Period.

Distributions to Allowed Investor Claims. On the Effective Date, or as soon thereafter as practicable, the holders of Allowed Investor Claims shall receive, in full and final satisfaction of such Allowed Investor Claims, the following:

Initial Cash Distribution. On the Initial Distribution Date, each holder of an Allowed Investor Claim shall receive such holder's Pro Rata share of Cash as approved by the Bankruptcy Court as part of the Confirmation Hearing.

Liquidation Certificate. Each holder of an Allowed Investor Claim shall receive a Liquidation Certificate, entitling the holder thereof to receive such holder's Pro Rata share of distributions from the orderly sale of Assets by the Liquidating Trust and the Platform Subsidiaries in accordance with the distribution provisions of the Plan and the Liquidating Trust Agreement. The Liquidation Certificate shall entitle the holder thereof to receive such holder's Pro Rata share of Cash equivalent to ninety percent (90%) of Net Distributable Cash, as determined on a quarterly basis, commencing on the last Business Day of the first full calendar quarter following the Effective Date. Following completion of the payments to Allowed General Unsecured Claims in accordance with the General Unsecured Claim Recovery Schedule, the holders of a Liquidation Certificate shall receive one hundred percent (100%) of the Net Distributable Cash from the Liquidating Trust.

General Litigation Certificate. Each holder of an Allowed Investor Claim shall receive a General Litigation Certificate, entitling the holder thereof to receive such holder's Pro Rata share of distributions of the Net Litigation Recovery.

Trust/IRA Litigation Certificate. Each holder of an Investor Claim relating to an investment in an IRA or trust shall receive, in addition to the Cash distribution on the Initial Distribution Date, the Liquidation Certificate and the General Litigation Certificate, a Trust/IRA Litigation Certificate, entitling the holder thereof to receive such holder's Share of distributions from the net recovery of litigation claims arising under or related to such IRA and trust activities conducted by the Debtors prior to the Petition Date.

Preference Settlement Option. Each holder of an Investor Claim who has received Cash distributions on account of such Claim during the Preference Period and elects the Preference Settlement Option, shall be entitled to receive the Preference Equalization Credit. The Preference Equalization Credit shall be calculated as follows:

$$\text{Preference Equalization Credit} = \frac{\text{Total Cash Received During Preference Period}}{6}$$

In addition, each Cash distribution that the holder of an Allowed Investor Claim is entitled to receive under the Plan shall be reduced by the Preference Equalization Credit until such reductions equal the total amount of the Cash, without interest, such holder received during the Preference Period. If the amount of Cash to be distributed to a holder of an Investor Claim on any Distribution Date is less than the Preference Equalization Credit determined for such Distribution Date, then such remaining amount of Preference Equalization Credit shall be credited against such holder's Cash distribution on the next succeeding Distribution Date (and if not fully utilized on such Distribution Date, on each succeeding Distribution Date until the remaining Preference Equalization Credit is fully utilized), in addition to any Preference Equalization Credit determined on the next succeeding Distribution Date.

Pursuant to Bankruptcy Rule 9019 and in consideration of the distributions and other benefits provided under the Plan, the provisions of this Section 0 constitute a good faith compromise and settlement of the claims the Debtors believe they have against the holder of an Investor Claim electing the Preference Settlement Option under Section 547 of the Bankruptcy Code. The entry of the Confirmation Order constitutes the Bankruptcy Court's approval of the compromise and settlement of such preference claim, and the Bankruptcy Court's finding that such compromise or settlement is in the best interests of the Debtors and their respective property and the holders of Claims and is fair, equitable and reasonable.

No Election. If the holder of an Investor Claim that has received Cash during the Preference Period does not elect the Preference Settlement Option, pursuant to Section 502(d) of the Bankruptcy Code, such Claim shall be deemed a Disputed Claim and all distributions that the holder of such Investor Claim is entitled to receive under the Plan shall be included in the Distribution Reserve by the Liquidating Trust pending the entry of a Final Order of the Bankruptcy Court resolving the Avoidance Actions.

Cancellation of Debt Instruments. As of the Effective Date, except to the extent provided otherwise in the Plan, all Debt Instruments and other documents evidencing Investor Claims, including any alleged or putative Lien securing such Investor Claims, shall be automatically canceled, extinguished, and deemed void (all without further action by any Person), and all obligations of any Person, including the Debtors and Non-Debtor Affiliates, and such instruments and documents shall be deemed fully and finally, released, satisfied and discharged.

Distribution Record Date. At the close of business on the Distribution Record Date, the ledgers of the Debtors shall be closed, and no further changes in the record holders of any Investor Claims shall be permitted. The Debtors and the Liquidating Trust shall have no further obligation to recognize any transfer of an Investor Claim occurring after the Distribution Record Date for purposes of distributions on the Initial Distribution Date. The Debtors and the Liquidating Trust shall be entitled to recognize and deal for all purposes under the Plan with only those record holders stated on the transfer ledger of the Debtors as of the close of business on the Distribution Record Date.

Delivery of Distribution to Holders of Investor Claim. All distributions to the holder of Allowed Investor Claims shall be made by the Liquidating Trust or the Disbursing Agent at the direction of the Liquidating Trustee in accordance with the Plan and the Liquidating Trust Agreement at the address contained in the records of the Debtors as of the Effective Date. If any holder's distribution is returned as undeliverable, no further distributions to such holder shall be made unless and until the Liquidating Trust is notified of such holder's then current address, at which time all missed distributions shall be made to such holder without interest. Undeliverable distributions shall be returned to the Liquidating Trust until such distributions are claimed. All claims for undeliverable distributions shall be made on or before one year following each Distribution Date. After the expiration of such period, all unclaimed distributions shall be included in the next distribution to the holders of all other Allowed Investor Claims as provided in the Plan and the Liquidating Trust Agreement. After such one-year period, the Claim of any holder of an Investor Claim for undeliverable distributions shall be discharged and forever barred notwithstanding any federal or state escheat laws to the contrary.

Interest. In the event the total distributions to the holders of Allowed Investor Claims as provided in the Plan exceed the amount of Allowed Investor Claims, the holders thereof shall be entitled to receive simple interest and payments on account thereof, up to the amount of any such excess distributions, at the rate of ten percent (10%) per year accruing from and after the Effective Date.

Class 4 – Miscellaneous Secured Claims

Impairment and Voting. Depending upon the option selected by the Debtors pursuant to the provisions below, the holders of Allowed Secured Claims in Class 4 may be impaired pursuant to the Plan. If a particular Allowed Secured Claim in Class 4 is impaired under the Plan, the holder of such Claim is entitled to vote on the Plan. For purposes of voting and receiving distributions under the Plan, each holder of an Allowed Secured Claim in Class 4 is considered to be in its own separate subclass within Class 4, and each such subclass is deemed to be a separate Class for purposes of the Plan.

Retention of Liens. The holders of Allowed Secured Claims shall retain their Liens on their Collateral, except as otherwise provided in Section 0.

Options; Treatment. On or before 10 Business Days following approval by the Bankruptcy Court of the Disclosure Statement Summary and the Disclosure Statement, with respect to each holder of an Allowed Secured Claim in Class 4, the Debtors shall elect one of the following alternative treatments for each such Allowed Secured Claim in a particular subclass.

Abandonment. Pursuant to the Plan, and on or before the Initial Distribution Date, the Debtors may abandon or surrender to the holder of such Allowed Secured Claim in Class 4 the Collateral securing such Allowed Secured Claim. Any Unsecured Deficiency Claim asserted by a holder of an Allowed Secured Claim in Class 4 shall be filed with the Bankruptcy

Court within 30 days following the date of the surrender or abandonment of such Creditor's Collateral. Any such Allowed Unsecured Deficiency Claim shall be treated in accordance with Section 5.4 of the Plan.

Cash. Pursuant to the Plan, on or before the Effective Date, the holder of an Allowed Secured Claim in Class 4 may receive, on account of such Allowed Secured Claim, Cash equal to its Allowed Secured Claims, or such lesser amount to which the holder of such Claims shall agree, in full satisfaction and release of such Claim.

No Impairment. The holder of an Allowed Secured Claim in Class 4 may be treated in accordance with the terms and conditions of all Debt Instruments evidencing such Claim and the legal, equitable, or contractual rights to which each holder of such Claim is entitled, except that the Collateral securing such Allowed Secured Claim may be transferred to one of the Platform Subsidiaries, subject to any Liens.

Cure; Reinstatement. Any default, other than a default of a kind specified in Section 365(b)(2) of the Bankruptcy Code, owed to a holder of an Allowed Secured Claim in Class 4 may be Cured or reinstated on or before the Initial Distribution Date, except that any Collateral may be transferred to one of the Platform Subsidiaries, subject to any Liens.

Collateral Transferred to Platform Subsidiaries. After selection of one of the options described above, to the extent that any Collateral securing the Allowed Secured Claims is not transferred to the holder of such Allowed Secured Claim, then such Collateral may be transferred to one of the Platform Subsidiaries, subject to any Liens.

Class 5 – General Unsecured Claims

Impairment and Voting. Class 5 is impaired by the Plan; consequently, all holders of Allowed General Unsecured Claims are entitled to vote on the Plan. As a result of the limitations upon substantive consolidation of the Debtors' Estates contained herein, each holder of a General Unsecured Claim may be considered to be its own separate subclass within Class 5 and, if applicable, each such subclass will be deemed to be a separate Class for purposes of the Plan.

Distributions. Each holder of an Allowed Claim in Class 5 shall be paid an amount equivalent to the General Unsecured Claims Distribution Percentage set forth in the General Unsecured Creditor Recovery Schedule. In full and final satisfaction of all General Unsecured Claims such holders of Allowed Claims in Class 5 shall receive the following.

Initial Cash Distribution. The holders of Allowed General Unsecured Claims in Class 5 shall receive their Pro Rata share of $1 million Cash in accordance with the General Unsecured Claims Recovery Schedule, unless such holder has filed with the Bankruptcy Court an objection to the amount of such Claim as provided herein. In that event, such holder's Claim shall be deemed to be a Disputed Claim, and any distributions to be made on account thereof shall be deposited in the Distribution Reserve.

GUC-Net Distributable Cash Payment. Commencing on the last Business Day of the first full calendar quarter following the Effective Date, the Liquidating Trust shall distribute the GUC-Net Distributable Cash Payment entitling the holder of an Allowed General Unsecured Claim to receive their Pro Rata share thereof until the General Unsecured Claim Distribution Percentage shall have been satisfied.

Class 6 – Excise Tax Claims.

To the extent the Class 6 Claim is an Allowed Excise Tax Claim, the holder thereof shall receive all distributions of Net Distributable Cash, if any, after payment in full of all Allowed Claims in Classes 1 through 5 under the Plan. The Debtors believe that the holders of Allowed Excise Tax Claims will not receive or retain any property under the Plan. Accordingly, Class 6 is impaired by the Plan and, for purposes of solicitation of votes to accept or reject the Plan, is deemed to have rejected the Plan.

Class 7 – Debt Securities Claims

Subordination. Pursuant to the Plan and Section 510 of the Bankruptcy Code, all Debt Securities Claims shall be subordinated, for distribution and all other purposes, to the Claims of all other Creditors in Classes 1 through 6 under the Plan.

Impairment; Distributions. The holders of Allowed Debt Securities Claims shall be entitled to receive all distributions of Net Distributable Cash, if any, after payment in full of all Allowed Claims in Classes 1 through 6. The Debtors believe that the holders of Allowed Debt Securities Claims shall not receive or retain any property under the Plan. Class 7 is impaired by the Plan and is deemed to have rejected the Plan.

Class 8 – Equity Interests and Equity Securities Claims

Cancellation; Subordination. All Equity Interests shall be cancelled and terminated as of the Effective Date. Pursuant to the Plan and Section 510 of the Bankruptcy Code, all Equity Securities Claims shall be subordinated, for distribution and all other purposes, to the Claims of all other Creditors.

Impairment; Distribution. The holders of Allowed Equity Interests and Allowed Equity Securities Claims shall not receive or retain any property under the Plan. Class 8 is impaired by the Plan and is deemed to have rejected the Plan.

Article 6. MEANS FOR IMPLEMENTATION OF THE PLAN

6.1 Creation of the Liquidating Trust; Transfer of Assets. On the Effective Date, the Liquidating Trust shall be established. Pursuant to Section 1123(a)(5)(B) of the Bankruptcy Code, on the Effective Date or as soon thereafter as practicable, the Assets shall be irrevocably transferred and assigned to the Liquidating Trust, to be held in trust for the benefit of all holders of Allowed Claims pursuant to the terms of the Plan and the Liquidating Trust Agreement. Following the Effective Date, the Liquidating Trust shall cause the transfer of Assets to the Platform Subsidiaries in consideration for all of the equity interests in such Platform Subsidiaries. The Liquidating Trust shall be entitled to cause the transfer of the Assets among the Platform Subsidiaries from time to time where such transfers will maintain or enhance the value of the Assets or facilitate the orderly management and administration of the Liquidating Trust or the Platform Subsidiaries. Except as otherwise provided in the Plan or in the Liquidating Trust Agreement, title to the Assets shall transfer to the Liquidating Trust and the Platform Subsidiaries free and clear of all Claims, Interests and Liens, including, without limitation, any alleged Lien of the holder of any Investor Claim in accordance with Section 1141 of the Bankruptcy Code, *except* for Liens on Assets held by holders of Allowed Secured Claims all of which will remain perfected without further order of the Bankruptcy Court. Pursuant to the Plan and the Confirmation Order, the transfer of the Assets to the Liquidating Trust and the Platform Subsidiaries shall be free and clear of any restrictions or prohibitions placed on such transfer in any contract or Debt Instrument.

6.2 Transfer of Litigation Claims. On the Effective Date or as soon thereafter as practicable, all Litigation Claims, Avoidance Actions and any D&O Policy shall be transferred and assigned to the Liquidating Trust. In accordance with Section 1123(b) of the Bankruptcy Code, the Liquidating Trust shall become vested with, in its capacity as the Estate representative under Section 1123(b)(3)(B) of the Bankruptcy Code, and may enforce, sue on, settle or compromise (or decline to do any of the foregoing) all claims, rights or causes of actions, suits and proceedings, whether in law or in equity, whether known or unknown, that the Debtors, their Estates, or the Non-Debtor Affiliates may hold against any Person or entity, including, without limitation, any Litigation Claims and Avoidance Actions.

6.3 Liquidating Trustee. The Liquidating Trust shall have one Liquidating Trustee. The Liquidating Trustee shall be selected by the Restructuring Committee and the Creditors' Committee prior to the Confirmation Hearing and shall be subject to approval by the Bankruptcy Court as part of the Confirmation Hearing. In the event that the Restructuring Committee and the Creditors' Committee cannot mutually agree upon a Person to be selected as Liquidating Trustee, the Bankruptcy Court shall resolve such dispute as part of the Confirmation Hearing. Pursuant to the Liquidating Trust Agreement, the Liquidating Trust Board shall have the power to fill any vacancy created by the death, resignation or removal of a Liquidating Trustee or remove a Liquidating Trustee. The Liquidating Trustee shall have the power to cause the formation of additional subsidiaries to hold some of the Assets pending sale, if such formation, in the reasonable business judgment of the Liquidating Trustee, is necessary to preserve or enhance the liquidation value of the Assets or assist in the orderly administration of the Liquidating Trust. The Liquidating Trustee shall, with the approval of a majority of the members of the Liquidating Trust Board: (i) sell any material Assets, (ii) approve the annual budget of the Liquidating Trust, (iii) approve the amount of reserves and operating expenses for the Liquidating Trust, (iii) create any entities, (iv) transfer any Assets to the Platform Subsidiaries or to any entity formed by the Liquidating Trust or the Platform Subsidiaries, (v) settle or pursue any Litigation Claims or Avoidance Actions or (vi) retain any professionals, the Disbursing Agent or any transfer agents. The Liquidating Trust shall provide the Liquidating Trustee, the members of the Liquidating Trust Board and such other officers and directors of the Liquidating Trust and the Platform Subsidiaries with indemnification rights and liability insurance in accordance with the Liquidating Trust Agreement. The Liquidating Trustee and the Disbursement Agent shall be compensated for their services in accordance with terms approved by the Bankruptcy Court as part of the Confirmation Hearing. The Bankruptcy Court shall retain jurisdiction to remove the Liquidating Trustee.

6.4 Liquidating Trust Board. Prior to the Confirmation Hearing, the Restructuring Committee and the Creditors' Committee shall select three Persons to serve on the Liquidating Trust Board, subject to approval by the Bankruptcy Court as part of the Confirmation Hearing. In the event that the Restructuring Committee and the Creditors' Committee cannot mutually agree upon the Persons to be selected to serve on the Liquidating Trust Board, the Bankruptcy Court shall resolve such dispute as part of the Confirmation Hearing. Each member of the Liquidating Trust Board shall sign a confidentiality agreement relating to any information they receive while acting as a member of the Liquidating Trust Board. The Liquidating Trust Board shall meet with the Investor Advisory Committee, at the request of the Investor Advisory Committee, on a reasonably periodic basis. The Liquidating Trust Board shall have the authority and responsibility to supervise, review, and direct the activities and performance of the Liquidating Trustee and shall have the authority to remove the Liquidating Trustee pursuant to the Plan and the Liquidating Trust Agreement. The affirmative vote of a majority of the members of the Liquidating Trust Board shall be the act of the Liquidating Trust Board, unless otherwise provided in the Plan or the Liquidating Trust Agreement. Pursuant to the Liquidating Trust Agreement, the remaining members of the Liquidating Trust Board shall have the power to fill any vacancy created by the death, resignation or removal of a member of the Liquidating Trust Board or remove a member of the Liquidating Trust Board for Cause (as defined in the Liquidating Trust Agreement) with the approval of the Bankruptcy Court. In the event of a vacancy in all of the positions of the Liquidating Trust Board due to the death or simultaneous resignation of all of the members of the Liquidating Trust Board, then the

Investor Advisory Committee shall nominate three Persons to fill such vacancies and such Persons shall be appointed, subject to the approval of the Bankruptcy Court and a majority vote of the holders of the Liquidation Certificates, the General Litigation Certificates and the Trust/IRA Litigation Certificates. The members of the Liquidating Trust Board shall be compensated for their services in accordance with terms approved by the Bankruptcy Court as part of the Confirmation Hearing. The Bankruptcy Court shall retain jurisdiction to remove any member of the Liquidating Trust Board.

6.5 Investor Advisory Committee. Prior to the Confirmation Hearing, the Creditors' Committee shall select three Holders of Allowed Investor Claims to serve on the Investor Advisory Committee, subject to approval by the Bankruptcy Court as part of the Confirmation Hearing. In the event that the Creditors' Committee cannot agree upon the Holders of Allowed Investor Claims to be selected to serve on the Investor Advisory Committee, the Bankruptcy Court shall resolve such dispute as part of the Confirmation Hearing. Each member of the Investor Advisory Committee shall sign a confidentiality agreement relating to any information they receive while acting as a member of the Investor Advisory Committee. The Investor Advisory Committee shall be entitled to request reasonably periodic meetings with the Liquidating Trust Board. The Investor Advisory Committee shall advise the Liquidating Trust Board as to the Investor Advisory Committee's position on any matters relating to the Trust Assets and the disposition thereof and any matters incidental thereto, including, without limitation, (i) the formation of the Platform Subsidiaries and other entities and (ii) the selection and retention of professional advisors. The Liquidating Trustee shall provide the Investor Advisory Committee with any information that it may reasonably request; *provided, however,* that such requests will not cause the Liquidating Trustee to incur significant expense. The Liquidating Trust Board shall have the power to fill any vacancy created by the death, resignation or removal of a member of the Investor Advisory Committee or remove a member of the Investor Advisory Committee for Cause (as defined in the Liquidating Trust Agreement) with the approval of the Bankruptcy Court. In the event of a vacancy in all of the positions of the Investor Advisory Committee due to the death or simultaneous resignation of all of the members of the Investor Advisory Committee, then the Liquidating Trust Board shall nominate three Persons to fill such vacancies and such Persons shall be appointed, subject to the approval of the Bankruptcy Court and a majority vote of the holders of the Liquidation Certificates, the General Litigation Certificates and the Trust/IRA Litigation Certificates. The members of the Investor Advisory Committee shall not be compensated. The Bankruptcy Court shall retain jurisdiction to remove any member of the Investor Advisory Committee.

6.6 Amendments to Liquidating Trust Agreement. The Liquidating Trust Agreement may be amended from time to time, without modifying the

Plan, by majority vote of the Liquidating Trust Board, except that the Liquidating Trust Agreement shall not be amended to materially alter the priority of Claims or distribution scheme under the Plan.

6.7 Formation of Platform Subsidiaries. As of the Effective Date and without any further action by the stockholders or directors of FAS or the Debtors, the FAS certificate of incorporation and by-laws shall be amended and restated substantially in the forms of the Restated New Residential Real Estate Subsidiary By-Laws and Restated New Residential Real Estate Certificate, which shall provide for, amount other things, the authorization of all acts necessary to implement the Plan, including, without limitation, the issuance of all of its capital stock to the Liquidating Trust. As of the Effective Date and without any further action by the stockholders or directors of the Debtors, the New Asset Subsidiary, LLC Operating Agreement and the New Asset Subsidiary, LLC Articles of Organization shall be executed and filed and the sole member of the New Asset Subsidiary, LLC shall be the Liquidating Trust.

6.8 Reporting Status. As a result of the nature of the Liquidating Trust, the certificates to be issued in connection therewith and the number of holders of record thereof, the Liquidating Trust will be a reporting company under the Exchange Act. Accordingly, the Liquidating Trust shall file periodic reports with the SEC, including financial statements audited in accordance with GAAP. Such reports and audited financial statements shall be made available to the holders of Investor Claims.

6.9 Sale of Assets. Following the Effective Date, the Liquidating Trust and the Platform Subsidiaries shall be entitled to manage and operate the Assets in a manner to maximize their value pending any orderly sale over time of such Assets. The Liquidating Trust and the Platform Subsidiaries shall seek to sell the Assets for the purpose of distributing the net proceeds thereof to those Creditors entitled thereto under the Plan. If the Liquidating Trustee concludes, in the exercise of reasonable business judgment, that it is appropriate to surrender or abandon to any Secured Creditor part or all of the balance of that Creditor's Collateral, in partial or complete satisfaction of the remaining Allowed Claims of that Secured Creditor, or to allow any Secured Creditor to enforce a Lien in accordance with applicable law, then the Liquidating Trustee may do so and the value of the Collateral so surrendered or with respect to which enforcement of Liens is permitted, shall be applied against the Creditors' Allowed Secured Claims. If the Liquidating Trust liquidates some or all of the Collateral for any Allowed Secured Claim, the Liquidating Trust shall promptly distribute the net sales proceeds of any such liquidation to the Secured Creditor with the senior-most Lien that secures an Allowed Claim that has not yet been fully satisfied. If allocation of the net sales proceeds among Secured Creditors is required, that allocation shall be made either by mutual agreement of all parties asserting a Lien against such net sale proceeds and the Liquidating Trust, or by Final Order of the Bankruptcy Court.

6.10 General Unsecured Claim Recovery Schedule. The Debtors shall file the General Unsecured Claim Recovery Schedule no later than 10 Business Days prior to the commencement of the Confirmation Hearing. Holders of Allowed General Unsecured Claims may object to the General Unsecured Claim Recovery Schedule, which objection shall be filed with the Bankruptcy Court and served on the Debtors' and Creditors' Committee counsel no later than five Business Days after the Effective Date. The Bankruptcy Court shall resolve any disputes or objections to the General Unsecured Claim Recovery Schedule. If such dispute resolution does not occur prior to the Initial Distribution Date, the Liquidating Trust shall segregate any distributions to holders of Allowed Claims in Class 5 in the Distribution Reserve as provided in the General Unsecured Claim Recovery Schedule.

6.11 Distributions; Proceeds From Asset Sales. The Liquidating Trust shall make interim distributions of Net Distributable Cash from the sale of Assets to all Classes then entitled to such a distribution at least on a quarterly basis, commencing on the last Business Day of the first full quarter following the Effective Date, except that the Liquidating Trust shall not be obligated to make any distributions of Net Distributable Cash in an amount less than $1 million except on the Final Distribution Date.

6.12 Special Distribution Procedures For Litigation Claims. The Liquidating Trust shall make distributions of the net recoveries (*i.e.*, recoveries after taking into account Professional Fees and expenses including any reserves for future litigation expenses as determined, in good faith, by the Liquidating Trust) from the Litigation Claims, the Avoidance Actions and, if applicable, any D&O Policy promptly upon receipt of such funds in accordance with the Plan and the Liquidating Trust Agreement. Any such recoveries shall be segregated and not co-mingled with any other Cash of the Liquidating Trust.

6.13 Termination of Liquidating Trust. Upon the distribution of all assets vested in the Liquidating Trust, including any recoveries from Litigation Claims, Avoidance Actions and any D&O Policy, and the preparation and filing of any tax returns, the Liquidating Trust shall be terminated, the Platform Subsidiaries dissolved, and the Liquidating Trustee shall have no further responsibilities or duties.

6.14 Dissolution of Debtors and Non-Debtor Affiliates. The Debtors and Non-Debtor Affiliates shall not continue to exist after the Effective Date as separate legal entities, in accordance with the applicable law in the respective jurisdictions in which they are formed or incorporated. The Plan and the Confirmation Order shall effectuate such dissolution for the Debtors and Non-Debtor Affiliates without further action on the part of shareholders or directors, and the dissolution will be deemed to be effectuated and taken by unanimous action of all necessary parties. To the extent the Debtors and Non-Debtor Affiliates deem it necessary or appropriate they may take any steps that will facilitate such dissolution.

6.15 Restructuring Committee; Officers. The existing officers of the Debtors and Non-Debtor Affiliates as of the Effective Date and the Restructuring Committee shall cease to serve in their current capacities at 11:59 p.m. on the Effective Date. The members of the Restructuring Committee and other officer entitled to indemnification under the Restructuring Committee By-Laws shall be indemnified by the Liquidating Trust and the Platform Subsidiaries for all actions taken while acting in such capacities for the Debtors and the Non-Debtor Affiliates in accordance with the indemnification provisions of the Restructuring Committee By-Laws and applicable state law on account of services provided from the Petition Date through and including the Effective Date.

6.16 Intercompany Claims. All Intercompany Claims shall be discharged and extinguished as of the Effective Date of the Plan, pursuant to the Substantive Consolidation Motion.

6.17 No Corporate Action Required. As of the Effective Date: (a) the adoption of the New Asset Subsidiary, LLC Operating Agreement, New Asset Subsidiary, LLC Articles of Organization, the Restated New Residential Real Estate Subsidiary By-Laws, the Restated New Residential Real Estate Subsidiary Certificate, the Liquidating Trust Agreement or similar constituent documents for the Liquidating Trust and the Platform Subsidiaries; (b) the initial selection of directors and officers for the Platform Subsidiaries and the appointment of the Liquidating Trustee; (c) the adoption, execution, delivery, and implementation of all contracts, leases, instruments, releases, and other agreements related to or contemplated by the Plan; and (d) the other matters provided for under, or in furtherance of, the Plan involving corporate or partnership action required of the Debtors, the Non-Debtor Affiliates, the Liquidating Trust or the Platform Subsidiaries shall be deemed to have occurred and become effective as provided in the Plan, and shall be deemed authorized and approved in all respects without further order of the Bankruptcy Court or any further action by the stockholders, directors, or partners of the Debtors, the Non-Debtor Affiliates, the Liquidating Trust and the Platform Subsidiaries.

6.18 Termination of Subordination Rights and Settlement of Related Investor Claims. The classification and manner of satisfying all Claims and Equity Interests under the Plan take into consideration all contractual, legal, and equitable subordination rights, whether arising under general principles of equitable subordination, Sections 510(b) and (c) of the Bankruptcy Code or otherwise, that a holder of a Claim or Equity Interest may have against other Claim or Equity Interest holders with respect to any distribution made in accordance with the Plan. As of the Effective Date, all contractual, legal, or equitable subordination rights that a holder of a Claim or Equity Interest may have with respect to any distribution to be made in accordance with the Plan shall be discharged and terminated, and all actions related to the enforcement of such subordination rights shall be permanently enjoined and distributions under the Plan shall not be subject to payment to any beneficiaries of such terminated subordination rights, or to levy, garnishment, attachment, or other legal process by any beneficiary of such terminated subordination rights. Pursuant to Bankruptcy Rule 9019 and in consideration of the distributions and other benefits provided under the Plan, the provisions of Sections 0 and 0 of the Plan constitute a good faith compromise and settlement of all claims or controversies relating to the termination of all contractual, legal, and equitable subordination rights that a holder of a Claim or Equity Interest may have with respect to any Allowed Claim or Allowed Equity Interest, or any distribution to be made on account of an Allowed Claim or an Allowed Equity Interest. The entry of the Confirmation Order constitutes the Bankruptcy Court's approval of the compromise and settlement of all such claims and controversies, including the Preference Settlement Option, and the Bankruptcy Court's finding that such compromise or settlement is in the best interests of the Debtors, the Non-Debtor Affiliates, and their respective property and holders of Claims and Equity Interests and is fair, equitable and reasonable.

6.19 Administration Pending Effective Date. Before the Effective Date, the Debtors shall continue to operate their businesses, subject to all applicable requirement of the Bankruptcy Code and the Bankruptcy Rules.

6.20 Post-Confirmation Fees; Final Decree. The Liquidating Trust shall be responsible for paying any post-confirmation fees under 28 U.S.C. § 1930(a)(6) and the filing of post-confirmation reports, until a final decree is entered. A final decree shall be entered as soon as practicable after distributions have commenced under the Plan.

Article 7. EXECUTORY CONTRACTS AND UNEXPIRED LEASES

7.1 Assumption or Rejection of Executory Contracts and Unexpired Leases. The executory contracts and unexpired leases between the Debtors and any Person are dealt with as follows:

Assumption Of Executory Contracts And Unexpired Leases and Assignment to Platform Subsidiaries. All executory contracts and unexpired leases set forth in the motion to assume executory contracts filed by the Debtors with the Bankruptcy Court prior to the Confirmation Hearing that exist between the Debtors and any Person shall be assumed by the Debtors and assigned to the Platform Subsidiaries as of the Effective Date, *except for* any executory contract or unexpired lease: (a) that has been rejected in accordance with an order of the Bankruptcy Court entered before the Confirmation Date; or (b) as to which a motion for approval of rejection of such executory contract or unexpired lease, if applicable, has been filed with the

Bankruptcy Court before the Confirmation Date.

Rejection of Executory Contracts And Unexpired Leases. All executory contracts and unexpired leases that exist between the Debtors and any Person and are set forth in the motion to reject executory contracts and unexpired leases filed with the Bankruptcy Court prior to the Confirmation Hearing shall be deemed rejected as of the Effective Date, *except for* any executory contract or unexpired lease that has been assumed or rejected in accordance with an order of the Bankruptcy Court entered before the Confirmation Date.

Approval of Assumption, Assignment, or Rejection. Entry of the Confirmation Order constitutes: (a) the approval under Section 365(a) of the Bankruptcy Code of the assumption and assignment of the executory contracts and unexpired leases assumed under the Plan or otherwise during the Chapter 11 Cases; and (b) the approval under Section 365(a) of the Bankruptcy Code of the rejection of the executory contracts and unexpired leases rejected under the Plan or otherwise during the Chapter 11 Cases. Notwithstanding anything contained in this Section to the contrary, the Debtors retain the right to add to, or delete from, the list of rejected executory contracts and unexpired leases any executory contract or unexpired lease that is initially an assumed executory contract or an assumed unexpired lease.

Cure of Defaults. On the Effective Date or as soon thereafter as practicable, the Liquidating Trust or the Platform Subsidiaries, as applicable, shall Cure any defaults under any executory contract or unexpired lease assumed and assigned under this Plan in accordance with Section 365(b)(1) of the Bankruptcy Code.

Post-Petition Date Contracts and Leases. Executory contracts and unexpired leases entered into, and other obligations incurred, after the Petition Date by the Debtors, shall be performed by the Debtors, the Liquidating Trust, or the Platform Subsidiaries, as applicable, in the ordinary course of business.

Bar Date. All proofs of claims relating to Claims arising from the rejection of any executory contract or unexpired lease under the Plan shall be filed with the Bankruptcy Court no later than thirty days after the Confirmation Date. Any such Claim not filed within that time shall be forever barred. With respect to any executory contract or unexpired lease rejected by the Debtors before the Confirmation Date, the deadline for filing such Claims shall be as set forth in the Bar Date Order.

Indemnification Obligations. Except with respect to the indemnification provisions contained in the Restructuring Committee By-Laws, any obligation of the Debtors to indemnify, reimburse, or limit the liability of any Person, including but not limited to, any Indemnification Obligation to any officer or director of the Debtors or any of the Non-Debtor Affiliates, or any agent, professional, financial advisor, or underwriter of any securities issued by the Debtors related to any acts or omissions occurring before the Petition Date: (a) are rejected, canceled, and discharged under the Plan as of the Confirmation Date; and (b) any and all Claims resulting from such obligations are disallowed under Section 502(e) of the Bankruptcy Code. Notwithstanding any of the foregoing, nothing contained in the Plan impacts, impairs or prejudices the rights of any Person covered by any applicable D&O Policy with respect to such policy or policies.

7.2 Retiree Benefits. Pursuant to Section 1114 of the Bankruptcy Code, payment of any Retiree Benefits shall be continued solely to the extent, and for the duration of the period, the Debtors or the Liquidating Trust are contractually or legally obligated to provide such benefits, subject to any rights of the Debtors or the Liquidating Trust under applicable law.

Article 8. CONFIRMATION WITHOUT ACCEPTANCE BY ALL IMPAIRED CLASSES

If any impaired Class is determined to have rejected the Plan in accordance with Section 1126 of the Bankruptcy Code, the Debtors may use the provisions of Section 1129(b) of the Bankruptcy Code to satisfy the requirements for Confirmation of the Plan.

Article 9. SECURITIES TO BE ISSUED IN CONNECTION WITH THE PLAN

9.1 Certificates. The Liquidating Trust shall issue for distribution, in accordance with the provisions of the Plan and the Liquidating Trust Agreement, the Liquidation Certificate, the General Litigation Certificate and the IRA/Trust Litigation Certificate.

9.2 Section 1145 Exemption. In accordance with Section 1145 of the Bankruptcy Code, the issuance of the Liquidation Certificate, the General Litigation Certificate and the IRA/Trust Liquidation Certificate under the Plan are exempt from the registration requirements of Section 5 of the Securities Act, and any state or local law requiring registration for offer or sale of a security or registration or licensing of an issuer of, underwriter of, or broker dealer in such securities and is deemed to be a public offer of such securities.

Article 10. CONDITIONS PRECEDENT

10.1 Conditions To Confirmation. The following are conditions precedent to confirmation of this Plan:

Approval of Disclosure Statement. The Bankruptcy Court enters a Final Order approving the Disclosure Statement and the Disclosure Statement Summary with respect to the Plan.

Form of Confirmation Order. The Confirmation Order has been entered in form and substance reasonably acceptable to the Debtors. If the Debtors are unable to reach an agreement with any party regarding the form and substance of the Confirmation Order, the Bankruptcy Court shall resolve all such disputes between the parties.

Substance of Confirmation Order. The Confirmation Order shall contain the following:

(a) The provisions of the Confirmation Order are nonseverable and mutually dependent;

(b) The approval of the Substantive Consolidation Motion;

(c) All executory contracts or unexpired leases assumed by the Debtors and assigned to the Platform Subsidiaries during the Chapter 11 Cases or under the Plan shall remain in full force and effect for the benefit of the Liquidating Trust and the Platform Subsidiaries notwithstanding any provision in such contract or lease (including those described in Sections 365(b)(2) and (f) of the Bankruptcy Code) that prohibits such assignment or transfer or that enables, permits or requires termination of such contract or lease;

(d) Except as expressly provided in this Plan, the Debtors are discharged as of the Confirmation Date from all Claims and any "debt" (as that term in defined in Section 101(12) of the Bankruptcy Code) that arose on or before the Confirmation Date, and the Debtors' liability in respect of such Claims and debts is extinguished completely, whether reduced to judgment or not, liquidated or unliquidated, contingent or noncontingent, asserted or unasserted, fixed or unfixed, matured or unmatured, disputed or undisputed, legal or equitable, or known or unknown, or that arose from any agreement of the Debtors that has either been assumed and assigned, or rejected in the Chapter 11 Cases or under this Plan, or obligation of the Debtors incurred before the Confirmation Date, or from the Debtors' conduct before the Confirmation Date, or that otherwise arose before the Confirmation Date including, without limitation, all interest, if any, on any such debts, whether such interest accrued before or after the Petition Date; and;

(e) The Confirmation Order, in accordance with Section 1123(b)(3)(B) of the Bankruptcy Code, specifically appoints the Liquidating Trust as a representative and agent of the Debtors and the Consolidated Estates to prosecute, compromise, or abandon the Litigation Claims in accordance with the Plan and the Liquidating Trust Agreement.

10.2 Conditions to Effectiveness. The following are conditions precedent to the occurrence of the Effective Date:

(a) The Confirmation Date has occurred;

(b) The Confirmation Order is a Final Order, *except that* the Debtors reserve the right to cause the Effective Date to occur notwithstanding the pendency of an appeal of the Confirmation Order, under circumstances that would moot such appeal;

(c) No request for revocation of the Confirmation Order under Section 1144 of the Bankruptcy Code has been made, or, if made, remains pending;

(d) The Bankruptcy Court in the Confirmation Order has approved the retention of jurisdiction provisions in 0 of the Plan;

(e) All documents necessary to implement the transactions contemplated by this Plan are made in form and substance reasonably acceptable to the Debtors and the Creditors' Committee;

(f) The Liquidating Trust has sufficient Cash on the Effective Date to make required distributions to holders of Allowed Claims on the Initial Distribution Date; and

(g) The Liquidating Trust and the Platform Subsidiaries receive all regulatory approvals, if any, which have become final and nonappealable or any period of objection by regulatory authorities has expired, as applicable, and all other material approvals, permits, authorization, consents, licenses, and agreements from other third parties necessary or appropriate to permit the transactions contemplated by the Plan and any related agreements and to permit the Liquidating Trust and the Platform Subsidiaries to conduct their business after the Effective Date in a manner consistent with the orderly sale of the Assets over time (collectively, the "Approvals"). The Approvals must not contain any condition or restriction that materially impairs the Liquidating Trust's or the Platform Subsidiaries' ability to conduct their business in a manner consistent in all respects with the manner as proposed to be carried on under the Plan.

10.3 Waiver Of Conditions. The conditions to Confirmation and the Effective Date may be waived in whole or in part by the Debtors at any time without notice, an order of the Bankruptcy Court, or any further action other than proceeding to Confirmation and consummation of the Plan.

Article 11. NON-ALLOWANCE OF PENALTIES AND FINES

Except as expressly provided for in the Plan, no distribution shall be made under this Plan on account of, and no Allowed Claim (whether Secured, Unsecured, Investor Claim, Priority or Administrative) shall include, any fine, penalty, or exemplary or punitive damages relating to or arising from any default or breach by the Debtors, and any Claim on account of such fine, penalty, or exemplary or punitive damages shall be deemed to be disallowed, whether or not an objection is filed to such Claim.

Article 12. TITLE TO PROPERTY; DISCHARGE; INJUNCTION

12.1 Transfer of Assets. Subject to the provisions of this Plan and the Liquidating Trust Agreement, the Assets, the Litigation Claims, the Avoidance Actions and any applicable D&O Policy shall be transferred to the Liquidating Trust and the Platform Subsidiaries, as applicable, on the Effective Date. As of the Effective Date, all such property shall be free and clear of all liens, Claims, and Equity Interests, except as otherwise provided in this Plan.

12.2 Discharge. Except as provided in the Plan or the Confirmation Order, the rights afforded under the Plan and the treatment of Claims and Equity Interests under the Plan are in exchange for and in complete satisfaction, discharge, and release of, all Claims including any interest accrued on General Unsecured Claims and Investor Claims from the Petition Date and the termination of all Equity Interests. Except as provided in the Plan or the Confirmation Order, confirmation: (a) discharges the Debtors, the Liquidating Trust and the Platform Subsidiaries from all Claims or other debts that arose before the Confirmation Date, and all debts of the kind specified in Sections 502(g), 502(h) or 502(i) of the Bankruptcy Code, whether or not: (i) a proof of claim based on such debt is filed or deemed filed under Section 501 of the Bankruptcy Code; (ii) a Claim based on such debt is Allowed under Section 502 of the Bankruptcy Code; or (iii) the holder of a Claim based on such debt has accepted the Plan; and (b) terminates all Equity Interests and other rights of Equity Interests in the Debtors except as expressly provided in the Plan.

12.3 Injunction. Except as provided in the Plan or the Confirmation Order, as of the Confirmation Date, all entities that have held, currently hold or may hold a Claim or other debt or liability that is discharged or an Equity Interest, or other right of an equity security holder that is terminated under the Plan are permanently enjoined from taking any of the following actions on account of any such discharged Claims, debts, liabilities, or terminated Equity Interests or rights: (a) commencing or continuing in any manner any action or other proceeding against the Debtors, the Restructuring Committee, the Liquidating Trust, and the Platform Subsidiaries; (b) enforcing, attaching, collecting or recovering in any manner any judgment, award, decree, or order against the Debtors, the Restructuring Committee, the Liquidating Trust, and the Platform Subsidiaries, or their respective property; (c) creating, perfecting, or enforcing any lien or encumbrance against the Debtors, the Liquidating Trust, the Platform Subsidiaries, or their respective property; (d) asserting a setoff, right of subrogation or recoupment of any kind against any debt, liability, or obligation due to the Debtors, the Liquidating Trust, the Platform Subsidiaries or their respective property; and (e) commencing or continuing any action, in any manner, in any place, that does not comply with or is inconsistent with the provisions of the Plan or the Bankruptcy Code.

12.4 Exculpation. None of the Debtors, the Liquidating Trust, the Platform Subsidiaries, the Restructuring Committee, the acting General Counsel of the Debtors (*i.e.*, Mark Dickerson), or the Creditors' Committee, or any of their respective professional advisors, attorneys, or agents, have or may incur any liability to any holder of a Claim or Equity Interest, including the holder of any Securities Claim or Investor Claim, or any other party in interest, or any of their respective members or former members, agents, employees, representatives, financial advisors, attorneys, or affiliates, or any of their successors or assigns, for any act or omission in connection with, relating to, or arising out of, the Chapter 11 Cases, the negotiation and execution of the Plan, the negotiation and pursuit of Confirmation of the Plan, or the consummation of the Plan, or the administration of the Plan, *except for* their acts or omissions constituting willful misconduct, as finally determined by a court of competent jurisdiction and in all respects are entitled to reasonably rely upon the advice of counsel with respect to their duties and responsibilities under the Plan or in the context of the Chapter 11 Cases. No holder of a Claim, Equity Interest, Investor Claim, or Securities Claim, or any other party in interest, including their respective agents, employees, representatives, financial advisors, attorneys, or affiliates, have any right of action against the Debtors, the Restructuring Committee, the acting General Counsel of the Debtors (i.e., Mark Dickerson), the Creditors' Committee or any of their respective professional advisors, attorneys, or agents, for any act or omission in connection with, relating to, or arising out of, the Chapter 11 Cases, the negotiation and pursuit of Confirmation of the Plan, the consummation of the Plan, or the administration of the Plan, *except for* their acts or omissions constituting willful misconduct as finally determined by a court of competent jurisdiction.

Article 13. PROCEDURES FOR RESOLVING DISPUTED, CONTINGENT, AND UNLIQUIDATED CLAIMS

13.1 Objection Deadline; Prosecution Of Objections. As soon as practicable, but in no event later than 90 days after the Effective Date, the Liquidating Trust shall file objections to Claims with the Bankruptcy Court and serve such objections upon the holders of each of the Claims to which objections are made. The Bankruptcy Court may extend the foregoing deadline.

13.2 No Distributions Pending Allowance. Notwithstanding any other provision of the Plan, no payments or distributions shall be made with respect to all or any portion of a Disputed Claim unless and until all objections to such Disputed Claim have been settled or withdrawn or have been determined by Final Order and the Disputed Claim, or some portion thereof, has become an Allowed Claim.

13.3 Distribution Reserve. The Liquidating Trust shall exclude the Distribution Reserve from Net Distributable Cash. As to any Disputed Claim, upon a request for estimation by the Liquidating Trust, the Bankruptcy Court shall determine what amount is sufficient to withhold as the Distribution Reserve. The Liquidating Trust may request estimation for every Disputed Claim that is unliquidated and the Liquidating Trust shall withhold the Distribution Reserve based upon the estimated amount of such Claim as set forth in a Final Order. If the Liquidating Trust elects not to request such an estimation from the Bankruptcy Court with respect to a Disputed Claim that is liquidated, the Liquidating Trust shall withhold the Distribution Reserve based upon the face amount of such Claim. Nothing in the Plan shall be deemed to entitle the holder of a Disputed Claim to post-petition interest on such Claim and such holder shall not be entitled to any such interest. If practicable, the Liquidating Trust shall invest any Cash that is withheld as the Distribution Reserve in a manner that shall yield a reasonable net return, taking into account the safety of the investment.

13.4 Distributions After Allowance. The Liquidating Trust shall make payments and distributions from the Distribution Reserve to each holder of a Disputed Claim that has become an Allowed Claim in accordance with the provisions of the Plan governing the Class of Claims to which such holder belongs. On the next succeeding interim distribution date after the date that the order or judgment of the Bankruptcy Court allowing all or part of such Claim becomes a Final Order, the Liquidating Trust shall distribute to the holder of such Claim any Cash or other property in the Distribution Reserve that would have been distributed on the Initial Distribution Date had such Allowed Claim been allowed on the Initial Distribution Date.

Article 14. RETENTION OF JURISDICTION

14.1 Jurisdiction. Notwithstanding the entry of the Confirmation Order and the occurrence of the Effective Date, the Bankruptcy Court retains such jurisdiction over the Chapter 11 Cases after the Effective Date as is legally permissible including, without limitation, jurisdiction to:

14.1.1 Allow, disallow, determine, liquidate, classify, estimate, or establish the priority or secured or unsecured status of any Claim, including the resolution of any request for payment of any Administrative Claim and the resolution of any and all objections to the allowance or priority of Claims;

14.1.2 Grant or deny any applications for allowance of compensation or reimbursement of expenses authorized under the Bankruptcy Code or the Plan;

14.1.3 Resolve any matters related to the assumption, assumption and assignment, or rejection of any executory contract or unexpired lease to which the Debtors is a party and to hear, determine and, if necessary, liquidate, any Claims arising from, or cure amounts related to, such assumption or rejection;

14.1.4 Ensure that distributions to holders of Allowed Claims are accomplished in accordance with the Plan;

14.1.5 Decide or resolve any motions, adversary proceedings, contested or litigated matters, and any other matters and grant or deny any applications or motions involving the Debtors that may be pending on the Effective Date;

14.1.6 Enter such orders as may be necessary or appropriate to implement or consummate the provisions of the Plan and all contracts, instruments, releases, and other agreements or documents created in connection with the Plan or the Disclosure Statement, except as otherwise provided in the Plan;

14.1.7 Resolve any cases, controversies, suits or disputes that may arise in connection with the consummation, interpretation or enforcement of the Plan or any Person's obligations incurred in connection with the Plan;

14.1.8 Modify the Plan before or after the Effective Date under Section 1127 of the Bankruptcy Code or modify the Disclosure Statement, the Disclosure Statement Summary or any contract, instrument, release, or other agreement or document created in connection with the Plan, the Disclosure Statement or the Disclosure Statement Summary; or remedy any defect or omission or reconcile any inconsistency in any Bankruptcy Court order, the Plan, the Disclosure Statement, the Disclosure Statement Summary, or any contract, instrument, release, or other agreement or document created in connection with the Plan, the Disclosure Statement, or the Disclosure Statement Summary, in such manner as may be necessary or appropriate to consummate the Plan, to the extent authorized by the Bankruptcy Code;

14.1.9 Issue injunctions, enter and implement other orders, or take such other actions as may be necessary or appropriate to restrain interference by any entity with consummation or enforcement of the Plan, except as otherwise provided in the Plan;

14.1.10 Enter and implement such orders as are necessary or appropriate if the Confirmation Order is for any reason modified, stayed, reversed, revoked, or vacated;

14.1.11 Determine any other matters that may arise in connection with or relate to the Plan, the Disclosure Statement, the Disclosure Statement Summary, the Confirmation Order or any contract, instrument, release, or other agreement or document created in connection with the Plan, the Disclosure Statement, the Disclosure Statement Summary or the Confirmation Order except as otherwise provided in the Plan;

14.1.12 Enter an order closing the Chapter 11 Cases;

14.1.13 Adjudicate, if applicable, the Avoidance Actions, the Litigation Claims (including those to be initiated and prosecuted by the Liquidating Trust as the Estate's representative under Section 1123(b)(3)(B) of the Bankruptcy Code), and any other cause of action or claims of the

Debtors and Non-Debtor Affiliates;

14.1.14 Adjudicate or otherwise resolve any disputes relating to the General Unsecured Claim Recovery Schedule as provided in the Plan and;

14.1.15 Approve, if applicable, the appointment or removal of any member of the Liquidating Trust Board, the Investor Advisory Committee or the Liquidating Trustee in accordance with the Plan and the Liquidating Trust Agreement.

Article 15. AMENDMENT AND WITHDRAWAL OF PLAN

15.1 Amendment of the Plan. At any time before the Confirmation Date, the Debtors may alter, amend, or modify the Plan under Section 1127(a) of the Bankruptcy Code. After the Confirmation Date and before substantial consummation of the Plan as defined in Section 1101(2) of the Bankruptcy Code, the Debtors may, under Section 1127(b) of the Bankruptcy Code, institute proceedings in the Bankruptcy Court to remedy any defect or omission or reconcile any inconsistencies in the Plan, the Disclosure Statement, the Disclosure Statement Summary, or the Confirmation Order, and such matters as may be necessary to carry out the purposes and effects of the Plan, *provided, however,* that prior notice of such proceedings shall be served in accordance with the Bankruptcy Rules or applicable order of the Bankruptcy Court.

15.2 Revocation or Withdrawal of the Plan. The Debtors reserve the right to revoke or withdraw this Plan at any time before the Confirmation Date. If the Plan is withdrawn or revoked, then the Plan shall be deemed null and void and nothing contained in the Plan shall be deemed a waiver of any Claims by or against the Debtors or any other Person in any further proceedings involving the Debtors or an admission of any sort, and this Plan and any transaction contemplated by this Plan shall not be admitted into evidence in any proceeding.

Article 16. MISCELLANEOUS

16.1 Filing of Objections to Claims. After the Effective Date, objections to Administrative Claims and all other Claims may be made and objections to Administrative Claims and Claims made before the Effective Date may be pursued by the Liquidating Trust or any other Person properly entitled to do so after notice to the Liquidating Trust and approval by the Bankruptcy Court. Any objections to Administrative Claims and Claims made after the Effective Date shall be filed and served on the holders of such Administrative Claims and Claims not later than 90 days after the Effective Date or such later date as may be approved by the Bankruptcy Court.

16.2 Settlement of Objections After Effective Date. From and after the Effective Date, the Liquidating Trust may litigate to Final Order, propose settlements of, or withdraw objections to, all pending or filed Disputed Claims, Disputed Equity Interests, Litigation Claims or Avoidance Actions and the Liquidating Trust may settle or compromise any Disputed Claim, Disputed Equity Interest, or Litigation Claim without notice and a hearing and without approval of the Bankruptcy Court.

16.3 Effectuating Documents; Further Transactions; Timing. The Debtors and the Non-Debtor Affiliates shall be authorized and directed to execute, deliver, file, or record such contracts, instruments, releases, and other agreements or documents, and to take such actions as may be necessary or appropriate to effectuate and further evidence the terms and conditions of the Plan, and any securities issued in accordance with the Plan. All transactions required to occur on the Effective Date under the terms of the Plan shall be deemed to have occurred simultaneously.

16.4 Exemption From Transfer Taxes. In accordance with Section 1146(c) of the Bankruptcy Code: (a) the issuance, distribution, transfer, or exchange of the Estate property, including the transfer and assignment of Assets to the Platform Subsidiaries and the assignment of Litigation Claims, Avoidance Actions and any D&O Policy to the Liquidating Trust; (b) the creation, modification, consolidation, or recording of any deed of trust or other security interest, the securing of additional indebtedness by such means or by other means in furtherance of, or connection with, this Plan or the Confirmation Order; (c) the making, assignment, modification, or recording of any lease or sublease; or (d) the making, delivery, or recording of a deed or other instrument of transfer under, in furtherance of, or in connection with, this Plan, the Confirmation Order, or any transaction contemplated above, or any transactions arising out of, contemplated by, or in any way related to, the foregoing shall not be subject to any document recording tax, stamp tax, conveyance fee, intangibles or similar tax, mortgage tax, stamp act or real estate transfer tax, mortgage recording tax or other similar tax or governmental assessment and the appropriate state or local government officials or agents shall be directed to forego the collection of any such tax or assessment and to accept for filing or recordation any of the foregoing instruments or other documents without the payment of any such tax or assessment.

16.5 Binding Effect. The Plan shall be binding on, and shall inure to the benefit of, the Debtors, the Non-Debtor Affiliates, the Liquidating Trust, the Platform Subsidiaries and the holders of all Claims and Equity Interests, including the holders of Investor Claims and Securities Claims, and their respective successors and assigns.

16.6 Governing Law. Except to the extent that the Bankruptcy Code or other federal law is applicable or as provided in any document implementing the Plan, the rights, duties and obligations of the Debtors, the Non-Debtor Affiliates and any other Person arising under the Plan shall be governed by, and construed and enforced in accordance with, the internal laws of the State of Arizona, without giving effect to Arizona's choice of law provisions.

16.7 Modification of Payment Terms. The Liquidating Trust shall have the right to modify the treatment of any Allowed Claim or Equity Interest in any manner adverse only to the holder of such Claim or Equity Interest at any time after the Effective Date upon the prior written consent of the holder whose Allowed Claim or Equity Interest treatment is being adversely affected.

16.8 Setoffs. The Debtors, the Non-Debtor Affiliates, the Liquidating Trust and the Platform Subsidiaries may, but are not required to, set off or recoup against any Claim or Equity Interest and the payments or other distributions to be made under the Plan in respect of such Claim, claims of any nature whatsoever that arose before the Petition Date that the Debtors may have against the holder of such Claim or Equity Interest to the extent such Claims may be set off or recouped under applicable law, but neither the failure to do so nor the Allowance of any Claim or Equity Interest under the Plan shall constitute a waiver or release by the Debtors, the Non-Debtor Affiliates, the Liquidating Trust and the Platform Subsidiaries of any such claim that it may have against such holder.

16.9 Notices. Any notice required or permitted to be provided under the Plan shall be in writing and served by either: (a) certified mail, return receipt requested, postage prepaid; (b) hand delivery; (c) reputable overnight courier service, freight prepaid; or (d) by fax; addressed as follows:

The Debtors: BAPTIST FOUNDATION OF ARIZONA
1313 East Osborn Road, Suite 250
Phoenix, Arizona 85014
Telephone: (602) 279-3587
Attn: Mark Dickerson, Esq.
Acting General Counsel

With a copy to: SQUIRE, SANDERS & DEMPSEY L.L.P.
40 North Central Avenue, Suite 2700
Phoenix, Arizona 85004
Telephone: (602) 528-4085
Facsimile: (602) 253-8129
Attn: Craig D. Hansen, Esq.
Email: Chansen@ssd.com

With a copy to: GALLAGHER & KENNEDY
2575 East Camelback Road
Phoenix, Arizona 85016-9225
Telephone: (602) 530-8000
Facsimile: (602) 530-8500
Attn: Charles R. Sterbach, Esq.
Email: CRS@gknet.com

With a copy to: HENDRICKSON & ASSOCIATES
4411 South Rural Road, Suite 201
Tempe, Arizona 85282
Telephone: (480) 345-7500
Facsimile: (480) 345-6406
Attn: Brian Hendrickson
Email: Hendricksonlaw@msn.com

Creditors' Committee: UNSECURED CREDITORS COMMITTEE
Darrel Srader and Steve Culp, Co-Chairmen
c/o Fennemore Craig
3003 North Central Avenue, Suite 2600
Phoenix, Arizona 85012
Telephone: (602) 916-5000
Facsimile: (602) 916-5999
Attn: Cathy Reece, Esq.
Email: Creece@fclaw.com

With a copy to: FENNEMORE CRAIG
3003 North Central Avenue, Suite 260
Phoenix, Arizona 85012
Telephone: (602) 916-5000
Facsimile: (602) 916-5999
Attn: Cathy Reece, Esq.
Email: Creece@fclaw.com

U.S. Trustee: Office of the United States Trustee
2929 North Central Avenue, Suite 700
Phoenix, Arizona 85012
Telephone: (602) 640-2100
Facsimile: (602) 640-2217
Attn: Richard Cuellar, Esq.
Elizabeth Amorosi, Esq.

16.10 Delivery of Notices. If personally delivered, such communication shall be deemed delivered upon actual receipt; if electronically transmitted in accordance with this Plan, such communication shall be deemed delivered by the next noon at point of arrival occurring on a Business Day following transmission; if sent by overnight courier in accordance with this Plan, such communication shall be deemed delivered within twenty-four hours of deposit with such courier or noon of the first Business Day following such deposit, whichever first occurs; and if sent by U.S. Mail in accordance with this Plan, such communication shall be deemed delivered as of the date of delivery indicated on the receipt issued by the relevant postal service; or, if the addressee fails or refuses to accept delivery, as of the date of such failure or refusal. Any party to this Plan may change its address for the purposes of this Plan by giving notice of such change in accordance with this section.

16.11 Termination of Statutory Committees. Any statutory committee or committees appointed in the Chapter 11 Cases and any examiner terminate on the Effective Date and thereafter shall have no further responsibilities in respect of the Chapter 11 Cases, except with respect to preparation of filing of applications for compensation and reimbursement of expenses.

16.12 Severability. If any provision of this Plan is found by the Bankruptcy Court to be invalid, illegal or unenforceable, if this Plan is found by the Bankruptcy Court to be invalid, illegal or unenforceable, or if this Plan cannot be Confirmed under Section 1129 of the Bankruptcy Code, the Bankruptcy Court, at the Debtors' request, shall retain the power to alter and interpret such term to make it valid or enforceable to the maximum extent practicable, consistent with the original purpose of the term or provision held be invalid, void or unenforceable, and such term or provision shall then be applicable as altered or interpreted. The Confirmation Order shall constitute a judicial determination and shall provide that each term and provision of this Plan, as it may have been altered or interpreted in accordance with the foregone, is valid and enforceable in accordance with its terms.

16.13 Withholding And Reporting Requirements. In connection with this Plan and all instruments and securities issued in connection with the Plan, the Debtors and the Liquidating Trust, as the case may be, shall comply with all withholding and reporting requirements imposed by any federal, state, local or foreign taxing authority, and all distributions under the Plan remain subject to any such withholding and reporting requirements. The Debtors and the Liquidating Trust, as the case may be, shall be authorized to take all actions necessary to comply with such withholding and recording requirements. Notwithstanding any other provision of this Plan, each holder of an Allowed Claim that has received a distribution, shall have sole and exclusive responsibility for the satisfaction or payment of any tax obligation imposed by any governmental unit, including income, withholding and other tax obligation on account of such distribution.

16.14 Quarterly Fees To The United States Trustee. The Liquidating Trustee shall pay all quarterly fees payable to the Office of the United States Trustee for the Debtors after Confirmation, consistent with applicable provisions of the Bankruptcy Code, Bankruptcy Rules, and 28 U.S.C. § 1930(a)(6).

16.15 Amendments to Exhibits. At any time prior to the commencement of the hearing on Confirmation of the Plan, the Debtors may make modifications to the Exhibits to the Plan without modifying the Plan, provided that such modifications do not materially alter the distribution provisions and the recoveries of Creditors pursuant to the Plan.

16.16 Method Of Payment. Payments of Cash required to be made under the Plan shall be made by check drawn on a domestic bank or by wire transfer from a domestic bank at the election of the Person making such payment. Whenever any payment or distribution to be made under the Plan is due on a day other than a Business Day, such payment or distribution may instead be made, without interest, on the immediately following Business Day.

Dated: Phoenix, Arizona
February 18, 2000

Respectfully submitted,

BAPTIST FOUNDATION OF ARIZONA, in its own capacity and on behalf of all of the Debtors

By: ______________________________
Jock Patton
Its: Chairman of the Restructuring Committee

SQUIRE, SANDERS & DEMPSEY L.L.P.

By: ______________________________
Craig D. Hansen, one of the attorneys for the **BAPTIST FOUNDATION OF ARIZONA**, et al., Debtors

GALLAGHER & KENNEDY

By: ______________________________
Charles R. Sterbach, one of the attorneys for **ARIZONA SOUTHERN NEW CHURCH VENTURES, INC.** et al., Debtors

HENDRICKSON & ASSOCIATES

By: ______________________________
Brian W. Hendrickson, attorneys for **ALO, INC., E.V.I.G., INC.,** et al., Debtors

APPENDIX P

SAMPLE PLAN—SALE TO THIRD PARTY

This Chapter 11 plan is from the reorganization of ***America West Airlines***. The bankruptcy was filed in 1991 and the reorganization was completed in 1994, when a new entity, AmWest Partners L.P. (formed by, among others, Continental Airlines and Mesa Airlines), agreed to purchase $115 million in common stock of the reorganized company and up to $130 million in new unsecured notes, thereby infusing the estate with new capital of up to $245 million for payments to creditors under the plan. AmWest acquired a 33.5 percent ownership interest and a 71.2 percent voting interest in the reorganized America West Airlines, with the remaining equity being issued to creditors in partial satisfaction of their claims. A small percentage of the new equity was given to current America West employees. Creditors were allowed to elect to receive cash in lieu of new common stock, and AmWest agreed to "purchase" the shares that would otherwise go to such electing creditors, further enhancing AmWest's ownership interest in the reorganized airline.

UNITED STATES BANKRUPTCY COURT
FOR THE DISTRICT OF ARIZONA

IN RE	)	
	)	
AMERICA WEST AIRLINES, INC.,	)	CASE NO.
	)	91-07505-PHX-RGM
	)	CHAPTER 11
Debtor.	)	

PLAN OF REORGANIZATION UNDER CHAPTER 11 OF THE UNITED STATES BANKRUPTCY CODE

AMERICA WEST AIRLINES, INC.
Martin J. Whalen, Esq.
4000 East Sky Harbor Blvd.
Phoenix, Arizona 85034

LEBOEUF, LAMB, GREENE & MACRAE
633 17th Street, Suite 2800
Denver, Colorado
(303) 291-2600

Of Counsel:
Carl A. Eklund
John Edward Maas

GALLAGHER & KENNEDY
2600 North Central Avenue
Phoenix, Arizona 85004
(602) 530-8000

Of Counsel:
Charles R. Sterbach

Co-Counsel to the Debtor and Debtor In Possession, Co-Proponent of this Plan of Reorganization

ARNOLD & PORTER
1200 New Hampshire Avenue, N.W.
Washington, D.C. 20036
(202) 872-6700

Of Counsel:
Richard P. Schifter
Samuel A. Flax
Brain P. Leitch

Counsel to AmWest Partners, L.P., Co-Proponent of this Plan of Reorganization

SQUIRE, SANDERS & DEMPSEY, L.L.P.
40 North Central Avenue, Suite 2700
Phoenix, Arizona 85004
(602) 528-4000

Of Counsel:
Thomas J. Salerno
Jordan A. Kroop
Craig D. Hansen

Co-Counsel to the Debtor and Debtor In Possession, Co-Proponent of this Plan of Reorganization

Dated: Phoenix, Arizona
June 28, 1994

TABLE OF CONTENTS

LIST OF EXHIBITS

Exhibit C – GPA Term Sheet

LIST OF SCHEDULES – **[OMITTED]**

Schedule 1 – Section 1110 Stipulations
Schedule 2 – Certain Final Orders Related to Settlements
Schedule 3 – Certain Assumed Agreements

PLAN OF REORGANIZATION UNDER CHAPTER 11 OF THE UNITED STATES BANKRUPTCY CODE

AMERICA WEST AIRLINES, INC., the Debtor and Debtor in Possession in the above-captioned Chapter 11 Case, and AMWEST PARTNERS, L.P., as co-proponents hereof, hereby jointly propose the following Plan of Reorganization pursuant to Section 1121(a), Title 11, United States Code for the resolution of the Debtor's outstanding creditor claims and equity interests. Reference is made to the Debtor's Disclosure Statement, filed contemporaneously with the Plan of Reorganization, for a discussion of the Debtor's history, business, properties, results of operations and projections for future operations and for a summary and analysis of the Plan of Reorganization and certain related matters.

ALL HOLDERS OF CLAIMS AGAINST AND EQUITY INTERESTS IN THE DEBTOR ARE ENCOURAGED TO READ THE PLAN OF REORGANIZATION AND THE DISCLOSURE STATEMENT IN THEIR ENTIRETY BEFORE VOTING TO ACCEPT OR REJECT THE PLAN.

ARTICLE 1

DEFINITIONS

As used in the Plan, the following terms shall have the respective meanings specified below:

1.1 Administrative Claim: A Claim for any cost or expense of administration of the Chapter 11 Case allowed under Section 503(b), Section 507(b), Section 546(c)(2) or Section 1114(e)(2) of the Bankruptcy Code and entitled to priority under Section 507(a)(1) of the Bankruptcy Code, including, without limitation, fees payable pursuant to Section 1930 of Title 28 of the United States Code, but not including the Post-Petition Agreement Claims. To the extent that a Claim is allowed as an administrative claim pursuant to Section 365(d)(3) of the Bankruptcy Code, such Claim shall also be deemed an Administrative Claim under this Section.

1.2 Allowed Claim and Allowed...Claim: Any Claim against the Debtor (i) proof of which, request for payment of which or application for allowance of which was filed or deemed to be filed on or before the Bar Date for filing proofs of claim or requests for payment for Claims of such type against the Debtor, (ii) if no proof of claim is filed, which has been or hereafter is listed by the Debtor in the Schedules as liquidated in amount and not disputed or contingent, or (iii) a Claim that is allowed in any contract, instrument, indenture or other agreement entered into in connection with the Plan and, in any case, a Claim as to which no objection to the allowance thereof has been interposed within the applicable period of limitation fixed by the Plan, the Bankruptcy Code, the Bankruptcy Rules or the

Bankruptcy Court. A Disputed Claim shall be an Allowed Claim if, and only to the extent that, such Disputed Claim has been Allowed by a Final Order or otherwise pursuant to Section 11.2. The term "Allowed," when used to modify a reference in the Plan to any Claim or class of Claims, shall mean a Claim (or any Claim in any such class) that is so Allowed, *e.g.*, an Allowed Secured Claim is a Claim that has been Allowed to the extent of the value, as determined by the Bankruptcy Court pursuant to Section 506(a) of the Bankruptcy Code, of any interest in property of the estate of the Debtor securing such Claim. Unless otherwise specified in the Plan, the Confirmation Order or in the Final Order of the Bankruptcy Court allowing such Claim, "Allowed Claim" shall not include interest on the amount of such Claim from and after the Petition Date.

1.3 AmWest: AmWest Partners, L.P., a Texas limited partnership, and, as the context requires, parties purchasing NewAWA Securities as part of the AmWest investment in NewAWA, even though such parties may or may not actually be partners or investors in AmWest itself.

1.4 Assumed Agreement: Each executory contract and unexpired lease of the Debtor which (i) has been assumed during the Chapter 11 Case prior to the Confirmation Date pursuant to Section 365 of the Bankruptcy Code, (ii) is the subject of a motion to assume pending on the Confirmation Date, or (iii) is listed on Schedule 3 hereto in accordance with Section 5.1.1, either without amendment, or with such amendments thereto as shall be agreed upon between the Debtor and the other parties thereto.

1.5 Avoidance Litigation: The Debtor's interest in any and all claims, rights and causes of action which have been or may be commenced by or on behalf of the Debtor to avoid and recover any transfers of property determined to be preferential, fraudulent or otherwise avoidable pursuant to Sections 544, 545, 547, 548, 549, 553(b) or 550 of the Bankruptcy Code.

1.6 AWA: America West Airlines, Inc., a Delaware corporation, as the Debtor and Debtor in Possession in the Chapter 11 Case, or, as the context may require, NewAWA.

1.7 AWA Common Stock: The duly authorized and validly issued shares of common stock of AWA, $.25 par value, which are outstanding immediately prior to the Effective Date.

1.8 AWA Debenture Claims: All Claims of the holders of AWA Debentures and the Indenture Trustee as of the Distribution Record Date for (i) payment, pursuant to the Indentures, of principal in the face amount of the AWA Debentures, plus interest accrued as of the Petition Date or (ii) the fees, costs and expenses of the Indenture Trustee pursuant to the Indentures, but excluding any Claims for damages in excess of the face amount of the AWA Debentures arising from the purchase or sale of such AWA Debentures, and excluding any Claims for equitable relief.

1.9 AWA Debentures: Collectively, the AWA 11½% Convertible Subordinated Debentures, the AWA 7¾% Convertible Subordinated Debentures, and the AWA 7½% Convertible Subordinated Debentures.

1.10 AWA 11½% Convertible Subordinated Debentures: The 11½% Convertible Subordinated Debentures due 2009, issued by AWA pursuant to the AWA 11½% Subordinated Indenture and outstanding immediately prior to the Effective Date.

1.11 AWA 11½% Subordinated Indenture: The Indenture of Trust dated December 15, 1986 between AWA and First Interstate Bank of Arizona, N.A.

1.12 AWA Preferred Stock: The duly authorized and validly issued shares of Series C 9¾% Convertible Preferred Stock of AWA, $.25 par value, outstanding immediately prior to the Effective Date.

1.13 AWA 7½% Convertible Subordinated Debentures: The 7½% Convertible Subordinated Debentures due 2011, issued by AWA pursuant to the AWA 7½% Subordinated Indenture and outstanding immediately prior to the Effective Date.

1.14 AWA 7½% Subordinated Indenture: The Indenture of Trust dated March 15, 1986 between AWA and First Interstate Bank of Arizona, N.A.

1.15 AWA 7¾% Convertible Subordinated Debentures: The 7¾% Convertible Subordinated Debentures due 2010, issued by AWA pursuant to the AWA 7¾% Subordinated Indenture and outstanding immediately prior to the Effective Date.

1.16 AWA 7¾% Subordinated Indenture: The Indenture of Trust dated August 1, 1985 between AWA and First Interstate Bank of Arizona, N.A.

1.17 AWA Warrants, Options and Other Equity Interests: All Equity Interest in AWA outstanding immediately prior to the Effective Date, except for the AWA Common Stock and the AWA Preferred Stock, but including without limitation all rights, options or warrants, authorized, adopted or distributed to holders of Equity Interests of officers, directors or employees of AWA, whether under one or more contracts or plans, to sell, purchase, grant or otherwise transfer any issued and outstanding or authorized but unissued Equity Interests of AWA under any and all applicable terms and conditions.

1.18 Ballot: The form for (i) acceptance or rejection of the Plan distributed to those holders of Claims or Equity Interests entitled to vote on the Plan and (ii) the election of (a) the option to purchase Equity Subscription Stock and Over-Subscription Stock and (b) the option to become an Electing Unsecured Creditor, as such form may be approved by the Bankruptcy Court and which shall otherwise comply with the requirements of the Bankruptcy Rule 3018(c).

1.19 Bankruptcy Code: The Bankruptcy Reform Act of 1978, Title 11, United States Code, as applicable to the Chapter 11 Case, as now in effect or hereafter amended.

1.20 Bankruptcy Court: The unit of the United States District Court for the District of Arizona having jurisdiction over the Chapter 11 Case.

1.21 Bankruptcy Rules: Collectively, the Federal Rules of Bankruptcy Procedure and the local rules of the Bankruptcy Court, as applicable to the Chapter 11 Case, as now in effect or hereinafter amended.

1.22 Bar Date: In the case of Claims other than Administrative Claims, February 28, 1992, and in the case of Administrative Claims (other than Preserved Ordinary Course Administrative Claims and Professional Fees), July 1, 1994.

1.23 Business Day: Any day other than a Saturday, Sunday or other day on which commercial banks in New York or Arizona are authorized or required by law to close.

1.24 Cash: Currency, checks and wire transfers of immediately available funds.

1.25 Chapter 11 Case: The case under Chapter 11 of the Bankruptcy Code in which AWA is the Debtor pending in the Bankruptcy Court with Case No. 91-07505-PHX-RGM, including all adversary proceedings pending in connection therewith.

1.26 Claim: Any right to payment from the Debtor, whether or not such right is reduced to judgment, liquidated, unliquidated, fixed, contingent, matured, unmatured, disputed, undisputed, legal, equitable, secured or unsecured arising at any time before the Effective Date or relating to any event that occurred before the Effective Date; or any right to an equitable remedy for breach of performance if such breach gives rise to a right of payment from the Debtor, whether or not such right to an equitable remedy is reduced to judgment, fixed, contingent, matured, unmatured, disputed, undisputed, secured or unsecured. Any alleged right to payment which is listed by the Debtor on the Schedules is disputed, unliquidated or contingent will not be a Claim hereunder if the holder thereof has not filed a timely proof of claim with regard thereto.

1.27 Class A: A category of holders of Claims or Equity Interest as classified in the Plan.

1.28 Confirmation: The entry by the Bankruptcy Court of the Confirmation Order.

1.29 Confirmation Date: The date upon which the Bankruptcy Court enters the Confirmation Order.

1.30 Confirmation Hearing: The duly noticed hearing held by the Bankruptcy Court on Confirmation of the Plan pursuant to Section *1128* of the

Bankruptcy Code. The Confirmation Hearing may be adjourned by the Bankruptcy Court from time to time without further notice other than the announcement of the adjourned date at the Confirmation Hearing.

1.31 Confirmation Order: An order of the Bankruptcy Court, in form and substance satisfactory to the Debtor and AmWest, confirming the Plan.

1.32 Contingent Claim: A Claim which is either contingent or unliquidated on or immediately before the Confirmation Date.

1.33 Convenience Claims: All Allowed General Unsecured Claims which are in an amount of five hundred dollars ($500) or less.

1.34 Creditors' Committee: The Official Committee of Unsecured Creditors appointed by the United States Trustee in the Chapter 11 Case pursuant to Section 1102(a)(1) of the Bankruptcy Code.

1.35 Debt Instrument: A debenture, promissory note or other transferable instrument evidencing a payment obligation.

1.36 Debtor and Debtor in Possession: AWA, as a debtor in possession in the Chapter 11 Case pursuant to Sections 1107 and 1108 of the Bankruptcy Code.

1.37 DIP Credit Agreement: The Third Amended and Restated Credit Agreement dated as of September 30, 1993, between AWA and the DIP Lenders, as approved by Final Order of the Bankruptcy Court dated September 29, 1993, together with all integrally related documents, schedules and exhibits, as such agreement and such integrally related documents, schedules and exhibits may be amended or amended and restated from time to time.

1.38 DIP Lenders: BT Commercial Corp., as Administrative Agent, GPA Leasing USA I, Inc., GPA Leasing USA Sub I, Inc., Kawasaki Leasing International, Inc., B&B Holdings, Inc. d/b/a Phoenix Cardinals, Bank of America Arizona, Bank One Arizona, N.A., Commerce and Economic Development Division, The Dial Corp., DMB Holding Limited Partnership, El Dorado Investment Company, First Interstate Bank of Arizona, N.A., Phelps Dodge Corporation, Phoenix Newspapers, Inc., and Phoenix Suns, Ltd. Partnership and each substitute or additional lender under any permitted assignment, amendment or amendment and restatement of the DIP Credit Agreement.

1.39 DIP Loan Claims: Any and all Claims, whether a Secured Claim or an Unsecured Claim, of the DIP Lenders, arising under the DIP Credit Agreement.

1.40 *Disclosure Statement :* The Disclosure Statement dated as of June 28, 1994, including exhibits and any supplements, amendments or modifications thereto, prepared pursuant to Sections 1125(a) and 1126(b) of the Bankruptcy Code, and Bankruptcy Rule 3018(b), as approved by the Bankruptcy Court.

1.41 Disputed Claim and Disputed . . . Claim: A Claim which is (i) the subject of a timely objection interposed by the Debtor, NewAWA or any party in interest (including the Creditors' Committee and the Equity Committee) in the Chapter 11 Case, if at such time such objection remains unresolved, (ii) a Claim that is listed by the Debtor as disputed, unliquidated or contingent in the Schedules or (iii) if no objection has been timely filed, a Claim which has been asserted in a timely filed proof of claim in an amount greater than or in a class different than that listed by the Debtor in the Schedules as liquidated in amount and not disputed or contingent; *provided, however,* that the Bankruptcy Court may estimate a Disputed Claim for purposes of allowance pursuant to Section 502(c) of the Bankruptcy Code. The term "Disputed," when used to modify a reference in the Plan to any Claim or class of Claims, shall mean a Claim (or any Claim in such class) that is a Disputed Claim as defined herein. In the event there is a dispute as to classification or priority of a Claim, it shall be considered a Disputed Claim in its entirety. Until such time as a Contingent Claim becomes fixed and absolute, such Claim shall be treated as a Disputed Claim and not an Allowed Claim for purposes related to allocations and distributions under the Plan.

1.42 Disputed Equity Interest: An Equity Interest which is the subject of a timely objection interposed by the Debtor, NewAWA or any party in interest (including the Equity Committee) in the Chapter 11 Case, if at such time such objection remains unresolved.

1.43 Distribution Agent: NewAWA or such disbursing agent(s) as NewAWA shall from time to time employ at its expense for the purpose of making distributions under the Plan.

1.44 Distribution Agent Charges: Any Taxes imposed upon or with respect to (i) the Distribution Agent in its capacity as such, or (ii) the assets held by the Distribution Agent in its capacity as such or any income realized thereon.

1.45 Distribution Date: With respect to any Allowed Claim or Equity Interest, each date on which a payment is made with respect to such Allowed Claim or Equity Interest.

1.46 Distribution Record Date: For the purposes under Bankruptcy Rules 3001 and 3021 for any distribution under the Plan to the holders of Claims or Equity Interests and for the determination of which Claims or Equity Interests may be disallowed, the Effective Date.

1.47 Effective Date: The last to occur of (i) the first Business Day that is at least eleven (11) days after the Confirmation Date and on which no stay of the Confirmation Order is in effect, and (ii) the Business Day on which all of the conditions set forth in Section 9.1 shall have been satisfied.

1.48 Electing Creditor Cash: The Cash to be received by Electing Unsecured Creditors in accordance with Section 3.5.

1.49 Electing Creditor Stock: The NewAWA Class B Common Stock to be distributed under certain circumstances to Electing Unsecured Creditors pursuant to Section 3.5.

1.50 Electing Unsecured Creditors: Holders of General Unsecured Claims who elect to receive Electing Creditor Cash instead of NewAWA Class B Common Stock in accordance with Section 3.5.

1.51 Employee Stock Purchase Notes: Any and all Debt Instruments executed and delivered by any current or former director, officer or employee of AWA under the Employee Stock Purchase Plan.

1.52 Employee Stock Purchase Plan: Any and all of the Debtor's stock purchase plan(s) whereby directors, officers or employees of AWA were authorized (whether on a mandatory or optional basis) to acquire or finance the purchase of AWA Common Stock on certain terms and conditions and subject to certain repayment obligations.

1.53 Equity Committee: The Official Committee of Equity Security Holders of AWA appointed in the Chapter 11 Case pursuant to Section 1102 (a)(2) of the Bankruptcy Code.

1.54 Equity Interest: Any interest in the Debtor represented by any class or series of common or preferred stock issued by the Debtor and any warrants, options or rights to purchase any such common or preferred stock. Equity Interests include, without limitation, all AWA Common Stock, AWA Preferred Stock and AWA Warrants, Options and Other Equity Interests.

1.55 Equity Interests Stock: The 2,250,000 shares of NewAWA Class B Common Stock to be issued to holders of AWA Common Stock as provided in Section 3.6.2.

1.56 Equity Interests Warrants: The NewAWA Warrants to purchase 6,230,769 shares of NewAWA Class B Common Stock to be issued to holders of AWA Common Stock as provided in Section 3.6.2.

1.57 Equity Subscription Stock: The up to 1,615,179 shares of NewAWA Class B Common Stock of which each holder of AWA Common Stock is entitled to purchase up to its Pro Rata Share as provided in Section 3.6.2.

1.58 ERISA: The Employee Retirement Income Security Act of 1974, as amended.

1.59 Escrow Agent: The bank, trust company or other organization independent of NewAWA, selected by AWA or NewAWA and retained pursuant to an agreement approved by order of the Bankruptcy Court, designated to act as escrow agent with respect to the Reserves as provided in Section 10.4, which entity may be the Distribution Agent, if the Distribution

Agent is not affiliated with NewAWA.

1.60 Fidelity: Fidelity Management Trust Company, its affiliates and funds and accounts managed by it and its affiliates.

1.61 Final Distribution Date: The Distribution Date for a Class after which the Reserve Amount for such Class will be zero.

1.62 Final Order: An order or judgment which has not been reversed, stayed, modified or amended and is no longer subject to appeal, *certiorari* proceeding or other proceeding for review or rehearing, and as to which no appeal, *certiorari* proceeding, or other proceeding for review or rehearing shall then be pending.

1.63 General Unsecured Claim: Any Unsecured Claim other than a Post-Petition Agreement Claim, an Administrative Claim, a Priority Wage Claim, a Priority Benefit Plan Contribution Claim, a Priority Tax Claim, a Convenience Claim or a Claim treated in accordance with Section 3.7 of the Plan.

1.64 GPA: GPA Group plc and affiliates thereof.

1.65 Indenture Trustee: Texas Commerce Bank, National Association (f/k/a Ameritrust Company of New York), as Successor Trustee to First Interstate Bank of Arizona, N.A., or any successor under the Indentures.

1.66 Indentures: Collectively, the AWA 11½% Subordinated Indenture, the AWA 7½% Subordinated Indenture and the AWA 7¾% Subordinated Indenture.

1.67 Interim Procedures Agreement. The Third Revised Interim Procedures Agreement dated April 21, 1994 between AWA and AmWest, as amended from time to time.

1.68 Investment Agreement: The Third Revised Investment Agreement, dated April 21, 1994, as amended from time to time, between AWA and AmWest, in the form of Exhibit A hereto, which is incorporated herein by reference.

1.69 IRS: The Internal Revenue Service.

1.70 Lehman: Lehman Brothers, Inc.

1.71 Net Proceeds: The gross proceeds received from the sale, lease, disposition, liquidation and collection of assets, less amounts actually incurred for (i) necessary and reasonable costs and expenses in connection with such sale, lease, disposition, liquidation or collection, including, but not limited to, attorneys' fees related thereto, and (ii) all liabilities, charges, Taxes, offsets and encumbrances required to be discharged with respect to such assets and in connection with the sale, lease, disposition, liquidation and collection thereof.

1.72 NewAWA: AWA on and after the Effective Date.

1.73 NewAWA By-laws: The Restated By-laws of NewAWA.

1.74 NewAWA Charter: The Restated Certificate of Incorporation of NewAWA.

1.75 NewAWA Class A Common Stock: The Class A Common Stock, par value $.01 per share, of NewAWA which NewAWA shall be authorized to issue on and after the Effective Date.

1.76 NewAWA Class B Common Stock: The Class B Common Stock, par value $.01 per share, of NewAWA which NewAWA shall be authorized to issue on and after the Effective Date.

1.77 NewAWA Common Stock: Collectively, the NewAWA Class A Common Stock and the NewAWA Class B Common Stock.

1.78 NewAWA Securities: Collectively, the NewAWA Common Stock, NewAWA Warrants and NewAWA Senior Unsecured Notes.

1.79 NewAWA Senior Unsecured Notes: The Senior Unsecured Notes which NewAWA shall be authorized to issue on or after the Effective Date.

1.80 NewAWA Warrants: The warrants to purchase shares of NewAWA Class B Common Stock which NewAWA shall be authorized to issue on or after the Effective Date.

1.81 Non-Electing Creditor Stock: The NewAWA Class B Common Stock to be distributed to NonElecting Unsecured Creditors in accordance with Section 3.5.2.

1.82 Non-Electing Unsecured Creditors: Holders of General Unsecured Claims that do not elect to be Electing Unsecured Creditors in accordance with Section 3.5.

1.83 Notice and a Hearing: This phrase shall have the same meaning as provided for in Section 102(1) of the Bankruptcy Code.

1.84 Official Service List: The then-current Official Service List in the Chapter 11 Case, as required by the Bankruptcy Court's "Order Establishing Notice Requirements With Respect to All Matters Herein" entered on June 28, 1991, and "Order Modifying Noticing Procedures and Requirements" entered on October 21, 1991.

1.85 Over-Subscription Stock: The shares of NewAWA Class B Common Stock which were available for purchase as Equity Subscription Stock and which were not so purchased. Over-Subscription Stock shall be available for sale to holders of AWA Preferred Stock in accordance with Section 3.6.1 and, if there are more than 250,000 such shares or if holders of AWA Preferred Stock subscribe for fewer shares than they are entitled to subscribe for, to Purchasing Stockholders in accordance with Section 3.6.2.

1.86 Person: An individual, a corporation, a limited liability company, a partnership, an association, a joint stock company, a joint venture, an estate, a trust, an unincorporated organization or a government, governmental unit or any subdivision thereof or any other entity.

1.87 Petition Date: June 27, 1991, the date on which the Debtor filed a voluntary petition commencing the Chapter 11 Case.

1.88 Plan: This Plan of Reorganization, either in its present form or as it may be amended, supplemented or modified from time to time, including all exhibits and schedules annexed hereto or referenced.

1.89 Plan Discount Rate: The rate of interest equal to eight percent (8%) per annum.

1.90 Post-Petition Agreement Claim: Any Claim against the Debtor of the type listed in Section 2.1 but not including an Administrative Claim arising as a result of the assumption of an executory contract or lease listed on Schedule 3 hereto.

1.91 Present Value: As the context requires, the present value as of the Effective Date of a stream of Cash payments computed using the Plan Discount Rate.

1.92 Preserved Ordinary Course Administrative Claim: Administrative Claims that are based on liabilities incurred in (a) AWA's purchase, lease or use of goods and services in the ordinary course of its business or (b) AWA's sale or provision of air transportation services (including the sale of tickets to passengers) in the ordinary course of its business, including Administrative Claims due on account of services provided to AWA after the Petition Date by its employees.

1.93 Prime Rate: The rate of interest which under current practice is listed as such under the heading "Money Rates" in the Eastern Edition of The Wall Street Journal and if a range of rates is listed, the lowest such rate. In the event that such a listing is not available, the Prime Rate shall be such other measure of the prime rate generally in effect as is reasonably selected by NewAWA. For purposes of the Plan and any notes or other instruments delivered pursuant hereto, the Prime Rate shall be deemed to adjust on and only on the last Business Day of each December, March, June and September to the Prime Rate then in effect.

1.94 Priority Benefit Plan Contribution Claim: Any Claim entitled to priority in payment under Section 507 (a)(4) of the Bankruptcy Code.

1.95 Priority Tax Claim: Any Claim entitled to priority in payment under Section 507 (a)(7) of the Bankruptcy Code.

1.96 Priority Wage Claim: Any Claim entitled to priority in payment under Section 507 (a)(3) of the Bankruptcy Code.

1.97 Professional Fees: The Administrative Claims for compensation and reimbursement submitted pursuant to Section 330, Section 331 or Section 503(b) of the Bankruptcy Code by Persons (i) employed pursuant to an order of the Bankruptcy Court under Section 327 or Section 1103 of the Bankruptcy Code or (ii) for whom compensation and reimbursement has been allowed by the Bankruptcy Court pursuant to Section 503(b) of the Bankruptcy Code.

1.98 Pro Rata Share: The ratio of an Allowed Claim or Equity Interest in a particular Class to the aggregate amount of all Allowed Claims or Equity Interests in that Class.

1.99 Purchasing Stockholder: A holder of AWA Common Stock who elects to purchase Equity Subscription Stock or Over-Subscription Stock as provided in Section 3.6.2.

1.100 Registration Rights Agreement: The Registration Rights Agreement to be entered into by and among NewAWA, AmWest and certain other parties pertaining to certain NewAWA Securities to be purchased or otherwise issued pursuant to the Investment Agreement or the Plan.

1.101 Rejected Agreement: Each executory contract or unexpired lease of Debtor that is rejected pursuant to Section 5.2.

1.102 Reserve: As to any Class, the amount held at any particular time by the Escrow Agent, as provided in Section 10.4, including the Reserve Amounts at such time, and any interest, dividends or other income earned upon investment of the Reserve Amount.

1.103 Reserve Amount: The NewAWA Securities and/or Cash reserved as of a particular date for the Disputed Claims or Disputed Equity Interests of a particular Class pursuant to Section 10.4.

1.104 Reserve Order: Any Final Order of the Bankruptcy Court establishing the Reserve Amount for any Reserve, as established in Section 10.4.

1.105 Schedules: The schedules of assets and liabilities and any amendments thereto filed by the Debtor with the Bankruptcy Court in accordance with Section 521(1) of the Bankruptcy Code.

1.106 Secured Claim: A Claim to the extent of the value of any interest in property of the Debtor's estate securing such Claim or to the extent of the amount of such Claim subject to setoff in accordance with Section 553 of the Bankruptcy Code, in either case as determined pursuant to Section 506(a) of the Bankruptcy Code. To the extent that the value of such interest or setoff is less than the amount of the Claim which has the benefit of such security or is subject to such setoff, such Claim is an Unsecured Deficiency Claim unless, in the case of a Claim secured by a lien on property of the Debtor's estate, the Class of which such Claim is a part makes a valid election under Section 1111 (b) of the Bankruptcy Code no later than the Voting Deadline to have such Claim treated as a Secured Claim to the extent allowed.

1.107 Securities Action: The presently uncertified class action lawsuit pending in the Superior Court of the State of Arizona for the County of Maricopa styled Clark v. Beauvais, Case No. CV 92-07197.

1.108 Stock Rescission or Damage Claim: Any Claim pursuant to Section 510 (b) of the Bankruptcy Code (i) for rescission of the purchase or sale of AWA Common Stock, (ii) for damages arising from the purchase or sale of AWA Common Stock, or (iii) for reimbursement, contribution or indemnification on account of such rescission or damage claim.

1.109 Stock Payment Escrow Account: The escrow account to be established in accordance with Section 10.2.2 to receive payment for Equity Subscription Stock and Over-Subscription Stock.

1.110 Stockholders' Agreement: The Stockholders' Agreement for America West Airlines, Inc., to be dated as of the Effective Date, substantially in the form of Exhibit B hereto, which is incorporated herein by reference.

1.111 Subordinated Claim: Any Claim or Equity Interest subordinated, for purposes of distribution, pursuant to Section 510(c) of the Bankruptcy Code.

1.112 Taxes: All income, franchise, excise, sales, use, employment, withholding, property, payroll or other taxes, assessments, or governmental charges, together with any interest, penalties, additions to tax, fines, and similar amounts relating thereto, imposed or collected by any federal, state, local or foreign governmental authority.

1.113 Unsecured Claim: A Claim not secured by a charge against or interest in property in which the Debtor's estate has an interest, including any Unsecured Deficiency Claim.

1.114 Unsecured Deficiency Claim: A Claim by a holder of a Secured Claim arising out of the same transaction as a Secured Claim to the extent that the value of such holder's interest in property of the Debtor's estate securing such Claim or subject to setoff is less than the amount of the Claim which has the benefit of such security or setoff, as provided by Section 506 (a) of the Bankruptcy Code.

1.115 Voting Deadline: The deadline for filing Ballots, as fixed by the Bankruptcy Court in the order approving the Disclosure Statement or otherwise.

1.116 Voting Record Date: June 8, 1994.

1.117 Other Definitions: Unless the context otherwise requires, any capitalized term used and not defined herein or elsewhere in the Plan but that is defined in the Bankruptcy Code or Bankruptcy Rules shall have the meaning set forth therein. Wherever from the context it appears appropriate, each term stated in either of the singular or the plural shall include the singular and the plural, and pronouns stated in the masculine, feminine or neuter gender shall include the masculine, the feminine and the neuter. The words "herein," "hereof," "hereto," "hereunder," and others of similar inference refer to the Plan as a whole and not to any particular Article, Section, subsection, or clause contained in the Plan.

ARTICLE 2

TREATMENT OF UNCLASSIFIED CLAIMS

The Claims against the Debtor covered in this Article 2 are not designated as Classes pursuant to Section 1123 (a)(1) of the Bankruptcy Code. The holders of such Claims are not entitled to vote on the Plan.

2.1 Treatment of Post-Petition Agreement Claims. This Section 2.1 contains provisions dealing with the Post-Petition Agreement Claims.

2.1.1 DIP Credit Agreement. The DIP Loan Claims will be paid in full, in Cash, by AWA on the Effective Date or such later date as may be agreed by AWA and the DIP Lenders, or shall be paid in such other manner as may be agreed to by AWA and the DIP Lenders.

2.1.2 Kawasaki Priority Facility. Any and all Claims arising from that certain Loan Restructuring Agreement, dated as of December 1, 1991, between AWA and Kawasaki Leasing International, Inc., as amended and supplemented from time to time, and as approved by Final Order of the Bankruptcy Court dated December 12, 1991, will be treated exclusively in accordance with the terms and conditions of such agreement or as otherwise agreed by the holder of such Claims and the Debtor or NewAWA.

2.1.3 Section 1110 Stipulations. Any and all Claims arising from the stipulations entered into pursuant to Section 1110 of the Bankruptcy Code between AWA and other parties during the Chapter 11 Case including, without limitation, the stipulations listed on Schedule 1 hereto, and as approved by Final Order of the Bankruptcy Court, shall in each case be treated exclusively in accordance with the terms and conditions of such stipulations and Final Orders, and such terms and conditions shall be binding upon NewAWA.

2.1.4 Settlement Stipulations and Other Post-Petition Orders. Any and all Claims arising from obligations of AWA which were or are the subject of settlement or other agreements entered into between AWA and other parties, whether prior to or after the Effective Date, which settlement or other agreements were or are approved by Final Order of the Bankruptcy Court, including, without limitation, those Final Orders listed on Schedule 2 hereto, shall be treated exclusively in accordance with the terms and conditions of such settlement and other agreements and Final Orders.

2.2 Treatment of Administrative Claims.

2.2.1. This Section 2.2 contains provisions dealing with the treatment of Administrative Claims. Such treatment is consistent with the requirements of Section 1129 (a)(9)(A) of the Bankruptcy Code.

2.2.2. Each Allowed Administrative Claim, other than Preserved Ordinary Course Administrative Claims, shall be paid in full in Cash (or otherwise satisfied in accordance with its terms) by NewAWA at such time or times as provided in Section 10.1 or as otherwise agreed by the holder of such Allowed Administrative Claim and the Debtor or NewAWA. Each Preserved Ordinary Course Administrative Claim shall be paid by NewAWA pursuant to the terms and conditions under which such Claim arose, without further action by the holder of such Claim.

2.2.3. All requests for payment of Administrative Claims, except for Professional Fees and Preserved Ordinary Course Administrative Claims, must be filed by the Bar Date or the holders thereof shall be forever barred from asserting such Administrative Claims against the Debtor. All final applications for allowance and disbursement of Professional Fees must be filed not later than sixty (60) days after the Effective Date. All such applications must be in compliance with all of the terms and provisions of any applicable order of the Bankruptcy Court, including the Confirmation Order, and all orders governing payment of Professional Fees. AWA will request the Bankruptcy Court to set the hearing on final allowance of Professional Fees in the Confirmation Order. Such applications may be later amended to include any fees and costs incurred after the Confirmation Date but prior to the Effective Date, or hearing date, as the case may be.

2.3 Allowed Priority Tax Claims. Each Allowed Priority Tax Claim, if any, will be paid in full in Cash by NewAWA at such time or times as provided in Section 10.1 hereof; provided, however, that NewAWA may elect to pay such Claims, in any such case, through deferred Cash payments over a period not exceeding six (6) years after the date of assessment of such Claim, of a value as of the Effective Date equal to the Allowed amount of such Claim, in each case unless otherwise agreed between NewAWA and the holder of such Allowed Priority Tax Claim. Such payments shall be made in equal annual installments of principal, plus simple interest accruing from the Effective Date at 6% per annum on the unpaid portion of Allowed Priority Tax Claim or such other rate as the Bankruptcy Court may approve. The first such payment shall be payable on the latest of: (i) the Effective Date; (ii) 60 days after the date on which an order allowing such Claim becomes a Final Order; and (iii) such other time as is agreed upon by the holder of such Claim and AWA or NewAWA; provided, however, that NewAWA shall have the right to prepay any such Allowed Priority Tax Claim, or any remaining balance of such Claim, in full or in part, at any time on or after the Effective Date, without premium or penalty. The foregoing treatment of Allowed Priority Tax Claims is consistent with the requirements of Section 1129 (a)(9)(C) of the Bankruptcy Code.

ARTICLE 3

DESIGNATION OF AND PROVISIONS FOR TREATMENT OF CLASSES OF CLAIMS AND EQUITY INTERESTS

All Claims and Equity Interests, except Post-Petition Agreement Claims, Administrative Claims and Priority Tax Claims are placed in the Classes described below. A Claim or Equity Interest is classified in a particular Class only to the extent that the Claim or Equity Interest qualifies within the description of that Class and is classified in other Classes only to the extent that any remainder of the Claim or Equity Interest qualifies within the description of such other Classes. A Claim is also classified in a particular Class only to the extent that such Claim is an Allowed Claim in that Class and has not been paid, released or otherwise satisfied prior to the Effective Date.

3.1 Class 1 — Allowed Priority Wage Claims. Each Allowed Priority Wage Claim shall be paid in full in Cash by NewAWA at such time or times as provided in Section 10.1 hereof. Class 1 is unimpaired under the Plan.

3.2 Class 2 — Allowed Priority Benefit Plan Contribution Claims. All Allowed Priority Benefit Plan Contribution Claims shall be paid in full in Cash by NewAWA at such time or times as provided in Section 10.1 hereof. Class 2 is unimpaired under the Plan.

3.3 Class 3 — Allowed Secured Claims

3.3.1 Class 3.1 — U.S. Leasing (Ford) Ramp Equipment Loan. This Class consists of any Secured Claims arising from that certain Promissory Note dated December 13, 1988, between AWA and Ford Equipment Leasing Co., as amended and supplemented from time to time and as in effect as of the Petition Date. The principal collateral securing this Claim consists of certain group transport support equipment and jetway equipment. On the Effective Date, the holder of the Allowed Class 3.1 Claim will receive a promissory note in the amount of such Allowed Claim, bearing interest at the Prime Rate plus 100 basis points per annum payable over a term of five years in level monthly principal installments, plus interest. The holder of such Claim will retain all of the liens securing such Claim as such liens may exist as of the Effective Date to the extent of the amount of the Note. Class 3.1 is impaired under the Plan.

3.3.2 Class 3.2 — Bank of America Revolver. This Class consists of any Secured Claims arising from that certain Revolving Loan Agreement dated April 17, 1990, among AWA, Bank of America National Trust & Savings Association, as Agent and for itself, First Interstate Bank of Arizona, the Industrial Bank of Japan Limited, Los Angeles Agency, The Valley National Bank of Arizona and First Hawaiian Bank, as amended and supplemented from time to time and as in effect as of the Petition Date. The principal collateral securing this Claim consists of Boeing 747 and 757 spare parts, certain expendable aircraft parts, inventory and six spare Pratt & Whitney Model JT8D-9A engines. On the Effective Date, the holder of the Allowed Class 3.2 Claim will receive a promissory note in the amount of such Allowed Claim, bearing interest at the Prime Rate plus 100 basis points per annum, payable over a term of four years in level quarterly principal installments, plus interest. The holder of such Claim will retain all of the liens securing such Claim as such liens may exist as of the Effective Date to the extent of the amount of the Note. Class 3.2 is impaired under the Plan.

3.3.3 Class 3.3 — Bank One of Arizona f/k/a Valley National Bank — Spare Parts Loan. This Class consists of any Secured Claims arising from (a) that certain Master Reimbursement Agreement, dated as of April 15, 1989 between AWA and Valley National Bank of Arizona, a national banking association, n/k/a Bank One of Arizona, N.A. ("BOAZ"), as amended and supplemented from time to time and as in effect as of July 25, 1991, and (b) that certain Amended and Restated Reimbursement Agreement, dated June 29, 1990 among AWA, BOAZ and Bank of America National Trust and Savings Association, as amended and supplemented from time to time and as in effect on the Petition Date. The principal collateral securing these Claims consists of certain spare rotable nonconsumable parts, accessories, appliances, equipment and other items that are appropriate for installation or use on, in or with any Boeing model 737 aircraft or any part thereof. On the Effective Date, the holder of such claim shall receive either (i) a cash payment in an amount equal to the sum of (A) $21,212,953.98, if the Effective Date occurs on June 10, 1994, $21,760,297.61, if the Effective Date occurs on August 1, 1994, $22,099,874.80, if the Effective Date occurs on September 1, 1994, $22,433,542.61, if the Effective Date occurs on November 1, 1994, provided that such amount shall be appropriately adjusted at an identical compounded rate if the Effective Date occurs on any other date other than as set forth above; plus (B) $65,000; plus (C) $1,976,000, if the Effective Date occurs on June 10, 1994, $2,027,998.16, if the Effective Date occurs on August 1, 1994, $2,059,645.79, if the Effective Date occurs on September 1, 1994, $2,090,742.69, if the Effective Date occurs on October 1, 1994, $2,123,369.47, if the Effective Date occurs on November 1, 1994, provided, that such amount shall be appropriately adjusted at an identical compounded rate if the Effective Date occurs on any other date other than as set forth above, and provided, further, that if an unexpired letter of credit expires at any time prior to the Effective Date, such amount shall be appropriately adjusted at an identical compounded rate such that interest shall have ceased to accrue on the principal amount represented by such expired letter of credit as of the date of such expiration; minus (D) $1,976,000; plus (E) the principal amount drawn under any unexpired letters of credit on or after June 10, 1994 and prior to the Effective Date; or (ii) such other treatment as shall be agreed upon by the Debtor and the holders of such Claims as is approved by the Bankruptcy Court. Class 3.3 is impaired under the Plan.

3.3.4 Class 3.4 — Hangar Facility Bonds. This Class consists of any Secured Claims arising from that certain Indenture of Trust dated August 1, 1986, between the Industrial Development Authority of the City of Phoenix, Arizona, and First Interstate Bank of Arizona, N.A., as Indenture Trustee, as amended and supplemented from time to time and as in effect as of the Petition Date and pursuant to which the Variable Rate Airport Facility Revenue Bonds (America West Airlines, Inc. Project) Series 1986 were issued. The principal collateral securing this Claim consists of the AWA maintenance and technical support facility located at Phoenix Sky Harbor International Airport. On the Effective Date, the holder of the Allowed Class 3.4 Claim will receive a promissory note in the amount of such Allowed Claim, bearing interest at the rate of 6% per annum, payable over a term of twelve years in level quarterly principal installments plus interest. The holder of such Claim will retain all of the liens securing such Claim as such liens may exist as of the Effective Date to the extent of the amount of the Note. Class 3.4 is impaired under the Plan.

3.3.5 Class 3.5 — Lockheed Finance No. 2. This Class consists of any Secured Claims arising from that certain Master Equipment Lease Agreement No. 0134 dated as of November 12, 1987, between AWA and Lockheed Finance Corporation, as amended and supplemented from time to time and as in effect as of the Petition Date. The principal collateral securing this Claim consists of certain ground support equipment. On the Effective Date, the holder of the Allowed Class 3.5 Claim will receive a promissory note in the amount of $750,000 bearing interest at the 30-day LIBOR rate (as provided for in such Master Lease Agreement) plus 200 basis points per annum, payable over a term of five years in level monthly principal installments, plus interest. The holder of such Claim will have no Unsecured Deficiency Claim and will retain all of the liens securing such Claim as such liens may exist as of the Effective Date to the extent of the amount of the Note. Class 3.5 is impaired under the Plan.

3.3.6 Class 3.6 — Other Secured Claims. This Class consists of Allowed Secured Claims not specifically provided for above. On the Effective Date, as to such Allowed Secured Claim, at AWA's option either:

(a) the holder of such Claim shall be treated in accordance with the terms and conditions of all documents respecting such Claim and the legal, equitable or contractual rights to which each holder of such Claim is entitled shall not otherwise be altered;

(b) (i) any default, other than a default of the kind specified in Section 365 (b)(2) of the Bankruptcy Code, shall be cured, provided that any accrued and unpaid interest, if any, which the Debtor may be obligated to pay with respect to such default shall be simple interest at the contract rate and not at any default or penalty rate of interest;

(ii) the maturity of the Claim shall be reinstated as such maturity existed before any default;

(iii) the holder of the Claim shall be compensated for any actual damages incurred as a result of any reasonable reliance by the holder on any contractual provision that entitled the holder to accelerate maturity of the Claim; and

(iv) the other legal, equitable or contractual rights to which the holder of the Claim is entitled shall not otherwise be altered; provided, however, that as to any Allowed Secured Claim which is a nonrecourse claim and exceeds the value of the collateral securing the Claim, the collateral may be sold at a sale at which the holder of such Claim has an opportunity to bid;

(c) on the Effective Date, or on such other date thereafter as may be agreed to by the Debtor and the holder of such Claim, the Debtor shall abandon the collateral securing such Claim, to the holder thereof in full satisfaction and release of such Claim;

(d) on the Effective Date, the holder of such Claim shall receive, on account of such Claim, Cash equal to its Allowed Secured Claim, or such lesser amount to which the holder of such Claim shall agree, in full satisfaction and release of such Claim;

(e) the holder of such Claim shall retain the liens securing such Claim and shall receive, on account of such Claim, deferred Cash payments, pursuant to Section 1129(b)(2)(A)(i)(II) of the Bankruptcy Code, totaling at least the Allowed amount of such Claim, of a Present Value, as of the Effective Date, of at least the value of such holder's interest in the Debtor's interest in the property securing such Claim;

(f) on the Effective Date, any property that is subject to the liens securing such Claim shall be sold, subject to Section 363(k) of the Bankruptcy Code, free and clear of such liens, with payment of the net proceeds thereof to the holder of such Claim to the extent of the value of such holder's respective interest in such property; or

(g) the holder of such Claim shall otherwise realize the indubitable equivalent of such Claim.

Each holder of an Allowed Claim in Class 3.6 shall be considered to be in its own separate subclass within Class 3.6, and each such subclass will be deemed to be a separate Class for purposes of this Plan. In the event that AWA does not make such designation, the holder of an Allowed Secured Claim shall, at any time prior to the Effective Date, be entitled to petition the Bankruptcy Court for an order requiring AWA to make such designation, but shall not be entitled to any other relief or to exercise any other remedies, except in accordance with such designation and any applicable Final Order(s) of the Bankruptcy Court.

3.4 Class 4 — Allowed Convenience Claims. This Class consists of Convenience Claims. Each Allowed Convenience Claim shall be paid by NewAWA Cash in the amount of such Allowed Convenience Claim to be distributed as provided in Section 10.1. Class 4 is not impaired under the Plan.

3.5 Class 5 — Allowed General Unsecured Claims. This Class consists of General Unsecured Claims.

3.5.1. Each holder of an Allowed General Unsecured Claim shall receive its Pro Rata Share of 26,775,000 shares of NewAWA Class B Common Stock; provided, however, that if the holder is an Electing Unsecured Creditor in accordance with Section 3.5.2, such holder shall receive Electing Creditor Cash equal to $8.889 for each share of NewAWA Class B Common Stock otherwise allocable to it under this sentence.

3.5.2. A holder of an Allowed General Unsecured Claim may become an Electing Unsecured Creditor only by providing notice of such election on the Ballot which such holder submits. Any holder of a Disputed General Unsecured Claim that wishes to become an Electing Unsecured Creditor must provide notice to the Debtor of the exercise of such right by no later than the Voting Deadline. Each such election by a holder of a General Unsecured Claim shall be irrevocable and must pertain to the entire amount of such holder's General Unsecured Claim. In the event that the aggregate amount of the Electing Creditor Cash would be in excess of $100,000,000, then each Electing Unsecured Creditor shall receive only its Pro Rata Share of $100,000,000 in Cash and shall also receive a number of shares of Electing Creditor Stock equal to the number of shares of NewAWA Class B Common Stock it would have received if it were a Non-Electing Unsecured Creditor minus the result of dividing the Electing Creditor Cash it receives by $8.889. For purposes of allocating Electing Creditor Cash among Electing Unsecured Creditors, each Disputed General Unsecured Claim held by an Electing Unsecured Creditor shall initially be valued at its face amount; provided, however, in the event that the aggregate amount of Electing Creditor Cash would exceed $100,000,000 and one or more holders of Disputed General Unsecured Claims have become Electing Unsecured Creditors, then any party in interest with regard thereto (including, without limitation, the Creditors' Committee), may seek an order of the Bankruptcy Court estimating the amount of any and all such Disputed General Unsecured Claims at a lower amount and, then, regardless of the amount at which such Disputed General Unsecured Claims are eventually Allowed, the holders thereof will be paid Electing Creditor Cash in an amount which does not exceed the amount of Electing Creditor Cash which would be payable for a Claim in the amount of such estimate and for any amount of the Disputed Claim which is Allowed in excess of such estimate, the holder shall receive Electing Creditor Stock in accordance with Section 10.4. NewAWA Class B Common Stock distributed to Non-Electing Unsecured Creditors, Electing Creditor Stock and Electing Creditor Cash shall be distributed in accordance with Section 10.2.

3.5.3. Any holder of an Unsecured Claim asserting that payment to any other holder of an Unsecured Claim should be subordinated to such first holder under Section 510(a) of the Bankruptcy Code, may only make such assertion by filing an adversary proceeding in the Chapter 11 Case on or before the Voting Deadline, or such other date as may be established by Final Order of the Bankruptcy Court. Any such subordination of one Unsecured Claim to another Unsecured Claim shall be made only upon Final Order of the Bankruptcy Court and no distribution hereby to any holder of an Allowed Claim which is the subject of such an adversary proceeding shall be delayed or withheld except upon Final Order of the Bankruptcy Court. Any such adversary proceeding involving holders of AWA Debenture Claims shall name as defendants the Debtor and on behalf of all such holders, the Indenture Trustee.

3.5.4. Class 5 is impaired under the Plan.

3.6 Class 6 — AWA Preferred and Common Stock

3.6.1 Class 6.1 — AWA Preferred Stock. This Class consists of AWA Preferred Stock. Each holder of shares of AWA Preferred Stock shall receive its Pro Rata Share of $500,000 in Cash plus the right to purchase as of the Effective Date its Pro Rata Share of the first 250,000 shares of Over-Subscription Stock at the price of $8.889 per share or such lesser amount of Over-Subscription Stock as is available after the purchase of Equity Subscription Stock in accordance with Section 3.6.2. Such Cash shall be distributed in accordance with Section 10.1. Payment for such Over-Subscription Stock shall be made no later than the Effective Date. Such Cash and rights shall be deemed to be in full satisfaction for all Claims and Equity Interests arising in connection with the AWA Preferred Stock including accrued and unpaid dividends thereon. Class 6.1 is impaired under the Plan. All shares of AWA Preferred Stock shall be deemed to be cancelled, annulled and extinguished on the Effective Date.

3.6.2 Class 6.2 — AWA Common Stock

(a) This Class consists of shares of AWA Common Stock other than shares of AWA Common Stock which are pledged as collateral for Employee Stock Purchase Notes. Each holder of such AWA Common Stock shall receive its Pro Rata Share of (i) the Equity Interests Stock and (ii) the Equity Interests Warrants, to be distributed in accordance with the procedure set forth in Section 10.2.

(b) Additionally, each such holder of AWA Common Stock other than the holder of a Disputed Equity Interest shall have the right to purchase its Pro Rata Share of the Equity Subscription Stock at the price of $8.889 per share; provided, however, that for purposes of determining such Pro Rata Share there shall be considered to be an aggregate of 22,100,000 shares of AWA Common Stock outstanding. Such right is not transferable and may only be exercised by the beneficial holder of such AWA Common Stock as of the Voting Record Date by the irrevocable indication thereof on the Ballot which such holder delivers or causes to be delivered. Each such holder may also indicate on the Ballot that it wishes to purchase Over-Subscription Stock, if available. The Over-Subscription Stock available to Purchasing Stockholders shall consist of the Equity Subscription Stock not subscribed for in accordance with the second preceding sentence and less the Over-Subscription Stock sold to holders of AWA Preferred Stock in accordance with Section 3.6.1. Each Purchasing Stockholder must irrevocably indicate on the Ballot the maximum number of shares of Equity Subscription Stock and Over-Subscription Stock which it desires to purchase. As set forth more fully in Section 10.2, either full payment or a satisfactory guarantee of payment for all Equity Subscription Stock and Over-Subscription Stock must be delivered by the Voting Deadline. The procedure for allocating Over-Subscription Stock is set forth in Section 10.2.

(c) Class 6.2 is impaired under the Plan. All shares of AWA Common Stock will be cancelled, annulled and extinguished on the Effective Date.

3.7 Class 7 — Certain Other Claims and AWA Warrants, Options and Other Equity Interests.

3.7.1 Class 7.1 — Employee Stock Purchase Note Claims and Certain AWA Common Stock. This Class consists of Stock Rescission or Damage Claims (including, without limitation, Claims by members of the putative plaintiff class in the Securities Action) which are held by Persons who are obligated under one or more Employee Stock Purchase Notes. This Class also includes AWA Common Stock pledged as collateral for Employee Stock Purchase Notes. Each holder of an Allowed Claim or Equity Interest in this Class shall receive in exchange for and in consideration of the dismissal with prejudice and permanent enjoinment of the Securities Actions, a release of any and all indebtedness incurred under the Employee Stock Purchase Plan, including the forgiveness, abandonment and cancellation of any liability under the Employee Stock Purchase Notes, but shall receive no other distribution under the Plan. In addition, all liens on AWA Common Stock securing Employee Stock Purchase Notes will be released and such AWA Common Stock will be returned to AWA and cancelled, annulled and extinguished as of the Effective Date and will not be entitled to any distribution under Section 3.6.2. Pursuant to Sections 1123(a)(5)(E), (F) and 1123(b)(3)(A) of the Bankruptcy Code, the treatment provided Class 7.1 Claims constitutes a compromise and settlement of the Securities Action and any and all objections to such Claims. The Debtor will either file appropriate pleadings seeking to effect the treatment provided Class 7.1 Claims in this Section 3.7.1 as a compromise and settlement prior to the Confirmation Hearing or request the Bankruptcy Court to approve this compromise and settlement at the Confirmation Hearing as in the best interests of the Debtor and holders of Claims and Equity Interests and fair, equitable and reasonable. Class 7.1 is impaired under the Plan.

3.7.2 Certain AWA Warrants, Options and Other Equity Interests and Other Claims. This Class consists of the following Claims and Equity Interests (except to the extent they are included in Class 7.1): (i) AWA Warrants, Options, and Other Equity Interests, (ii) Stock Rescission or Damage Claims, (iii) Subordinated Claims and (iv) all Claims, if any, arising from the cancellation or rejection (to the extent they constitute executory contracts) of AWA Warrants, Options and Other Equity Interests. Holders of such Claims and Equity Interests will not be entitled to receive or retain any property under the Plan on account of such Claims or Equity Interests, and pursuant to Section 1126(g) of the Bankruptcy Code, are deemed not to have accepted the Plan. Class 7.2 is impaired under the Plan. All AWA Warrants, Options and Other Equity Interests will be cancelled, annulled and extinguished on the Effective Date.

ARTICLE 4

PROVISIONS OF NEW AWA SECURITIES ISSUED PURSUANT TO THE PLAN

4.1 NewAWA Class A Common Stock. Principal provisions of the NewAWA Class A Common Stock are summarized as follows:

(a) *Authorization.* The NewAWA Charter shall authorize the issuance of 1,200,000 shares of NewAWA Class A Common Stock.

(b) *Par Value.* The NewAWA Class A Common Stock shall have a par value of $.O1 per share.

(c) *Rights.* The NewAWA Class A Common Stock shall have such rights with respect to dividends, liquidation, voting and other matters as are set forth in the NewAWA Charter and as provided under applicable law, including, without limitation, the right to fifty votes per share which shall be voted together as a single class with the NewAWA Class B Common Stock.

(d) *Convertibility.* Each share of NewAWA Class A Common Stock will be convertible, at the option of the holder, into one share of NewAWA Class B Common Stock.

4.2 NewAWA Class B Common Stock. Principal provisions of the NewAWA Class B Common Stock are summarized as follows:

(a) *Authorization.* The NewAWA Charter shall authorize the

issuance of 100,000,000 shares of NewAWA Class B Common Stock.

(b) *Par Value.* The NewAWA Class B Common Stock shall have a par value of $.01 per share.

(c) *Rights.* The NewAWA Class B Common Stock shall have such rights with respect to dividends, liquidation, voting and other matters as are set forth in the NewAWA Charter and as provided under applicable law, including, without limitation, the right to one vote per share which shall be voted together as a single class with the NewAWA Class A Common Stock.

(d) *Exchange Listing.* NewAWA will seek a listing of the NewAWA Class B Common Stock on a national securities exchange or automated quotation system and will use its reasonable efforts to obtain such listing prior to the distribution to holders of Allowed Claims and Equity Interests of NewAWA Class B Common Stock.

4.3 NewAWA Warrants. Principal provisions of the NewAWA Warrants are as follows:

(a) *Authorization.* The Plan hereby authorizes the issuance of NewAWA Warrants to purchase 10,384,615 shares of NewAWA Class B Common Stock.

(b) *Exercise Price.* The proponents of the Plan will seek to have the exercise price for the NewAWA Warrants determined in the Confirmation Order or otherwise pursuant to a Final Order of the Bankruptcy Court to be issued before the Effective Date or as soon thereafter as possible, which exercise price shall equal the aggregate amount of Allowed General Unsecured Claims on the date of such order plus the Bankruptcy Court's estimate of the Disputed General Unsecured Claims which will become Allowed General Unsecured Claims, which sum shall be multiplied by 1.1 and divided by 26,775,000.

(c) *Exercise.* The NewAWA Warrants will be exercisable by the holder thereof at any time on or prior to the fifth anniversary of the Effective Date.

(d) *Rights.* The NewAWA Warrants will not be redeemable. The number of shares of NewAWA Class B Common Stock purchasable upon exercise of each NewAWA Warrant will be adjusted upon (i) payment of a dividend payable in, or other distribution of, NewAWA Class B Common Stock to all of the then-current holders of NewAWA Class B Common Stock, (ii) a combination, subdivision or a reclassification of NewAWA Class B Common Stock, and (iii) a rights issuance. The holders of the NewAWA Warrants will not have any voting rights in respect thereof.

(e) *Exchange Listing.* NewAWA will seek a listing of the NewAWA Warrants on the same securities exchange or automated quotation system as the NewAWA Class B Common Stock is listed.

4.4 NewAWA Senior Unsecured Notes. Principal provisions of the NewAWA Senior Unsecured Notes are as follows:

(a) *Authorization.* The Plan hereby authorizes the issuance of the NewAWA Senior Unsecured Notes in a maximum principal amount of $100,000,000.

(b) *Maturity.* The NewAWA Senior Unsecured Notes will mature seven years from issuance.

(c) *Interest Rate.* The NewAWA Senior Unsecured Notes will bear interest, payable semiannually, in arrears at a fixed rate equal to 425 basis points over the yield of seven-year United States Treasury Notes as of the Effective Date, but not to exceed 11.5% per annum.

(d) *Ranking.* The NewAWA Senior Unsecured Notes will rank pari passu with all existing and future senior unsecured indebtedness of NewAWA.

(e) *Mandatory Redemption.* If within three years after the Effective Date, NewAWA completes an underwritten public offering of primary equity, NewAWA shall use 50% of the Net Proceeds thereof to redeem up to $20,000,000 in principal amount of the NewAWA Senior Unsecured Notes at 104% of the principal amount plus accrued interest, provided, however, that in the event that at the time of such offering the unrestricted cash balance of NewAWA is less than $100,000,000, then such redemption will be at the option of NewAWA. Thereafter, the NewAWA Senior Unsecured Notes will be redeemable at NewAWA's option, in whole or in part. The redemption price will be equal to the following percentage of the principal amount redeemed in each of the following years plus accrued interest:

Year 4:	105.0%
Year 5:	103.3%
Year 6:	101.7%
Year 7 and thereafter	100.0%

(f) *Special Redemption.* During the first three years after the Effective Date, the New AWA Senior Unsecured Notes will be callable by NewAWA (i) as a whole, without regard to the source of funding, at 105% of the principal amount redeemed plus accrued interest or (ii) in part, out of the proceeds of a primary equity offering at 105% of the principal amount plus accrued interest, less the $20 million in principal amount redeemed of NewAWA Senior Unsecured Notes subject to Mandatory Redemption as described above.

ARTICLE 5

EXECUTORY CONTRACTS AND UNEXPIRED LEASES

5.1 *Assumption of Certain Executory Contracts and Unexpired Leases*

5.1.1 Except as otherwise provided in the Plan or in any contract, instrument, release, indenture or other agreement or document entered into in connection with the Plan, on the Effective Date, pursuant to Section 365 of the Bankruptcy Code, AWA shall assume or assume and assign, as indicated, each of the Assumed Agreements including, without limitation, the executory contracts and unexpired leases listed on Schedule 3 hereto; provided, however, that AWA or NewAWA shall have the right, at any time prior to the Effective Date, to amend Schedule 3: (a) unless indicated otherwise on Schedule 3, to delete any executory contract or unexpired lease listed therein, thus providing for its rejection pursuant to Section 5.2; or (b) to add any executory contract or unexpired lease, thus providing for its assumption or assumption and assignment pursuant to this Section 5.1.1. The Debtor or NewAWA shall provide notice of any amendments to Schedule 3 to the parties to the executory contracts or unexpired leases affected thereby and, if such amendments are made before the Effective Date, to the parties on the Official Service List. Pursuant to Section 1123 (b)(2) of the Bankruptcy Code, the Confirmation Order shall constitute an order of the Bankruptcy Court approving the assumptions and assignments described in this Section 5.1.1, pursuant to Section 365 of the Bankruptcy Code, as of the Effective Date.

5.1.2 Unless otherwise agreed by AWA and the counterparty to any such Assumed Agreement, (i) all cure payments which may be required by Section 365 (b)(1) of the Bankruptcy Code under any Assumed Agreement, if not previously made, shall be made on the Effective Date or promptly thereafter, and (ii) in the event of a dispute regarding the amount or timing of any cure payments, the ability of NewAWA to provide adequate assurance of future performance, or any other matter pertaining to assumption or assignment, such dispute shall be resolved by the Bankruptcy Court and NewAWA shall make such cure payments, if any, or provide such assurance as may be required by the Final Order resolving such dispute on the terms and conditions of such Final Order.

5.1.3 Except as otherwise provided in the Plan (including any such provision on Schedule 3) or in any contract, instrument, release or indenture or other agreement or document entered into in connection with the Plan, each Assumed Agreement shall, at AWA's option, be assumed only to the extent that any such contract or lease constitutes an executory contract or unexpired lease. Listing a contract or lease on Schedule 3 shall not, in and of itself, constitute an admission by the Debtor or NewAWA that such contract or lease is an executory contract or unexpired lease or that the Debtor or NewAWA has any liability thereunder. Contracts and leases which are within the definition of Assumed Agreements and which are later determined to have not been in fact executory contracts or unexpired leases, shall be treated in accordance with the provisions in the Plan for the treatment of that type of Claim which properly arises from the true nature of the legal relationship between the parties as determined by the Bankruptcy Court or by settlement; provided, however, that either the Debtor or NewAWA may in its sole discretion amend the Plan to provide for different treatment of any such Claim after Notice and a Hearing.

5.1.4 Except as otherwise provided in the Plan (including any such provision on Schedule 3) or in any contract, instrument, release or indenture or other agreement or document entered into in connection with the Plan, all assumptions of executory contracts and unexpired leases under the Plan shall be without prejudice to the rights of the Debtor or NewAWA to assign later such assumed executory contracts or unexpired leases, notwithstanding any prohibition to the contrary in any such contract or lease.

*5.2 Rejection of Certain Executory Contracts and Unexpired Leases.*_On the Effective Date, except for every Assumed Agreement, each executory contract and unexpired lease entered into by AWA prior to the Petition Date that has not previously expired or terminated pursuant to its own terms and (to the extent they are executory contracts) all AWA Warrants, Options and Other Equity Interests shall be rejected pursuant to Sections 365 and 1123 (b)(2) of the Bankruptcy Code and considered a Rejected Agreement hereunder.

5.3 Claims Based on Rejection of Executory Contracts or Unexpired Leases. All proofs of claim with respect to Claims arising from the rejection of any Rejected Agreement shall be filed with the Bankruptcy Court within the later to occur of thirty (30) days after the Effective Date. Any Claims not filed within such time shall be forever barred from assertion against the Debtor, its estate and property, or NewAWA.

ARTICLE 6

IDENTIFICATION OF CLASSES OF CLAIMS NOT IMPAIRED BY THE PLAN AND THE CLASS OF CLAIMS AND EQUITY INTERESTS DEEMED TO HAVE REJECTED THE PLAN

6.1 Unimpaired Classes. Claims in Classes 1, 2 and 4 are not impaired under the Plan. Any Class not specifically designated in the Plan as unimpaired is impaired under the Plan. Claims in unimpaired Classes are not entitled to vote on the Plan.

6.2 Class Deemed to Have Rejected the Plan. Claims and Equity Interests in Class 7.2 are not entitled to receive or retain any property under the Plan and are therefore deemed not to have accepted the Plan, and such Class shall not be entitled to vote on the Plan.

6.3 Other Impaired Classes. Claims in Classes 3.1, 3.2, 3.3, 3.4, 3.5, 3.6, 5, 6.1, 6.2 and 7.1 are impaired under the Plan and shall be entitled to vote on the Plan.

ARTICLE 7

ACCEPTANCE OR REJECTION OF THE PLAN; EFFECT OF REJECTION BY ONE OR MORE CLASSES

7.1 Impaired Classes to Vote. Except as otherwise required by the Bankruptcy Code or the Bankruptcy Court, each holder of a Claim or Equity Interest that is impaired under the Plan is entitled to vote to accept or reject the Plan if, as of the Voting Record Date, (i) its Claim is an Allowed Claim, (ii) its Claim has been temporarily allowed for voting purposes only by order of the Bankruptcy Court pursuant to Bankruptcy Rule 3018 (in which case such Claim may be voted in such temporarily allowed amount), (iii) its Claim has been scheduled by the Debtor (but only if such Claim is not scheduled as disputed, contingent or unliquidated) and no objection to such Claim has been filed, (iv) it has filed a proof of claim on or before the Bar Date (or such later date as the Bankruptcy Court may have established with respect to any particular Claim, but not later than the date of the order approving such Disclosure Statement), and such Claim is not a Disputed Claim, or (v) its Equity Interest is registered on the stock ledger or equivalent of the Debtor. Notwithstanding the foregoing, a holder of a Disputed Claim which has not been temporarily allowed as provided above may nevertheless vote such Disputed Claim in an amount equal to the portion, if any, of such Claim which is not disputed and is shown as fixed, liquidated and undisputed in the Debtor's Schedules or such amount which the Debtor concedes is Allowed in a filing made by the Debtor in the Bankruptcy Court. Each holder of an AWA Debenture Claim, and not the Indenture Trustee with respect to such Claim, shall have the right to vote to accept or reject the Plan.

7.2 Acceptance by Class of Holders of Claims or Equity Interests. A Class of holders of Claims shall have accepted the Plan if the Plan is accepted by at least two-thirds in amount and more than one-half in number of the Allowed Claims of such Class that have voted to accept or reject the Plan. A Class of Equity Interests shall have accepted the Plan if acceptance is voted for by the holders of at least two-thirds in amount of the Equity Interests of such Class who have voted to accept or reject the Plan.

7.3 Cramdown. Inasmuch as Class 7.2 is deemed not to have accepted the Plan in accordance with Section 1129 (a) of the Bankruptcy Code, and in the event that one or more other Classes of impaired Claims or Equity Interests does not accept or is deemed not to have accepted the

Plan, the Debtor requests that the Bankruptcy Court confirm the Plan in accordance with Section 1129(b) of the Bankruptcy Code. AWA and AmWest reserve the right to modify the Plan to the extent, if any, that confirmation pursuant to Section 1129(b) of the Bankruptcy Code requires or permits such modification.

ARTICLE 8

MEANS FOR IMPLEMENTATION OF THE PLAN

8.1 Investment Agreement. On the Effective Date, the investment and sale of securities contemplated by the Investment Agreement shall be consummated in accordance with such agreement. In the event of conflict between the terms of the Plan and of the Investment Agreement, the terms of the Plan shall control.

8.2 Stockholders' and Registration Rights Agreements. On the Effective Date, the Stockholders' Agreement and Registration Rights Agreement shall become effective.

8.3 Delivery of Alliance Agreements. On or before the Effective Date, AWA, Continental Airlines, Inc., and Mesa Airlines, Inc., as applicable, shall enter into the Alliance Agreements, as such term is defined in the Investment Agreement.

8.4 GPA Settlement. On the Effective Date, NewAWA and GPA will consummate the transactions described in the term sheet attached hereto as Exhibit C and incorporated herein by reference.

8.5 Corporate Governance. On or as of the Effective Date, the NewAWA Charter shall be filed with the Secretary of State of the State of Delaware and the NewAWA By-laws shall take effect, each containing such provisions as are necessary to satisfy the terms of the Plan and Section 1123 (a)(6) of the Bankruptcy Code.

8.6 Release of Certain Claims and Actions.

8.6.1. On the Effective Date, in consideration for services rendered in the Chapter 11 Case, the Debtor shall be deemed to have finally and irrevocably waived, released and relinquished any and all claims and causes of action, if any, that it has or may have against the Creditors' Committee, the Equity Committee or any member thereof or against their respective professional advisors arising out of or related to each such Person's actions or omissions to act in all of such Person's capacities in connection with the Chapter 11 Case, including the formulation, preparation, dissemination, implementation or confirmation of the Plan or the Disclosure Statement or any contract, instrument, release or other agreement or document created or entered into, or any other act taken or omitted to be taken in connection therewith, and the Debtor is enjoined from asserting any such claim or cause of action in any court or forum; provided, however, that this provision shall not operate as a release, waiver or relinquishment of, or injunction against asserting, any such claims or causes of action (i) provided in or contemplated by the Plan or (ii) arising from any actual fraud (but not constructive fraud) or willful misconduct of any such Person.

8.6.2. On the Effective Date, in consideration for benefits realized in the Chapter 11 Case, the Debtor shall be deemed to have finally and irrevocably waived, released and relinquished any and all claims and causes of action, if any, that it has or may have against AmWest, any of AmWest's partners, Fidelity or Lehman or their respective partners, affiliates, employees or professional advisors arising out of or related to such Person's actions or omissions to act in connection with the Chapter 11 Case, including the formulation, preparation, dissemination, implementation or confirmation of the Plan or the Disclosure Statement or any contract, instrument, release or other agreement or document created or entered into, or any other act taken or omitted to be taken in connection therewith, and the Debtor is enjoined from asserting any such claim or cause of action; provided, however, that this provision shall not operate as a release, waiver or relinquishment of, or injunction against asserting, any such claims or causes of action (i) provided in or contemplated by the Plan, (ii) arising from any actual fraud (but not constructive fraud) or willful misconduct of any such Person, and (iii) reserved to the Debtor pursuant to the Investment Agreement or the Interim Procedures Agreement.

8.6.3. On the Effective Date, the Creditors' Committee and each member thereof, the Equity Committee and each member thereof, AmWest and each of its partners, Fidelity and Lehman shall be deemed to have finally and irrevocably waived, released and relinquished any and all claims and causes of action, if any, that any of them have or may have against the Debtor or its professional advisors arising out of or related to such Person's actions or omissions to act in connection with the Chapter 11 Case, including the formulation, preparation, dissemination, implementation or confirmation of the Plan or the Disclosure Statement or any contract, instrument, release or other agreement or document created or entered into, or any other act taken or omitted to be taken in connection therewith, and such Persons are enjoined from asserting any such claims or causes of action; provided, however, that this provision shall not operate as a release, waiver or relinquishment of, or injunction against asserting any such claims or causes of action (i) provided in or contemplated by the Plan, (ii) arising from any actual fraud (but not constructive fraud) or willful misconduct of the Debtor, and (iii) reserved to AmWest and/or any of its partners pursuant to the Investment Agreement or the Interim Procedures Agreement; and, provided, further, this Section 8.6.3 shall not apply to any claims made against the Debtor arising from third party claims against the Creditors' Committee or any member thereof or the Equity Committee or any member thereof. Any Person who as of the Effective Date is or was an officer or director of

AWA, shall be a beneficiary of the releases provided under Section 8.6.3 if such Person, no later than the Effective Date, delivers a release in substantially the form of Sections 8.6.1 and 8.6.2.

8.7 Indemnification Obligations

8.7.1. Upon, and at all times after the Effective Date, the NewAWA Charter shall contain provisions which (i) eliminate the personal liability of AWA's former, present and future directors for monetary damages resulting from breaches of their fiduciary duties to the fullest extent permitted by applicable law and (ii) require NewAWA, subject, to appropriate procedures, to indemnify AWA's former, present and future directors and executive officers to the fullest extent permitted by applicable law.

8.7.2. On or as of the Effective Date, NewAWA shall enter into written agreements with each person who is a director or executive officer of AWA as of the date of the Investment Agreement providing for similar indemnification of such person and providing that no recourse or liability whatsoever with respect to the Investment Agreement, the Plan or the consummation of the transactions contemplated hereby or thereby shall be had, directly or indirectly, by or in the right of AWA against such person.

8.7.3. For purposes of the Plan, except as limited hereinafter, any obligations of the Debtor to indemnify its current and former directors, officers, employees, and any officer, director or employee serving as a fiduciary of any employee benefit plan or program of AWA, pursuant to charter, by-laws, contract or applicable state law shall be deemed to be, and may be treated as though they are, executory contracts that are Assumed Agreements under the Plan, and such obligations (subject to any defenses thereto) shall survive confirmation of the Plan and remain unaffected thereby, irrespective of whether indemnification is owed in connection with a pre-Petition Date or post-Petition Date occurrence; provided however, that the foregoing assumption shall not affect any release of such obligations given to the Debtor before the Effective Date or to NewAWA on or after the Effective Date.

8.8 Exemption from Certain Taxes. Pursuant to Section 1146(c) of the Bankruptcy Code, none of the transactions contemplated to take place on the Effective Date shall subject the Debtor or NewAWA to any state or local sales, use, transfer, documentary, recording or gains tax.

8.9 Directors and Officers. A list of the initial post-Effective Date directors and officers of NewAWA shall be filed by the Debtor with the Bankruptcy Court prior to the Confirmation Date.

8.10 Revesting of Assets; No Further Supervision. The assets of the Debtor and all property of the Debtor's estate (including without limitation, all rights of the Debtor to recover property under Sections 542, 543, 550 and 553 of the Bankruptcy Code, all Avoidance Litigation and all proceeds thereof) and any property acquired by AWA or NewAWA under or in connection with the Plan shall vest or revest in NewAWA, in each case free and clear of all Claims, liens, charges, encumbrances or Equity Interests, other than as specifically set forth in the Plan. The Plan does not contain any restrictions or prohibitions on the conduct of the business of NewAWA and NewAWA shall have all of the powers of a corporation under the Delaware General Corporation Law, consistent with its obligations under the Stockholders' Agreement. From and after the Effective Date, NewAWA may use, operate and deal with its assets, and may conduct and change its business, without any supervision by the Bankruptcy Court or the Office of the United States Trustee, and free of any restrictions imposed on the Debtor by the Bankruptcy Code or by the Bankruptcy Court during the Chapter 11 Case. Nothing contained in this Section shall be construed to prohibit, limit, restrict or condition the Debtor's authority in any lawful manner to sell or otherwise dispose of any other assets.

8.11 Implementation. The Debtor and AmWest shall be authorized and are directed to take all necessary steps, and perform all necessary acts, to consummate the terms and conditions of the Plan, including, without limitation, the Investment Agreement.

8.12 Cancellation of Securities. As of the Effective Date, all previously issued and outstanding securities of the Debtor, including without limitation: all AWA Common Stock, all AWA Preferred Stock, all AWA Warrants, Options and Other Equity Interests and all AWA Debentures; any certificate or other instrument evidencing any such security; except as otherwise specifically provided in Section 10.3 hereof, any indenture relating to any of the foregoing; and the Debtor's obligations thereunder shall be deemed void, cancelled, and of no further force or effect, without any further action on the part of any Person. Holders of Allowed Claims and Equity Interests represented by such securities shall have such rights to receive distributions as are set forth in the Plan.

ARTICLE 9

CONDITIONS PRECEDENT TO THE EFFECTIVE DATE

9.1 Effectiveness of the Plan. The effectiveness of the Plan, and the occurrence of the Effective Date, shall be subject to the satisfaction of the following conditions precedent:

(a) The Confirmation Order shall have been entered and no stay of the Confirmation Order shall be in effect;

(b) Each of the conditions precedent to the obligations of AmWest under the Investment Agreement shall have been satisfied or waived by AmWest and the purchase and sale of securities and the other transactions contemplated by the Investment Agreement shall have been simultaneously consummated; and

(c) Each of the conditions precedent to the obligations of the Debtor under the Investment Agreement shall have been satisfied or waived by the Debtor and the purchase and sale of securities and other transactions contemplated by the Investment Agreement shall have been simultaneously consummated.

ARTICLE 10

PROVISIONS COVERING DISTRIBUTIONS AND PAYMENTS

10.1 Making of Distributions and Payments. NewAWA, or a Distribution Agent on its behalf, shall make the payments and distributions expressly required to be made by it in respect of the Post-Petition Agreement Claims, Allowed Administrative Claims (other than Preserved Ordinary Course Administrative Claims), Allowed Priority Wage Claims, Allowed Priority Benefit Plan Contribution Claims, Allowed Priority Tax Claims, Allowed Convenience Claims and AWA Preferred Stock upon the latest of (i) the Effective Date, or as soon thereafter as practicable, (ii) such date as may be fixed by the Bankruptcy Court, or as soon thereafter as practicable, (iii) the fifth Business Day after such Claim is Allowed, or as soon thereafter as practicable, and (iv) such date as the holder of such Claim and NewAWA have agreed or shall agree.

10.2 Distributions by the Distribution Agent

10.2.1. On the Effective Date, NewAWA will issue in the name of the Distribution Agent, as trustee, the Non-Electing Creditor Stock for distribution to Non-Electing Unsecured Creditors in accordance with Section 3.5, and the Electing Creditor Stock for distribution to Electing Unsecured Creditors in accordance with Section 3.5. Additionally, NewAWA will deliver to the Distribution Agent the Electing Creditor Cash for distribution to Electing Unsecured Creditors in accordance with Section 3.5. As promptly as practicable after the issuance of such NewAWA Securities and delivery of Electing Creditor Cash to the Distribution Agent, the Distribution Agent will distribute such securities and Cash to the holders of Allowed Claims entitled thereto in accordance with Section 3.5, but shall reserve from such distributions the Reserve Amount as required by Section 10.4.

10.2.2. Not later than thirty (30) days after the Voting Deadline, the Debtor shall allocate among the Purchasing Stockholders, the Equity Subscription Stock and the Over-Subscription Stock in accordance with this Section 10.2.2 and advise the Distribution Agent of such allocation. Each Purchasing Stockholder shall be allocated initially the lesser of (i) the number of shares for which it has made a valid purchase election on its Ballot and (ii) its Pro Rata Share of the Equity Subscription Stock. Holders who hold shares of AWA Common Stock for the account of others such as brokers, trustees or depositories may only exercise the right to purchase Equity Subscription Stock and Over-Subscription Stock upon receipt of instructions and appropriate payment or guarantee of payment from the beneficial owners of such shares as of the Voting Record Date. The shares of Equity Subscription Stock not allocated as above will be considered Over-Subscription Stock and will be allocated first to holders of AWA Preferred Stock in accordance with Section 3.6.1 and then to holders of AWA Common Stock who have indicated on the Ballot that they wish to acquire more than their Pro Rata Share of the Equity Subscription Stock. If sufficient shares of Over-Subscription Stock are available, all subscriptions therefor will be honored in full. If sufficient shares of Over-Subscription Stock are not available to honor all such subscriptions, the available shares of Over-Subscription Stock will be allocated among those who subscribed based on their proportional number of shares of AWA Common Stock. The allocation process may involve a series of allocations in order to assure that the total number of shares of Over-Subscription Stock is distributed on a Pro Rata Share basis. The right to purchase Equity Subscription Stock and Over-Subscription Stock may be exercised through a holder's broker, who may charge such holder a servicing fee in connection with such exercise. No such fees shall be paid by the Debtor or NewAWA. The Debtor shall establish the Stock Payment Escrow Account for the purpose of receiving payment for Equity Subscription Stock and Over-Subscription Stock, which shall be held by the Escrow Agent or another bank, trust company or other organization independent of AWA and designated by the Debtor and approved by the Bankruptcy Court. Purchasing Stockholders may choose one of the following methods of payment:

(a) The Purchasing Stockholder may deliver full payment for the Equity Subscription Stock and the Over-Subscription Stock, together with its Ballot, with the check made payable to AWA Subscription Stock Escrow Account, by no later than the Voting Deadline. The Debtor shall deposit all such checks in the Stock Payment Escrow Account with any interest thereon to accrue to the benefit of Debtor or NewAWA pending distribution of the Equity Subscription Stock and Over-Subscription Stock; or

(b) The Purchasing Stockholder may deliver or cause to be delivered to the Escrow Agent, by no later than the Voting Deadline, a notice of guaranteed delivery by telegram or otherwise, from a bank or trust company or a New York Stock Exchange member firm, guaranteeing delivery of payment of the full price of the subscribed for Equity Subscription Stock and Over-Subscription Stock. In such case, full payment for the Equity Subscription Stock and the Over-Subscription Stock (as such amount may be reduced as set forth below) must be received by the Escrow Agent by no later than 5:00 p.m. on the fifth Business Day after the Confirmation Date.

Promptly after completing the allocation required by the first sentence of this Section 10.2.2, a confirmation will be sent to each Purchasing Stockholder showing the number of shares of Equity Subscription Stock and the number of shares, if any, of Over-Subscription Stock allocated to such holder. In the event that such number of shares of Over-Subscription Stock is less than the number of shares of Over-Subscription Stock for which such holder has either paid for or guaranteed payment for, such notice shall also state such fact and if full payment shall have already been made for such stock, such notice shall also include a check representing the excess payment. Whichever of the two above methods of payment is used, issuance and delivery of the Equity Subscription Stock, the Over-Subscription Stock and any refunds of payments therefor shall be subject to collection of checks and actual payment pursuant to any notice of guaranteed delivery. All offers to purchase Equity Subscription Stock and Over-Subscription Stock shall be irrevocable. In the event that the Effective Date has not occurred by the date the Interim Procedures Agreement is terminated, all amounts in the Stock Payment Escrow Account (other than interest accrued thereon) shall be returned to the Purchasing Stockholders who have made payment for the Equity Subscription Stock and/or Over-Subscription Stock.

10.2.3. On the Effective Date, NewAWA will issue in the name of the Distribution Agent, as trustee, (i) the number of shares of Equity Subscription Stock and Over-Subscription Stock to be issued to Purchasing Stockholders and holders of AWA Preferred Stock in accordance with Sections 3.6.1, 3.6.2 and 10.2.2, and (ii) the Equity Interests Stock and the Equity Interests Warrants for distribution to holders of AWA Common Stock as provided in Section 3.6.2. As promptly as practicable after the Effective Date, but in any event within fifteen (15) Business Days, the Distribution Agent will distribute (i) to each holder of AWA Preferred Stock, the number of shares of Over-Subscription Stock purchased in accordance with Section 3.6.1, (ii) to each Purchasing Stockholder, the number of shares of Equity Subscription Stock and Over-Subscription Stock purchased by such Purchasing Stockholder pursuant to Section 3.6.2 and (iii) to each holder of AWA Common Stock as of the Distribution Record Date other than the holder of a Disputed Equity Interest, such holder's Pro Rata Share of the Equity Interests Stock and of the Equity Interests Warrants, less any Reserve Amount required pursuant to Section 10.4; *provided, however*, that holders of AWA Common Stock whose stock is held of record by Cede or by any other depository or nominee on their behalf or their broker-dealer's behalf will have their NewAWA Securities credited to the account of Cede or such other depository or nominee.

10.2.4. The Distribution Agent in its capacity as trustee holding issued but undistributed NewAWA Securities and Electing Creditor Cash shall (i) similarly hold in trust for distribution pursuant to this Section 10.2 any dividend or distribution made thereon, and (ii) whenever any matter (including election of directors) is presented for a vote by holders of such

NewAWA Securities, vote all of the NewAWA Securities so held by it in trust in the same manner and proportion as the shares of NewAWA Class B Common Stock are voted.

10.2.5. If, after the Effective Date, NewAWA (i) pays a dividend or makes a distribution on the outstanding NewAWA Securities held by the Distribution Agent, (ii) subdivides the outstanding shares of NewAWA Securities held by the Distribution Agent into a greater number of shares or units, (iii) combines the outstanding shares or units of NewAWA Securities held by the Distribution Agent into a smaller number of shares or units, (iv) issues by reclassification of the outstanding NewAWA Securities held by the Distribution Agent any shares of its capital stock, or (v) is a party to a consolidation, merger or transfer of assets providing for any change in or exchange of the outstanding NewAWA Securities held by the Distribution Agent, then the Distribution Agent's obligation to distribute NewAWA Securities to any holder of an Allowed Claim or Equity Interest arising after the record date in the case of a dividend or distribution and after the Effective Date of any of the other foregoing transactions shall be adjusted so as to take into account such dividend, distribution or other event. Any such distribution shall be made net of any Distribution Agent Charges incurred in connection with such event.

10.2.6. The duties of the Distribution Agent (including its duties as trustee pursuant to this Section 10.2) are expressly limited to the ministerial functions set forth in this Article 10. The Distribution Agent shall incur no liability for its actions (or failure to act) or conduct as Distribution Agent, or as trustee holding issued but undistributed NewAWA Securities or Cash except to the extent attributable to the gross negligence or willful misconduct of the Distribution Agent. The Distribution Agent shall at all times maintain a segregated account for any Cash being held in trust, and shall deposit or invest all such Cash in (i) direct obligations of the United States of America or obligations for which the full faith and credit of the United States of America is pledged, (ii) certificates of deposit and interest bearing deposits with banks having a long-term bond rating of AA or better and capital, surplus and undivided profits of not less than $100,000,000, or (iii) commercial paper having one of the two highest ratings by Standard & Poor's, Inc. or Moody's Investor Services, Inc., except as otherwise authorized by the Bankruptcy Court; *provided, however*, that no such deposit or investment shall have a maturity of more than 90 days. All Distribution Agent Charges shall be deducted from the applicable NewAWA Securities or Cash held by the Distribution Agent. All Cash and NewAWA Securities held by or transferred to the Distribution Agent for distribution to holders of Allowed Claims or Equity Interests pursuant to the Plan shall be held by the Distribution Agent (including NewAWA in its capacity as Distribution Agent) solely as trustee of an express trust and shall not be or constitute property of the Distribution Agent (including NewAWA as Distribution Agent) for any purpose whatsoever, and the Distribution Agent shall not have any right or interest to any such Cash or stock for its own account, except as expressly provided in the Plan.

10.2.7. AWA shall deliver to the Distribution Agent its stock ledger for the AWA Common Stock or provide access thereto, which ledger shall reflect the cancellation of certain AWA Common Stock in accordance with Section 3.7.1. The Distribution Agent shall cause a register for the transfer of Allowed Claims (other than Allowed AWA Debenture Claims) and of AWA Common Stock to be maintained. Transfers after the Distribution Record Date shall be registered only (i) upon Final Order of the Bankruptcy Court directing such transfer or (ii) in the event of a transfer by operation of law.

10.3 Service of Indenture Trustee

10.3.1. Subject to the right of the Indenture Trustee to resign and terminate an Indenture as set forth in Section 10.3.2, the Indenture Trustee shall receive and act as disbursing agent for all distributions to each holder of record of an Allowed AWA Debenture Claim. Unless terminated pursuant to Section 10.3.2 below, the Indentures shall continue in effect after the Effective Date for the sole purpose of allowing the Indenture Trustee to make the distributions to be made on account of such Allowed AWA Debenture Claims under the Plan and for defending any subordination action brought under Section 3.5. AWA and NewAWA shall be required to reimburse the Indenture Trustee solely for fees, costs and expenses (including reasonable costs of counsel associated therewith) in connection with activities required under this Section 10.3.1. Any fees, costs, or expenses incurred by the Indenture Trustee for any other activities it may undertake shall be collectible solely from the holders of AWA Debentures. Notwithstanding anything to the contrary herein, the Indenture Trustee shall retain any and all charging liens or similar rights provided in the Indentures for so long as it is Indenture Trustee.

10.3.2. Notwithstanding the foregoing, the Indenture Trustee may at any time terminate any or all of the AWA Indentures and all of the Indenture Trustee's duties and obligations and authority to act thereunder, with or without cause, by giving fifteen (15) days written notice of termination to NewAWA and the Distribution Agent and by turning over to the Distribution Agent a list of record holders of Debentures under such Indenture as of the Distribution Record Date, together with such other information and documents as may be reasonably necessary in order to permit the Distribution Agent to make distributions to holders of Allowed AWA Debenture Claims arising out of the AWA Debentures issued pursuant to such Indenture. If distributions under the Plan have not been completed at the time of termination of such Indenture, the Distribution Agent shall thereafter act in place of such Indenture Trustee, and all references in the Plan to the Indenture

Trustee for purposes of making distributions under the Plan with regard to such Indenture shall be deemed to apply to such Distribution Agent. Any actions taken by the Indenture Trustee not for a purpose authorized in the Plan shall be of no force or effect.

10.3.3. For purposes of any distributions under the Plan to holders of AWA Debenture Claims, the Indenture Trustee (or if the Indenture Trustee has resigned in accordance with Section 10.3.2, the Distribution Agent as its successor) shall be deemed to be the sole holder of all AWA Debenture Claims evidenced by the AWA Debentures issued under each Indenture. Accordingly, all distributions provided for in the Plan on account of Allowed AWA Debenture Claims shall be distributed to the Indenture Trustee as disbursing agent or, if the Indenture Trustee has resigned pursuant to Section 10.3.2, to the Distribution Agent as its successor, for further distribution to individual holders of Allowed AWA Debenture Claims pursuant to the Plan. The transfer books of the Indenture Trustee for the Debentures shall close as of the Distribution Record Date and no further transfers shall be recognized.

10.3.4. Any provision of the Plan to the contrary notwithstanding, no distribution under the Plan shall be required to be made by the Indenture Trustee or the Distribution Agent to any holder of an AWA Debenture Claim until such time as the certificate representing the AWA Debenture in respect of which such AWA Debenture Claim is made shall have been surrendered in accordance with Section 10.3.5. Notwithstanding any provision of this Section 10.3.4 to the contrary, any holder of an AWA Debenture Claim based on a certificate representing an AWA Debenture that has been lost, stolen, mutilated or destroyed may, in lieu of surrendering such certificate as provided in this Section 10.3, deliver to the Indenture Trustee, or if the Indenture Trustee has resigned, to the Distribution Agent as its successor, (i) evidence satisfactory to the Indenture Trustee or the Distribution Agent, as the case may be, of the loss, theft, mutilation or destruction of such certificate and (ii) such security or indemnity as may reasonably be required by the Indenture Trustee or the Distribution Agent, as the case may be, to save the Indenture Trustee or the Distribution Agent, as the case may be, harmless with respect thereto, and upon providing such evidence and such security or indemnity the holder of such AWA Debenture Claim shall, for all purposes under the Plan, be deemed to have surrendered such certificate.

10.3.5. A holder of record on the Distribution Record Date of a certificate relating to an AWA Debenture Claim shall surrender such holder's certificate representing such AWA Debenture Claim to the Indenture Trustee, or if the Indenture Trustee has resigned in accordance with Section 10.3.2, to the Distribution Agent as its successor, in accordance with written instructions given not more than thirty (30) days after the Effective Date to such holder by the Indenture Trustee or the Distribution Agent, as the case may be. Upon receipt of any certificate relating to such AWA

Debenture Claim, the Indenture Trustee or the Distribution Agent shall cancel such certificate and deliver such canceled certificate to such Person as the Distribution Agent shall designate.

10.3.6. On the Final Distribution Date, all rights under the Plan of any holder of an Allowed AWA Debenture Claim which has not surrendered its certificate representing such AWA Debenture Claim in accordance with this Section 10.3 shall lapse and be automatically terminated without any further action and the Indenture Trustee or the Distribution Agent as its successor shall at such time return to the Distribution Agent any funds or property it then holds in respect of such unsurrendered certificate to be treated as unclaimed property pursuant to Section 10.6 and, upon such return, the Indenture Trustee or the Distribution Agent as its successor shall have no further obligation in respect of such funds or property.

10.4 Reserves for Distributions for Disputed Claims and Disputed Equity Interests

10.4.1. Except as may be otherwise agreed with respect to any Disputed Claim or Disputed Equity Interest and as approved by the Bankruptcy Court, no distributions shall be made with respect to all or any portion of a Disputed Claim or Disputed Equity Interest unless and until such Disputed Claim or Disputed Equity Interest (or portion thereof) shall have become an Allowed Claim or Equity Interest and such Allowed Claim or Equity Interest is otherwise entitled to distributions hereunder.

10.4.2. Prior to making any distribution to holders of Allowed Claims or Equity Interests in Class 5 or Class 6.2 in accordance with Section 10.2, the Distribution Agent shall deposit in a Reserve established separately for each such Class an amount of NewAWA Securities and/or Cash equal to the amount of such distribution that would have been distributed to holders of Disputed Claims or Disputed Equity Interests in such Class if such Disputed Claims or Equity Interests were Allowed Claims or Equity Interests in their full face amount at the time of the calculation of such distribution. A separate Reserve shall be established and thereafter maintained for each Class as to which any Claims or Equity Interests remain Disputed as of the Effective Date. The Distribution Agent shall at all times until any Disputed Claim or Disputed Equity Interest is resolved by Final Order, retain in the Reserve all amounts that would have been distributed to the holder of such Disputed Claim or Disputed Equity Interest had such Claim or Equity Interest been an Allowed Claim or Equity Interest in its full face amount on the Effective Date. Notwithstanding the foregoing, upon motion by the Debtor or NewAWA, the Bankruptcy Court may enter a Reserve Order, establishing a Reserve Amount to be escrowed in the Reserve for any Class which may be less than the amount otherwise required hereunder, which amount shall reflect the Bankruptcy Court's estimate of the level of Reserves for a particular Class reasonably required to protect the legitimate rights and interests of holders of Disputed Claims or Disputed Equity Interests in such Class. In the event a Reserve Order is entered, the Distribution Agent shall deposit or retain in the Reserve with respect to any Class subject to such order only the Reserve Amount required by such Reserve Order. Any amount not so deposited or retained shall be distributed to all holders of Allowed Claims or Equity Interests in the Class for which such Reserve Amount was established as provided for in the Plan. The date of each such distribution shall be a Distribution Date.

10.4.3. As soon as practicable after a Disputed Claim or Disputed Equity Interest, or portion thereof, becomes an Allowed Claim or Equity Interest, the Distribution Agent shall make a distribution to the holder of such Allowed Claim or Equity Interest from the Reserve in the amount of (i) the portion of the NewAWA Securities or Cash in the Reserve that should be distributed pursuant to the terms of the Plan in view of the amount of the Allowed Claim or Equity Interest; plus (ii) the proportional share of any interest, earnings or dividends actually earned and received on such Reserve; less (iii) the proportional share of any Distribution Agent Charges incurred on account of such escrowed assets. To the extent that sufficient New AWA Securities or Cash are not available to make the full distribution required by the preceding sentence, in view of the then-appearing rights of the holders of other Disputed Claims and Disputed Equity Interests, the Distribution Agent shall make such lesser distribution as shall then be ordered by the Bankruptcy Court. No holder of a Disputed Claim or Disputed Equity Interest shall have any claim against the Reserve for the Class in which such Disputed Claim or Disputed Equity Interest is included until such Disputed Claim or Disputed Equity Interest shall become an Allowed Claim or Equity Interest. In no event shall any holder of any Disputed Claim or Disputed Equity Interest have any recourse against or be entitled to receive (under the Plan or otherwise) or recover from the Debtor, NewAWA, the Distribution Agent or any Reserve, any payment (in Cash, NewAWA Securities or other property) in the event that the Reserve therefor is insufficient to pay an Allowed Claim or Equity Interest in full. In no event shall the Distribution Agent, the Debtor or NewAWA have any responsibility or liability for any loss to or of any Reserve.

10.4.4. The Reserve for a Class shall be terminated when all Disputed Claims and Disputed Equity Interests are finally resolved in such Class. All remaining assets, if any, in the Reserve shall be distributed, first, to holders, if any, who received less than a proportionate distribution pursuant to order of the Bankruptcy Court under Section 10.4.3 and thereafter to all holders of Allowed Claims or Equity Interests in the Class for which such Reserve was established, on a pro rata basis. The date of such distribution shall be the Final Distribution Date with regard to such Class.

10.5 Fractional Interests; Odd Lots; De Minimis Distributions

10.5.1. Fractional shares or units of NewAWA Securities shall not be issued or distributed and no Cash payments shall be made in respect thereof. All holders of Allowed Claims or Equity Interests in such Class which would otherwise be entitled to a fractional interest in such NewAWA Security shall be placed on a list in descending order according to the size of the fractional interest in the NewAWA Security to be distributed. For purposes of the preceding sentence, Electing Unsecured Creditors and Non-Electing Unsecured Creditors shall be placed on separate lists. In the event that two or more holders of Allowed Claims or Equity Interests are entitled to the same fractional portion (rounded to six decimal places) in such NewAWA Security, their relative ranking on any such list shall be determined by lot. The fractional shares or units which each such holder would have received will be aggregated. Then, one share or unit, as applicable, will be distributed to each of the holders on such list in descending order until the total amount of aggregated shares or units is exhausted.

10.5.2. In the event that any holder of an Allowed Claim or Equity Interest would receive fewer than ten (10) shares or units of NewAWA Securities in a distribution made under this Article 10, the Distribution Agent may instead sell such NewAWA Securities on behalf of any or all of such holders and then distribute to each such holder its pro rata share of the Net Proceeds of such sale. Such sale may be either a private sale or through a securities exchange or automated quotation system on which such NewAWA Securities are listed and absent manifest error or intentional wrongdoing on the part of the Distribution Agent in connection with such sale, the Net Proceeds realized from such sale shall be conclusively determined to be reasonable. The distribution of a pro rata share of such Net Proceeds to each such holder shall be deemed to be in full satisfaction of the payment to be made to such holder of Allowed Claims or Equity Interests in such distribution. These procedures are intended to result in the affected holders receiving appropriate distributions while saving expenses in the administration of the Debtor's estate that would be associated with maintaining such holders as stockholders of NewAWA.

10.6 Delivery of Distributions; Unclaimed Property. Distributions and deliveries to holders of (i) Allowed General Unsecured Claims shall be made at the addresses set forth on the proofs of claim filed by such holders (or at the last known addresses of such holders if no proof of claim is filed or if NewAWA has been notified of a change of address), (ii) AWA Debenture Claims shall be made at the address contained in the records of the Indenture Trustee (or, if the Indenture Trustee has resigned pursuant to Section 10.3.2 of the Plan, in such records it has delivered to the Distribution Agent as its successor) and (iii) Equity Interests shall be made to the address shown on the stock ledger of AWA. If any holder's distribution is returned as undeliverable, no further distributions to such holder shall be made unless and until the Distribution Agent, NewAWA or the Indenture Trustee is notified in writing of such holder's then-current address, at which time all missed distributions shall be made to such holder without interest (except to the extent that such missed distributions have become unclaimed property). Amounts in respect of undeliverable distributions made through the Distribution Agent or through the Indenture Trustee, shall be returned to NewAWA until such distributions are claimed. All claims for undeliverable distributions shall be made on or before the second (2nd) anniversary of the applicable Distribution Date, and after such date, such undeliverable distributions shall be unclaimed property. All unclaimed property attributable to any Claim or Equity Interest shall revert to the Reserve, if any, then existing with regard to Claims or Equity Interests of such Class and, if none exists, to NewAWA, and the Claim of any holder with respect to such property shall be discharged and forever barred and shall no longer be deemed an Allowed Claim or Equity Interest.

10.7 Method of Payment. Payments of Cash required to be made pursuant to the Plan shall be made by check drawn on a domestic bank or by wire transfer from a domestic bank at the election of the Person making such payment.

10.8 Payment Dates. Whenever any payment or distribution to be made under the Plan shall be due on a day other than a Business Day, such payment or distribution shall instead be made, without interest, on the immediately following Business Day.

10.9 Compliance with Tax Requirements. In connection with the Plan, to the extent applicable, the Distribution Agent and the Indenture Trustee shall comply with all tax withholding and reporting requirements imposed on it by any governmental unit, and all distributions pursuant to the Plan shall be subject to such withholding and reporting requirements. The Distribution Agent and Indenture Trustee shall be authorized to take any and all actions that may be necessary or appropriate to comply with such withholding and reporting requirements. Notwithstanding any other provision of the Plan, (i) each Person (including holders of Allowed Claims and Equity Interests) receiving a distribution of Cash or NewAWA Securities pursuant to the Plan shall have sole and exclusive responsibility for the satisfaction and payment of any tax obligations imposed by any governmental unit, including income, withholding and other tax obligations, on account of such distribution and (ii) at the option of NewAWA, no distribution pursuant to the Plan shall be made to or on behalf of such entity unless and until such entity has made arrangements satisfactory to NewAWA for the satisfaction and payment of such tax obligations. At the option of NewAWA, any Cash or NewAWA Securities to be distributed pursuant to the Plan shall, pending the implementation of such arrangements, be treated as an undeliverable distribution pursuant to Section 10.6 above.

ARTICLE 11

PROCEDURES FOR RESOLVING DISPUTED CLAIMS OR EQUITY INTERESTS

11.1 Filing of Objections to Claims or Equity Interests. After the Effective Date, objections to Claims or Equity Interests shall be made and objections to Claims or Equity Interests made previous thereto shall be pursued only by NewAWA and, upon leave of the Bankruptcy Court for good cause shown, the Creditors' Committee (if it is then still in existence). Any objections made by NewAWA or the Creditors' Committee after the Effective Date shall be served and filed not later than 180 days after the Effective Date; *provided, however*, that such period may be extended by order of the Bankruptcy Court for good cause shown.

11.2 Settlement of Objections to Claims or Equity Interests After Effective Date. From and after the Effective Date, NewAWA may litigate to judgment, propose settlements of, or withdraw objections to, all pending or filed Disputed Claims or Disputed Equity Interests, and NewAWA may settle or compromise any Disputed Claim or Disputed Equity Interest, without notice and a hearing and without approval of the Bankruptcy Court; *provided, however*, notice of any settlement or compromise involving the allowance of a General Unsecured Claim in excess of $100,000 shall be provided to the Indenture Trustee (if the AWA Indentures have not been previously terminated) and to the Creditors' Committee (if still then in existence), who shall each have ten (10) days to object to such settlement or compromise and in such case, such settlement or compromise must be approved by the Bankruptcy Court.

11.3 Payment or Distribution to Holders of Disputed Claims or Equity Interests. Except as the Debtor or NewAWA, as applicable, may otherwise agree with respect to any Disputed Claim or Disputed Equity Interest, no payments or distributions shall be made with respect to any portion of a Disputed Claim or Disputed Equity Interest unless and until all objections to such Disputed Claim or Disputed Equity Interest have been settled or determined by a Final Order of the Bankruptcy Court. Payments and distributions to each holder of a Disputed Claim or Disputed Equity Interest to the extent that it ultimately becomes an Allowed Claim or Equity Interest shall be made in accordance with Section 10.4. A Disputed Claim or Disputed Equity Interest that is estimated for purposes of allowance and distribution pursuant to Section 502(c) of the Bankruptcy Code and which is estimated and Allowed at a fixed amount by Final Order of the Bankruptcy Court shall thereupon be an Allowed Claim or Equity Interest for all purposes in the amount so estimated and Allowed.

11.4 Reserves for Disputed Claims and Disputed Equity Interests. Appropriate Reserves for Disputed Claims and Disputed Equity Interests shall be established and maintained as provided in Section 10.4.

ARTICLE 12

MISCELLANEOUS PROVISIONS

12.1 Modification of Payment Terms. NewAWA reserves the right to modify the treatment of any Allowed Claim in any manner adverse only to the holder of such Claim at any time after the Effective Date upon the consent of the holder whose Allowed Claim treatment is being adversely affected.

12.2 Discharge of Debtor. The rights afforded and the treatment of Claims and Equity Interests under the Plan shall be in exchange for and in complete satisfaction, discharge, release and termination of all Claims of any nature whatsoever against the Debtor or any of its assets or properties and all Equity Interests in the Debtor; and upon the Effective Date (i) the Debtor shall be deemed discharged and released pursuant to Section 1141(d)(1)(A) of the Bankruptcy Code from any and all Claims, including but not limited to demands and liabilities that arose before the Effective Date, all debts of the kind specified in Section 502(g), 502(h) or 502(i) of the Bankruptcy Code, whether or not (a) a proof of claim based upon such debt is filed or deemed filed under Section 501 of the Bankruptcy Code, (b) a Claim based upon such debt is allowed under Section 502 of the Bankruptcy Code or (c) the holder of a Claim based upon such debt has accepted the Plan; and (ii) all rights and interests of holders of Equity Interests in the Debtor shall be terminated pursuant to Section 1141(d)(1)(B) of the Bankruptcy Code. The Confirmation Order shall be a judicial determination of discharge and termination of all liabilities of and all Claims against, and all Equity Interests in, the Debtor, except as otherwise specifically provided in the Plan. On the Effective Date, as to every discharged debt, Claim and Equity Interest, the holder of such debt, Claim or Equity Interest shall be permanently enjoined and precluded from asserting against NewAWA or against its assets or properties or any transferee thereof, any other or further Claim or Equity Interest based upon any document, instrument or act, omission, transaction or other activity of any kind or nature that occurred prior to the Effective Date, except as expressly set forth in the Plan or the Confirmation Order.

12.3 Termination of Subordination Rights. Except as specifically provided elsewhere herein, on the Confirmation Date, all contractual, legal or equitable subordination rights that a holder of a Claim or Equity Interest may have with respect to any distribution to be made pursuant to the Plan shall be discharged and terminated, and all actions related to the enforcement of such subordination rights shall be permanently enjoined. Accordingly, distributions pursuant to the Plan to holders of Allowed Claims and Equity Interests shall not be subject to payment to a beneficiary of such terminated subordination rights, or to levy, garnishment, attachment or other legal process by any beneficiary of such terminated subordination rights. Pursuant to Bankruptcy Rule 9019 and in consideration for the distribution and other benefits provided under the Plan, the provisions of this Section 12.3 shall constitute a good faith compromise and settlement of all claims or controversies relating to the termination of all contractual, legal and equitable subordination rights that a holder of a Claim or Equity Interest may have with respect to any Allowed Claim or Equity Interest, or any distribution to be made on account of such Allowed Claim or Allowed Equity Interest.

12.4 Termination of the Creditors' and Equity Committees

12.4.1. The Creditors' Committee shall, unless theretofore terminated, terminate on the Effective Date and shall thereafter have no further responsibilities in respect of the Chapter 11 Case except (i) with respect to preparation and filing of applications for compensation and reimbursement of expenses in accordance with Section 2.2.3, (ii) with respect to any contested matter or adversary proceeding commenced prior to the Effective Date in which the Creditors' Committee is an indispensable litigant or any appeal of an order in the Chapter 11 Case in which the Creditors' Committee is an indispensable litigant and if, in each case, the Creditors' Committee's participation in such proceeding is consistent with the orders of the Bankruptcy Court establishing the Creditors' Committee and with Section 1103 of the Bankruptcy Code, and (iii) with respect to monitoring and participating in matters and proceedings which could give rise to General Unsecured Claims (including, without limitation, Avoidance Litigation, rejection of executory contracts and unexpired leases and resolution of Unsecured Deficiency Claims and Disputed General Unsecured Claims) for a period of five months after the Effective Date, unless such period is extended by the Bankruptcy Court for good cause shown. In connection with such activities, the Creditors' Committee may continue the retention of its counsel, its local counsel and its accountants and may replace one or more of such professional advisors, if necessary, but shall not retain additional professional advisors. NewAWA shall pay the reasonable fees and expenses of the Creditors' Committee incurred in connection with such activities, *provided, however*, that the aggregate fees related to matters and proceedings which could give rise to General Unsecured Claims shall not exceed an average of $75,000 per month for the first two months after the Effective Date and an average of $50,000 per month for any subsequent month. All such fees and expenses shall be paid only in accordance with the fee and expense guidelines promulgated by the Debtor in the Bankruptcy Case and shall be paid by NewAWA within thirty (30) days of receipt of invoice therefor, except in the case of an objection to any such fees and expenses, which, if not resolved by NewAWA and the Creditors' Committee, may be noticed by either such entity for a hearing before the Bankruptcy Court. Notwithstanding anything to the contrary in this Section 12.4.1, all such activities shall cease when the aggregate amount of Disputed Claims is less than $3,000,000 or one year after the Effective Date, whichever occurs first, except in a case where the Creditors' Committee is an indispensable litigant as contemplated by clause (ii) above.

12.4.2. The Equity Committee shall, unless theretofore terminated, terminate on the Effective Date and shall thereafter have no further responsibilities in respect of the Chapter 11 Case except (i) with respect to preparation and filing of a final application for compensation and reimbursement of expenses in accordance with Section 2.2.3 and (ii) with respect to any contested matter or adversary proceeding commenced prior to the Effective Date in which the Equity Committee is an indispensable litigant or any appeal of an order in the Chapter 11 Case in which the Equity Committee is an indispensable litigant and, in each case, if the Equity Committee's participation in such proceeding is consistent with the orders of the Bankruptcy Court establishing the Equity Committee and with Section 1103 of the Bankruptcy Code.

12.5 Setoffs. The Debtor and NewAWA may, but shall not be required to, set off or recoup against any Claim and the payments or other distributions to be made pursuant to the Plan in respect of such Claim, claims of any nature whatsoever which the Debtor or NewAWA may have against the holder of such Claim to the extent such Claim may be set off or recouped under applicable law, but neither the failure to do so nor the allowance of any Claim hereunder shall constitute a waiver or release by the Debtor or NewAWA, of any such claim that it may have against such holder.

12.6 Opt-Out. Pursuant to Section 203(b)(3) of the Delaware General Corporation Law, AWA elects, as of the Effective Date, that it will no longer be governed by the provisions of Section 203 of the Delaware General Corporation Law.

12.7 Section Headings. The Section headings contained in the Plan are for reference purposes only and shall not affect in any way the meaning or interpretation of the Plan.

12.8 Severability. If any provision of the Plan is found by the Bankruptcy Court to be invalid, illegal or unenforceable, then, at the option of the Debtor or NewAWA, such provision shall not affect the validity or legality of any other provisions of the Plan which shall remain effective.

12.9 Computation of Time. In computing any period of time prescribed or allowed by the Plan, the provisions of Bankruptcy Rule 9006(a) shall apply.

12.10 Governing Law. Except to the extent that the Bankruptcy Code, the Bankruptcy Rules or any other statutes, rules or regulations of the United States are applicable, and subject to the provisions of any contract, instrument, release, indenture or other agreement or document entered into in connection with the Plan, the rights and obligations arising under the Plan shall be governed by, and construed and enforced in accordance with, the laws of the State of Arizona, without giving effect to the principles of conflicts of law thereof. Notwithstanding anything to the contrary herein, the laws of escheat and abandoned property of no state shall be applicable to any property distributed or abandoned hereunder.

ARTICLE 13

PROVISIONS FOR EXECUTION AND SUPERVISION OF THE PLAN

13.1 Retention of Jurisdiction. Except as otherwise provided herein, from and after the Effective Date, the Bankruptcy Court shall retain and have exclusive jurisdiction over the Chapter 11 Case for all legally permissible purposes, including, without limitation, the following purposes:

(a) to determine any and all objections to the allowance of Claims;

(b) to resolve any and all matters related to the rejection, assumption, or assumption and assignment, as the case may be, of executory contracts or unexpired leases to which the Debtor is a party or with respect to which the Debtor may be liable, and to hear and determine, and if need be to liquidate, any and all Claims arising therefrom;

(c) to determine any and all applications for the determination of any priority of any Claim including without limitation Claims arising from any event that occurred prior to the Petition Date or from the Petition Date through the Effective Date and for payment of any alleged Administrative Claim, Priority Tax Claim, Priority Benefit Plan Contribution Claim or Priority Wage Claim;

(d) to determine any and all applications, motions, adversary proceedings and contested or litigated matters that may be pending on the Effective Date;

(e) to determine all controversies, suits and disputes that may arise in connection with the interpretation, enforcement or consummation of the Plan or in connection with the obligations of the Debtor, NewAWA or AmWest under the Plan, or in connection with the performance by any Distribution Agent of its duties hereunder, and to enter such orders as may be necessary or appropriate to implement any distributions to holders of Allowed General Unsecured Claims;

(f) to consider any modification, remedy any defect or omission, or reconcile any inconsistency in the Plan or any order of the Bankruptcy Court, including the Confirmation Order, all to the extent authorized by the Bankruptcy Code;

(g) to issue such orders in aid of execution of the Plan to the extent authorized by Section 1142 of the Bankruptcy Code;

(h) to determine such other matters as may be set forth in the Confirmation Order or as may arise in connection with the Plan or the Confirmation Order,

(i) to determine any suit or proceeding brought by NewAWA on behalf of the Debtor's estate to recover property under Section 542, 543 or 553 of the Bankruptcy Code or any Avoidance Litigation;

(j) to consider and act on the compromise and settlement of any Claim against or cause of action by or against the Debtor's estate;

(k) to estimate Claims for purposes of allowance pursuant to Section 502(c) of the Bankruptcy Code;

(1) to hear and determine any dispute or controversy relating to any Allowed Claim or any Claim alleged or asserted by any Person to be an Allowed Claim;

(m) to determine any and all applications for allowances of compensation and reimbursement of expenses and any other fees and expenses authorized to be paid or reimbursed under the Bankruptcy Code or the Plan;

(n) to determine any issues arising in connection with elections made on a Ballot by a holder of a Claim or Equity Interest;

(o) to determine the appropriate Reserve Amounts;

(p) to determine whether the payment of any Claims hereunder should be subordinated to the payment of other Claims;

(q) to hear and determine any tax disputes concerning AWA, including the amount and preservation of AWA's tax attributes, to determine and declare any tax effects under the Plan, and to determine any Taxes which the Debtor's bankruptcy estate may incur as a result of the transactions contemplated herein, pursuant to Sections 346, 505 and 1146 of the Bankruptcy Code; and

(r) to enter a final decree closing the Chapter 11 Case.

13.2 Amendment of Plan. The Plan may be amended by the Debtor before the Effective Date and by NewAWA thereafter as provided in Section 1127 of the Bankruptcy Code.

13.3 Post-Effective Date Notice. From and after the Effective Date, any notice to be provided under the Plan shall be sufficient if provided to (i) the Official Service List as contained in the records of the Bankruptcy Court on the Effective Date; or (ii) all parties whose rights may be affected by the action which is the subject of the notice; or (iii) in any case, such notice as is approved as sufficient by order of the Bankruptcy Court.

13.4 Revocation of Plan. Subject to the approval of AmWest as required by the Investment Agreement, the Debtor reserves the right to revoke and withdraw the Plan prior to entry of the Confirmation Order. If the Debtor revokes or withdraws the Plan, then the Plan shall be deemed null and void and nothing contained herein shall be deemed to constitute a waiver or release of any Claims by or against the Debtor or any other person or to prejudice in any manner the rights of the Debtor or any Person in any further proceedings involving the Debtor.

Dated: Phoenix, Arizona
June 28, 1994

Respectfully submitted,

AMERICA WEST AIRLINES, INC.

By: /s/ WILLIAM A. FRANKE
William A. Franke
Chairman of the Board and Chief Executive Officer

AMWEST PARTNERS, L.P.

By: /s/ AMWEST GENPAR, INC.,
its general partner

By: /s/ JAMES G. COULTER
James G. Coulter
Vice President

PLAN OF REORGANIZATION

EXHIBIT A

INVESTMENT AGREEMENT

[Exhibits to Investment Agreement omitted]

EXHIBIT A

[Certain terms of the following Investment Agreement have been modified by the Plan of Reorganization to which this Exhibit A is attached.]

THIRD REVISED INVESTMENT AGREEMENT

April 21, 1994

America West Airlines, Inc.
4000 East Sky Harbor Boulevard
Phoenix, AZ 85034

Attention: William A. Franke
Chairman of the Board

Gentlemen:

This letter agreement (this "*Agreement*") sets forth the agreement between America West Airlines, Inc., a Delaware corporation (including, on or after the effective date of the Plan, as defined herein, its successors, as reorganized pursuant to the Bankruptcy Code, as defined herein) (the "*Company*"), and AmWest Partners, L.P., a Texas limited partnership ("*Investor*").

The Company will issue and sell to Investor, and Investor hereby agrees and commits to purchase from the Company, a package of securities of the Company for $244,857,000 in cash (subject to adjustment as herein provided), consisting of (i) shares of Class A Common Stock of the Company ("*Class A Common*"), (ii) shares of Class B Common Stock of the Company ("*Class B Common*" and, together with the Class A Common, "*Common Stock*"), (iii) senior unsecured notes of the Company ("*Notes*") and (iv) warrants to purchase shares of Class B Common ("*Warrants*"), all on the terms and subject to the terms and conditions hereinafter set forth.

Investor's purchase of the securities referred to above (the "*Investment*") will be made in connection with and as part of the transactions to be consummated pursuant to a joint Plan of Reorganization of the Company (the "*Plan*") and an order (the "*Confirmation Order*") confirming the Plan issued by the Bankruptcy Court, as defined herein. The Plan will contain provisions called for by, or otherwise consistent with, this Agreement.

In consideration of the agreements of Investor hereunder, and as a precondition and inducement to the execution of this Agreement by Investor, the Company has entered into the Third Revised Interim Procedures Agreement with Investor, dated the date hereof (the "*Procedures Agreement*").

SECTION 1.*Definitions*. For purposes of this Agreement, except as expressly provided herein or unless the context otherwise requires, the following terms shall have the following respective meanings:

"*Affiliate*" shall mean (i) when used with reference to any partnership, any Person that, directly or indirectly, owns or controls 10% or more of either the capital or profit interests of such partnership or is a partner of such partnership or is a Person in which such partnership has a 10% or greater direct or indirect equity interest and (ii) when used with reference to any corporation, any Person that, directly or indirectly, owns or controls 10% or more of the outstanding voting securities of such corporation or is a Person in which such corporation has a 10% or greater direct or indirect equity interest. In addition, the term "Affiliate," when used with reference to any Person, shall also mean any other Person that, directly or indirectly, controls or is controlled by or is under common control with such Person. As used in the preceding sentence, (A) the term "control" means the possession, directly or indirectly, of the power to direct or cause the direction of the management and policies of the entity referred to, whether through ownership of voting securities, by contract or otherwise and (B) the terms "controlling" and "controls" shall have meanings correlative to the foregoing. Notwithstanding the foregoing, the Company will be deemed not to be an Affiliate of Investor or any of its partners or assignees.

"*Alliance Agreements*"shall have the meaning specified in Section 5.

"*Approvals*" shall have the meaning specified in Section 8(b).

"*Bankruptcy Code*" shall mean Chapter 11 of the United States Bankruptcy Code.

"*Bankruptcy Court*" shall mean the United States Bankruptcy Court for the District of Arizona.

"*Business Combination*" means:

(i) any merger or consolidation of the Company with or into Investor or any Affiliate of Investor;

(ii) any sale, lease, exchange, transfer or other disposition of all or any substantial part of the assets of the Company to Investor or any Affiliate of Investor;

(iii) any transaction with or involving the Company as a result of which Investor or any of Investor's Affiliates will, as a result of issuances of voting securities by the Company (or any other securities convertible into or exchangeable for such voting securities) acquire an increased percentage ownership of such voting securities, except pursuant to a transaction open on a pro rata basis to all holders of Class B Common; or

(iv) any related series or combination of transactions having or which will have, directly or indirectly, the same effect as any of the foregoing.

"*Class A Common*" shall have the meaning specified in the second paragraph of this Agreement.

"*Class B Common*" shall have the meaning specified in the second paragraph of this Agreement.

"*Common Stock*" shall have the meaning specified in the second paragraph of this Agreement.

"*Company*" shall have the meaning specified in the first paragraph of this Agreement.

"*Confirmation Date*" shall mean the date on which the Confirmation Order is entered by the Bankruptcy Court.

"*Confirmation Order*" shall have the meaning specified in the third paragraph of this Agreement.

"*Continental*" shall mean Continental Airlines, Inc.

"*Creditors' Committee*" shall mean the Official Committee of the Unsecured Creditors of America West Airlines, Inc. appointed in the Company's Chapter 11 case pending in the Bankruptcy Court.

"*Disclosure Statement*" shall mean a disclosure statement with respect to the Plan.

"*Effective Date*" shall mean the effective date of the Plan; provided that in no event shall the Effective Date be (a) earlier than 11 days after the Bankruptcy Court approves and enters the Confirmation Order providing for the confirmation of the Plan or (b) before all material Approvals are obtained.

"*Electing Party*" shall have the meaning specified in Section 4(a)(2)(ii).

"*Equity Committee*" shall mean the Official Committee of Equity Holders of America West Airlines, Inc. appointed in the Company's Chapter 11 case pending in the Bankruptcy Court.

"*Equity Holders*" shall mean the Company's equity security holders (including holders of common stock and preferred stock) of record as of the applicable record date fixed by the Bankruptcy Court.

"*Governance Agreements*" shall have the meaning specified in Section 6.

"*GPA*" shall mean GPA Group plc or, if applicable, any direct or indirect subsidiary thereof.

"*GPA Put Agreement*" shall have the meaning specified in Section 7(j).

"*Independent Directors*" shall have the meaning specified in Section 6(a).

"*Initial Order*" shall have the meaning specified in Section 8(a).

"*Investment*" shall have the meaning specified in the third paragraph of this Agreement.

"*Investor*" shall have the meaning specified in the first paragraph of this Agreement.

"*Mesa*" shall mean Mesa Airlines, Inc.

"*Monthly Targets*" shall mean the amounts specified in the Monthly Targets Schedule.

"*Monthly Targets Schedule*" shall mean the letter agreement between the Company and Investor dated the date hereof.

"*Notes*" shall have the meaning specified in the second paragraph of this Agreement. The Notes shall be subject to the terms and conditions set forth in Exhibit B hereto.

"*Outside Date*" shall mean August 31, 1994; provided that Investor shall have the right from time to time to irrevocably extend the Outside Date to a date not later than November 30, 1994, but only if Investor gives the Company prior written notice of its election to extend the then current Outside Date (which notice shall specify the new Outside Date) and then only if, at the time of the giving of such notice, Investor is not in breach of any of its representations, warranties, covenants or obligations under this Agreement, the Procedures Agreement or any Related Agreement (excluding any breach by Investor which is not willful or intentional and which is capable of being cured on or before the new Outside Date). Unless waived by the Company, any notice given pursuant to this definition shall be delivered to the Company not less than 15 days prior to the then current Outside Date except that, in the event the Effective Date has not occurred for any reason arising within such 15-day period not due to a breach by Investor of any of its representations, warranties, covenants or agreements hereunder, such notice shall be given as soon as practicable but in no event later than the then current Outside Date.

"*Person*" means a natural person, a corporation, a partnership, a trust, a joint venture, any Regulatory Authority or any other entity or organization.

"*Plan*" shall have the meaning specified in the third paragraph of this

Agreement.

"*Plan 9*" means the Company's Plan Revision No. 9 which consists of the Summary Pro Forma Financial Statements: June 1993 Through December 1994, dated July 15, 1993.

"*Plan R-2*" shall mean the Company's Summary Pro Forma Financial Statements, 5 Year Plan: 1994 Through 1998, Plan No. R-2, dated January 13, 1994.

"*Procedures Agreement*" shall have the meaning specified in the fourth paragraph of this Agreement.

"*Projections*" shall mean the projections set forth in Plan 9 on pages 15 and 18 of Tab E and pages 7 and 8 of Tab F.

"*Purchase Price*" shall have the meaning specified in Section 2.

"*Regulatory Approvals*" shall mean all approvals, permits, authorizations, consents, licenses, rulings, exemptions and agreements required to be obtained from, or notices to or registrations or filings with, any Regulatory Authority (including the expiration of all applicable waiting periods, if any, under the Hart-Scott-Rodino Antitrust Improvements Act of 1976, as amended) that are necessary or reasonably appropriate to permit the Investment and the other transactions contemplated hereby and by the Related Agreements and to permit the Company to carry on its business after the Investment in a manner consistent in all material respects with the manner in which it was carried on prior to the Effective Date or proposed to be carried on by the reorganized Company.

"*Regulatory Authority*" shall mean any authority, agency, commission, official or other instrumentality of the United States, any foreign country or any domestic or foreign state, county, city or other political subdivision.

"*Related Agreements*" shall have the meaning specified in Section 3.

"*Securities*" shall mean the securities of the Company issued to the Unsecured Parties, Investor and its assigns and GPA under this Agreement. The Securities are described in Section 4.

"*Unsecured Creditors*" shall mean, as of any date, the Persons holding of record as of such date the allowed or allowable prepetition unsecured claims without priority of the Company.

"*Unsecured Parties*" shall mean the Equity Holders and the Unsecured Creditors.

"*Warrants*" shall have the meaning specified in the second paragraph of this Agreement.

SECTION 2.*Commitment to Make Investment.* Subject to the terms and conditions of this Agreement and the Procedures Agreement, on the Effective Date, the Company shall issue and sell and Investor shall purchase Securities in accordance with this Agreement and the Plan. Such Securities shall be issued, sold and delivered to Investor, its designees and/or one or more third party investors, and the $244,857,000 purchase price therefor, as such purchase price may be adjusted pursuant hereto (the "*Purchase Price*"), shall be paid by wire transfer of immediately available funds on the Effective Date.

SECTION 3.*Related Agreements.* The agreements necessary to effect the Investment (the "*Related Agreements*," such term to include the Alliance Agreements and the Governance Agreements) shall be in form and substance reasonably satisfactory to Investor and the Company, and shall contain terms and provisions, including representations, warranties, covenants, warranty termination periods, materiality exceptions, cure opportunities, conditions precedent, anti-dilution provisions (as appropriate), and indemnities, as are in form and substance reasonably satisfactory to such parties; provided, however, that the Related Agreements shall contain provisions called for by, or otherwise consistent with, this Agreement.

SECTION 4.*Capitalization.* (a) Upon consummation of the Plan, the capitalization of the Company shall be as follows:

(1) *Class A Common.* There shall be 1,200,000 shares of Class A Common, all of which shares shall, in accordance with the Plan, be issued to Investor. Investor shall pay $8,960,400 for the Class A Common. At the option of the holders thereof, shares of Class A Common shall be convertible into shares of Class B Common on a share for share basis.

(2) *Class B Common.* There shall be 43,800,000 shares of Class B Common, all of which shares shall, in accordance with the Plan, be issued as follows:

(i) *Investor.* Investor shall be issued 13,875,000 shares plus the number of shares (if any) to be acquired by Investor pursuant to clause (ii) below minus the number of shares, if any, purchased by the Equity Holders pursuant to the second sentence of clause (iii) below. For each share of Class B Common issued to it, Investor shall pay $7.467; provided that (A) for each share acquired by Investor pursuant to clause (ii) below and (B) for each share not purchased by the Equity Holders pursuant to clause (iii) below, Investor shall pay $8.889.

(ii) *Unsecured Creditors.* The Unsecured Creditors (or a trust created for their benefit) shall be issued 26,775,000 shares. Notwithstanding the foregoing, each Unsecured Creditor shall have the right to elect to receive cash equal to $8.889 for each share of Class

B Common otherwise allocable to it under this clause (ii). The election of each such Person (the "*Electing Party*") must be made on or before the date fixed by the Bankruptcy Court for voting with respect to the Plan; provided, however, that in the event that such elections of all Electing Parties aggregate to more than $100 million, then (A) the amount of cash so paid shall be limited to $100 million and (B) the Electing Parties shall each receive proportionate amounts of cash and Class B Common in accordance with the Plan. Subject to the foregoing proviso, Investor shall increase the Investment by the amount necessary to pay all Electing Parties the cash amounts payable to them under this clause (ii) in respect of the shares of Class B Common specified in their elections and, upon payment of such amounts, such shares shall be issued to Investor without further consideration. Notwithstanding the foregoing, Investor's acquisition of shares of Class B Common pursuant to this clause (ii) shall, if permitted by applicable securities and other laws, be consummated immediately after the issuance of such shares to the Electing Parties on the Effective Date. If such shares are not so acquired post-consummation of the Plan, all shares of Class B Common acquired by Investor pursuant to this clause (ii) shall, for all purposes hereof, be deemed to be part of the Securities acquired by Investor hereunder.

(iii) *Equity Holders*. The Equity Holders (or a trust created for their benefit) shall be issued 2,250,000 shares. In addition, the Equity Holders shall have the right to purchase up to 1,615,179 shares allocable to Investor pursuant to clause (i) above at $8.889 per share. Such election must be made by each Equity Holder on or before the date fixed by the Bankruptcy Court for voting with respect to the Plan. The Plan shall set forth the terms and conditions on which the foregoing rights may be exercised.

(iv) *GPA*. 900,000 shares shall be issued to GPA.

(3) *Warrants*. There shall be Warrants to purchase 10,384,615 shares of Class B Common at the exercise price as specified in and subject to the terms of Exhibit A hereto, and such Warrants shall, in accordance with the Plan, be issued as follows:

(i) Warrants to purchase up to 2,769,231 shares of Class B Common shall be issued to Investor; and

(ii) Warrants to purchase up to 6,230,769 shares of Class B Common shall be issued to the Equity Holders or a trust or trusts created for their benefit; and

(iii) Warrants to purchase up to 1,384,615 shares of Class B Common shall be issued to GPA.

(4) *Senior Unsecured Notes*. Investor shall, in accordance with

the Plan and subject to the terms of Exhibit B hereto, be issued $100 million principal amount of Notes against payment in cash of not less than 100% of the principal amount thereof to the Company; provided, however, that the Company shall have the right, exercised at any time prior to the date fixed by the Bankruptcy Court for voting with respect to the Plan, to increase the principal amount of the Notes to be so purchased by Investor to up to $130 million. GPA shall, in accordance with the Plan, be issued $30,525,000 principal amount of Notes; provided, however, that GPA shall have the right to elect to receive cash in lieu of all or any portion of the Notes otherwise issuable to it under this paragraph (4), such election to be made on or before the date fixed by the Bankruptcy Court for voting with respect to the Plan.

(b) Holders of the Class A Common shall have fifty votes per share. Holders of Class B Common shall have one vote per share. Holders of Class A Common and holders of Class B Common shall vote together as a single class except as otherwise required by law or the provisions of this Agreement. Investor may elect, with respect to any shares of Class B Common held by it, to suspend the voting rights relating to such shares by giving prior written notice to the Company, which notice shall describe such shares in reasonable detail and state whether or not the voting suspension is permanent or temporary and, if temporary, specify the period thereof.

(c) Neither Investor nor any Affiliate of Investor or of any partner of Investor will transfer or otherwise dispose of any Common Stock (other than to an Affiliate of the transferor) if, after giving effect thereto and to any concurrent transaction, the total number of shares of Class B Common beneficially owned by the transferor is less than 200% of the total number of shares of Class A Common beneficially owned by the transferor, provided, however, than nothing in this paragraph (c) shall prohibit any Person from transferring or otherwise disposing, in a single transaction or a series of concurrent transactions, of all shares of Common Stock owned by such Person.

SECTION 5.*Business Alliance Agreements*. Continental and the Company shall enter into mutually acceptable business alliance agreements on the Effective Date, which agreements may include, but shall not be limited to, agreements to share ticket counter space, ground handling agreements, agreements to link frequent flier programs, and combined purchasing agreements, and schedule coordination and code sharing agreements. On the Effective Date, Mesa shall enter into agreements with the Company extending the existing contractual arrangements between the Company and Mesa for five years from the Effective Date and modifying the termination provisions thereof consistent with such extension. Such agreements with Continental and Mesa are herein collectively referred to as the "*Alliance Agreements*".

SECTION 6.*Governance Agreements.* On the Effective Date, the Company, Investor and Investor's partners (other than any such partner holding shares of Class B Common the voting rights with respect to which have been suspended as contemplated by Section 4(b)) shall enter into one or more written agreements (the "*Governance Agreements*") effectively providing as follows:

(a) At all times during the three-year period commencing on the Effective Date, the Company's board of directors shall consist of 15 members designated as follows:

(i) nine members (at least 8 of whom are U.S. citizens) shall be designated by Investor, with certain of the partners of Investor having the right to designate certain of Investor's designated directors;

(ii) three members (at least two of whom are U.S. citizens) shall be designated by the Creditors Committee; provided that each such member shall be reasonably acceptable to Investor at the time of his or her initial designation;

(iii) one member shall be designated by the Equity Committee; provided that such member shall be a U.S. citizen reasonably acceptable to Investor at the time of his or her initial designation;

(iv) one member shall be designated by the Company's board of directors as constituted on the date preceding the Effective Date; provided that such member shall be a U.S. citizen reasonably acceptable to Investor at the time of his or her initial designation; and

(v) one member shall be designated by GPA for so long as GPA shall own at least 2% of the voting equity securities of the Company; provided that such member shall be reasonably acceptable to Investor at the time of his or her initial designation.

The directors (and their successors) referred to in clauses (ii), (iii) and (iv) above are hereinafter referred to collectively as the "*Independent Directors*."

(b) In the case of the death, resignation, removal or disability of an Independent Director after the Effective Date, his or her successor shall be designated by the Stockholder Representatives, except that if such Independent Director was initially designated by the Creditors' Committee or the Equity Committee and if, at the time of such Independent Director's death, resignation, removal or disability (as the case may be), the Creditors' Committee or the Equity Committee (as the case may be) remains in effect, the successor to such Independent Director shall be designated by the Creditors' Committee or the Equity Committee (as the case may be). As used herein, "*Stockholder Representatives*" shall mean, collectively, (A) one individual who, on the date hereof, is serving as a director of the Company, (B) one individual who, on the date hereof, is serving as a member of the Creditors' Committee and (C) one individual who, on the date hereof, is serving as a member of the Equity Committee. The initial Stockholder Representatives shall be selected on or before the Effective Date (x) by the Company's board of directors in the case of the individual referred to in clause (A) above, (y) by the Creditors' Committee in the case of the individual referred to in clause (B) above and (z) by the Equity Committee in the case of the individual referred to in clause (C) above. In case of the death, resignation, removal or disability of a Stockholder Representative after the Effective Date, his or her successor shall be designated by the remaining Stockholder Representatives.

(c) Until the third anniversary of the Effective Date, Investor will vote and cause to be voted all shares of Common Stock (other than those the voting rights of which have been suspended) owned by Investor or any of its partners or by the assignees or transferees of all or substantially all of the Common Stock owned by Investor or any of its partners (other than a Person who acquires such stock pursuant to a tender or exchange offer open to all stockholders of the Company) in favor of the election as directors of any and all individuals designated for such election as contemplated by clauses (ii), (iii), (iv) and (v) of paragraph (a) above.

(d) No director nominated by Investor shall be an officer or employee of Continental. All Company directors, if any, who are selected by, or who are directors of, Continental shall recuse themselves from voting on, or otherwise receiving any confidential Company information regarding, matters in connection with negotiations between Continental and the Company (including, without limitation, those relating to the Alliance Agreements) and matters in connection with any action involving direct competition between Continental and the Company. All Company directors, if any, who are selected by, or who are directors, officers or employees of, Mesa shall recuse themselves from voting on, or otherwise receiving any confidential Company information regarding, matters in connection with negotiations between Mesa and the Company (including, without limitation, those relating to the Alliance Agreements) and matters in connection with any action involving direct competition between Mesa and the Company.

(e) During the three-year period commencing on the Effective Date, the Company will not consummate any Business Combination unless such transaction shall be approved in advance by at least three Independent Directors or by a majority of the stock voted at the meeting held to consider such transaction which is owned by stockholders of the Company other than Investor or any of its Affiliates; provided, however, that neither Mesa nor any fund or account managed or advised by Fidelity Management Trust Company or its Affiliates (or any of their non-

Affiliated transferees) will be deemed an Affiliate of Investor for purposes of voting on any Business Combination involving Continental.

SECTION 7.*Plan of Reorganization.* The Plan shall (i) be proposed jointly by the Company and Investor, (ii) contain terms and conditions reasonably satisfactory to Investor and the Company, and (iii) include the following provisions; provided that Investor and the Company may, by mutual agreement, modify the Plan or otherwise restructure the Investment in a manner consistent with the contemplated economic consequences to the Company, Investor, the Unsecured Parties and GPA in order to enable the Company, as reorganized, to more fully utilize its existing tax attributes:

(a) *Debtor-in-Possession Financing.* The Company's debtor-in-possession financing shall be repaid in full in cash on the Effective Date.

(b) *Administrative Claims.* All allowed administrative claims shall be paid as required pursuant to Section 1129(a) of the Bankruptcy Code, provided that such claims do not exceed the amount set forth in Plan R-2 plus $15 million, and provided further that payment of such claims in excess of those set forth in Plan R-2 would not, if payment was to be made in the month immediately preceding the Effective Date, cause the Company to fail to meet any of the Monthly Targets for such month.

(c) *Tax Claims.* All priority tax claims shall be paid over the maximum term permitted by the Bankruptcy Code, as determined by the Bankruptcy Court, with interest accruing at a rate determined by the Bankruptcy Court, provided that such claims do not exceed the amounts set forth in Plan R-2 plus $8.5 million, and provided further that payment of such claims in excess of those set forth in Plan R-2 would not, if payment was to be made in the month immediately preceding the Effective Date, cause the Company to fail to meet any of the Monthly Targets for such month.

(d) *Non-tax Priority Claims.* All non-tax priority claims shall be paid as required pursuant to Section 507 of the Bankruptcy Code, provided that such claims do not exceed the amounts set forth in Plan R-2.

(e) *Secured Claims.* Secured debt claims shall be treated as provided in Plan R-2 subject to (i) modification based on updated appraisals of collateral values to be conducted by the Company and consistent with the applicable provisions of the Bankruptcy Code, or (ii) such other terms as shall be reasonably satisfactory to the Company and Investor.

(f) *Unsecured Creditors.* In consideration for the shares and cash issued or paid, as the case may be, to the Unsecured Creditors pursuant to Section 4(a)(2)(ii), the unsecured claims of the Unsecured Creditors shall be cancelled as specified in the Plan.

(g) *Equity Holders.* In consideration for (A) the right to purchase shares pursuant to Section 4(a)(2)(iii), (B) the shares issued to the Equity Holders pursuant to Section 4(a)(2)(iii), and (C) the Warrants issued to the Equity Holders pursuant to Section 4(a)(3)(ii), the equity interests of the Equity Holders shall be cancelled as specified in the Plan.

(h) *Leases*. All aircraft leases which have been assumed prior to the date hereof will be honored by the Company in accordance with their terms and without reduction of rentals thereunder, provided that with the consent of the Company, Investor and any applicable lessor, any such lease may be amended to reduce the rentals payable thereunder, it being understood that, in consideration of any such amendment and with the consent of the Creditors' Committee, securities of the Company may be issued to such lessors from securities otherwise allocable to the Unsecured Parties to the extent consistent with any agreement in writing entered into by Investor and the Equity Committee on or before the date hereof.

(i) *Kawasaki*. The contractual right of Kawasaki Leasing International Inc. ("*Kawasaki*") to require the Company to lease certain aircraft and aircraft engines shall be modified on terms satisfactory to the Company, Investor and Kawasaki or, in the absence of such modification, honored.

(j) *GPA*. In consideration for (A) the shares issued to GPA pursuant to Section 4(a)(2)(iv), (B) the Warrants issued to GPA pursuant to Section 4(a)(3)(iii), (C) the Notes and cash issued or paid, as the case may be, to GPA pursuant to Section 4(a)(4) and (D) the granting to GPA on the Effective Date of the right (the "*New GPA Put*") to require the Company to lease from GPA on or prior to June 30, 1999, up to eight aircraft of types consistent with the fleet currently operated by the Company, GPA shall, as specified in the Plan, cancel and waive all rights to put any aircraft to the Company which it may have pursuant to the Put Agreement between GPA and the Company, dated as of June 25, 1991 (the "*GPA Put Agreement*") and/or the related Agreement Regarding Rights of First Refusal for A320 Aircraft, dated as of September 1, 1992 (the "*First Refusal Agreement*") and all other claims of any kind or nature arising out of or in connection with the GPA Put Agreement and/or the First Refusal Agreement (other than claims for reimbursement of expenses incurred by GPA in connection therewith). Each such lease shall provide for the payment by the Company of a fair market rental (determined at or about the time of delivery of the related aircraft to the Company on the basis of rentals then prevailing in the marketplace for comparable leases of comparable aircraft to lessees of comparable creditworthiness); and each such lease shall have such other terms and provisions and be in such form as is agreed upon by the Company and GPA with the approval of Investor (which approval shall not be unreasonably withheld or delayed) and attached to the agreement pursuant to which GPA is granted the New GPA Put.

(k) *Prepetition Aircraft Purchase Contracts*. The prepetition contract for the purchase of aircraft between the Company and The Boeing Company shall either be modified on terms satisfactory to Investor, the Company and The Boeing Company or, in the absence of such agreement, rejected. The Company's aircraft purchase contract with ANSA, S.A.R.L. ("*Airbus*") shall be amended on terms consistent with the provisions of the AmWest-A320 Term Sheet, dated as of February 23, 1994 by and between Investor and Airbus.

(l) *Employees*. The Company shall have the right to release employees from all currently existing obligations to the Company in respect of shares of Company stock purchased by such employees pursuant to the Company's stock purchase plan, such release to be in consideration for the cancellation of such shares.

(m) *Exculpation*. The Plan will contain customary exculpation provisions for the benefit of the Creditors' Committee and the Equity Committee and their respective professionals.

SECTION 8.*Conditions to Investor's Obligations Relating to the Investment*. The obligations of Investor to consummate the Investment and the other transactions contemplated herein shall be subject to the satisfaction, or the written waiver by Investor, of the following conditions:

(a) an initial order approving the Procedures Agreement, which order shall be in form and substance reasonably satisfactory to Investor (the "*Initial Order*"), shall have been entered by the Bankruptcy Court on or prior to May 6, 1994 and, once entered, shall be in effect and shall not be modified in any material respect or stayed;

(b) subject to Section 10(b), the Company and Investor, as applicable, shall have received all Regulatory Approvals, which shall have become final and nonappealable or any period of objection by Regulatory Authorities shall have expired, as applicable, and all other material approvals, permits, authorizations, consents, licenses and agreements from other third parties that are necessary or appropriate to permit the Investment and the other transactions contemplated hereby and by the Related Agreements and to permit the Company to carry on its business after the Effective Date in a manner consistent in all material respects with the manner in which it was carried on prior to the Effective Date (collectively with Regulatory Approvals, the "*Approvals*"), which Approvals shall not contain any condition or restriction that, in Investor's reasonable judgment, materially impairs the Company's ability to carry on its business in a manner consistent in all material respects with prior practice or as proposed to be carried on by the reorganized Company;

(c) the certificate of incorporation and bylaws of the Company shall contain the terms contemplated by this Agreement and shall otherwise be reasonably satisfactory to Investor;

(d) there shall be in effect no injunction, stay, restraining order or decree issued by any court of competent jurisdiction, whether foreign or domestic, staying the effectiveness of any of the Approvals, the Initial Order or the Confirmation Order, and there shall not be pending any request or motion for any such injunction, stay, restraining order or decree; provided, however, that the foregoing condition shall not apply to any such injunction, stay, order or decree requested, initiated or supported by Investor or any of its partners or other Affiliates or to any such request or motion made, initiated or supported by Investor or any its partners or other Affiliates;

(e) there shall not be threatened or pending any suit, action, investigation, inquiry or other proceeding (collectively, "*Proceedings*") by or before any court of competent jurisdiction or Regulatory Authority (excluding the Company's bankruptcy case, but including adversary proceedings and contested matters in such bankruptcy case, and excluding any such Proceedings fully and accurately disclosed by the Company in Schedule 1 hereto), or any adverse development occurring since December 31, 1993 in any such Proceedings, which Proceedings or development, singly or in the aggregate, in the good faith judgment of Investor, are reasonably likely to have a material adverse effect on the Company's ability to carry on its business in a manner consistent in all material respects with prior practices or are reasonably likely to impair in any material respect Investor's ability to realize the intended benefits and value of this Agreement, the Procedures Agreement or any Related Agreement; provided, however, that the foregoing condition shall not apply to any such Proceeding or development requested, initiated or supported by Investor or any of its partners or other Affiliates;

(f) the Company shall have delivered to Investor appropriate closing documents, including the instruments evidencing the Securities being issued to Investor, certifications of the Company officers (including, but not limited to, incumbency certificates, and certificates as to the truth and correctness of statements made in the Disclosure Statement or any other offering document distributed in connection with any securities issued in respect of this Agreement or the Related Agreements) and opinions of legal counsel, all of which shall be reasonably satisfactory to Investor;

(g) by no later than March 31, 1994, the Company shall have delivered to Investor audited financial statements as of December 31, 1993, and for the year then ended, which statements shall reflect a financial performance and a financial position of the Company consistent in all material respects with the unaudited results previously announced by the Company for such year, and, if requested by Investor, the Company shall have discussed such financial statements with Investor and provided an opportunity for Investor to discuss such financial statements with the Company's auditors;

(h) since December 31, 1993, except for the matters disclosed in Schedule I hereto, no material adverse change in the Company's condition (financial or otherwise), business, assets, properties, operations or relations with employees or labor unions shall have occurred and no matter (except for the matters disclosed in Schedule I hereto) shall have occurred or come to the attention of Investor that, in the reasonable judgment of Investor, is likely to have any such material adverse effect;

(i) the following shall be true in all material respects (in each case based on the Company's actual monthly or daily financial statements, which shall be prepared by the Company in a manner consistent in all material respects with its historical monthly and daily financial statements previously furnished to Investor): (A) the Company's actual monthly Operating Cash Flow (as defined on the Monthly Targets Schedule) shall not, in any month, be less than the minimum amount therefor established as part of the Monthly Targets, (B) the Company's actual 4 month Rolling Cash Flow (as defined on the Monthly Targets Schedule) shall not be less, as of the end of any four calendar month period, than the minimum amount therefor established as part of the Monthly Targets, (C) the Company's actual end of month Reported Cash Balance (as defined in the Monthly Targets Schedule) shall not, as of the end of any calendar month, be less than the minimum amount therefor established as part of the Monthly Targets, (D) the Company's actual five-day average Minimum Cash Balance (as defined in the Monthly Targets Schedule) shall not be, as of the end of any five day period, less than the minimum amount therefor established as part of the Monthly Targets; (E) the Company shall not have taken any actions which the Company knew or reasonably should have known would likely impair or hinder in any material respect the Company's ability to achieve the Projections; (F) the amount and nature of the obligations and liabilities (including, without limitation, tax liabilities and administrative expense claims) required to be paid by the Company on the Effective Date or to be paid by the Company following the Effective Date pursuant to obligations assumed by the Company during the course of its bankruptcy proceedings shall not be in excess of the amounts reflected in Plan R-2 plus any additional allowances provided in Section 7 (as reduced by any repayments of the existing debtor-in-possession loan made on or prior to the Effective Date) and shall not be materially different in nature than those specified in Plan R-2 (except with respect to administrative claims not known to the Company when Plan R-2 was developed); and (G) the Company shall have paid all fees and expenses due Investor under the Procedures

Agreement;

(j) since the date hereof, there shall have occurred no outbreak or escalation of hostilities or other international or domestic calamity, crisis or change in political, financial or economic conditions or other adverse change in the financial markets that impairs (or could reasonably be expected to impair in any material respect the Company's ability to carry on its business in a manner consistent in all material respects with prior practice or impairs (or could reasonably be expected to impair) in any material respect Investor's ability to realize the intended benefits and value of this Agreement or any Related Agreement;

(k) the Related Agreements, including all Alliance Agreements, to be executed by the Company shall have been executed by the Company on or before the Effective Date and, once executed, shall not have been modified without the consent of Investor, shall be in effect and shall not have been stayed;

(1) the Company shall have performed in all material respects all obligations on its part required to be performed on or before the Effective Date under this Agreement, the Procedures Agreement and the Related Agreements and all orders of the Bankruptcy Court in respect thereof that are consistent with the provisions of such instruments;

(m) all representations and warranties of the Company under this Agreement, the Procedures Agreement and the Related Agreements shall be true in all material respects as of the Effective Date;

(n) the Plan and Disclosure Statement each shall have been filed by the Company on or prior to May 15, 1994, and, once filed, shall have been served by the Company on all appropriate parties and, once served, shall not have been modified in any material respect without the prior consent of Investor (which consent shall not be unreasonably withheld), withdrawn by the Company or dismissed;

(o) the Disclosure Statement (in the form approved by the Bankruptcy Court and as amended or supplemented, if applicable) shall have been true and correct in all material respects as of the date first mailed to Unsecured Parties and as of the date fixed by the Bankruptcy Court for voting on the Plan and such Disclosure Statement shall not contain any untrue statement of a material fact or omit to state any material fact necessary in order to make the statements made therein (taken as a whole), in light of the circumstances under which they were made, not misleading; provided, however, that the foregoing condition shall not apply to statements or other information furnished or provided by Investor or any of its Affiliates for use in the Disclosure Statement;

(p) the order approving the Disclosure Statement shall have been entered by the Bankruptcy Court on or prior to June 30, 1994, and, once entered, shall not have been modified in any material respect, shall be in effect and shall not have been stayed;

(q) the Plan (including all securities of the Company to be issued pursuant thereto and all contracts, instruments, agreements and other documents to be entered into in connection therewith), the Disclosure Statement and the Confirmation Order shall be consistent with the terms of this Agreement and otherwise reasonably satisfactory in form and substance to Investor;

(r) the Confirmation Order shall have been entered by the Bankruptcy Court in form reasonably satisfactory to Investor on or before August 15, 1994, and, once entered, shall not have been modified in any material respect, shall be in effect and shall not have been stayed and shall not be subject to any appeal;

(s) the Effective Date shall have occurred on or prior to the Outside Date unless the reason therefor shall be attributable to the breach by Investor or its Affiliates of any of their respective representations, warranties, covenants or obligations contained herein or in the Procedures Agreement or any Related Agreement;.

(t) either pursuant to the Confirmation Order or otherwise, the Bankruptcy Court shall have established one or more bar dates for administrative expense claims pursuant to an order reasonably acceptable to Investor, which bar date or dates shall occur on or before dates reasonably acceptable to Investor; and

(u) the Securities and Exchange Commission shall have declared effective a shelf registration statement with respect to the Securities issuable to Investor.

In the event any of the conditions set forth in clause (a)-(n), (p) or (r) is not satisfied by the date specified in such clause (the "*Deadline*"), then, on the 15th day following the then current Deadline, the Deadline shall be automatically extended on a day-to-day basis unless the Company and Investor otherwise agree in writing or unless Investor gives a notice of termination to the Company pursuant to Section 20(b) of the Procedures Agreement within such 15-day period. If any Deadline is automatically extended as aforesaid, Investor may thereafter establish a new Deadline by giving notice to the Company specifying the new Deadline, provided that the new Deadline may not be sooner than 30 days after the date of such notice.

SECTION 9. *Conditions to Company's Obligations Relating to Investment.* The Company's obligations to consummate or to cause the consummation of the issuance and sale of the Securities and the other transactions contemplated by this Agreement shall be subject to the satisfaction, or to the effective written waiver by the Company, of the condition described in Section 8(b) and the following additional conditions:

(a) payment of the Purchase Price;

(b) Investor shall have delivered to the Company appropriate closing documents, including, but not limited to, executed counterparts of the Related Agreements and certifications of officers, and opinions of legal counsel, all of which shall be reasonably satisfactory to the Company;

(c) there shall be in effect no injunction, stay, restraining order or decree issued by any court of competent jurisdiction, whether foreign or domestic, staying the effectiveness of any of the Approvals, the Initial Order or the Confirmation Order, and there shall not be pending any request or motion for any such injunction, stay, restraining order or decree; provided, however, that the foregoing condition shall not apply to any such injunction, stay, order or decree requested, initiated or supported by the Company or to any such request or motion made, initiated or supported by the Company;

(d) the Related Agreements to be executed by Investor or any of its partners shall have been executed by such parties on or before the Effective Date and, once executed, shall not have been modified without the consent of the Company, shall be in effect and shall not have been stayed;

(e) Investor, Continental and Mesa shall have performed in all material respects all obligations on their part required to be performed on or before the Effective Date under this Agreement, the Procedures Agreement and the Related Agreements and all orders of the Bankruptcy Court in respect thereof that are consistent with the provisions of such instruments;

(f) all representations and warranties of Investor, Continental and Mesa under this Agreement, the Procedures Agreement and the Related Agreements shall be true and correct in all material respects as of the Effective Date;

(g) the Company shall be reasonably satisfied that the Alliance Agreements, when fully implemented, shall result in an increase to the Company's pretax income of not less than $40 million per year; provided, however, that Investor shall have no liability for any failure of the Company to achieve any such increase in net income except to the extent such failure results from a default by Investor or its partners pursuant to the terms of such Alliance Agreements;

(h) since the date hereof, there shall have occurred (A) no outbreak or escalation of hostilities or other international or domestic calamity, crisis or change in political, financial or economic conditions or other adverse change in the financial markets or (B) any adverse change in the condition (financial or otherwise), business, assets, properties or prospects of Continental or Mesa, in each case that materially impairs the ability of either Continental or Mesa to perform its obligations under the Alliance Agreements or the Company's ability to realize the intended benefits and value of this Agreement, the Alliance Agreements (as contemplated by clause (g) above) or the other Related Agreements;

(i) since the time of their initial filing by the Company, neither the Plan nor the Disclosure Statement shall have been modified in any material respect without the prior consent of the Company (which consent shall not be unreasonably withheld or delayed), withdrawn by Investor or dismissed;

(j) the certificate of incorporation and bylaws of the Company shall contain the terms contemplated by this Agreement and shall otherwise be reasonably satisfactory to the Company;

(k) the Plan (including all Securities to be issued pursuant thereto and all contracts, instruments, agreements and other documents to be entered into in connection therewith), the Disclosure Statement and the Confirmation Order shall be consistent with the terms of this Agreement and otherwise reasonably satisfactory in form and substance to the Company;

(l) the Confirmation Order shall have been entered by the Bankruptcy Court in form reasonably acceptable to the Company and, once entered, shall not have been modified in any material respect, shall be in effect and shall not have been stayed and shall not be subject to any appeal; and

(m) the Effective Date shall have occurred on or prior to the Outside Date unless the reason therefor shall be attributable to the breach by the Company of any of its representations, warranties, covenants or obligations contained herein or in the Procedures Agreement or any Related Agreement.

SECTION 10. *Cooperation.* (a) The Company and Investor will cooperate in a commercially reasonable manner, and will use their respective commercially reasonable efforts, to consummate the transactions contemplated hereby, including all commercially reasonable efforts to satisfy the conditions specified in this Agreement. The Company will use commercially reasonable efforts, and Investor will cooperate in a commercially reasonable manner in seeking, to obtain all Approvals.

(b) Notwithstanding anything in Section 8 or 9 to the contrary, if prior to the Outside Date, the Department of Justice or any other Regulatory Authority raises any antitrust objection to the consummation of the Investment or the implementation of any Alliance Agreement, which objection has not been resolved on or before the Outside Date, Investor nevertheless shall be required to consummate the Investment and, to that end, agrees to timely make such adjustment to the composition of its partnership and to the

Alliance Agreements as required to resolve such antitrust objection; provided, however, that nothing in this paragraph (b) shall affect the rights of the Company under Section 9(g) or obligate the Company to enter into or approve any adjustment or modification of the Alliance Agreements which, in the Company's reasonable judgment, is prejudicial to the Company or the Unsecured Parties in any material respect and which, if entered into or approved, would materially impair the Company's ability to realize the reasonably anticipated benefits of such Alliance Agreements.

SECTION 11. *Registration Rights Agreement.* Investor and the Company will enter into a registration rights agreement on terms acceptable to Investor and the Company. The registration rights agreement will reflect the understanding of the parties with respect to their registration rights and obligations and will provide that Investor, its partners and any assignees and transferees, shall have the right to cause the Company to (i) include the Securities issuable to Investor pursuant to the Plan (including any such Securities issued or issuable in respect of the Warrants or by way of any stock dividend or stock split or in connection with any combination of shares, merger, consolidation or similar transaction), on customary terms, in "piggyback" underwritings and registrations and (ii) to effect, on customary terms, one demand registration under the Securities Act for the public offering and sale of the Securities issued to Investor under the Plan at any time after the third anniversary of the Effective Date.

SECTION 12. *Applicable Provisions of Law and Regulations.* It is understood and agreed that this Agreement shall not create any obligation of, or restriction upon, the Company or Investor or the partners of Investor that would violate applicable provisions of law or regulation relating to ownership or control of a U.S. air carrier. At all times after the Effective Date, the certificate of incorporation of the Company shall provide that, in the event persons who are not U.S. citizens shall own (beneficially or of record) or have voting control over shares of Common Stock, the voting rights of such persons shall be subject to automatic suspension as required to ensure that the Company is in compliance with applicable provisions of law or regulation relating to ownership or control of a U.S. air carrier.

SECTION 13. *Representations and Warranties of the Company.* The Company represents and warrants to Investor as follows:

(a) The Company has complied in all material respects with the terms of all orders of the Bankruptcy Court in respect of the Investment, this Agreement and the Procedures Agreement.

(b) The Company has delivered to Investor copies of the audited balance sheets of the Company as of December 31, 1992 and the statements of income, stockholders equity and cash flows for the years then ended, together with the notes thereto. Such financial statements, and when delivered to Investor the financial statements of the Company referred to in Section 8(g) will, present fairly, in accordance with generally accepted accounting principles (applied on a consistent basis except as disclosed in the footnotes thereto), the financial position and results of operations of the Company as of the dates and for the periods therein set forth.

(c) When delivered to Investor, the unaudited financial statements of the Company referred to in Section 15 (b)(ii) will (i) present fairly, in accordance with generally accepted accounting principles (applied on a consistent basis except as disclosed therein and subject to normal year-end audit adjustments), the financial position and results of operations of the Company as of the date and for the period therein set forth, it being understood and agreed, however, that the foregoing representation relating to conformity with generally accepted accounting principles is being made only to the extent such principles are applicable to interim unaudited reports and (ii) reflect a financial position and results of operations not materially worse than those set forth in the pro forma financial statements contained in Plan 9.

(d) The Projections and the Monthly Targets were prepared in good faith on a reasonable basis, and when prepared represented the Company's best judgment as to the matters set forth therein, taking into account all relevant facts and circumstances known to the Company. Nothing has come to the Company's attention since the dates on which the Projections and the Monthly Targets, respectively, were prepared which causes the Company to believe that any of the projections and other information contained therein were misleading or inaccurate in any material respect as of such dates. It is specifically understood and agreed that the delivery of the Projections and the Monthly Targets shall not be regarded as a representation, warranty or guarantee that the particular results reflected therein will in fact be achieved or are likely to be achieved.

(e) No written statement, memorandum, certificate, schedule or other written information provided (or to be provided) to Investor or any of its representatives by or on behalf of the Company in connection with the transactions contemplated hereby, when viewed together with all other written statements and information provided to Investor and its representatives by or on behalf of the Company, in light of the circumstances under which they were made, (i) contains or will contain any materially misleading statement or (ii) omits or will omit to state any material fact necessary to make the statements therein not misleading.

(f) The board of directors of the Company has approved the Investment and Investor's acquisition of Securities hereunder for purposes of, and in accordance with the provisions and requirements of, Section 203 (a)(1) of the General Corporation Law of the State of Delaware and, as a consequence, Investor will not be subject to the provisions of such Section with respect to any "business combination" between Investor and the Company (as such term is defined in said Section 203).

SECTION 14. *Representations and Warranties of Investor.* Investor represents and warrants to the Company as follows:

(a) The general and limited partners of Investor (other than one such partner which will elect to suspend the voting rights of its Securities as contemplated by Section 4(b)) are U.S. citizens within the meaning of Section 101(16) of the Federal Aviation Act of 1958, as amended.

(b) Investor has, or has commitments for, sufficient funds to pay the Purchase Price and otherwise perform its obligations under this Agreement.

(c) No written statement, memorandum, certificate, schedule or other written information provided (or to be provided) to the Company or any of its representatives by or on behalf of Investor in connection with the transactions contemplated by the Alliance Agreements, when viewed together with all other written statements and information provided to the Company and its representatives by or on behalf of Investor, in light of the circumstances under which they were made, (i) contains or will contain any materially misleading statement or (ii) omits or will omit to state any material fact necessary to make the statements therein not misleading.

SECTION 15. *Covenants.* (a) Investor covenants (i) to support, subject to management's recommendation, increases in employee compensation through 1995 at least equal to those set forth in Plan R-2 and (ii) after the Effective Date, to cause the board of directors of the Company to consider implementation of a broad based employee incentive compensation plan and a management stock incentive plan.

(b) The Company covenants (i) to use commercially reasonable efforts to cause the shelf registration statement referred to in Section 8(u) to remain effective for three years following its effective date and (ii) as soon as available, to deliver to Investor a copy of the unaudited balance sheet of the Company as of the end of each fiscal quarter of the Company prior to the Effective Date and the unaudited statements of income and cash flows for the periods then ended.

SECTION 16. *Certain Taxes.* The Company shall bear and pay all transfer, stamp or other similar taxes (if any are not exempted under Section 1146 of the Bankruptcy Code) imposed in connection with the issuance and sale of the Securities.

SECTION 17. *Administrative Expense.* All amounts owed to Investor or its assignees by the Company under this Agreement, the Related Agreements, the Procedures Agreement and all orders of the Bankruptcy Court in respect thereof shall be treated as an allowed administrative expense priority claim under Section 507 (a)(1) of the Bankruptcy Code.

SECTION 18. *Incorporation by Reference*. The provisions set forth in the Procedures Agreement, including, but not limited to, the provisions regarding confidentiality, liability indemnity and termination, are hereby incorporated by reference and such provisions shall have the same force and effect herein as if they were expressly set forth herein in full.

SECTION 19. *Notices*. All notices, requests and other communications hereunder must be in writing and will be deemed to have been duly given only if delivered personally or by facsimile transmission or mailed (first class postage prepaid) or by prepaid express courier to the parties at the following addresses or facsimile numbers:

If to the Company:	America West Airlines, Inc. 4000 East Sky Harbor Boulevard Phoenix, Arizona 85034 Attention: William A. Franke and Martin J. Whalen Fax Number: (602) 693-5904
with a copy to:	LeBoeuf, Lamb, Greene & MacRae 633 17th Street, Suite 2800 Denver, Colorado 80202 Attention: Carl A. Eklund Fax Number: (303) 297-0422
and a copy to:	Andrews & Kurth L.L.P. 4200 Texas Commerce Tower Houston, Texas 77002 Attention: David G. Evans Fax Number: (713) 220-4285
and a copy to:	Murphy, Weir & Butler 101 California Street, 39th Floor San Francisco, California 94111 Attention: Patrick A. Murphy Fax Number: (415) 421-7879
and a copy to:	Lord, Bissell and Brook 115 South LaSalle Street Chicago, IL 60603 Attention: Benjamin Waisbren Fax Number: (312) 443-0336

If to Investor:	AmWest Partners, L.P. 201 Main Street, Suite 2420 Fort Worth, Texas 76102 Attention: James G. Coulter Fax Number: (817) 871-4010
with a copy to:	Arnold & Porter 1200 New Hampshire Ave., N.W. Washington, D.C. 20036 Attention: Richard P. Schifter Fax Number: (202) 872-6720
and a copy to:	Jones, Day, Reavis & Pogue North Point 901 Lakeside Avenue Cleveland, Ohio 44114 Attention: Lyle G. Ganske Fax Number: (216) 586-7864
and a copy to:	Goodwin, Procter & Hoar Exchange Place Boston, MA 02109 Attention: Laura Hodges Taylor, P.C. Fax Number: (617) 523-1231
and a copy to:	Murphy, Weir & Butler 101 California Street, 39th Floor San Francisco, California 94111 Attention: Patrick A. Murphy Fax Number: (415) 421-7879
and a copy to:	Lord, Bissell and Brook 115 South LaSalle Street Chicago, IL 60603 Attention: Benjamin Waisbren Fax Number: (312) 443-0336

All such notices, requests and other communications will (i) if delivered personally to the address as provided in this Section, be deemed given upon delivery, (ii) if delivered by facsimile transmission to the facsimile number as provided in this Section, be deemed given upon receipt, and (iii) if delivered by mail or by express courier in the manner described above to the address as provided in this Section, be deemed given upon receipt (in each case regardless of whether such notice is received by any other person to whom a copy of such notice, request or other communication is to be delivered pursuant to this Section). Either party from time to time may change its address, facsimile number or other information for the purpose of notices to that party by giving notice specifying such change to the other party hereto.

SECTION 20. *Governing Law.* Except to the extent inconsistent with the Bankruptcy Code, this Agreement shall in all respects be governed by and construed in accordance with the laws of the State of Arizona, without reference to principles of conflicts or choice of law under which the law of any other jurisdiction would apply.

SECTION 21. *Amendment.* This Agreement may only be amended, waived, supplemented or modified by a written instrument signed by authorized representatives of Investor and the Company. Investor may extend the time for satisfaction of the conditions set forth in Section 8 (prior to or after the relevant date) by notifying the Company in writing. The Company may extend the time for satisfaction of the conditions set forth in Section 9 (prior to or after the relevant date) by notifying Investor in writing.

SECTION 22. *No Third Party Beneficiary.* This Agreement and the Procedures Agreement are made solely for the benefit of the Company and Investor and their respective permitted assigns, and no other Person (including, without limitation, employees, stockholders and creditors of the Company) shall have any right, claim or cause of action under or by virtue of this Agreement or the Procedures Agreement, except to the extent such Person is entitled to protection as contemplated by Section 28(b) or to expense reimbursement pursuant to the Procedures Agreement or may assert a claim for indemnity pursuant to the Procedures Agreement.

SECTION 23. *Assignment.* Except as otherwise provided herein, Investor may assign all or part of its rights under this Agreement to any of its partners (each of whom may assign all or part to its Affiliates) or to any fund or account managed or advised by Fidelity Management Trust Company or any of its Affiliates and may assign any Securities (or the right to purchase any Securities) to any lawfully qualified Person or Persons, and the Company may assign this Agreement to any Person with which it may be merged or consolidated or to whom substantially all of its assets may be transferred in facilitation of the consummation of the Plan and the effectuation of the issuance and sale of the Securities as contemplated hereby or by the Related Agreements. None of such assignments shall relieve the Company or Investor of any obligations hereunder, under the Procedures Agreement or under the Related Agreements.

SECTION 24. *Counterparts.* This Agreement may be executed by the parties hereto in counterparts and by telecopy, each of which shall be deemed to constitute an original and all of which together shall constitute one and the same instrument. With respect to signatures transmitted by telecopy, upon request by either party to the other party, an original signature of such other party shall promptly be substituted for its facsimile.

SECTION 25. *Invalid Provisions.* If any provision of this Agreement is held to be illegal, invalid or unenforceable under any present or future laws, rules or regulations, and if the rights or obligations of Investor and the Company under this Agreement will not be materially and adversely affected thereby, (a) such provision will be fully severable, (b) this Agreement will be construed and enforced as if such illegal, invalid or unenforceable provision had never comprised a part hereof, (c) the remaining provisions of this Agreement will remain in full force and effect and will not be affected by the illegal, invalid or unenforceable provision or by its severance herefrom, and (d) in lieu of such illegal, invalid or unenforceable provision, there will be added automatically as a part of this Agreement a legal, valid and enforceable provision as similar in terms to such illegal, invalid or unenforceable provision as may be possible. If the rights and obligations of Investor or the Company will be materially and adversely affected by any such provision held to be illegal, invalid or unenforceable, then unless such provision is waived in writing by the affected party in its sole discretion, this Agreement shall be null and void.

SECTION 26. *Tagalong Rights.* On the Effective Date, Investor shall enter into a written agreement for the benefit of all holders of Class B Common (other than Investor and its Affiliates) whereby Investor shall agree, for a period of three years after the Effective Date, not to sell, in a single transaction or related series of transactions, shares of Common Stock representing 51% or more of the combined voting power of all shares of Common Stock then outstanding unless such holders shall have been given a reasonable opportunity to participate therein on a pro rata basis and at the same price per share and on the same economic terms and conditions applicable to Investor, provided, however, that such obligation of Investor shall not apply to any sale of shares of Common Stock made by Investor (i) to any Affiliate of Investor, (ii) to any Affiliate of Investor's partners, (iii) pursuant to a bankruptcy or insolvency proceeding, (iv) pursuant to judicial order, legal process, execution or attachment, (v) in a widespread distribution registered under the Securities Act of 1933, as amended ("*Securities Act*") or (vi) in compliance with the volume limitations of Rule 144 (or any successor to such Rule) under the Securities Act.

SECTION 27. *Stock Legend.* All securities issued to Investor pursuant to the Plan shall be conspicuously endorsed with an appropriate legend to the effect that such securities may not be sold, transferred or otherwise disposed of except in compliance with (i) Section 26 and (ii) applicable securities laws.

SECTION 28. *Directors' Liability and Indemnification.* (a) Upon, and at all times after, consummation of the Plan, the certificate of incorporation of the Company shall contain provisions which (i) eliminate the personal liability of the Company's former, present and future directors for monetary damages resulting from breaches of their fiduciary duties to the fullest extent permitted by applicable law and (ii) require the Company, subject to appropriate procedures, to indemnify the Company's former, present and future directors and executive officers to the fullest extent permitted by applicable law. In addition, upon consummation of the Plan, the Company shall enter into written agreements with each person who is a director or executive officer of the Company on the date hereof providing for similar indemnification of such person and providing that no recourse or liability whatsoever with respect to this Agreement, the Procedures Agreement, the Related Agreements, the Plan or the consummation of the transactions contemplated hereby or thereby shall be had, directly or indirectly, by or in the right of the Company against such person. Notwithstanding anything contained herein to the contrary, the provisions of this Section 28 (a) shall not be applicable to any person who ceased being a director of the Company at any time prior to March 1, 1994.

(b) Investor agrees, on behalf of itself and its partners, that no recourse or liability whatsoever (except as provided by applicable law for intentional fraud, bad faith or willful misconduct) shall be had, directly or indirectly, against any person who is a director or executive officer of the Company on the date hereof with respect to this Agreement, the Procedures Agreement, the Related Agreements, the Plan or the consummation of the transactions contemplated hereby or thereby, such recourse and liability, if any, being expressly waived and released by Investor and its partners as a condition of, and in consideration for, the execution and delivery of this Agreement.

SECTION 29. *Jurisdiction of Bankruptcy Court.* The parties agree that the Bankruptcy Court shall have and retain exclusive jurisdiction to enforce and construe the provisions of this Agreement.

SECTION 30. *Interpretation.* In this Agreement, unless a contrary intention appears, (i) the words "herein", "hereof" and "hereunder" and other words of similar import refer to this Agreement as a whole and not to any particular Section or other subdivision and (ii) reference to any Section means such Section hereof. The Section headings herein are for convenience only and shall not affect the construction hereof. No provision of this Agreement shall be interpreted or construed against either party solely because such party or its legal representative drafted such provision.

SECTION 31. *Termination.* This Agreement shall terminate concurrently with the termination of the Procedures Agreement.

SECTION 32. *Entire Agreement.* The Agreement supersedes any and all other agreements (oral or written) between the parties in respect to the subject matter hereof other than the Procedures Agreement.

AMWEST PARTNERS, L.P.

AMWEST PARTNERS, L.P.

By: AmWest Genpar, Inc.,
its General Partner

By: ____________________

Title: ____________________

Accepted and Agreed to
this 21st day of April, 1994.

AMERICA WEST AIRLINES, INC.
as Debtor and Debtor-in-Possession

By: ______________________

Title: ______________________

PLAN OF REORGANIZATION

EXHIBIT B

STOCKHOLDERS' AGREEMENT

STOCKHOLDERS' AGREEMENT FOR AMERICA WEST AIRLINES, INC.

THIS STOCKHOLDERS' AGREEMENT FOR AMERICA WEST AIRLINES, INC. (this "*Agreement*") is entered into as of this __________ day of __________, 1994 by and among AmWest Partners, L.P., a Texas limited partnership ("*AmWest*"), GPA Group plc, a corporation organized under the laws of Ireland ("*GPA*"), __________ and __________ (collectively, the "*Stockholder Representatives*"), and America West Airlines, Inc., a Delaware corporation (the "*Company*").

RECITALS:

WHEREAS, on June 27, 1991, the Company filed a case seeking relief under Chapter 11 of the Bankruptcy Code in the United States Bankruptcy Court for the District of Arizona (the "*Bankruptcy Court*"); and

WHEREAS, on December 8, 1993, the Bankruptcy Court entered an Order on Motion to Establish Procedures for Submission of Investment Proposals (the "*Procedures Order*"); and

WHEREAS, pursuant to the Procedures Order, AmWest and the Company have entered into that certain Third Revised Investment Agreement dated April 21, 1994 (the "*Investment Agreement*"), contemplating an investment by AmWest in the Company (the "*Investment*") and providing for the consummation of the Company's Plan of Reorganization (the "*Plan*"); and

WHEREAS, on __________, 1994, the Bankruptcy Court entered an order confirming the Plan; and

WHEREAS, in consideration of the Investment, the Company has issued common stock of the Company ("*Common Stock*") consisting of Class A Common Stock ("*Class A Common*") and Class B Common Stock ("*Class B Common*") and warrants to purchase Class B Common to AmWest; and

WHEREAS, in exchange for the release and modification of certain agreements and claims, the Company has issued shares of Class B Common and warrants to purchase Class B Common to GPA; and

WHEREAS, pursuant to Section 6(b) of the Investment Agreement, the Official Committee of Equity Holders of America West Airlines, Inc., appointed in the Company's Chapter 11 case (the "*Equity Committee*") has appointed __________ as a Stockholder Representative; and

WHEREAS, pursuant to Section 6(b) of the Investment Agreement, the Official Committee of Unsecured Creditors of America West Airlines, Inc., appointed in the Company's Chapter 11 case (the "*Creditors' Committee*") has appointed __________ as a Stockholder Representative; and

WHEREAS, pursuant to Section 6(b) of the Investment Agreement, the Board of Directors of the Company, as constituted prior to consummation of the Plan, has appointed __________ as a Stockholder Representative; and

WHEREAS, the parties hereto have agreed to enter into this Agreement pursuant to Section 218(c) of Title 8 of the Delaware Code (the "*General Corporation Law*").

NOW, THEREFORE, in consideration of the premises herein and other good and valuable consideration, the receipt and sufficiency of which are hereby acknowledged, the parties hereto agree as follows:

1. Definitions.

"Affiliate" shall mean (i) when used with reference to any partnership, any person or entity that, directly or indirectly, owns or controls ten percent (10%) or more of either the capital or profit interests of such partnership or is a partner of such partnership or is a person or entity in which such partnership has a ten percent (10%) or greater direct or indirect equity interest and (ii) when used with reference to any corporation, any person or entity that, directly or indirectly, owns or controls ten percent (10%) or more of the outstanding voting securities of such corporation or is a person or entity in which such corporation has a ten percent (10%) or greater direct or indirect equity interest. In addition, the term "Affiliate," when used with reference to any person or entity, shall also mean any other person or entity that, directly or indirectly, controls or is controlled by or is under common control with such person or entity. As used in the preceding sentence, (A) the term "control" means the possession, directly or indirectly, of the power to direct or cause the direction of the management and policies of the entity referred to, whether through ownership of voting securities, by contract or otherwise and (B) the terms "controlling" and "controls" shall have meanings correlative to the foregoing. Notwithstanding the foregoing, neither the Company nor any Fidelity Fund will be deemed to be an Affiliate of AmWest or any of its partners.

"Alliance Agreements" shall have the meaning set forth in the Investment Agreement.

"AmWest Director" shall mean a director of the Company designated by AmWest pursuant to Section 2.1(a).

"Annual Meeting" shall mean an annual meeting of the shareholders of the Company.

"Board" shall mean the Company's Board of Directors.

"Bylaws" shall mean the Restated Bylaws adopted by the Company in accordance with Section 303 of the General Corporation Law pursuant to the Plan.

"Citizens of the United States" shall have the meaning set forth in Section 1301, Title 49, United States Code, as now in effect or as it may hereafter from time to time be amended.

"Continental" shall mean Continental Airlines, Inc. or any successor.

"Creditors' Committee Director" shall mean a director of the Company designated by the Creditors' Committee or otherwise pursuant to Section 2.1(b).

"Effective Date" shall mean the date upon which the Restated Certificate of Incorporation becomes effective in accordance with the Plan and the General Corporation Law.

"Equity Committee Director" shall mean a director of the Company designated by the Equity Committee or otherwise pursuant to Section 2.1(b).

"Fidelity Fund" shall mean a fund or account managed or advised by Fidelity Management Trust Company or any of its Affiliates or successor(s).

"GPA Director" shall mean a director of the Company designated by GPA pursuant to Section 2.1(c).

"Independent Company Director" shall mean a director of the Company designated pursuant to Section 2.1(b).

"Independent Directors" shall mean, collectively, the Creditors' Committee Directors, the Equity

Committee Director, and the Independent Company Director.

"Mesa" shall mean Mesa Airlines, Inc. or any successor.

"Public Offering" shall have the meaning set forth in Section 4.2.

"Restated Certificate of Incorporation" shall mean the Restated Certificate of Incorporation adopted by the Company in accordance with Section 303 of the General Corporation Law pursuant to the Plan.

"Stockholder Representatives" shall mean the persons identified as such in the recitals set forth above; provided that in the case of the death, resignation, removal or disability of a Stockholder Representative, his or her successor shall be designated by the remaining Stockholder Representatives, and upon providing a written acknowledgment to such effect to all other parties hereto and agreeing to be bound and subject to the terms hereof, shall become a Stockholder Representative.

"Third Annual Meeting" shall mean the first Annual Meeting after the third anniversary of the Effective Date.

2. Designation and Voting for Company Directors.

2.1 Until the Third Annual Meeting, subject to the exception set forth in Section 4.7(a), the Board shall consist of up to fifteen (15) persons, of whom nine (9) persons shall be AmWest Directors, five (5) persons shall be

Independent Directors and up to one (1) person shall be a GPA Director, all designated in accordance with the following procedure:

(a) The AmWest Directors designated on Exhibit A hereto shall serve until the first Annual Meeting following the Effective Date and until the successor to each such director shall be duly elected and qualified, or until their death, disability, removal or resignation. No less than thirty (30) days in advance of each Annual Meeting prior to (but not including) the Third Annual Meeting, and no less than five (5) days in advance of any other meeting of the Board at which a director will be elected to sit on the Board in a seat vacated by an AmWest Director because of death, disability, removal, resignation, or otherwise, AmWest shall give written notice to the other parties hereto designating the individual or individuals to serve as AmWest Directors. For so long as AmWest and/or its Affiliates holds at least five percent (5%) of the voting equity securities of the Company, GPA agrees to vote the Common Stock held and controlled by it and to cause the GPA Director to vote or provide written consents in favor of such designees and to take any other action necessary to elect such designees. The Stockholder Representatives agree to recommend to the Independent Directors to vote or provide written consents in favor of such designees and to take any other action necessary to elect such designees.

(b) Three (3) Creditors' Committee Directors, one (1) Equity Committee Director, and one (1) Independent Company Director, each as designated on Exhibit A hereto, shall serve until the first Annual Meeting following the Effective Date and until the successor to each such director shall be duly elected and qualified, or until their death, disability, removal or resignation. Until the Third Annual Meeting, the Company shall nominate for reelection, and AmWest and GPA shall vote the Common Stock held and controlled by them in favor of, each Independent Director designated on Exhibit A for so long as he or she continues to serve on the Board. No less than five (5) days in advance of any meeting of the Board at which a director will be elected to sit on the Board in a seat vacated by an Independent Director because of death, disability, removal, resignation or otherwise (a "Successor Independent Director"), and no less than thirty (30) days in advance of an Annual Meeting prior to (but not including) the Third Annual Meeting at which the term of any Successor Independent Director will expire, the Stockholder Representatives shall give written notice to the other parties hereto designating the individuals to serve as Independent Directors; except that if the Creditors' Committee or the Equity Committee remain in effect, they shall have the right to designate the Creditors' Committee Directors and the Equity Committee Director, respectively, or the individuals to fill vacancies thereof, by giving written notice to the other parties hereto in accordance with the terms set forth above and provided that the Stockholder Representatives shall select any Successor Independent Director to replace the Independent Company Director from among the executive officers of the Company. Each of AmWest and GPA agrees to vote the Common Stock held and controlled by them and to cause the AmWest Directors and the GPA Director, respectively, to vote or provide written consents in favor of such designees and to take any other action necessary to elect such designees; provided that each Independent Director shall be reasonably acceptable to AmWest at the time of his or her initial designation.

(c) The GPA Director designated on Exhibit A hereto shall serve until the first Annual Meeting following the Effective Date and until the successor to such director shall be duly elected and qualified or until his or her death, disability, removal, or resignation. No less than thirty (30) days in advance of each Annual Meeting prior to (but not including) the Third Annual Meeting, and no less than five (5) days in advance of any other meeting of the Board at which a director will be elected to sit on the Board in a seat vacated by the GPA Director because of death, disability, removal, resignation or otherwise, GPA shall give written notice to the other parties hereto designating the individual to serve as GPA Director. Unless the rights of GPA hereunder have been terminated pursuant to Section 6.2, AmWest agrees to vote the Common Stock held and controlled by it, and to cause the AmWest Directors, and the Stockholder Representatives agree to recommend to the Independent Directors, to vote or provide written consents in favor of such designee and to take any other action necessary to elect such designee; provided that the GPA Director shall be reasonably acceptable to AmWest at the time of his or her initial designation.

(d) Except as otherwise provided herein, each of AmWest, the Stockholder Representatives, and GPA agrees to nominate or cause the nomination of the AmWest Directors, the Independent Directors, and the GPA Director, respectively, in accordance with the Bylaws.

(e) Notwithstanding the foregoing, no party hereto shall be obligated to vote any shares for which the voting rights have been suspended, whether voluntarily or involuntarily.

(f) In the event that AmWest, the Creditors' Committee or Equity Committee (for so long as each is in existence and has the ability to designate a director as herein provided), the Stockholder Representatives, or GPA shall fail or refuse to designate a nominee to the Board for a position allocated to and to be filled by such group or entity as herein provided, such position shall not be filled and shall remain vacant unless and until such designation shall be made as herein provided.

(g) In the event that the rights and obligations of GPA with respect to this Agreement are terminated in accordance with Section 6.2, GPA agrees to cause the resignation of, or provide notice to the other parties hereto as provided in subsection (h)(i) below requesting removal of the GPA Director, at which time the Board shall be reduced to fourteen (14) persons.

(h) The parties hereto agree to (i) vote the Common Stock held and controlled by them in favor of the removal from the Board, upon notice by the group or entity having the right to designate such director under this Section 2.1 and requesting such removal, of any person or persons designated to the Board by such group or entity, and (ii) to vote the Common Stock held and controlled by them (other than stock held individually by any Stockholder Representative) and to cause (or in the case of the Stockholder Representatives, recommend to) the directors designated by them to vote or take such action as may be required under the General Corporation Law or otherwise to implement the provisions of this Agreement. The group or entity who has nominated any director in accordance with this Agreement shall have the exclusive right to remove or replace such director by written notice as herein provided; except that nothing in this agreement shall be construed to limit or prohibit the removal of any director for cause.

2.2 Until the Third Annual Meeting, at least eight of the AmWest Directors, at least two of the Creditors' Committee Directors, the Equity Committee Director, and the Independent Company Director shall each be Citizens of the United States.

2.3 AmWest agrees that no AmWest Director shall be an officer or employee of Continental.

3. Voting on Certain Matters.

3.1 Any Director who is selected by, or who is a director of, Continental shall recuse himself or herself from voting on, or otherwise receiving any confidential information regarding, matters in connection with negotiations between Continental and the Company (including, without limitation, negotiation between Continental and the Company of the Alliance Agreements) and matters in connection with any action involving direct competition between Continental and the Company. Any Director who is selected by, or who is a director, officer or employee of, Mesa shall recuse himself or herself from voting on, or otherwise receiving any confidential information regarding, matters in connection with negotiations between Mesa and the Company (including, without limitation, negotiation between Mesa and the Company of the Alliance Agreements) and matters in connection with any action involving direct competition between Mesa and the Company.

3.2 Until the Third Annual Meeting, the affirmative vote of the holders of a majority of the voting power of the outstanding shares of each class of common stock of the Company entitled to vote (excluding any shares owned by AmWest or any of its Affiliates, but not, however, excluding shares owned, controlled or voted by Mesa or any of its transferees that are not otherwise Affiliates of AmWest), voting as a single class, shall be required to approve, adopt or authorize:

(a) Any merger or consolidation of the Company with or into AmWest or any Affiliate of AmWest;

(b) Any sale, lease, exchange, transfer, or other disposition by the Company of all or any substantial part of the assets of the Company to AmWest or any Affiliate of AmWest;

(c) Any transaction with or involving the Company as a result of which AmWest or any of AmWest's Affiliates will, as a result of issuances of voting securities by the Company (or any other securities convertible into or exchangeable for such voting securities), acquire an increased percentage ownership of such voting securities, except for (i) the exercise of Warrants issued under the Plan, (ii) the conversion of Class A Common held by it to Class B Common, or (iii) otherwise pursuant to a transaction in which all holders of Class B Common may participate on a pro rata basis at the same price per share and on the same economic terms, including, without limitation, (A) a tender or exchange offer for all shares of the Common Stock and (B) a Public Offering; or

(d) Any related series or combination of transactions having or which will have, directly or indirectly, the same effect as any of the foregoing.

At the request of any party proposing such a transaction and subject to approval by the Board, the Company agrees to put to a vote of the shareholders the approval of any transaction referred to in subparagraphs (a) through (d) above (excluding the excepted transactions referred to in clauses (i), (ii), and (iii) of subparagraph (c)) at the next regular or any duly convened special meeting of the shareholders of the Company. The voting requirements specified above shall not be applicable to a proposed action which has been approved or recommended by at least three Independent Directors.

4. Further Covenants.

4.1 Neither AmWest nor any partner or Affiliate of AmWest or of any partner of AmWest shall sell or otherwise transfer any Common Stock (other than to an Affiliate of the transferor) if, after giving effect thereto and to any related transaction, the total number of shares of Class B Common beneficially owned by the transferor is less than twice the total number of shares of Class A Common beneficially owned by the transferor; *provided, however*, that nothing contained in this Section 4.1 shall prohibit any owner of Common Stock from selling or otherwise transferring, in a single transaction or related series of transactions, all shares of Common Stock owned by it, subject to the remaining provisions of this Agreement.

4.2 AmWest agrees that its constituent documents shall at all times require that this Agreement be binding upon all general and limited partners of AmWest and any Affiliate of AmWest or such partners who hold or receive shares of the Company for their own account or direct the voting of any shares held by AmWest and upon any assignees or transferees in a single transaction or a related series of transactions of all or substantially all of the Common Stock owned by AmWest or any of its partners or Affiliates of AmWest or any of their partners; *except* any assignment or transfer made contemporaneous with the consummation of the Plan to any Fidelity Fund or Funds; and *except* any assignee or transferee who acquires such Common Stock pursuant to (i) a tender or exchange offer open to all shareholders of the Company on a pro rata basis at the same price per share and on the same economic terms, (ii) a distribution registered under the Securities Act of 1933 (as amended, the "Securities Act") (a "Public Offering"), or (iii) a transfer made pursuant to Rule 144 (as amended, "Rule 144") under the Securities Act. AmWest shall not sell or transfer (including upon dissolution of AmWest) any Common Stock held by it to any of its general or limited partners, to any Fidelity Fund, or to any Affiliate of AmWest or such partners and AmWest shall not sell or transfer all or substantially all of the Common Stock held by it in a single transaction or a related series of transactions, except in accordance with clauses (i), (ii) or (iii), above, unless and until it causes any assignee or transferee to provide a written acknowledgment to the other parties hereto that it accepts and is bound and subject to the terms of this Agreement.

4.3 AmWest covenants and agrees that it shall not sell, in a single transaction or a related series of transactions, shares of Common Stock representing fifty one percent (51%) or more of the combined voting power of all shares of Common Stock then outstanding, other than (i) pursuant to or in connection with a tender or exchange offer for all shares of Common Stock and for the benefit of all holders of Class B Common on a pro rata basis at the same price per share and on the same economic terms, (ii) to any Affiliate of AmWest, (iii) to any Affiliate of AmWest's partners, (iv) pursuant to a bankruptcy or insolvency proceeding, (v) pursuant to a judicial order, legal process, execution or attachment, or (vi) in a Public Offering.

4.4 Within ten (10) days of the Effective Date, AmWest shall file with the Securities and Exchange Commission, a Schedule 13D pursuant to Regulation 13D-G ("Regulation 13D-G") under the Securities Exchange Act of 1934 (as amended, the "Exchange Act"), and shall amend such filing as required by Regulation 13D-G. Each other party hereto covered by such filing covenants and agrees to promptly provide to AmWest all information pertaining to such party and necessary to make such amendments and to notify AmWest of any changes in facts or circumstances pertaining to such party that would require any amendments under Regulation 13D-G.

4.5 AmWest agrees that it shall not cause any amendment to the provisions of the Restated Certificate of Incorporation or the Bylaws or otherwise take any action that supersedes or materially adversely affects or impairs the rights and obligations of the parties under this Agreement or is contrary to the provisions of this Agreement.

4.6 (a) Each certificate evidencing shares of Common Stock issued to AmWest or any of its partners, GPA and any of their respective Affiliates, and any assignee or transferee bound by the terms hereof, including shares of Common Stock issued in connection with the exercise of any warrant, so long as such Common Stock is held by them and prior to the termination or expiration of this Agreement, shall be conspicuously stamped or marked with a legend including substantially as follows:

> THE RIGHTS AND OBLIGATIONS OF THE HOLDER OF THIS CERTIFICATE SHALL BE SUBJECT TO THE TERMS AND PROVISIONS OF THAT CERTAIN STOCKHOLDERS' AGREEMENT DATED   , 1994, COPIES OF WHICH ARE ON FILE AT THE PRINCIPAL OFFICE OF AMERICA WEST AIRLINES, INC.

and each such certificate, for so long as such certificate is held by AmWest or any of its partners and any of their respective Affiliates and any assignee or transferee bound by the terms hereof and prior to the termination or expiration of this Agreement, shall include in such legend the following:

> THIS CERTIFICATE AND ANY INTEREST HEREIN MAY NOT BE SOLD, TRANSFERRED OR OTHERWISE DISPOSED OF EXCEPT IN ACCORDANCE WITH THE AFORESAID STOCKHOLDERS' AGREEMENT.

(b) All certificates evidencing shares of Common Stock and warrants of the Company that have not been registered pursuant to the Securities Act of 1933, as amended, and that are not exempt from registration under Section 1145 of the Bankruptcy Code, shall at all times be conspicuously stamped or marked with a legend including substantially as follows:

> THE SECURITIES REPRESENTED BY THIS CERTIFICATE HAVE NOT BEEN REGISTERED UNDER THE SECURITIES ACT OF 1933, AS AMENDED, AND THE RULES AND REGULATIONS THEREUNDER (THE "SECURITIES ACT") OR UNDER THE SECURITIES LAWS OF ANY STATE; AND SUCH SECURITIES MAY NOT BE SOLD OR TRANSFERRED OTHER THAN IN ACCORDANCE WITH THE REGISTRATION REQUIREMENTS OF THE SECURITIES ACT OR AN EXEMPTION THEREFROM AND FROM ANY APPLICABLE STATE SECURITIES LAWS.

(c) Upon the termination of this Agreement, the Company shall, without charge and upon surrender of certificates by the holders thereof and written request cancel all certificates evidencing shares of Common Stock bearing the legend described in subparagraph (a) above and issue to the holders thereof replacement certificates that do not bear such a legend for an equal number of shares held by such holders. Upon the transfer of any Common Stock bearing the legend described in subparagraph (a) above to a party not bound and subject to by this Agreement, the Company shall, without charge and upon the surrender of certificates by the holders thereof and written request cancel all certificates evidencing such shares of Common Stock and issue to the transferee thereof replacement certificates that do not bear such a legend.

4.7 During the term of this Agreement, AmWest shall not cause the issuance of any preferred stock that would (a) increase the number of directors in excess of the number provided in Section 2.1 (except for increases caused by a provision allowing holders of preferred stock to elect additional directors in the event of nonpayment of dividends) or (b) eliminate or reduce the number of Creditors' Committee Directors, Equity Committee Director, Independent Company Director, or GPA Director.

5. Rights Upon Breach.

5.1 Each party hereto recognizes and agrees that a violation of any term, provision, or condition of this Agreement may cause irreparable damage to the other parties which is difficult or impossible to quantify or ascertain and that the award of any sum of damages may not be adequate relief to such other parties. Each party hereto therefore agrees that in the event of any breach of this Agreement, the other party or parties shall, in addition to any remedies at law which may be available, have the right to obtain appropriate equitable (including, but not limited to, injunctive) relief. All remedies hereunder shall be cumulative and not exclusive.

5.2 In addition to any other remedies available at law or in equity, each party hereto agrees that the Company shall have the right (a) to withhold transfer, and to instruct any transfer agent for securities of the Company to withhold transfer, of any certificates evidencing shares of Common Stock held by AmWest or any partner or Affiliate of AmWest or transferee if the Company reasonably believes that such transfer would not be in material compliance with the terms and provisions of this Agreement, unless the transferee provides to the Company an opinion of legal counsel reasonably acceptable to the Company that such transfer will be in material compliance with the terms and provisions hereof, and (b) to require any person requesting such transfer to provide such information as may reasonably be requested by the Company regarding ownership of securities, affiliations, if any, between AmWest and the transferee and such other matters pertaining to the transfer as may be appropriate to enable the Company to determine the compliance of the proposed transfer of securities with the terms and provisions of this Agreement.

6. Termination.

6.1 This Agreement shall automatically terminate without any action by any party on the day immediately preceding the Third Annual Meeting and shall not be extended except in accordance with Section 7.3. Upon such termination, the rights and obligations of each party hereunder shall terminate and the provisions of this Agreement shall be of no force and effect; *provided* that no such termination shall relieve any person or entity from liability for breach or default of this Agreement prior to such termination.

6.2 GPA's rights and obligations under this Agreement (other than its obligations under Section 2.1 (g)) shall terminate immediately and without notice upon the earlier of (a) termination of this Agreement under Section 6.1, (b) the sale or transfer by GPA of equity securities of the Company resulting in the holding by GPA of less than two percent (2%) of the voting equity securities of the Company (on a fully diluted basis), or (c) any occurrence, other than as described in clause (b) above, resulting in the holding by GPA of less than two percent (2%) of the voting equity securities of the Company (on a fully diluted basis) if (i) the Company files a Form 10-Q under the Exchange Act, or other written report or statement, that is delivered to GPA and a copy to the party designated in Section 7.1, reflecting information as to the Company's total issued and capital stock from which GPA can determine whether it holds less than two percent (2%) of the voting equity securities of the Company (on a fully diluted basis) and (ii) GPA continues to hold less than two percent (2%) of the voting equity securities (on a fully diluted basis) for greater than thirty-five (35) days after delivery of such Form 10-Q, or provision of such report or statement to GPA. GPA acknowledges that the Company's continuing with its existing procedures for the distribution of Form- 10-Qs constitutes delivery to GPA within the meaning of this Section 6.2.

7. Miscellaneous.

7.1 All notices, requests and other communications hereunder must be in writing and will be deemed to have been duly given only if delivered personally or by facsimile transmission or mailed (first class postage prepaid) or by prepaid express courier at the following addresses or facsimile numbers:

If to AmWest:	AmWest Partners, L.P. 201 Main Street, Suite 2420 Fort Worth, Texas 76102 Attention: James G. Coulter Fax Number: (817) 871-4010
with a copy to:	Arnold & Porter 1200 New Hampshire Ave., N.W. Washington, D.C. 20036 Attention: Richard P. Schifter Fax Number: (202) 872-6720

and a copy to:	Jones, Day, Reavis & Pogue North Point 901 Lakeside Avenue Cleveland, Ohio 44114 Attention: Lyle G. Ganske Fax Number: (216) 586-7864
If to GPA:	GPA Group plc GPA House Shannon, Ireland Attention: Patrick H. Blaney Fax Number: 353 61 360220
with a copy to:	Paul, Hastings, Janofsky & Walker 399 Park Avenue, 31st Floor New York, New York 10022 Attention: Marguerite R. Kahn Fax Number: (212) 319-4090

If to ____________:
If to ____________:
If to ____________:

If to the Company:	America West Airlines, Inc. 4000 East Sky Harbor Boulevard Phoenix, Arizona 85034 Attention: General Counsel Fax Number: (602) 693-5904
with a copy to:	Andrews & Kurth, L.L.P. 4200 Texas Commerce Tower Houston, Texas 77002 Attention: David G. Elkins Fax Number: (713) 220-4285

All such notices, requests and other communications will (i) if delivered personally to the address as provided in this Section 7.1, be deemed given upon delivery, (ii) if delivered by facsimile transmission to the facsimile number as provided in this Section 7.1, be deemed given upon receipt, and (iii) if delivered by mail or by express courier in the manner described above to the address as provided in this Section 7.1, be deemed given upon receipt (in each case regardless of whether such notice is received by any other person to whom a copy of such notice, request or other communication is to be delivered pursuant to this Section 7.1). Any party from time to time may change its address, facsimile number or other information for the purpose of notices to that party by giving notice as provided in this Section 7.1 specifying such change to the other parties hereto. Nothing in this Section 7.1 shall be deemed or construed to alter the notice provisions contained in the Bylaws.

7.2 This Agreement shall in all respects be governed by and construed in accordance with the laws of the State of Delaware without reference to principles of conflicts or choice of law under which the law of any other jurisdiction would apply.

7.3 This Agreement may only be amended, waived, supplemented, modified or extended by a written instrument signed by authorized representatives of each party hereto.

7.4 This Agreement shall inure to the benefit of and be binding upon each of the parties hereto and their respective successors and permitted assigns.

7.5 This Agreement may be executed by the parties hereto in counterparts and by telecopy, each of which shall be deemed to constitute an original and all of which together shall constitute one and the same instrument.

7.6 If any term or provision of this Agreement shall be found by a court of competent jurisdiction to be illegal, invalid or unenforceable to any extent, the remainder of this Agreement shall not be affected thereby and shall be enforced to the greatest extent permitted by law.

7.7 The parties hereto intend that in the case of any conflict or inconsistency between this Agreement and the Restated Certificate of Incorporation or the Bylaws, that this Agreement shall control, and therefore in the event that any term or provision of this Agreement is rendered invalid, illegal or unenforceable by the Restated Certificate of Incorporation or the Bylaws, the parties agree to amend the Restated Certificate of Incorporation or the Bylaws (as the case may be) so as to render such term or provision valid, legal and enforceable, if and to the extent possible.

IN WITNESS WHEREOF, the parties hereto, by their respective officers thereunto duly authorized, have executed this Agreement as of the date first written above.

AMWEST PARTNERS, L.P.

By: AmWest Genpar, Inc., its General Partner

By: ______________________________
Name:
Title:

GPA GROUP PLC

By: ____________________________________
Name:
Title:

____
[Stockholder Representative]

____
[Stockholder Representative]

____
[Stockholder Representative]

AMERICA WEST AIRLINES, INC.

By: ____________________________________
Name:
Title:

PLAN OF REORGANIZATION

EXHIBIT C

GPA TERM SHEET

GPA TERM SHEET

This Term Sheet, dated as of June 13, 1994, sets forth the principal terms and conditions (the "Terms and Conditions") of the treatment to be afforded to the claims and interests of GPA Group plc and its affiliates (individually and collectively, "GPA") pursuant to a joint plan of reorganization (the "Plan") of America West Airlines, Inc. (the "Company") to be proposed and sponsored by the Company in conjunction with AmWest Partners, L.P. ("AmWest") under and in accordance with the Third Revised Investment Agreement, dated as of April 21, 1994, between the Company and AmWest (the "Investment Agreement") and the Third Revised Interim Procedures Agreement, dated as of April 21, 1994, between the Company and AmWest (the "Interim Procedures Agreement"). Except as otherwise defined herein, capitalized terms used herein have the meanings stated in the Investment Agreement.

Termination of Put Agreement .... On the Effective Date, GPA shall (i) cancel all rights of GPA to put any aircraft to the Company pursuant to the A320 Put Agreement, dated as of June 25, 1991, between the Company and GPA, as amended by the First Amendment thereto, dated as of September 1, 1992 (as so amended, the "Put Agreement") and the related Agreement Regarding Rights of First Refusal for A320 Aircraft, dated as of September 1, 1992 (the "First Refusal Agreement"), among the Company, GPA and Kawasaki Leasing International Inc., and (ii) waive, and covenant not to seek or assert, any and all claims of any kind or nature arising out of or in connection with the Put Agreement and/or the First Refusal Agreement, other than claims for reimbursement of expenses incurred by GPA in connection therewith. As of the date of this Term Sheet, GPA has been fully reimbursed by the Company for all expenses incurred by GPA in connection with the Put Agreement and the First Refusal Agreement.

Aircraft and Engine Subleases .... On the Effective Date, the Company shall ratify (without modification or amendment) all of its obligations (including, without limitation, rental obligations) under and in connection with (i) the sixteen separate Aircraft Sublease Agreements between the Company and GPA, and (ii) the three separate Engine Sublease Agreements between the Company and GPA (in each case, as such Sublease Agreement is more fully described on Schedule I to the Put Agreement and, in each case, as such Sublease Agreement was assumed by the Company pursuant to Section 365 of the Bankruptcy Code).

DIP Financing .... On the Effective Date, all amounts due and owing by the Company under the debtor-in-possession financing provided to the Company by GPA and other debtor-in-possession lenders shall be paid in full (it being understood that, upon receipt of such amounts, GPA shall take all such actions as are required to be taken by GPA pursuant to the documents relating to such financing to cause and evidence the release of all liens securing such financing and the termination of the transactions relating to such financing).

Common Stock .... On the Effective Date, GPA shall receive 900,000 shares of the Class B Common Stock of the Company (the "Class B Common Stock"), which shares shall represent two percent of the total amount of the Common Stock of the Company (without giving effect to exercise of the warrants described below and in the Investment Agreement) and which Class B Common Stock shall have the terms and provisions contemplated in the Investment Agreement.

Warrants .... On the Effective Date, GPA shall receive warrants to purchase up to 1,384,615 shares of Class B Common Stock, which shares shall represent 2.5% of the Common Stock of the Company on a fully diluted basis and which warrants shall be exercisable at a price determined in accordance with, and have such other terms and provisions as are described in, the Plan.

Cash .... On the Effective Date, GPA shall receive $30,525,000 in cash.

Board Seat .... Pursuant to and in accordance with the terms, provisions and conditions to be contained in a Stockholders' Agreement to be entered into among the reorganized Company, AmWest, GPA and certain other parties, and for so long as GPA owns at least two percent of the voting equity securities of the Company (on a fully diluted basis), GPA shall be allocated one seat, out of a total of fifteen seats, on the Board of Directors of the reorganized Company. The member of the Board of Directors of the reorganized Company designated by GPA shall be reasonably acceptable to AmWest at the time of his or her initial designation (it being understood that each of the persons currently serving as "independent directors" of AWA, Patrick Blaney, John Tierney and Declan Traecy shall be acceptable to AmWest for such purposes). AmWest and GPA will execute a voting agreement or similar arrangement pursuant to which (i) AmWest will agree to vote in favor of GPA's nominee to the Board of Directors of the reorganized Company, and (ii) GPA will agree to vote in favor of AmWest's nine nominees to the Board of Directors of the reorganized Company, in each case, for so long as (a) AmWest owns at least five percent of the vesting equity securities of the Company (on a fully diluted basis), and (b) GPA owns at least two percent of the voting equity securities of the Company (on a fully diluted basis).

New Puts .... GPA will be granted the right to deliver or put to the Company, and the Company will be obligated to lease from GPA, during the period beginning not later than June 30, 1995 and ending on June 30, 1999 (the "New Put Period"), up to eight new or used aircraft of types consistent with the Company's fleet plan and requirements (such right being referred to herein as the "New Put Right").

Each lease entered into by the Company in connection with the exercise by GPA of the New Put Right shall provide for the payment by the Company of a fair market rental for the related aircraft, taking into consideration whether the related aircraft is new or used, the specifications and condition of the related aircraft and all provisions of such lease that are relevant to the overall cost to the Company of the related aircraft, and determined at or about the time of delivery of such aircraft to the Company on the basis of operating lease rentals then prevailing in the marketplace for comparable operating leases of comparable aircraft to airlines of comparable creditworthiness to the Company (at or about the time of delivery of such aircraft to the Company and without regard to the prior pendency of the Case); each such lease will be for a lease term determined as hereinafter described; and each such lease shall have such other terms and provisions and be in such form as is agreed upon by the Company and GPA and attached to the agreement between the Company and GPA pursuant to which GPA is granted the New Put Right (such agreement being referred to herein as the "New Put Agreement").

The specific number, types and delivery dates for the aircraft which GPA will be entitled to deliver to the Company (and which the Company will be obligated to lease from GPA) in a particular year during the New Put Period (as well as whether such aircraft will be new or used aircraft) will be determined on the basis of mutual agreement by the Company and GPA, taking into account the Company's fleet requirements for such year, the availability to GPA for purposes of the New Put Agreement (in light of applicable commercial constraints) of aircraft during such year and the number of aircraft theretofore delivered and thereafter remaining to be delivered by GPA to the Company under the New Put Agreement; *provided, however*, that if, on or prior to the Mutual Agreement Deadline (as such term is hereinafter defined) for a particular year, the Company and GPA shall not have mutually agreed upon the specific number, types and delivery dates for the aircraft which GPA will be entitled to deliver to the Company (and which the Company will be obligated to lease from GPA) during such year (as well as whether such aircraft will be new or used aircraft), GPA will have the right to put to the Company (and the Company will be obligated to lease from GPA without any necessity for further agreement of the Company) up to the Maximum Number (as such term is hereinafter defined) of aircraft for such year, with (i) the specific types of such aircraft being selected by GPA from among the Eligible Types (as such term is hereinafter defined), (ii) such aircraft being new or used aircraft as selected by GPA, and (iii) the specific delivery dates for such aircraft being selected by GPA, in each case, upon at least 150 days' prior written notice by GPA to the Company; and *provided further, however*, that, unless GPA and the Company shall otherwise agree in writing (whether by reason of mutual agreement relevant to a particular year or otherwise), GPA will not have the right to put to the Company more than five used aircraft during the New Put Period. As used herein, the term "Mutual Agreement Deadline" means (i) with respect to each of 1995 and 1996, January 31, 1995, and (ii) with respect to each ensuing year during the New Put Period, January 1st of the preceding year. As used herein, the term "Maximum Number" means (i) with respect to 1995, two, and (ii) with respect to each ensuing year during the New Put Period, three. As used herein, and unless GPA and the Company shall otherwise agree in writing, the term "Eligible Types" means, with respect to the types of aircraft which GPA will be entitled to put to the Company without the necessity for further agreement of the Company, Boeing 737-300 aircraft, Boeing 757 aircraft and Airbus A320 aircraft...

The aircraft which GPA will be entitled to deliver or put to the Company (and which the Company will be obligated to lease from GPA) may be new or used aircraft; *provided, however*, that unless GPA and the Company shall otherwise agree in writing, GPA will not have the right to deliver or put to the Company more than five used aircraft during the New Put Period; and *provided further, however*, that any such aircraft which is an Airbus A320 aircraft will (i) be new *ex factory* or like-new having no greater than 100 flight hours of commercial service, (ii) have IAE V250OA-5 engines if (a) the Company has or is scheduled to have IAE V250OA-5 engines in its fleet on the delivery date for such aircraft, (b) the Company is scheduled to have IAE V250OA-5 engines in its fleet within 24 months of the delivery date for such aircraft, or (c) if new A320 aircraft powered with IAE V250OA-1 engines are not or are not scheduled to be generally available from the airframe and engine manufacturers on the delivery date for such aircraft, or have IAE V250OA-1 Engines (upgraded to maximum performance) if any of the conditions described in the preceding clauses (a), (b) and (c) is not fulfilled, and (iii) have such other specifications (including configuration) as are substantially the same as those of other A320 aircraft in the Company's fleet or as are otherwise mutually agreed upon by GPA and the Company and, in either case, incorporated in the New Put Agreement; and *provided further, however*, that any such aircraft which is not an A320 aircraft will have such specifications (including configuration and engines) as are substantially the same as those of other aircraft of the same type in the Company's fleet or as are otherwise mutually agreed upon by GPA and the Company and, in either case, incorporated in the New Put Agreement; and *provided further, however*, that any such aircraft which is a used aircraft will (i) be fresh from (or have no more than 150 flight hours beyond) "C" or annual check, (ii) if maintained under a program involving block "D" check, be in at least half-time condition or if maintained under a program involving segmentation of "D" check, be no more than 12 months from next scheduled major check on airframe and engines, and (iii) be in such other condition (consistent with operating lease return conditions currently prevailing in the operating lease marketplace) as is mutually agreed upon by GPA and the Company and incorporated in the New Put Agreement. .....

The lease term shall be (i) not more than eighteen years and not less than (a) ten years for any new A320 aircraft, or (b) seven years for any other new aircraft, and (ii) not more than seven years and not less than three years for any used aircraft. Unless otherwise mutually agreed in writing by the Company and GPA, (i) the lease term for a new aircraft shall be the minimum term applicable to such aircraft, and (ii) the lease term for a used aircraft shall be five years.

Conditions .... The obligation of GPA to consummate the transactions contemplated by this Term Sheet (including, without limitation, the cancellation of GPA's rights and claims under and in respect of the Put Agreement and the First Refusal Agreement) shall be subject to the satisfaction of the following conditions: (i) the Plan shall provide for, and be consummated in accordance with, all of the Terms and Conditions (it being understood that all of the Terms and Conditions are integral to the treatment of GPA's claims and interests and that no one Term or Condition is of greater significance than any other Term or Condition); (ii) the Plan shall provide for, and be consummated with, the capital structure of the reorganized Company being as described in the Investment Agreement, the consideration distributed pursuant to the Plan being as described in the Investment Agreement (except for changes approved in writing by GPA and Permitted Reallocations (as such term is hereinafter defined), and the economic interests of GPA not being diluted from those contained in the Investment Agreement and this Term Sheet; (iii) the Company shall have paid or reimbursed GPA for all expenses reasonably incurred by GPA in connection with the transactions contemplated by this Term Sheet, including, without limitation, the reasonable fees and expenses of GPA's counsel and financial advisor (other than the fees of such financial advisor that are in the nature of "success fees"); (iv) there shall have been executed and delivered, in form and substance reasonably satisfactory to GPA, all such definitive documentation as is necessary or reasonably advisable to implement the transactions contemplated by this Term Sheet (including, without limitation, documentation providing to GPA such registration rights as are reasonably acceptable to GPA with respect to the securities of the reorganized Company that are acquired by GPA in the transactions contemplated by this Term Sheet); and (v) the Board of Directors of GPA (or an appropriate committee thereof) shall have approved the execution and delivery by GPA of the aforesaid definitive documentation (it being understood that, within ten business days following the date of this Term Sheet, GPA shall deliver to AmWest and the Company a certified copy of a resolution evidencing the approval by the Board of Directors of GPA (or an appropriate committee thereof) of this Term Sheet and the transactions contemplated hereby). As used herein, the term "Permitted Reallocation" shall mean changes in the allocation among the Unsecured Creditors, AmWest (and its Affiliates) and the Equity Holders of the aggregate consideration payable to such persons and entities as set forth in the Investment Agreement, without (i) increase or decrease in the aggregate amount thereof, or (ii) change in the terms and conditions of such considerati on from those set forth in the Investment Agreement unless, in any such case, AmWest shall have obtained the prior written consent of GPA.

The obligations of the Company and AmWest to consummate the transactions contemplated by this Term Sheet shall be subject to the satisfaction of the following conditions: (i) the transactions contemplated by the Investment Agreement (other than those contemplated by this Term Sheet) shall have been consummated; (ii) there shall have been executed and delivered, in form and substance reasonably satisfactory to the Company and AmWest, all such definitive documentation as is necessary or reasonably advisable to implement the transactions contemplated by this Term Sheet; and (iii) there shall have been delivered to the Company and AmWest a certified copy of a resolution evidencing the approval by the Board of Directors of GPA (or an appropriate committee thereof) of this Term Sheet and the transactions contemplated hereby.

Other .... Nothing contained in this Term Sheet shall limit, restrict or impair in any manner or to any extent the treatment afforded by the Plan to any allowed administrative claim of GPA arising from the fulfillment by GPA of its deficiency guarantee obligations to General Electric Capital Corporation with respect to aircraft formerly leased by the Company from General Electric Capital Corporation (it being acknowledged that such treatment shall be in accordance with Section 1129(a)(9)(A) of the Bankruptcy Code).

APPENDIX Q

DIP FACILITY PRICING STUDY ©

DIP Facility Pricing

Houlihan Lokey Howard & Zukin Capital
Proprietary & Confidential Analysis

Company	Effective Date	Amount ($ millions)	Libor + Spread (bps)	Base + Spread (bps)	Unused Line Fee (bps)	Facility Fee (bps)	Term (Months)	Agent
Acme Metals, Inc.	10/98	100.0	175-300	50-100	37.5	80.0	24	BankAmerica Business Credit
APS Holdings	2/98	327.0	250 - 275	150	50.0	125.0	18	Chase
Axiohm Transaction Solutions, Inc.	11/99	20.0	Not offered	250	50.0	200.0	7	Lehman Commercial Paper
Brazos Sportswear	4/99	62.5	350	150	25.0	100.0	14	Fleet Capital
Breed Technologies	10/99	125.0	350	100	50.0	350.0	12	BankAmerica
Bruno's	2/98	200.0	225	125	50.0	75.0	24	Chase
Cityscape Financial Corp.	10/98	250.0	275	275	37.5 - 50	175.0	6	Greenwich Capital/CIT

© These materials were prepared by the investment banking and financial advisory firm of ***Houlihan Lokey Howard & Zukin*** with offices in Los Angeles, New York, Chicago, San Francisco, Washington, D.C., Minneapolis, Dallas, Atlanta, Toronto and Seoul. The authors appreciate the permission of Houlihan Lokey Howard & Zukin in the use of these materials.

Company	Effective Date	Amount ($ millions)	Libor + Spread (bps)	Base + Spread (bps)	Unused Line Fee (bps)	Facility Fee (bps)	Term (Months)	Agent
Crown Books	7/98	40.0	Not offered	100	25.0	200.0	12	Paragon Capital/Foothill
Fruit of the Loom	12/99	625.0	250	100	50.0	$10.6 million	18	Bank of America
Golden Books	3/99	55.0	Not offered	62.5	50.0	150.0	24	CIT
Goss Graphic Systems	8/99	50.0	325	225	50.0	200.0	9	Bankers Trust/Stonington
Harnischfeger	6/99	750.0	275	175	50.0	$7.5 million	24	Chase
Harvard Industries	1/98	175.0	350	150-175	50.0	$1.375 million	24	CIT
Hechinger Co.	6/99	700.0	250-300	50-100	37.5	75.0	24	BankBoston Retail Finance
Hvide Marine	9/98	300.9	Not offered	300-750	50.0	$3.7 million	8	Citibank
Integrated Health Services	2/00	300.0	300	200	37.5	165.0	12	Citibank
Laclede Steel Company	12/98	85.0	400	200	50.0	$210,000	12	BankAmerica/Bank of New York
Levitz Furniture	9/97	260.0	375	150	50.0	$2.6 million	18	BT
Loewen Group	6/99	200.0	275	125	50.0	$1.8 million	24	First Union
Long John Silver's	6/98	65.0	300	200	50.0	12.0	12	Chase
Mariner Post-Acute Network	1/00	50.0	Not offered	250 - 300	25 - 75	250.0	12	First Union/PNC Bank
Mobile Media Communications	2/97	200.0	250	150	50.0	50.0	12	Chase

Company	Effective Date	Amount ($ millions)	Libor + Spread (bps)	Base + Spread (bps)	Unused Line Fee (bps)	Facility Fee (bps)	Term (Months)	Agent
NextWave Personal Communcations	7/98	25.0	Not offered	200	100.0	50.0	24	Cellexis International
Optel	12/99	60.0	Not offered	100-200	50.0	175.0	12	CIT/Foothill
PennTraffic	3/99	300.0	250 - 275	150	50.0	75.0	12	Fleet Bank
Philip Services	6/99	100.0	350	250	50.0	150.0	5	BT
Purina Mills	10/99	50.0	300	200	50.0	100.0	12	Chase Bank of Texas
Service Merchandise	4/99	750.0	225	125	37.5	225.0	26	Citicorp
SGL Carbon Corp.'s	1/99	60.0	200	100	50.0	N/A	24	Citicorp
Trism	10/99	42.4	225 - 250	25 - 50	25.0	65.0	6	CIT
United Companies Financial	3/99	300.0	275	75	25.0	$4.25 million	12	Greenwich Cap./CIT/Nomura
Vencor	10/99	100.0	250 - 450	50	25 - 75	200.0	12	Morgan Guaranty Trust Co.

APPENDIX R

SUMMARY OF EMPLOYEE INCENTIVE PLANS ©

SUMMARY OF EMPLOYEE INCENTIVE PLANS

Summary of Employee Incentive Plans

Company	Type of Plan	Plan Elements	Employees Covered and Payment Thereto	Terms of Payout	FYE Sales	Max Plan Cost
Fruit of the Loom, Inc. March 2000	Retention and Emergence Payment Program And Executive Severance Program		Retention and Emergence Bonuses Tier 1 Key Employees (Executive Officers and Key Employees) -- 100% of base salary (9 Employees). Tier II Key Employees (VPs, Plant Managers, and Key Employees) – 62.5% of base salary (49 Employees) Tier III Key Employees (Directors and Salaried Direct Support) – 15.625% - 31.25% of base salary (77 Employees) A total of 135 employees are covered under the retention and emergence payments Executive Severance Tier I – 200% of salary Tier II – Existing Program in Place Tier III – Existing Program in Place Estimated Total Cost of Plan: Tier I: $3.0 million Tier II: $3.7 million Tier III: $1.8 million Total: $8.5 million	Retention and Emergence Bonuses Retention and emergence payments will be made in 3 installments: 180 days and 360 days after initial filing date, and on the effective date of the plan. Tier I – Each of the first two installments equal 25% of base pay and the final installment, payable on the effective date of the plan, equals 50% of base pay. Tier II - Each of the first two installments equal 18.75% of base pay and the final installment, payable on the effective date of the plan, equals 25% of base pay. Tier III - Each of the first two installments equal 4.6875% to 9.375% of base pay and the final installment, payable on the effective date of the plan, equals 6.12% to 12.5% of base pay. Severance benefits paid upon a qualifying termination of employment.	2.0 billion	Retention and Emergence Bonuses $8.4M (0.42% of sales)

©These materials were prepared by the investment banking and financial advisory firm of ***Houlihan Lokey Howard & Zukin*** with offices in Los Angeles, New York, Chicago, San Francisco, Washington, D.C., Minneapolis, Dallas, Atlanta, Toronto and Seoul. The authors appreciate the permission of Houlihan Lokey Howard & Zukin in the use of these materials.

Mondi of America November 1999	Retention Plan		<u>Retention Plan</u> CEO - $300,000 retention payment Sr. VP Retail Operations - $150,000 retention payment Corporate Office Employees (15) and Warehouse Employees (20) – 1 month's pay per month employee remains with Company post-petition (minimum one months pay, maximum 3 months pay). Cost of program to be $165,000	<u>Retention Plan</u> 50% upon filing of disclosure statement and 50% on effective date of the plan.	N/A	
Sun Healthcare Group, Inc. October 1999	Retention Plan Severance Program		<u>Retention Plan</u> 930 Key Employees – Corporate, regional, and facility managers and employees $6 million discretionary pool Allocation of retention payment pool not disclosed <u>Severance Plan:</u> Key Executives - Top 5 managers – up to 24 months 930 Key Employees – Corporate, regional, and facility managers and employees – 4 to 12 months	<u>Retention Plan</u> $2 million may be paid through 12/31/99 Up to $4 million may be paid through 4/1/00 Any remaining amount to be distributed on 9/30/00 <u>Severance Program</u> Key Executives - Top 5 managers - Payments will be made on same schedule as salary payments. 930 Key Employees – Lump sum at the date of termination	$3.1 billion	<u>Retention Bonuses</u> $6.0M (0.19% of sales)

London Fog Industries, Inc. September 1999	Retention Plan Severance Plan		Retention Plan Restructuring Team Executives (16) –50% of prorated monthly base pay for period of employment with Company ($975,625 is maximum retention payout amount). Turnaround Team Key Executives (13) – 75% of bonus target amount ($104,231 is maximum retention payout amount). Middle Management Team (120) – 25%, 50%, or 75% (as applicable) of prorated monthly base pay, with no guaranteed minimum ($1,336,655 is maximum retention payout amount). Retail Field Team Employees at 108-125 retail stores - $350,000 discretionary retention payment tool. Allocation of retention payment pool not disclosed. Transition Team Employees (26) - $292,743 maximum retention payments. Allocation of retention pool not disclosed. Offshore Team Employees in Sri Lanka (4) - $3,879 maximum retention payments. Allocation of retention pool not disclosed. Total maximum retention payments = $3,063,133 Severance Plan Restructuring Team Executives (16) – 6 months Turnaround team (13) – 6 months Transition team employees (26) – 1 to 3 months (subject to level of employment and years of service). Offshore team employees in Sri Lanka (4)	Retention Plan Restructuring Team Executives – 25% of 11/19/99 (target termination date). 75% on termination date. Turnaround Team Key Executives – 20% on 12/1/99; 30% on 5/1/00; 50% on 9/1/00 All others – Payable by 6/1/00 or sooner at discretion of company. Accrues monthly for duration of covered employee's employment with the Company.	N/A	
Vencor, Inc. September 1999	Retention Plan		Key Employees (most senior officers of operational departments) – 50% to 125% of base pay. $7,325,000 discretionary pool funds retention payments	1/3 on approval date 1/3 date plan becomes effective 1/3 three months following effective date	$3.0 billion	Retention Bonuses $7.325M (0.24% of sales)
Zenith Electronics Corp. August 1999	Retention Plan Severance Plan		Retention Plan Engineering and Technical Employees- $182,013 paid on 8/31/99 $299,003 paid on 9/30/99 Severance Plan Certain Executives and key employees – severance benefits greater than basic package but details not disclosed. General employee population – two weeks pay for each year of service up to 28 weeks		$1.2 billion	Retention Bonuses $0.5M (0.04% of sales)

Harnischfeger June 1999	Retention Plan Severance Plan Change of Control Plan		<u>Retention Plan</u> The retention plan is a 2 year program and covers approximately 150 people Tier I -Executive management positions- 60-70% of base pay (at management's discretion) Tier II - Executive management positions (Corporate & Subsidiary Vice Presidents) – 40-50% of base pay Tier III – Select Corporate managers and profess – 30% of base pay CEO Discretionary Fund – needed to provide retention incentives to employees hired subsequent to the approval of the Retention Plan. An additional $500,000 will be available on an as needed basis for key executives, managers, and technical/professional staff. <u>Severance Plan</u> Tier I Executives – 24 months CEO – continuation of benefits EVP, Subsidiary President, Subsidiary Chief Operating Officer – Outplacement Service Tier II – Executive management positions – 12 months, continuation of benefits, outplacement assistance Tier III – Select Corporate managers and professionals – 6 months, continuation of benefits, outplacement assistance. <u>Change of Control Plan</u> President, EVP, and COO – 3 times salary + target bonus Other Executive Management positions – 2 times salary + target bonus	<u>Retention Plan</u> Tier I - 50% of year 1 bonus at/or before 6/7/00 and 50% of year 1 bonus and 100% of year 2 bonus upon emergence Tier II – 67% of year 1 bonus in year 1, 33% of year 2 bonus in year 2, and the remaining 33% of year 1 bonus and 67% of year 2 bonus to be paid upon emergence. Tier III – 100% of year 1 bonus paid in year 1, 50% of year 2 bonus paid in year 2 and 50% of year 2 bonus paid upon emergence.	$2.0 billion	
Loewen Group International, Inc. June 1999	Retention Plan Severance Plan		<u>Retention Plan</u> Senior Corporate Executives (14) – 15%-25% of base pay Corporate Staff (74) – 10% of base pay Operations Country Management (4) – 15-25% of base pay Cemetery Regional Operations Management (33) – 15-20% of base pay Funeral Home Regional Operations Management (46) – 5% of base pay Undisclosed - $500,000 discretionary pool in addition to foregoing payment. Allocation of discretionary pool not disclosed. <u>Severance Plan</u> Senior management team (11) – 24 months Other executives at the VP level – 12 months Directors and Controllers – 6 months Funeral Home Managers – 3 months Other Employees – up to 4 weeks	<u>Retention Plan</u> Senior Corporate Executives – 12/31/99 Corporate Staff –12/31/99 Operations Country Management –12/31/99 Cemetery Regional Operations Management –5% of base pay paid on 9/30/99; 10-15% of base pay paid on 12/31/99 Funeral Home Regional Operations Management –9/30/99 $500,000 discretionary pool –undisclosed <u>Severance Plan</u> Payable in installments according to payroll schedule	$1.1 billion	

Starter Corporation April 1999	Retention Plan		Designated managers (CFO, SVP-HR, SVP ops, National Sales Manager) - $290,000 discretionary pool. Allocation of discretionary pool not disclosed. Proceeds pool – based on gross proceeds of asset sales and liquidations. Proceeds pool payments range from 0% to 150% of fixed payments under discretionary pool. VP National Sales – Shares in discretionary pool above. Proceeds pool is the same as above, except may choose between sales commissions or proceeds pool payments. Operating employees - $920,000 discretionary pool. Allocation of discretionary pool not disclosed.	Designated managers (CFO, SVP-HR, SVP ops, National Sales Manager) – Fixed payments made under discretionary payments on release date or 7/26/99. Proceeds payments made on release date, 7/26/99, 9/27/99, and on emergence. Other: Upon voluntary termination or termination with cause, terminating employee will not be entitled to receive any unpaid retention payments.	N/A	
The Cosmetic Center, Inc. April 1999	Retention Plan		Store managers – 4 weeks pay Assistant Store manager – 2 weeks pay Designated store and corporate headquarters employees and warehouse management who stay with company until terminated – ½ week per full or partial week worked from 7/9/99 through termination date	Payable within 45 days of store closing sales termination. Note: This retention program is an amended program. The initial program is unavailable.	N/A	
Service Merchandise Corp March 1999	Retention Plan		CEO, President, and Chief Operating Officer– 80% of base pay Chief Administrative Officer – 60% of base pay Senior Vice Presidents – 50% of base pay Vice Presidents – 36% of base pay Assistant Vice Presidents – 30% of base pay Key Employees – 24% of base pay Assistant Store managers/Jewelry managers – 12% of base pay	CEO, President, and Chief Operating Officer; Chief Administrative Officer; Senior Vice Presidents ; Vice Presidents — – 25% paid on 7/31/99; 75% paid on 1/31/00 All others same as above except last payment made on January 2001. Note: Key employees also participate in an annual incentive program. Payouts determined by attainment of EBITDA goals and several unidentified performance measures.	$3.2 billion	

Brazo's Sportswear, Inc. January 1999	Retention Plan		90 Critical employees - \$1.0 to \$1.1 million discretionary pool. Allocation of retention payment pool not disclosed.	Upon the earlier to occur, the completion of the critical employee's assignment of 12/31/99	N/A	
Boston Chicken, Inc. October 1998	Retention Bonus Plan Severance Plan	Company planned to severely reduce store count and structure an agreement with key vendors and franchisees.	***CEO voluntarily excluded himself from the retention bonus plan. Top executives receive 50% to 100% of base salary.*** ***Other key employees receive 20% to 50% of base salary under the plan.*** <u>Retention Bonus Plan</u> - CEO voluntarily excluded from plan (separate annual bonus program). - CFO and Division President and Vice Presidents receive 50% of salary. - Area Managers receive 46% of salary. - General Managers receive 45% of salary. - Other corporate directors and managers receive 20% to 33% of salary. <u>Severance</u> - CEO - 400% of salary. - CFO - 200% of salary. - Division President and Vice Presidents -- 100% of salary. - No others receive severance packages.	1. Retention bonuses paid to employees remaining with the company through confirmation. Paid upon confirmation. 2. Severance available in change of control (lump sum payment) or if terminated without cause (over time).	\$761.6M	Est. \$3.1M (0.40% of sales)
Westbridge Capital May 1998	Incentive Plan Equity Plan		***Incentive Plan entitled CEO and Executive VPs to 74% of salary plus a share in 0.50% of new common stock.*** ***Other Key managers received 0% to 60% of base salary.*** <u>Incentive Plan</u> - 74% of salary paid to CEO and EVPs. Other managers receive 0% to 60% of base salary. Most senior managers receive 60%. <u>Equity Plan</u> - CEO and EVPs share in 0.50% of new common stock of the reorganized company. Approximately 32,500 shares based on 6.5 million issued (priced at \$4/share).	Bonuses payable as follows: <u>Incentive Plan</u> - 1/2 in cash at the effective date of a plan of reorganization. - 1/2 in cash upon the first anniversary of the effective date. <u>Equity Plan</u> - All stock is payable on the effective date of a plan.	\$188.9M	Est. 1.6M (Inc. Equity, 0.85% of sales)

Bruno's Inc. February 1998	Retention Plan Severance Plan		Retention Plan Senior Officers – 125% of base pay Other covered officers – 55% of base pay Severance Plan Senior Vice Presidents – 12 months Vice Presidents (16) – Continuation of benefits Directors (17) – 6 months, continuation of benefits Other salaries, non-contract employees (77) – 3 months, continuation of benefits.	Other – If employee resigns for good reason or is terminated without cause, the retention bonus is payable on a pro-rata basis. Non store level managers are eligible for an AI based on corporate EBITDA goals (Officers under retention bonus plan do not qualify for the annual incentive). If employee resigns for good reason or it terminated without cause, in contemplation or, on or after a change in control, the retention bonus is payable in full.	$2.9 billion	
HomePlace Stores, Inc. January 1998	Retention Program Severance Package		***Retention payments ranging from 10% to 50% of base salary*** Retention Plan - CEO (1) volunteered not to participate in the Retention Program. - President (1) 50% of salary - VP's, high-level managers & directors, district mangers and buyers (40) 40% of salary - Mid-level directors and managers (12) 15% of salary - Store managers, asst buyers, replenishers and low-level mngrs (136) 10% of salary Severance Package - 52 weeks of salary each for the CEO and President ($225,000 each) - 1 week salary for every 4 months of service, up to 26 weeks for VPs and high-level managers ($1.5 M total) - 1 month's salary for mid-level directors and managers ($500,000 total) - 1 to 2 weeks for store managers and low-level managers ($2.4 M total)	Retention Plan - President's retention bonus to be paid at emergence from Ch. 11. - VP's retention bonuses to be paid 15% quarterly for first three-quarters, remainder paid at emergence. - Mil-level and low -level managers bonuses paid out on a quarterly basis over one year. - Total cost ($2.2 million) Severance Package - Paid only in change of control or termination without cause.	$500.0M	Retention $2.2M (0.44% of sales) Severance $4.9M (0.98% of sales)
Venture Stores, Inc. January 1998	Retention Bonus	Plan formulated to incentivize key executives to remain despite a likely liquidation of retail locations.	***Key employees 25% to 100% of base salary*** Retention Bonuses 1. Tier 1 Key Employees (Executive VP's and above) -- 100% of base salary. 2. Tier 2 Key Employees (Vice Presidents) -- 50% of base salary. 3. Tier 3 Key Employees (Manager level) -- 25% of base salary.	Retention bonus to be paid upon plan confirmation earned if the employee remained with the company through confirmation. The maximum amount of retention bonuses awarded under the plan was $3.37 million. Under a severance arrangement, the maximum paid if all executives were terminated without cause would be $1.9 million.	$1,107.9M	Retention $3.4M (0.30% of sales) Severance $1.9M (0.14% of sales)

Levitz Furniture, Inc. September 1997	Emergence Bonus Liquidation Severance Package	Structured to provide senior management with an incentive to confirm a plan of reorganization expeditiously. Plan was modified to reflect hiring of new CEO.	***Senior executives emergence bonus varies based upon creditor recoveries and date of emergence.*** ***Other key employees receive between 20% and 100% of base salary upon emergence.*** Emergence Bonus - CEO -- 0.45% of the amount by which the value of distributions made under a plan of reorganization exceed the market value of claims as of the filing date, adjusted by the date upon which a plan is filed. Adjusted 125% if filed before 12 months, 100% if filed between 12 and 18 months, and 75% if filed after 18 months, but in no case less than 25% of annual salary. Distributed 50% in cash and 50% in securities received by unsecured creditors. Minimum -- $81,250 (no unsecured recovery); maximum -- $920,000 (100% recovery). - CFO -- Same as CEO, except percentage is 0.40%. Minimum - $68,750 (no unsecured recovery); maximum -- $818,000 (100% recovery) - EVP, General Counsel - 100% of base salary. - Vice Presidents (H.R., Controller, MIS, Treasurer) - 75% of base salary. - Other Key executives (13) - 42.5% of base salary. - Regional Managers and other Senior staff (48) - 20% of base salary. - Store Managers (55) -- 20% of base salary. Liquidation - In the event of liquidation, CEO receives 40% of annual salary; CFO receives 25%. Severance Package - CEO and CFO -- equal to 18 months base salary. - Other senior management - 12 months base salary.	Emergence Bonus - Payable upon emergence subject to formula for emergence date for senior executives. Severance Package - Paid only if terminated without cause or in the case of a change of control. In the case of a change of control, severance is to be paid in lump sum within 30 days, otherwise in equal monthly installments.	$966.0M	Est. $4.0M (0.41% of sales)
Montgomery Ward July 1997	Incentive Bonus Plan Severance Plan		Incentive Bonus Plan - Senior Executives (Chairman and Division CEOs)- 125% of base salary if confirmation occurs before 18 months, 100% if before 24 months, 50% thereafter. - All executives above Vice President (26) - 75% of annualized base salary. - High-level managers (119) - 50% of annualized base salary. - Lower-level managers (355) - 33% of annualized base salary. Severance Plan - All executives above Vice President (26) - 78 weeks of pay. - High-level managers (119) - 52 weeks of pay. - Lower-level managers (355) - 1 week for each full year of continuous service with a minimum of 4 weeks and a maximum of 39 weeks.	Incentive Bonus Plan - Retention payment is earned if the employee remains employed through December 31, 1998 and paid at confirmation in cash. Severance Plan - Earned only if terminated without cause.	$5,386.0M	Not Available

Payless Cashways, Inc July 1997	Severance Plan	No stay bonus plan was implemented during the pre-packaged Ch. 11 filing period.	***12 Months Severance to senior executives.***	12 months severance would be paid at termination without cause or in the event of a change of control.	$2,490.9M	None
Best Products Co., Inc. September 1996	Retention Plan	Independent, annual retention plans were approved for FY 1992 - FY 1993. Plans were reinstatement of pre-Chapter 11 incentive plans. Plan outlined here is FY 1992 retention plan.	***Key employees receive 10% - 60% of base salary*** 1. Bonuses based on target performance for debtor 28% higher than FY 1991 performance (the "Goal"). 2. Bonus ranges, expressed as a percentage of annual salary, depended on the performance of the debtor in relation to the Goal, as follows: a. Meet Goal: i. Officers: 30% - 40% ii. Directors: Greater of (i) 20% or (ii) $15,000 (for both i. and ii., the "Objective Bonus Level"). b. Exceed Goal: Bonuses were increased by two-times the percentage by which the debtor exceeded the goal, up to a maximum of 150% of the Objective Bonus Level (e.g., 110% of Goal resulted in a bonus of 120% of Objective Bonus Level). i. Officers: 45% - 60% ii. Directors: Greater of (i) 30% or (ii) $22,500. c. 90% - 100% of Goal: At 90% of goal bonuses were reduced to 50% of the Objective Bonus Level: any additional percentage of performance over 90% was multiplied by five to increase the payable bonuses, up to a maximum of 100% of the Objective Bonus Level (e.g., 92% of Goal resulted in a bonus of 60% of the Objectives Bonus Level). i. Officers: 15% - 20% ii. Directors: Greater of (i) 10% or (ii) $7,500.	At close of fiscal year.	$1,495.2M	$1.7M (0.11% of sales)

Color Tile, Inc. January 1996	Retention Program	Debtors propose to create a fund of $600,000 (the "Fund") to provide retention incentive compensation (a "Retention Bonus") to certain of Debtor's key employees.	***Key employees, as determined by CEO, receive Retention Bonuses in amounts to be proposed by CEO, to be paid from a $600,000 fund. A committee consisting of the CEO, a Bank Group representative, a Creditors' Committee representative, and a representative of the Franchise Committee shall, by majority vote, approve or reject any such proposal.*** Severance: Exec. Officers (2) – 1.1yrs. salary effective 2 years Managers (7) – 1.0 year of salary effective 1 year	1. Terms of Payout are as follows: - 50% of bonus on the earliest of (i) December 31, 1996, (ii) date of non-cause related termination, (iii) one week after consummation of plan of reorganization. - 50% paid 90 days after first distribution. 2. Severance: - payable (i) on termination w/o cause, (ii) material reduction in annual base salary, (iii) material reduction of duties, or (iv) appointment of trustee under Chapter 7 of Bankruptcy Code.	$673.5M	Not Available
Edison Brothers Stores, Inc. November 1995	Retention Bonus Annual Operational Bonus	Retention and Bonus plan consisted of payments to 4 groups of senior executives and a provision for annual bonuses to middle level managers.	***Retention Bonuses of three to four times highest monthly salary to senior executives. Middle level managers staying with the debtor receive annual 10% bonuses.*** Senior Executive Retention Bonuses: Twelve top executives, CEO to Senior VP's, receive retention bonus of four times their highest monthly salary (roughly 33% of annual). Nine VP's and other senior executives receive three times their highest monthly salary (roughly 25% of annual). Each executive is also granted severance of 12 times his/her highest monthly salary. Middle Level Manager Annual Bonuses: A bonus equal to 10% of base salary for each middle manager staying with the debtor during the entire fiscal year.	Senior Executive Retention Bonus: Two payments of 2 or 1.5 times highest monthly salary at year-end and once thereafter. Middle Level Manager Bonuses: Bonus paid at end of the fiscal year for continuing managers.	$1,500M	$2.0M (0.1% of sales)

Forstmann & Company, Inc. October 1995	Incentive Plan	<u>$1.5M maximum pool size</u> - $1.03M by formula based upon EBITDAR performance. - $407K: Discretionary portion based on individual performance. Results justified by CEO prior to confirmation with Board of Directors and Creditor's Committee. This discretionary portion is available to Tiers II through V.	Tier I: CEO Tier II: Senior Management Team (7) Tier III: Management Team (10) Tier IV: Management Team (19) Tier V: All others <u>Tier</u> — <u>Fixed target Bonus</u> — <u>Average % of Base Salary</u> I — To Be Determined — NA II — $50,000 — 28.6% III — $30,000 — 40.0% IV — $20,000 — 26.0% V — possible discretionary awards — NA	Pool Determined By Achieving EBITDAR Run Rate at Confirmation EBITDAR <u>Increment</u> — <u>Pool Increment</u> <$20M EBITDAR — $0 First $2M>$20M EBITDAR — $200K Second $2M>$22M EBITDAR — $400K Each $1M>$24M EBITDAR — $200K Note: maximum amount for fixed pool equals $1,030K and is achieved at an EBITDAR level of $25.9M	$222.6M	$1.5M (0.67% of sales)
	Termination Award	<u>Termination Award:</u> - Due to (1) change of control (including confirmation) and (2) termination without cause. - Amount: 1.5 times salary for Tiers II & III - This plan continues two years after confirmation of a plan of reorganization. - Payment under this plan is in lieu of any other severance payments.	Note: A 100% funding of the "Pool" is achieved when the designated amount reaches $1,030,000. At that point, 100% of the "Target" awards are earned. Levels of total fixed pool below maximum are awarded to recipients pro rata. Pool decreases if covered employee leaves voluntarily. Calculation of EBITDAR run rate at confirmation will be detailed by Company management and will be reviewed and verified by the financial advisors to Creditors' Committee.	<u>Payment:</u> - 50% one month after Effective Date - 50% six months after Effective Date		
Elder Beerman October 1995	Retention Program		<u>Retention Program</u> CEO, Chairman, and President – 25% of base pay. Additional 10% of base pay if target exceeded. EVPs and SVPs – 20% of base pay. Additional 10% of base pay if target exceeded. VP/DMM – 15% of base pay. Additional 10% of base pay if target exceeded. Store managers and buyers – 15% of base pay (received only year end bonus) Key Corporate Staff – 15% of base pay (receive mid-year bonus (5%) to stay) OtherCorporate Staff – 10% of base pay (receive mid-year bonus (5%) to stay)	Other – Annual bonus payable subject to (1) company achievement of financial goals established by the company after consultation wit creditors' committees & (2) continued employment through end of bonus year.	$0.5 billion	
	Severance Plan		<u>Severance Plan</u> Chief Executive Office, Vice Chairman, President, Executive Vice Presidents, Senior Vice Presidents – 12 months VP, DMM, Subsidiary Director of Stores – 9 months Store managers, buyers, Day Corporate Staff – 6 months Subsidiary VP HR, Buyers, Director of Planning – 4 months Other Corporate Staff – 3 months			

Caldor, Inc. August 1995	Incentive Bonus Program	Implemented to address problem with management defections given below-market pay scale.	***Bonuses would vary between approximately 10% and 70% of the employee's annual salary*** - CEO, Executive Vice Presidents, District Managers, Buyers, Store Managers, Operating Vice Presidents, Managers and Directors all participate. - For the top three levels of employees, bonuses would be measured by the debtor's EBITDAR performance in the season prior to the plan of confirmation and paid 75% in cash and 25% in restricted stock. If met target CEO, President - 140% of base; 2 ExecVPs - 110% of base; if not was reduced by 1/2. - The other five levels of employees would be paid in cash and receive bonuses regardless of EBIDTAR performance: VPs - 40% of base, High level managers - 25% of base, Lower level key employees - 10-20% of base. - CEO provided with a discretionary $500,000 fund to reward all but the top two levels of employees. Such discretionary awards could be made at any time, but were limited to $100,000 per employee.	- Bonuses payable in two installments: one at the effective date of the plan and one six months following the effective date. - In the event of a liquidation, the retention award would be offset against any severance benefits accruing to the employee. - Receipt of any award would be contingent on a satisfactory evaluation.	$2,765.5M	Not Available
Bidermann Industries, Inc. June 1995	Retention following notice of eventual termination	Debtor planned to eliminate 111 of 257 corporate and administrative positions in its offices in NY and NJ. The layoffs were part of major consolidation of debtor's operations and a plan to relocate certain of the debtor's offices into smaller, less expensive space. Debtor estimated that it would save $2.5M the first year and $3M on a normalized basis.	***Employees to be severed receive 2% - 5% of base salary for each month or partial month the employee remained with the debtor following notice of termination.*** - 75% receive 2% stay bonus payment - 25% receive 3% - 5% stay bonus payment	1. Required to remain with debtor until date of terminate established by debtor. 2. Sign waiver and release of claims against debtor 3. Effective nine months post-consideration.	Not Available	$550,000

Bradlees Stores, Inc. June 1995	Retention Program Incentive Bonus Program	<u>Severance without Cause</u>: CEO – (i) lump sum payment equal to accrued salary & target bonus for remainder of contract; (ii) immediate vesting Equity Incentive Awards; and (iii) continuation of benefits. COO – similar to CEO EVP – similar to CEO <u>Following "change of control"</u>: CEO – (i) lump sum payment equal to salary and target bonus for greater of 3 years or remainder of contract term; (ii) full vesting Equity Incentive Awards; (iii) continuation of benefits; and (iv) parachute excise tax gross payment. COO – similar to CEO EVP – similar to CEO	<u>Retention Bonus Program</u> CEO – Retention bonus of 65% of base salary and 6% of appreciation in gross enterprise value from petition date to date of valuation (the "Time Span"). COO – 50% of base salary and 3% of appreciation in gross enterprise value over Time Span. EVP – 40% of base salary. Other Senior Management (10) -- 33% of base salary. Key Management (15 Officers) -- 28% of base salary. Middle Management (56) -- 20% of base salary. Managers Group -- 15% of base salary. All Others (Buyers, Planners, Store Managers) -- 12.5% of base salary. <u>Incentive Bonus Program</u> - Participants include CEO and COO. - Benefits vest at a rate of 20% per annum over five-year period. - Benefits accelerated in the event of termination without cause, change in control "for good reason." CEO -- Incentive award of $2M after five years from contract date with an annual non-refundable advance of $300,000 minimum against such amount. COO – Incentive award of $1M after five years from contract date.	<u>Incentive Bonus Program</u> Contingent on growth in the "gross enterprise value" of Bradlees from the date of entry into the program until the cash out date, subject to five year vesting provision.	$1,840.9M	Not Available

ENDNOTES

Chapter One

Introduction

[1] Recapitalization funds are certainly available. By way of example, in 1999 private equity funding reached $95.5 billion (a new record for the sixth consecutive year); venture capital fund-raising reached $35.6 billion (a record and an 87 percent increase from 1998); mezzanine fund-raising jumped 53 percent from 1998 levels to a record $4.3 billion; and domestic merger and acquisition activity reached a staggering $1.4 trillion (up from $1.2 trillion in 1998). Source: John Rose, *Tretwith Securities* (February 1, 2000). *See also* Miller, "Looming Financial Or Business Failure: Fix Or File—A Legal Perspective," *Workouts & Turnarounds II* (Wiley 1999) at 21 (hereafter "*Workouts & Turnarounds*").

[2] U.S. Constitution, Article I, § 8, provides:

> The Congress shall have the Power . . .
>
> * * *
>
> To establish . . . uniform Laws on the subject of Bankruptcies throughout the United States.

[3] *See* Symposium, "100 Years Of Bankruptcy: Looking Forward By Looking Back," 15 *Bankruptcy Developments Journal* 253 (Summer 1999); Warren, *Bankruptcy In United States History* (Beard Books 1999); Coleman, *Debtors And Creditors In America* (Beard Books 1999); Sullivan, Warren & Westbrook, *As We Forgive Our Debtors: Bankruptcy And Consumer Credit In America* (Beard Books 1998).

[4] *See* Salerno, Hansen, Meyer, *et al. Pre-Bankruptcy Planning For The Commercial Reorganization: A Brief Guide For The CEO, CFO/COO, General Counsel And Tax Advisor* (American Bankruptcy Institute 1997) at iii ("*Pre-Bankruptcy Planning*").

[5] The figures for Chapter 11 filings since 1982 are as follows:

1982	14,058	1987	19,901	1992	22,634	1997	10,765
1983	21,206	1988	17,690	1993	21,400	1998	8,386
1984	20,023	1989	18,281	1994	20,123	1999	9,412
1985	21,420	1990	19,951	1995	13,904	2000	9,884
1986	24,740	1991	23,989	1996	11,911		

Source: Bankruptcy Division, Administrative Office for U.S. Courts.

Even though the number of filings is down, the size of the cases (in terms of both debt and assets) is enormous. For example, the twelve largest Chapter 11 cases filed in 1999 involved a staggering ***$30.774 billion*** in assets! *See* "Special Reports—Largest Bankruptcies—1999," *Turnarounds & Workouts* at 5 (January 15, 2000). Nor does it look like the wave will abate any time soon. The nine largest Chapter 11 filings for the month of January 2000 involved in the aggregate over ***$3.7 billion*** in listed assets and over ***$5.3 billion*** in liabilities. *See* "January's Top Chapter 11 Filings And Emergencies," *Daily Bankruptcy Review* at 9 (February 2, 2000).

[6] Interestingly, many industrialized nations outside of the United States are rethinking the nature of their bankruptcy laws, and looking at the more "debtor friendly" U.S. laws. Thailand and Germany have recently revamped their laws to allow for bankruptcy proceedings involving something other than liquidation. Costa Rica, the Czech Republic, and Romania are also considering such changes.

[7] If your company has public debt securities, you can be sure the marketplace is watching your company even if you aren't. This scrutiny goes beyond the normal financial reporting required by securities laws. There are numerous "tracking services" keeping tabs on companies with public debt, and they rate them (usually by a scale showing how close to a bankruptcy filing they are). *See, e.g.,* "Companies To Watch," *Dow Jones Newsletters* (Federal Filings, Inc.). For a company with public debt or equity securities, financial difficulties are like the "neon cat in the cellophane bag."

[8] *See* "The Retail Industry—Trends In The Next Century," *Workouts & Turnarounds* at 399.

[9] The literature abounds with the lurid tales of some of the more high-profile restructurings. *See* Bernstein, *Grounded: Frank Lorenzo And The Destruction Of Eastern Airlines* (Beard Books 1996); Moore & Simendinger, *Hospital Turnarounds: Lessons In Leadership* (Beard Books 1998); Petzinger, *Oil & Honor: The Texaco-Pennzoil Wars* (Beard Books 1995); Daughen & Blinzen, *The Wreck Of The Penn Central* (Beard Books 1993); *Ling: The Rise, Fall, And Return Of A Texas Titan* (Beard Books 1996) (regarding the LTV collapse).

[10] Numerous "cottage industries" are thriving by acquiring the equity in restructured companies (the so-called "turnaround funds," or "vulture funds," depending on your perspective), acquiring assets from those same businesses, or buying trade claims or other debt (such as bonds) for either a profitable return or as a means to acquire the equity in the company when it emerges. All one needs is access to the Internet to play in this game. For example, accessing BankruptcyData.Com (at *www.bankruptcydata.com/prices.htm*) will give the bid and asked-on bonds and trade debt for companies in Chapter 11. Indeed, in 2000 approximately 20% of the total trading volume was in the distressed market. *Loan Pricing Corp. Report* (march 2001).

The number of books written on this area is indicative of just how prevalent an endeavor it is. *See* Altman, *Bankruptcy & Distressed Restructurings; Analytical Issues And Investment Opportunities* (Beard Books 1998); Platt, *Why Companies Fail: Strategies For Detecting,*

Avoiding And Profiting From Bankruptcy (Beard Books 1997); Branch and Ray, *Bankruptcy Investing: How To Profit From Distressed Companies* (Beard Books 1997); Altman, *Distressed Securities: Analyzing And Evaluating Market Potential And Investment Risk* (Beard Books 1997); Altman, "Market Dynamics And Investment Performance Of Distressed And Defaulted Debt Securities," *Workouts & Turnarounds* at 238.

[11] *See* Altman, *The High Yield Debt Market: Investment Performance And Economic Impact* (Beard Books 1996).

Chapter Two

The Reorganization Process

[12] Sometimes lawyers will refer to an "Act Case." This is a term of art used to distinguish an older case that was initiated before 1978 under the Bankruptcy Act of 1898. As one might imagine, essentially all of those cases are out of the federal judicial system at this point, although amazingly some live on in appellate stages.

[13] Specifically, Congress added a Chapter 12 to the Bankruptcy Code pursuant to the Bankruptcy Judges, U.S. Trustees And Family Farmer Bankruptcy Act of 1986, which was intended to have a limited life to help small farms and farmers in times of particular economic stress in the mid-1980s. This Chapter 12 was supposed to "sunset" in a short period of time, but has been extended on a regular basis. In any event, it is a very specialized section of the Bankruptcy Code and not directly relevant to the subject matter of this book.

[14] Certain bankruptcy professionals, and usually most management members, bristle at the "DIP" acronym. At least one bankruptcy judge in California regularly admonishes counsel not to use the term. It's ultimately a losing battle.

[15] For example, the largest failure of a non-profit organization in U.S. history is the case of the *Baptist Foundation of Arizona* and its ninety affiliated entities, which was filed in the U.S. Bankruptcy Court for the District of Arizona in November 1999. The Baptist Foundation was a non-profit organization whose original purpose was to invest in Baptist ventures and causes. It soon embarked on more tenuous and risky endeavors, and is currently being liquidated under the auspices of a Chapter 11 bankruptcy proceeding.

[16] *See* Daggett, *Railroad Reorganization* (Beard Books 1991).

[17] For example, anyone who saw the movie *The Rainmaker,* adapted from the John Grisham novel of the same name, might note that after the hero obtains a huge verdict against the evil insurance company, all of his efforts are thwarted because the insurance company files a bankruptcy petition. While making for good literature and cinema, in fact the insurance company

in question would not have been allowed to file a bankruptcy petition under U.S. laws, but would have had to resort to a liquidation under the applicable state law that handles insurance receiverships and liquidations. Mr. Grisham should be excused for his ignorance of federal bankruptcy law—after all, he was a litigator in practice. That having been said, insurance holding companies can (and do) file bankruptcy (such as *Home Holdings, ICH,* and *Penn. Corp.*).

[18] *See* Spero, *The Failure Of The Franklin National Bank* (Beard Books 1990). For history buffs, *see also* DeRoover, *The Rise And Decline Of The Medici Bank (1397-1494)* (Beard Books 1992).

[19] The fees are periodically increased by Congress. The filing fee for Chapter 11 is $830.00 for each petition as of January 2000. The discussions regarding where this bankruptcy can or should be filed, and the strategic thoughts that go into that, are dealt with in Chapter Four.

[20] Once a public reporting company makes the decision to file a bankruptcy, or even if that enterprise is seriously considering the filing of a bankruptcy, it is always appropriate to issue press releases or make public filings to avoid securities fraud claims once the bankruptcy is actually filed. Securities counsel can and should coordinate with bankruptcy counsel to ensure that the public is kept appropriately informed because securities fraud actions against individual directors and officers can and must be considered as part of this process.

[21] Under the current version of the Bankruptcy Code, if a business enterprise has fewer than twelve creditors, any one creditor who is owed $10,000.00 and is unsecured can commence an involuntary bankruptcy petition. If the business enterprise has more than twelve creditors, three creditors who are owed in the aggregate $10,000.00 are necessary. These creditors (called ***petitioning creditors***) must assert (and prove) that the company is not paying its debts as they come due. *See* Bankruptcy Code § 303. In any event, once an involuntary proceeding is filed (with all its attendant adverse publicity and the like), many (but not all) businesses opt to convert the proceeding to a voluntary proceeding to take control of the process.

[22] Under the old Bankruptcy Act, the debtor was identified by the less-flattering term of "the bankrupt." In some older form loan documents you may still see references to "being adjudicated a bankrupt"—this was the term of art under the Bankruptcy Act.

[23] *See* Bankruptcy Code § 101(32). The full definition is:

(32) "insolvent" means —

(A) with reference to an entity other than a partnership and a municipality, financial condition such that the sum of such entity's debts is greater than all of such entity's property, at a fair valuation, exclusive of —

(i) property transferred, concealed, or removed with intent to hinder, delay, or defraud such entity's creditors; and

(ii) property that may be exempted from property of the estate under section 522 of this title;

(B) with reference to a partnership, financial condition such that the sum of such partnership's debts is greater than the aggregate of, at a fair valuation—

(i) all of such partnership's property, exclusive of property of the kind specified in subparagraph (A)(i) of this paragraph; and

(ii) the sum of the excess of the value of each general partner's nonpartnership property, exclusive of property of the kind specified in subparagraph (A) of this paragraph, over such partner's nonpartnership debts.

[24] *See* Bankruptcy Code § 109(a). Actually, the other prerequisite is that the debtor pay the filing fee—without it, the clerk's office won't accept the petition. As such, the interesting irony exists that while a company can never be too rich to file bankruptcy, it can be too poor.

[25] *See* Petzinger, *Oil And Honor: The Texaco-Pennzoil Wars* (Beard Books 1992).

[26] Notwithstanding this, there are examples where Chapter 11 cases have been dismissed as being filed in "bad faith." For example, the Third Circuit Court of Appeals recently held that an economically healthy business that files a "preemptive" bankruptcy to avoid potentially costly litigation may lack the "valid reorganizational purpose" needed to invoke the protection of the bankruptcy laws. *See In re SGL Carbon Corp.*, 200 F.3d 154 (3rd Cir. 1999).

[27] There are numerous law review articles that deal with this matter, and it is a confusing mess for lawyers, courts, and business people. *See generally* Roache, "The Fiduciary Obligations Of A Debtor In Possession," 1993 *U. Ill. L. Rev.* 133; Bienenstock, "Conflicts Between Management And The Debtor In Possession's Fiduciary Duties," 61 *Cin. L. Rev.* 543 (1992); Roberts, "The Conundrum Of Directors' Duties Of Nearly Insolvent Corporations," 23 *Mem. St. U. L. Rev.* 273 (1993). *See also* Salerno, Hansen & Meyer, *Advanced Chapter 11 Bankruptcy Practice—Second Edition* at Section 5.10 *et seq.* (Aspen Law And Business, 1997) (hereafter "*Advanced Chapter 11*").

[28] *See* Fortgang, Gardner & Caro, "At The Front Line: The Secured Creditor," *Workouts & Turnarounds* at 108.

[29] *See* Bankruptcy Code § 507.

[30] As to securities claims against officers and directors, these are discussed

in Chapter Four.

[31] *See* Bankruptcy Code § 510(b).

[32] The Bankruptcy Code defines a "debt" as "liability on a *claim*." Bankruptcy Code § 101(12). A "creditor" is an "entity that has a *claim* against the debtor. . . ." Bankruptcy Code § 101(10). Finally, the Bankruptcy Code (§ 101(5)) defines "*claim*" as:

"[C]laim" means—

(A) right to payment, whether or not such right is reduced to judgment, liquidated, unliquidated, fixed, contingent, matured, unmatured, disputed, undisputed, legal, equitable, secured, or unsecured; or

(B) right to an equitable remedy for breach of performance if such breach gives rise to a right to payment, whether or not such right to an equitable remedy is reduced to judgment, fixed, contingent, matured, unmatured, disputed, undisputed, secured, or unsecured.

[33] The authors gratefully acknowledge Professor Tom Jackson, formerly of the University of Virginia Law School, who so perceptively pointed out this metaphor when he taught bankruptcy law at that school.

[34] For example, one can only imagine the problems of the Dow Corning Corporation in defending the thousands of Dalkon Shield cases pending in courts all over the country; or the nationwide personal injury asbestos litigation that hounded Johns-Manville.

[35] *See* Jensen-Conklin, "Do Confirmed Chapter 11 Plans Consummate? The Results Of A Study And Analysis Of The Law," 97 *Comm. L. J.* 297, 317 (Fall 1992) ("Conklin"). A study done in the Conklin article involved a postconfirmation analysis of forty-five Chapter 11 cases. The less complex the reorganization proceeding, the more likely it is to emerge quickly. Some bankruptcies that are in the nature of "prepackaged bankruptcies" (discussed later in the chapter) do emerge quickly from bankruptcy proceedings, although the bulk of the negotiations were done in the months and months preceding the filing of the bankruptcy.

[36] *See* Conklin at 317.

[37] *See* Conklin at 323.

[38] *See Pre-Bankruptcy Planning* at (iii); *Advanced Chapter 11* at Chapter 9.

[39] A lien that is not properly perfected or not timely perfected will be subject to attack under the "strong arm" provisions discussed in Chapter Four.

[40] The fiduciary duties of Creditors Committees are taken seriously by courts. If a Creditors Committee member violates its fiduciary duty (such as by trading on inside information or taking actions that benefit that creditor to

the detriment of other creditors), it faces liability like any fiduciary. Creditors Committee members have been removed from Committee membership because of conflicts of interest. In fact there is E&O insurance available to Creditors Committee members to cover negligence in the discharge of their duties (but not obviously fraud or intentional breaches of fiduciary obligations). *See also* discussion on "Chinese Walls" and Confidentiality Agreements in Chapter Three; Kurtz, Linstrom & Pohl, "Representing The Unsecured Creditors' Committee In Insolvency Restructurings," *Workouts & Turnarounds* at 156.

[41] This is not true in all instances. For example, in the *America West Airlines* case, a substantial portion of the equity was held by employees ("Your hometown, employee-owned airline!"). The company was clearly insolvent—creditors were not paid in full. Nonetheless, the employee-stockholders were given, in the aggregate, a small percentage of stock in the company when it emerged from Chapter 11 to keep their goodwill on a going- forward basis. It was a nice try, but probably ultimately unsuccessful. Within a year after emergence from Chapter 11, the employees (who before bankruptcy were the lowest paid in the industry—hey, they were "owners") unionized, and America West now has the same labor costs as its competitors.

[42] Payment for the professionals representing these Committees where equity is clearly out of the money is a touchy subject. If the Equityholder Committee decides to launch a legal war to extract something for its constituency, it better win because the chances of having the bankruptcy court approve fees if it loses is realistically pretty slim. In the *Megafoods* Chapter 11 case, the equity was acknowledged as being out of the money at the outset of the case. Public equityholders formed a Committee nonetheless, and hired counsel. The bankruptcy court appointed the professionals, but admonished them that they were going to need to show a tangible benefit to their constituency before fees would be paid. The Equityholder Committee was very cooperative in that case.

[43] *See* Bankruptcy Code § 503(b)(3)(D).

[44] In fact, it is common when a company has public debt securities that an Indenture Trustee sits on the Creditors Committee.

[45] The Bankruptcy Code sets a sixty-day deadline from the filing of the case. *See* Bankruptcy Code §§ 365(d)(2), (4). This is illusory, however, since in almost all Chapter 11 cases of any size the bankruptcy court regularly extends this time period, and the ultimate decision is usually made at plan confirmation.

[46] Certain types of contracts can't be assumed. For example, "personal services" contracts are not assumable, nor are contracts to buy or sell securities of the debtor, or contracts to make "financial accommodations" (usually loan commitments). *See* Bankruptcy Code § 365(c).

[47] There are special Bankruptcy Code provisions for leases of airport landing slots, shopping centers, time-share arrangements, and licenses for intellectual property. The basic premise is the same. *See* discussion in Chapter Four.

[48] At the risk of offending some readers, an irreverent joke among bankruptcy practitioners goes as follows:

> The CEO of Coors Brewing Co. seeks an audience with the Pope. The Pope receives him, and the CEO states the basis for his visit.
>
> "Your Eminence, I have a request. Coors will donate $100 million to charitable causes if you'll change the words of the Lord's Prayer from 'Give us this day our daily bread' to 'Give us this day our daily beer.'"
>
> The Pope is stunned, and declines. The CEO is not easily discouraged and returns again and again with the same request, each time upping the ante. After three weeks, the CEO makes his final offer—$1 billion for a one word change.
>
> The Pope tells the CEO to come back the following day while he considers the request. As soon as the CEO leaves, the Pope hurriedly picks up the phone.
>
> "Get me the Vatican bankruptcy lawyer right away! That executory contract with Pepperidge Farms is killing us!"
>
> Bankruptcy lawyers find this humorous, but then again they don't get out too often.

[49] Even under these mandatory appointment circumstances, the bankruptcy court still has discretion over the precise scope of the examiner's duties.

[50] This is a good way for a proactive debtor to discharge its fiduciary duties and increase its credibility with its creditors. For example, in *Revco, Circle K, Interco,* and *Unison HealthCare Corporation*, the debtors either initiated or acquiesced in the appointment of an examiner to investigate financial transactions between the companies and its officers and directors. While increasing costs for the estate, at least the debtors did not appear to be protecting insiders.

[51] To guard against an examiner finding fraud so that he or she can then become the trustee, the Bankruptcy Code precludes an examiner from being appointed a trustee in the case in which he served as examiner. *See* Bankruptcy Code § 321(b).

[52] *See* discussion in Chapter Four.

[53] A number of years ago the FBI investigated the antics of certain bankruptcy practitioners and judges in Chicago who manipulated the system to draw certain judges. It was called "Operation Greylord," and resulted in

numerous indictments. Now most assignments are done by computerized random selection.

[54] *See Pre-Bankruptcy Planning* at 21. If a company has long-standing outside general counsel, use of that firm to do the reorganization work may be precluded because the Bankruptcy Code requires attorneys to be "disinterested." This means that the firm cannot be a creditor (although the firm can cure this problem by waiving its prebankruptcy claim) or, have partners who are serving or who recently served on the board or as an officer, who have ongoing representation of affiliates that may not be filing bankruptcy (due to intercompany transactions), or who have ongoing representation of some of the major creditor groups in the case. Exploring potential conflicts with prospective reorganization counsel is important to avoid possible disqualification side battles with the U.S. Trustee or possibly creditors once the case is filed.

[55] As one wry bankruptcy judge was heard to comment, the only "disinterested" bankruptcy lawyer is one who is not being paid.

[56] *See* Bankruptcy Code §§ 35, 328, and 329 and Bankruptcy Rules 2014 and 2016. The duty to disclose conflicts (and potential conflicts) is ongoing—if a conflict comes up after the case is commenced, counsel have an obligation to timely supplement their disclosures with the bankruptcy court.

[57] For example, at the outset of a case all creditors may not be known (other than the largest). Once all creditors are known, counsel will need to update the conflicts check. The lawyers also have their own sets of issues. Failure to fully and candidly disclose connections can lead to a loss of some or all fees by counsel, (such as occurred to Weil, Gotshal & Manges in the *Leslie Faye* Chapter 11 in New York), or worse. John Gellene, a New York partner at Milbank, Tweed, Hadley & McCloy, was convicted of making fraudulent bankruptcy oaths and is currently serving a fifteen- month sentence in a federal prison resulting from incomplete disclosure of conflicts in the *Bucyrus Erie* Chapter 11 that was filed in Wisconsin. *See U.S. v. Gellene*, 182 F.3d 578 (7th Cir. 1999). As you might imagine, being in prison for lying about conflicts is probably not the sort of crime that engenders much respect in the prison yard.

[58] *See* Bankruptcy Code § 1129(a)(7).

[59] In cases where debt or equity securities will be given to creditors for payment of their claims, those securities may need to be valued for plan confirmation purposes.

[60] *See* Millon & Pratt, "Valuation Of Companies Within Workout And Turnaround Situations," *Workouts & Turnarounds* at 225.

[61] The players in this area may change. For example, Salomon Brothers and Merrill Lynch were at one time big players in this industry, but have now ceased their activities.

[62] *See* Gray, "The Accountant's Role In The Workout Environment—Beyond 'Bean Counting,'" *Workouts & Turnarounds* at 303.

[63] *See Pre-Bankruptcy Planning* at 23-24. A good article on the utility of these specialists is found in Sitrick, "Public Relations in a Chapter 11," *B.C.D. Newsletter* at A-7 (LRP Publications, December 10, 1992). *See also* Sitrick, "Stabilizing the Work Force Controlling the Information Flow," *Workouts and Turnarounds* at 329 (Price Waterhouse 1991); Sitrick, "Spin Control: Managing Internal And External Communications," *Workouts & Turnarounds* at 74. *See also* Lubove, "Gotcha!" *Forbes* at 145 (November 15, 1999) (article discussing uses of crisis public relations firms such as Sitrick & Company in the Chapter 11 cases of *America West Airlines; Barney's New York; Circle K Corp;, Gillette Holdings/Vail Associates; Greyhound Lines, Inc.; Hawaiian Airlines;* and *L.J. Hooker Corp;* and the *Orange County* Chapter 9 proceeding). *See also* Sitrick and Mayer, *Spin—How To Turn The Power Of The Press To Your Advantage* (Regnery Publ. 1998).

[64] *See* "Corporate Insurer to Cover Cost of Spin Doctors," *The New York Times* at C-1 (September 10, 1996).

[65] The use of Web sites to disseminate information in reorganization cases is clearly both a curse and a blessing. While it is a wonderful medium for public information, there is no quality control, nor is there any restriction as to who can put information (or misinformation, as the case may be) on Web sites. Any fourteen-year-old with a PC and a modem can create a Web page, and to the uninformed these can look like "official" sites. For example, in the *Baptist Foundation of Arizona* case, an unidentified creditor created a "BFA Recovery Web Site" that reports some useful information (dates and times of hearings, addresses of the court and the like), and some misinformation (advice on how to legally protect interests in the cases, sample forms and letters for a letter-writing campaign to the bankruptcy judge, etc.). Since there is no way to prescreen information or assure its accuracy, unknowing creditors will likely look to the Web site as the unvarnished truth and act on the advice given in the site. Indeed, the bankruptcy court received over 400 letters in the first 10 days of the case! Such are the benefits and disadvantages of technology. *See also* Johnson, "What They're Saying On The Internet *Can* Affect Your Bankruptcy," 35 *Bankruptcy Court Decisions, Weekly News & Comment* at A-1 (February 29, 2000).

[66] Nor is there any lack of literature on the subject. *See, e.g.,* "Special Report: Industry Executives Doing Turnarounds," *Turnarounds & Workouts* at 7 (August 15, 1999); Bibeault, *Corporate Turnaround: How Managers Turn Losers Into Winners* (Beard Books 1999); Moore & Simendinger, *Hospital Turnarounds: Lessons In Leadership* (Beard Books 1999); Whitney, *Taking Charge: Management Guide To Troubled Companies And Turnarounds* (Beard Books 1999); DiNapoli & Fuhr, "Trouble Spotting:

Assessing The Likelihood Of A Turnaround," *Workouts & Turnarounds* at 1; Pate, "Business Regeneration: Early Detection—Early Intervention," *Workouts & Turnarounds* at 54. Turnaround specialists even have their own trade group—the Turnaround Managers Association, or TMA.

[67] This is not to suggest that the creditors themselves sit on the board, but rather that they supply resumes of third-party independent candidates who will then go through the normal director scrutiny process before being appointed to the board. It is possible that sometimes a turnaround manager is placed on the board at the insistence of a creditor group, although the board as a general rule does not exercise operational decision- making powers. This was done in the *Megafoods* and *Loewen Group International* cases.

[68] *See, e.g.,* "Special Report: Nation's Largest Industrial Auctioneers," *Turnarounds & Workouts* at 5 (March 15, 2000).

[69] Professionals in bankruptcy cases can only be paid after submitting fee applications, which must be approved by the bankruptcy court after parties have the right to object. Many jurisdictions have what are called "interim fee procedures" that allow professionals to be paid every thirty days, usually with a percentage "holdback" (usually 20 percent of fees). At the end of the case they will file "final" fee applications for final approval of fees and costs. At that point they will get their "holdbacks" (if the court so orders). Conversely, if for some reason the court doesn't finally approve the fees in the full amount, they may have to "disgorge" (pay back) some of the interim fees they've already been paid. *See, e.g., In re Circle K Corp.*, 191 B.R. 426 (Bankr. D. Ariz. 1996) (ordering a professional to disgorge over $1.3 million; the court's order was ultimately overturned on appeal).

[70] Presumably cash would be acceptable as well, although generally speaking only drug runners (and perhaps politicians) keep that sort of cash handy.

[71] In 1992, the Supreme Court changed the way professionals took retainers in *Barnhill v. Johnson*, 503 U.S. 393 (1992). Before then, in some jurisdictions, mere delivery of a retainer check on Monday, with a bankruptcy filing on Tuesday and the bank honoring the check on Thursday, was fine. This is no longer so.

[72] *See Pre-Bankruptcy Planning* at 8-9. The so-called "mega cases" may have their own dynamics and realities, and may succeed absent a prepetition exit strategy because of their sheer size. In essence, everyone has too much to lose if the case fails. There are, of course, exceptions, such as the demise of Eastern Airlines. Nonetheless, the larger cases usually have some sort of an exit strategy formulated upon filing.

[73] The phrase was first used by Patrick Murphy, Esq., of Murphy, Sheneman & Rogers in San Francisco.

[74] *Pre-Bankruptcy Planning* at iv.

[75] If you think LBOs were an '80s phenomenon, think again. The LBO

volume in the United States for 1999 exceeded ***$62 billion***, its highest level of the decade. *Trenworth Securities* (February 1, 2000). Maybe someone can revive the *Predator's Ball.*

[76] The essential terms of the restructuring may be memorialized in a term sheet or reorganization agreement, the final implementation of which will need to be done through a confirmed plan.

[77] Examples of other successful prepackaged deals were *Crystal Oil Corporation* (filed in 1996—three months in Chapter 11), *Republic Health Corporation* (filed in 1989—four months in Chapter 11, *LaSalle Energy Corporation* (filed in 1990—three months in bankruptcy), *Circle Express* (filed in 1990—two months in bankruptcy); *J.P.S. Textile* (filed in 1991—three months in Chapter 11), *TIE Communications* (filed in 1991—two and a half months in bankruptcy), *Edgell Communications* (1991—one month), *Anglo Energy* (1990—three months), and *14 Wall Street Associates* (1990—two months in bankruptcy). *See also* Altman at 415-416.

[78] *See* Salerno and Hansen, "A Bankruptcy Strategy," *The Journal Of Business Strategy* at 15 (January/February 1991); Henry, " Bankruptcy Works For Those Who Have Money And Vision," *Turnarounds & Workouts* at 1 (February 1, 1991); *Advanced Chapter 11* at Chapter 9; Saggese & Ranney-Marinelli, *A Practical Guide To Out Of Court Restructurings And Plans Of Reorganization* (Matthew Bender 1993); Altman, *Bankruptcy And Distressed Restructurings: Analytical Issues And Investment Opportunities* at 401 (Beard Books 1999) (discussing prepackaged bankruptcies in the article entitled "Emerging Trends In Bankruptcy Reorganization").

[79] *See* Salerno & Hansen at 15; Altman at 413.

[80] *See* McConnell, "The Economics Of Bankruptcy," *Journal of Applied Corporate Finance* 93 (1991). *See also Pre-Bankruptcy Planning* at 25.

[81] *See* Salerno & Hansen at 16; Altman at 413.

Chapter Three

The New Realities

[82] Hence the importance of determining where a company should file (discussed in Chapter Four). There are many jurisdictions where bankruptcy judges understand business realities, and have consequently become havens for Chapter 11 filings. The most obvious is Wilmington, Delaware.

[83] An interesting perspective from a non-lawyer is found in *A Feast For Lawyers* (Beard Books 1999) by Sol Stein, a former principal of Stein & Day Publishers. Mr. Stein detailed the contentious Chapter 11 (and ultimate liquidation) of his publishing company in the Southern District of New York in the late 1980s. It's a short book, with some useful non-legal insight into the process. For example, Mr. Stein warns prospective debtors about the

"10 big lies of bankruptcy." Perhaps he's just a bit bitter. *See also* Rutberg, *Ten Cents On The Dollar – Or The Bankruptcy Game* (Beard Books 1999).

[84] Professionals will sit in on board meetings, and weekly (if not daily) meetings with professionals will be common. At the end of this process you will either love or hate your professionals—or maybe both. *See* Kruger & Keller, "The Lawyer's Role In Representing The Distressed Company," *Workouts & Turnarounds* at 85.

[85] At the same time, sophisticated creditors (such as bondholders) in large cases fully understand the need to adequately compensate management during the Chapter 11 case. *See* discussion in Chapter Four on *Golden Parachutes*.

[86] For example, the granting of large bonuses and other perks to senior management caused a major disruption in the *A. H. Robins* Chapter 11 in Virginia.

[87] As discussed in Chapter Two, it may be a public relations specialist.

[88] *See* discussion in Chapter Four regarding *Golden Parachutes*.

[89] As is discussed in Chapter Four more thoroughly, the company's obligation to indemnify its officers and directors (whether by statute or bylaw) is considered an executory contract in a bankruptcy proceeding. As such, unless the debtor specifically assumes that obligation it will have no obligation to indemnify officers and directors for any personal liability that may be incurred as a result of actual or threatened securities litigation that almost always arises in financially troubled companies with public debt or equity. This does not impact applicable D&O insurance coverage, which remains in effect to protect the officers and directors.

In the *UDC Homes* Chapter 11 that was filed in Delaware in 1995, the debtor's plan assumed this liability. After the company emerged with a healthy balance sheet, huge judgments were taken against individual officers and directors (as well as accountants and others), all of which had to ultimately be reimbursed and indemnified by the reorganized company because of the assumption. As a practical matter, it almost never makes any sense for a company to assume these types of obligations because they are subordinated to essentially all other creditors as a matter of law. *See* Bankruptcy Code § 510(b).

[90] Of course, because much of the heat will be focused on lawyers, it's hard to garner too much sympathy for them. It's not unlike the old joke: "Why did labs switch from rats to lawyers for testing purposes? The technicians didn't get attached to the lawyers."

[91] In many reorganization cases, good advice to management is that it has a period of time (maybe sixty to ninety days) to build credibility with key constituencies.

[92] For example, in the *Megafoods Stores* Chapter 11 bankruptcy, the company (which ran warehouse style supermarkets in a four-state area) was the darling of Wall Street with its initial public offering, and followed that up with two public debt offerings raising approximately $160 million. Approximately eighteen months later, the company was in bankruptcy with no cash reserves and no appreciable EBITDA. The CFO was the first to resign (at the urging of the Creditors Committee), and the Board was reconstituted to include three outside, independent directors (which were drawn from a number of candidates, including some proffered by the Creditors Committee). Approximately four or five months later, the CEO was asked to resign and did. All of the machinations turned out to be for naught, however, as the company liquidated anyway about a year after that.

[93] Bankruptcy Rule 2004 provides in pertinent part as follows:

(a) Examination on Motion. On motion of any party in interest, the court may order the examination of any entity.

(b) Scope of Examination. The examination of an entity under this rule or of the debtor . . . may relate only to the acts, conduct, or property or to the liabilities and financial condition of the debtor, or to any matter which may affect the administration of the debtor's estate, or to the debtor's right to a discharge. In a family farmer's debt adjustment case under chapter 12, an individual's debt adjustment case under chapter 13, or a reorganization case ***under chapter 11*** of the Code, other than for the reorganization of a railroad, ***the examination may also relate to the operation of any business and the desirability of its continuance, the source of any money or property acquired or to be acquired by the debtor for purposes of consummating a plan and the consideration given or offered therefor, and any other matter relevant to the case or to the formulation of a plan.***

(c) Compelling Attendance and Production of Documentary Evidence. The attendance of an entity for examination and the production of documentary evidence may be compelled in the manner provided in Rule 16 for the attendance of witnesses at a hearing or trial.

[94] *See, e.g., In re Continental Forge Co.*, 73 B.R. 1005 (Bankr. W.D. Pa. 1987); *In re Nixon Electric Supply, Inc.*, 85 B.R. 988 (Bankr. W.D. Tex. 1988).

[95] *See, e.g., In re Continental Forge Co.*, 73 B.R. 1005 (Bankr. W.D. Pa. 1987). This doesn't happen in the majority of cases, but has occurred in contested confirmations where business- plan performance is critical to valuation.

[96] In certain circumstances creditors or other parties in interest can file plans of reorganization, with or without the debtor's consent. *See* discussion in Chapter Four on *Keeping Control—Exclusivity Rules!*

[97] *See Revlon, Inc. v. MacAndrews & Forbes Holdings, Inc.*, 506 A.2d 173 (Del. 1986). *See also Paramount Communications, Inc. v. Time, Inc.*, 571 A.2d 1140 (Del. 1989); *Paramount Communications, Inc. v. QVC Network, Inc.*, 637 A.2d 34 (Del. 1993).

[98] *See* Dunne, "The *Revlon* Duties And The Sale Of Companies In Chapter 11," 52 *The Bus. Law.* 1333 (August 1997).

[99] This is not to suggest there's anything unlawful or improper about this tactic. In an insolvent company, creditors have leverage. The "raiders" know the process and how to play the game, and they do it well. Instructive late-night reading is *The Vulture Investors* by Hilary Rosenberg. Although you may lie awake, tired and troubled, after this exercise, you will nevertheless have a greater appreciation for the personalities, dynamics, and possible consequences of the reorganization process.

[100] *See In re Johns-Manville Corp.*, 801 F.2d 60 (2nd Cir. 1986). *See also Advanced Chapter 11* at Chapter 14.

[101] The phrase "Chinese Wall" has an interesting origin. The use of the phrase is intended to convey an impenetrable barrier so that information would not pass from one person to the other, such as a company that holds bonds for its own account but which also trades bonds for its customers. The trading desk cannot talk to the arm of the entity that holds the debt. The phrase Chinese Wall is used because the Great Wall of China is the only man-made structure that can be seen from space. As such, the metaphysical "wall" to prevent information transfer is so apparent it can be seen for miles.

Chapter Four

Surviving To Plan Confirmation

[102] The venue provisions relating to the Bankruptcy Code are contained in 28 U.S.C. § 1408. The section provides in pertinent part as follows:

Except as provided in section 1410 of this title, a case under title 11 may be commenced in the district court for the district –

> (1) in which the domicile, residence, principal place of business in the United States, or principal assets in the United States, of the person or entity that is the subject of such case have been located for the one hundred and eighty days immediately preceding such commencement, or for a longer portion of such one-hundred-and-eighty-day period than the domicile, residence, or principal place of business, in the United States, or principal assets in the United States, of such person were located in any other district; or
>
> (2) in which there is pending a case under title 11 concerning such person's affiliate, general partner, or partnership.

[103] This leads to the unusual situation where a case is not immediately iden-

tified by its commonly recognized name. For example, the steel giant *LTV Corporation*'s Chapter 11 case filed in New York was officially known as *In re Chateaugay Corp.* because it was an LTV affiliate that filed in New York to obtain venue there. The *Eastern Airlines* Chapter 11 was officially known as *In re Ionosphere Club* for the same reason.

"Affiliate" is broadly defined in Bankruptcy Code § 101(2) as follows:

"affiliate" means –

(A) entity that directly or indirectly owns, controls, or holds with power to vote, 20 percent or more of the outstanding voting securities of the debtor, other than an entity that holds such securities –

(i) in a fiduciary or agency capacity without sole discretionary power to vote such securities; or

(ii) solely to secure a debt, if such entity has not in fact exercised such power to vote;

(B) corporation 20 percent or more of whose outstanding voting securities are directly or indirectly owned, controlled, or held with power to vote, by the debtor, or by an entity that directly or indirectly owns, controls, or holds with power to vote, 20 percent or more of the outstanding voting securities of the debtor, other than an entity that holds such securities –

(i) in a fiduciary or agency capacity without sole discretionary power to vote such securities; or

(ii) solely to secure a debt, if such entity has not in fact exercised such power to vote;

(C) person whose business is operated under a lease or operating agreement by a debtor, or person substantially all of whose property is operated under an operating agreement with the debtor; or

(D) entity that operates the business or substantially all of the property of the debtor under a lease or operating agreement.

[104] For example, this was considered by *America West Airlines* when it filed its Chapter 11 in 1991 in Phoenix, Arizona. It was the largest national airline based in Phoenix, and was a major employer in Arizona. While America West was a Delaware corporation (and could have filed in Delaware), the "home court advantage" was ultimately determined to be very important to the company. In fact, it was aided in coming out of its reorganization by community support led by business leaders in Arizona so Phoenix could keep its "home town airline."

[105] *See* Salerno, "Seventh Circuit Sounds a Death Knell for Reorganizations of Toxic Polluters," *American Bankruptcy Institute Journal* at 8 (September 1992).

[106] Lawyers for a high-profile debtor in the mid-1990s, with operations throughout Orange County, Los Angeles County, and Santa Barbara, California (all in the Central District of California), advised the debtor to avoid Los Angeles altogether and file its Chapter 11 in Santa Barbara. Ultimately, while the judge displayed the desired business sophistication, the case failed, and those same lawyers were denied substantial amounts of their fees.

[107] For example, in Delaware there are currently only two judges, so the personalities and proclivities of the possible judges are easier to assess. This observation is not meant to disparage any particular judge or jurisdiction, but it is a reality you will hear your bankruptcy lawyers discuss (if not with you, then with each other).

[108] The issue of appropriate venue for Chapter 11 filings is coming under intense scrutiny by the National Bankruptcy Review Commission established as part of the Bankruptcy Reform Act of 1994, with many commentators taking the position that a true business presence should be a prerequisite for establishing venue (as compared with a purely legal presence, such as a state of incorporation). *See, e.g., The Biased Business of Revenue Shopping* (ABI Bankruptcy Reform Study Project, July 21, 1995). *See also Pre-Bankruptcy Planning* at 24-25. In the end, perhaps because Sen. Joseph Biden of Delaware is the former chairman and still a powerful member of the Senate Judiciary Committee, which oversees bankruptcy law, Congress made no changes to the bankruptcy venue provisions.

[109] In companies with publicly traded debt or equities, bankruptcy filings are usually timed to occur either before the market opens for trading or after. On the west coast, for example, which is three hours earlier than New York, arrangements frequently can be and are made with clerk's offices to open early so that a filing can occur prior to the markets opening. This way, a press release can be put out immediately so that anyone who is trading is trading with knowledge (or at least constructive knowledge if they would read the press releases) that the company is in bankruptcy. The same can happen by filing after the market closes so that the word is out in the public domain to warn people who wish to trade in the public debtor's equities.

[110] The Bankruptcy Code's definition of "property of the estate" is found in Bankruptcy Code § 541. This section provides in pertinent part as follows:

(a) The commencement of a case under section 301, 203, or 303 of this title creates an estate. Such estate is comprised of all the following property, wherever located and by whomever held:

(1) Except as provided in subsections (b) and (c)(2) of this section, all legal or equitable interests of the debtor in property as of the commencement of the case.

* * *

(3) Any interest in property that the trustee recovers under sec-

tion 329(b), 363(n), 543, 550, 553, or 723 of this title.

(4) Any interest in property preserved for the benefit of or ordered transferred to the estate under section 510(c) or 551 of this title.

* * *

(6) Proceeds, product, offspring, rents, or profits of or from property of the estate. . . .

(7) Any interest in property that the estate acquires after the commencement of the case.

(b) Property of the estate does not include—

(1) Any power that the debtor may exercise solely for the benefit of an entity other than the debtor;

(2) Any interest of the debtor as a lessee under a lease of non residential real property that has terminated at the expiration of the stated term of such lease before the commencement of the case under this title, and ceases to include any interest of the debtor as a lessee under a lease of nonresidential real property that has terminated at the expiration of the stated term of such lease during the case;

* * *

(4) Any interest of the debtor in liquid or gaseous hydrocarbons to the extent that –

(A) (i) the debtor has transferred or has agreed to transfer such interest pursuant to a farmout agreement or any written agreement directly related to a farmout agreement; and

(ii) but for the operation of this paragraph the state could include the interest referred to in clause (i) only by virtue of section 365 or 544(a)(3) of this title; or

(B) (i) the debtor has transferred such interest pursuant to a written conveyance of a production payment to an entity that does not participate in the operation of the property from which such production payment is transferred; and

(ii) but for the operation of this paragraph, the estate could include the interest referred to in clause (i) only by virtue of section 542 of this title.

(c) (1) Except as provided in paragraph (2) of this subsection, an interest of the debtor in property becomes property of the estate under subsection (a)(1) . . . of this section not with standing any provision in an agreement, transfer instrument, or applicable nonbankruptcy law–

(A) That restricts or conditions transfer of such interest by the debtor; or

(B) that is conditioned on the insolvency or financial condition of the debtor, on the commencement of a case under this title, or on the appointment of or taking possession by a trustee in a case under this title or a custodian before such commencement and that effects or gives an option to effect a forfeiture, modification, or termination of the debtor's interest in property.

(2) A restriction on the transfer of a beneficial interest of the debtor in a trust that is enforceable under applicable nonbankruptcy law is enforceable in a case under this title.

(d) Property in which the debtor holds, as of the commencement of the case, only legal title and not an equitable interest, such as a mortgage secured by real property, or an interest in such a mortgage, sold by the debtor but as to which the debtor retains legal title to service or supervise the servicing of such mortgage or interest, becomes property of the estate under subsection (a)(1) . . . this section only to the extent of the debtor's legal title to such property, but not to the extent of any equitable interest in such property that the debtor does not hold.

[111] *See* note 110, in particular Bankruptcy Code § 541(d).

[112] *See* Bankruptcy Code § 362(a).

[113] Likewise, the Bankruptcy Code cannot completely silence a creditor in light of the First Amendment's grant of freedom of speech. Thus, while a creditor, a lessor of billboards, who superimposes "BEWARE, THIS COMPANY DOES NOT PAY ITS BILLS" on one of the debtor's leased billboard advertisements may not win the corporate citizen of the year award, he doesn't violate the automatic stay. *See In re National Service Corp.*, 724 F.2d 859 (5th Cir. 1984). This type of spiteful behavior is not unheard-of, particularly in certain industries, and can heighten the need for both excellent public relations advisors and powerful headache medicines. When *Stuart Entertainment*, the manufacturer of bingo supplies and devices, filed its Chapter 11 petition in August 1999, several of its competitors attempted to take over some of Stuart's local bingo hall accounts and distributors by circulating rumors about Stuart's demise. Because Stuart was able to successfully implement public relations strategies (using its own distributors to quell the fears of bingo hall operators), the competitors' strategy did not work. Stuart successfully reorganized and emerged from bankruptcy only four months later.

[114] *See In re Minoco Group of Cos., Ltd.*, 799 F.2d 517 (9th Cir. 1986).

[115] Banks can—and often do—place administrative freezes on a debtor's bank account in order to preserve the bank's *postpetition* set-off rights. While the bank must obtain relief from the automatic stay from the bankruptcy court before exercising its rights to set off, the bank could lose the right altogether if it relinquishes possession of estate property. The U.S. Supreme Court ruled in 1995 that banks do not violate the automatic stay by placing an administrative freeze on bank accounts while seeking relief from the stay. *Citizens Bank of Maryland v. Strumpf,* 516 U.S. 16 (1995).

[116] In the *McCulloch Corporation* bankruptcy in Tucson, Arizona, a Mexican trucking company seized millions of dollars in the debtor's inventory located in Mexico and refused to complete shipment until its prepetition claim was paid in full. The act was in obvious violation of the automatic stay. Despite the bankruptcy judge's stern warning to the creditor's lawyer (using such terms as "extortion") and order to return the goods immediately, the Mexican company essentially thumbed its nose at the court's order, saying that it had no force under Mexican law. The debtor was able to obtain its goods only after agreeing to pay the Mexican company more than 50 percent of its unsecured, prepetition claim in cash. Virtually no other unsecured creditor in that case has yet been paid, and it is unlikely that any will receive more than 5 percent of its claim. The lesson—never use a creditor based outside the United States to ship property of the estate.

[117] Courts currently disagree about whether and under what legal authority a corporate debtor may also obtain punitive damages for intentional stay violations but, as a practical matter, circumstances when punitive damages would seem appropriate are relatively rare.

[118] *See* Bankruptcy Code § 362(b).

[119] Such action also constitutes impermissible discrimination. *See* Bankruptcy Code § 525(a).

[120] This last exception has a wrinkle, however: any tax lien that would have otherwise attached to property of the estate by reason of the tax assessment—for example, liens on a debtor's personal property to secure payment of assessed *ad valorem* taxes are ubiquitous in Texas municipalities—does not attach unless the tax would not be discharged and the property is sold during the bankruptcy proceedings. If the automatic stay were to prevent the attachment of such liens, secured lenders would benefit, since the lenders would otherwise be subordinated to those liens. With this exception to the automatic stay, unless the property is sold, local governments—who rely heavily on such taxes for sources of revenue—will have their liens, and those liens will trump existing liens on that property.

[121] Those are the practical concerns. Legally, courts apply a balancing test to determine whether "cause" exists to allow pending litigation to proceed

in another court. The test is whether or not: (1) any "great prejudice" to either the bankruptcy estate or the debtor will result from continuation of the lawsuit; (2) the hardship of the stay to the plaintiff considerably outweighs the hardship of lifting the stay to the debtor; (3) the plaintiff has a probability of prevailing on the merits of its case.

[122] The single-asset scenario looks like this: the debtor (a limited partnership or an LLC, usually) owns essentially one asset—a piece of real property. The property is secured by a mortgage or deed of trust, the underlying loan is in monetary default, and the lender-mortgagee is readying a foreclosure. The debtor files a Chapter 11 petition on the eve of the foreclosure sale, thereby putting a stop to the foreclosure, thwarting (at least temporarily) the lender's ability to obtain the benefit of its security interest. Many courts hold that if the debtor has only one asset and one real creditor (the lender), real reorganization is a virtual impossibility and the stay should be lifted for cause. The petition is said to have been filed in "bad faith," and the practical effect of lifting the stay in these cases is to dismiss the bankruptcy case, since nothing is left to reorganize once the lender forecloses.

[123] Bankruptcy Code § 101(51B) defines "single-asset real estate" as "real property constituting a single property or project, other than residential real property with fewer than 4 residential units, which generates substantially all of the gross income of a debtor and on which no substantial business is being conducted by a debtor other than the business of operating the real property and activities incidental thereto having aggregate noncontingent, liquidated secured debts in an amount no more than $4,000,000." Obviously, large commercial real estate assets fall outside this category, so the special provisions in the Bankruptcy Code dealing with "single- asset real estate" cases do not apply in many circumstances. *See also* Bankruptcy Code § 362(d)(3). This ninety-day period can be extended by the bankruptcy court "for cause."

[124] *See* note 26.

[125] *See* Bankruptcy Code § 361.

[126] For some years, there was pointed disagreement as to what constituted "fair market value." Some courts preferred a value based on a supposed distressed sale of the collateral, others preferred a value based on what it would cost to replace the collateral on the open market, and still others preferred a value based on wholesale value, retail value, or an average of the two. The Supreme Court resolved this dispute in *Associates Commercial Corp. v. Rash,* 520 U.S. 953 (1997) by establishing that value is to be determined with reference to the "replacement value" – that is, the price a willing buyer in the debtor's trade, business, or situation would pay to a willing seller to obtain comparable property of like age and condition.

[127] This formulation is found in the important Supreme Court case *United Savings Ass'n. v. Timbers of Inwood Forest Associates, Ltd.,* 484 U.S. 365 (1988).

[128] At one time there was a difference of opinion among courts as to when the check was considered "transferred" by the debtor. Was it when it was delivered by the debtor, or when the bank honored it? In 1992 the Supreme Court resolved the issue by ruling that a check is considered "transferred" when the bank honors it, not when it's delivered. *See Barnhill v. Johnson*, 503 U.S. 393 (1992). This has significance, especially to the company's restructuring lawyers who will want a retainer that they don't have to give back! *See* discussion in Chapter Two on *The Professional Team.*

[129] *See, e.g., In re Adams Apple, Inc.,* 829 F.2d 1484 (9th Cir 1987); *In re Ionosphere Clubs, Inc.,* 98 B.R. 174 (Bankr. S.D.N.Y. 1989). *See also Advanced Chapter 11*, Chapter 7.

[130] Hence the importance of choosing the right venue!

[131] Of course, this has also been done. In the Chapter 11 proceeding of *Stuart Entertainment, Inc.*, which was filed in Delaware in 1999, the bankruptcy court did in fact enter a first day order that allowed the debtor to pay approximately $3,000,000 to $5,000,000 in prebankruptcy trade debt. No prepetition trade creditors were left out of this relief. With the trade taken care of, the plan of reorganization essentially amounted to a conversion of publicly held bond debt to equity in the reorganized entity. Interestingly, the Unsecured Creditors Committee (which is really designed to watch out for the interest of all unsecured creditors) objected to payment of prebankruptcy unsecured debt. The court overruled the objection. Such are the interesting side dramas that one sees in bankruptcy cases.

[132] One way that creative debtor counsel can try to deal with essential vendors is to get court permission to pay them their prebankruptcy claim, but only to the extent that they agree to extend normal trade terms postbankruptcy on the same basis they did prebankruptcy. For example, once a bankruptcy is filed many vendors' knee-jerk reaction is to put the debtor on C.O.D. terms. This has a devastating effect on the cash of a business enterprise. Accordingly, debtors (or their professionals) will negotiate deals with these creditors that they will pay them their prebankruptcy claims as long as they are extended customary trade terms on a postbankruptcy basis.

[133] *See* Bankruptcy Code § 102(1)(A).

[134] *See* Bankruptcy Code § 102(1)(B)(ii).

[135] To be fair, courts may limit how much in prebankruptcy wages can be paid or impose other restrictions during the interim period of the order.

[136] Generally debtors will negotiate these with the key employees, and then run them by major secured creditors and Committees to get their support before seeking bankruptcy court approval.

[137] For example, retention bonuses and severance packages for non-senior-level people in liquidation cases were proposed and approved in the

liquidations of *McCulloch Corp.* and *Nationsway Trucking*, both of which liquidated through Chapter 11 proceedings.

[138] There are also certain circumstances where management seeks to obtain bankruptcy court approval of severance and termination packages without the consent of the creditors, which makes for a very ugly dynamic. In these cases, creditors don't want management around and view executive attempts to obtain court approval of severance packages as a way to entrench themselves into the company.

[139] *See* discussion in Chapter Three under *Just Whom Does My Lawyer Represent Anyway?*

[140] For example, this occurred in the Chapter 11 case of *In re Stuart Entertainment, Inc.*, which was confirmed in December 1999 in the District of Delaware.

[141] This was the protocol utilized in the Chapter 11 restructuring of *In re Unison HealthCare Corp.*, which was confirmed in 1999 in the District of Arizona.

[142] The motion, supporting declaration, and accompanying order authorizing the package were taken from the Chapter 11 case of *In re Unison HealthCare Corp.*, which was filed in 1999 in the District of Arizona. The provisions are fairly typical of those found in Chapter 11 cases.

[143] *See also* Bankruptcy Code § 552(b).

[144] Bankruptcy Code § 363(a) defines "cash collateral" as "cash, negotiable instruments, documents of title, securities, deposit accounts, or other cash equivalents whenever acquired in which the estate and an entity other than the estate have an interest and includes the proceeds, products, offspring, rents, or profits of property and the fees, charges, accounts or other payments for the use or occupancy of rooms and other public facilities in hotels, motels, or other lodging properties subject to a security interest . . . whether existing before or after the commencement of a case under [the Bankruptcy Code]."

[145] *See* Bankruptcy Code § 364(a).

[146] *See* Bankruptcy Code § 364(c)(1).

[147] *See* Bankruptcy Code § 364(c)(2).

[148] Recall the discussion on "negative notice" earlier in this chapter. In financing cases (which would include both cash collateral and DIP financing) the negative-notice process is used frequently although bankruptcy courts will generally put some limit on how much can be lent (or spent) during the negative-notice period so that other creditors are not completely left out of the process.

[149] For example, *Turnarounds & Workouts* periodically prints a "Special Report" entitled "*Sources of Debtor-In-Possession Financing*," which

lists the companies, the contacts, the telephone numbers, and recent DIP loans and amounts. In its December 15, 1999, "Special Report," *Turnarounds & Workouts* listed Ableco Finance, LLC; Bank Boston Retail Finance Inc.; Chase Manhattan Bank; Citibank; GECC; the CIT Group/Business Credit; Congress Financial Corporation; DDJ Capital Management, LLC; Deutsche Banc Alex Brown; Foothill Capital Corporation; Jefferies & Company, Inc.; PPM Finance, Inc.; and Rothschild Recovery Fund, LLP, all as sources of potential DIP financing.

150 A good discussion on DIP financing is found in Altman, *Bankruptcy and Distressed Restructurings: Analytical Issues and Investment Opportunities* at 408 (Beard Books 1999). *See also* Fitch Investors Service, Inc., *Special Debtor-In-Possession Loans Report* (March 25, 1991).

151 What generally happens is the prebankruptcy lender offers a DIP facility that is a continuation of the prebankruptcy line. Due to borrowing base formulas under the existing loan documents, the debtor will collect $100 (which will go to the lender), and the lender will lend back $30.

152 For example, in the *Megafoods Stores* Chapter 11 proceeding, a primary supplier of groceries refused to load trucks until the company wired transferred funds to pay for the delivery. It does not take an economics major to understand the hugely detrimental impact this had on cash flow for the business.

153 As part of most first day orders, debtors usually seek (and obtain) bankruptcy court permission to continue to use their existing checking accounts and checks. The normal rule is that old accounts are shut down, and new checks are printed showing the payor as "ABC, Inc., DIP."

154 *See* Bankruptcy Rules 1007, 1008, and 1009; Official Bankruptcy Forms 6 and 7.

155 Individual debtors and debtors in Chapter 7 cases must file certain additional Statements not relevant to business reorganizations.

156 Schedules I (Current Income Of Individual Debtors) and J (Current Expenditures Of Individual Debtors) are inapplicable in business cases.

157 At a bare minimum, you should be sure to footnote the schedules to disclose the basis for valuation of assets (book value, estimates of fair market values, etc.), thereby giving yourself "wiggle room" later in the case.

158 As of December, 2000, Quarterly U.S. Trustee fees under 28 U.S.C. § 1930(a)(6) were as follows:

Total Quarterly Disbursements	Quarterly Fee
Less than $15,000	$250
$15,000-$74,999.99	$500

$75,000-$149,999.99	$750
$150,000-$224,999.99	$1,250
$225,000- $299,999.99	$1,500
$300,000-$999,999.99	$3,750
$1,000,000-$1,999,999.99	$5,000
$2,000,000-$2,999,999.99	$7,500
$3,000,000-$4,999,999.99	$8,000
$5,000,000 or more	$10,000

These fees are periodically adjusted (always upwards).

[159] The Bankruptcy Code does not define what is or is not a "utility." In practice, not much time is spent arguing about whether a particular entity is a utility. Most bankruptcy courts know a utility when they see one, and companies are rarely inclined to dispute a debtor's designation of it as a utility, mostly because the company will be able to exact from the estate a security deposit or other adequate assurance of payment postpetition. Other trade creditors do not have statutory authority to demand such adequate assurance.

[160] *See* Bankruptcy Code § 366, which provides:

(a) Except as provided in subsection (b) of this section, a utility may not alter, refuse, or discontinue service to, or discriminate against, the trustee or the debtor solely on the basis of the commencement of a case under this title or that a debt owed by the debtor to such utility for service rendered before the order for relief was not paid when due.

(b) Such utility may alter, refuse, or discontinue service if neither the trustee nor the debtor, within 20 days after the date of the order for relief, furnishes adequate assurance of payment, in the form of a deposit or other security, for service after such date. On request of a party in interest and after notice and a hearing, the court may order reasonable modification of the amount of the deposit or other security necessary to provide adequate assurance of payment.

[161] For example, in the *Baptist Foundation of Arizona* case, even though the company was exempt from federal and state securities filings and regulations because it was a non-profit organization, the SEC still monitored the case on a regular basis.

[162] *See Pre-Bankruptcy Planning* at 17.

[163] *See In re Minoco Group of Companies, Ltd.*, 799 F.2d 517 (9th Cir. 1986). The interesting distinction is usually that while the *policy* is an asset

of the estate, the *proceeds* of the policy are not. Nonetheless, the policy is protected as an estate asset.

[164] *See, e.g., In re Circle K Corp.*, 121 B.R. 257 (Bankr. D. Az. 1990).

[165] These distinctions regarding injunctive relief arose over the years largely in environmental contexts, but have since been relied on by courts to analyze the automatic stay's effect on many different types of judicial injunctions.

[166] The intersection between environmental laws and bankruptcy laws are complex and the subject of numerous legal commentaries. *See, e.g.*, Salerno, Ferland & Hansen, "Environmental Law And Its Impact On Bankruptcy Law—The Saga Of Toxins-R-Us," 25 *Real Property Probate and Trust J.* 261 (Summer 1990); Salerno & Miller, "The Co-PRP Dilemma: Disallowance Of Contingent Claims Under Code § 502," *Turnarounds & Workouts Survey Of Environmental Law* (December 15, 1993); Salerno, "And The Beat Goes On—The Seventh Circuit Espouses The 'Greater Fool' Theory As A Solution For Environmental Contamination Problems," *American Bankruptcy Institute J.* 8 (September 1992); Salerno, "Future Claimants In Mass Tort Bankruptcy Cases—Good News And Bad News For Debtors And Reorganization Cases From The Southern District Of Florida," *American Bankruptcy Institute J.* 8 (September 1994); *Advanced Chapter 11* at §§ 14.34 *et seq.*

[167] Recently, the U.S. Supreme Court declined to review a Tenth Circuit Court of Appeals ruling that held that: (1) the present value of future unfunded benefit liabilities had to be calculated not by PBGC's regulatory procedures but rather based on a "prudent investor" standard; and (2) the claim for future unfunded benefit liabilities was not entitled to priority status. *See Pension Benefit Guaranty Corp. v. Reorganized CF&I Fabricators of Utah Inc.*, 150 F.3d 1293 (10th Cir. 1998), in which the PBGC had submitted a claim for $328 million. The Tenth Circuit's opinion agrees with virtually every other case in the country on these issues. Despite losing everywhere, the PBGC still claims priority status in each new case.

[168] 7 U.S.C. §§ 499(a) *et seq.*

[169] 7 U.S.C. § 499(e)(C)(2).

[170] It's not always clear whether certain goods fall within the statutory definition of "perishable agricultural commodities." When is a potato not a potato—what does one have to do to a potato before it no longer is a "commodity"? For an interesting case involving PACA, french fries, and something referred to as a "suspension of batter solids in a slurry of water," *see In re Long John Silver's Restaurants Inc.,* 230 B.R. 29 (Bankr. D. Del. 1999). For a humorous review of that case, *see* Salerno, "You Want Fries With That? Or, How to 'Batter' Yourself Out of PACA Protections," *American Bankruptcy Institute J.* 32 (May 1999).

[171] *See Begier v. IRS*, 496 U.S. 53 (1990).

172 Internal Revenue Code § 6672.

173 *See* Bankruptcy Code § 1146(c). In the *14 Wall Street L.P.* Chapter 11 done in the Southern District of New York (Manhattan), the debtor transferred a large downtown office building (located at—you guessed it—14 Wall Street) to the secured lender using a prepackaged Chapter 11 bankruptcy filing, essentially to avoid notoriously high New York State transfer taxes.

174 The Uniform Commercial Code in most states allows a seller to reclaim goods that were sold to an insolvent buyer provided they make a written demand for the goods within ten days of the receipt of the goods by the buyer. This comes up most frequently when goods are sold and delivered on normal thirty-day trade terms, and five days after the debtor receives the goods it files a bankruptcy petition.

175 *See* Bankruptcy Code § 546(c).

176 This protocol was used, for example, in the *Circle K* and *Megafoods Stores* bankruptcy proceedings. While it is a drain on cash flow, it is a good leverage device to help a debtor get its vendors to extend ordinary trade terms postbankruptcy.

177 *See* Bankruptcy Code § 1114.

178 *See* Bankruptcy Code § 1113.

179 Large sales also may raise the bankruptcy court's concern that the debtor is attempting to implement a "*sub rosa* plan"—or a disguised plan—without complying with the plan process. "*Sub rosa*" means literally "under the rose," and is the phrase used in legal decisions.

180 *See* Bankruptcy Code §§ 363(f) and (h). Specifically, those sections provide in pertinent part as follows:

> (f) The trustee may sell property . . . free and clear of any interest in such property of an entity other than the estate, only if—
>
> > (1) applicable nonbankruptcy law permits sale of such property free and clear of such interest;
> >
> > (2) such entity consents;
> >
> > (3) such interest is a lien and the price at which such property is to be sold is greater than the aggregate value of all liens on such property;
> >
> > (4) such interest is in bona fide dispute; or
> >
> > (5) such entity could be compelled, in a legal or equitable proceeding, to accept a money satisfaction of such interest.
>
> * * *
>
> (h) Notwithstanding subsection (f) of this section, the trustee may sell

both the estate's interest . . . and the interest of any co-owner in property in which the debtor had, at the time of the commencement of the case, an undivided interest as a tenant in common, joint tenant, or tenant by the entirety, only if—

(1) partition in kind of such property among the estate and such co-owners is impracticable;

(2) sale of the estate's undivided interest in such property would realize significantly less for the estate than sale of such property free of the interests of such co-owners;

(3) the benefit of the estate of a sale of such property free of the interests of co-owners outweighs the detriment, if any, to such co-owners; and

(4) such property is not used in the production, transmission, or distribution, for sale, of electric energy or of natural or synthetic gas for heat, light, or power.

[181] *See* Bankruptcy Code § 363(k).

[182] For example, in the *McCulloch Corporation* Chapter 11, which occurred in Tucson, all of the debtor's intellectual property and manufacturing rights for manufacturing chainsaws and other items in Europe were being auctioned. The first potential acquirer in the door was an Italian entity and it bid approximately $10.3 million for all of the rights. As part of that offer, the potential buyer requested and obtained bankruptcy court approval for a $400,000 bust up fee. After a duly-noticed auction, the asset sold for approximately $33 million, and the original offer was not the successful offer. As such, the Italian entity was paid $400,000 for being the "stalking horse" in the case. *See also* Houlihan, Lokey, Howard & Zukin, *1998 Transaction Termination Fee Study*, (July 1999).

[183] For example, in the *UDC Homes* Chapter 11 in Wilmington, Delaware, the bankruptcy court did approve such "window shop" provisions.

[184] Aggressive buyers sometimes request "lock up provisions" precluding a debtor from even considering any other offers. These are rarely approved, and are really not appropriate in bankruptcy cases.

[185] Of course, to the extent that due diligence for potential asset sales involve the review of confidential or proprietary information, potential offerors will need to sign confidentiality letters as discussed in Chapter Three.

[186] *See* Salerno & Kroop, *Bankruptcy Litigation And Practice: A Practitioner's Guide—3rd Edition* at § 8.68 (Aspen Law Publishers 2000) (hereafter "*Bankruptcy Litigation And Practice*"). The exact elements of a preference are found in Bankruptcy Code § 547(b):

any transfer of an interest of the debtor in property—

(1) to or for the benefit of a creditor;

(2) for or on account of an antecedent debt owed by the debtor before such transfer was made;

(3) made while the debtor was insolvent;

(4) made—

(A) on or within days before the date of the filing of the petition; or

(B) between days and one year before the date of the filing of the petition, if such creditor at the time of such transfer was an insider; and

(5) that enables such creditor to receive more than such creditor would receive if—

(A) the case were a case under chapter 7 of this title;

(B) the transfer had not been made; and

(C) such creditor received payment of such debt to the extent provided by the provisions of this title.

[187] The reason for this is because it's assumed that an insider (such as an officer or director) has inside information about the financial condition of the company, and is likely to use that information to his or her advantage.

[188] This created quite a stir in the *Megafoods Stores* bankruptcy. The debtor brought preference litigation against hundreds of creditors—essentially everyone that received a check within ninety days of the filing. Some of these creditors were lessors of assumed leases. The action was dismissed against them, and sanctions against the debtor were sought (and denied).

[189] *See* Bankruptcy Code § 502(d). Some debtors take the position that all they need to do is file a preference lawsuit against a creditor and the creditor's claim will be "disallowed." This is incorrect—the disallowance occurs after the bankruptcy court determines a preference has occurred (after a trial or other hearing). *See, e.g., In re Davis*, 889 F.2d 658 (5th Cir. 1989); *In re Parker North American Corp.*, 24 F.3d 1145, 1155 (9th Cir. 1994).

[190] The defenses to avoidance of a preference are found in Bankruptcy Code § 547(c)(1) through (8). It is important to understand that these exceptions are to *avoidance* of a preference—they assume that all elements of a preference in § 547(b) are already proved.

[191] Be sure not to confuse this "new value" defense with the "new value corollary" to the absolute priority rule, which is discussed in Chapter Five.

[192] The reasoning for this is that the creditor has not bettered its position with respect to the estate, it has simply traded an older debt for a newer debt. But in bankruptcy, unsecured debt is unsecured debt irrespective of when it was incurred. The even exchange of debt means that the creditor is not better off in relation to the estate or other creditors. It's important to

remember that the creditor must actually extend the new credit—not simply make it available. Credit card companies tried this line of defense in defending credit card preference payments, and lost. They said if a cardholder had a $5,000 credit limit, had a $5,000 balance, and made a $1,000 payment, there was no preference because the card issuer extended another $1,000 in available credit. That has not been considered new value, but merely replacing one obligation for another. *See also* Bankruptcy Code § 547(c)(2).

[193] Creditors need to be vigilant and properly perfect whatever liens they get, however. If on Day 1 the company signs the note and security agreement, the lender doesn't get around to recording or filing the form UCC-1 as required by applicable state law until Day 40, and a bankruptcy is filed on Day 85, the recordation of the lien will be voidable as a preference. *See, e.g., In re Vance*, 721 F.2d 259 (9th Cir. 1985); *Advanced Chapter 11* at § 6.78.

[194] Prior to 1984, the Bankruptcy Code had a forty-five-day time limit on "ordinary course" transactions—payments on invoices over forty-five days old were automatically considered outside of the ordinary course of business. The Bankruptcy Code was changed in 1984 to do away with the forty-five-day limit. The Supreme Court has held that the ordinary course of business defense is not limited to trade debt, but also applies to long-term debt. *Union Bank v. Wolas*, 502 U.S. 151 (1991).

[195] For example, on Day 1 the vendor got $100 on a past due invoice; on Day 4 it delivers goods worth $50, for which the invoice is unpaid. The preference exposure is $50, not $100. Bankruptcy Code § 547(c)(4).

[196] The precise definition of a "fraudulent transfer" is found in Bankruptcy Code § 548(a)(1):

> Any transfer of an interest of the debtor in property, or any obligation incurred by the debtor, that was made or incurred on or within one year before the date of the filing of the petition, if the debtor voluntarily or involuntarily—
>
> (A) made such transfer or incurred such obligation with actual intent to hinder, delay, or defraud any entity to which the debtor was or became, on or after the date that such transfer was made or such obligation was incurred, indebted; or
>
> (B) (i) received less than a reasonably equivalent value in exchange for such transfer or obligation; and
>
> (ii) (I) was insolvent on the date that such transfer was made or such obligation was incurred, or became insolvent as a result of such transfer or obligation;
>
> (II) was engaged in business or a transaction, or was about to engage in business or a transaction, for which any prop-

erty remaining with the debtor was an unreasonably small capital; or

(III) intended to incur, or believed that the debtor would incur, debts that would be beyond the debtor's ability to pay as such debts matured.

[197] *See* Bankruptcy Code § 548.

[198] *See* Bankruptcy Code § 544(a).

[199] An example of this would be if a debtor, on the eve of bankruptcy, transferred all its assets to another company for very little consideration or value in exchange in order to prevent the debtor's creditors from having any assets from which to seek a recovery. Individual debtors and closely held companies are far more prone to this type of behavior ("gifts" to family members on the eve of bankruptcy) than larger companies, although these types of things have happened even in larger companies (usually involving related-party transactions).

[200] *See* Queenan, "The Collapsed Leveraged Buyout And The Trustee In Bankruptcy," 11 *Cardozo L. Rev.* 1 (1989); *Advanced Chapter 11* at §§ 6.140 *et seq. See also* note 74.

[201] Bankruptcy Code § 544(a)(1) establishes the DIP as a hypothetical judicial lien creditor—"a creditor that extends credit to the debtor at the time of the commencement of the case, and that obtains, at such time and with respect to such credit, a judicial lien on all property on which a creditor on a simple contract could have obtained such a judicial lien, whether or not such a creditor exists . . ."

[202] Another type of "secret lien" is the so-called "constructive trust." For example, a company defrauds a person out of assets or money, and then files a bankruptcy. The creditor takes the position that although the assets are titled in the company's name, because of the prebankruptcy fraud the assets really are held in "constructive trust" for the benefit of the defrauded creditor. Unless the creditor has received a judgment from a court prebankruptcy determining it has a constructive trust, the DIP "trumps" this claim (although the fraud may give rise to other problems, such as the appointment of a Chapter 11 trustee). *See, e.g., In re Tleel*, 876 F.2d 769 (9th Cir. 1989); *In re North American Coin & Currency, Ltd.*, 767 F.2d 1573 (9th Cir. 1985); *Belisle v. Plunkett*, 877 F.2d 512 (7th Cir. 1989); *In re General Coffee Corp.*, 828 F.2d 699 (11th Cir. 1987). *But see In re Howard's Appliance Corp.*, 874 F.2d 88 (2nd Cir. 1989); Weintraub & Resnick, "Bankruptcy Trustee's Strong Arm Power Balked By Constructive Trust," 22 *U.C.C.L.J.* 367 (1990).

[203] Bankruptcy Code § 544(a)(3) establishes the DIP as "a bona fide purchaser of real property, other than fixtures, from the debtor, against whom applicable law permits such transfer to be perfected, that obtains the status

of a bona fide purchaser and has perfected such transfer at the time of the commencement of the case, whether or not such a purchaser exists."

[204] *See* Bankruptcy Code § 544(a).

[205] Bankruptcy Code § 549 sets forth the ability of the DIP to avoid certain postpetition transfers.

[206] *See* Bankruptcy Code § 546(a). Specifically, the Bankruptcy Code provides that actions on certain avoidance powers have to be brought the later of two years after the bankruptcy filing (or "entry of the order for relief") or one year after the appointment of a trustee if a Chapter 11 trustee is appointed, provided such appointment occurs before the two years.

[207] This is precisely what happened in the rocky Chapter 11 proceeding of *Megafoods Stores*. In that case, the stabilization of the business was taking much longer than anticipated (and indeed, it never occurred as the case ultimately wound up in liquidation), and the debtor filed preference litigation against hundreds of defendants very shortly before the time period expired. Unfortunately, included as defendants were people that would clearly be deemed not to have received preferences, such as lessors on real property leases that had been assumed. The bankruptcy court dismissed out many of the defendants who sought sanctions against the debtors and their professionals (which the bankruptcy court declined to impose).

[208] Executory contracts and unexpired leases, and the DIP's ability to assume and reject them, are covered in Bankruptcy Code § 365. This section is (aside from the definitional § 101) the longest section of the Bankruptcy Code. Given the relative simplicity of the basic concepts of assumption and rejection, it is surprising that the section should be so long and involved, until one realizes that it has become one of Congress's favorite places to stick special interest legislation (along with the exceptions to the automatic stay found in Bankruptcy Code § 362(b), and the treatment of union contracts and retiree benefits found in Bankruptcy Code §§ 1113 and 1114, discussed later). Special provisions regarding intellectual property licenses, shopping center leases, and other specialized types of contracts have been included in § 365 in response to some very effective lobbying by special interest groups such as airlines, shopping center landlords, and technology licensors.

[209] Bankruptcy Code § 365(e) specifically provides that the filing of a bankruptcy petition does not permit the other party to an executory contract or unexpired lease to terminate or modify the debtor's rights under the contract or lease, even when the terms of the contract or lease so provide. To do so would violate the automatic stay. *See, e.g., In re Minoco Group Of Cos., Ltd.*, 799 F.2d 517 (9th Cir. 1986). Provisions in leases and other contracts denominating a bankruptcy of a party as an event of default, giving rise to a termination of the lease or contract, is referred to as an "ipso facto" clause, and these are never enforceable in a bankruptcy proceeding except with respect to the making of a loan or other financial accommoda-

tion or to issue a security of the debtor.

[210] *See, e.g., Moody v. Amoco Oil Co.*, 734 F.2d 1200 (7th Cir. 1984). *See also* Bankruptcy Code § 541(b)(2) (excluding from definition of property of the estate any unexpired lease of real property that has terminated by its own terms prebankruptcy, or which expires during the case).

[211] Countryman, "Executory Contracts in Bankruptcy: Part I," 57 *Minn. L. Rev.* 439, 460 (1973). For an excellent review of what makes a contract "executory," *see In re Columbia Gas System, Inc.*, 50 F.3d 233 (3d Cir. 1995).

[212] This is particularly true in cases in which a retailer is going to be closing certain stores or liquidating altogether. In the *Ernst Home Centers* bankruptcy in Seattle, a regional hardware and home center chain was liquidating and it was the tenant under many long-term, below-market leases in very desirable shopping center locations. Since the sale of the debtor's inventory was accomplished through a liquidator and benefited the secured lender almost exclusively, the estate was without much in the way of assets for unsecured creditors without the value inherent in the leases. The debtor succeeded in "selling" the leasehold interests to a third-party investor called FADCO, who then marketed the leases and collected cash premiums that new tenants would agree to pay to take over the remaining term of the attractive, below-market leases. FADCO paid the estate $16 million in cash for the leases, cash that was the primary source of recovery for unsecured creditors and the main reason that a Chapter 11 plan of liquidation was possible. Otherwise, the case would have likely been converted to a Chapter 7 and unsecured creditors would have been essentially wiped out.

[213] Or so it's supposed to be. In the *R.H. Macy's* Chapter 11 case in Manhattan in the early 1990s, the debtor assumed scores of leases in various shopping centers around the country prior to plan confirmation, and a year or so later decided it didn't want many of those sites. The plan essentially terminated the leases and treated the claims like prebankruptcy breach claims. In 1996, the Second Circuit Court of Appeal (the decisions of which are controlling law in the Southern District of New York) would have made that plan unconfirmable as a matter of law. *See* discussion in note 214, below.

[214] *See, e.g., In re Klein Sleep Products, Inc.*, 78 F.3d 18 (2nd Cir. 1996).

[215] *See* Bankruptcy Code § 365(d)(3). All rent payable under the lease in this context is typically referred to in bankruptcy circles as "administrative rent." *See In re Pacific-Atlantic Trading Co.*, 27 F.3d 40, (9th Cir. 1994).

[216] Circuit-level courts have begun to cause problems with respect to cure of non-monetary defaults. Bankruptcy Code § 365(b)(2)(D) provides that the debtor does not need to cure a default relating to "the satisfaction of any penalty rate or provision relating to a default arising from any failure by the debtor to perform nonmonetary obligations under the executory contract or

unexpired lease." Nearly all bankruptcy professionals and judges assumed for years that this provision meant that the debtor was not required to pay penalties or cure any non-monetary default provision in a contract or lease before assuming the contract or lease. The Ninth Circuit, however, held in *In re Claremont Acquisition Corp.,* 113 F.3d 1029 (9th Cir. 1997) that a debtor-franchisee was not permitted to assume and assign its executory franchise agreement because § 365(d)(2)(D) does **not** excuse the debtor from having to cure non-monetary defaults such as the continuous-operations clause in the franchise agreement. This decision is, to be blunt, ridiculous. Not only is it based on a tortured interpretation of the lack of a comma in § 365(d)(2)(D), but the rule would prevent countless retail debtors from ever assuming and assigning any of their valuable below-market leases for closed stores because a debtor cannot go back in time and continuously operate. If these retail debtors cannot assume and assign their leases—perhaps the most valuable assets left in a liquidating debtor's estate—then any Chapter 11 liquidation is likely doomed, and unsecured creditors will be left holding the bag.

[217] These restrictions are found in Bankruptcy Code § 365(c). A hot area of dispute at the time of this writing is whether § 365(c) is to be interpreted to prevent a debtor from even assuming a contract that it could not assign under § 365(c), even when the debtor has no actual intention of assigning the contract. Some courts have adopted a "hypothetical" test, and prohibit the debtor from assuming a contract if it could not also assign it, while other courts have adopted an "actual" test that would allow a debtor to assume a contract that could not be assigned, so long as the debtor does not actually intend to assign it to a third party. The dispute is important, particularly in relation to government contracts, certain franchise contracts, loan servicing agreements, and intellectual property licenses that often provide the very foundation of a debtor's continued business operations but cannot be assigned. If the hypothetical test were to apply, a debtor's reorganization (dependent on assumption of the contracts) could be doomed, even if the debtor had no intention of assigning the contract. *Cf. In re Catapult Ent., Inc.*, 165 F.3d 747 (9th Cir. 1999) and *In re Leroux*, 69 F.3d 608 (1st Cir. 1995).

[218] Much like learned theologians debating how many angels can dance on the head of a pin, legal scholars have been debating for over twenty years what the full implication of "rejection" is. Does the contract disappear? What about covenants not to compete and other specifically enforceable post-termination rights? The cases are all over the board on this issue.

[219] *See* Bankruptcy Code § 502(b)(6). Even this cap may be subject to mitigation.

[220] *See* Bankruptcy Code § 365(n). Hansen, Salerno & Brown, "Technology Licenses Under Section 365(n) Of The Bankruptcy Code: The Protections Afforded The Technology User," 95 *Comm. L.J.* 170 (Summer 1990). This provision is modeled after § 365(h), which deals with the effect of a

debtor-lessor's rejection of an unexpired real property lease. If the DIP is the lessor under such a lease, it may reject the lease, but the lessee may elect to retain its rights to possession and enjoyment of the leased property so long as it continues to pay rent as required in the lease. The lessee also may elect to treat the lease as terminated and vacate the premises with no further obligation to the lessor.

[221] Some very large retail businesses have gone through Chapter 11 reorganizations over the last ten to fifteen years: *Macy's; Federated Department Stores (Bloomingdales, Burdines, etc.); Herman's Sports; Woodward & Lothrop; Caldor; Montgomery Ward; Ames; Ernst Home Center; Rickel Home Center*; and more recently, *Just for Feet*.

[222] *See* Bankruptcy Code § 365(b)(3).

[223] Shopping center leases typically require that the tenant conduct only a particular sort of business in a particular location in the center, largely because the landlord wants to ensure that no one tenant will unduly compete with another tenant or that any tenant's business will not be incompatible with other businesses being conducted in the center. It would make little economic sense for a mall to have no women's clothing stores but eight Orange Julius stands. That having been said, apparently shopping center landlords don't care how many Gaps they have—Gap Kids, Baby Gap, regular Gap, Gap Senior, Dog Gap, Lawyer Gap . . .

[224] Remember Braniff? People's Express? Eastern? Pan Am? They're all gone, having liquidated in bankruptcy. Other airlines have reorganized in Chapter 11 proceedings, including *TWA*, *America West*, and *Continental* (twice).

[225] *See* Bankruptcy Code § 365(d)(5) through (9).

[226] Another peculiar provision of the Bankruptcy Code involving airlines is § 1110, granting special rights to lessors and those holding security interests in aircraft equipment and vessels, which essentially gives them the right to recover the equipment within sixty days unless all defaults are cured or the court orders otherwise.

[227] *See* Bankruptcy Code § 365(h)(2).

[228] *See* Bankruptcy Code § 365(i).

[229] The procedure is set forth in Bankruptcy Code § 1113.

[230] Courts disagree on what precise standards to apply in this inquiry. *See Bankruptcy Litigation & Practice* for a review of the relevant case law. *See also In re American Provision Co.,* 44 B.R. 7 (Bankr. D. Minn. 1984), in which the court adopted a nine-element test for rejection of a collective bargaining agreement: (1) the DIP must make a proposal to the union to modify the collective bargaining agreement; (2) the proposal must be based on the most complete and reliable information available; (3) the proposed

modifications must be necessary to permit the reorganization of the debtor; (4) the proposed modifications must assure that all creditors, the debtor, and all affected parties are treated fairly; (5) the DIP must provide to the union such relevant information as is necessary to evaluate the proposal; (6) between the time of the making of the proposal and the time of the hearing on approval of the rejection of the existing collective bargaining agreement, the debtor must meet at reasonable times with the union; (7) at the meetings the debtor must confer in good faith in attempting to reach mutually satisfactory modifications of the collective bargaining agreement; (8) the union must have refused to accept the proposal without good cause; and (9) the balance of the equities must clearly favor rejection of the collective bargaining agreement.

[231] *See* Bankruptcy Code § 1114.

[232] *See* Bankruptcy Code § 1129(a)(13).

[233] *See* 28 U.S.C. § 1334(c). This is called "*in rem*" jurisdiction if you want to impress your friends with Latin phrases.

[234] Perhaps one of the more noteworthy international insolvency circumstances involved the *Maxwell Communications* case where insolvency proceedings were ongoing simultaneously in New York and England.

[235] These roadblocks include requests to remove the matter to other courts such as state courts, requests for jury trials, withdrawal of the dispute to the federal District Court, and other procedural tactics. These are highly legalistic matters and are raised here only because they may affect the ability of a debtor to get things resolved quickly in a bankruptcy court.

[236] *See* 28 U.S.C. § 157(b)(2)(O). The personal injury plaintiff's bar had a pretty strong lobby when Congress amended the bankruptcy laws to add 28 U.S.C. § 157 in 1984.

[237] 517 U.S. 44 (1996).

Chapter Five

The Plan of Reorganization

[238] *See Defining Success In Business Bankruptcy* (ABI Bankruptcy Reform Study Project, May 6, 1995).

[239] The company will be aware of its obvious creditors such as bondholders, unpaid trade creditors, and the like. It is sometimes the less obvious creditors that can create problems.

[240] *See* Bankruptcy Rule 2002(l).

[241] For example, in public issuances of debt, the indenture trustee would generally be allowed to file a proof of claim on behalf of all of the holders of the bonds.

[242] Notwithstanding going to extraordinary lengths to notice the world of a bar date, there are times when creditors will simply ignore it and come into

the bankruptcy court later pleading for mercy in allowing them to assert claims. This happens. There are also courts that have an interesting view of what is a "claim" that must be filed by a bar date. This has come up in situations involving the Environmental Protection Agency in contamination claims (particularly in places such as the Seventh Circuit Court of Appeals, which encompasses Chicago in Illinois) and also pops up in product-liability type claims. *See* note 103, above. Sometimes Committees representing potential future claimants are established (as was done in *Johns-Manville* and *A.H. Robins*). To the extent those claims or potential claims are material to a company, counsel will need to be consulted as to the best way to ensure they get notice of the reorganization so they don't pop up later.

[243] A common phenomena is that creditors will file inflated claims just to preserve their rights. There is a ***claims objection*** process to weed out these types of claims that is discussed later in this chapter.

[244] For example, in the reorganization process involving *Circle K,* the primary debt consisted of $300 million in senior secured debt and about $500 million in subordinated bond debt. The case lasted for three years, and ultimately the secured lenders insisted that the debtor sell off the company. The sales price that was ultimately negotiated after a shopping process was enough to take care of the secured debt and a small amount of the senior unsecured debt, but did not leave as much as a dime for the half a billion dollars in subordinated debentures. They were obviously not happy about this. The debtor filed its plan anyway, and after a contested and lengthy confirmation battle royale, the bankruptcy court approved the debtor's plan that froze out over $500 million in bond debt. The debtor clearly would have preferred to reach an agreement with the bondholders, but the economics of the case were such that it was not feasible to do so. Accordingly, the debtor chose its ally (the class of senior secured lenders) and filed a plan with its support.

[245] The Bankruptcy Code was amended in 1984 to require that a plan have at least one accepting "impaired" class in order to be confirmed. In other words, a debtor can't attempt to cramdown every class of creditors under the plan. This is discussed in more detail in the section on *Step Four: The Plan Confirmation Process*.

[246] What's more, the professionals (to the extent that they didn't know each other either personally or professionally before) will become pretty close during this process. While they may scream at each other in court, they'll be friendly outside of the courtroom. Indeed, they are probably involved in other cases simultaneously (sometimes in different roles). This is not a bad thing—in fact it helps the process because good professionals who know and trust one another can help get companies through the difficult first few months of a case.

[247] The judge presiding over the *Megafoods* bankruptcy remarked when

he looked out over his courtroom full of high priced lawyers that, "the sound of all these meters running is deafening."

[248] Of course, the authors as professionals themselves think this is a laudable aim, but clients for some reason differ.

[249] *See* Bankruptcy Code § 1121(b) and (c).

[250] If a trustee is appointed, the exclusivity period automatically terminates, and it's a free-for-all. Any creditor can file a plan. *See* Bankruptcy Code § 1121(c).

[251] On February 2, 2000, the bankruptcy court in the *Service Merchandise* Chapter 11 case pending in Nashville extended the debtor's exclusivity period for fourteen months (until April 2001). This is rumored to be the longest single extension of exclusivity in Bankruptcy Code history. *See* Arsenault, "Exclusivity Period Is Longest Ever," 14 *Turnarounds & Workouts* at 1 (March 15, 2000).

[252] For example, this type of problem occurred in the Chapter 11 case of *In re Quorum International, Ltd.*, a nationwide multi-level marketing company. The Creditors Committee sought to have exclusivity terminated so it could file a plan. The primary basis asserted was that the debtor was not conducting the case in the best interests of the creditors, but rather for the benefit of insiders and entrenched management. The debtor fought the motion, and was successful in defeating it. Thereafter, the Creditors Committee objected to confirmation of the debtor's plan (which it contended was being pursued for the benefit of management and insiders), and also asked that the bankruptcy court appoint a trustee to take over the operations. After lengthy litigation, the bankruptcy court informed the parties it was "inclined" to deny confirmation of the plan and appoint a trustee. The debtor then settled with the Creditors Committee and gave a reasonable distribution to the unsecured creditors in the case (collateralized by a letter of credit). It was an expensive exercise for all concerned.

[253] Both of these situations were present in the *Stratosphere Corporation* Chapter 11 case, which was filed in Las Vegas. The primary debt in the case was bond debt secured by the company's primary asset—its casino—a good portion of which had been acquired by Carl Icahn. At the end of the case, the secured bonds remained secured for a portion of the debt on the casino, and essentially all of the equity was given to the bondholders in satisfaction of the portion of the secured debt that was not supported by the value of the casino.

[254] The Bankruptcy Code allows a debtor to deal with certain small trade creditors by creating what is called an "***administrative convenience class***." Creating this class allows a debtor to get small trade creditors cashed out shortly after plan confirmation (usually with an up-front cash payment). This not only keeps their support for the debtor, but also takes care of an

administrative burden because debtors don't want to have to send out 2,000 checks for $2.15 to small creditors.

[254] Even if a company has its debt or equity delisted or suspended by the SEC, debt can continue to trade on the over-the-counter market or even between private investors that are sophisticated in these transactions. What frequently occurs is that a holder of some of the public debt wishes to consolidate its debt holdings by acquiring other debt. This has the dual benefit of giving that holder a greater say in the process, as well as allowing that holder to average out its holdings such that its aggregate holding cost is lower. For example, if the holder originally acquired its debt at 70¢ on the dollar (when the press releases were not horrible), that same holder may wish to acquire more debt when it's trading at 30¢ on the dollar, so that its average holding price in total is lower. This is sometimes a good thing for a debtor in that it consolidates the players that must be negotiated with.

[256] *See* Bankruptcy Code § 1145(a)(1). This is commonly referred to as a "transactional exemption."

[257] *See* Bankruptcy Code § 1145(a)(2). The recipients of the securities issued under the plan will not themselves have the benefit of the Bankruptcy Code's exemption on subsequent resales of those securities, so in order to trade the securities they will have to rely on some other exemption to securities laws (such as the private placement exemption). *See, e.g., In re Standard Oil & Exploration of Delaware*, 136 B.R. 141, 151-152 (Bankr. W.D. Mich. 1992); *In re Frontier Airlines, Inc.*, 93 B.R. 1014 (Bankr. D. Col. 1988).

[258] The plan will generally contain language to the effect that the reorganized company will use its best efforts to register the equity securities issued under the plan on a national security exchange or automated quotation system prior to, or as soon as practicable after, the distribution to holders of claims entitled to receive the equity securities.

[259] "**Demand registration**" rights, often found in tandem with piggyback registration rights, are rights that a company grants to a shareholder who has acquired shares from the company in a private placement. In other words, the shareholder holds restricted securities and may not freely trade such shares without doing so pursuant to an effective registration statement. Demand registration rights enable the person who holds these rights to require the company to file a registration statement with the SEC so that such shareholder can freely sell his or her shares in the company. "**Tag-along**" rights are rights that are triggered when one or more shareholders give notice to the other parties to a shareholder agreement (*i.e.,* the other shareholders) that such shareholders intends to sell their shares to a third party. Tag-along rights allow the shareholder(s) receiving this notice to include their shares in the sale (hence the term "tag along"), usually on a *pro rata* basis (and thereby carving back the number of shares that the selling

shareholder can sell). The provisions granting these rights are typically lengthy and set forth the mechanics for how the rights become operable. "**Drag-along**" rights are basically the same as tag-along rights, only now the selling shareholder can require that the other shareholders sell their shares along with such shareholder (*i.e.,* drag them along). Major shareholders in a company might require that the other shareholders agree to such a provision so they can effectively sell your interest in the company. Why? Because an acquirer might not want to have minority shareholders to get in the way. Drag-along rights would most likely have some sort of fair market value requirement with respect to the proposed sale price, as well as the other protections that would ensure that those shareholders who are drug along are treated "fairly."

260 Moreover, the Trust Indenture Act of 1939 doesn't apply to any notes issued under the plan if they mature before one year. *See* Bankruptcy Code § 1145(c).

261 Of course, this assumes the reorganized debtor would meet the requirements for registration and listing on a recognized national market (such as NASDAQ, NYSE or AMEX). There are times that bondholders insist that a debtor give some equity to trade creditors so the requisite number of shareholders for listing is met.

262 An interesting phenomena in distressed or insolvent companies is the fundamental disconnect between the public debt and equity markets. Public debt may be trading at 40 percent, and at the same time the stock is still trading (albeit in the 7/16ths range). Amazingly, trading in stock may continue even after the Chapter 11 is filed (assuming the company has not been delisted or suspended), though it is done primarily by wildcat speculators. Amazingly, in the *America West* bankruptcy, convertible debentures were still converting to equity after the filing!

263 There are some unusual circumstances where some stock in the reorganized debtor will be set aside to be issued to certain equityholders. For example, in the *America West Airlines* reorganization case, many of the stockholders were employees whose stockholdings were going to be wiped out in the reorganization. Notwithstanding that, in an effort to maintain the goodwill of the employees, the confirmed plan of reorganization allowed for a small minority position (about 5 percent) to be issued to employees.

264 In the unlikely event that the debtor proposed a plan that was to pay all creditors, in full, with interest (such as occurred in the *Dow Corning* case), there would be no need to dilute or extinguish existing equity.

265 The Bankruptcy Code *requires* that a plan contain the following seven things: (1) classes of claims; (2) specify which classes are not impaired under the plan; (3) specify the treatment of claims and interests; (4) provide the same treatment for all creditors within a class (unless they agree or have agreed prior to the bankruptcy to less favorable treatment, such as in

contractual subordination agreements); (5) provide adequate means to implement a plan (sales of assets, mergers, etc.); (6) preclude the issuance of non-voting securities; and (7) provide for things that are consistent with the interests of creditors, equity security holders and with public policy with respect to selection of officers or directors in the reorganized company. *See* Bankruptcy Code § 1123(a).

[266] An exception would be where secured creditors hold an undivided portion of a secured claim, such as secured bondholders issued under one indenture or participants in a loan.

[267] Something else that may be done in the plan is to ***substantively consolidate***, or merge, the assets and liabilities of numerous related companies. This was done in the *Circle K* and *Unison HealthCare* cases, where the parent companies and numerous subsidiaries (between twenty-four and thirty-five in those cases) were merged together. This is generally viewed as an extraordinary remedy, and will only be done under exceptional circumstances. *See* Gilbert, "Substantive Consolidation In Bankruptcy: A Primer," 43 *Vand. L. Rev.* 245 (1990); *Advanced Chapter 11* at §§ 4.68 *et seq.* This is the reason why in all structured finance transactions "bankruptcy remote" borrowers are required, and "substantive consolidation opinions" of counsel are standard.

[268] *See* discussion on *Bar Date Orders* earlier in this chapter.

[269] For example, in the *Circle K* Chapter 11 bankruptcy, the plan was confirmed in April 1993 and the claims-objection process is still ongoing as of March 2000.

[270] That is not to say that the debtor is not able to negotiate with creditors about treatment that they would find acceptable in a plan. Some persnickety lawyers looking to disrupt the process like to take the position that the debtor is unable to negotiate acceptable plan treatment because to do so would violate the Bankruptcy Code prohibition on soliciting acceptances of a plan without a court-approved Disclosure Statement. This is simply not true. The process is designed to reach consensus, and the only way to do that is to negotiate prior to filing a plan of reorganization.

[271] Picture an unsecured trade creditor owed $10,000 in a huge restructuring getting in the mail a Disclosure Statement, plan, ballots, and all other sorts of documents the copying of which was responsible for denuding an acre of Brazilian rain forest. The creditor will generally not read any of it, and will pick up the phone to call the debtor's lawyer to find out how much he or she is going to get. The people who would otherwise read a Disclosure Statement (such as sophisticated investors and bondholders) generally know a lot of what they need to know about the company as a result of the negotiating process. Nonetheless, the Disclosure Statement is a required step under the Bankruptcy Code and must be dealt with.

[272] *See* Bankruptcy Code § 1125(a)(1).

[273] *See, e.g., Advanced Chapter 11* at §§ 9.8 *et seq.*; *In re Metrocraft Publishing Service, Inc.*, 39 B.R. 567, 568 (Bankr. N.D. Ga. 1984); *In re Malek*, 35 B.R. 443 (Bankr. E.D. Mich. 1983).

[274] This is a disclosure where plan proponents are pretty consistent in how they deal with it. If you look at the tax discussion in a Disclosure Statement, for the most part it tends to say that the state of the tax law is unclear and all creditors should check with their own tax advisor.

[275] In addition, the U.S. Trustee's Office for certain jurisdictions also attempts to implement checklists. *See, e.g., Guidelines By U.S. Trustee For The Central District Of California*, which also requires a discussion of efforts to market assets and a description of future management compensation.

[276] The case law is clear that projections and discussions of ability to make payments under plans as part of the confirmation process are not, and should not be, regarded as guarantees, but only good faith estimates by a debtor. *See, e.g., In re Drexel Burnham Lambert Group, Inc.*, 138 B.R. 723 (Bankr. S.D.N.Y. 1992); *see also* Reehl, "Plan Feasibility: A Quantitative Approach," 21 *Cal. Bankr. J.* No. 2 at 29 (1993); *Advanced Chapter 11* at §§ 11.13 *et seq.*

[277] In financially regulated businesses, such as banks and some others, book values may relate to fair market values as they may be required to periodically "mark to market" for financial statement purposes.

[278] *See* Bankruptcy Code § 1125 and Bankruptcy Rules 2002(b), 3016, and 3017. In "small business" reorganizations (which are defined as companies that do not have aggregate non-contingent liquidated secured and unsecured debt as of the date of the petition of over $2 million—that pretty much leaves out most normal bankruptcies), the courts will combine the hearing on the Disclosure Statement with the hearing on plan confirmation. That really doesn't make much conceptual sense, but Congress did it as a way to shortcut the process in very small cases.

[279] *See* Bankruptcy Rules 2002(b) and 9006(c)(1).

[280] *See* Bankruptcy Code § 1125(a)(1).

[281] Soliciting via the Internet is not a viable option at this point since ballots must be signed. Electronic signatures for non-lawyers is not in place in any jurisdiction as of the date of this book.

[282] An example of an overly complex ballot was the one used in *Southland Corporation's* prepackaged Chapter 11 case. The ballot was characterized by the bankruptcy judge as looking like a "Chinese menu" due to all of the elections. The court ultimately found the prebankruptcy ballot and balloting process so complex that it required the debtor to do it again postbankruptcy.

[283] *See* Bankruptcy Code § 1126(a).

[284] The filing of a proof of claim creates an evidentiary presumption that that claim is valid and enforceable as filed unless and until the debtor or another party in the bankruptcy case objects to that plan. As such, even if a creditor is listed as disputed in the debtor's Schedules, but it files a proof of claim by the bar date, if the debtor takes no further action the creditor's filing of a proof of claim creates the presumption that that claim is valid and therefore an "allowed claim." *See* Bankruptcy Rule 3001(f).

[285] *See* Bankruptcy Code § 506(a). There are certain elections an undersecured creditor can make in a plan process under a special provision of the Bankruptcy Code that allows an undersecured creditor to waive its unsecured deficiency claim and have its entire claim treated as secured. *See* Bankruptcy Code § 1111(b)(2). This is beyond the scope of this book. *See generally* Salerno, Hansen, Haydon & Owens, "The 1111(b)(2) Election: A Primer," *Bankruptcy Dev. J.* 99 (Winter 1996).

[286] *See* Bankruptcy Rules 3007 and 3018(a).

[287] An interesting issue arises with a claim that is temporarily allowed for one amount, but after a full trial is determined to have a higher value. Under the bankruptcy law, that creditor can have its claim reconsidered, although the reconsideration won't impact any other creditor that has received money under the plan. *See* Bankruptcy Code § 502(j).

[288] *See* Bankruptcy Code § 1124.

[289] *See* Bankruptcy Code § 1126(f). Conversely, classes of claims or creditors that will receive any payment or property under a plan also do not need to be solicited because they are deemed to reject the plan. *See* Bankruptcy Code § 1126(g). Interestingly, the Bankruptcy Code states that there is a conclusive presumption that unimpaired creditors have voted for the plan, but the same conclusive presumption does not apply with respect to creditors who are deemed to reject the plan. As such, presumably a creditor that is receiving no distribution under a plan (such as, for example, a subordinated debtholder) could still vote to accept the plan and that ballot could be counted. The benefit of the presumptions of acceptance or rejection simply goes to who actually must be given the plan, Disclosure Statement, and ballot when the solicitation process ensues. While these nuances excite bankruptcy lawyers, interjecting them in cocktail party conversation is a sure way to break up a party.

[290] Interestingly, it has been determined that even a creditor that has its legal rights *improved* may be deemed impaired under the Bankruptcy Code! *See In re L&J Anaheim Assoc.*, 995 F.2d 940 (9th Cir. 1993).

[291] *See* Bankruptcy Code § 1126(g).

[292] *See* Bankruptcy Code § 1126(c).

[293] As such, creditors can't veto a plan simply by failing to vote. Under some insolvency laws (such as the Czech Republic Insolvency Act), the

voting requirements relate to all claims in the class, not just the claims voting. Accordingly, creditors can kill a plan by simply not voting.

294 *See* Bankruptcy Code § 1126(e).

295 *See* 18 U.S.C. § 152(5) and (6).

296 *See, e.g., In re Revere Copper & Brass, Inc.*, 58 B.R. 1 (Bankr. S.D.N.Y. 1985); *Advanced Chapter 11*, §§ 14.73 *et seq.*

297 *See* Bankruptcy Rule 3018(a).

298 *See* Bankruptcy Code § 1129(a)(1)-(13).

299 *See* Bankruptcy Code § 1129(a)(1) and (2).

300 *See, e.g.,* note 26 regarding the Third Circuit Court of Appeal's determination that a company that files Chapter 11 to avoid major litigation may lack the "valid reorganization purpose" needed to invoke the protection of the bankruptcy laws. *See In re SGL Carbon Corp.*, 200 F3d 154 (3rd Cir. 1999).

301 Perhaps the most liberal definition of good faith was promulgated by the Seventh Circuit in *In re 203 North LaSalle Partnership*, 126 F3d 955 (7th Cir. 1997). In that case, the bankruptcy and appellate courts found that even if a bankruptcy were initially filed for reasons other than purely good intentions (in that case to avoid depreciation recapture from the foreclosure of real estate), if a plan is proposed that ultimately is consistent with the Bankruptcy Code (such as maximizing value for all creditors), then the good faith requirement is met.

302 *See* Bankruptcy Code § 1129(a)(4).

303 *See* Bankruptcy Code § 1129(a)(5).

304 *See* Bankruptcy Code § 1129(a)(6).

305 *See* Bankruptcy Code § 1129(a)(7).

306 *See* Bankruptcy Code § 1129(a)(8).

307 In those cases, it is still necessary for the bankruptcy court to have an evidentiary basis to confirm the plan. What plan proponents do (depending upon the court) is to submit an affidavit or declaration of some officer of the company that essentially lists, in fairly conclusory fashion, that the plan complies with all of the thirteen requirements found in the Bankruptcy Code. Since no one objects, the debtor will offer the declaration in lieu of testimony by that officer. The court will generally ask if anyone has any objection to this process, and if no one does, the court will accept the declaration just as if that officer got on the stand and testified under oath. At that point, when the bankruptcy court makes its findings as required by the Bankruptcy Code, it will have an evidentiary basis upon which to do so. To the extent that a particular creditor may have rejected the plan but does not object to this process being followed, that creditor can't later gripe about the evidentiary

basis used by the court in making its findings under the bankruptcy law. This is important because, on appeal, a bankruptcy court's factual determinations must be respected unless they are "clearly erroneous"— a very difficult standard to overcome.

[308] *See* Bankruptcy Code § 1129(a)(9).

[309] *See* Bankruptcy Code § 1129(a)(9)(C).

[310] *See* Bankruptcy Code § 1129(a)(10).

[311] *See* discussion on classifications found in *Step Two: Drafting The Plan of Reorganization*.

[312] *See* Bankruptcy Code § 1129(a)(11).

[313] *See* Bankruptcy Code § 1129(a)(12). These fees are generally not material. *See* discussion in Chapter Four on *Reporting Requirements And Other Annoyances*.

[314] *See* Bankruptcy Code § 1129(a)(13).

[315] *See* Bankruptcy Code § 1123 (a) (6). *See also Advanced Chapter 11* at § 10.21.

[316] *See* Collier On Bankruptcy ¶ 1123.01[6] (15th ed. 1997). *See also In re Acequia, Inc.*, 787 F.2d 1352 (9th Cir. 1986). Separate and apart from the prohibition upon the issuance of non-voting equity securities, Bankruptcy Code § 1123(a)(7) requires the bankruptcy court to independently scrutinize a plan of reorganization that alters voting rights. This obligation exists regardless of whether the plan of reorganization provides for the issuance of equity securities.

[317] *See, e.g., In re Acequia*, 787 F.2d 1352, 1361-62 (9th Cir. 1986); *In re Quaker City Cold Storage Co.*, 71 F. Supp. 124 (E.D. Pa. 1941).

[318] *See* Eppling, "Fun With Nonvoting Stock," 10 *Bankruptcy D. J.* 17 (1993). *See also* 12 U.S.C. §1843(a), which prohibits a bank holding company from acquiring direct or indirect ownership or control of any voting shares of any company which is not a bank. There are certain limited exceptions to this prohibition. For example, 12 U.S.C. §1843(c) permits a bank holding company to acquire voting shares in exchange for debt, except that the holding company must dispose of the shares within a two-year period. In view of the timing associated with a turnaround of a troubled company as well as the typical discount so-called reorganized securities trade at following completion of the bankruptcy, this requirement may require the holding company to sell at a significantly distressed price.

[319] *See, e.g.,* Klee, "Adjusting Chapter 11: Fine Tuning The Plan Process," 69 *Am. Bankr. L.J.* 551 (1995); *see also* Krotinger, "Management And Corporate Reorganizations," 41 *Col. L. Rev.* 646 (1941).

[320] *See* Internal Revenue Code § 382. Indeed, in certain situations, the NOL

is the only thing a company has! There are instances when businesses are bought primarily for the NOL. In addition, bankruptcy courts have recognized that the NOL is a valuable asset of the estate and that the automatic stay prohibited a postpetition stock transfer that would have a negative impact on the preservation of the NOL. *See In re Prudential Lines*, 928 F.2d 565 (2d Cir. 1991).

321 *See Advanced Chapter 11* at Chapter 13; Sheinfeld, Witt & Hyman, *Collier On Bankruptcy Taxation* (Matthew Bender 1999).

322 *See, e.g., In re Consul Restaurant Corp.*, 146 B.R. 979 (Bankr. D. Minn. 1992); *In re Resorts International, Inc.*, 145 B.R. 412 (Bankr. D. N.J. 1990); *In re Jartran, Inc.*, 44 B.R. 331 (Bankr. N.D. Ill. 1984). The plan need not guarantee success but must present a workable scheme that shows a reasonable likelihood of success. *See In re Drexel Burnham Lambert Group, Inc.*, 138 B.R. 723 (Bankr. S.D.N.Y. 1992). *See also Advanced Chapter 11* at §§ 11.13 and 11.14.

323 *See, e.g., In re Clarkson*, 767 F2d 417 (11th Cir. 1985).

324 *See* Bankruptcy Code § 1129(b)(2)(A).

325 *See Advanced Chapter 11* at § 11.26 *et seq.*

326 *See Advanced Chapter 11* at § 11.27. For a compilation of pre-1989 cases in this area, *see* Depperschmidt & Kratzke "The Proper Interest Rate For Allowed Secured Claims In Bankruptcy Proceedings," 21 *Toledo L. Rev.* 459 (1990).

327 *See* Bankruptcy Code § 506(a). It is beyond the scope of this book to get into a discussion of a secured creditor's rights under Bankruptcy Code § 1111(b)(2). In any event, to the extent that this is an issue, counsel should be consulted. *See also* Haydon, Owens, Salerno & Hansen, "The 1111(b)(2) Election: A Primer," 13 *Bankr. Dev. J.* at 99 (Winter 1996). *See also Advanced Chapter 11* at § 11.30.

328 In single-asset or real-estate-related cases, when overleveraged properties do not sufficiently cash flow to pay a market rate of interest, debtors toy with the idea of floating interest rates as well as ***negative amortization*** plans. Negative amortization plans accrue a market rate of interest, but capitalize it to the end of the loan because the cash flow from the properties is not sufficient to pay the interest on a current basis. These types of plans are harshly scrutinized by bankruptcy courts because they put a significant risk on the secured lender in the event that there is a default under the plan. *See Advanced Chapter 11* at § 11.28.

329 *See* Bankruptcy Code § 1129(b)(2)(B). On the issue of providing property of a value equal to the unsecured creditors' claims, this is where expert testimony on valuation of securities is important. *See* discussion in Chapter Two on *The Players And Their Roles*.

[330] Of course, to the extent that there were contractual subordination provisions prebankruptcy, those subordinated creditors could be behind the unsecured creditors as well. In a cramdown in this context, the junior claims would be the subordinated creditors who could not receive or retain anything until the senior claims were paid in full, with interest.

[331] This happened in the *America West Airlines* case, for example.

[332] There has been a big ruckus over whether or not old equity can get around the absolute priority rule by agreeing to buy stock in the reorganized debtor at some amount even when senior creditors are not being paid in full. This is known as the "new value" corollary to the absolute priority rule. It is a result of judicial decisions from the late 1930s, and there has been a big debate as to whether or not this judicially created concept survived the enactment of the Bankruptcy Code in 1978. This issue went to the Supreme Court not once but three times (most recently resulting in a decision in May 1999), and the Supreme Court has yet to finally resolve the conflict among the various Circuits. *See In re 203 North LaSalle Street Partnership*, 526 U.S. 434 (1999). *See, also* Salerno, Hansen & Kroop, "Urgent Message To The Supreme Court: 'Just Do It!'," 34 *B.C.D. Weekly News & Comment* 1 (May 25, 1999). In large commercial cases, this is not an issue that arises.

[333] *See* Bankruptcy Code § 1129(b)(2)(C).

[334] There are unfortunate examples of where a debtor believes it has dealt with claims only to find that those claims are not effectively discharged in the bankruptcy. This comes up most frequently in the environmental contamination area and with successor liability in the products-liability area. These are very technical areas and must be explored in depth with counsel. *See, e.g.*, Salerno, "Future Claimants In Mass Tort Bankruptcy Cases—Good News And Bad News For Debtors In Reorganization Cases From The Southern District Of Florida," *American Bankruptcy Institute Journal* 8 (September 1994); Salerno, "Seventh Circuit Sounds A Death Knell For Reorganization Of Toxic Polluters," *American Bankruptcy Institute Journal* 8 (September 1992); Salerno, "When Does An Environmental Claim Arise? Introducing The Eleventh Circuit's 'Piper Test'," *American Bankruptcy Institute Journal* 8 (October 1995); *Advanced Chapter 11 Bankruptcy*, Chapter 14.

[335] *See* Bankruptcy Code § 1141(d)(3).

[336] For example, in the *Baptist Foundation Of Arizona* Chapter 11, it is anticipated that the liquidation will take between two and five years given the numerous and interrelated assets held by the corporate entities.

[337] One of the reasons there is this ambiguity is because of the Bankruptcy Code's use of the word "consummation" in § 1141(d)(3)(B), which states that the corporate debtor will be denied a discharge if it "does not engage in business after consummation of the plan." The Bankruptcy Code does not

define "consummation." Accordingly, some courts have looked at the word consummation and defined it as the beginning of performance under the plan, but not the completion of all acts that must be done under the plan. As such, those courts have determined that a corporate debtor that is going to liquidate over a period of time postconfirmation is indeed engaging in business after "consummation of the plan" in that the consummation under the plan occurs when the reorganized debtor begins its liquidation efforts. *See e.g., In re River Capital Corporation*, 155 B.R. 382 (Bankr. E.D. Va. 1991).

[338] *See* Bankruptcy Code § 524(e).

[339] *See* discussion in Chapter Four on *The Venue Game*.

[340] *See* Bankruptcy Code § 1125(e). This has generally been interpreted as protecting people from federal or state securities fraud actions with respect to offers of securities under plans, again provided that they were acting in good faith and in accordance with the Bankruptcy Code.

[341] An example of such a provision in a plan is found in the confirmed plan in *Unison HealthCare Corporation*, which provides in pertinent part as follows:

> Neither the Debtors, Reorganized Unison, the Creditors Committee, the Ad Hoc Committee . . . nor any of their respective officers, directors, employees, advisors, attorneys, or agents, shall have or incur any liability to any holder of a Claim or Equity Interest, including the holder of any Equity Interest Related Claim, or any other party in interest, or any of their respective members or former members, agents, employees, representatives, financial advisors, attorneys, or Affiliates, or any of their successors or assigns, for any act or omission in connection with, relating to, or arising out of, the Chapter 11 Cases, the negotiation and pursuit of confirmation of the Plan, or the consummation of the Plan, or the administration of the Plan *except for* their acts or omissions constituting willful misconduct, as finally determined by a court of competent jurisdiction and in all respects shall be entitled to reasonably rely upon the advice of counsel with respect to their duties and responsibilities under the Plan or in the context of the Chapter 11 Cases. No holder of a Claim, Equity Interest or Equity Interest Related Claim, or any other party in interest, including their respective agents, employees, representatives, financial advisors, attorneys or Affiliates, shall have any right of action against the Debtors, Reorganized Unison, the Creditors Committee, the Ad Hoc Committee . . . or any of their respective officers, directors, employees, advisors, attorneys, or agents, for any act or omission in connection with, relating to, or arising out of, the Chapter 11 Cases, the negotiation and pursuit of confirmation of the Plan, the consummation of the Plan, or the administration of the Plan, *except for* their acts or omissions consti-

tuting willful misconduct as finally determined by a court of competent jurisdiction.

[342] Some cases provide that, for example, official Committees may enjoy certain immunity from suit as to actions taken in their official capacities assuming that those actions were taken in good faith. *See, e.g., In re Tucker Freight Lines, Inc.*, 62 B.R. 213 (Bankr. W.D. Mich. 1986); *Pan American Corp. v. Delta Airlines, Inc.*, 175 B.R. 438 (S.D.N.Y. 1994).

[343] *See, e.g., In re Lowenschuss*, 67 F.3d 1394 (9th Cir. 1995); *Landsing Diversified Properties-II v. First National Bank & Trust Co. of Tulsa*, 922 F.2d 592 (10th Cir. 1990); In *re Continental Airlines, Inc.*, 203 F.3d 203 (3rd Cir. 2000).

[344] *See, e.g., In re Specialty Equipment Company*, 3 F.3d 1043 (7th Cir. 1993) (third- party release in plan is enforceable as to creditors voting to accept the plan); *In re West Coast Video Enterprises*, 174 B.R. 906 (Bankr. E.D. Penn. 1994); *Republic Supply Company v. Shoaf*, 815 F.2d 1046 (5th Cir. 1987) (confirmed plan of reorganization order is *res judicata* as to releases and cannot be challenged subsequently if not appealed in the bankruptcy case); *In re Drexel Burnham Lambert Group, Inc.*, 960 F.2d 285 (2nd Cir. 1992); *In re A.H. Robins Co.*, 880 F.2d 694 (4th Cir. 1989). *See also* Feldstein, "Reinterpreting Bankruptcy Code § 524(e): The Validity Of Third Party Releases In A Plan," 22 *Cal. Bankr. J.* 25 (1994).

[345] For example, trust fund withholding taxes are deducted from employee payroll and should be periodically deposited in a trust fund account. In companies where payroll is handled in-house, the temptation to use this money for temporary cash flow needs can be tempting.

[346] *See* Internal Revenue Code § 6672.

[347] *See, e.g., U.S. v. Energy Resources Company, Inc.*, 495 U.S. 545 (1990); *In re Deer Park, Ltd.*, 10 F.3d 1478 (9th Cir. 1993).

[348] *See, e.g., In re American Bicycle Association*, 895 F.2d 1277 (9th Cir. 1990).

[349] Under the Bankruptcy Rules, there is a very short time period for a party to file a notice of appeal—in fact, it is the shortest in the entire federal judicial system. Specifically, a party only has ten calendar days from the date that the court enters the confirmation order to file a notice of appeal. *See* Bankruptcy Rule 8002(a). Failure to timely file a notice of appeal moots out the appeal.

[350] For example, in the casino industry individuals who will wind up owning more than a certain percentage of equity in a gaming company must go through an investigation and approval process by the relevant gaming authorities. This may have to occur postconfirmation. As such, it may be a condition to the Effective Date of a casino restructuring that individuals receiving stock as a result of the plan be approved by the appropriate gaming regulatory board.

[351] This particular ploy was used in the sale of the *Dunes Hotel & Casino* in Las Vegas in the mid-1980s. The plan that was confirmed was a liquidating plan, and the sale process was going to occur postconfirmation. As such, the debtor provided that the Effective Date in that case would not occur until three months after the plan was actually confirmed, at the time when the casino would be sold. No one griped in that particular case, so the debtor got away with it. It's unclear whether a debtor would get away with this sort of extended Effective Date in other cases.

[352] Under the Bankruptcy Code, the discharge is deemed effective on the confirmation date "except as otherwise provided . . . in the plan, or in the order confirming the plan . . . ." *See* Bankruptcy Code § 1141(d)(1). Accordingly, the plan and the order confirming the plan can specifically provide when a discharge will occur.

[353] The reason it is not technically a contract is because numerous cases that have looked at the nature of a discharge as a result of bankruptcy law have stated that the discharge comes about by operation of law, and not by reason of any consideration being given between the debtor and the creditors. *See, e.g., Underhill v. Royal*, 769 F.2d 1426 (9th Cir. 1985). While an interesting technical point, for purposes of conceptual understanding the analogy to a binding contract between the debtor and creditors is still an apt one (albeit not technically legally correct).

[354] The amounts to be deposited into the trust fund were originally a result of statistical analysis done by experts to determine how many people would ultimately get sick, and what their damages would likely be. The reason this was necessary is because asbestosis (the disease one gets when exposed to asbestos) can take many years to manifest itself (sometimes up to thirty years). Interestingly (and unfortunately) the trust fund wound up being underfunded and itself filed a bankruptcy many years after the original *Manville* bankruptcy was completed.

[355] When *Manville* filed its Chapter 11 it was a named defendant in 12,500 lawsuits, and experts estimated that another 50-100,000 such lawsuits could be expected with potential total liability of about $2 billion. *See* 140 Cong. Rec. H. 10,765 (October 4, 1994).

[356] *See* Bankruptcy Code § 524(g). *See also Kane v. Johns-Manville Corp.*, 843 F.2d 636 (2nd Cir. 1988).

[357] *See* Bankruptcy Code § 1127(b).

[358] *See* Bankruptcy Code § 1101(2).

[359] *See In re Heatron, Inc.*, 34 B.R. 526 (Bankr. W.D. Mo. 1983) (in a total liquidation plan, all or substantially all of the assets to be liquidated must be sold prior to a finding of "substantial consummation").

[360] *See In re Hayball Trucking, Inc.*, 67 B.R. 681 (Bankr. E.D. Mich. 1986); *In re H&L Developers, Inc.*, 178 B.R. 77 (Bankr. E.D. Pa. 1994);

In re Antiquities Of Nevada, Inc., 173 B.R. 926 (Bankr. 9th Cir. 1994) ("substantial consummation" requires completion or near completion of transfers of property from a debtor to the reorganized debtor, but only commencement of payments to be made to creditors under the plan). Technically speaking, even if the debtor keeps its same name, once the plan is confirmed and effective, it is considered a new entity (albeit a legal continuation of the previous entity). A "transfer" of assets is deemed to take place from the debtor entity to the reorganized debtor, although no formal transfer instruments and the like need to be drafted and recorded.

[361] *See* Bankruptcy Code § 1144.

[362] Fraud on a federal bankruptcy court is not looked on kindly, and it is a federal offense. Criminal repercussions and disbarment proceedings would likely flow from such a finding by the bankruptcy court.

[363] *See, e.g., In re Ernst*, 45 B.R. 700 (Bankr. D. Minn. 1985) (stay is terminated even if plan provides for default remedies); *In re Pan American School Of Travel, Inc.* 47 B.R. 242 (Bankr. S.D.N.Y. 1985).

[364] This occurred, for example, in the Chapter 11 case of *Shepherd Oil, Inc.* Shepherd Oil owned an ethanol refinery in Arizona, and went through a Chapter 11 bankruptcy that resulted in a confirmed plan. Approximately two years later, Shepherd Oil (as reorganized) defaulted, and certain creditors commenced an involuntary bankruptcy against it (resulting in the second *Shepherd Oil* bankruptcy). The ethanol refinery was ultimately liquidated through the second bankruptcy proceeding.

[365] The reorganized debtor will still need to pay the U.S. Trustee's quarterly fees (discussed in Chapter Four) until the case is formally closed.

Chapter Six

Ten Myths About Reorganization

[366] Not unlike an in-law who, after a few drinks at a family gathering, recounts how he or she found a bone fragment in a hot dog and wound up with the "huge settlement" from Hormel Foods.

[367] *See* discussion in Chapter Four.

[368] *See* discussion in Chapter Five on *Prohibition On Total "Cramdown" Plans.*

[369] *See* discussion in Chapter Five.

[370] *See* discussion in Chapter Four on *Financing The Preconfirmation Operations.*

[371] *See* discussion in Chapter Four on *Stabilizing The Business Operations.*

[372] *See* discussion in Chapter Two on *The Players And Their Roles* and *Public Relations Specialists.*

[373] *See* discussion in Chapter Four on *The Automatic Stay.*

[374] *See* discussion in Chapter Four on *Bankruptcy Court Jurisdiction (And Limitations On That Jurisdiction).*

[375] *See* discussion in Chapter Four on *Dealing With Executory Contracts And Unexpired Leases.*

[376] *See* discussion in Chapter Two involving *What's This "Insolvency" Thing?. See also* discussion in Chapter Five on *Step Five: The Plan Confirmation Process.*

[377] *See* discussion in Chapter Two on *The DIP.*

[378] *See* discussion in Chapter Four on *The Strong Arm Powers.*

[379] *See* discussion in Chapter Three on *The Personal Toll, The "Sacrificial Lambs," Life In A Fishbowl* and *Your New Business Partners.*

[380] *See* discussion in Chapter Five on *Keeping Control—Exclusivity Rules!*

[381] *See* discussion in Chapter Three on *The Company IS In Play—Live With It.*

[382] *See* discussion in Chapter Three on *Making The Transitions—Attitudinal Adjustments.*

[383] *See* discussion in Chapter Two on *The Pecking Order—Payment Priorities In Reorganization Cases.*

[384] *See* discussion in Chapter Five on *The "Holy Grail"—Discharge.*

[385] *See* discussion in Chapter Four on *Dealing With The "Special Claims." See also* discussion in Chapter Five on *Exculpation And Releases.*

[386] For example, *Texaco*, *Johns-Manville, A.H. Robins, R.H. Macy's, America West Airlines, Continental Airlines,* and *Dow Corning* all used the bankruptcy process to deal with otherwise crippling debt that enabled them to emerge as healthy, viable companies.

[387] When an individual files a bankruptcy, that bankruptcy will generally be reported on his or her personal credit reports for a period of seven to ten years depending upon the credit reporting agency. That can have an adverse impact on obtaining personal unsecured credit for individuals. The same is not true of corporations, and acting as an officer or director of a company that has filed bankruptcy does not show up on that officer's or director's individual credit rating or reports (although it is a disclosure item in public filings in the future under Regulation S-K). Item 401 of Regulation S-K requires the disclosure of the business experience of directors and executive officers for the past five years. This regulation also requires the disclosure of such person's involvement in certain specified legal proceedings, including, without limitation, if such person was an executive officer of a company that filed a petition under the federal bankruptcy laws or any state insolvency law.

[388] *See* discussion in Chapter Four on *Financing The Preconfirmation Operations.*

[389] *The Iliad*, XVIII, line 328 (700 BC). Homer was undeniably a sexist, as a more politically correct adage would have been that "Zeus doesn't bring all *persons*' plans to fulfillment." The authors chose not to take liberal editorial license with Homer's classic work, and request appropriate dispensation.

INDEX

Printed in the United States
67512LVS00003B/1

9 781587 980268